T0211989

Lecture Notes in Computer Science 12937

More information about this subseries at http://www.springer.com/series/7407

Zhe Liu · Fan Wu · Sajal K. Das (Eds.)

Wireless Algorithms, Systems, and Applications

16th International Conference, WASA 2021
Nanjing, China, June 25–27, 2021
Proceedings, Part I

 Springer

Editors
Zhe Liu
Nanjing University of Aeronautics
and Astronautics
Nanjing, China

Fan Wu
Shanghai Jiao Tong University
Shanghai, China

Sajal K. Das
Missouri University of Science
and Technology
Rolla, MO, USA

ISSN 0302-9743 ISSN 1611-3349 (electronic)
Lecture Notes in Computer Science
ISBN 978-3-030-85927-5 ISBN 978-3-030-85928-2 (eBook)
https://doi.org/10.1007/978-3-030-85928-2

LNCS Sublibrary: SL1 – Theoretical Computer Science and General Issues

This Springer imprint is published by the registered company Springer Nature Switzerland AG
The registered company address is: Gewerbestrasse 11, 6330 Cham, Switzerland

Preface

The 16th International Conference on Wireless Algorithms, Systems, and Applications WASA 2021 and its workshops was held in Nanjing Dongjiao State Guest House during June 25–27, 2021. The conference was hosted by the Nanjing University of Aeronautics and Astronautics and co-organized by the Beijing University of Posts and Telecommunications, Tsinghua University, Southeast University, Nanjing University, Hohai University, Shandong University, and the Collaborative Innovation Center of Novel Software Technology and Industrialization. WASA is an international conference on algorithms, systems, and applications of wireless networks. WASA is designed to be a forum for theoreticians, system and application designers, protocol developers, and practitioners to discuss and express their views on the current trends, challenges, and state-of-the-art solutions related to various issues in wireless networks. Topics of interests include, but are not limited to, effective and efficient state-of-the-art algorithm design and analysis, reliable and secure system development and implementations, experimental study and testbed validation, and new application exploration in wireless networks.

The conference received 315 submissions. Each submission was reviewed by at least three Program Committee members or external reviewers. The Program Committee accepted 97 full papers and 63 workshop papers which were included in the conference program. The Program Committee also selected the three best papers: "Deep Reinforcement Learning Based Intelligent Job Batching in Industrial Internet of Things" by Chengling Jiang, Zihui Luo, Liang Liu, and Xiaolong Zheng, "A Robust IoT Device Identification Method with Unknown Traffic Detection" by Xiao Hu, Hong Li, Zhiqiang Shi, Nan Yu, Hongsong Zhu, and Limin Sun, and "TS-Net: Device-free Action Recognition with Cross-modal Learning" by Biyun Sheng, Linqing Gui, and Fu Xiao.

We thank the Program Committee members and the external reviewers for their hard work in reviewing the submissions. We thank the Organizing Committee and all volunteers from the Nanjing University of Aeronautics and Astronautics for their time and effort dedicated to arranging the conference.

July 2021

Zhe Liu
Fan Wu
Sajal K. Das

Organization

General Co-chairs

Bing Chen   Nanjing University of Aeronautics and Astronautics,
                              China
Huadong Ma   Beijing University of Posts and Telecommunications,
                              China
Junzhou Luo   Southeast University, China
Ke Xu   Tsinghua University, China

Program Co-chairs

Zhe Liu   Nanjing University of Aeronautics and Astronautics,
                              China
Fan Wu   Shanghai Jiao Tong University, China
Sajal K. Das   Missouri University of Science and Technology, USA

Local Co-chairs

Baoliu Ye   Nanjing University, China
Fu Xiao   Nanjing University of Posts and Telecommunications,
                              China
Shuai Wang   Southeast University, China
Kun Zhu   Nanjing University of Aeronautics and Astronautics,
                              China

Web Co-chairs

Yanchao Zhao   Nanjing University of Aeronautics and Astronautics,
                              China
Bin Tang   Hohai University, China

Organizing Co-chairs

Lei Xie   Nanjing University, China
Liming Fang   Nanjing University of Aeronautics and Astronautics,
                              China

Publicity Co-chairs

Haipeng Dai   Nanjing University, China
Chi (Harold) Liu   Beijing Institute of Technology, China

Zhibo Wang   Zhejiang University, China
Chenren Xu   Peking University, China

Publication Co-chairs

Weizhi Meng   Technical University of Denmark, Denmark
Junlong Zhou   Nanjing University of Science and Technology, China

Steering Committee

Xiuzhen Cheng   American University of Sharjah, UAE
Zhipeng Cai   Georgia State University, USA
Jiannong Cao   Hong Kong Polytechnic University, Hong Kong, China
Ness Shroff   Ohio State University, USA
Wei Zhao   University of Macau, China
PengJun Wan   Illinois Institute of Technology, USA
Ty Znati   University of Pittsburgh, USA
Xinbing Wang   Shanghai Jiao Tong University, China

Technical Program Committee

Ran Bi   Dalian University of Technology, China
Edoardo Biagioni   University of Hawaii at Manoa, USA
Salim Bitam   University of Biskra, Algeria
Azzedine Boukerche   University of Ottawa, Canada
Zhipeng Cai   Georgia State University, USA
Srinivas Chakravarthi   Amazon, USA
  Thandu
Sriram Chellappan   University of South Florida, USA
Quan Chen   Guangdong University of Technology, China
Xianfu Chen   VTT Technical Research Centre of Finland, Finland
Xu Chen   Sun Yat-sen University, China
Songqing Chen   George Mason University, USA
Soufiene Djahel   Manchester Metropolitan University, UK
Yingfei Dong   University of Hawaii, USA
Zhuojun Duan   James Madison University, USA
Luca Foschini   University of Bologna, Italy
Jing Gao   Dalian University of Technology, China
Xiaofeng Gao   Shanghai Jiao Tong University, China
Jidong Ge   Nanjing University, China
Chunpeng Ge   Nanjing University of Aeronautics and Astronautics,
                          China
Daniel Graham   University of Virginia, USA
Ning Gu   Fudan University, China
Deke Guo   National University of Defense Technology, China
Bin Guo   Northwestern Polytechnical University, China

Meng Han	Kennesaw State University, USA
Suining He	University of Connecticut, USA
Zaobo He	Miami University, USA
Pengfei Hu	Shandong University, China
Yan Huang	Kennesaw State University, USA
Yan Huo	Beijing Jiaotong University, China
Holger Karl	University of Paderborn, Germany
Donghyun Kim	Kennesaw State University, USA
Hwangnam Kim	Korea University, South Korea
Bharath Kumar Samanthula	Montclair State University, USA
Abderrahmane Lakas	UAE University, UAE
Sanghwan Lee	Kookmin University, South Korea
Feng Li	Shandong University, China
Feng Li	Indiana University-Purdue University Indianapolis, USA
Ruinian Li	Bowling Green State University, USA
Wei Li	Georgia State University, USA
Zhenhua Li	Tsinghua University, China
Zhetao Li	Xiangtan University, China
Peng Li	University of Aizu, Japan
Qi Li	Tsinghua University, China
Yaguang Lin	Shaanxi Normal University, China
Zhen Ling	Southeast University, China
Weimo Liu	George Washington University, USA
Jia Liu	Nanjing University, China
Fangming Liu	Huazhong University of Science and Technology, China
Liang Liu	Beijing University of Posts and Telecommunications, China
Hongbin Luo	Beihang University, China
Jun Luo	Nanyang Technological University, Singapore
Liran Ma	Texas Christian University, USA
Jian Mao	Beihang University, China
Bo Mei	Texas Christian University, USA
Hung Nguyen	Carnegie Mellon University, USA
Pasquale Pace	University of Calabria, Italy
Claudio Palazzi	University of Padova, Italy
Junjie Pang	Qingdao University, China
Javier Parra-Arnau	University of Ottawa, Canada
Tie Qiu	Tianjin University, China
Ruben Rios	University of Malaga, Spain
Kazuya Sakai	Tokyo Metropolitan University, Japan
Omar Sami Oubbati	University of Laghouat, Algeria
Kewei Sha	University of Houston - Clear Lake, USA
Hao Sheng	Beihang University, China
Bo Sheng	University of Massachusetts Boston, USA

Tuo Shi	Harbin Institute of Technology, China
Sukhpal Singh Gill	Queen Mary University of London, UK
Junggab Son	Kennesaw State University, USA
Riccardo Spolaor	Shandong University, China
Chunhua Su	University of Aizu, Japan
Violet Syrotiuk	Arizona State University, USA
Guoming Tang	National University of Defense Technology, China
Bin Tang	Hohai University, China
Xiaohua Tian	Shanghai Jiaotong University, China
Luis Urquiza	Universitat Politècnica de Catalunya, Spain
Tian Wang	Huaqiao University, China
Yawei Wang	George Washington University, USA
Yingjie Wang	Yantai University, China
Zhibo Wang	Wuhan University, China
Leye Wang	Peking University, China
Wei Wei	Xi'an University of Technology, China
Alexander Wijesinha	Towson University, USA
Mike Wittie	Montana State University, USA
Kaishun Wu	Shenzhen University, China
Xiaobing Wu	University of Canterbury, New Zealand
Wei Xi	Xi'an Jiaotong University, China
Yang Xiao	University of Alabama, USA
Kun Xie	Hunan University, China
Kaiqi Xiong	University of South Florida, USA
Kuai Xu	Arizona State University, USA
Wen Xu	Texas Woman's University, USA
Lei Yang	The Hong Kong Polytechnic University, China
Panlong Yang	University of Science and Technology of China, China
Changyan Yi	Nanjing University of Aeronautics and Astronautics, China
Wei Yu	Towson University, USA
Dongxiao Yu	Shandong University, China
Sherali Zeadally	University of Kentucky, USA
Deze Zeng	China University of Geosciences, China
Bowu Zhang	Marist College, USA
Yong Zhang	Shenzhen Institutes of Advanced Technology, China
Yang Zhang	Nanjing University of Aeronautics and Astronautics, China
Cheng Zhang	George Washington University, USA
Xu Zheng	University of Science and Technology of China, China
Yanwei Zheng	Shandong University, China
Lu Zhou	Nanjing University of Aeronautics and Astronautics, China
Jindan Zhu	Amazon Web Service, USA
Tongxin Zhu	Harbin Institute of Technology, China
Yifei Zou	University of Hong Kong, China

Contents – Part I

Algorithms

IoT and Edge Computing

Scheduling and Optimization I

Contents – Part II

Data Center Networks and Cloud Computing

Privacy-Aware Computing

Internet of Vehicles

Contents – Part III

Wireless Communications

Layer Based Fast Data Collection in Battery-Free Wireless Sensor Networks

Jin Zhang[1], Hong Gao[1(✉)], Dan Yin[2], and Kaiqi Zhang[1]

[1] School of Computer Science and Technology, Harbin Institute of Technology, Harbin, China
{zhangjinhit,honggao,zhangkaiqi}@hit.edu.cn
[2] School of Electrical and Information Engineering, Beijing University of Civil Engineering and Architecture, Beijing, China
yindan@bucea.edu.cn

Abstract. Battery-free Wireless Sensor Networks (BF-WSNs) is a promising technology of Wireless Sensor Networks (WSNs). Nodes in BF-WSNs are able to harvest ambient energy, so they have eternal life in theory. Although many works in this field study data collection, few works are concerned about latency. Moreover, some of them adopt unrealistic centralized scheduling manner, others are trapped in performance degradation. Thus, in this paper, we propose a distributed minimum latency data collection algorithm for BF-WSNs—Layer Based Fast Data Collection (LBFDC) Algorithm. LBFDC is distributed so it is able to deal with dynamic situations in BF-WSNs. Because it adopts an adaptive routing strategy and allocates more chances to nodes to transmit, the latency of LBFDC is significantly reduced.

Keywords: Battery-Free Wireless Sensor Networks · Data collection · Latency · Distributed algorithm

1 Introduction

The finite battery energy of nodes limits the lifetime of Wireless Sensor Networks (WSNs). Once energy is exhausted, users have to spend a lot of time and effort on replacing batteries. WSNs were plagued by this problem for years. In recent years, the developments of low-power devices and energy harvesting technologies bring us Battery-free Wireless Sensor Networks (BF-WSNs). Nodes in BF-WSNs can harvest energy from the environment. So they can work perpetually in theory. For this reason, BF-WSNs attracts many researchers' interest.

People are interesting about sensing data generated by WSNs. Many sensing data analysis, processing and repairs algorithms have been proposed [1,3,4,9,12]. And many pieces of literature about BF-WSNs study how to gather data from BF-WSNs, such as data collection. Data collection is: every node delivers its data to the sink directly or through relays of other nodes. Most related works concentrate on maximizing the volume of collected data by the sink [2,11] or maximizing the network utility [10,14]. Although latency is a critical metric of

© Springer Nature Switzerland AG 2021
Z. Liu et al. (Eds.): WASA 2021, LNCS 12937, pp. 3–15, 2021.
https://doi.org/10.1007/978-3-030-85928-2_1

performance, few works aim to reduce latency so far [13,15]. In [13], the authors proposed a protocol for minimum latency data collection in a WSN powered by wireless energy transfers. The protocol works in a centralized manner and it can hardly deal with unstable energy sources. In [15], the authors proposed two distributed algorithms for minimum latency data collections in line topology and general topology, respectively. However, in their algorithms, the routing is fixed and few nodes are allocated chances to transmit in every time slot. Therefore, its performance is far from the optimum.

In Battery Powered WSNs (BP-WSNs), many works study this problem [6,7]. However, due to the differences between BF-WSNs and BP-WSNs, they are unsuitable to BF-WSNs. First, battery-free nodes usually need to accumulate energy before transmissions. While nodes always have enough energy for transmission before death in BP-WSNs. Second, due to the fluctuation of ambient energy, BF-WSNs desire distributed algorithms much more than centralized.

In this paper, we propose a distributed algorithm for minimum latency data collection in BF-WSNs—Layer Based Fast Data Collection (LBFDC). First, we divide networks into layers, distinguish cross-layer collisions and in-layer collisions. Next, we propose a cross-layer scheduling algorithm and an in-layer scheduling algorithm solving two types of collisions, respectively. These two algorithms take adaptive routing strategy and allocate more chances to nodes to transmit every time slot, so they accelerate the data collection. Combining two algorithms, we get a distributed data collection algorithm for BF-WSNs. The contributions of this paper are:

1. A novel distributed algorithm for minimum latency data collection in BF-WSNs is proposed. To achieve low latency, it takes an adaptive routing strategy and allocates more chances to nodes to transmit.
2. The theoretical latency bound of the proposed algorithm is analyzed and proved. And it is much less than the bound of the existing method. Moreover, we verify that the bound is quite accurate through simulations.
3. We conduct extensive simulations to evaluate our algorithm. The results show that it outperforms the existing algorithm signally.

The sections of this paper are organized as follows. In Sect. 2, we introduce the models and define the problem. In Sect. 3, we propose LBFDC algorithm. In Sect. 4, we analyze its latency bound. In Sect. 5, we evaluate LBFDC through extensive simulations. Finally, we conclude this paper in Sect. 6.

2   Problem Definition

We consider a network of n battery-free nodes and a sink s. The transmission range of all nodes is r, i.e., node v can successfully receive the signal from node u only if $dist(u,v) \leq r$, where $dist(u,v)$ is the Euclidean distance between them. Time is slotted to slots with τ seconds. Every node can only transmit or receive one data packet in a time slot. We adopt the protocol interference model where the interference range equals the transmission range r as [5,7]. In this model, node v receives data from node u successfully in time slot t only if u is the only transmitting node within r from v in the time slot.

The energy consumptions of transmitting and receiving a data packet are e_t and e_r, respectively. The harvesting rate within a time window of T_p slots can be predicted accurately in advance by plenty of technologies, such as [8]. For example, if the predicted energy harvesting rate of node u in time slots during $[t, t+T_p]$ is $\hat{e}_u(t)$, it means that at time slot t, battery-free node u predicts that it will harvest $\hat{e}_u(t)$ energy in each time slot during $[t, t+T_p]$. The harvested energy is stored in equipped capacitor. The energy level of node u in time slot t is $E_u(t)$. And it is limited by the energy capacity e_{max} of capacitor, i.e., $E_u(t) \leq e_{max}$. The overflowed energy is wasted directly.

Without loss of generality, the data collection starts at time slot 0. In this time slot, every node generates a data packet. These data packets are supposed to be delivered to the sink as soon as possible. If the sink s collects all data packets at time slot l, the latency of data collection is l time slots. S_t is the set of schedules in time slot t. It is comprised of 2-tuples, e.g., $(u, v) \in S_t$ means that node u transmits a data packet to node v in time slot t. The schedules in S_t should satisfy:

1. $\forall (u, v) \in S_t, dist(u, v) \leq r$;
2. $\forall (u, v) \in S_t, E_u(t) \geq e_t \wedge E_v(t) \geq e_r$;
3. $\forall (u, v) \in S_t$ and $(x, y) \in S_t, dist(u, y) > r$ and $dist(x, v) > r$.

Thus, the data collection schedule $\mathcal{S}$ is $\{S_1, S_2, \ldots, S_l\}$. Our objective is to minimize l.

3 Layer Based Fast Data Collection Algorithm

In the 1st subsection, we partition the network into layers according to the shortest path tree (SPT) rooted at the sink s. In the 2nd subsection, we propose a *cross-layer* collision-free scheduling algorithm. Then in the 3rd subsection, we propose a *in-layer* collision-free scheduling algorithm.

3.1 Network Layering

We leverage SPT to partition the network into layers. SPT can be constructed by breath-first searching algorithm. We omit its details to save space.

We use R to denote the depth of the SPT, use L_i to denote the set of nodes in the ith layer from root s. Specially, $L_0 = \{s\}$. Then, we use N_u to represent neighbors of node u, use $N_{u,i} = L_i \cap N_u$ to represent node u's neighbors in layer L_i. Obviously, if $u \in L_i$, its neighbors are in three disjoint layers L_{i-1}, L_i and L_{i+1}. We restrict that data packets can only be transmitted from higher layers to lower layers, which means node $u \in L_i$ can only transmit to its neighbors in L_{i-1}. We name this restriction *forward transmission restriction*.

Then, we divide collisions into two categories—*cross-layer collisions* and *in-layer collisions*. Cross-layer collisions are collisions that occur between two transmissions from two different layers and in-layer collisions are collisions that occur

---

Algorithm 1: Cross-layer Scheduling

Input: Topology of the network; e_t, e_r and e_b; T_f, the lengh of time frames.
Output: A data collection schedule S
1 Partition the network into layers $L_1, L_2, \ldots, L_R$ using shortest path tree;
2 Divide the layers into three groups, $\mathcal{L}_0 = \{L_i | i \mod 3 = 0\}$, $\mathcal{L}_1 = \{L_i | i \mod 3 = 1\}$ and $\mathcal{L}_2 = \{L_i | i \mod 3 = 2\}$;
3 $S \leftarrow \emptyset$;
4 $k \leftarrow 0$;
5 **while** *sink s hasn't received all data packets* **do**
6   **for** $\delta = 0, 2, 1$ **do**
7   Generate in-layer schedules $S_t, t = kT_f + 1, \ldots, (k+1)T_f$ for transmissions from layers in $\mathcal{L}_\delta$ in $(k+1)$th time frame;
8          $S \leftarrow S \cup \{S_t | t = kT_f + 1, \ldots, (k+1)T_f\}$;
9          $k \leftarrow k + 1$;
10   **end**
11 **end**
12 **return** S

---

between two transmissions from the same layer. In the next two subsections, we will propose a cross-layer collision-free scheduling algorithm and an in-layer collision-free scheduling algorithm. Combining them together, we can obtain a collision-free scheduling algorithm.

3.2 Cross-layer Scheduling

We observe that due to spatial separation, transmissions from two different layers are collision-free if they are far from each other. Thus, we get Lemma 1 as follows.

Lemma 1. *Under forward transmission restriction, a transmission from $L_i, i \geq 1$ cannot collide with another transmission from $L_j, j \geq i + 3$.*

This lemma can be easily proved so we omit its proof to save space.

Then, we partition layers into three disjoint groups—$\mathcal{L}_0 = \{L_i | i \mod 3 = 0\}$, $\mathcal{L}_1 = \{L_i | i \mod 3 = 1\}$ and $\mathcal{L}_2 = \{L_i | i \mod 3 = 2\}$. We can easily get the following corollary according to Lemma 1.

Corollary 1. *Under forward transmission restriction, transmissions from the group $\mathcal{L}_\delta$ are cross-layer collision-free, $\delta = 0, 1, 2$.*

Corollary 1 tells us that there is no cross-layer collision if we let nodes in only one group transmit simultaneously. What we only need to concern about is how to avoid in-layer collisions.

The algorithm for cross-layer scheduling is provided in Algorithm 1. Notice that from Line 6 to Line 10, every loop generates schedules for T_f time slots, i.e., a time frame. Here, we define *time frame* as:

Definition 1 *(Time Frame). A time frame consists of $T_f = (b + w)$ time slots. The length of time frames is smaller than the length of prediction time window of the energy harvesting rate, i.e., $T_f \leq T_p$, so nodes can predict their energy harvesting rates accurately in a time frame. The first b time slots comprise the beacon phase. It is for nodes to exchange beacons. The last w time slots comprise the transmission phase. Nodes transmit in the transmission phase according to schedules generated in the beacon phase. To keep model simple, we assume that every node consumes e_b energy in the beacon phase. e_b is the upper bound of energy consumption in the beacon phase.*

In Line 7 of Algorithm 1, we should embed an in-layer scheduling algorithm, which will be proposed in the next subsection. The latency of data collection schedule generated by Algorithm 1 is $l = kT_f$ time slots finally.

3.3   In-Layer Scheduling

In this subsection, first, we introduce in-layer scheduling briefly. Second, since the schedules of nodes are interdependent, we should generate the scheduling order for them. Third, we introduce the data structures used in the beacon phase. Finally, we explain the in-layer scheduling in detail. Without loss of generality, we discuss this problem in a subgraph of two adjacent layers, L_i and L_{i-1}. For convenience, we name nodes in L_i (L_{i-1}) transmitters (receivers), name L_i (L_{i-1}) transmitter layer (receiver layer).

Brief Introduction to In-Layer Scheduling. In the beacon phase of every time frame, nodes exchange beacons to generate schedules for the transmission phase. Thus, we focus on the beacon phase in the following.

The beacon phase is comprised of many turns for receiver layers and transmitter layers to exchange information. At the beginning of each turn, receivers inform transmitters of their status using *status beacons* (the first turn) or their schedules using *receiver beacons* (the other turns). After hearing information from receivers, transmitters decide their schedules, generate *transmitter beacons* and broadcast to receivers. After receiving transmitter beacons, receivers update their schedules, and wait for broadcasting beacons in the next turn. Every node can generate its schedules before the end of the beacon phase. In the transmission phase, it will transmit or receive according to the schedules.

Two transmitters can't decide schedules in the same turn if they have common receivers. For instance, if both u_1 and u_2 can transmit to v, u_1 can't eliminate the possibility of collisions with u_2 without knowledge about schedules of u_2. Hence, u_1 and u_2 should decide their schedules in different turns to let the latter one avoid collisions with the previous one. Thus, we need a *scheduling order* for transmitters to generate schedules sequentially. In the next subsection, we will propose an algorithm to generate a scheduling order.

Algorithm 2: Schedule Order Generating

    Input: Layer L_i, layer L_{i-1} and edges between them;
    Output: Scheduling Order $\mathcal{O}_i$;
1 $\mathcal{L} \leftarrow L_i$;
2 $\mathcal{O}_i \leftarrow \emptyset$;
3 **while** $\mathcal{L} \neq \emptyset$ **do**
4      $O \leftarrow \emptyset$;
5      $R \leftarrow \emptyset$;
6   **while** $\mathcal{L} \setminus N_{R,i} \neq \emptyset$ **do**
7          $u \leftarrow$ select a node from $\mathcal{L} \setminus N_{R,i}$;
8          $O \leftarrow O \cup \{u\}$;
9          $R \leftarrow R \cup N_{u,i-1}$;
10   **end**
11      $\mathcal{O}_i \leftarrow \mathcal{O}_i \cup \{O\}$;
12      $\mathcal{L} \leftarrow \mathcal{L} \setminus O$;
13 **end**
14 **return** $\mathcal{O}_i$;

Generating Scheduling Order for Transmitters. A naive scheduling order is to let transmitters decide their schedules one by one. However, the length of this order is $O(L_i)$, which increases with the scale of the network in general. To accelerate the beacon phase, we should shorten the length of the scheduling order. We find that transmitters with no common receivers can decide their schedules without collision possibility. Actually, if we add edges between transmitter pairs that have common receivers, finding the shortest scheduling order is transformed to the minimum vertex coloring problem in graph theory. It is using the least number of colors to label the graph's vertexes so that no two adjacent vertexes have the same color. Since it's NP-hard, we propose a heuristic algorithm to generate scheduling order in Algorithm 2.

In Line 1 of Algorithm 2, left transmitters set $\mathcal{L}$ is used to contain the transmitters that haven't been determined scheduling order. In Line 2, $\mathcal{O}_i = \{O_i^1, O_i^2, \ldots, O_i^{|\mathcal{O}_i|}\}$ is the generated scheduling order, where O_i^k is the transmitters in the kth turn. Line 3 to 13 runs until all nodes' scheduling order are determined. In Line 4, O is the transmitters set in the new turn. And in Line 5, R is the neighboring receivers set of O. Line 6 to 10 finds the maximal subset from left transmitters set $\mathcal{L}$ for the new turn. In Line 6, we check whether there is a transmitter in $\mathcal{L}$ can decide schedules with O together. If so, we insert it into O and update neighboring receivers set R (Line 7 to 9); else, O is the maximal, so we insert it into scheduling order $\mathcal{O}_i$ as a new turn and update left transmitters set $\mathcal{L}$. For convenience, we use R_i^k to denote neighboring receivers of O_i^k, i.e., the receivers in the kth turn.

We provide a concrete example of Algorithm 2 in Fig. 1. In Fig. 1, the red nodes are the transmitters in the new turn, the blue nodes are their receivers, and the black nodes are neighboring transmitters of blue nodes that can't decide schedules in this turn. The generated scheduling order is $\mathcal{O}_i = \{\{u_1, u_4, u_5\},$

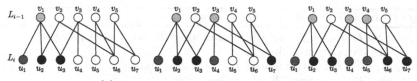

(a) Finding transmitters in the 1st turn.

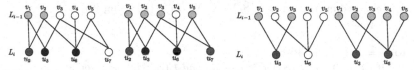

(b) Finding transmitters in the 2nd turn. (c) Finding transmitters in the 3rd turn.

Fig. 1. Example of scheduling order generating. (Color figure online)

$\{u_2, u_7\}, \{u_3, u_6\}\}$. This means the schedules of layer L_i can be generated after 3 turns in this example. The length of generated scheduling order is much less than the layer size $|L_i| = 7$.

The scheduling order can be generated after deploying the network. It won't change until the topology of network changes.

Data Structures for In-Layer Scheduling. In this part, we introduce three beacons and two other data structures used in in-layer scheduling.

Schedule Array: The schedule array $\tilde{S}_u$ of node u is an array of w bits. We use $\tilde{S}_u[j]$ to denote its jth bit. If node u is a transmitter (receiver) in the current frame and $\tilde{S}_u[j] = 1$, it will transmit (receive) in the jth time slot in transmission phase; otherwise, it will idle.

$$\hat{E}(\tilde{S}_u)[j] = \begin{cases} \min\{e_{max}, E_u(t) + b\hat{e}_u(t)\}, & \text{if } j = 1 \\ \min\{e_{max}, \hat{E}(\tilde{S}_u)[j-1] + \hat{e}_u(t) - e_t\}, & \text{if } u \in L_i \wedge \tilde{S}_u[j-1] = 1 \\ \min\{e_{max}, \hat{E}(\tilde{S}_u)[j-1] + \hat{e}_u(t) - e_r\}, & \text{if } u \in L_{i-1} \wedge \tilde{S}_u[j-1] = 1 \\ \min\{e_{max}, \hat{E}(\tilde{S}_u)[j-1] + \hat{e}_u(t)\}, & \text{if } \tilde{S}_u[j-1] = 0 \end{cases} \quad (1)$$

Stored Energy Array: The stored energy array $\hat{E}(\tilde{S}_u)$ of node u with schedule array $\tilde{S}_u$ is an array of w elements. Each element is the predicted stored energy level in the corresponding time slot in transmission phase. We use $\hat{E}(\tilde{S}_u)[j]$ to denote its jth element. It can be calculated using Eq. (1), in which we assume the first time slot in the current frame is time slot t.

Status Beacon: The status beacon of node v is a 2-tuple $(E_v(t), \hat{e}_v(t))$. $E_v(t)$ is its stored energy in the first time slot of the frame, and $\hat{e}_v(t)$ is its predicted energy harvesting rate.

Transmitter Beacon: The transmitter beacon TB_u of node u is an array of w elements. Every element in TB_u is either an ID of a receiver or *NULL*.

Algorithm 3: Transmitter Beacon Generating

Input: $\tilde{S}_v, \tilde{F}_v, v \in N_{u,i-1}$, schedule arries and F2R arries of neighboring receivers of transmitter u.

Output: The transmitter beacon TS_u of transmitter u;

1 Initialize TB_u by setting $TB_u[j] = Null, j = 1, 2 \ldots, w$;

2 Initialize $\tilde{S}_u$ by setting $\tilde{S}_u[j] = 0, j = 1, 2, \ldots, w$;

3 Calculate stored energy array $\hat{E}(\tilde{S}_a), a \in N_{u,i-1} \cup \{u\}$ using Eq. (1);

4 $D_u \leftarrow D_u(t)$;

5 **for** $v \in N_{u,i-1}$ **do**

6   **for** $j = 1, 2, \ldots, w$ **do**

7   **if** $D_u > 0$ *and* $\hat{E}(\tilde{S}_u)[j] \geq e_t + e_b$ *and* $\hat{E}(\tilde{S}_v)[j] \geq e_r + e_b$ *and* $\forall v' \in N_{u,i-1}, \tilde{F}_{v'}[j] = 0$ **then**

8              $\tilde{S}_v' \leftarrow \tilde{S}_v$;

9              $\tilde{S}_v'[j] \leftarrow 1$;

10   Calculate stored energy array $\hat{E}(\tilde{S}_v')$;

11   **if** $\forall j \in [1, w], \hat{E}(\tilde{S}_v') \geq 0$ **then**

12                  $TB_u[j] \leftarrow ID_v$;

13                  $\tilde{S}_a[j] \leftarrow 1, a \in \{u, v\}$;

14   Calculate stored energy array $\hat{E}(\tilde{S}_a), a \in \{u, v\}$;

15   Set $\tilde{F}_a[j] = 1, a \in N_{u,i-1}$;

16                  $D_u \leftarrow D_u - 1$;

17   **end**

18   **end**

19   **end**

20 **end**

21 **return** TB_u;

For instance, if $TB_u[j] = ID_v$, u will transmit a data packet to v in the jth time slot of the transmission phase. If $TB_u[j] = NULL$, node u will idle.

Receiver Beacon: The receiver beacon of node v is a 2-tuple $(\tilde{S}_v, \tilde{F}_v)$. $\tilde{S}_v$ is its schedule array. $\tilde{F}_v$ is a Forbidden-to-Transmit (F2T) array of w bits. $\tilde{F}_v[j] = 1$ indicates that some neighboring transmitter of v will transmit in the jth time slot of the transmission phase so v can't receive in this time slot; vice versa.

Turns in Beacon Phase. The first turn in the transmission phase is different from the others. At the beginning of the first turn, all transmitters and receivers initialize schedule arrays $\tilde{S}_u[j] = 0, j = 1, 2 \ldots, w, u \in L_i \cup L_{i-1}$, and receivers initialize F2R array $\tilde{F}_v[j] = 0, j = 1, 2 \ldots, w, v \in L_{i-1}$. Then, receivers inform transmitters of theirs status using status beacons. After all receivers broadcasting status beacons sequentially, it's time for transmitters in O_i^1 to generate and broadcast transmitter beacons. They don't need information about receivers' schedules and F2R time slots because they know receivers have no schedules and all time slots are available. In the meanwhile, receivers in R_i^1 keep listening to transmitter beacons. After listening, they update their receiver beacons.

In the kth turn, $k > 1$, receivers in R_i^k should broadcast their receiver beacons firstly. After receiving beacons from R_i^k, transmitters in O_i^k generate and broadcast their transmitter beacons. Meanwhile, receivers in R_i^k listen to transmitter beacons, update their receiver beacons and wait for their next turns.

Transmitter beacons are generated as Algorithm 3. Line 1 to 4 does initialization. D_v records the number of left packets on node u after transmissions of existing schedules. Line 5 to 20 checks every receiver v of u and every time slot j in the transmission phase: whether u can transmit to v in time slot j. If so, they should satisfy the following 4 conditions: 1) u has data packet according to existing schedules (Line 7); 2) u (v) has enough energy for transmitting (receiving) and beacon phase (Line 7); 3) no neighboring receiver of u is scheduled to receive (Line 7); 4) if v receive in time slot j, it still has enough energy to finish existing schedules (Line 8 to 11). If they satisfy above conditions, we schedule u to transmit to v in time slot j by doing updating in Line 12 to 16. Otherwise, we move to check the next time slot (Line 6) or the next receiver (Line 5).

4 Performance Analysis

In this section, we analyze the latency bound theoretically. We modify LBFDC to Modified LBFDC (MLBFDC) with performance degradation, so the latency of MLBFDC can be used as the upper latency bound of LBFDC. Then we apply MLBFDC in the worst energy situation to obtain its upper latency bound. In this case, the latency bound of MLBFDC is also the bound of LBFDC.

We use e_l to denote the lower bound of the energy harvesting rate. In the worst energy situation, all nodes harvest ambient energy at this rate. In this case, every ($\lceil \frac{e_l + e_r}{T_f e_l - e_b} \rceil + 3$) frames comprise a round in MLBFDC. In a round, all nodes can only harvest energy in the first $\lceil \frac{e_l + e_r}{T_f e_l - e_b} \rceil$ frames. After that, they would have energy for transmitting once and receiving once respectively. In the last 3 frames, we schedule nodes using LBFDC algorithm with restriction that each node can only transmit and receive at most one data packet. We use S_M to denote the schedule of MLBFDC under this setting, and use $l(S_M)$ to denote its latency. We have the following lemma.

Lemma 2. *The data collection latency of schedule S is no more than the data collection latency of schedule S_M, i.e., $l(S) \leq l(S_M)$.*

Without loss of generality, we assume $R \mod 3 = 0$ while analyzing $l(S_M)$.

Lemma 3. *In schedule S_M, after k rounds, if there are data packets in layers from L_{3i+1} to L_{3i+3}, $i \in [1, \frac{R}{3} - 1]$, there must be data packets in layers from L_{3j+1} to L_{3j+3}, $j \in [1, i]$.*

Proof. First, we claim: if there are data packets in layers from $L_{3i'+1}$ to $L_{3i'+3}$ at the end of the $(k-1)$th round, they must transmit at least one data packet to layers from $L_{3i'-2}$ to $L_{3i'}$ in the kth round according to the strategy of S_M.

Then we prove this lemma from contradiction. Suppose that there is no packet in layers from L_{3j+1} to L_{3j+3}, $j \in [1, i]$ at the end of the kth round. According to our claim, they received no data packet in the kth round. Thus there must be no data' packet in layers from L_{3j+4} to L_{3j+6}, $j = [1, i]$ at the end of the $(k-1)$th round. Continue this induction, we come to a conclusion that there is no data packet in layers from L_{3j+1} to L_R at the end of the kth round. Thus there is no data packet in layers from L_{3i+1}, L_{3i+2} or L_{3i+3} as well, which is in conflict with the precondition. Therefore, the lemma is proved.   □

Lemma 4. *The latency bound of the schedule* S_M *generated by MLBFDC is* $n(\lceil \frac{e_t + e_r}{T_f e_l - e_b} \rceil + 3)T_f$, *i.e.,* $l(S_M) \leq n(\lceil \frac{e_t + e_r}{T_f e_l - e_b} \rceil + 3)T_f$.

Proof. According to Lemma 3, in schedule S_M, sink s receives at least one data packet every round until it receives all data packets. Since there are n data packets in the network, the latency bound of S_M is $n(\lceil \frac{e_t + e_r}{T_f e_l - e_b} \rceil + 3)T_f$.   □

Theorem 1. *The latency bound of the schedule* S *generated by LBFDC is* $n(\lceil \frac{e_t + e_r}{T_f e_l - e_b} \rceil + 3)T_f$, *i.e.,* $l(S) \leq n(\lceil \frac{e_t + e_r}{T_f e_l - e_b} \rceil + 3)T_f$.

Proof. The theorem can be proved easily by Lemma 2 and Lemma 4.   □

The previous work for this problem proposed DCoSG (Data Collection for General BF-WSNs) [15]. If taking SPT to partition the network, its latency is bounded by $12n(\lceil \frac{e_t + e_r}{T_f e_l - e_b} \rceil + 1)T_f$ under the interference model in this paper. Thus, the latency bound improvement of LBFDC is significant.

5   Evaluation

We conduct simulations using C++ and Python on a Windows PC to evaluate our algorithm in this section.

5.1   Simulation Configurations

By default, we simulate 300 battery-free nodes randomly deployed in a 150 m × 150 m area. We set the length of a time slot to $\tau = 40\,\mu$s. In our simulations, the beacon phase is 2 time slots and consumes 5μJ energy, i.e., $b = 2$ and $e_b = 5\,\mu$J. We evaluate various lengths of the transmission phase in our simulations. The energy consumptions of transmitting and receiving a data packet are $e_t = 100\,\mu$J and $e_r = 80\,\mu$J, respectively. The energy harvesting rates of nodes vary from 25 μJ/s to 400 μJ/s. They are sampled from distributions generated by Perlin Noise as Fig. 2. The default energy capacity is 200 μJ.

We compare our algorithm with the state-of-art distributed low latency data collection algorithm for BF-WSNs—DCoSG [15]. Actually, it's the only algorithm solving this problem. The configurations of DCoSG is set referring to the simulations in [15]. The length of beacon phase in DCoSG is set to 1 time slot. The energy consumption is 1 μJ.

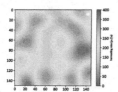 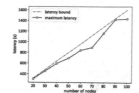 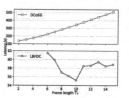

Fig. 2. Harvesting rate distribution example.

Fig. 3. Evaluation of latency bound.

Fig. 4. Impact of frame length.

5.2 Evaluation of Latency Bound

First, we evaluate the theoretical latency bound of LBFDC proved in Sect. 4. We vary the network size from 20 nodes to 100 nodes. In each network size, we simulate 100 networks, then pick the maximum latency to compare it with the upper latency bound. The results are shown in Fig. 3. We can see that the theoretical upper latency bound is very close to the maximum practical latency of LBFDC, which means our bound is accurate.

5.3 Evaluation of LBFDC

Impact of Frame Length. It takes 1 time slot for DCoSG, 5 for LBFDC to harvest enough energy for beacon phase. Thus, the minimum frame lengths of DCoSG and LBFDC are 2 time slots and 6 time slots in Fig. 4, respectively. Every point is the average result of 100 simulations. The latency of DCoSG rises proportionally with increasing frame length. While the latency of LBFDC fluctuates around 58 s. Which means in DCoSG, nodes can't make use of the extended frame length. However in LBFDC, all nodes in transmitter layers have chances to transmit. Thus they can make more use of the extended frame length.

In the following, we set the frame length of DCoSG to 2 time slots, and three different time frame lengths—6, 10 and 15, of LBFDC.

Impact of Network Size. To evaluate the impact of network size, we change the number of nodes from 50 to 550 with a step of 50 in Fig. 5. Every data point is the average result of 100 networks. Both latencies of DCoSG and LBFDC are increasing proportionally as the number of nodes increasing. The latencies of LBFDC with different frame lengths are nearly identical. They outperform DCoSG throughout the simulations. The improvement of LBFDC gets larger in networks with more nodes. In large-scale network with more than 250 nodes, the improvement reaches about 60%. Among LBFDC with three frame lengths, the latencies of $T_f = 10$ and $T_f = 15$ are almost the same. They are smaller than the latency of LBFDC with $T_f = 6$, and the improvement is getting apparent with increasing number of nodes.

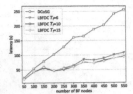
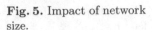
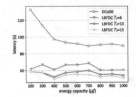
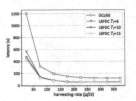

Fig. 5. Impact of network size.

Fig. 6. Impact of energy capacity.

Fig. 7. Impact of energy harvesting rate.

Impact of Energy Capacity. We vary the energy capacity of all nodes in Fig. 6 to evaluate its impact. The latency of DCoSG falls when the energy capacity is lower than $500\,\mu J$, then becomes stable at 90 s. The reason is that when the energy capacity is small, nodes waste much energy due to overflow. When the energy capacity is great, it's enough for nodes to save energy before transmitting or receiving. Thus extra energy capacity reduce the latency of DCoSG. The latency of LBFDC is quite stable when the energy capacity changes. The reason is that nodes in LBFDC can use their harvested energy timely. Although LBFDC performs best with $T_f = 15$, the latencies of LBFDC with three different frame lengths are very close. They all fluctuate around 60 s.

Impact of Energy Harvesting Rate. To evaluate the impact of the energy harvesting rate, we adopt uniform energy harvesting rates varying from $25\,\mu J = s$ to $375\,\mu J = s$ in Fig. 7. Both the latencies of DCoSG and LBFDC decrease quickly when the energy harvesting rate increases from $25\,\mu J = s$ to $125\,\mu J = s$. Then they become stable when the energy harvesting rate is higher than $125\,\mu J = s$. When the energy harvesting rate is great enough, the bottleneck of the energy supply disappears. In this situation, the latency of LBFDC is still about half the latency of DCoSG. Because every time frame, LBFDC allocates more chances to nodes to transmit. Under low energy harvesting rate, the latency of LBFDC with $T_f = 6$ is much higher than LBDC with $T_f = 10$ and $T_f = 15$. When the energy harvesting rate increases, they have nearly the same performance.

6   Conclution

In this paper, we propose a novel distributed algorithm to reduce data collection latency in BF-WSNs—LBFDC. LBFDC contains a cross-layer scheduling algorithm to avoid cross-layer collisions, and an in-layer scheduling algorithm to avoid in-layer collisions. In the meanwhile, LBFDC leverages an adaptive routing strategy so transmitters can select receivers adaptively according to their status. And LBFDC allocates more chances to nodes to transmit every time frame. As a consequence, the latency of LBFDC is much improved compared with the existing method. In the future, we want to study data processing while data collection in BF-WSNs, such as data aggregation and top-k data query.

Acknowledgment. This work is supported by the National Natural Science Foundation of China under Grant NO. 61632010.

References

1. Cai, Z., Chen, Q.: Latency-and-coverage aware data aggregation scheduling for multihop battery-free wireless networks. IEEE Trans. Wirel. Commun. **20**, 1770–1784 (2020)
2. Che, Y.L., Duan, L., Zhang, R.: Spatial throughput maximization of wireless powered communication networks. IEEE J. Sel. Areas Commun. **33**(8), 1534–1548 (2015)
3. Cheng, S., Cai, Z., Li, J.: Curve query processing in wireless sensor networks. IEEE Trans. Veh. Technol. **64**(11), 5198–5209 (2014)
4. Cheng, S., Cai, Z., Li, J., Gao, H.: Extracting kernel dataset from big sensory data in wireless sensor networks. IEEE Trans. Knowl. Data Eng. **29**(4), 813–827 (2016)
5. Choi, H., Wang, J., Hughes, E.A.: Scheduling for information gathering on sensor network. Wireless Netw. **15**(1), 127–140 (2009)
6. Gong, D., Yang, Y.: Low-latency SINR-based data gathering in wireless sensor networks. In: Proceedings of the IEEE INFOCOM 2013, Turin, Italy, 14–19 April 2013, pp. 1941–1949. IEEE (2013)
7. Huang, S.C., Du, H., Park, E.K.: Minimum-latency gossiping in multi-hop wireless networks. In: Jia, X., Shroff, N.B., Wan, P. (eds.) Proceedings of the 9th ACM International Symposium on Mobile Ad Hoc Networking and Computing, MobiHoc 2008, Hong Kong, China, 26–30 May 2008, pp. 323–330. ACM (2008)
8. Kansal, A., Hsu, J., Zahedi, S., Srivastava, M.B.: Power management in energy harvesting sensor networks. ACM Trans. Embedded Comput. Syst. (TECS) **6**(4), 32-es (2007)
9. Li, J., Cheng, S., Cai, Z., Yu, J., Wang, C., Li, Y.: Approximate holistic aggregation in wireless sensor networks. ACM Trans. Sens. Netw. (TOSN) **13**(2), 1–24 (2017)
10. Liu, R., Sinha, P., Koksal, C.E.: Joint energy management and resource allocation in rechargeable sensor networks. In: 29th IEEE International Conference on Computer Communications, Joint Conference of the IEEE Computer and Communications Societies, INFOCOM 2010, San Diego, CA, USA, 15–19 March 2010, pp. 902–910. IEEE (2010)
11. Mehrabi, A., Kim, K.: General framework for network throughput maximization in sink-based energy harvesting wireless sensor networks. IEEE Trans. Mob. Comput. **16**(7), 1881–1896 (2017)
12. Miao, D., Cai, Z., Li, J., Gao, X., Liu, X.: The computation of optimal subset repairs. Proc. VLDB Endow. **13**(12), 2061–2074 (2020)
13. Yao, Q., Huang, A., Shan, H., Quek, T.Q.S., Wang, W.: Delay-aware wireless powered communication networks - energy balancing and optimization. IEEE Trans. Wirel. Commun. **15**(8), 5272–5286 (2016)
14. Zhang, Y., He, S., Chen, J.: Data gathering optimization by dynamic sensing and routing in rechargeable sensor networks. IEEE/ACM Trans. Netw. **24**(3), 1632–1646 (2016)
15. Zhu, T., Li, J., Gao, H., Li, Y.: Latency-efficient data collection scheduling in battery-free wireless sensor networks. ACM Trans. Sens. Netw. **16**(3), 25:1–25:21 (2020)

OD-PPS: An On-Demand Path Planning Scheme for Maximizing Data Completeness in Multi-modal UWSNs

Tao Yu, Chunfeng Liu, Wenyu Qu$^{(\boxtimes)}$, and Zhao Zhao

Tianjin Key Laboratory of Advanced Networking, College of Intelligence and Computing, Tianjin University, Tianjin, China
`wenyu.qu@tju.edu.cn`

Abstract. Data collection based on autonomous underwater vehicle (AUV) brings significant advantages for underwater wireless sensor networks (UWSNs) to save and balance energy consumption. For some marine monitoring applications, not only the value of information (VoI) of the event but also the timeliness of the event needs to be considered in order to collect the sensed event data as comprehensively as possible to ensure the data completeness in the monitoring area. However, existing research works often ignore the latter, which may lead to inaccurate decisions made by marine applications due to missing data completeness. Therefore, in response to the on-demand scenario where events generate dynamically, we propose an on-demand path planning scheme (OD-PPS) to maximize the completeness of the data collected by the AUV. In the scheme, we first apply iterative local search method to obtain a collection order of the nodes. After optimizing the visiting points of the nodes to shorten the path length, a node re-insert algorithm is proposed to reduce the data loss. Then, for new collection requests generated during the AUV collection process, we update the AUV path according to the location of the node that sent the request. Finally, extensive simulations verify the effectiveness of the proposed scheme.

Keywords: Underwater wireless sensor networks · Autonomous underwater vehicle · Data collection · Path planning · Data completeness

1 Introduction

As an effective underwater environment sensing and data transmission technology, underwater wireless sensor networks (UWSNs) have been widely used in environmental monitoring and resource exploration [13]. Compared with traditional UWSNs using single communication method, the transmission performance of UWSNs equipped with multi-modal communication method [4,15] is more prominent. It can take advantage of multiple communication technologies to improve network performance. Common communication technology combinations in multi-modal UWSNs include long-distance low-frequency underwater acoustic communication (UAC) and short-distance high-frequency UAC or

© Springer Nature Switzerland AG 2021
Z. Liu et al. (Eds.): WASA 2021, LNCS 12937, pp. 16–28, 2021.
https://doi.org/10.1007/978-3-030-85928-2_2

underwater wireless optical communication. Making full use of the multi-modal communication capabilities of UWSNs and designing reasonable data collection strategies has become a current research focus.

The sensor nodes that undertake the monitoring tasks have limited energy and are difficult to charge. Therefore, for the multi-hop network structure, the network lifetime cannot be guaranteed. Fortunately, by adopting AUV to collect data without using sensor nodes to undertake the task of forwarding data, the energy consumption of nodes can be effectively reduced. At the same time, with the increasing of marine applications, the diversity of data transmission requirements makes transmission strategies in UWSNs need to have the ability to meet multiple transmission requirements. Therefore, the AUV-assisted collection strategy combined with application requirements has aroused wide interest among researchers.

However, there are still some problems that have not been considered by existing work. In terms of the scenarios of data collection, path planning methods of AUV in the deterministic scenario have been extensively studied [6], where the AUV plans a global data collection path and collects data periodically according to this path during the network operation. These methods of path planning are inefficient in the on-demand data collection scenario [7]. In on-demand scenario, sensor nodes sense randomly generated events in the environment, which requires the AUV to dynamically plan the data collection path according to network demand. From the perspective of data, the transmission delay of data is the most frequently considered factor in the existing AUV path planning research [16]. To reflect the importance of data, AUV path planning based on the value of information (VoI) has also been proposed in recent years [1,4]. Maximizing the VoI is the research focus of these works. However, in some emergency events monitoring applications, data of events not only has VoI but also often has a deadline. If the AUV fails to collect data before the deadline, the data will become meaningless and unnecessary to collect. In this case, the VoI-based path planning method can only enable some high VoI data to be collected in time, but the data completeness of the network application cannot be guaranteed.

Compared to data collection oriented by data VoI, data collection that considers data timeliness requires a shorter path to collect data faster. The moving distance of the AUV can be effectively shortened by utilizing the node communication range, which does not require the AUV to collect data at the location of the node. Based on this consideration, we propose an on-demand path planning scheme (OD-PPS) for the on-demand data collection scenario where sensor nodes sense randomly generated events in the underwater environment. The AUV dynamically plans and updates the collection path according to the data collection requirements in the network. The main goal of the scheme is to enable data to be collected as much as possible before the deadline to ensure data completeness. The main contributions of this paper are as follows:

1) Taking into account the deadline and VoI of the data, the node collection order is constructed by modeling iterative local search algorithm. And a visiting points optimization algorithm utilizing communication range is applied to shorten the AUV path length.

2) For new requests generated during the AUV data collection process, we update the AUV path by performing node insertion on the existing path, which effectively improves the data collection performance.
3) We implemented extensive simulations to validate the effectiveness of our proposed method compared with the other two typical methods.

The remainder of this paper is organized as follows: Sect. 2 gives the system model and problem definition. Our path planning scheme is presented in detail in Sect. 3. In Sect. 4, we evaluate the performance of the scheme proposed in this paper. Finally, Sect. 5 concludes the paper.

2   System Model and Problem Definition

2.1   System Model

In Network Aspect: As illustrated in Fig. 1, a 3D UWSN containing a set S of sensor nodes $\{s_1, s_2, \cdots, s_{|S|}\}$, an AUV and a surface buoy are deployed. To make the network work more efficiently, what we consider is a multi-modal acoustic network [15]. Low-frequency UAC has the characteristics of low transmission rate but long transmission distance. The transmission distance of high-frequency UAC is shorter but the transmission rate is higher [5]. Therefore, short control information can be transmitted by low-frequency UAC, and high-frequency UAC can be used for the node to transmit sensed data to the AUV at a short distance.

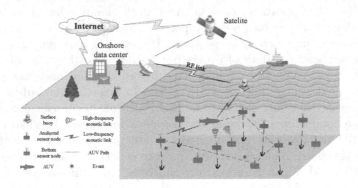

Fig. 1. UWSN model of AUV-based event data collection.

According to network demand, the sensor nodes are equipped with a high-frequency UAC modem H and a low-frequency UAC modem L_1. AUV is equipped with two low-frequency UAC modems L_1, L_2 (orthogonal to each other), and a high-frequency UAC modem H. The communication range of the low-frequency UAC modem covers the entire monitoring area to ensure that request packets and data processing results can be directly transmitted. The communication radius of high-frequency UAC modem is smaller, which defined as R_c. The transmission rate of high-frequency UAC modem is denoted as B.

In Node Aspect: The network consists of two different types of nodes: sensor nodes and AUV. They will complete different tasks according to their role in the network and select the appropriate modem to transmit data.

Sensor Nodes: the nodes perceive event data according to application requirements and send short request packets to the AUV through low-frequency UAC modem L_1. When the AUV approaches the node, the node transmits the data packets of events to the AUV through high-frequency UAC modem H.

AUV: The AUV receives the collection requests sent by nodes through low-frequency UAC modem L_1 and plan a path to collect event data through the high-frequency UAC modem H. Then the AUV processes the event data and sends the processing results to the surface buoy through the low-frequency UAC modem L_2. We denote the initial velocity of the AUV as V_0, and its direction can be controlled by the AUV. However, the actual velocity and movement trajectory of the AUV is usually affected by the ocean current velocity V_c. To control the AUV to move along the shortest straight path, the velocity synthesis method can be adopted [17]. As shown in Fig. 2, O and A represent AUV and target respectively. The velocity of AUV and ocean current can be decomposed into velocity parallel to OA and velocity perpendicular to OA. To keep the AUV moving in the straight path, we need to determine the velocity direction of V_0 in the plane where V_c and OA are located so that $|V_0| * sin(\theta_1)$ is equal to $|V_c| * sin(\theta_2)$, but in the opposite direction. Then, the actual velocity V_{auv} of the AUV moving along the OA is:

$$V_{auv} = V_0 * cos(\theta_1) + V_c * cos(\theta_2) \tag{1}$$

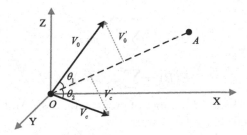

Fig. 2. Velocity synthesis of AUV and ocean current

In Data Aspect: If an event k occurs, the node s_i closest to the event will sense and collect relevant data $p_{i,k}$ about the event. Data $p_{i,k}$ has a value of VoI $V_{i,k}$ to indicate the importance of the event data. It also has a deadline $l'_{i,k}$, which indicates the timeliness of data. If the data is not collected by AUV before the deadline, the completeness of event information in this area will be missing. Once the sensor senses and collects the data of a new event, it will send a data collection request (including node id, data id, VoI and deadline information) to the AUV. According to the received data collection requests, the AUV maintains a set W_s of nodes waiting to be collected. Different events may occur near the same node and be sensed by that node. Therefore, the node in W_s may have more than one event data to be collected. Different event data of each node also has different VoI and deadline. We define Γ^i_{min} as the minimum deadline and Γ^i_{max} as the maximum deadline for the data in s_i. If the arrival time of AUV to s_i is greater than Γ^i_{max}, the AUV cannot collect any data from s_i in time.

2.2   Problem Definition

Due to the unpredictability of future events, when planning the path of AUV, only the nodes in W_s can be used in the current state. We use $P = <v_0, (s_1, v_1), \cdots, (s_i, v_i), \cdots, (s_n, v_n)>$ to represent a possible collection path of nodes in W_s, where v_0 represents the starting position of the AUV. s_i is node to be collected, and v_i is a visiting point within the communication range R_c of s_i, from which AUV can collect the data generated by s_i. Then, the time for AUV to reach s_i in P can be calculated as follows:

$$T_i = T_{i-1} + \frac{size(p_{i-1})}{B} + \frac{d(v_{i-1}, v_i)}{V_{auv}}, i = 1, 2, \ldots, n \qquad (2)$$

where $size(p_{i-1})$ is the volume of data collected by the AUV at the previous node. $d(v_{i-1}, v_i)$ represents the distance between v_{i-1} and v_i. V_{auv} is the actual velocity calculated by the velocity synthesis method based on the ocean current velocity. When $i = 1$, T_{i-1} denotes the departure time of the AUV. Then, we define binary variable $w_{i,k}$ to indicate whether the data $p_{i,k}$ of the event k sensed by s_i can be collected before the deadline. When $T_i \leq \Gamma_{i,k}$, $w_{i,k} = 1$, otherwise $w_{i,k} = 0$. Therefore, the number of event data that AUV can collect in time from s_i and P are:

$$\varphi(s_i) = \sum_{k=1}^{m_i} w_{i,k} \qquad (3)$$

$$E(P) = \sum_{i=1}^{n} \varphi(s_i) \qquad (4)$$

where m_i represents the total number of event data in s_i. And $E_{max} = \sum_{i=1}^{n} m_i$ is the maximum value that $E(P)$ can reach.

According to the analysis, three cases need to be considered when planning the data collection path:

- case 1: All data can be collected in time under any path $E(P) = E_{max}$.
- case 2: No matter how the path is planned, there will always be some data that cannot be collected in time $E(P) < E_{max}$.
- case 3: Some data cannot be collected in time under some paths, but after reasonable path planning, all data can be collected in time.

In case 1, when all the data can be collected in time, a shorter path should be planned to reduce the time spent in collecting data. To collect as much data as possible in time is the objective considered in case 2. Case 3 is a transition from case 2 to case 1. In order to unify the three cases, the objective function is defined as:

$$\max \left(E(P) + \alpha * (1 - \frac{D(P)}{D_{max}}) + (1 - \alpha) * \frac{V(P)}{V_{max}} \right) \tag{5}$$

where $\alpha = 1$ or 0. $D(P) = \sum_{i=1}^{n} d(v_{i-1}, v_i)$ denotes the total length of path P. $D_{max} = \sum_{i=1}^{n} d_{max}$ is the theoretical maximum length of path P. $V_{max} = \sum_{i=1}^{n} \sum_{k=1}^{m_i} V_{i,k}$ is the total VoI when all data is collected in time. $V(P) = \sum_{i=1}^{n} \sum_{k=1}^{m_i} V_{i,k} * w_{i,k}$ represents the total VoI of the event data collected by the AUV under path P.

Both $1 - D(P)/D_{max}$ and $V(P)/V_{max}$ belong to $[0, 1]$. If there is event data that can be collected in time, then $E(P) \geq 1$. Therefore, $E(P)$ is the main factor in the objective function. When $\alpha = 1$, the objective function is applicable to case 1. In the process of iterative local search, it can make the path evolve in a shorter direction while ensuring that all data can be collected in time. When $\alpha = 0$, the objective function is applicable to case 2. $E(P)$ ensures that the path improves in the direction of collecting more data in time. The effect of $V(P)/V_{max}$ is that when $E(P_1) = E(P_2)$ of two paths, the path with larger VoI will be selected.

3   Proposed OD-PPS Scheme

Our scheme includes two parts. In Sect. 3.1, a low-complexity strategy based on the iterative local search is designed to plan the collection path of existing nodes in W_s. In Sect. 3.2, we describe the processing of new data collection requests received by the AUV during the data collection process.

3.1   Path Planning of Existing Nodes

In this part, a method for planning a path to collect data from existing nodes is proposed, which includes three steps: node collection order, path length optimization, and node re-insert.

Node Collection Order: We take the location of each sensor node as the visiting point for AUV to collect the data of the node, and obtain the data collection order of the nodes in W_s based on iterative local search [9]. Two low-complexity local search algorithms or-opt [11] and 2-opt [3] are adopted. The or-opt local search moves a chain of consecutive nodes to the middle of the other two nodes to get the neighborhood path of the current path P. In 2-opt, the neighborhood path of P can be obtained by replacing edges (s_i, s_{i+1}) and (s_j, s_{j+1}) with edges (s_i, s_j) and (s_{i+1}, s_{j+1}), and reversing the order of nodes between nodes s_{i+1} and s_j.

Based on these two local search methods, the node collection order is optimized by iteration. As shown in Algorithm 1, an initial collection order P_{init}

Algorithm 1. Iterative Local Search Algorithm

1: **Input:** location of AUV, set W_s of nodes to be collected;
2: **Output:** a nodes collection order P_{basic};
3: **Initialization:** sorting Γ^i_{min} of each node in W_s in ascending order to construct an initial path P_{init};
4: Set $P_0 = P_{init}$ and $t = 0$;
5: **for** $i = 1$ to 2 **do**
6: **repeat**
7:   **if** $i = 1$ **then**
8:    Search all neighborhood paths $N(P_t)$ of P_t through *or-opt*;
9:   **else**
10:   Search all neighborhood paths $N(P_t)$ of P_t through *2-opt*;
11: **end if**
12: Find the path P'_t with the maximum OFV in $N(P_t)$;
13: **if** $OFV(P'_t) > OFV(P_t)$ **then**
14:   Set $P_{t+1} = P'_t$ and $t = t + 1$;
15: **end if**
16: **until** no improvement
17: **end for**
18: $P_{basic} = P_t$;
19: **return** P_{basic};

---

is constructed by sorting the minimum deadline Γ^i_{min} of each node in W_s from small to large. In each iteration, we first apply or-opt to get all the neighborhood paths $N(P_t)$ of the current path P_t. Then, path P'_t with the largest Objective Function Value (OFV) in $N(P_t)$ is selected and compared with the OFV of the current path P_t. If it is better than P_t, current path is replaced. Otherwise, it indicates that a local optimal path has been reached through or-opt iterative local search. To explore whether there is a better path, we use 2-opt local search to repeat the previous process based on the results of or-opt.

Path Length Optimization: As shown in Fig. 3, the length of a path can be effectively shortened by finding a visiting point within the communication range of each node as the visiting location of the AUV. Despite the distance for the node to transmit data to the AUV may increase and thus may lead to more attenuation of communication signal, the side effect for the data transmission is still negligible within the communication range.

For an initial path $P_b = \ <v_0, (s_1, v_1), \cdots, (s_i, v_i), \cdots, (s_n, v_n)>$, where v_i represents the initial visiting point corresponding to each node. In order to shorten the path length, we improve the method in [10] to update v_i to the optimal position. On the local path, there are two cases for calculating the optimal visiting points of the nodes. In case 1, each node s_i from s_1 to s_{n-1} has a visiting point v_{i-1} in front and an visiting point v_{i+1} behind it. The optimal location of visiting point v_i is to minimize $d(v_{i-1}, v_i) + d(v_i, v_{i+1})$ while satisfying

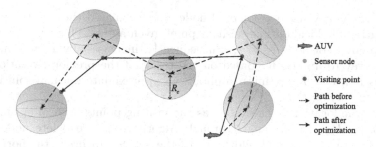

Fig. 3. Utilize visiting points to shorten the path. Dotted line: path with nodes as the visiting points. Solid line: path after optimizing the visiting points.

that v_i is within the communication range of s_i. It can be obtained by solving the following nonlinear programming:

$$\min \quad d(v_{i-1}, v_i) + d(v_i, v_{i+1}) \tag{6}$$

$$s.t. \quad d(v_i, s_i) \leq R_c \tag{7}$$

In case 2, there is no node after the last node s_n in the path. The optimal position of v_n is obtained by solving $min\ d(v_{n-1}, v_n)$ with constraint $d(v_n, s_n) \leq R_c$.

On the global path, Algorithm 2 is executed on the given initial path P_b to shorten the total distance. The basic idea of Algorithm 2 is to optimize node by node and perform multiple iterations. The process of each iteration is as follows:

Algorithm 2. Visiting Points Optimization Algorithm

1: **Input:** initial path P_b;
2: **Output:** path P_{opt} after optimizing visiting points;
3: **for** $k = 1$ to I_{num} **do**
4:     **for** $i = 1$ to n **do**
5:         **if** $i \leq n - 1$ **then**
6:             $v_i' = CalculateVisitingPoint(v_{i-1}, s_i, v_{i+1}, R_c)$;
7:         **else**
8:             $v_i' = CalculateVisitingPoint(v_{i-1}, s_i, R_c)$;
9:         **end if**
10:        $v_i = v_i'$;
11:    **end for**
12: **end for**
13: $P_{opt} = P_b$;
14: **return** P_{opt};

First, set the initial loop variable $i = 1$ to optimize for the first visiting point. Taking the triple information (v_{i-1}, s_i, v_{i+1}) and the communication radius R_c

as input, the new visiting point v_i' of node s_i is calculated through the method of calculating the local optimal visiting point given above. Then, we update the visiting point v_i of node s_i to v_i'. Subsequently, increase i by 1 in turn, using the same way to update v_i. Based on the result of the previous iteration, the process is repeated I_{num} times to obtain an approximate optimal solution for the visiting points.

Taking the location of each node as the visiting points, a local optimal collection order P_{basic} is obtained through Algorithm 1. We delete nodes with $\varphi(s_i) = 0$ from P_{basic}, and add them to the set S_r. In order to shorten the path length, we take P_{basic} as the input and execute Algorithm 2 to optimize the visiting point of each node. The optimization result is recorded as P_{opt}.

Node Re-insert: The path length of P_{opt} is shorter than P_{basic}, which means that the data of nodes in P_{opt} can be collected earlier. If $S_r \neq \emptyset$, the nodes in S_r can be re-inserted into P_{opt}. Based on the consideration that the node with a larger deadline is more likely to be re-inserted into the path, each time we take out the node s_x with the largest Γ_{max}^i from S_r. Insert s_x between two adjacent nodes s_{i-1} and s_i in P_{opt}, and record it as P_{opt}'. The location of node s_x is used as the visiting point of s_x, and the visiting points of other nodes in the path remain unchanged. Then we take P_{opt}' as input and execute Algorithm 2 to update the visiting points to obtain the path P_{opt}''. If P_{opt}'' satisfies the following two conditions: (1) $\varphi(s_x) \geq 1$; (2) $E(P_{opt}'') > E(P_{opt})$, then it is feasible. Among all the feasible paths, we choose the one with the smallest increase in path length and use it as the current path P_{opt}. Conversely, if there is no feasible insertion position, s_x is discarded. Then repeat the process until the set S_r is empty.

After executing the path planing algorithm in this section, we get a path P_{opt} based on the nodes in W_s. Then, the AUV collects data following this path.

3.2   Processing of New Requests

In the process of AUV collecting data according to the planned path P_{opt}, new events may generate in the environment. They will be sensed by nodes, so new data collection requests will be sent to AUV.

If a new request comes from a node s_i that will be collected in the current path P_{opt}, no changes are required for the data collection path. When the AUV reaches node s_i in P_{opt}, the data of new event will be collected by the way. Another type of new request comes from a node s_{new} that is not in the current path P_{opt}. Although s_{new} is not in P_{opt}, its position may be close to the path. Therefore, inserting it into a suitable position in the path will not increase the length of the AUV movement too much, and may not affect the data collection of other nodes in the P_{opt}.

For s_{new}, we need to insert it into the best position in P_{opt} with the smallest path length increase and update the visiting points, which can be achieved through the node insertion method described in Sect. 3.1. If there are no feasible insertion positions, the node s_{new} is added to the set W_s for the next round of data collection.

4   Performance Evaluation

In this section, two typical data collection schemes MWSF [14] and GAAP [4] are compared with the scheme OD-PPS proposed in this paper.

4.1   Simulation Scenario and Settings

According to the results in [14], the weight in MWSF is set to 0.1 to get its best performance. To make simulation more realistic, a multi-layer current model [8,12] that can simulate thermohaline circulation and deep ocean currents is used. In this model, the water flow is impelled by the density and temperature gradient to flow at a constant velocity and direction at a certain depth. And as the depth increases, the current velocity gradually decreases. In the simulation, we divide the network into 5 layers with 2000 m as a layer and set the maximum current velocity to 0.8 m/s.

In each run, we generate 200 events in the monitoring area one by one in a Poisson process with parameter λ. Therefore, the time interval between adjacent events obeys an exponential distribution with mean equal to $1/\lambda$. $1/\lambda$ reflects the generation speed of event. For simplicity, we assume that among all nodes that perceive the same event, only the node closest to the event will record the data of event and send a data collection request. Based on the feature that the generation probability of important data is smaller [2], for each event data, we assign a VoI value from $\{20, 10, 5, 2\}$ with the corresponding probability $\{0.1, 0.2, 0.3, 0.4\}$. Other detailed parameters are summarized in Table 1.

Table 1. Simulation parameters

Parameter	Value	Parameter	Value
Deployment area size	2 km * 2 km * 1 km	Data volume of event $p_{i,k}$	128 kbit
Number of nodes $|S|$	40–140	Communication rate B	31.2 kbit/s
Number of iterations I_{num}	10	Deadline of data $\Gamma_{i,k}$	80 min
Transmission radius R_c	200 m–400 m	Initial velocity of AUV V_0	1.8 m/s

4.2   Simulation Results

Our result is an average of 300 experiments. And we evaluate the performance of all schemes from the following three metrics:

Completeness Ratio: It is defined as the ratio of the number of event data collected by AUV in time to the total number of events generated.

Total VoI: It is the total VoI of the data collected by AUV.

Throughput: The number of event data collected by AUV in a given time.

Figure 4 shows the completeness ratio of the three methods under different network parameters. The results of different $1/\lambda$ are shown in Fig. 4(a). We can see that OD-PPS achieves the best completeness ratio among the three methods. This is because our method always plans a global path according to the requests under the current network state and optimizes the visiting points of the path. Moreover, the completeness ratio of the three methods increases as the generation speed of the event decreases. The reason is that the waiting time of the requests is shorter when the event generation speed is slow.

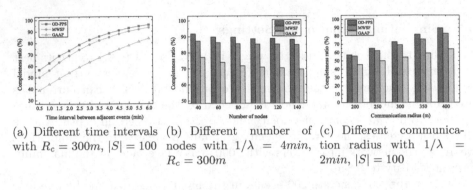

(a) Different time intervals with $R_c = 300m$, $|S| = 100$

(b) Different number of nodes with $1/\lambda = 4min$, $R_c = 300m$

(c) Different communication radius with $1/\lambda = 2min$, $|S| = 100$

Fig. 4. Performance of completeness ratio under different parameters

Figure 4(b) presents the results under different number of nodes. OD-PPS achieves a data completeness ratio of at least 3% more than MWSF and 14% more than GAAP under all the number of nodes. It is worth noting that the performance of the three methods only slightly decreases as the node density increases. The reason is that when the node density decreases, the distance between nodes increases, so the number of nodes that AUV can visit in a given time decreases. At the same time, the possibility of a node having data of multiple events increases, so the average number of event data collected by the AUV from one node increases. Two factors interact to cause this result.

In Fig. 4(c), we observe that OD-PPS has the best completeness ratio performance under all communication radius. The completeness ratio of OD-PPS is about 11.4% higher than that of GAAP at $R_c = 200$ m. This gap increases to 25.2% at $R_c = 400$ m. This is because our method optimizes the visiting points in the path. Therefore, compared with MWSF and GAAP, the effect of shortening the path of OD-PPS is better as the communication radius increases.

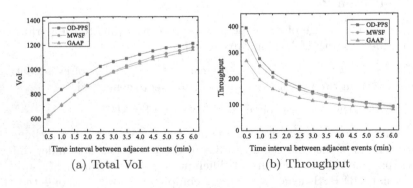

(a) Total VoI

(b) Throughput

Fig. 5. Performance of VoI and throughput under different $1/\lambda$

In addition to the completeness ratio, we also explored the effectiveness of our method from the perspective of VoI and throughput. The results are shown in Fig. 5, where the settings of R_c and $|S|$ are the same as those in Fig. 4(a). Figure 5(a) shows that OD-PPS also performed best on the total VoI. The total VoI collected by OD-PPS is 19% higher than MWSF and GAAP at $1/\lambda = 0.5$. The reason why MWSF collects more data than GAAP (Fig. 4(a)) but the total VoI is similar to GAAP is due to different strategies. GAAP always collects node with higher VoI first, while MWSF plans the path based on node distance and data deadline. Figure 5(b) shows the throughput of data collected by AUV. The unit of throughput is expressed as the number of event data that can be collected by AUV in 10 h. We notice that the throughput of the three methods increases as the generation speed of the event increases. This is because the distance between nodes with data decreases. Moreover, compared with the greedy methods of MWSF and GAAP, our method plans the path from a global perspective. Therefore, the performance gap between the other two methods and OD-PPS is greater under high generation speed of event. Conversely, the slower the event generation, the collection capability of AUV gradually approaches the generation speed of event. Therefore, the throughput of the three methods is also gradually approaching.

5 Conclusions

In this paper, by considering the data completeness, we proposed an AUV path planning scheme that collects data in on-demand scenario. In detail, we applied iterative local search, visiting points optimization algorithm, and nodes re-insert to obtain the AUV path with good collection order and shorter length. In addition, new requests are handled appropriately based on the location of the node. Simulation is performed to compare our proposed method with the other two typical methods. The simulation results show that our method is higher than the comparison algorithm in the completeness ratio, VoI, and throughput. In future work, we will consider the energy factor based on this work.

Acknowledgment. This research was supported in part by the National Natural Science Foundation of China-Guangdong Joint Fund under Grant No. U1701263, the National Natural Science Foundation of China (NSFC) under Grant No. 61871286, and Tianjin Key Laboratory of Advanced Networking (TANK).

References

1. Basagni, S., Bölöni, L., Gjanci, P., Petrioli, C., Phillips, C.A., Turgut, D.: Maximizing the value of sensed information in underwater wireless sensor networks via an autonomous underwater vehicle. In: IEEE Conference on Computer Communications, pp. 988–996. IEEE (2014)
2. Cheng, C.F., Li, L.H.: Data gathering problem with the data importance consideration in underwater wireless sensor networks. J. Netw. Comput. Appl. **78**, 300–312 (2017)

3. Croes, G.A.: A method for solving traveling-salesman problems. Oper. Res. **6**(6), 791–812 (1958)
4. Gjanci, P., Petrioli, C., Basagni, S., Phillips, C.A., Bölöni, L., Turgut, D.: Path finding for maximum value of information in multi-modal underwater wireless sensor networks. IEEE Trans. Mob. Comput. **17**(2), 404–418 (2017)
5. Hajenko, T., Benson, C.: The high frequency underwater acoustic channel. In: OCEANS 2010 IEEE SYDNEY, pp. 1–3. IEEE (2010)
6. Han, G., Long, X., Zhu, C., Guizani, M., Zhang, W.: A high-availability data collection scheme based on multi-AUVs for underwater sensor networks. IEEE Trans. Mob. Comput. **19**(5), 1010–1022 (2019)
7. He, L., Yang, Z., Pan, J., Cai, L., Xu, J., Gu, Y.: Evaluating service disciplines for on-demand mobile data collection in sensor networks. IEEE Trans. Mob. Comput. **13**(4), 797–810 (2013)
8. Liu, C., Zhao, Z., Qu, W., Qiu, T., Sangaiah, A.K.: A distributed node deployment algorithm for underwater wireless sensor networks based on virtual forces. J. Syst. Architect. **97**, 9–19 (2019)
9. Lourenço, H.R., Martin, O.C., Stützle, T.: Iterated local search: framework and applications. In: Gendreau, M., Potvin, J.-Y. (eds.) Handbook of Metaheuristics. ISORMS, vol. 272, pp. 129–168. Springer, Cham (2019). https://doi.org/10.1007/978-3-319-91086-4_5
10. Nesamony, S., Vairamuthu, M.K., Orlowska, M.E., Sadiq, S.W.: On optimal route computation of mobile sink in a wireless sensor network. Technical report 465, School of ITEE, The University of Queensland (2006)
11. Or, I.: Traveling salesman-type combinatorial problems and their relation to the logistics of regional blood banking. Ph.D. thesis, Northwestern University, Evanston, IL (1976)
12. Pompili, D., Melodia, T., Akyildiz, I.F.: Three-dimensional and two-dimensional deployment analysis for underwater acoustic sensor networks. Ad Hoc Netw. **7**(4), 778–790 (2009)
13. Qiu, T., Zhao, Z., Zhang, T., Chen, C., Chen, C.P.: Underwater internet of things in smart ocean: system architecture and open issues. IEEE Trans. Industr. Inf. **16**(7), 4297–4307 (2019)
14. Somasundara, A.A., Ramamoorthy, A., Srivastava, M.B.: Mobile element scheduling for efficient data collection in wireless sensor networks with dynamic deadlines. In: IEEE International Real-Time Systems Symposium, pp. 296–305. IEEE (2004)
15. Zhao, Z., Liu, C., Qu, W., Yu, T.: An energy efficiency multi-level transmission strategy based on underwater multimodal communication in UWSNs. In: IEEE Conference on Computer Communications, pp. 1579–1587. IEEE (2020)
16. Zheng, H., Wang, N., Wu, J.: Minimizing deep sea data collection delay with autonomous underwater vehicles. J. Parallel Distrib. Comput. **104**, 99–113 (2017)
17. Zhu, D., Huang, H., Yang, S.X.: Dynamic task assignment and path planning of multi-AUV system based on an improved self-organizing map and velocity synthesis method in three-dimensional underwater workspace. IEEE Trans. Cybern. **43**(2), 504–514 (2013)

Improving WiFi Fingerprint Positioning Through Smartphone Built-In Sensors Based Trajectory Estimation

Zhenjie Ma, Ke Shi[✉] [iD], Xiaomei Song, and Aihua Zhang

School of Computer Science and Technology, Huazhong University of Science and Technology, Wuhan 430074, China
keshi@hust.edu.cn

Abstract. Wireless indoor localization is fundamental to many smartphone applications, appealing to a great deal of research efforts in the past decades. Among them, RSSI based fingerprinting using existing WiFi infrastructures has become an increasingly popular technique. However, WiFi fingerprinting still suffers from the vulnerable and changeable wireless signal transmissions. To address this issue, we propose a novel smartphone built-in sensors assisted WiFi fingerprinting method. The data generated from the smartphone built-in sensors such as accelerometer and gyroscope is utilized to estimate the user's trajectory. Then an integrated probability model combining the RSSI fingerprint and users' trajectory is established to implement fingerprint-location match. Performance evaluation results show that the proposed method has higher location accuracy and better adaption to changeable environment.

Keywords: RSSI fingerprint · Built-in sensors · Trajectory estimation · Integrated probability model · Indoor Positioning

1 Introduction

The popularity of mobile and pervasive computing stimulates extensive research on wireless indoor localization. Now the solutions based on pervasive WiFi infrastructure has dominated this field. Received Signal Strength Indicator (RSSI) [1] based localization technique is one of the cheapest and easiest methods to implement. However, RSSI is extracted from the radio frequency signal at a per packet level and tends to fluctuate according to changes in the environment or multipath fading.

To address this issue, RSSI-based fingerprinting [2, 3] is proposed, which uses a two-stage mechanism. In offline phase, the signal strengths at the predefined RP (Reference Point) from several access points are recorded and stored in a database along with their coordinates. During the online locating, the current RSSI vector at an unknown location is compared to those stored in the database and the user location is estimated though some close match.

WiFi fingerprinting still suffers from the vulnerable and changeable wireless signal transmissions. Any changes of the environment may change the fingerprint, which make

© Springer Nature Switzerland AG 2021
Z. Liu et al. (Eds.): WASA 2021, LNCS 12937, pp. 29–40, 2021.
https://doi.org/10.1007/978-3-030-85928-2_3

the fingerprint obtained in online location different with the fingerprint stored in the database during the offline survey.

Nowadays, smartphones are equipped with various functional built-in sensors such as IMU (inertial measuring unit). An IMU usually consists of the sensors like accelerometer, gyroscope, and compass, which respectively reveal the acceleration, rotational velocity, and direction of user motion. From IMU measurements, user's moving trajectory can be estimated.

The main idea of this paper is to improve the localization accuracy of WiFi fingerprinting by leveraging the user's trajectory information obtained from the built-in sensors to determine the best location match during the online location. Besides fingerprint similarity, user's trajectory is used to evaluate the location result to prevent possible deviation caused by unstable RSSI information. An integrated probability model is proposed, which utilizes the results and estimated errors of RSSI matching and trajectory estimation to give the final position.

2 Related Work

Many approaches have been proposed to implement the WiFi fingerprinting matching process such as RADAR [2] and Horus [3]. Machine learning technique such as SVM (Support Vector Machines) is also proposed, which utilize data filtering rules obtained through statistical analysis to improve the quality of training samples and thus improve the quality of positioning model [4].

Multi-sensor infusion based methods are proposed to improve the positioning accuracy, especially utilizing the IMU already embedded in the most smartphones. Kalman filter [5] and its extension [6] are proposed to combine WiFi positioning with PDR (Pedestrian Dead Reckoning) positioning. It is hard for these methods to adapt the complex indoor environment.

Particle filter based methods [7, 8] are proposed to add motion constrains to the positioning model. However, the particle filter is unsuitable for real-time smartphone positioning as it is computationally expensive and time-consuming.

Besides RSSI, many researches use CSI (Channel State Information) [9] fingerprint to improve positioning accuracy. Compared with RSSI, CSI can provide multi-channel subcarrier phase and amplitude information to better describe the propagation path of the signal. However, collecting CSI needs modifying operating system kernel and customizing hardware drivers, which limits its applications significantly.

Motivated by recent advances in deep learning, some researchers utilize deep learning based models such as CNN to overcome limitations of fingerprint-based localization approaches [10, 11]. But these approaches suffer from the limitation of training labels and only work well at the certain scenario.

Therefore, we still focus on utilizing RSSI and IMU measurements that are widely available to improve the positioning accuracy. We build an integrated probability model combining the RSSI-based positioning with user's trajectory in a lightweight way that makes it more suitable for resource-limited smartphones. It can improve the positioning accuracy and adapt the changeable environment.

3 Proposed Method

3.1 Overview

Figure 1 Trajectory estimation assisted WiFi Fingerprinting. shows the framework of trajectory estimation assisted WiFi Fingerprinting, which consists of three modules, RSSI matching, trajectory estimation, and integrated probability model.

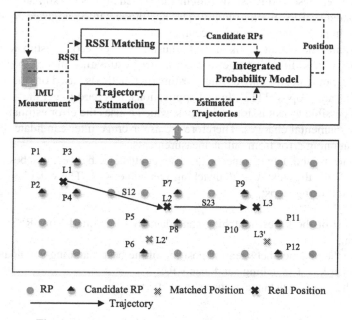

Fig. 1. Trajectory estimation assisted WiFi fingerprinting.

RSSI matching module takes RSSI vector as input and outputs a list of candidate RPs with corresponding probabilities. As shown in Fig. 1, when a user is at location *L1*, *L2*, and *L3*, RSSI matching module outputs candidate RPs list {*P1*, *P2*, *P3*, *P4*}, {*P5*, *P6*, *P7*, *P8*}, and {*P9*, *P10*, *RP11*, *RP12*} respectively. Due to signal fluctuation, some RPs that have large deviations from the actual positions may be selected as candidate RPs. For example, *P6* is selected as candidate RP, which cause the estimated position *L2'* and the actual location *L2* have a large deviation. There is also a large deviation between *L3'* and *L3* since *P12* is selected.

Trajectory estimation modules utilizes the IMU measurements to get the user's trajectory between the consecutive positions. As shown in Fig. 1, *S12* is the estimated trajectory between *L1* and *L2* and *S23* is the estimated trajectory between *L2* and *L3*.

Integrated probability model uses estimated trajectory to amend the selected candidate RPs list and determines the final position. The reachability of selected RP can be evaluated based on estimated trajectory. We can remove the RP with low reachability from candidate list or reduce its contribution to the final positioning result according its reachability. For example, given the trajectory *S12*, a user is unlikely to reach *P6*. Its probability can be reduced greatly, which makes the final positioning result is closer to the actual position.

3.2 RSSI Matching

Trajectory estimation assisted WiFi Fingerprinting does not require a specialized RSSI matching algorithm. The only demand is the matching outcome should be a likelihood of various RPs given observed RSSI measurements, which allows to estimate the centroid of the all candidate RPs as the solution. The likelihood can be adjusted by trajectory estimation to improve the positioning accuracy.

To determine the extent of likelihood adjustment, we need to estimate the RSSI matching error. It is difficult to get a precise error estimating model in changeable environments. Some positioning accuracy estimating methods based on offline training data analyzing are proposed [12]. In real applications, it is hard to get the training data covering all possible transmission conditions, which causes the error estimation cannot adapt to environmental changes. Therefore we use average inter-candidate distance to infer the positioning error from online measurements.

Average inter-candidate distance is the average distance between the best matching candidate RP and the next $k - 1$ matching candidate RPs. The calculating process contains the following steps:

1. Get the list of the k best matching candidate RPs outputted from RSSI matching algorithm;
2. Compute the distance between the position of the best matching candidate RP and all the other $k - 1$ matching candidate RPs;
3. Return the average distance as the estimated error, ε_{fp}.

3.3 Trajectory Estimation

Nowadays almost all smartphones have built-in IMU. Users' orientation and velocity can be determined with the measurements provided by accelerometers and gyroscopes, and then the relationships between the users' position and a known starting point can be derived. It is known as inertial navigation, which can be used to track user's trajectory.

The built-in sensors are noisy, which brings tiny errors in the measurement of acceleration in inertial navigation. What's more, errors are integrated into progressively large errors in velocity and even larger in position. This process is called integration drift. In order to avoid errors accumulation caused by integration drift, instead of directly integrating acceleration twice over time, we count the steps through analyzing the acceleration changing pattern when user walking. The step length is proportional to acceleration changing in the direction that is perpendicular to the moving direction. This relation can be utilized to determine the length of each step. The distance can be obtained by estimating the number of steps and the length of each step. Owing to high sampling frequency of gyroscope, integrating its measuring value over time to get orientation only causes small errors, so we utilize the gyroscope to estimate the user's orientation.

Obviously, it is inevitable that there will be deviations in the estimation of walking distance and orientation, which cause the error between estimated trajectory and real trajectory. We use ε_{dis} to represent this error. From previous research [13] and our own experiments, the estimation errors are decided by users' motion smoothness. We can define motion smoothing factor ϕ as follows:

$$\phi = \frac{\mu}{\delta} \tag{1}$$

where μ represents user's average speed and δ represents the mean square variation of user's speed. By using data fitting, ε_{dis} can be derived as follows:

$$\varepsilon_{\mathrm{dis}} = \frac{a}{\phi} + b \tag{2}$$

The values of a and b can be calculated by using the result of data fitting as shown in Fig. 2. Relationship between error and smoothing factor.

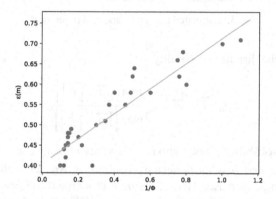

Fig. 2. Relationship between error and smoothing factor.

3.4 Integrated Probability Model

After obtaining the user's trajectory and its error, we propose an integrated probability model fusing the estimated trajectory and RSSI to improve the localization accuracy.

Integrating the Estimated Trajectory from Previous Location to Current Location As shown in the left part of Fig. 3, there may be deviations between the real trajectory $\vec{b}$ and the estimated trajectory $\vec{a}$, we need to compute the conditional probability of the real trajectory given the estimated trajectory, $P_{dsp}\left(\vec{b}\,/\,\vec{a}\right)$, which consists of two parts, the distance probability $P_{dst}\left(\vec{b}\,/\,\vec{a}\right)$ and the orientation probability $P_{dir}\left(\vec{b}\,/\,\vec{a}\right)$.

First, there are some constraints that the proposed distance probability model must conform to:

1. The distance difference $\|\vec{a}\| - \|\vec{b}\|$ is positively related with the distance probability.

2. When the value of $\|\vec{a}\| - \|\vec{b}\|$ is fixed, the longer the distance is, the larger the probability is.
3. Since the error of the estimated distance is mainly derived from the estimation of strides, the positive difference has the same probability with the negative difference. Thus, we can get the formula as: $P_{dst}\left(\vec{b} \big/ \vec{a}\right) = P_{dst}\left(\vec{a} \big/ \vec{b}\right)$.

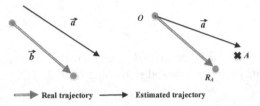

Real trajectory ⟶ Estimated trajectory

Fig. 3. Estimated trajectory and real trajectory.

We can define the distance probability as:

$$P_{dst}\left(\vec{b} \big/ \vec{a}\right) = \frac{\min\left\{\left|\vec{a}\right|, \left|\vec{b}\right|\right\}}{\max\left\{\left|\vec{a}\right|, \left|\vec{b}\right|\right\}} \tag{3}$$

Similarly, the probability of orientation also has the following constraints: the smaller the angle between $\vec{a}$ and $\vec{b}$ is, the larger the probability is. And the probability decreases rapidly while the angle increases. Hence, $\cos\langle a, b\rangle$ is adopted to indicate the probability of orientation. When angle difference is greater than 90°, it could lead to the negative value. So we set the probability value to 0 to avoid negative value in this situation. It isM reasonable since this situation occurs very rarely. Therefore, the orientation probability can be calculated as:

$$P_{dir}\left(\vec{b} \big/ \vec{a}\right) = \begin{cases} \cos\langle a, b\rangle, & \langle a, b\rangle \in \left[0, \frac{\pi}{2}\right] \\ 0, & \langle a, b\rangle \notin \left[0, \frac{\pi}{2}\right] \end{cases} \tag{4}$$

Since distance information is derived from accelerator and orientation information is stemmed from gyroscope, we can assume distance probability and orientation probability are independent. Thus, $P_{dsp}\left(\vec{b} \big/ \vec{a}\right)$ can be calculated as:

$$P_{dsp}\left(\vec{b} \big/ \vec{a}\right) = \begin{cases} \frac{\min\left\{\left|\vec{a}\right|, \left|\vec{b}\right|\right\}}{\max\left\{\left|\vec{a}\right|, \left|\vec{b}\right|\right\}} \cos\langle\vec{a}, \vec{b}\rangle, & \langle a, b\rangle \in \left[0, \frac{\pi}{2}\right] \\ 0, & \langle a, b\rangle \notin \left[0, \frac{\pi}{2}\right] \end{cases} \tag{5}$$

As depicted in the right part of Fig. 3, when a user walks from a known location O to destination A, we can get an estimated trajectory $\vec{a}$ by using the method proposed in previous section. Through RSSI matching, we also can get a candidate RP R_A and its matching probability $P_{pf}\left(\overrightarrow{OR_A}\right) = P_{pf}\left(R_A/s_A\right)$ where s_A is the RSSI vector measured and collected at A. The integrated probability can be defined as:

$$P_{com}\left(\overrightarrow{OR_A}\right) = (1 - \alpha)P_{pf}\left(\overrightarrow{OR_A}\right) + \alpha P_{dsp}\left(\overrightarrow{OR_A}\Big/\vec{a}\right) \qquad (6)$$

where α represents the contribution of the estimated trajectory probability to the integrated probability. Its value is determined by the ratio of the accuracy of estimated trajectory versus the accuracy of RSSI matching. Since we use ε_{fp} and ε_{dis} to represent the error of RSSI matching and estimated trajectory respectively, α should satisfy:

$$\frac{\varepsilon_{fp}}{\varepsilon_{dis}} = \frac{\alpha}{1 - \alpha} \qquad (7)$$

Integrating the Estimated Trajectory Containing Multiple Locations

The positioning accuracy can be improved by integrating the estimated trajectory from previous location to current location. However, if there is a large error in previous location, the improvement may be limited. We now utilize the historical path containing multiple locations to improve the positioning accuracy further.

In RSSI-based positioning, the k candidate RPs with the highest matching probability can be obtained from each measurement at the online phase, it may lead to multiple candidate paths as shown in Fig. 4. One candidate path can be represented by the points gathered from each measurement at online phase, $[p_1, p_2, ..., p_n]$, where p_i is the candidate RP for the ith measurement. We can express a path as a vector $path = [\overrightarrow{p_1 p_2}, \overrightarrow{p_2 p_3}, ..., \overrightarrow{p_{n-1} p_n}]$, where $\overrightarrow{p_{i-1} p_i}$ represents the path segment corresponding to the estimated trajectory p_{i-1} to p_i.

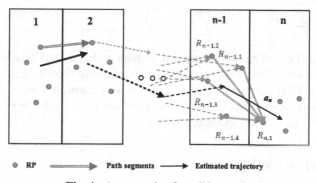

Fig. 4. An example of candidate paths

Considering the measurement is independent of each other, every segment of path can also be regarded as independent. Consequently, the probability of candidate path is

$$P_{com}(path) = P_{pf}\left(p_1/s_1\right) \prod_{i=2}^{n} P_{com}\left(\overrightarrow{p_{i-1} p_i}\right) \qquad (8)$$

where n represents the total times of measurement, and represents the matching probability of RP p_1. By setting a virtual predecessor p_0 to the first RP p_1, the above equation can be generalized as:

$$P_{com}(path) = \prod_{i=1}^{n} P_{com}(\overrightarrow{p_{i-1}p_i}) \tag{9}$$

where $P_{com}(\overrightarrow{p_0p_1}) = P_{gf}(p_0/s_1)$.

After defining probability of candidate path, the next step is to compute the probability of candidate points. Intuitively, current candidate point can be reached through many paths from prior RP when user is walking in the indoor environment. Thus, the probability of current candidate point can be deduced as:

$$P(R) = \sum_{path \in PATH(R)} P_{com}(path) \tag{10}$$

where $PATH(R)$ is the set of paths ended with R. As depicted in Fig. 4, we take an assumption that $R_{n-1,j}$ and $R_{n,j}$ are the candidate points for the $n\text{-}1^{th}$ and n^{th} measurement respectively. The above equation can be simplified as:

$$\begin{aligned}
P(R_{n,j}) &= \sum_{i=1}^{k} \sum_{path \in PATH(R_{n-1,i})} P_{com}(path)P_{com}(\overrightarrow{R_{n-1,i}R_{n,j}}) \\
&= \sum_{i=1}^{k} \left(P_{com}(\overrightarrow{R_{n-1,i}R_{n,j}}) \sum_{path \in PATH(R_{n-1,i})} P_{com}(path) \right) \\
&= \sum_{i=1}^{k} P(R_{n-1,i})P_{com}(\overrightarrow{R_{n-1,i}R_{n,j}})
\end{aligned} \tag{11}$$

Since the RSSI matching probability and the path probability of the k RPs should be stored at each measurement, the space complexity of above algorithm is $O(kn)$. Moreover, the $P(R_{n-1,j})$ has been calculated in $n\text{-}1^{th}$ measurement, the time complexity of getting $P(R_{n,j})$ is reduced to $O(k)$. Considering that there are k candidate points, the time complexity of getting current location is $O(k^2)$.

4   Performance Evaluation

4.1   Setup

The experimental environment is illustrated in Fig. 5. There are 6 APs (indicated by yellow dots) deployed in the experiment area. The grid of RPs in the operation area includes 78 points with a spacing of 1.5 m. Wherein the blue spots represent the positions of the RPs, and the red spots represent the test positions during online period. During offline phase, we measured 110 RSS training samples at each RP to build the radio map.

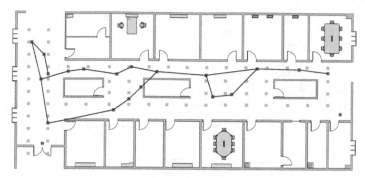

Fig. 5. Experimental environment.

During online phase, we collected 10 real-time RSS vectors at each test position with a sampling period of 250 ms.

Considering the user's trajectory, we generate 200 movement paths through an algorithm simulating the real human movement. We walk along the generated path 10 times to obtain the sensor data.

The positioning accuracy is calculated by the following equation:

$$E = \sqrt{(x - x_0)^2 + (y - y_0)^2} \tag{12}$$

where *(x, y)* represents the positioning coordinate, and (x_0, y_0) represents the real coordinate.

4.2 Results and Analysis

We first compare the positioning accuracy of our method with other methods like RADAR, Horus and PF + IKNN. As seen in Fig. 6, our method has the best performance. The mean localization errors of RADAR, Horus and PF + IKNN are 2.57 m, 1.18 m and 1.05 m respectively, our method reduces the mean localization error to 0.97 m. RADAR uses the KNN algorithm to determine candidate RPs, and simply take the average value of these RPs' coordinates as positioning results. That's why RADAR performs the worst. Horus and our method adopt statistical probability to build a radio map and look for the fittest fingerprint during the online phase. Compared with Horus, our method performs better because it reduces the contribution of RSSI-based results with high matching probability but large deviation to the final positioning results. The performance improvement is more significant when the location error is higher than 1.5 m.

PF + IKNN also has a close performance. Although the improved KNN reduces the positioning time, particle filter is computationally expensive, which is unsuitable for real-time positioning. Instead of using complex filtering mechanism, our method uses a lightweight probability mechanism to adjust the contribution of fingerprinting and IMU to the final results. The time complexity of particle filter is $O(n^2)$, where *n* indicates the number of particles and is set to 700 in the compared research. And the time complexity

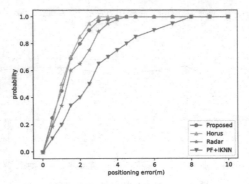

Fig. 6. Cumulative distribution function of positioning error.

of our proposed method is $O(k^2)$, where k indicates the number of candidate RPs, which is usually less than 10.

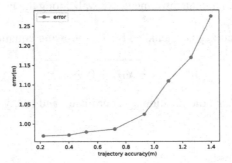

Fig. 7. Positioning error versus the accuracy of estimated trajectory.

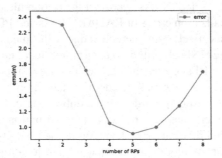

Fig. 8. Positioning error versus the number of RPs.

We also analyse the effects of the accuracy of estimated trajectory on final positioning results. We generate 8 estimated trajectories and then give them different accuracy. Figure 7 shows that as the accuracy of estimated trajectory improve, the final positioning result is more accurate. This can be easily explained according to Eq. 7 that the more accurate the estimated trajectory is, the higher the corresponding weight is.

Figure 8 shows how the number of RPs affects the positioning accuracy. The proposed method performs the worst when only one RP is matched per measurement. WiFi signal is vulnerable to the changeable environment, if only one RP is selected, it is quite possible to select a RP with significant deviation, which has bad influence on the final result. When the number of matched RPs increases, the most selected RPs with high matching probabilities have low deviation, which have a positive impact on accuracy. The accuracy decreases when the number of RPs exceeds the number of 6, which is similar with the case described in the literature [2]. That is because, with the number of RPs increasing, the RPs with the larger deviation may be selected and contribute to the calculation of final probability and furthermore, have a negative impact on final result. Therefore, the number of RPs should be determined empirically according to the actual environment.

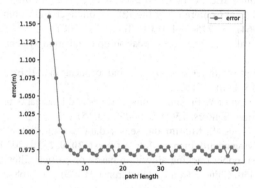

Fig. 9. Positioning error versus the path length

The relationship between the path length and the positioning accuracy is shown in Fig. 9. When we set the path length to 0, which means there is only one RP contained in the candidate path, the sensor data makes no contribution to the final probability, and the positioning result is only determined by the classical RSSI-based algorithm. So it is vulnerable to the labile environment and have the worst performance. With the increase of path length, the estimated trajectory makes contribution to the final probability. We also find the positioning accuracy stays around 0.97 m when the length of path exceeds 8. It means the integrated probability model can ease the adverse effects of changeful environment when the length of candidate path is long enough.

5   Conclusions and Future Directions

RSSI-based location is vulnerable to dynamic environment, which may introduce large deviation to final result. To deal with this issue, an integrated probability model combining the RSSI fingerprint and users' trajectory is proposed to improve online positioning accuracy. Experimental results show that the proposed method can greatly reduce the adverse effects of inconstant environment and meanwhile, it's computationally lightweight enough to be utilized in the smart phones.

The error of users' trajectory estimating and RSSI matching has great impact on the performance of our method because it decides the contribution of a certain candidate RP to the final positioning result. We will continue to develop more precise error model that can adapt to dynamic human motions in different environment. New deep learning methods will be considered. Now our method selects a fix number of candidate RPs. To improve the accuracy, we also will study on adaptive candidate RPs selection.

References

1. Guo, X., et al.: A survey on fusion-based indoor positioning. IEEE Commun. Surv. Tutorials **22**(1), 566–594 (2020)
2. Bahl, P., Padmanabhan, V.N.: RADAR: an in-building RF-based user location and tracking system. In: Proceedings IEEE INFOCOM 2000. Conference on Computer Communications. Nineteenth Annual Joint Conference of the IEEE Computer and Communications Societies (Cat. No.00CH37064), pp. 775–784. IEEE, Tel Aviv (2000)
3. Youssef, M., Agrawala, A.: The horus location determination system. Wirel. Netw. **14**(3), 357–374 (2008)
4. Shi, K. et al.: Support vector regression based indoor location in IEEE 802.11 environments. Mob. Inf. Syst. **2015**, 1–14 (2015)
5. Chen, Z., et al.: Fusion of WiFi, smartphone sensors and landmarks using the kalman filter for indoor localization. Sensors. **15**(1), 715–732 (2015)
6. Sansano-Sansano, E., et al.: Multimodal sensor data integration for indoor positioning in ambient-assisted living environments. Mob. Inf. Syst. **2020**, 1–16 (2020)
7. Li, N., et al.: A fast indoor tracking algorithm based on particle filter and improved fingerprinting. In: 2016 35th Chinese Control Conference (CCC), pp. 5468–5472. IEEE, Chengdu (2016)
8. Qian, Y., Chen, X.: An improved particle filter based indoor tracking system via joint Wi-Fi/PDR localization. Meas. Sci. Technol. **32**(1), 014004 (2021)
9. Liu, W., et al.: Survey on CSI-based indoor positioning systems and recent advances. In: 2019 International Conference on Indoor Positioning and Indoor Navigation (IPIN), pp. 1–8. IEEE, Pisa (2019)
10. Dai, P., et al.: Combination of DNN and improved KNN for indoor location fingerprinting. Wirel. Commun. Mob. Comput. **2019**, 1–9 (2019)
11. Wang, X., et al.: Deep convolutional neural networks for indoor localization with CSI images. IEEE Trans. Netw. Sci. Eng. **7**(1), 316–327 (2020)
12. Nikitin, A., et al.: Indoor localization accuracy estimation from fingerprint data. In: 2017 18th IEEE International Conference on Mobile Data Management (MDM), pp. 196–205. IEEE, Daejeon (2017)
13. Kang, W., Han, Y.: SmartPDR: smartphone-based pedestrian dead reckoning for indoor localization. IEEE Sens. J. **15**(5), 2906–2916 (2015)

Wi-Tracker: Monitoring Breathing Airflow with Acoustic Signals

Wei Liu, Shan Chang$^{(\boxtimes)}$, Shizong Yan, Hao Zhang, and Ye Liu

School of Computer Science and Technology, Donghua University, Shanghai, China
liuwei628@mail.dhu.edu.cn, changshan@dhu.edu.cn

Abstract. Continuous and accurate breathing monitoring during sleep plays a critical role in early warning and health diagnosis of diseases. To extract breathing patterns, there exist three categories of solutions, i.e., using camera to collect image data, wearing sensor devices or deploying dedicated hardware to record sensor data. However, video-based schemes raise privacy concerns and sensor-based schemes are intrusive. Deploying dedicated hardware incurs high cost. In addition, most of the existing solutions focus on sensing chest/abdomen movement to detect breathing. However, chest/abdomen movement is not a good indicator for breathing monitoring due to existing false body movement. To overcome the above limitations, we propose Wi-Tracker, a contactless and nonintrusive breathing monitoring system, which exploits ultrasound signals generated by smartphone to sense Doppler effect caused by exhaled airflow on the reflected sound waves to detect breathing. By analyzing the data collected from real sleep environments, we find that Power Spectral Density (PSD) of acoustic signals can be utilized to sense breathing procedures. Specifically, Wi-Tracker first adopts a Cumulative PSD method to eliminate frequency interference and extract breathing patterns. Then, Wi-Tracker designs a CPSD-based peak detection algorithm to detect breathing events. Finally, Wi-Tracker applies a fake peak removal algorithm to further improve its performance. We evaluate Wi-Tracker with six volunteers over a one-month period. Extensive experiments show that Wi-Tracker can achieve a Mean Estimation Error (MEE) of 0.17 bpm for breathing rate estimation, which is comparable or even better as compared to existing WiFi-based or RF-based approaches.

Keywords: Breathing monitoring · Acoustic sensing · Airflow detection

1 Introduction

Vital signs, such as breathing rate, is an important factor affecting an individual's health. Therefore, accurate breathing monitoring is critical to collect vital data for early warning and treatment of many respiratory diseases. Traditionally, vital signs of breathing rate during sleep can be detected and recorded by special devices such as capnometer [1] or pulse oximeter [2]. Although these technologies can obtain high accuracy, the users are usually required to wear a dozen of sensors, which are intrusive and uncomfortable for long-term monitoring.

© Springer Nature Switzerland AG 2021
Z. Liu et al. (Eds.): WASA 2021, LNCS 12937, pp. 41–52, 2021.
https://doi.org/10.1007/978-3-030-85928-2_4

Recently, some works use the data recorded by camera [3–5], Radar [6–8], customized acoustic devices [9], RFID readers/tags [10–13], commodity WiFi [14–18] or built-in microphone of the smartphone [19,20] to extract vital signs during sleep without wearing sensors. However, video-based solutions may raise privacy concerns and require good lighting conditions. Deploying dedicated hardware (e.g., Radar, RFID readers/tags, commodity WiFi) and customized devices incurs high cost and low development efficiency. In addition, these works including smartphone-based solutions typically monitor breathing by detecting the displacement of human chest/abdomen. However, chest/abdomen movement is not a good indicator of recording breathing patterns when user is covered by thick obstacles (e.g., blanket, quilt). Particularly, for people suffering from obstructive sleep apnea (OSA), their chest/abdomen can still move as if they are breathing normally while they are going into respiratory arrest [9]. Therefore, current research works based on chest/abdomen movement detection cannot monitor breathing accurately due to existing false body movement. To overcome the above limitations, we study whether it is feasible to utilize acoustic signals generated by smartphone to sense exhaled airflow rather than chest/abdomen movement. Specifically, we first transform the smartphone into an active sonar system. Then, we transmit inaudible sound waves (i.e., not disturbing) from the smartphone speaker and receive their reflections at the microphone. Finally, the exhaled airflow from breathing may cause Doppler effect to the reflected sound waves so that breathing events can be detected.

In order to build an acoustic-based contactless breathing monitoring system using smartphone, we face many challenges in practice. First, the system needs to sense breathing procedures from the reflected sound waves recording shallow exhaled airflows. Second, the system needs to extract fine-grained breathing patterns to detect breathing events accurately. Third, the system needs to eliminate body movement interference during sleep in order to enhance its robustness.

To tackle the above challenges, we first study the feasibility of utilizing ultrasound signals generated by smartphone to sense Doppler effect caused by exhaled airflow to capture breathing patterns, and find that Power Spectral Density (PSD) of acoustic signals can be utilized to sense breathing procedures. Based on our empirical study, we present a contactless and nonintrusive breathing monitoring system named Wi-Tracker, which directly leverages acoustic devices (i.e., speaker and microphone) on smartphone to detect breathing. Wi-Tracker first uses a high-pass filter to filter out the ambient noise. Second, Wi-Tracker computes PSD with Short-Time Fourier Transform (STFT) method. Third, Wi-Tracker accumulates all PSD along the frequency dimension to eliminate frequency interference and sense breathing procedures. Finally, Wi-Tracker applies a Cumulative PSD (CPSD) based peak detection algorithm to detect breathing events and a fake peak removal algorithm to further improve detection performance.

The contributions of Wi-Tracker are summarized as follows.

- We propose Wi-Tracker, a continuous contactless and intrusive breathing monitoring system, which directly leverages acoustic devices on smartphone to sense exhaled airflow rather than chest/abdomen movement. To the best of our knowledge, Wi-Tracker is the first attempt for breathing monitoring by detecting exhaled airflow using smartphone.

- We find that PSD of acoustic signals can be utilized to sense breathing procedures, and further design a CPSD-based peak detection algorithm to eliminate frequency interference and detect breathing events.
- We find that variation of Doppler frequency shift caused by body movement is larger than breathing naturally, and design a fake peak removal algorithm to eliminate body movement interference to improve detection performance.
- We implement Wi-Tracker with smartphone and evaluate the performance with extensive experiments involving six volunteers over one month period. Experimental results show that Wi-Tracker can achieve a mean estimation error (MEE) of 0.17 bpm for breathing rate estimation, which is comparable or even better as compared to WiFi-based or RFID-based approaches.

The rest of the paper is organized as follows. Section 2 introduces the preliminary findings and results. Section 3 presents the system design of Wi-Tracker. The evaluation results are shown in Sect. 4. Section 5 concludes the paper.

2   Preliminary Findings and Results

Theoretically, the exhaled airflow from breathing can be regarded as turbulence, which can cause Doppler frequency shift on the reflected sound waves [9]. Therefore, we could utilize acoustic signals generated by smartphone to sense Doppler effect caused by exhaled airflow to capture breathing patterns. In this section, we conduct preliminary experiment to verify this theory.

Specifically, we utilize the speaker of smartphone to generate continuous inaudible ultrasound waves at 20 kHz and receive their reflections at the microphone of smartphone. The reason why we choose this frequency is that the frequency cannot be heard by people and can reduce noise interference. The sampling rate of the microphone is set at 48 kHz. Figure 1 shows our Wi-Tracker deployment. The smartphone is placed above the volunteer's head at a distance of 20 cm (i.e., position P0), and speaker at the bottom of the smartphone points toward the effective sensing area where the exhaled airflow passes. The volunteer breathes naturally first, and then is asked to wear a face mask during breathing. Figure 2 shows the variation of Doppler frequency shift under different breathing conditions. As shown in Fig. 2(a), we can observe that the echo PSD shows periodic micro-Doppler frequency shift (i.e., 200 Hz) around 20 kHz with each breathing when the volunteer breathes naturally without a face mask. But when volunteer breathes with a face mask, the exhaled airflow is blocked and the micro-Doppler frequency shift disappears shown in Fig. 2(b). The preliminary experiment results demonstrate that we can utilize ultrasound signals generated by smartphone to sense Doppler effect caused by exhaled airflow to detect breathing.

3   System Design

Figure 3 shows the architecture of Wi-Tracker. The whole system is composed of three modules that work in a pipelined manner. Data collection module has been briefly introduced in Sect. 2. Therefore, we focus on introducing the following two modules in this section.

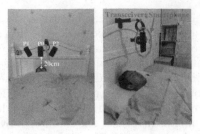

Fig. 1. Wi-Tracker deployment in a bedroom.

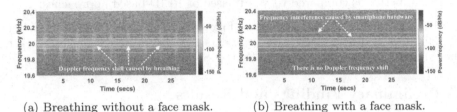

(a) Breathing without a face mask.   (b) Breathing with a face mask.

Fig. 2. Variation of Doppler frequency shift under different breathing conditions.

3.1   Data Processing

High-Pass Filtering and PSD Computing. Original acoustic signals received by microphone contain ambient noises which could come from environment-related interferences including talking in a loud voice, playing video, moving around, etc. Note that the frequencies of all these ambient noises are far below the 20 kHz [9]. Therefore, we first use a high-pass filter to filter out acoustic signals below 18 kHz. After that, we transform the filtered acoustic signals into time-frequency domain using Short Time Fourier Transform (STFT). Then, PSD of received signals can be calculated by:

$$PSD_{R(t)} = \frac{STFT_N(R(t))^2}{N}, \tag{1}$$

$$R(t) = \sum_{i \in \Omega} A_i \sin(2\pi f t + \varphi_i), \tag{2}$$

Where t and f are the time and frequency of received signals $R(t)$, respectively. Ω denotes the set of all paths of acoustic signals, A_i is the coefficient representing the amplitude reduction of the acoustic signal of path i, φ_i is corresponding to the initial phase φ and the phase change during the propagation in path i, N is the points of Discrete Fourier Transform (DFT) [20]. Figure 2(a) shows the result of PSD computing in the time-frequency domain when volunteer breathes naturally. We can see that the echo PSD presents periodic micro-Doppler frequency shift around 20 kHz with each breathing. The main frequency of the echo PSD is 20 kHz which is the same as transmitted ultrasound waves. But we observe from Fig. 2(b) that there are four interference frequency points (i.e., around 19.88, 19.94, 20.06 and 20.12 kHz) with high PSD. We speculate

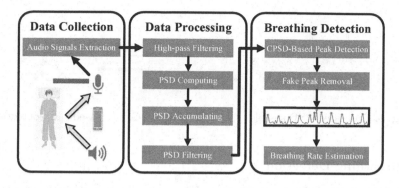

Fig. 3. System architecture of Wi-Tracker.

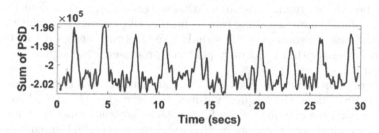

Fig. 4. Accumulated PSD signals.

that the reason is the received acoustic signals are disturbed by the internal complicated hardware units of smartphone. Note that we only retain the PSD of the frequency band from 19.6 kHz to 20.4 kHz. The reason is the amplitude change of PSD around 20 kHz is limited (i.e., lower 200 Hz in practice) due to weak exhaled airflow.

PSD Accumulating and Filtering. Considering the change of frequency interference shown in Fig. 2(b) is relatively stable with time, we adopt a Cumulative PSD (CPSD) method to eliminate frequency interference and extract coarse-grained breathing patterns. Specifically, Wi-Tracker first accumulates all PSD along the frequency dimension from 19.6 kHz to 20.4 kHz. Figure 4 shows the result of accumulated PSD signals. We observe that all breathing related events shown in Fig. 2(a) can be roughly extracted. Although CPSD-based method can eliminate frequency interference and extract coarse-grained breathing patterns, there is always noise existed in the PSD signals. Then, Wi-Tracker uses a moving average filter with a Gaussian window to further filter out the noise to extract fine-grained breathing patterns. Finally, Wi-Tracker normalizes filtered PSD signals for breathing detection. Figure 5 displays the PSD signals after applying moving average filter. It can be seen that the processed PSD signals are more neat and smooth, and the breathing events can be observed by PSD amplitude variations.

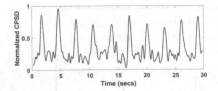

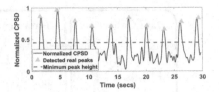

Fig. 5. Processed PSD signals.   **Fig. 6.** CPSD-based peak detection.

3.2   Breathing Detection

CPSD-Based Peak Detection. From Fig. 5, we clearly observe the processed PSD signals present a periodic ripple-like pattern over the time which corresponds to breathing events. This observation suggests that we can detect breathing events and calculate breathing rate by finding all peaks and calculating peak-to-peak intervals of processed PSD signals. We thus first design a CPSD-based peak detection algorithm to identify peaks of processed PSD signals, described as Algorithm 1.

Specifically, as shown in lines 1–9 of Algorithm 1, Wi-Tracker first accumulates all PSD along the frequency dimension from f_1 kHz to f_E kHz. Then, Wi-Tracker applies a moving average filter with a Gaussian window with window length of *len* to filter out the noise existed in accumulated PSD signals, as shown in line 10 of Algorithm 1. Next, Wi-Tracker normalizes filtered PSD signals and sets a minimum peak height based on minimum possible PSD amplitude variation caused by breathing events to further eliminate environmental interference, as shown in lines 11–12 of Algorithm 1. Finally, Wi-Tracker uses a typical peak finding method to find peaks of processed PSD signals, as shown in lines 13–19 of Algorithm 1. In our experiment, we empirically set f_1, f_E, *len* and α as 19.6, 20.4, 10 and 1.4, respectively. Figure 6 illustrates the peaks found by applying Algorithm 1 to the processed PSD signals. The red dotted line represents the calculated minimum peak height, which is able to differentiate breathing events from external environment. It can be seen from Fig. 6 that all the real peaks reflecting breathing events shown in Fig. 2(a) are detected accurately.

Fake Peak Removal and Breathing Rate Estimation. Although Algorithm 1 can detect breathing events by identifying the peaks of processed PSD signals, it is almost inevitable that some body movements (e.g., hands/legs movement, body rolling) exist during sleep. To observe the influence of body movement, we ask a volunteer to move his body one time during breathing naturally. The result is shown in Fig. 7. We can observe that body movement causes a larger Doppler frequency shift than breathing. This observation suggests that we can filter out body movement interference by removing the fake peak which causes Doppler frequency shift at a relatively lower frequency band. We thus design a fake peak removal algorithm to remove fake peaks of processed PSD signals to improve detection performance, described as Algorithm 2.

Specifically, as shown in lines 1–7 of Algorithm 2, for each local peak identified by Algorithm 1, Wi-Tracker first accumulates PSD at the peak's position

---

Algorithm 1. CPSD-Based Peak Detection.

Require: Given a segment of PSD signals: $PSD_{([t_1,t_e],[f_1,f_E])} =$ $\{PSD_{(t_1,f_1)}, ..., PSD_{(t_1,f_E)}, ..., PSD_{(t_e,f_1)}, ..., PSD_{(t_e,f_E)}\}$;

Ensure: Local peak set: $LocalPeakSet$;

1: $AccuPSD, FilterPSD, NormPSD \leftarrow \emptyset, \emptyset, \emptyset$;

2: $LocalPeakSet \leftarrow \emptyset$; /*Initialize local peak set*/

3: **for** $i = 1{:}e$ **do**

4:    $sumPSD_{t_i} \leftarrow 0$;

5:    **for** $j = 1{:}E$ **do**

6:       $sumPSD_{t_i} \leftarrow sumPSD_{t_i} + PSD_{(t_i,f_j)}$; /*PSD accumulating*/

7:    **end for**

8:    Add $sumPSD_{t_i}$ into $AccuPSD_{t_i}$;

9: **end for**

10: $FilterPSD \leftarrow Filter(AccuPSD, len)$; /*PSD filtering*/

11: $NormPSD \leftarrow Normalize(FilterPSD)$; /*PSD normalization*/

12: $P_{height} \leftarrow \alpha * Mean(NormPSD)$; /*Minimum peak height setting*/

13: $MaxSet \leftarrow FindLocalMaxs(NormPSD)$; /*$MaxSet = \{m_k, 1 \leq k \leq K\}$*/

14: **for** $k = 1{:}K$ **do** /*Finding local peak set*/

15:    **if** $amplitude(m_k) > P_{height}$ **then**

16:       add m_k into $LocalPeakSet$;

17:    **end if**

18: **end for**

19: **Return** $LocalPeakSet$.

---

along a relatively lower frequency band from $f_{S'}$ kHz to $f_{E'}$ kHz. Then, Wi-Tracker compares the accumulated PSD with a threshold δ used to discriminate the fake peak. Finally, Wi-Tracker only retains the peaks which have a low accumulated PSD at a relatively lower frequency band, as shown in lines 8–12 of Algorithm 2. Particularly, we set $f_{S'}$ and $f_{E'}$ as 19 and 19.5, respectively. In our experiment, we observe that a low threshold of $-1.3 * 10^5$ (i.e., $\delta = -1.3 * 10^5$) is good enough to discriminate real peaks caused by breathing from others. Figure 8 illustrates the real peaks and fake peak found by applying Algorithm 2 to the processed PSD signals. It can be seen from Fig. 8 that the fake peak reflecting body movement shown in Fig. 7 is removed and all the real peaks reflecting breathing events are also detected accurately. The results demonstrate the effectiveness of our Algorithm 2. Once all the real peaks are detected by our algorithms, the breathing rate R^E can be estimated as follow:

$$R^E = \frac{N}{T_E - T_S} * 60, \tag{3}$$

where N is the total number of the detected real peaks, T_S and T_E are the start time and end time (in seconds) of the processed PSD signals, respectively.

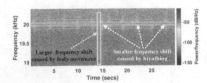

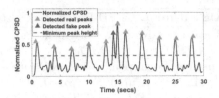

Fig. 7. Doppler frequency shift under different activities.

Fig. 8. Illustration of fake peak removal.

Algorithm 2. Fake Peak Removal.

Require: Local peak set: $LocalPeakSet = \{p_k, 1 \leq k \leq K\}$;
  PSD signals of lower frequency band: $PSD_{([t_1,t_e],[f_{S'},f_{E'}])} = \{PSD_{(t_1,f_{S'})}, ..., PSD_{(t_1,f_{E'})}, ..., PSD_{(t_e,f_{S'})}, ..., PSD_{(t_e,f_{E'})}\}$;
Ensure: Real peak set: $RealPeakSet$;
 1: $T_{sum} \leftarrow \delta$; /*A threshold used to discriminate the fake peak*/
 2: **for** $k = 1{:}K$ **do**
 3:   $loc \leftarrow location(p_k)$; /*Location of the peak*/
 4:   $sumPSD_{t_{loc}} \leftarrow 0$;
 5:   **for** $j = S'{:}E'$ **do** /*PSD accumulating of lower frequency band */
 6:     $sumPSD_{t_{loc}} \leftarrow sumPSD_{t_{loc}} + PSD_{(t_{loc},f_j)}$;
 7:   **end for**
 8:   **if** $sumPSD_{t_{loc}} < T_{sum}$ **then** /*Removing the fake peak*/
 9:     add p_k into $RealPeakSet$;
10:   **end if**
11: **end for**
12: **Return** $RealPeakSet$.

---

4   Evaluation

In this section, we first introduce the implementation of Wi-Tracker. Then we evaluate the overall performance of Wi-Tracker and compare it with the state-of-the-art methods. Finally, we evaluate the performance of Wi-Tracker under various factors.

4.1   Implementation

Hardware/Software Implementation. Wi-Tracker is implemented using commodity smartphone (i.e., XIAOMI MIX2) shown in Fig. 1. The speaker of smartphone is programmed to transmit inaudible ultrasound waves at 20 kHz continuously, and the microphone of smartphone receives their reflections at 48 kHz sampling rate. We use a laptop with 1.8 GHz CPU and 8 GB memory for data processing. The proposed method is programmed in MATLAB R2018b.

Participants. We conduct the experiments by recruiting six volunteers, including four adults (three males and one female) and two children (one boy and one girl). Their ages are in the range of 9 to 30 years. During the one-month experiment, we ask each of the volunteer to test for 20 min per day, and another volunteer seated beside him/her records the ground truth manually by watching the video stream.

Performance Metrics. To evaluate the performance of Wi-Tracker, we calculate the Mean Estimation Error (MEE) between the estimated breathing rate and the actual breathing rate. The breathing rate is in the form of *bpm* (i.e., breath per minute).

$$MEE = \frac{\sum_{i=1}^{k} |R_k^E - R_k^A|}{k}, \qquad (4)$$

where R_k^E and R_k^A correspond to the estimated and the actual breathing rate of the volunteer, respectively.

4.2 Overall Performance

Performance of Wi-Tracker for Different Volunteers. Figure 9(a) illustrates the performance of Wi-Tracker in terms of breathing rate estimation for each individual volunteer. We can observe that the MEE of Wi-Tracker is less than 0.4 bpm for all volunteers and the standard deviations (black error bar) are under 0.03 bpm. The average MEE of all volunteers is about 0.17 bpm. Particularly, we find the MEEs of volunteer 2 and 4 are slightly higher than other volunteers. The reason is that these two volunteers are children who cause relatively smaller Doppler frequency shift than adults due to their weaker exhaled airflow.

In Comparison to the State-of-the-Art Systems. We further compare Wi-Tracker with the state-of-the-art breathing monitoring systems. Specifically, we compare our Wi-Tracker with VitalSigns [15], PhaseBeat [16] and RobustRFID [12], and summarize the MEE of breathing rate estimation reported in each system as shown in Fig. 9(b). We can observe that Wi-Tracker outperforms RFID-based system (i.e., RobustRFID) with an average 0.33 bpm improvement of the breathing rate estimation. Compared with WiFi-based systems (i.e., VitalSigns and PhaseBeat), Wi-Tracker can achieve comparable performance without deploying any dedicated devices. Particularly, Wi-Tracker senses exhaled airflow rather than chest/abdomen movement other systems sensed, which is a better indicator for breathing monitoring. Overall, Wi-Tracker can achieve comparable or even better performance as compared to existing WiFi-based or RFID-based approaches and provide a novel method to monitor breathing by sensing exhaled airflow using acoustic signals generated by smartphone.

4.3 Impact of Various Factors

Smartphone Positions. We study the impact of smartphone positions for Wi-Tracker by placing the smartphone at three different places, i.e., P0, P1

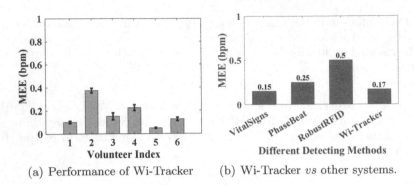

(a) Performance of Wi-Tracker   (b) Wi-Tracker *vs* other systems.

Fig. 9. Overall performance

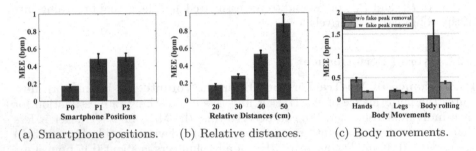

(a) Smartphone positions.   (b) Relative distances.   (c) Body movements.

Fig. 10. Impact of various factors

and P2 shown in Fig. 1. For each position, we randomly invite two volunteers to test for 30 min. The results are shown in Fig. 10(a), we can observe that the MEEs of Wi-Tracker for the three positions are 0.17 bpm, 0.48 bpm and 0.50 bpm, respectively. In particular, the MEEs of placing smartphone at P1, P2 are slightly higher than P0. The reason is when the smartphone is inclined, a part of acoustic signals could be blocked and interfered by the user's head and the effective sensing area where the exhaled airflow passes becomes smaller. Overall speaking, Wi-Tracker is not very sensitive to smartphone positions as long as the speaker of smartphone points toward exhaled airflow from breathing. The results show that Wi-Tracker can provide accurate breathing monitoring (i.e., lower than 0.50 bpm) under different smartphone positions.

Relative Distances. In this experiment, we vary relative distance between smartphone and user's head, ranging from 20 cm to 50 cm with an interval of 10 cm. For each distance, we also randomly invite two volunteers to test for 30 min to evaluate the performance of Wi-Tracker. Figure 10(b) shows the MEE as distance varies. It can be seen that when we increase the relative distances, the MEE of Wi-Tracker is also increased. The reason is the received acoustic signals become weaker with longer distance, which cause a smaller change of Doppler frequency shift. Overall, although the MEE of Wi-Tracker increases a bit as the relative distance increases, it can still achieve satisfactory performance (i.e., lower than 0.53 bpm) within 40 cm.

Body Movements. As mentioned above, body movements cause a larger Doppler frequency shift and further influence the performance of Wi-Tracker. To evaluate the impact, we also randomly invite two volunteers to test for 30 min, and the volunteers move their whole body (i.e., body rolling) or limbs (i.e., hands movement or legs movement) several times during the test. Figure 10(c) shows the MEEs of Wi-Tracker under different body movement interferences and the change trend of MEE before/after applying fake peak removal algorithm. It can be seen that when the fake peak removal algorithm is applied, the MEE of Wi-Tracker is lower than 0.38 bpm even existing body rolling interference. On the contrary, the MEE of Wi-Tracker is higher than 1.45 bpm. In addition, as shown in Fig. 10(c), we find that the legs' movement causes slight influence on the performance of Wi-Tracker because it is beyond the sensing area of Wi-Tracker. The results demonstrate that Wi-Tracker works well (i.e., lower than 0.38 bpm) under different body movement interferences and fake peak removal algorithm we designed is effective.

5 Conclusion

In this paper, we introduce a new method to monitor breathing during sleep by using acoustic signals generated by smartphone, without requiring the user to wear any sensor devices. In particular, we propose Wi-Tracker, a contactless and nonintrusive breathing monitoring system, which exploits Doppler effect caused by the exhaled airflow on the reflected sound waves to detect breathing. Wi-Tracker first senses the breathing procedures leveraging the PSD of acoustic signals, then Wi-Tracker proposes a CPSD-based peak detection algorithm to eliminate frequency interference and extract breathing events. Finally, Wi-Tracker applies a fake peak removal algorithm to eliminate body movement interference and further improve its performance. The experimental results demonstrate the performance of Wi-Tracker for breathing monitoring.

Acknowledgements. This work was supported in part by the National Natural Science Foundation of China (Grant No. 61972081, 61772340), DHU Distinguished Young Professor Program, Fundamental Research Funds for the Central Universities (Grant No. 2232020A-12).

References

1. Jaffe, M.B.: Infrared measurement of carbon dioxide in the human breath: "breathe-through" devices from Tyndall to the present day. Anesthes. Analg. **107**(3), 890–904 (2008)
2. Shariati, N.H., Zahedi, E.: Comparison of selected parametric models for analysis of the photoplethysmographic signal. In: Proceedings of International Conference on Computers, Communications and Signal Processing, pp. 169–172 (2005)

3. Bartula, M., Tigges, T., Muehlsteff, J.: Camera-based system for contactless monitoring of respiration. In: Proceedings of Annual International Conference of the IEEE Engineering in Medicine and Biology Society, pp. 2672–2675 (2013)
4. Aarts, L.A.M., et al.: Non-contact heart rate monitoring utilizing camera photoplethysmography in the neonatal intensive care unit-a pilot study. Early Hum. Dev. **89**(12), 943–948 (2013)
5. Oh, K.T., Shin, C.S., Kim, J., Yoo, S.K.: Level-set segmentation-based respiratory volume estimation using a depth camera. IEEE J. Biomed. Health Inf. **23**(4), 1674–1682 (2019)
6. Lee, Y.S., Pathirana, P.N., Steinfort, C.L., Caelli, T.: Monitoring and analysis of respiratory patterns using microwave doppler radar. IEEE J. Transl. Eng. Health Med. **2**, 1–12 (2014)
7. Adib, F., Mao, H., Kabelac, Z., Katabi, D., Miller, R.C.: Smart homes that monitor breathing and heart rate. In: Proceedings of ACM CHI, pp. 837–846 (2015)
8. Nguyen, P., Zhang, X., Halbower, A., Vu, T.: Continuous and fine-grained breathing volume monitoring from afar using wireless signals. In: Proceedings of IEEE INFOCOM, pp. 1–9 (2016)
9. Wang, T., Zhang, D., Wang, L., et al.: Contactless respiration monitoring using ultrasound signal with off-the-Shelf audio devices. IEEE Internet Things J. **6**(2), 2959–2973 (2019)
10. Yang, Y., Cao, J., Liu, X.: ER-rhythm: coupling exercise and respiration rhythm using lightweight COTS RFID. Proc. ACM IMWUT **3**(4), 1–24 (2019)
11. Chen, L., Xiong, J., Chen, X., Lee, S.I., Fang, D.: Lungtrack: towards contactless and zero dead-zone respiration monitoring with commodity RFIDs. Proceedings of ACM IMWUT **3**(3), 1–22 (2019)
12. Yang, Y., Cao, J.: Robust RFID-based respiration monitoring in dynamic environments. In: Proceedings of IEEE SECON, pp. 1–9 (2020)
13. Yang, C., Wang, X., Mao, S.: Respiration monitoring with RFID in driving environments. IEEE J. Sel. Areas Commun. **39**(2), 500–512 (2021)
14. Liu, X., Cao, J., Tang, S., Wen, J.: Wi-Sleep: contactless sleep monitoring via WiFi signals. In: Proceedings of IEEE RTSS, pp. 346–355 (2014)
15. Liu, J., Wang, Y., Chen, Y., Yang, J., Cheng, J.: Tracking vital signs during sleep leveraging off-the-shelf WiFi. In: Proceedings of ACM MobiHoc, pp. 267–276 (2015)
16. Wang, X., Yang C., Mao, S.: PhaseBeat: exploiting CSI phase data for vital sign monitoring with commodity WiFi devices. In: Proceedings of IEEE ICDCS, pp. 1230–1239 (2017)
17. Yang, Y., Cao, J., Liu, X., Xing, K.: Multi-person sleeping respiration monitoring with COTS WiFi devices. In: Proceedings of IEEE MASS, pp. 37–45 (2018)
18. Zeng, Y., Liu, Z., Wu, D., Liu, J., Zhang, J., Zhang, D.: Demo: a multi-person respiration monitoring system using COTS WIFI devices. In: Proceedings of ACM IMWUT, pp. 195–198 (2020)
19. Nandakumar, R., Gollakota, S., Watson, N.: Contactless sleep apnea detection on smartphones. In: Proceedings of ACM MobiSys, pp. 45–57 (2015)
20. Xu, X., Yu, J., Chen, Y., Zhu, Y., Kong, L., Li, M.: BreathListener: fine-grained breathing monitoring in driving environments utilizing acoustic signals. In: Proceedings of ACM MobiSys, pp. 54–66 (2019)

Low-Cost Wi-Fi Fingerprinting Indoor Localization via Generative Deep Learning

Jiankun Wang[1], Zenghua Zhao[1(✉)] (iD), Jiayang Cui[1], Yu Wang[2] (iD), YiYao Shi[3],
and Bin Wu[1]

[1] College of Intelligence and Computing, Tianjin University, Tianjin, China
`zenghua@tju.edu.cn`
[2] Department of Computer and Information Sciences, Temple University,
Philadelphia, Pennsylvania, USA
`wangyu@temple.edu`
[3] Zhejiang Information Technology Center, China Post Group Corporation,
Zhejiang, China

Abstract. Wi-Fi fingerprinting indoor localization has been studied in past decades producing many outstanding work. However, few has been deployed in real-world scenarios. One of the pain points is time-consuming and effort-intensive fingerprint mapping. In this paper, we leverage a large number of low-cost fingerprints without location tags (unlabeled fingerprints) and only a small number of high-cost fingerprints with location tags (labeled fingerprints) to construct a low-cost yet high-accuracy virtual fingerprint map. Specifically, we propose a novel semi-supervised deep generative model, SCVAE (Semi-supervised Conditional Variational AutoEncoder). It generates virtual fingerprints at any given location by learning the underlying probability distribution of Wi-Fi RSS through collected fingerprints, especially the unlabeled ones. A regressor is adopted providing pseudo labels for unlabeled fingerprints. Two efficient training strategies are further designed to improve its performance. Moreover, based on SCVAE, we design and implement a Wi-Fi fingerprinting indoor localization system, DeepPrint (Deep learning of fingerPrinting). It is evaluated extensively in real indoor environments with a total area about 8,400 m². The results show that DeepPrint makes Wi-Fi fingerprinting indoor localization deployed at a low cost in large-scale venues.

Keywords: Indoor localization · Mobile sensing · Wi-Fi fingerprinting · Generative deep learning · Semi-supervised learning

1 Introduction

Wi-Fi fingerprinting indoor localization has attracted many researchers' attentions in recent years due to pervasive AP (Access Point) deployments and popular

This research was supported in part by the National Natural Science Foundation of China (NSFC) under grant No. 61832013.
Y. Shi—Did this work when she was a master student in Tianjin University.

portable Wi-Fi devices [7]. Although fruitful work has been produced in academia, few has been deployed in real-world large-scale venues such as shopping malls. One primary reason is the high cost of fingerprint mapping. Fingerprint mapping is to associate Wi-Fi fingerprints with location tags by collecting fingerprints at reference points. Site survey of reference points is very time-consuming and effort-intensive, and usually needs professional work from trained workers. Moreover, localization accuracy depends heavily on the density and accurate locations of reference points [11], which further increases the cost to achieve high accuracy. Therefore, Wi-Fi fingerprinting achieves high accuracy at a high cost.

On the other hand, fingerprint collection without location tags is much easier, and thus efficient and inexpensive. For instance, without location constraint, fingerprints can be collected by any workers or even ordinary customers in a shopping mall by crowdsourcing [21,24]. Then it is natural to ask a question: shall we leverage inexpensive fingerprints to facilitate fingerprint mapping so as to achieve high localization accuracy yet at a low cost?

If we take location information associated with fingerprints as labels, then the above question becomes: shall we use a large number of unlabeled fingerprints (without location tags) and a small number of labeled fingerprints (with location tags) to generate high-accuracy fingerprint map while reducing cost? This can be further divided into two sub-problems: (1) how to generate high quality fingerprint map from known fingerprints, and (2) how to leverage unlabeled fingerprints when few labels are available? For the former, deep generative models are promising on reconstructing original data by learning their underlying features [8]. Among them, CVAE [19] is notable for enabling data generation with some given labels. The latter sub-problem falls into the scope of semi-supervised learning [15]. However, existing deep generative models cannot be directly applied to generate fingerprints, since most of them focus on classification tasks, and are supervised which cannot process unlabeled data. We take fingerprint generation as a regression problem due to continuous locations. It needs a semi-supervised solution to leverage a large number of unlabeled fingerprints.

In this paper, we first develop a novel semi-supervised deep generative model SCVAE (Semi-supervised Conditional Variational Auto-Encoder) to generate high-accuracy VFPs (Virtual FingerPrints). The basic idea is to learn the underlying probability distribution of Wi-Fi RSS (Received Signal Strength) using a large number of unlabeled fingerprints and a small number of labeled ones, based on which dense and accurate VFPs are generated. Different from supervised CVAE [19], SCVAE stacks a regressor to the endec (encoder and decoder), providing pseudo labels for unlabeled fingerprints which are input to and reconstructed by the endec together with labeled fingerprints. We then propose efficient pre-training and joint-training strategies to improve the performance of SCVAE. Afterwards, the well-trained decoder is used as a generator to generate high-accuracy VFPs.

Based on SCVAE, we design and implement a Wi-Fi fingerprinting localization system DeepPrint (Deep learning of fingerPrinting). DeepPrint estimates a location for a Wi-Fi RSS sample by running KNN (K-Nearest Neighbor) against the VFP map. We carry out extensive experiments to evaluate the performance of DeepPrint in real-world deployments including three corridors in an office building and a large shopping mall, with a total area about $8,400\,m^2$. The performance of DeepPrint is compared with those of well-known counterparts: CVAE [19], RADAR [2], and Modellet [11]. Results show that DeepPrint outperforms them in all scenarios. In particular, DeepPrint yields an average localization accuracy about 3.0 m with only 6 reference points (60 m apart from each other) in the office building. While in the shopping mall, the average accuracy of DeepPrint is 5.1 m at a reference point interval of 30 m. With a comparable accuracy, the reference point interval for Modellet and RADAR is 10 m. DeepPrint achieves comparable localization accuracy to RADAR and Modellet with a small number of reference points, thus reducing fingerprint mapping cost significantly (by cutting down 40%–81.7% of the number of required reference points).

In summary, our contributions are two-fold:

- We propose a novel semi-supervised deep generative model SCVAE to generate high-accuracy VFP map at a low cost. Unlike existing work using either unlabeled or labeled ones, it leverages a large number of inexpensive unlabeled fingerprints and only a small number of expensive labeled ones. To the best of our knowledge, this is the first systematic work that solves Wi-Fi fingerprinting problem using deep generative model leveraging unlabeled fingerprints.
- We design and implement DeepPrint, a Wi-Fi fingerprinting indoor localization system based on SCVAE. Performance of DeepPrint is evaluated extensively in real scenarios with a total area about $8,400\,m^2$. Results show that DeepPrint can achieve comparable localization accuracy with a small number of reference points, which significantly decreases the fingerprint mapping cost.

The rest of the paper is organized as follows. Section 2 reviews related work. We present DeepPrint and SCVAE in Sect. 3. Section 4 evaluates the performance of DeepPrint, and Sect. 5 concludes the paper.

2 Related Work

There are numerous studies on Wi-Fi indoor localization [23], we only review those close to our work from three aspects: fingerprint based, model based and deep learning based approaches.

Fingerprint-Based Approaches. In fingerprinting localization, through deterministic [2, 4] or probabilistic algorithms [12, 26], a location is estimated based on a fingerprint map. In addition to Wi-Fi RSS, CSI (Channel State Information) is also used as fingerprint to achieve sub-meter accuracy [20]. Since CSI is only available on specified wireless interface cards [25], we only consider RSS in this paper. Generally, for fingerprint-based approaches, time-consuming and labor-intensive site survey is a big hurdle for practical deployments. Fingerprint crowdsourcing has recently been promoted to relieve the burden of site survey by allowing unprofessional users to participate fingerprint collection [17,18,21,22]. However, designing a high-quality fingerprint annotation of crowdsourcing remains as a challenge.

Model-Based Approaches. Model-based approaches usually leverage RF propagation model LDPL (Log-Distance Path Loss) to derive RSS at various locations [3,6]. However, most of them assume known AP locations, which are rarely available in practice. EZ [3] and its upgraded EZPerfect [14] relax the assumptions by leveraging a genetic algorithm to solve LDPL equations using fingerprints. The state-of-the-art Modellet [11] integrates RADAR [2] and EZPerfect to improve localization accuracy in large-scale venues by generating VFPs. To capture locality of fingerprint in Modellet, VFPs have to be created by modeling APs one-by-one across the area of interest.

Deep-Learning-Based Approaches. Deep Learning is a powerful machine learning paradigm [10]. Various deep learning models have been investigated to denoise Wi-Fi RSS received [1,27]. In addition, Gan *et al.* [5] use LDPL model and ray tracing method to construct a large sample data for weights training. Unfortunately, it requires indoor GIS (Geographic Information System) and AP locations which are difficult to obtain in practice. Zhang *et al.* [27] leverage deep neural network to fuse magnetic field and Wi-Fi signal.

3   Design of DeepPrint

We address the above challenges through the design of a systematic way to generate high-accuracy VFP map via generative deep learning, thus achieving high localization accuracy at a low cost.

3.1   DeepPrint Overview

We first propose a semi-supervised deep generative model SCVAE to generate virtual Wi-Fi fingerprints by leveraging a large number of unlabeled fingerprints and a small number of labeled ones. Based on SCVAE, we then design DeepPrint, a WiFi fingerprinting indoor localization system. As shown in Fig. 1, DeepPrint consists of three phases: training phase, generating phase and on-line localizing phase.

Training Phase. In the training phase, SCVAE is trained by a small number of labeled Wi-Fi RSS fingerprints x_l and a large number of unlabeled ones x_u. We design two training strategies, pre-training and joint training, to improve model accuracy and to make training efficient with fast convergence.

Generating Phase. After training, the well-trained decoder serves as a **generator** to generate VFPs at dense locations. The dense VFPs and sparse RFPs (Real Fingerprints, i.e., labeled fingerprints) are combined to construct the Wi-Fi fingerprint map.

Localizing Phase. In the on-line localizing phase, Wi-Fi RSS collected by a user is transmitted to the backend server running the localization module. The location is then estimated and fed back to the user. We adopt a simple algorithm KNN in order to highlight the performance of DeepPrint.

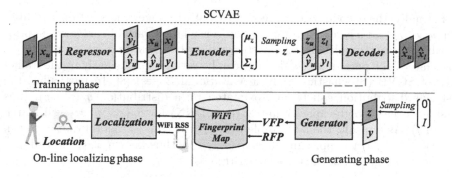

Fig. 1. System framework of DeepPrint.

3.2 SCVAE Model

We consider Wi-Fi RSS $x = (rss_1, rss_2, \ldots, rss_N)$ received at a location y in the area of interest, where rss_i is the RSS from the ith AP, N is the total number of APs, and $y = (y_1, y_2)$ denotes the coordination of a location on the floor plan. Labeled fingerprints are Wi-Fi RSS collected at reference points, denoted as x_l, which are associated with locations (labels) y_l. Unlabeled fingerprints are RSS collected randomly without site survey, denoted as x_u.

The goal of SCVAE is to reconstruct the input Wi-Fi RSS x given their location y by learning their underlying probability distribution at only sparse labeled fingerprints x_l and yet plenty of unlabeled fingerprints x_u. To this end, SCVAE stacks a regressor to the endec to leverage unlabeled fingerprints. In what follows, we first discuss the endec and then the regressor.

Endec (Encoder and Decoder). The architecture of the endec is shown in Fig. 2. The encoder seeks to represent input Wi-Fi fingerprint x with location y in a latent variable space $\mathbb{Z}$, which is isotropic Gaussian $\mathcal{N}(\mu_z, \Sigma_z)$. The decoder aims to reconstruct the original x from $\mathbb{Z}$ conditioned on location y. The process is known as conditional variational autoencoder (CVAE) [19].

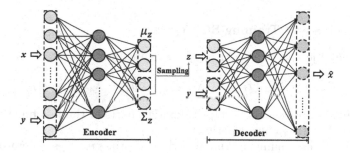

Fig. 2. Architecture diagram of the endec.

Formally, the decoder tries to reconstruct Wi-Fi fingerprints x from distribution $p_\theta(x|z,y)$ for a given location y, where z is a latent variable drawn from prior distribution $p_\theta(z|y)$. Usually, the posterior distribution $p_\theta(z|x,y)$ is intractable. Fortunately, the parameters of decoder can be estimated efficiently in the framework of SGVB (Stochastic Gradient Variational Bayes) [8]. In particular, the posterior distribution can be approximated by a distribution $q_\phi(z|x,y)$. It is possible to use a high-capacity model (e.g., DNN) for $q_\phi(z|x,y)$ to well match $p_\theta(z|x,y)$. As a result, the intractable $p_\theta(z|x,y)$ becomes tractable since we can just use $q_\phi(z|x,y)$ to approximate it. $q_\phi(z|x,y)$ is thus known as the encoder.

The loss function of the endec is written as:

$$\mathcal{L}_{ED}(\phi,\theta;x,y) = -D_{KL}(q_\phi(z|x,y)||p_\theta(z|y)) + \mathbb{E}_{q_\phi(z|y)}[\log p_\theta(x|z,y)], \quad (1)$$

where D_{KL} is the KL (Kullback-Leibler) divergence measuring the difference between two probability distributions [13]. The objective is to minimize the difference between $q_\phi(z|x,y)$ and $p_\theta(z|y)$, and the difference between the reconstructed $\hat{x}$ and the original x. Leveraging reparameterizing trick as in [8], the loss function can be optimized using standard stochastic gradient ascent techniques. Thus we can learn the model parameters efficiently, with parameter updating in small batches. This enables DeepPrint to scale to large scenarios with big volume of data.

Unfortunately, unlabeled Wi-Fi fingerprints x_u cannot be input to the encoder, since the location y_u is unknown. However, we have to leverage x_u to learn the underlying distribution of Wi-Fi fingerprints since there are only limited x_l available. Therefore, we design a regressor to predict pseudo location $\hat{y}_u$ for x_u, and thus x_u with $\hat{y}_u$ can be reconstructed by the endec.

Regressor. The task of regressor $R(\cdot)$ is to predict location $\hat{y}$ for Wi-Fi fingerprint x, i.e., $\hat{y} = R(x)$. The regressor is trained with labeled fingerprints. Considering location y is continuous real-valued data, we use negative log-likelihood as the loss function of the regressor $\mathcal{L}_R$:

$$\mathcal{L}_R(x,y) = -\mathbb{E}_{x,y\sim P(x,y)}\left[\log\left[\frac{1}{\sqrt{2\pi}\sigma_y}e^{-\frac{||\hat{y}-y||_2}{2\sigma_y^2}}\right]\right]. \quad (2)$$

3.3 Objective and Training Strategies

All in all, the objective of SCVAE $\mathcal{L}_{total}$ is defined as:

$$\mathcal{L}_{total} = \mathcal{L}_{ED}(x_l,y_l) + \lambda_1\mathcal{L}_{ED}(x_u,\hat{y}_u) + \lambda_2\mathcal{L}_R(x_l,y_l), \quad (3)$$

where λ_1 and λ_2 are weights to adjust different parts in the loss function. They are set by experience in our experiments.

Recall that a large number of unlabeled fingerprints enables generator to generate high accuracy fingerprints in areas where there are only sparse RPs. On the other hand, the errors of pseudo labels impact the performance of generator significantly. To reduce the prediction error of regressor and improve the performance of generator, we design two training strategies: pre-training and joint training.

Pre-training. The regressor and the endec are trained independently before joint training, called by pre-training. Only labeled fingerprints are used in the pre-training. Since labeled fingerprints are associated with real locations, the regressor and the endec can learn real data feature through pre-training.

Since the number of labeled fingerprints is usually small, it leads to overfitting problem and thus deteriorates the prediction accuracy of the regressor. To cope with this problem, we leverage the endec to generate pseudo fingerprints to enlarge the set of labeled fingerprints. In particular, after the endec is pre-trained with labeled fingerprints, the decoder, acting as a generator, generates pseudo fingerprints at given locations. Then the pseudo fingerprints together with the labeled ones are used to pre-train the regressor. Although the pseudo fingerprints are not so accurate as the real ones, they alleviate the overfitting problem for the regressor.

Joint Training. After pre-training, the regressor and endec are trained jointly with both labeled and unlabeled fingerprints. Parameters of the regressor and the endec obtained by pre-training are saved as initial parameters for joint training. In this way, what learned in pre-training is transferred to SCVAE, thus improving the performance.

3.4 Virtual Fingerprint Generation

After training SCVAE, we use the generator (the well-trained decoder) to generate VFPs at dense locations except reference points in the area of interest. Unlike the decoder, the generator takes input z sampled from Gaussian distribution $\mathcal{N}(0, I)$ instead of $\mathcal{N}(\mu_z, \Sigma_z)$, where I is the identity matrix. Given a position y, we generate N_v VFPs by varying z, where N_v is the number of VFPs. The VFP at position y is obtained by averaging N_v VFPs. The densely generated VFPs and the sparsely original RFPs (the labeled fingerprints training SCVAE) are combined to construct the high-density Wi-Fi fingerprint map.

4 Evaluation

In this section, we evaluate the localization accuracy of DeepPrint with data collected from real large-scale deployments, and compare it with existing Wi-Fi fingerprinting localization approaches.

4.1 Implementation

The sensing functionality of DeepPrint is implemented on Android smartphones. The training, generating, and localizing are deployed at a server with CPU Intel

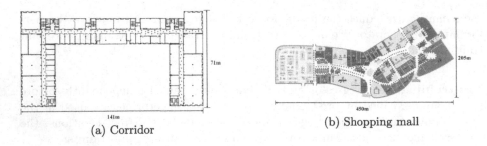

(a) Corridor   (b) Shopping mall

Fig. 3. Floor maps of two experiment sites. Dots are reference points.

Core Processor I7-7700K and GPU GeForce GTX 1080Ti. We implement SCVAE using the deep learning platform of Pytorch 1.4.0 [16].

The encoder, decoder, and regressor are DNNs with 3 hidden layers. The encoder and regressor share the same network structure with 256, 128, and 32 neurons for each layer, respectively. The decoder has the reverse structure. We use ReLU as the activation function for all the hidden layers of DNNs, and Adam as the optimizer [9]. The dimension of the latent variable z is set to 8, which has little impact on the performance of SCVAE.

4.2   Experiment Setup

We conduct extensive experiments in two typical indoor environments (Fig. 3): one corridor in an office building, and one floor in a shopping mall. The total size is about $8,400\,\text{m}^2$. Reference points (dots in Fig. 3) are about 5 m apart from each other along corridors, and distributed uniformly on the floor. The high density of reference points allows us to downsample for sparser densities. The reference point interval varies between 5 m, 10 m, 20 m, 30 m, and 60 m. Take the shopping mall as an example, there are 399 reference points under 5 m interval and 33 reference points under 60 m interval. Test points are disjoint with reference points and also distributed uniformly on the floor. Labeled fingerprints are collected at reference points (for training) and at test points (for testing). Unlabeled fingerprints are collected by randomly walking on the floor. The sampling rate is 5 Hz. There are 772 and 7642 VFPs in the office building and the shopping mall respectively.

Benchmark. We use CVAE, Modellet, and RADAR as benchmarks. CVAE [19] is a supervised deep generative model designed for image generation. To make it fit Wi-Fi fingerprinting localization, we modify its neural network from CNN to DNN, also from classification to regression. We only use labeled fingerprints to train CVAE. To show the benefits from unlabeled fingerprints in DeepPrint, we train DeepPrint using the same number of labeled fingerprints as in CVAE but leveraging a large number of unlabeled data. Modellet [11] is a state-of-the-art Wi-Fi fingerprinting localization system, which also generates virtual fingerprints to improve localization accuracy in large-scale complicated scenarios (shopping malls). RADAR [2] is a well-known Wi-Fi fingerprinting localization system. It is also a benchmark used by Modellet.

The benchmarks and SCVAE all use KNN as the fingerprint matching algorithm. The values of K are selected according to the density of the fingerprint map. We set $K = 9$ for SCVAE and CVAE, set $K = 3$ for modellet and RADAR.

4.3 Accuracy of VFP Generated by SCVAE

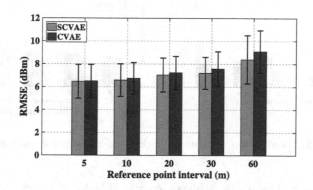

Fig. 4. VFP accuracy in corridor under various reference point intervals.

We first carry out experiments to evaluate the accuracy of VFP generated by SCVAE. To examine the impact of labeled fingerprints, SCVAE is trained under all various reference point intervals. VFPs are then generated at test points by the generator under each setup. We calculate the RMSE (Root-Mean-Square Error) between VFPs and RFPs at each test point. To show the important role of unlabeled fingerprints playing in SCVAE, we also calculate the RMSE of VFPs generated by CVAE for comparison. Since there is no unified model in modellet to generate VFP at test points, we don't compare with modellet.

Results in the corridor are shown in Fig. 4. Similar results hold in the mall. We can see that at the same reference point interval, SCVAE always outperforms CVAE. Therefore, benefiting from unlabeled fingerprints, SCVAE learns the underling structure of Wi-Fi RSS well, and generates VFPs with higher accuracy compared with CVAE.

4.4 Localization Accuracy

We then evaluate DeepPrint in both scenarios in Fig. 3. To show the impact of labeled fingerprints, the experiments are performed under various reference point intervals. Figure 5 shows the average localization error distance for both scenarios. We can see that DeepPrint always outperforms other three approaches in both scenarios tested, especially when labeled fingerprints are sparse. Taking the reference point interval of 60 m for example. In the corridor, the average localization error of DeepPrint is 3.1 m, and decreases by 1.4 m, 6.6 m and 9.4 m compared with CVAE, Modellet, and RADAR, respectively. In the shopping

mall, the average accuracy error of DeepPrint is 6.5 m, decreasing by 2.0 m, 2.3 m
and 7.5 m compared with others. This is because DeepPrint leverages unlabeled
fingerprints, which facilitates learning the underlying probability distribution of
Wi-Fi RSS in the area of interest. Therefore the generated VFPs achieve high
accuracy, which in turn improves the performance of DeepPrint.

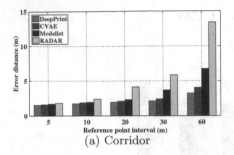
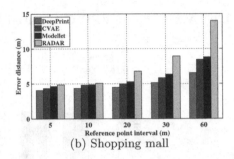

(a) Corridor   (b) Shopping mall

Fig. 5. Localization error under various reference point intervals.

Cost Efficiency. DeepPrint achieves comparable localization accuracy with
extremely sparse RPs. To show its cost efficiency, we calculate the decreasing rate
of the number of RPs used by DeepPrint, Modellet, and RADAR at comparable
localization accuracy. Suppose n_1 is the number of RPs used by DeepPrint, and
n_2 the number of RPs used by a counterpart at comparable accuracy. Then the
decreasing rate r is calculated by $r = (1 - n_1/n_2) \times 100\%$. From Fig. 6, we can
see that compared with other Wi-Fi localization systems, DeepPrint decreases
the number of RPs by 40%–81.7% at comparable accuracy. The results show
that DeepPrint achieves high accuracy at low cost.

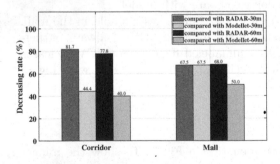
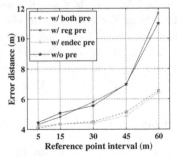

Fig. 6. The decreasing rate of the number of
reference points used by DeepPrint compared
with counterparts at comparable localization
accuracy.

Fig. 7. Localization accuracy with
different pre-training strategies
under various reference point intervals.

4.5   Effect of Pre-training

We pre-train the regressor and endec independently before joint training. To evaluate the effect of pre-training, we carry out joint training with four pre-training strategies: 1) w/ both pre: with both regressor and endec pre-training (what DeepPrint uses), 2) w/ reg pre: with only regressor pre-training, 3) w/ endec pre: with only endec pre-training, and 4) w/o pre: without pre-training. The experiments are performed at various reference point intervals: 5 m, 30 m, and 60 m.

To check the impact of training strategies on localization accuracy of Deep-Print, we generate VFPs by the generator under the four training strategies, and then perform localization. The results are shown in Fig. 7. We can see that the strategy with both pre-training outperforms all the other three. The strategy without pre-training performs the worst. The results verify the effect of pre-training.

5   Conclusions

We proposed a semi-supervised deep generative model SCVAE to generate high-quality virtual fingerprints with only a small number of reference points, by leveraging a large number of easily-collected unlabeled fingerprints. Based on SCVAE, a WiFi fingerprint indoor localization system DeepPrint was designed and deployed in real-world large-scale indoor scenarios with a total area about 8,400 m^2. Experimental results show that DeepPrint achieves comparable localization accuracy to the state-of-the-art counterparts and significantly reduces the fingerprint collection cost.

References

1. Abbas, M., Elhamshary, M., Rizk, H., Torki, M., Youssef, M.: WiDeep: WIFI-based accurate and robust indoor localization system using deep learning. In: PerCom, pp. 1–10 (2019)
2. Bahl, P., Padmanabhan, V.N.: RADAR: an in-building RF-based user location and tracking system. In: Proceedings IEEE INFOCOM 2000, vol. 2, pp. 775–784 (2000)
3. Chintalapudi, K., Padmanabha Iyer, A., Padmanabhan, V.N.: Indoor localization without the pain. In: Mobicom 2010, New York, NY, USA, pp. 173–184. ACM (2010)
4. Feng, C., Au, W.S.A., Valaee, S., Tan, Z.: Received-signal-strength-based indoor positioning using compressive sensing. IEEE Trans. Mob. Comput. 11(12), 1983–1993 (2012)
5. Gan, X., Yu, D., Huang, L., Li, Y.: Deep learning for weights training and indoor positioning using multi-sensor fingerprint. In: IPIN 2017, pp. 1–7, September 2017
6. Gwon, Y., Jain, R.: Error characteristics and calibration-free techniques for wireless LAN-based location estimation. In: MobiWac 2004, pp. 2–9. ACM (2004)
7. He, S., Chan, S.H.G.: Wi-fi fingerprint-based indoor positioning: recent advances and comparisons. IEEE Commun. Surv. Tutor. 18(1), 466–490 (2016)

8. Kingma, D.P., Welling, M.: Auto-encoding variational Bayes. In: ICLR (2014)
9. Kingma, D., Ba, J.: Adam: a method for stochastic optimization. In: ICLR, San Diego, USA (2015)
10. LeCun, Y., Bengio, Y., Hinton, G.: Deep learning. Nature **521**(7553), 436–441 (2015)
11. Li, L., Shen, G., Zhao, C., Moscibroda, T., Lin, J.H., Zhao, F.: Experiencing and handling the diversity in data density and environmental locality in an indoor positioning service. In: MobiCom 2014, New York, NY, USA, pp. 459–470. ACM (2014)
12. Madigan, D., Einahrawy, E., Martin, R.P., Ju, W., Krishnan, P., Krishnakumar, A.S.: Bayesian indoor positioning systems. In: INFOCOM 2015, vol. 2, pp. 1217–1227, March 2005
13. Murphy, K.P.: Machine Learning: A Probabilistic Perspective. The MIT Press, Cambridge (2012)
14. Nandakumar, R., Chintalapudi, K.K., Padmanabhan, V.N.: Centaur: locating devices in an office environment. In: Mobicom 2012, New York, NY, USA, pp. 281–292. ACM (2012)
15. Oliver, A., Odena, A., Raffel, C., Cubuk, E.D., Goodfellow, I.J.: Realistic evaluation of deep semi-supervised learning algorithms. In: NIPS 2018, Red Hook, NY, USA, pp. 3239–3250. Curran Associates Inc. (2018)
16. Paszke, A., et al.: Automatic differentiation in PyTorch. In: NIPS 2017 Workshop on Autodiff (2017)
17. Rai, A., Chintalapudi, K.K., Padmanabhan, V.N., Sen, R.: Zee: zero-effort crowdsourcing for indoor localization. In: Proceedings of ACM MobiCom, pp. 293–304 (2012)
18. Shen, G., Chen, Z., Zhang, P., Moscibroda, T., Zhang, Y.: Walkie-Markie: indoor pathway mapping made easy. In: NSDI 2013, Berkeley, CA, USA, pp. 85–98. USENIX Association (2013)
19. Sohn, K., Lee, H., Yan, X.: Learning structured output representation using deep conditional generative models. In: NIPS 2015, pp. 3483–3491 (2015)
20. Vasisht, D., Kumar, S., Katabi, D.: Decimeter-level localization with a single WIFI access point. In: NSDI 2016, Berkeley, CA, USA, pp. 165–178. USENIX Association (2016)
21. Wang, B., Chen, Q., Yang, L.T., Chao, H.C.: Indoor smartphone localization via fingerprint crowdsourcing: challenges and approaches. IEEE Wirel. Commun. **23**(3), 82–89 (2016)
22. Wu, C., Yang, Z., Liu, Y., Xi, W.: WILL: wireless indoor localization without site survey. IEEE Trans. Parallel Distrib. Syst. **24**(4), 839–848 (2013)
23. Xiao, J., Zhou, Z., Yi, Y., Ni, L.M.: A survey on wireless indoor localization from the device perspective. ACM Comput. Surv. **49**(2), 1–31 (2016)
24. Yang, Z., Wu, C., Liu, Y.: Locating in fingerprint space: Wireless indoor localization with little human intervention. In: Mobicom 2012, New York, NY, USA, pp. 269–280. ACM (2012)
25. Yang, Z., Zhou, Z., Liu, Y.: From RSSI to CSI: indoor localization via channel response. ACM Comput. Surv. **46**(2), 25:1–25:32 (2013)
26. Youssef, M., Agrawala, A.: The Horus WLAN location determination system. In: MobiSys 2005, New York, NY, USA, pp. 205–218. ACM (2005)
27. Zhang, W., Sengupta, R., Fodero, J., Li, X.: DeepPositioning: intelligent fusion of pervasive magnetic field and WIFI fingerprinting for smartphone indoor localization via deep learning. In: IEEE ICMLA 2017, pp. 7–13 (2017)

Winfrared: An Infrared-Like Rapid Passive Device-Free Tracking with Wi-Fi

Jian Fang$^{(\boxtimes)}$, Lei Wang$^{(\boxtimes)}$, Zhenquan Qin, Yixuan Hou, Wenbo Zhao, and Bingxian Lu

Dalian University of Technology, Dalian, China
fangjian@mail.dlut.edu.cn, lei.wang@dlut.edu.cn

Abstract. Accurate and fast target tracking is the basis of many intelligent applications and is therefore widely discussed and researched. The existing methods have many disadvantages, such as dead zone, high costs, and long delays. Combining the advantages of many methods, we propose an infrared-like rapid passive target tracking method with Wi-Fi. By analyzing and utilizing the feature of the Line of Sight and channel state information, we build a net that can track the moving target with a small number of transceivers. The evaluation result shows that our method can achieve rapid target tracking with low overhead.

Keywords: Passive tracking · Device-free · Wi-Fi

1 Introduction

Target tracking, which is an important branch of indoor localization, has been widely used in many wireless network applications, such as access control, activity recognition, and security monitoring. It usually asks for accurate and real-time location information and the moving direction of the target with the help of dedicated or generic devices. This problem was addressed by camera or infrared-based methods in the early stage. However the existence of "dead zone" and the optical solution in the famous movie *Once a Thief* invalidate those methods. Otherwise, the cost of deployment and maintenance of dedicated equipment is unbearable for many scenarios.

In recent years, we have witnessed an exponential growth in wireless network devices, and they have been widely used in a variety of applications including location-related works. Therefore, Wi-Fi-based tracking and localization methods were proposed. They solved the "dead zone" and cost problems largely, and

The work was supported by NSFC with No. 61902052, "National Key Research and Development Plan" with No. 2017YFC0821003-2, "Science and Technology Major Industrial Project of Liaoning Province" with No. 2020JH1/10100013, "Dalian Science and Technology Innovation Fund" with No. 2019J11CY004 and 2020JJ26GX037, and "the Fundamental Research Funds for the Central Universities" with No. DUT20ZD210 and DUT20TD107.

Z. Liu et al. (Eds.): WASA 2021, LNCS 12937, pp. 65–77, 2021.
https://doi.org/10.1007/978-3-030-85928-2_6

have achieved high accuracy due to ubiquitous and abundant features of Wi-Fi signals. These methods, however, always ask targets to wear or take devices like smartphones or sensors which incurs obvious inconvenience. In security monitoring, for example, you can not ask an intruder to work with you. Also, privacy protection and organizing devices of different standards are thorny issues.

Recent technologies have boosted the development of Device-free Localization (DfL), which does not ask for any accessories on the targets. DfL has a much broader range of applicability and flexibility and attracted much attention from researchers. Traditional Received Signal Strength (RSS) based DfL methods are usually coarse-grained and limited by multipath effect, incurring unsatisfactory localization accuracy. Other works either build a complex CSI fingerprint database [15] or a map from the location of the target to CSI dynamics [9]. They will increase the accuracy but sacrifices many human efforts and scalabilities since it is a high-overhead and repeated process for collecting data in dynamic scenarios. Otherwise, offline training takes much time which makes it a failure in real-time systems like security protection.

Although there are many pitfalls for traditional camera and infrared-based approaches, however, their basic principles provide us a novel way to utilize Wi-Fi since there are serval commonalities. For example, an LoS path between a pair of Wi-Fi transceivers is just like an enhanced and featured infrared beam with Fresnel zone [21]. Can we just imagine that a Wi-Fi transmitter is an infrared generator to help us localize or track targets? A lot of research shows that differences in characteristics of wireless signals are obvious when if or not there is a block on the Line of Sight (LoS) path of the link. With enough link, we can form a Wi-Fi infrared net, and by using the structure of points and lines, we can track the target by identifying them when and how to go through the LoS.

In this paper, we present Winfrared, a rapid passive device-free localization method with COTS Wi-Fi, we build an infrared-like system with Wi-Fi link. Winfrared does not request any complex fingerprint database or off-line training. We made full use of the fact that AP has existed on a large scale on many occasions. With only a limited number of transceivers, Winfrared could divide the covered area into nearly square level parts. We utilize *phase difference* as the metric to track the route of one or more targets rapidly.

The main contributions of this paper are as follows.

1. We analyze the relationship of different features of CSI and the movement of targets crossing the LoS path between transceivers and give an optimal combination that can accurately judge this behavior.
2. We propose a tracking method based on an infrared-like net with Fresnel zones of Wi-Fi which can achieve a meter-level tracking accuracy with a small number of transceivers.
3. We prototype Winfrared on commercial off-the-shelf devices and validate its performance in various environments. The experiments result demonstrate the effectiveness of Winfrared in different scenarios.

2   Related Work

Indoor Localization with the device has been discussed for quite a long time and has achieved quite a satisfactory accuracy. However, *Passive Device-Free Localization* is an emerging issue. Compared with traditional camera [3] and infrared-based [5] methods, there is no request on light and human effort with Wi-Fi-based localization, and it can cover most of the area and reduce "dead zone" [6,17]. Therefore, the device-free Wi-Fi-based method which consists of RFID, RSS, and CSI solution is gradually occupying the mainstream.

RSS-based is a common method while it can achieve acceptable accuracy with low cost on hardware. Youssef in his inspiring work proposes fingerprinting localization methods based on RSS [18] and opens a new research direction. E-HIPA [11] and FitLoc [1] apply compressive sensing which enables localization of one or more targets with very little RSS data and human efforts. Rass [19] divide tracking fields into several triangle areas and build relationships between signal dynamics and positions.

With the development of physical layer research, CSI-based localization schemes and applications have attracted lots of attention from researchers. PhaseU [14] propose a real-time LoS identification scheme in various scenarios with smart sensors on targets. Widar [9] can estimates velocity and location by building a CSI dynamics model and achieves decimeter accuracy without statistical learning. LiFS [12] pre-process all the subcarriers and find someone who is less or not affected by the multipath effect to determine the location of the target by a set of power fading equations. IndoTrack [7] proposes Doppler-MUSIC and Doppler-AoA methods to extract and estimate velocity and location information from CSI with only commodity Wi-Fi. Zhang *et al.* from Peking University [8,10,21] groundbreakingly introduces the theory of Fresnel zone into passive human sensing and obtains fine-grained respiration detection and localization results, Their work has a theoretical and practical explanation for the phenomenon that the perception results of different positions are significantly different and provides a new approach to explore human sensing and target localization. [3] tries to integrate various technologies to obtain a better tracking effect while LPWAN provides the possibility of tracking and identifying targets in a larger area [2,16,20].

Most of existing works model the features of signal with the location of targets, which will take much time for data processing no matter how high the computational complexity is. In some scenarios like security, there is no request on decimeter level accuracy and no time for processing, with only limited equipment, Winfrared can achieve close to square magnitude partition to the area and acceptable localization accuracy, while saving much time.

3   Background

3.1   Channel State Information and Subcarriers

The relationship of signal at transmitter and receiver is $Y = HX + N$, where X, Y, N are transmitted signal, received signal, and Gaussian noise, respectively.

On the level of subcarriers, $Y(k) = H(k)X(k)+N(k)$, where $k \in \{1, 2, \cdots, K\}$ is the subcarrier index, $H = \{H(k)\}, k \in 1, 2, \cdots, K$ is the CSI matrix, represents combined effect of fading, reflection of the link *etc.*. CSI can provide finer-grained channel descriptions than RSS for different types of wireless signals [4,13]. In this paper, we do all the experiments on COTS Intel 5300 NIC. We can get $K = 30$ subcarrier information, which is about one group for every 2 subcarriers at 20 MHz or one in 4 at 40 MHz [4]. And $H(f) = \|H(f)\|e^{j\angle H(f)}$, where $\| * \|$ and $\angle*$ are amplitude and phase, respectively.

3.2 Line of Sight and Fresnel Zone

In complex indoor scenarios, Wi-Fi signals travel through multiple paths due to rich reflection, refraction, scattering caused by barriers. Even in an empty room, reflection paths caused by the ceiling and floor still exist. However, among all the paths of Wi-Fi signals between transceivers, there is a most strong, stable path called the Line of Sight (LoS) path, which means signals propagating directly from the transmitter to receiver just like the human eyes can see.

The Fresnel zone is a concept proposed to study the directional diffraction of light, and it is one of a series of concentric prolate ellipsoidal regions of space between and around a pair of the transceivers antenna system. Since the nature of wireless signals and light are both waves, the concept of the Fresnel zone is now widely used in the study of electromagnetic signals. Studies have shown that in wireless signal transmission, over 70% of energy is concentrated in the first Fresnel zone, so we need to ensure that there are no obstacles in this area in practice. However, it is for this reason that when an object appears in this area, the characteristics of the signal will changes significantly, which can be exploited by us to do some identification works.

For a given wavelength of the wireless signal, these concentric ellipses are expressed like $|P_1E_n| + |P_2E_n| - |P_1P_2| = \frac{1}{2}n\lambda$, where E_n is the boundary of the n_{th} frensel zone. Therefore, reflection path is $\frac{1}{2}n\lambda$ larger than the LoS path when there is a target on the $n = 1$ fresnel zone (First Fresnel zone, FFZ). The calculations of the radius of the Fresnel zone at point P are as: $F_n = \sqrt{\frac{n\lambda d_1 d_2}{d_1+d_2}}$, $d_1, d_2 \gg n\lambda$, where d_1 is the distance between transmitter and point P, d_2 is the distance between receiver and point P, $D = d_1 + d_2$ is distance between transceivers, and $\lambda = \dfrac{c}{f}$ is the wavelength.

4 Winfrared Design and Evaluation

4.1 Overview

In a traditional infrared security system, due to the physical characteristics of the infrared beam, large areas are remained uncovered although many infrared transceivers are deployed in the monitoring area. The Wi-Fi link has similar but more flexible characteristics than infrared. We can determine that targets are moving through the LoS path of a Wi-Fi Link by modeling its characteristics just like an infrared security system. Therefore, we propose Winfrared, an infrared-like system using Wi-Fi. Winfrared works in three folds and the structure of it is shown as Fig. 1.

- We first analyze the relationship between characteristics of CSI dynamics and targets moving through the LoS path. And we choose phase difference, the most significant characteristic, as the metric.
- Then, we form a Wi-Fi link net with several transceivers and divide the monitoring area into as many as small areas. We also analyze the error of the tracking location based on the properties of the graph as shown in Fig. 2.
- We utilize phase difference and MAC address to judge through which LoS path the target moving. And with the help of timestamps and the topology, we can know the order of the movements. Therefore, we can track the route of one or more targets rapidly with low overhead.

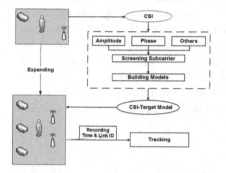

Fig. 1. Structure of Winfrared.

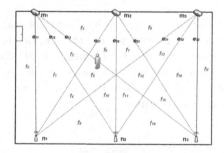

Fig. 2. A 3 × 3 case.

4.2   CSI Variation Model of a Target Going Through the LoS Path

To sum up all the existed works, we found that CSI variation of the link is closely related to interferences between transceivers. However, the same interference, usually a movement of the target, has different on subcarriers since CSI may also strongly affected by multipath, noise, and the relative position of the targets and transceivers, *etc.*. As depicted by Wang *et al.* in [12], we also would like to find the most "neat" subcarrier that least affected by noises and choose the simplest and clearest characteristic to build a CSI variation model of targets moving through the link.

To find a universal metric under different scenarios, we take height, distance, size of the target, and degree of the movement into consideration comprehensively. We first set one pair of transceivers apart 1 m to 10 m on the planet of

0.5 m, 0.8 m, and 1 m, respectively. We invite two volunteers, a 1.85 m height male and a 1.7 m height female respectively, and let them walk through the LoS path of Wi-Fi Link at a normal walking speed of 0.5 m/s from three directions, perpendicular to the LoS path (90°), 60°, and 30°. We would like to find the most "neat" subcarrier and the most prominent characteristic of the CSI by exploring the CSI dynamic of one target and one link first. Then, we will expand it to multiple targets and multiple links. Therefore, we time and record the whole process of volunteers moving through transceivers and finally determine the exact time point by slow-motion playback.

Figure 3 shows the result of part of our pre-experiments, we can see three distinct yellow high energy bars in the spectrograms framed by red as shown in Fig. 3(a), which matched the male volunteer moving through one pair of transceivers apart 2 m from three directions, respectively. And Fig. 3(b) and 3(c) are amplitude and phase difference change over packets (duration between packets is 0.03 s). While Fig. 3(e) and 3(f) are the female volunteer moving 4 times. In all these figures, there is a corresponding number of fluctuations to the movement. By slow-motion playback, we can approximately determine that the parts in the red rectangle are the key parts. By comparing Fig. 3(b) and 3(c), Fig. 3(e) and 3(f), the most significant difference between them is the duration of fluctuation, we noticed that the red rectangle in Fig. 3(c) and 3(f) are more slender, in other words, the amplitude may have been affected by interference besides the target movement, while changes in phase difference are more pronounced, precise, and matching time and movement more accurately. Therefore, we would like to select phase difference to be the metric due to its higher stability and less volatility.

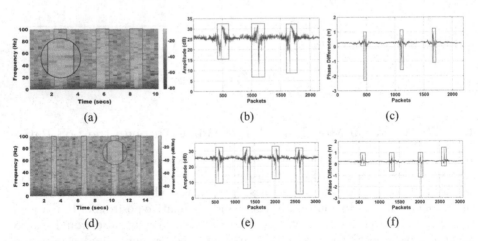

(a)   (b)   (c)

(d)   (e)   (f)

Fig. 3. Realtime amplitude and phase difference of one target moving through the LoS path. (Color figure online).

Since we select phase difference as the metric, here comes a new problem. We know that IWL 5300 can provide information on 3 antennas and 30 subcarriers,

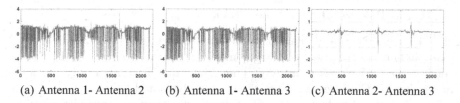

(a) Antenna 1- Antenna 2   (b) Antenna 1- Antenna 3   (c) Antenna 2- Antenna 3

Fig. 4. Phase different of three combinations of antennas.

based on our previous work, we have reasons to believe that the same interference has a different effect on a different combination of antennas and 30 subcarriers. So we do another selection as shown in Fig. 4, Fig. 4(a), 4(b), and 4(c) shows phase difference of three combinations of antennas, we can find that oscillograph of combination antenna 1–2 and antenna 1–3 are very messy, we can hardly find any useful characteristics in them. However, it is very clear to see a good match with the known movement in Fig. 4(c). Therefore, we would like to use the combination of Antenna 2 and 3 in this paper. However, this combination is not necessarily fixed. Through experiments, we found that the optimal combination will change significantly when it in different environments or when the devices are replaced.

So far, we selected phase difference as the metric and the best combination of the antenna according to our devices and the environment. We determined a threshold through many times of experiments and experience. To verify the validity of the threshold, we randomly selected and tested 300 sets of data in different scenarios (different volunteers, height and distance of the transceivers, etc.). The test results are shown in Table 1:

Table 1. Classification accuracy of our model

TP	TN	FP	FN
0.985	0.967	0.033	0.015
Precision	Recall	Accuracy	
0.968	0.985	0.976	

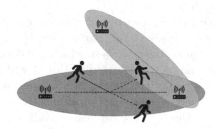

Fig. 5. Use the Fresnel zone to determine the "stop and turn" and direction of movement.

The accuracy can meet the detection requirements on a single link in most scenarios. We will explain how Winfrared can further improve the tracking robustness by forming a net.

4.3   Rapid Passive Device-Free Tracking

A Wi-Fi Link Net for Tracking the Target. As depicted in Subsect. 4.2, we can judge the progress of a target moving through a single Wi-Fi link by modeling the CSI phase accurately. Therefore, we can continuously track the target using MAC address-distinguished transceivers and links.

Considering a simple scenario G in which deployed m transmitters and n receivers like Fig. 2. All the transceivers are equally spaced along the longer side of the room, and we assume that the location of the door is always known. We define the set of all the transceivers as Vertices Set $V(G)$ and the link between them are Edges Set $E(G)$. Edge Tx$_i$ to Rx$_j$ is e_{ij}. And we define the area nearest to the door as planet 0 (P_0). In Winfrared, we have two basic claims.

Claim 1. *The route of a target is continuous, which means that the target will not jump or teleport from one place to another.*

A target could only appear in two adjacent areas divided by e_{ij} at two adjacent time points. In other words, any two adjacent locations have at least one common edge.

Claim 2. *The target can only move through one LoS path of the link at the same time point.*

Base on Claim 1, we further assume that a target could only change its location by moving through *one* link, not the intersection of two links. Otherwise, when there is more than one affected link recognized at the same time, we need to distinguish it whether caused by multiple targets or a narrow-angle between two links.

Winfrared combines the advantages of Wi-Fi networks and infrared, forming an infrared-like net with Wi-Fi links, we treat the Fresnel zone of the Wi-Fi link as an infrared beam and track how the target moving in the net utilizing CSI phase difference.

We take a $m = n = 3$ case for example as shown in Fig. 2. We tag all the area as $f_1, f_2, \cdots, f_{16}$, partitioned by $e_{ij}, 0 \leq i, j \leq 2$. In a tracking progress, the target appears in f_0 in which the door locate first. It will cross e_{11} and enter f_1 first no matter which direction it will go. And then, if the target wants to go from f_1 to f_2, it must through e_{12} and match the model.

We use a bunch of 9-bit binary code to represent the area which the target in, and the $0 \sim 8_{th}$ bit respectively correspond to e_{11} to e_{13}, e_{21} to e_{23}, and e_{31} to e_{33}. It is obvious that each e_{ij} divides the area into two parts alone, and we define the part which is nearer to the door as 0, while the other part is 1. Therefore, for example, we use 000000000 to represent the location of target when it is in f_0, and 001011111 for f_{12}. We can treat the route of a target in the room as a trail on the dual graph G^* of G. For each move, there will be only a one-bit change in theory. However, when there is a two (or more) bits change or two (or more) consecutive unrelated bits change (means two disjoint links, like e_{11} and e_{32}), it reveals that the tracking process is wrong and we can correct the error by utilizing the structure of the G.

Consider a more general condition, and relax the conditions without limiting the placement of transceivers, we can get a more complex and common topology of the network. We still set the number of transmitter and receiver as m and n, respectively. In the best case, each Tx_i and Rx_j forms a link and they are non-coincident.

Theorem 1. *The total number of Winfrared link is no more than $\dfrac{(m+n)(m+n-1)}{2}$, and effective link is no more than $m \times n$. While m, n is the number of transmitter and receiver, respectively.*

Proof. $m+n$ transceivers could form a $(m+n) - order\ complete\ graph$, we assume all the equipment are actived and duplex, the link of this system is $\binom{2}{m+n} = \dfrac{(m+n)(m+n-1)}{2}$. And if they are simplex only from transmitter to receiver, they form a *bigraph*, and set of transmitter and receiver are its two subgraph, so the number of effective link is $m \times n$.

Lemma 1. *The number of areas divided by LoS Wi-Fi links K is larger than $m \times n$.*

Proof. We use $K_{i,j}$ to represent the number of area when $m = i$ and $n = j$.

- When $m = 1, n = 1$, it is easy to get $K_{1,1} = 2$. Since $2 > 1 \times 1$, conclusion established.
- We assume conclusion established when $m = m_0, n = n_0$, we get $K_{m_0,n_0} > m_0 \times n_0$.
- When $n = n_0 + 1$, the newly added point will connect with the m_0 points to form m_0 new links, and $m_0 \times n_0$ intersection points are generated with the existing links to divide the original K_{m_0,n_0} regions and generate at least new $m_0 \times n_0$ regions. Therefore, $K_{m_0,n_0+1} > K_{m_0,n_0} + m_0 \times n_0 > m_0 \times n_0 + n_0 = m_0 \times (n_0 + 1)$.

Time Synchronization. Since target tracking is a continuous progress, and the locations of it are in time-order, there should be a tight time synchronization among all the equipment. Therefore, we design a simple mechanism which enables all the equipment could synchronize their clock once in a while.

Theorem 2. *Every two vertexes of G (Tx_i, Rx_j, $1 \leq i, j \leq 3$) could be synchronized in no more than 2-time slots.*

Proof. G is a connected graph, and it is 3-connected. The diameter of G is $d(G) = max\ \{d(u,v)|u, v \in V(G)\} = \lceil \log_{\Delta-1} \dfrac{N(\Delta - 2) + 2}{\Delta} \rceil = 2$, where maximum degree $\Delta = 3$ and order $N = 6$. Without loss of generality, we assume $m > n$, so $d(G) = \lceil \log_{m-1} \dfrac{(m+n)(m-2) + 2}{m} \rceil < \lceil \log_{m-1} \dfrac{2m(m-2)+2}{m} \rceil = \lceil \log_{m-1} \dfrac{2(m-1)^2}{m} \rceil$. When $m \geq 2, m - 1 \geq 1, \dfrac{2}{m} \leq 1, f(m) = d(G)$ is monotonically increasing, so $d(G) < \log_{m-1}(m-1)^2 = 2$. If there are more points in G, that is, if m and n are any value, the same argument can be made.

We set m_1 as the standard clock, and it can synchronize $n_1 \sim n_3$ when transmitting data to them with only one hop since they are adjacent. And m_2, m_3 could be synchronized by n_j with ACK frame. We set a maximum time slot T_m to be a default interval to start synchronization.

Some Details to Improve the Tracking Accuracy and Robustness. In the experiment, we find an interesting unsolved problem which we called "stop and turn around problem" as shown in Fig. 5. Considering a scenario that the target just happened to stop at the LoS path and turn around, it is likely that it will cause a very similar effect on the CSI as the target move through the path normally. However, the location of the target remains unchanged actually, which will cause significant localization errors. We can solve this problem by utilizing the characteristics of graph structure based on Claim 1 and 2. But it is a time delay method that takes effect after one or more movements. Can we just find a real-time and more intuitive approach to address this problem?

We found that the most significant difference between a person normally passing through a LOS path and "stop and turn around" is that the person has an approximately 180° turn. According to our preliminary experiment in Sect. 4.2, this turn is reflected in Fig. 3(c) and 3(f) by an increase in the phase difference and a widening of the time domain. Based on multiple measurements and analysis of the person's walk, we set a threshold to distinguish "stop and turn around", so that we can correct the track in the first place.

Then, we utilize an FZ-based solution that can further detect the direction and trend of the target moving through the Fresnel zone of transceivers. As we know, the Fresnel zone is a series of the ellipse with the same focus at transmitter and receiver, and as the number of the Fresnel zone increases, the long axis length of the ellipse also increases. If a target walks from afar, it will through the n_{th} fresnel zone to the FFZ orderly, and the movement of the target will cause a different effect on different fresnel zone. Therefore, we would like to utilize this characteristic to figure out whether a target has crossed the LoS path.

According to the periodic characteristics of wireless signals, we know that if the phase difference of two superimposed signals is $2k\pi$, it will produce an enhanced signal, while the signal will be weakened when the phase difference is $2k\pi + \pi$, where k is a constant. The phase difference caused by the reflection of a target on the boundary of FFZ is π according to the Sect. 3. And there is a π phase shift caused by reflection itself, therefore, the superimposed phase difference on FFZ is 2π, which will produce an enhanced signal. However, when the target is on the boundary of the 2_{nd} fresnel zone, the phase difference will be $2\pi + \pi$, which will produce a weakened signal.

Therefore, the signal will show a state close to a sinusoid when targets moving through the multiple fresnel zones continuously from outside to the LoS path, while the period of the x-axis (time or distance covered) is decreasing because the radius difference of the Fresnel zone is gradually reducing (we assume the target is moving along the short axis of the ellipse), and vice versa. We can use this method to determine when a person approaches or leaves the LoS path, and infer the angle between the path and the LoS path, namely the direction of the movement, according to the distance between the peaks of the sinusoid-like signal. While as shown in Fig. 5, thanks to the multiple cross Fresnel zones formed by transceivers of Winfrared, a walking process may affect multiple links. For example, a person walks toward the blue LoS and turns around toward the green LoS, the two links can judge his/her walking trend and direction respectively. It is significantly different from that the person goes straight through the blue LoS. The more complex his/her route, the better Winfrared's tracking performance.

4.4   Measurement of Localization Error

Among all the localization and tracking works, the two most important evaluation indicators are response speed and error. Since Winfrared does not ask for off-line training and only judges the behavior of the target crossing the LoS path, its response time is relatively small. However, as shown in Fig. 2, we use area divided by LoS between transceivers as the unit of location, but we still need to take a specified point as the result of the localization. And we find that most of the f_n is a triangle or a simple convex quadrilateral made up of triangles, We take the center of gravity as the coarse-grained location of $f_k, 1 \leq k \leq K = 16$, therefore, we can get a polyline as the route of the targets. But how to measure the error of localization?

In this paper, we first transfer f_n to a round with same area, then take its radius as the localization error of this region, and we take the average of all regions as the global positioning error. We noticed that the network topology we designed is highly symmetrical, satisfying axisymmetric and central symmetry. This property is very helpful in improving the uniformity of localization errors since we only need to calculate 5 different radiuses in Fig. 2. And if the sides of the monitored area rectangle are a and b, respectively. Therefore, the area of f_n are $S(f_1, f_{16}) = \frac{ab}{8}$, $S(f_2, f_4, f_{13}, f_{15}) = \frac{ab}{24}$, $S(f_3, f_8, f_9, f_{14}) = \frac{ab}{12}$, $S(f_5, f_{12}) = \frac{ab}{24}$, $S(f_6, f_7, f_{10}, f_{11}) = \frac{ab}{24}$. The radius of the corresponding circle of the same area are $r(f_{1,16}) = \sqrt{\frac{ab}{8\pi}}, r(f_{2,4,13,15}) = \sqrt{\frac{ab}{24\pi}}, r(f_{3,8,9,14}) = \sqrt{\frac{ab}{12\pi}}, r(f_{5,12}) = \sqrt{\frac{ab}{24\pi}}, r(f_{6,7,10,11}) = \sqrt{\frac{ab}{24\pi}}$. We assume there is a room with the area of $a \times b = 100\,\mathrm{m}^2$, then the average location error is 1.35 m. The CDF of the error of tracking location is shown in Fig. 6. And the average error will be reduced to 0.83 m if one pair of transceivers are added. Even without the addition of equipment, the variation of the error is gradually reduced with the increase of the monitoring area as shown in Fig. 7.

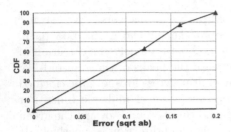

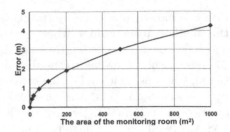

Fig. 6. CDF of the error of the tracking location when using a 3×3 deployment.

Fig. 7. The error variation of the tracking location with the area of the monitoring room when using a 3×3 deployment.

5   Conclusion and Discussion

In this paper, we propose a Wi-Fi-based passive tracking method, we first analyze the relationship between moving across the LoS of the transceiver and characteristics of wireless signals, then we build a Winfrared net, evaluation result shows that with a small number of transceivers, Winfrared can track targets accurately and rapidly. We believe that our method does not only work well with Wi-Fi devices on the ground. In future work, we need to solve some more detailed problems, such as the simultaneous occurrence of multiple targets. And we need to design a more reasonable topology to reduce the error. We also would like to combine Winfrared with LPWAN and introduce it into larger area tracking. Long-range communication and localization have been hard issues for a long time because of the complex environment. We believe the concept of Winfrared will also outperform any other methods in the long range.

References

1. Chang, L., et al.: FitLoc: fine-grained and low-cost device-free localization for multiple targets over various areas. IEEE/ACM Trans. Netw. **25**, 1994–2007 (2017)
2. Chen, L., et al.: LungTrack: Towards contactless and zero dead-zone respiration monitoring with commodity RFIDs. Proc. ACM Interact. Mob. Wear. Ubiquit. Technol. **3**(3), 1–22 (2019)
3. Fang, S., Munir, S., Nirjon, S.: Fusing Wifi and camera for fast motion tracking and person identification: demo abstract. In: Proceedings of the 18th Conference on Embedded Networked Sensor Systems, pp. 617–618 (2020)
4. Halperin, D., Hu, W., Sheth, A., Wetherall, D.: Tool release: Gathering 802.11 n traces with channel state information. ACM SIGCOMM Comput. Commun. Rev. **41**(1), 53–53 (2011)
5. Hijikata, S., Terabayashi, K., Umeda, K.: A simple indoor self-localization system using infrared LEDs. In: 2009 Sixth International Conference on Networked Sensing Systems (INSS), pp. 1–7. IEEE (2009)

6. Kotaru, M., Joshi, K.R., Bharadia, D., Katti, S.: SpotFi: decimeter level localization using WiFi. ACM Spec. Interest Group Data Commun. **45**(4), 269–282 (2015)
7. Li, X., et al.: IndoTrack: device-free indoor human tracking with commodity Wi-Fi. Proc. ACM Interact. Mob. Wear. Ubiquit. Technol. **1**(3), 1–22 (2017)
8. Niu, K., Zhang, F., Xiong, J., Li, X., Yi, E., Zhang, D.: Boosting fine-grained activity sensing by embracing wireless multipath effects. In: Proceedings of the 14th International Conference on emerging Networking EXperiments and Technologies, pp. 139–151 (2018)
9. Qian, K., Wu, C., Yang, Z., Yang, C., Liu, Y.: Decimeter level passive tracking with WiFi. In: Proceedings of the 3rd Workshop on Hot Topics in Wireless, pp. 44–48. ACM (2016)
10. Wang, H., et al.: MFDL: A multicarrier Fresnel penetration model based device-free localization system leveraging commodity Wi-Fi cards. arXiv preprint arXiv:1707.07514 (2017)
11. Wang, J., et al.: E-HIPA: an energy-efficient framework for high-precision multi-target-adaptive device-free localization. IEEE Trans. Mob. Comput. **16**(3), 716–729 (2017)
12. Wang, J., et al.: LiFS: low human-effort, device-free localization with fine-grained subcarrier information. In: Proceedings of the 22nd Annual International Conference on Mobile Computing and Networking, pp. 243–256 (2016)
13. Wang, Y., Lu, H., Sun, H.: Channel estimation in IRS-enhanced mmWave system with super-resolution network. IEEE Commun. Lett. **25**(8), 2599–2603 (2021)
14. Wu, C., Yang, Z., Zhou, Z., Qian, K., Liu, Y., Liu, M.: PhaseU: real-time LOS identification with WiFi. In: 2015 IEEE Conference on Computer Communications (INFOCOM), pp. 2038–2046. IEEE (2015)
15. Xiao, J., Wu, K., Yi, Y., Wang, L., Ni, L.M.: Pilot: passive device-free indoor localization using channel state information. In: 2013 IEEE 33rd International Conference on Distributed Computing Systems (ICDCS), pp. 236–245. IEEE (2013)
16. Xie, B., Xiong, J.: Combating interference for long range LoRa sensing. In: Proceedings of the 18th Conference on Embedded Networked Sensor Systems, pp. 69–81 (2020)
17. Xie, Y., Xiong, J., Li, M., Jamieson, K.: XD-track: leveraging multi-dimensional information for passive Wi-Fi tracking. In: Proceedings of the 3rd Workshop on Hot Topics in Wireless, pp. 39–43 (2016)
18. Youssef, M., Mah, M., Agrawala, A.: Challenges: device-free passive localization for wireless environments. In: Proceedings of the 13th Annual ACM International Conference on Mobile Computing and Networking, pp. 222–229. ACM (2007)
19. Zhang, D., Liu, Y., Guo, X., Ni, L.M.: RASS: a real-time, accurate, and scalable system for tracking transceiver-free objects. IEEE Trans. Parallel Distrib. Syst. **24**(5), 996–1008 (2013)
20. Zhang, F., Chang, Z., Niu, K., Xiong, J., Jin, B., Lv, Q., Zhang, D.: Exploring LoRa for long-range through-wall sensing. Proc. ACM Interact. Mob. Wear. Ubiquit. Technol. **4**(2), 1–27 (2020)
21. Zhang, F., et al.: From Fresnel diffraction model to fine-grained human respiration sensing with commodity Wi-Fi devices. Proc. ACM Interact. Mob. Wear. Ubiquit. Technol. **2**(1), 53 (2018)

Fusing Directional and Omnidirectional Wi-Fi Antennas for Accurate Indoor Localization

Kunxin Zhu, Yongxin Hu, Ning Liu, and Qun Niu[✉]

Sun Yat-sen University, Guangzhou, China
{zhukx3,huyx57}@mail2.sysu.edu.cn, {liuning2,niuq3}@mail.sysu.edu.cn

Abstract. Wi-Fi fingerprint-based indoor localization has attracted much attention due to the pervasiveness of Wi-Fi access points (APs). However, the localization accuracy could be degraded due to signal fluctuations and noises of omnidirectional antennas. Some researches propose to leverage the signal distribution of different APs to enhance the localization accuracy. Nevertheless, they are either sensitive to signal errors or computationally costly.

In this paper, we propose a directional AP guided indoor localization system, where we incorporate directional APs to constrain the spatial space of clients. Based on the observation that signals of different APs fluctuate similarly, we study *signal correlation* between multiple APs. Consequently, we can identify anomalous APs (signal changes drastically compared with others) and filter them to reduce the adverse impact on the localization accuracy. Based on the correlation estimation, we model the localization problem with Dempster-Shafer (DS) theory and directional AP guidance to estimate the confidence values of AP signals adaptively. Furthermore, we remove the division in DS theory to avoid the paradox problem. We have implemented our algorithm and conducted extensive experiments in two different trial sites. Experimental results show that we can improve the localization accuracy by at least 27% compared with the state-of-the-art competing schemes.

Keywords: Indoor localization · Directional antenna · Fusion theory

1 Introduction

Indoor location-based service (ILBS) has attracted much attention due to its great commercial value. It has a wide range of applications, such as indoor navigation, public security and so on. The quality of these applications, however, is largely dependent on the accuracy of localization algorithms.

To achieve sufficient accuracy, researchers have studied various signals for indoor localization, such as Wi-Fi [4], vision [14], magnetic field [13], light [11], etc. Among these signals, Wi-Fi fingerprint has received considerable attention

© Springer Nature Switzerland AG 2021
Z. Liu et al. (Eds.): WASA 2021, LNCS 12937, pp. 78–91, 2021.
https://doi.org/10.1007/978-3-030-85928-2_7

due to the pervasiveness of Wi-Fi APs. A target[1] receives signals from different APs and predicts its position. This method has two phases [5,19]: an offline phase followed by an online phase. In the offline phase, researchers construct a fingerprint database of the area. They collect received signal strength indicators (RSSIs) from different APs at each reference point (RP), which is a known location point. These RSSIs form a unique vector of each RP, termed Wi-Fi fingerprint. All fingerprints form a map saved in the database. In the online phase, a user collects a Wi-Fi fingerprint vector. Then, the localization algorithm compares it with the map and calculates the position.

Despite extensive research efforts, recent arts have a few limitations:

- *Location ambiguity with omnidirectional antennas*: Previous approaches [8,10] leverage omnidirectional antennas (OAs) for indoor localization. However, these APs emit wireless signals in all directions, which could lead to location ambiguity due to multipath fading in the complicated indoor environment.
- *Erroneous location estimation with anomalous AP signals*: Due to environmental changes and temporal obstruction, some AP signals could be anomalous, leading to large localization errors. However, many approaches [6,7] do not identify anomalous AP signals, which could lead to large localization errors.
- *Non-uniform confidence of AP signals*: AP signals could be noisy due to various environmental (e.g., multipath fading) and temporal (e.g., moving pedestrians) factors. Therefore, the confidence value of different AP signals vary spatially and temporally. However, many approaches (e.g., [15]) compare the AP RSSI with uniform confidence values, which could lead to noisy location estimations.

To address these problems, we propose to fuse directional and omnidirectional signals for accurate localization, termed *FDOLoc*. Our key contributions are as follows:

- *Directional AP-guided indoor localization system*: In order to reduce the impact of signal ambiguity, we propose to incorporate directional antennas (DAs) into our localization system, where we constrain the spatial space of users to reduce the impact of fingerprint ambiguity.
- *Correlation evaluation for anomalous AP identification*: According to our experimental results, AP signals are *correlated* indoors, i.e., fluctuation levels are similar without drastic environmental changes or obstructions. Based on the observation, we propose to evaluate the correlation of AP signals, where we model the correlation by conducting pair-wise comparisons. Consequently, we are able to identify anomalous APs automatically.
- *DS-based adaptive AP confidence estimation*: We propose Dempster-Shafer theory-based AP confidence estimation algorithm, where we estimate

---

[1] We use "client" and "target" interchangeably in this paper.

the confidence value of each AP adaptively using the query fingerprint. Additionally, we propose a refining algorithm, where we remove the division to avoid the paradox issue due to signal noises.

The rest of this paper is organized as follows. After reviewing related works in Sect. 2, we show the signal correlation, the characteristics of DAs and the basic concept of DS theory in Sect. 3. Then we elaborate our framework in Sect. 4, followed by illustrative experimental results in Sect. 5. Finally, we conclude in Sect. 6.

2   Related Work

We briefly review recent arts that are most related to ours as follows.

In order to reduce the impact of multipath fading and fingerprint ambiguity, some researches [3,16] propose to leverage DAs to achieve sufficient accuracy. However, they need to move DAs to localize a fixed user, which is tedious in practice. Bigler et al. [2] propose an algorithm that estimates the position based on the DA's RSSI. Despite the high accuracy, they have to build an accurate propagation model for DAs, which is prone to the environmental noises.

Jun et al. [9] propose a method for localization using Wi-Fi sequences. They divide the test site into small regions and assign a unique sequence to each region directly as a fingerprint. TileJunction [6] calculates the possible areas (called tiles) of the target for each AP, and estimates the fine-grained location in the overlapped area of tiles. Despite the extensive research efforts, many of them do not consider the signal correlation between different APs, leading to compromised localization accuracy with noises.

Some works employ DS theory in indoor localization. For example, Zhang et al. [18] fuse OA signals with the Gaussian model for accurate localization. Furthermore, Lohan et al. [12] optimize the mass function to reduce the positioning error. Although accurate in specific scenarios, many of them do not consider the paradox of DS theory, leading to large localization errors when the conflict between data sources is serious. DST [1] proposes a complex combination method to avoid the paradox problem. Although the localization accuracy is high, the computational cost is also higher.

3   Preliminary

Based on DS theory, FDOLoc models the signal correlation between APs and filters the noise for indoor positioning. In addition, directional antennas are used to increase the positioning accuracy. We discuss the correlation among APs, characteristics of DAs and introduce Dempster-Shafer theory in this section.

3.1   Correlation of AP Signals

In this section, we analyze the correlation of AP signals. As shown in Fig. 1, we deploy four OAs in a room and collect Wi-Fi fingerprints at RP1 both in the online and offline stage. Additionally, we collect fingerprints with noises (e.g., pedestrian walking around). We present the RSSI values in Table 1, where $-33(5)$ dBm indicates the mean RSSI value (-33) and the standard deviation (5), respectively.

If the impact of noises is marginal, the deviation of the online fingerprint from each AP is similar to that in the offline stage. For example, the online vector at $RP1$ is $\{-30, -42, -55, -47\}$. Each AP value falls within one standard deviation of the offline vector $\{-33(5), -43(2), -52(7), -45(6)\}$.

However, if the impact of noises is significant, the deviation of RSSIs in the online stage is different from that in the offline stage and the impact of noise on each AP signal is different. Some AP signals are less affected by noise and the signal distribution is similar. When a pedestrian walks around AP3, the fluctuation of RSSIs from this AP is more significant than others (AP1, AP2 and AP4). Based on this motivation, we propose to leverage the signal correlation to remove signal noises for more accurate localization.

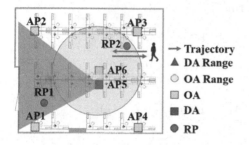

Fig. 1. Floor plan of a test site.   **Fig. 2.** Illustration of RSSI fluctuation.

Table 1. RSSI from each AP.

	AP1	AP2	AP3	AP4
Offline RP1	$-33(5)$	$-43(2)$	$-52(7)$	$-45(6)$
Online RP1	-30	-42	-55	-47
Online (trajectory) RP1	-34	-41	-67	-43

3.2   Characteristics of Directional Antenna

Figure 1 illustrates the radiated ranges of the DA (AP5) and the OA (AP6). We collect the RSSI of $AP5$ and $AP6$ at $RP1$ (radiated area) and $RP2$ (non-radiated are) over a period of time, respectively. Figure 2 shows that the RSSI of the DA is more stable than that of the OA. Additionally, the signal strength of the DA in its radiated area is stronger. Last, the RSSI of the DA in its radiated and non-radiated areas are more differentiable. To summarize, signals from a DA are more stable and distinguishing at different positions. Therefore, they can be exploited to improve the localization accuracy.

3.3 DS Theory

We briefly explain the basic concept of DS theory, which fuses multi-source data to make a decision. Γ is denoted as a finite set of n mutually exclusive atomic hypotheses, i.e., $\Gamma = \{\theta_1, ..., \theta_n\}$. $\Theta = 2^{\Gamma}$ is denoted as the power set of Γ. A basic probability assignment (BPA) over Γ is defined as a function $m\colon \Theta \to [0, 1]$, which can be regarded as distribution probabilities of each hypothesis in Θ. BPA functions should satisfy the following conditions:

$$m(\emptyset) = 0, \quad \sum_{A \subseteq \Theta} m(A) = 1. \tag{1}$$

L independent sources bring L BPA functions of a hypothesis A in Θ and we denote these functions as $m_1, m_2, .., m_L$. The fused BPA value (probability) m_c is calculated by Dempster's combination rule:

$$m_c(A) = (m_1 \oplus m_2 \oplus \cdots \oplus m_L)(A) =$$
$$\frac{1}{1 - K} \{ \sum_{A_1 \cap A_2 \cap \cdots \cap A_L = A} m_1(A_1) \cdot m_2(A_2) \cdots m_L(A_L) \}, \tag{2}$$

$$K = 1 - \sum_{A_1 \cap A_2 \cap \cdots \cap A_L \neq \emptyset} m_1(A_1) \cdot m_2(A_2) \cdots m_L(A_L), \tag{3}$$

where $A, A_1, \cdots, A_L$ are hypotheses in Θ and $K \in [0, 1]$ is a conflict indicator (as K approaches 1, the conflict level is high).

4   Design of FDOLoc

In this section, we present the design of FDOLoc in Fig. 3. It has two phases: an offline phase and an online phase. In the offline phase, we collect the RSSI data, preprocess and save them. In the online phase, users upload the collected RSSI data to FDOLoc. At first, FDOLoc preprocesses these raw data. Second, FDOLoc compares signal sequences to reduce the searching space and selects the candidate point. Last, an improved DS algorithm with paradox correction is applied to fuse signals and estimate the position.

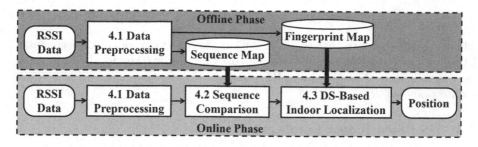

Fig. 3. Overview of the proposed FDOLoc.

4.1 Data Preprocessing

In the offline phase, given L APs and N RPs, we let AP_l $(1 \leq l \leq L)$ and RP_n $(1 \leq n \leq N)$ denote the lth AP and the nth RP, respectively. To construct the fingerprint map, we collect the RSSI at each RP within a period of time. Let Y_l^n be the RSSI from AP_l collected at RP_n in the offline stage. Multiple RSSI samples are collected at different time τ, indexed by $1, 2$ and so on. Denote samples as $\{Y_l^n(\tau)|1 \leq \tau \leq T_l^n\}$, where T_l^n is the total number of samples. The average μ_l^n and the standard deviation σ_l^n are given by:

$$\mu_l^n = \frac{1}{T_l^n} \sum_{\tau=1}^{T_l^n} Y_l^n(\tau), \ \sigma_l^n = \sqrt{\frac{1}{T_l^n - 1} \sum_{\tau=1}^{T_l^n} (Y_l^n(\tau) - \mu_l^n)^2}. \qquad (4)$$

We preprocess $\{Y_l^n(\tau)\}$ to remove the outlier that lies outside $3\sigma_l^n$ and then recalculate until there is no outlier. Finally, the fingerprint of RP_n is a vector:

$$F^n = \{\mu_l^n \pm \sigma_l^n | 1 \leq l \leq L\}. \qquad (5)$$

To construct a sequence map, we walk along survey paths and collect the RSSI sequence from a DA. We denote the sequence of the pth survey path as follows:

$$S^p = \{Y_D^p(\tau)|1 \leq \tau \leq T_D^p\}, \qquad (6)$$

where $Y_D^p(\tau)$ means the RSSI data from a DA collected along the pth path and T_D^p is the corresponding sample number. The sequence data are also preprocessed by the above method (remove the outlier) and saved into the database.

In the online phase, when the user is walking, the client collects an RSSI sequence from a DA. Once the user stops walking and stands in a position, RSSI samples from a DA and multiple OAs are collected. All raw data are preprocessed by the method mentioned above and we get an online sequence $S = \{Y_D(\tau)|1 \leq \tau \leq T_D\}$ (Y_D is the DA's RSSI) and an online fingerprint $F = \{Y_l|1 \leq l \leq L\}$ (Y_l is the AP_l's RSSI).

4.2 Sequence Comparison

After preprocessing, we use Dynamic Time Warping (**DTW**) algorithm to compare the online RSSI sequence S with the offline sequences S^p. This step determines whether the user's current active area is in DA radiated area or not, i.e.:

$$p_{min} = \arg\min_{p} \mathbf{DTW}(S, S^p), \tag{7}$$

where p_{min} is the path that the user is most likely to walk along. Consequently, FDOLoc can reduce the computational cost and improve the localization accuracy significantly. The remaining RP points in the positioning area form a candidate point set R.

4.3   DS-Based Indoor Localization

We propose an adaptive fusing algorithm based on DS theory with paradox correction to fuse the RSSI data. Given the RSSI from AP_l at a candidate point $RP_n \in R$, we have two discriminating hypotheses: I and N. I means a state that the user is at RP_n and N means otherwise. Hence, $\Gamma = \{I, N\}$ and we define Θ as follows:

$$\Theta = 2^\Gamma = \{\emptyset, I, N, \{I, N\}\}. \tag{8}$$

Hypothesis $\{I,N\}$ in Eq. (8) means an uncertain state that we cannot determine whether the user is at RP_n by AP_l signals, i.e., the signal from AP_l is abnormal, the noise is large and the data reliability is low.

Before we define BPA functions, we give the following preconditions:

- In the initial phase, we assume all APs work normally, i.e., there is no abnormal signal and the reliability is high.
- The distribution of RSSI from an AP in a fixed position within a period of time follows Gaussian distribution [18].

We denote $m_l^n(I)$, $m_l^n(N)$ and $m_l^n(\{I, N\})$ as BPA functions of RP_n according to AP_l. Since there is no abnormal data initially, we set $m_l^n(\{I, N\})$ to zero, i.e.:

$$m_l^n(\{I, N\}) = 0. \tag{9}$$

$m_l^n(I)$ represents the confidence value that the user is at RP_n based on the RSSI from AP_l. If the user is closer to RP_n, the online RSSI from AP_l should be more similar to the offline RSSI in the database, hence $m_l^n(I)$ should be higher. As the RSSI exhibits a Gaussian distribution, we define $m_l^n(I)$ as follow:

$$m_l^n(I) = \exp(-\frac{(Y^l - \mu_n^l)^2}{2(\sigma_n^l)^2}), \tag{10}$$

where Y^l is the online RSSI from AP_l, μ_n^l is the average of the offline RSSI from AP_l collected at RP_n and σ_n^l is the standard deviation. Note that we determine the confidence value of $m_l^n(I)$ using both offline and online fingerprints without manual calibrations. Therefore, it is adaptable to our test sites.

At last, according to the Eq. (1), we calculates $m_l^n(N)$ and $m_l^n(\emptyset)$ as follows:

$$m_l^n(\emptyset) = 0 , \ m_l^n(N) = 1 - m_l^n(I). \tag{11}$$

In our localization problem, the original combination rules (2) and (3) are specifically defined as follows:

$$K^n = 1 - \prod_{l=1}^{L} m_l^n(I) - \prod_{l=1}^{L} m_l^n(N), \tag{12}$$

$$m_c^n(A) = \frac{1}{1 - K^n} \prod_{l=1}^{L} m_l^n(A), \ A = I, N, \{I, N\}. \tag{13}$$

However, the above original combination rules may lead to a paradox result when the data conflict is serious. Once K^n approaches 1, Eq. (13) has a divide-by-zero error, leading to erroneous combination probability (we will show the paradox simulation results in Sect. 5). To address the problem, we propose to refine DS theory to achieve sufficient accuracy and design a new combination rule based on [17], which removes the division $1 - K^n$.

We first give the following definitions:

$$k_{ij}^n = m_i^n(I)m_j^n(N) + m_i^n(N)m_j^n(I), \tag{14}$$

$$\hat{k}^n = \frac{1}{L(L-1)/2} \sum_{i<j} k_{ij}^n, \tag{15}$$

$k_{ij}^n \in [0, 1]$ is a conflict indicator of the data between AP_i and AP_j, where larger values indicate higher degree of conflict. In addition, $\hat{k}^n$ denotes the average conflict degree between each pair of APs.

To reduce the impact of noises, we smooth $\hat{k}^n$ and give a new variable ϵ^n, which represents the average belief about each pair of APs. ϵ^n is given by Eq. (16):

$$\epsilon^n = e^{-\hat{k}^n}. \tag{16}$$

Next, we get the average probability of hypothesis A by the following equation:

$$Q(A) = \frac{1}{L} \sum_{l=1}^{L} m_l^n(A), \ A = A, N. \tag{17}$$

Then, $\epsilon^n Q(A)$ represents the average belief of hypothesis A.

At last, we define the new fusion probabilities as w^n and calculate them as follows:

$$w^n(A) = (1 - K^n)m_c^n(A) + K^n \epsilon^n Q(A), \ A = I, N, \tag{18}$$

$$w^n(\{I, N\}) = 1 - w^n(I) - w^n(N). \tag{19}$$

In Eq. (18), $K^n \to 0$ and $w^n(A) \to m_c^n(A)$ when the conflict is not serious. Otherwise, $K^n \to 1$ and the proportion of $\epsilon^n Q(A)$ increases. $w^n(\{I, N\})$ means the uncertainty of user at RP_n based on the fused probability.

In order to evaluate the confidence of AP_l, we design a local noise indicator G_l^n, which measures the degree of noises based on the conflict indicator between AP_l and all other APs at RP_n. Then, we calculate the global noise degree of AP_l using the local noise indicator at all RPs. Formally, we define G_l^n and G_l as follows:

$$G_l^n = \sum_{j=1, j \neq l}^{L} k_{lj}^n / (L-1), G_l = \sum_{n=1}^{N} G_l^n / N. \tag{20}$$

If G_l is sufficiently large (say, larger than a threshold G_t), we conclude that AP_l is anomalous. Consequently, we filter it out and recalculate combination probabilities with the remaining APs.

For each RP_n in candidate set R, we have the following combination probabilities: $w^n(I), w^n(N)$ and $w^n(\{I, N\})$. We set a threshold α and if $w^n(\{I, N\})$ is larger than α, useful information is obscured by the noise and cannot be extracted. In this case, we reset the corresponding $w^n(I)$ to 0.5, which means discarding the RSSI data at RP_n.

Finally, after fusing the RSSI data, we calculate the weight of each RP and estimate the user position $\hat{x}$ as follows:

$$W_i = \frac{w^i(I)}{\sum_{i=1}^{|R|} w^i(I)}, \quad \hat{x} = \sum_{i=1}^{|R|} x_i * W_i, \tag{21}$$

where R denotes the candidate set and x_i denotes the coordinate of RP_i.

5 Experimental Evaluation

We present the experimental settings in Sect. 5.1 and show illustrative experimental results in Sect. 5.2.

5.1 Experimental Settings and Performance Metrics

We have conducted experiments in two typical sites, a laboratory and an office. The laboratory covers around 140 m^2 and the office room covers 70 m^2. The floor plans are shown in Fig. 4, where red circles denote RPs, blue rectangle denotes the AP with DAs, yellow rectangle denotes the AP with OAs, yellow circles denote the OA radiated range and blue triangles denote the DA range.

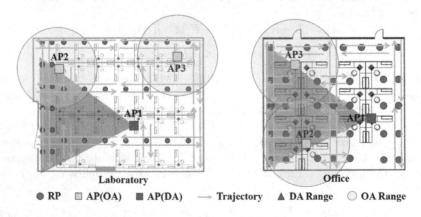

Fig. 4. Floor plans of our test sites. (Color figure online)

We collect 48 samples of RSSI vectors at each RP to construct the offline fingerprint map. For the offline signal sequence, we design dense survey paths (denoted by yellow solid arrows in Fig. 4). When we walk along these paths, RSSIs are collected continuously. The sampling frequency is 10 Hz and the length of sequences is 30. We have 33 and 36 RPs in the laboratory and office area, respectively. In each trial site, we have one DA and two OAs. The sequence length is 30 in both sites. G_t and α are 0.7 and 0.6, respectively.

We compare the proposed FDOLoc with the following state-of-the-art competing methods:

- DST [1] does not use a traditional RSSI model based on the signal propagation. It employs an arctangent function to model the probability density function of distance and uses it to calculate BPA values.
- INTRI [7] forms possible signal contours while considering signal noises. It minimizes the distance between user position and contours by LP-based formulation to find the coordinate.
- Lohan [12] considers the relationship between signal strength and reliability by DS theory and proposes a new method of BPA functions.

Additionally, to evaluate the effectiveness of the DA, we also compare with our model's without DAs, termed *FDOLoc-O*. We replace the DA with an OA.

We evaluate the performance using the mean localization error: $e = \frac{1}{U}\sum_{n=1}^{U} \| \hat{x}_n - x_n \|_2$, where $\| \cdot \|_2$ indicates L_2 norm, U indicates the number of test cases, x_n denotes the ground truth and $\hat{x}_n$ is the estimated location of the user.

Furthermore, we evaluate the time consumption with different numbers of OAs. The running time is defined as the time elapsed from the input data to the output result. For each method, we repeat the test 20 times and take the average as the final result.

5.2   Illustrative Experimental Results

Before we start the real experiments, we design a simulation to compare combination probabilities with different DS fusion algorithms. Suppose there are three APs (AP_1, AP_2 and AP_3) emitting signals. For a candidate point RP_c, three APs predict whether the user is at RP_c and give the corresponding BPA values (m_1, m_2, m_3), which are presented in Table 2. From this table, AP_1 and AP_3 give high probabilities to hypothesis I. Based on AP_1 and AP_3, the user is very likely to be at RP_c. However, when there is a pedestrian walking around AP_2, AP_2 may be blocked, the probability of hypothesis I is low, which indicates serious data conflict. K is calculated by Eq. (3) and gets close to one. The original combination BPA value $m_c(I)$, $m_c(N)$ and $m_c(I, N)$ are given by Eq. (13) and shown in Table 2.

While two APs gives high probabilities that the user is at RP_c, the combined probability is low. Consequently, this is a paradox problem because of the original combination rule (2). With erroneous readings (e.g., noisy readings from AP_2), the RSSIs from all APs do not provide sufficient information for user localization. On the contrary, our proposed method considers the conflict between each pair of APs and only discards abnormal APs, thus achieving higher accuracy. We present the results in Table 2. $w(I)$ is higher than $m_c(I)$ and $w(\{I, N\})$ indicates the degree of uncertainty.

Based on Table 2, we add a new AP_4. While more and more APs supports the high probability of hypothesis I, $w(I)$ is higher and $w(\{I, N\})$ is lower as $m_c(I)$ and $m_c(\{I, N\})$ are almost unchanged. It shows our algorithm is robust to noises (Table 3).

Table 2. BPA value with 3 APs.

Θ	BPA				
	m_1	m_2	m_3	m_c	w
I	0.7	0.001	0.8	0.009	**0.25**
N	0.3	0.999	0.2	0.991	**0.31**
{I,N}	0	0	0	0	**0.44**

Table 3. BPA value with 4 APs.

Θ	BPA					
	m_1	m_2	m_3	m_4	m_c	w
I	0.7	0.001	0.8	0.7	0.021	**0.31**
N	0.3	0.999	0.2	0.3	0.979	**0.26**
{I,N}	0	0	0	0	0	**0.43**

Figure 5 illustrates the CDF of localization error in the office. Both FDOLoc and FDOLoc-O outperform Lohan and INTRI. Compared with Lohan, FDOLoc-O makes a paradox correction. Thus the algorithm is more robust to environmental noises. It uses the correlation between signals and fuses RSSI values from multiple APs to estimate the reliability. DST uses more complicated BPA function models and DS combination rules. Therefore, it achieves comparable accuracy with higher time overhead. When the DA is introduced, FDOLoc performs better than other schemes. It reduces the mean localization error by more than 27% compared with other methods. This is because our method takes the advantage of stable DA signals and constrains the position of the user based on the coverage of the DA, thus reducing the impact of temporal noises from OA signals.

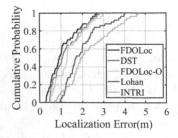

Fig. 5. CDF of localization error (office).

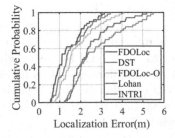

Fig. 6. CDF of localization error (lab).

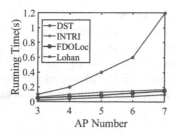

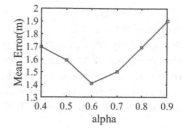

Fig. 7. Running time v.s. AP number.   **Fig. 8.** Localization error v.s. α.

Figure 6 illustrates the CDF of localization error in the laboratory. As the area increases, the signal strength decreases and the proportion of noise increases on the area edge, which leads to larger localization error. Therefore, the localization accuracy decreases in the laboratory. FDOLoc outperforms competing schemes. This is mainly due to the introduction of the DA and the DS fusing algorithm. By removing the division, we are able to avoid the paradox and achieve sufficient accuracy.

Figure 7 presents the time overhead. It shows that the overall time consumption increases with more OAs. This is because all algorithms need to calculate the position based on the RSSI value of each AP, and the algorithm complexity is positively correlated with the number of APs. The time consumption of Lohan is low. Since Lohan does not make a paradox correction, the running time is lower than that of FDOLoc. The computational complexity of INTRI is linear. Therefore, its time consumption is relatively low. However, as we introduce the DA and the DS fusion model, FDOLoc achieves higher localization accuracy with environmental and sensor noises. At last, DST has the highest computational time because it uses a complex fusion rule. As the number of APs increases, the computational overhead increases drastically.

Figure 8 illustrates the mean localization error v.s. α. It shows that the mean localization error decreases as α increases. The reason is that our algorithm can identify and discard noisy APs and localize the target with stable ones, thus achieving higher accuracy. If, however, α grows larger than 0.6, the localization error begins to increase. This is because more noisy APs are considered in the localization process. To achieve sufficient accuracy, we set α to 0.6 in our experiment.

6 Conclusion

In this paper, we propose a directional AP guided indoor localization algorithm to achieve sufficient localization accuracy. In order to enhance the distinctiveness of Wi-Fi fingerprints, we propose to incorporate directional APs, where we are able to constrain the location of a client to a smaller area. In order to reduce the impact of drastic signal changes, we propose to leverage the correlation between AP signals. Then, we identify anomalous AP signals based on their deviations from other APs. Based on the correlation evaluation, we model the localization problem with DS theory, where we estimate the confidence values of AP signals adaptively and fuse their independent estimations attentively to achieve sufficient accuracy. Furthermore, we refine the model by removing the division part to avoid the paradox in the localization process. Extensive experimental results in two different trial sites show that our approach is able to reduce the localization error by more than 27%.

Acknowledgement. This work is supported by the National Natural Science Foundation of China (61972433), the Natural Science Foundation of Guangdong Province (2021A1515012242), and the Fundamental Research Funds for the Central Universities (19lgjc11).

References

1. Achroufene, A., Amirat, Y., Chibani, A.: RSS-based indoor localization using belief function theory. IEEE Trans. Autom. Sci. Eng. **16**(3), 1163–1180 (2018)
2. Bigler, T., Treytl, A., Kienmayer, C.: Increasing localization robustness using directional antennas. In: 2017 22nd IEEE ETFA, pp. 1–4. IEEE (2017)
3. Chang, Y.J., Ou, C.H., Ssu, K.F.: A cluster analysis-based localization scheme for wireless sensor networks using mobile anchor nodes with directional antennas. In: 2018 IEEE ICASI, pp. 1156–1158. IEEE (2018)
4. Chen, Z., et al.: M^3: multipath assisted Wi-Fi localization with a single access point. IEEE Trans. Mobile Comput. **20**(2), 588–602 (2021)
5. Choi, J., Lee, G., Choi, S., Bahk, S.: Smartphone based indoor path estimation and localization without human intervention. IEEE Trans. Mobile Comput. (2020). https://doi.org/10.1109/TMC.2020.3013113
6. He, S., Chan, S.H.G.: Tilejunction: mitigating signal noise for fingerprint-based indoor localization. IEEE Trans. Mobile Comput. **15**(6), 1554–1568 (2015)
7. He, S., Chan, S.H.G.: INTRI: contour-based trilateration for indoor fingerprint-based localization. IEEE Trans. Mobile Comput. **16**(6), 1676–1690 (2016)
8. Huang, B., Li, X., Mao, G., Jia, B., Li, W.: On the pedestrian flow analysis through passive WiFi sensing. In: 2019 IEEE GLOBECOM, pp. 1–6. IEEE (2019)
9. Jun, J., et al.: Low-overhead WiFi fingerprinting. IEEE Trans. Mobile Comput. **17**(3), 590–603 (2017)
10. Laoudias, C., Moreira, A., Kim, S., Lee, S., Wirola, L., Fischione, C.: A survey of enabling technologies for network localization, tracking, and navigation. IEEE Commun. Surv. Tutor. **20**(4), 3607–3644 (2018)
11. Li, L., Xie, P., Wang, J.: Enabling 3D ambient light positioning with mobile phones and battery-free chips. IEEE Trans. Mobile Comput. **20**(3), 952–964 (2021)
12. Lohan, E.S., Talvitie, J., Granados, G.S.: Data fusion approaches for WiFi fingerprinting. In: 2016 IEEE ICL-GNSS, pp. 1–6. IEEE (2016)
13. Niu, Q., He, T., Liu, N., He, S., Luo, X., Zhou, F.: MAIL: multi-scale attention-guided indoor localization using geomagnetic sequences. Proc. ACM Interact. Mob. Wearable Ubiquitous Technol. **4**(2), 1–23 (2020)
14. Niu, Q., Li, M., He, S., Gao, C., Gary Chan, S.H., Luo, X.: Resource-efficient and automated image-based indoor localization. ACM Trans. Sen. Netw. **15**(2), 1–31 (2019)

15. Pan, M.S., Li, K.Y.: ezNavi: an easy-to-operate indoor navigation system based on pedestrian dead reckoning and crowdsourced user trajectories. IEEE Trans. Mobile Comput. **20**(2), 488–501 (2021)
16. Singh, M., Bhoi, S.K., Khilar, P.M.: Geometric constraint-based range-free localization scheme for wireless sensor networks. IEEE Sens. J. **17**(16), 5350–5366 (2017)
17. Sun, Q., Ye, X., Gu, W.: A new combination rules of evidence theory. Acta Electron. Sin. **8**, 117–119 (2000)
18. Zhang, M., Zhang, S., Cao, J.: Fusing received signal strength from multiple access points for WLAN user location estimation. In: 2008 IEEE ICICSE, pp. 173–180. IEEE (2008)
19. Zhu, X., Qu, W., Qiu, T., Zhao, L., Atiquzzaman, M., Wu, D.O.: Indoor intelligent fingerprint-based localization: principles, approaches and challenges. IEEE Commun. Surv. Tutor. **22**(4), 2634–2657 (2020)

Blockchain

Rewarding and Efficient Data Sharing in EHR System with Coalition Blockchain Assistance

Suhui Liu[1], Jiguo Yu[1,2,3]([⊠]), and Liquan Chen[4,5]

[1] School of Computer Science, Qufu Normal University, Rizhao, China
jiguoyu@sina.com
[2] School of Computer Science and Technology, Qilu University of Technology
(Shandong Academy of Sciences), Jinan, China
[3] Shandong Laboratory of Computer Networks, Jinan, China
[4] School of Cyber Science and Engineering, Southeast University, Nanjing, China
Lqchen@seu.edu.cn
[5] Purple Mountain Laboratories for Network and Communication Security,
Nanjing, China

Abstract. Internet of things is and will revolutionize our society and life tremendously. And data, generated by tons of IoT devices, is the foundation of all that. It is equatable to say that sharing enables data to play its due value and even makes it more valuable. While it is impractical for data owners to share for free, especially in terms of electronic health records (EHR) contain private information. Many data sharing schemes were proposed and very few of them can fulfil efficient sharing and fair payment simultaneously. One vital issue to achieve fair payment is how to verify the effectiveness of participants' behaviours, such as the integrity of data stored in the third-party server. Furthermore, in most existed data sharing systems, each access is authorized by the data owner, which requires the data owner to be online in real time and leads to too many interactions and high overlheads. In this paper, we design a blockchain-assisted data sharing scheme by combining the attribute-based encryption (ABE) primitive. Our scheme achieves efficient one-to-many data sharing, fine-grained access control, efficient decryption, user-level revocation, fairness payment and reliable data integrity verification.

Keywords: Data sharing system · Blockchain technology · Attribute-based encryption · Electronic health records

1 Introduction

Electronic Health Records (EHRs) changed the medicinal services framework from a paper-based industry to a digitalized format which has both financial

This work was partially supported by NSF of China under Grants 61832012, 61672321, 61771289 and 61373027, and the Science, Education and Industry Integration Innovation Program of Qilu University of Technology (Shandong Academy of Science) under Grant 2020KJC-ZD02.

and operational benefits. For example, it improves medical quality and decreases medical errors [17]. On the one hand, it is life-saving for patients if some chronic diseases can be detected in the early stage by monitoring and analysing their medical data. On the other hand, EHRs are attracting huge interest from a number of stakeholders, such as pharmaceutical companies, data analysis companies, hospitals and insurance companies, etc. In fact, the sharing of medical data is becoming an industry worth tens of billions of dollars. Thus, it is unrealistic and unfair to expect data owners to share their data for free.

The first hinder we confront when it comes to EHRs is give consideration to both data confidentiality and access control. As the cloud storage server can not be trusted in most times or it can be sabotaged by adversaries, it is necessary for data owners to encrypt their data before uploading them to the public cloud. However, conventional symmetric encryptions and public key encryptions impede people of sharing data and create values. A novel primitive, attribute-based encryption (ABE) [9,12,22], can ensure data confidentiality and achieve one-to-many data sharing simultaneously. Thus, implying ABE in EHRs system to achieve efficient and secure data sharing is becoming an interesting area.

Sine patients do not have physical control of their data as long as those data are stored in the cloud server, it becomes dangerous if the malpracticed doctors collude with the cloud. Due to the favorable characteristics of the blockchain [23], such as decentralization, persistency, auditability and anonymity, some works have explored how to apply it to EHRs systems to ensure data integrity, such as [1,3,4]. Besides, the blockchain is a promising method to realize user-centric and secure access control in EHRs systems by utilizing the smart contract [6,10].

However, how to monitor and control the life circle of medical data and achieve efficient data sharing and fairness payment is still a difficult issue to tackle. In this paper, we propose an comprehensive data sharing system by utilizing the blockchain technology and the attribute-based encryption (ABE) primitive for EHRs systems. The main challenges we handled are: data life-cycle monitoring, data confidentiality, data integrity verification, one-to-many data sharing, efficient decryption and user management.

Firstly, the complete life-cycles of medical data, including data encryption, data uploading [2], data storage, data search, data sharing and data updating, are monitored by the blockchain. Thus, the data ownership is determined when the data is uploaded. And it is unchangeable and traceable due to the superior characteristics of blockchain ledger. As a result, the fairness payment is easy to be implemented, that is, the user who uses the data must pay and cannot escape, the owner who contributes the data will be paid according to their contributions, and even the cloud cannot deceive users and owners to obtain benefits.

Secondly, our system combines ABE primitive, which can achieve data confidentiality, fine-grained access control and sharing. As any data user can access and decrypt as long as its attribute set satisfies the access stricture defined by the data owner, there is no need for data owners to be online for every data access authorization. More importantly, the ABE scheme we adopted, which are designed in our formal work [13], inherited several practical functions which are suitable for our data sharing system properly, for instance, distributed user management, efficient user revocation and user decryption. Furthermore, we designed a delicate smart contract to verify the correctness of the outsourced decryption. In this way, it is easy to fulfil rewarding cloud decryption service for data users.

Finally, one of the fundamental goals of cryptography, data integrity, can be ensured by several primitives, such as digital signatures and message authentication codes (MACs). However, when it comes to semi-trusted remote storage servers as cloud, it cannot be relied blindly on the integrity verification function controlled by non-data owners as those servers might cover data lose or even data tempering. Moreover, it cannot be guaranteed that a third party audition will not act maliciously. In our system, the hash of data is stored in the unchangeable ledger and the integrity verification is performed by smart contracts before data sharing and payment. Besides, the associated monetary punishment and data update are designed by smart contracts if the data stored in the cloud is tempered or missed.

2 Related Works

Blockchain was first introduced by Nakamoto [18] to support distributed records of money-related transactions which were not dependent on centralized authorities or financial institutions. Due to its incomparable characters, several blockchain-assisted data sharing schemes were proposed for EHRs system. Wang et al.'s scheme supports granular access authorisation and it improves computational performance as it requires no public key infrastructure (PKI) [20]. Chen et al. [5] harnessed smart contract-based blockchain to perform distributed search for EHR system, which is suitable only for self-to-self data sharing. Cao et al. [4] harnessed the blockchain to ensure secure storage in cloud for eHealth systems. Their scheme designed an efficient way to manage encryption keys by a password-based key agreement mechanism. Machado et al. [15] proposed a data integrity verification system by utilizing the blockchain, which relies on trustful communication. Yet, their scheme did not consider the data confidentiality and payable data sharing issue.

El et al. [7] proposed a blockchain-assisted architecture for EHR systems, while their system requires interactions between the data owner and the data user during accessing data which is not user-friendly. Dagher et al. [6] proposed a blockchain-assisted EHR sharing system where patients have direct control of who can access their data by utilizing smart contracts. In this way, the patients take too much responsibility and leads to impractical implement. More, this system uses re-encryption primitive to avoid encrypting once for each data user. However, this kind of sharing is not efficient enough in reality.

Those blockchain-assisted sharing systems mentioned above have one common problem, too heavy responsibility is landed on the patients as they have to authorize every access to their data even though the cloud-assisted eHealth system can provide the patient-centric approach [19]. Several previous works have explored using ABE, a cryptography primitive which can achieve fine-grained access control, to solve the fore-mentioned problem. Liu et al. [14] proposed a data sharing system with ABE for mobile health networks, which ensures two-way anonymity by a pseudoidenity method. However, this system did not consider the data integrity and payment. The data sharing system proposed by Maganti et al. [16] uses identity-based broadcast encryption. In the meanwhile, it relies on a central server to verify the integrity of data. Wei et al. [21] added three functionalities, user revocation, secret key delegation and ciphertext update, to the original ABE to secure data sharing of EHR system while dismissing data integrity issue. Joshi et al. [11] utilized attribute-based access control to transfer the management overhead from the patients to the organization.

Table 1. Function comparison.

Scheme	OtM and FGDS	BC-KG	BC-IV	AP-P	EVO	ER	BC-T& A
[15]	–	×	✓	–	–	–	×
[16]	IBBE(CP AB proxy)	×	Central	–	×	×	×
[20]	✓	×	✓	–	× heavy	× KGC	× ×
[21]	✓	×	×	–	×	✓	×
Ours	✓	✓	✓	✓	✓	✓	✓

Abbreviations: OtM: one-to-many. FGDS: fine-grained data sharing. BC-KG: BC assisted (distributed) key generation. BC-IV: BC assisted (distributed) integrity verification. AP-P: autonomic payment (rewarding data sharing) and punishment. EVO: efficient and verifiable outdec. ER: efficient revocation. BC-&TA: BC assisted data trace and audit.

Despite the advantages arose from the ABE, all works mentioned above only focused on data confidentiality and sharing while did not consider data integrity problem. Wang et al. [20] combined ABE, IBS and blockchain to achieve confidentiality, authentication and integrity of medical data. Although their scheme fulfils fine-grained access control and one-to-many sharing, it requires heavy computational overheads which lead to long latency. Liu et al. [13] proposed a efficient blockchain-aided data sharing system by utilizing searchable attribute-based encryption, where the blockchain directly handles key generation and user revocation. More importantly, it achieves fine-grained keyword-based search and outsourced decryption for data consumers. Eltayieb et al. [8] combined the blockchain and the attribute-based signcryption to fulfil data confidentiality and unforgeability while using the blockchain to check the correctness of the results returned from the cloud.

Some comparison between our blockchain-assisted data sharing system and other related works are summarized in Table 1.

3   System Definition

3.1   System Model

In our BC-assisted EHR sharing system, there are four stakeholders which are described as follows:

1) **Data Owners (DO):** or patients and their data-generating devices, which are responsible for generating and encrypting electric health records and then uploading them to the cloud. Our system provides a patient-centric method to manage personal medical records which establishes the basis for subsequent payments. In practical applications, patients can use an authorization mechanism or smart devices (based on artificial intelligence) to encrypt and upload their data. This part is beyond the scope of this paper.

2) **Cloud Storage Server:** stores all the ciphertext, including the associated search indexes. Thus, it performs keyword-based search for data users. In our system, the cloud also performs verifiable outsourced decryption for security and better efficiency. Note that we assume the cloud is honest but curious, which means it will serve users well but users cannot trust it fully as it might leak users' data for economy benefit actuation or it might be compromised or invaded.

3) **Data User (DU):** can be researchers, institutions and other people who want to access and utilize owners' records stored in the cloud. Each data user needs to request its decryption key first and half of its key will be controlled by the blockchain for outsourced decryption and efficient revocation. In this way, our system achieves backward security (revoked users cannot access subsequently encrypted records).

4) **Blockchain:** is consisted with a bunch of nodes, which ensures data integrity and fairness payment by smart contracts and the underlying consensus mechanism.

Figure 1 shows the basic system model of our data sharing system. A data owner encrypts and uploads its data to the cloud and sends the associated hash value to the blockchain. Any user can request access to the cloud, the cloud will perform search and out-decrypt for the user as long as its attribute set satisfies the access structure in the ciphertext. To ensure the integrity of the data, the user requests integrity verification to the blockchain. If no error occurs, the blockchain will pay the cloud and the associated data owners for incentives.

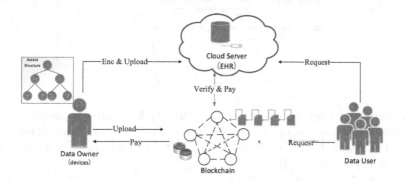

Fig. 1. System model

3.2   System Process

Our data sharing system contains the following five procedures:

(1) System Initialization: Each data owner, data user and the cloud has to register to the blockchain to get an unique account (address), which is used to share data and accomplish payment.

Besides, the blockchain is responsible for ABE system set up and key generation. This part is similar to our formal work [13].

(2) Encryption and Uploading: To ensure data confidentiality and sharing, a data owner encrypts the medical files and generates search indexes. Before uploading the ciphertexts to the cloud, it sends the hash value in the blockchain for later verification.

Then it uploads the ciphertexts to the cloud server. The cloud signs the cloud and sends the signature to the blockchain. Finally, the blockchain verifies the signature and store the file information in the ledger.

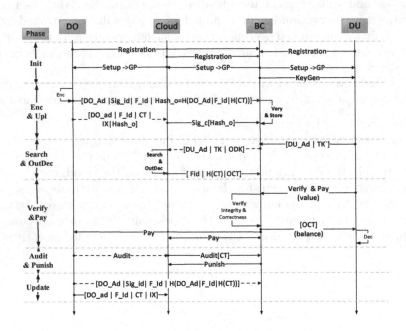

Fig. 2. Architecture flow

(3) Search and OutDec: A data user requests for search by sending a partial token to the blockchain. Then the blockchain generates the complete token for the user. And, the blockchain sends the token and the user's outsourced decryption key to the cloud.

Next, the cloud performs search and oursourced decryption if the user's attribute set in its decryption key satisfies the access structure in the ciphertext. Finally, the cloud sends the decryption results along with information of related data owners and hash values of files to the blockchain.

Note: the cloud will search for files with the specified keyword as many as possible because the search fee is linearly related to the number of resulted files.
(4) Verification and Payment: The data user calls the verification smart contract to accomplish distributed integrity verification.

Moreover, our scheme enables outsourced decryption by the cloud assistance. Thus, a smart contract is utilized to verify the correctness of the out-decrypted result. Next, decryption results which pass the verification will be send to the data user.

There are two conditions in reality. One is that the data owner requested data is a medical server provider, like a doctor, who wants to utilize the patient's data to diagnose. In this condition, no value (money) need to be attached to the smart contract which will perform the verification only. Another condition is that the data user is a data consumer, such as a research institution, who will analysis patients' data and earn profit from it. Then, they need to pay a certain fee to incentive data owners and the cloud service provider.

Finally, the associated data owners and the cloud will be paid for their sharing and works by the smart contracts.
(5) Audition, Punishment and Update: On the other hand, if the integrity verification fails, the associated data owner will receive a message implies that its data might be tempered or missed. Then the data owner will call for the smart contract to audit and perform the punishment if the data is changed indeed.

Next, the data owner can update its data by sending a new file hash to the blockchain.

Figure 2 illustrates the detailed architecture flow of our data sharing system.

3.3   Security Model

In our blockchain-assisted data sharing system, there are three types of adversaries.

(1) External adversary I. This type of adversary tries to impersonate a data owner to change data. As our system utilizes a signature mechanism to authenticate data owners, the adversaries may implement signature forgery attack to break the security of the underlying signature scheme.

(2) External adversary II. This type of adversary tries to access data illegally. Data users have to generate the related partial search token to access data in our system, thus the adversaries have to perform token forgery attack to break the security of the searchable attribute-based encryption scheme if they want to access corresponding data successfully.

(3) Internal adversary - honest but curious cloud storage server. We assume that the cloud server performs data storage, data search and data decryption in a honest way. However, some adversaries may corrupt the cloud server to modify or replace data. Notice that the external adversaries may want to modify data either, this attack can be resisted easier because the external adversaries own less sources than the cloud server.

Based on the adversary model defined above, our blockchain-assisted data sharing system should satisfies the following security requirements:

- Confidentiality. The encrypted data (ciphertext) cannot be recovered by illegal users (including internal and external adversaries).
- Integrity. No adversary can delete, modify or update data without being spotted by the blockchain.
- Unforgeability. The search token cannot be forged by adversaires without associated private key.
- Non-repudiation. External adversary I cannot impersonate a data owner by forging the signature without the related private key.

4   Concret Construction

Based on Liu et al.'s scheme [13], this paper designed a verifiable and rewarding data sharing system. Recall that Liu's scheme contains twelve algorithms, named **Al1 – Al12**.

I: System Initialization

1) Consensus nodes perform the **Al1** (Setup($1^\lambda, \varrho$) $\rightarrow$ GP) algorithm and get the public parameter GP where $para1 = e(g, g)^\alpha$.

Assume there are n consensus nodes in the blockchain, more than t nodes work together by performing the Pedersen (k,n) Secret Sharing scheme [13] to reconstruct the global private parameter α which is not available to any one nodes. Each consensus node owners a sub-secret α_i and the global public parameter $para1$ is constructed as follows:

$$e(g, g)^\alpha = \prod_{i=1}^{k} (e(g, g)^{\alpha_i})^{L(i)}$$
$$= e(g, g)^{\sum_{i=1}^{k} L(i) \cdot \alpha_i}$$

2) Each participant, including data owners, data users and the cloud, runs the **Al2** (IdKeyGen(GP, UID) $\rightarrow$ (PK$_{UID}$, SK$_{UID}$)) algorithm to get an unique key pair.

For example, a data user's private key SK_{UID} and its public key (also its account address) PK_{UID}:

$$SK_{UID} = \beta_{UID}$$
$$DU\_Ad = PK_{UID} = g^{\beta_{UID}}$$

Similarly, the cloud can get its key pair (CL_{PK}, CL_Ad) and a data owner can get its key pair (SK_{OID}, DO_Ad).

3) Then, a data user request for decryption key (ODK, DK). The BC runs the **Al3** (PubDecKeyGen(GP, UID, PK$_{UID}$, U$_{UID}$, st) $\rightarrow$ (PDKey$_{UID}$, st)), **Al4** (UpdKeyGen(GP, t, rl, st) $\rightarrow$ (UK$_t$, st)) and **Al5** (OutDecKeyGen(GP, UID, U$_{UID}$, PDKey$_{UID}$, UK$_t$) $\rightarrow$ PreDecK$_{UID,t}$) algorithms.

Note: the outsourced decryption ODK is stored in the ledger, which creates condition for cloud outsourced decryption and efficient user revocation.

II: Encryption and Uploading

A DO owns the right to control who can access its data by defining a specific access structure. Then it runs the **A16** $(\mathsf{Enc}(\mathsf{GP},(\mathbb{D},\delta),\mathsf{t},\mathsf{SymKey}) \to CT)$ and **A17** $(\mathsf{IdxGen}(\mathsf{GP},(\mathbb{D},\delta),\{\mathsf{kw}\}) \to \mathsf{IX})$ algorithms to encrypt a file with an unique id F_Id. It gets the ciphertext CT and the search index IX where $para2 = g^s$, $s \in \mathbb{Z}_p^*$. Next it calculates a hash value by a collision-resisted hash function:

$$Hash\_o = hash(DO\_Ad|F\_Id|H(CT))$$

where DO_Ad is the public address of the data owner, F_Id is the identity of the file and $H(CT)$ is the hash of the file.

The DO signs the whole message with its private identity key and generates a signature Sig_id for resisting message forgery attack. Then it sends $[DO\_Ad|Sig_id|F\_Id|Hash\_o]$ to the blockchain before uploading $[DO\_Ad|F\_Id|CT|IX]$ to the cloud.

After receiving the ciphertext from the data owner, the cloud computes $Hash' = hash(DO\_Ad|F\_Id|H(CT))$ with the ciphertext and signs $Hash'$ with its private key. Then it sends the signature to the blockchain. The file information will be recorded in the ledger if both signatures are verified.

III: Search and OutDecryption

1) A DU runs the **A18** $(\mathsf{PTokGen}(\mathsf{GP},\mathsf{SK}_{\mathsf{UID}},\mathsf{kw}) \to \mathsf{TK}')$ algorithm and sends $[DU\_Ad|TK']$ to the BC, where DU_Ad is the public address of the data user and TK' is the partial search token. Then the consensus nodes run the **A19** $(\mathsf{TokenGen}(\mathsf{GP},\mathsf{UID},\mathsf{U}_{\mathsf{UID}},\mathsf{Token}') \to \mathsf{TK})$ algorithm to generate the complete token TK. Finally, the blockchain sends $[DU\_Ad|TK|ODK]$ to the cloud, where ODK is the associated decryption key of the data user stored in the ledger.

2) The cloud runs the **A10** $(\mathsf{Search}(\mathsf{GP},\mathsf{U}_{\mathsf{UID}},\mathsf{Token},\mathsf{Index}) \to CT/\bot)$ and **A11** $(\mathsf{PreDec}(\mathsf{GP},\mathsf{UID},\mathsf{U}_{\mathsf{UID}},\mathsf{PreDecK}_{\mathsf{UID},\mathsf{t}},CT,\mathsf{t}) \to OCT/\bot)$ algorithms to search and out-decrypt for the user. Sends a set of compliant results $[DO\_Ad|F\_Id|H(CT)|OCT]$ to the blockchain as follows:

$$OCT = (OCT_1, OCT_2) = (e(g,g)^{\alpha \cdot s \cdot \beta_{UID}}, g^s)$$

IV: Verification and Payment

1) Right after sending the search request to the cloud, the DU creates a smart contract for verification (data integrity and outdec correctness) and payment.

2) The smart contract performs distributed verification for the user. For the first kind of data user, such as doctors and hospitals, a notification message will be send if no error occurs. For business participants like research companies or insurance institutions, the payment will be performed autonomically according to some pre-defined rules if no error occurs.

Firstly, the smart contract get the address of related data owner, then it calculates the following value to verify the integrity:

$$hash(DO\_Ad|F\_Id|H(CT))$$

Then, it broadcasts a message to calculate the following value to verify the correctness of the outsourced decryption:

$$e(g,g)^{\alpha \cdot s \cdot \beta_{UID}} = \prod_{i=1}^{k}(e(OCT_2, DU\_Ad)^{\alpha_i})^{L(i)}$$

$$= \prod_{i=1}^{k}(e(g^s, g^{\beta_{UID}})^{\alpha_i})^{L(i)}$$

$$= e(g,g)^{s \cdot \beta_{UID} \cdot \sum_{i=1}^{k} L(i) \cdot \alpha_i}$$

If OCT passes the verification, the user gets it and performs the **Al12** $(\mathsf{Dec}(\mathsf{GP}, \mathsf{SK}_{\mathsf{UID}}, \mathsf{CT'}) \to \mathsf{SymKey}/ \perp)$ algorithm to get the plaintext. Finally, the user will pay through the smart contract.

V: Audition and Punishment

1) The verification algorithm in the smart contract will return a set of file identity which failed the verification. And it will send a message to the associated data owners. Then each data owner will call for the audition algorithm to check the integrity of its files.
2) If the files are altered, the smart contract will penalize the cloud automatically. Next, the DO might update its data if he/she wants.

5   Analysis

5.1   Security Analysis

Secure Against Chosen-Ciphertext Attacks: The security against chosen-ciphertext attacks of our sharing system follows the ciphertext indistinguishability of scheme [13].

Secure Against EHR Forgery or Modification Attacks:

(1) For an adversary who tries to forge an EHRs ciphertext. This adversary cannot modify the corresponding ledger-stored file hash. Thus, this forgery will be caught by the auditor during the audition as the blockchain is untamable. Moreover, the cloud server cannot implement this attack successfully either.
(2) For an adversary who corrupts the cloud server to replace an EHRs ciphertext. If an adversary wants to replace an existing record with a new one, he/she has to fork the blockchian successfully. In other words, the security against data forgery of our sharing system is based on the security of the blockchain.

Secure Against Token Forgery Attacks: The security against token forgery attacks of our system follows the index indistinguishability of scheme [13].

Secure Against Impersonation Attacks:

(1) A data owner who attempts to convince that an EHR is generated by other data owner.
(2) An external adversary who performs private key guessing attacks and impersonate the victim to generate illegal data, and even to perform attacks such as Distributed Denial of Service (DDoS).

When it comes to either conditions described above, our sharing system can resist it with the signature scheme as long as this signature is unforgeable.

5.2   Performance Analysis

Simulation environment: Desktop (Dell Inspiron 15-5548) i5-5200U 2.20 GHZ, 16.0 GB RAM, Windows 10.

We use the Remix, an online compiler, to write and compile our smart contract and then deploy it in the Ropsten test network, which costs only 0.000 857GAS (0.0000061704ETH, 0.010232USD). The transaction fee for one record of the five functions in our smart contract are summarized in Table 2, which are based on 1 ETH = 1658.3 USD, 1 GAS = 0.007200 ETH rates (3/23/2021). The time costs of all five functions are less than 1 s.

Table 2. Costs of different functions.

Function	Storinge	Search	Inte_Verif	Payment	Audit&Punish
Gas Fee	0.000105	0.000225	0.000052	0.000026	0.000047
ETH	0.000000756	0.00000162	0.0000003744	0.0000001872	0.0000003384
USD	0.001254	0.002686	0.000621	0.000310	0.000561

6   Conclusion

In this paper, we proposed a blockchain-assisted data sharing system for EHRs by implementing a searchable attribute-base encryption scheme which supports distributed key management, outsourced decryption and efficient user revocation. The whole life circle of data are monitored and recored by the blockchain and smart contracts are used to verify the integrity of out-stored data and the correctness of out-decryption. More importantly, data tracing and audition, autonomic identity verification and fairness payment are achieved.

References

1. Cai, Z., Zheng, X.: Privacy-preserved data sharing towards multiple parties in industrial IoTs. IEEE J. Sel. Areas Commun. (JSAC) **38**(5), 968–979 (2020)
2. Cai, Z., Zheng, X.: A private and efficient mechanism for data uploading in smart cyber-physical systems. IEEE Trans. Netw. Sci. Eng. (TNSE) **7**(2), 766–775 (2020)
3. Cao, S., Zhang, G., Liu, P., Zhang, X., Neri, F.: Cloud-assisted secure eHealth systems for tamper-proofing EHR via blockchain. Inf. Sci. **485**, 427–440 (2019)
4. Cao, S., Zhang, X., Xu, R.: Toward secure storage in cloud-based eHealth systems: a blockchain-assisted approach. IEEE Netw. **34**(2), 64–70 (2020)
5. Chen, L., Lee, W.K., Chang, C.C., Choo, K.K.R., Zhang, N.: Blockchain based searchable encryption for electronic health record sharing. Future Gener. Comput. Syst. **95**, 420–429 (2019)
6. Dagher, G.G., Mohler, J., Milojkovic, M., Marella, P.B.: Ancile: privacy-preserving framework for access control and interoperability of electronic health records using blockchain technology. Sustain. Cities Soc. **39**, 283–297 (2018)
7. El Sayed, A.I., Abdelaziz, M., Megahed, M.H., Azeem, M.H.A.: A new supervision strategy based on blockchain for electronic health records. In: 2020 12th International Conference on Electrical Engineering (ICEENG), pp. 151–156. IEEE (2020)
8. Eltayieb, N., Elhabob, R., Hassan, A., Li, F.: A blockchain-based attribute-based signcryption scheme to secure data sharing in the cloud. J. Syst. Archit. **102**, 101653 (2020)
9. Goyal, V., Pandey, O., Sahai, A., Waters, B.: Attribute-based encryption for fine-grained access control of encrypted data. In: Proceedings of the 13th ACM Conference on Computer and Communications Security, pp. 89–98 (2006)
10. Guo, H., Li, W., Nejad, M., Shen, C.C.: Access control for electronic health records with hybrid blockchain-edge architecture. In: 2019 IEEE International Conference on Blockchain (Blockchain), pp. 44–51. IEEE (2019)
11. Joshi, M., Joshi, K.P., Finin, T.: Delegated authorization framework for EHR services using attribute based encryption. IEEE Trans. Serv. Comput. (2019)
12. Liu, S., Yu, J., Hu, C., Li, M.: Outsourced multi-authority ABE with white-box traceability for cloud-IoT. In: Yu, D., Dressler, F., Yu, J. (eds.) WASA 2020. LNCS, vol. 12384, pp. 322–332. Springer, Cham (2020). https://doi.org/10.1007/978-3-030-59016-1_27
13. Liu, S., Yu, J., Xiao, Y., Wan, Z., Wang, S., Yan, B.: BC-SABE: blockchain-aided searchable attribute-based encryption for cloud-IoT. IEEE Internet Things J. **7**(9), 7851–7867 (2020)
14. Liu, X., Luo, Y., Yang, X.: Traceable attribute-based secure data sharing with hidden policies in mobile health networks. Mobile Inf. Syst. **2020** (2020)
15. Machado, C., Fröhlich, A.A.M.: IoT data integrity verification for cyber-physical systems using blockchain. In: 2018 IEEE 21st International Symposium on Real-Time Distributed Computing (ISORC), pp. 83–90. IEEE (2018)
16. Maganti, P.K., Chouragade, P.: Secure health record sharing for mobile healthcare in privacy preserving cloud environment. In: 2019 IEEE International Conference on Electrical, Computer and Communication Technologies (ICECCT), pp. 1–4. IEEE (2019)
17. Menachemi, N., Collum, T.H.: Benefits and drawbacks of electronic health record systems. Risk Manage. Healthc. Policy **4**, 47 (2011)
18. Nakamoto, S.: Bitcoin: A peer-to-peer electronic cash system. Technical Report, Manubot (2019)

19. Narayan, S., Gagné, M., Safavi-Naini, R.: Privacy preserving EHR system using attribute-based infrastructure. In: Proceedings of the 2010 ACM Workshop on Cloud Computing Security Workshop, pp. 47–52 (2010)
20. Wang, H., Song, Y.: Secure cloud-based EHR system using attribute-based cryptosystem and blockchain. J. Med. Syst. **42**(8), 152 (2018)
21. Wei, J., Chen, X., Huang, X., Hu, X., Susilo, W.: RS-HABE: revocable-storage and hierarchical attribute-based access scheme for secure sharing of e-health records in public cloud. IEEE Trans. Dependable Secure Comput. (2019)
22. Yu, J., Liu, S., Wang, S., Xiao, Y., Yan, B.: LH-ABSC: a lightweight hybrid attribute-based signcryption scheme for cloud-fog-assisted IoT. IEEE Internet Things J. **7**(9), 7949–7966 (2020)
23. Zhu, S., Cai, Z., Hu, H., Li, Y., Li, W.: zkCrowd: a hybrid blockchain-based crowdsourcing platform. IEEE Trans. Ind. Inform. (TII) **16**(6), 4196–4205 (2020)

Temporal Networks Based Industry Identification for Bitcoin Users

Weili Han[1]($\boxtimes$), Dingjie Chen[1], Jun Pang[2], Kai Wang[1], Chen Chen[1], Dapeng Huang[1], and Zhijie Fan[1]

[1] School of Software, Fudan University, Shanghai, China
wlhan@fudan.edu.cn
[2] Department of Computer Science, University of Luxembourg, Esch-sur-Alzette, Luxembourg

Abstract. With the development of Bitcoin, many thriving activities have developed into stable industries, such as Miner. Identifying and analyzing the transaction behaviors of users within these industries helps to understand the Bitcoin ecosystem from a macro perspective. Currently, industry identification mainly faces two issues. First, the anonymity of Bitcoin makes it difficult to identify the industry identifiers of users who participate in activities through different addresses. Second, since users usually engage in multiple industries at different periods, both the identification of their dynamically changing industry identifiers and the detection of their mostly engaged industry are challenging research tasks.

In this paper, we propose an industry identification approach for Bitcoin users. First, we develop a fine-grained address clustering method to mine the relationship between addresses and their owners. Compared with existing methods, this method improves 0.18 in accuracy and 0.60 in recall. Based on temporal networks, we then train a multi-label classification model to identify the dynamically changing industry identifiers of users with an average accuracy of 0.92. With respect to multi-industry users, we further propose a major industry identifier detection method to identify the industry where users are mostly engaged. Applying this approach, we reproduce the major activity trajectories of users across the industries, which provides us with an opportunity to analyze the transaction behaviors of users within the industries.

Keywords: Bitcoin activity · Address clustering · Industry identifier identification · Temporal network

1 Introduction

The Bitcoin system (Bitcoin for short) has attracted a large number of users to participate in various activities, generating over 600 million transactions in total. Up to January 2021, the digital currency bitcoin has become the fifth-largest world currency [1]. As the number and value of transactions have grown rapidly, many thriving activities have developed into relatively stable modular structures.

© Springer Nature Switzerland AG 2021
Z. Liu et al. (Eds.): WASA 2021, LNCS 12937, pp. 108–120, 2021.
https://doi.org/10.1007/978-3-030-85928-2_9

By constructing a large-scale transaction network, we observe that Bitcoin users with similar activity purposes exhibit tighter connectivity, resulting in stable modular structures for these activities. Referring to the classification of activities in macroeconomics [2], we define these modular structures as Bitcoin industries, i.e., the Bitcoin industry is a group of activities with similar purposes. Here, we introduce five Bitcoin industries, including Darknet, Exchange, Gambling, Investment and Miner. For example, the Exchange industry provides digital currency exchange activities for Bitcoin users. Identifying and analyzing the transaction behaviors of users in such modular structures can deepen the understanding of Bitcoin from a macro perspective [3].

Currently, there are mainly two issues with industry identification. First, the anonymity of Bitcoin allows users to participate in various activities through different addresses, which makes it challenging to accurately identify their industry identifiers. Before identifying the industry identifiers of users, we shall first master the many-to-one relationship between addresses and their owners. However, existing address clustering methods indiscriminately apply coarse-grained heuristic rules to different transaction patterns, which mistakenly associates the addresses of multiple Bitcoin users into a single cluster, i.e., causing the problem of over-merging.

Second, since users can engage in various industries at different periods, it is difficult to identify their dynamically changing industry identifiers and detect the industry where they are mostly engaged (i.e., major industry). Driven by personal interests, the activity participation of Bitcoin users presents similar overlaps and migrations to that of social network users [4]. More specifically, they may change their current activities or perform activities in various industries, leaving their industry identifiers uncertain. Therefore, it is unpractical to classify the changing activity patterns into a single fixed industry identifier. However, in a short period (such as a week), a Bitcoin user tends to focus on certain industries and exhibits a relatively stable activity pattern, which provides us with an opportunity to accurately identify their dynamic industry identifiers and major industry identifier.

To solve these issues, we propose an industry identification approach based on temporal networks. We cluster addresses into users, classify the dynamically changing industry identifiers of users, and detect the industry where users are mostly engaged. Based on this approach, we can reproduce the major activity trajectories of users across the industries.

The main contributions of this paper are summarized below:

- We develop a fine-grained address clustering method to mine the relationship between addresses and Bitcoin users. Compared with existing address clustering methods, our method has improved precision by 0.18 and recall by 0.60, mitigating the problem of over-merging.
- Based on temporal networks, we train a multi-label classification model to identify the dynamic industry identifiers of users with an average accuracy of 0.92. Among them, about a quarter (23.35%) of users have multiple industry identifiers within a short period, called *multi-industry users*.

– For multi-industry users, we propose a major industry identifier detection method. By comparing the active scores of users in different industries, this method identifies the industry where users are mostly engaged.

The rest of the paper is organized as follows. First, we present the background knowledge in Sect. 2. Next, we discuss the collection and preparation of datasets in Sect. 3 and introduce industry identification in Sect. 4. The related work is discussed in Sect. 5. Finally, we conclude the paper in Sect. 6.

2   Background

2.1   Transaction Patterns in Bitcoin

Bitcoin supports users to complete transactions in an open computing environment. In a typical transaction pattern, the sender sends bitcoins from his addresses to the recipients and pays some bitcoins to the miners as miner fees. When the number of bitcoins sent exceeds the sum of the recipients' expectation and the miner fee, the extra bitcoins will be sent back to the address predefined by the sender. The extra bitcoins are called *changes* and the predefined address is called *change address*. In addition to the typical transaction pattern, the following four special transaction patterns are also considered in our work.

- *Coinbase transaction*: Bitcoin uses the transaction to reward miners who submit new blocks, thus all recipients of this transaction can be regarded as miners.
- *Mixing transaction*: This transaction packages multiple remittance transactions into one single transaction to obfuscate the address association among different Bitcoin users. Some Bitcoin mixers offer this type of service, such as Bitblender.
- *Peeling chain transaction*: The transaction consists of one input address and two output addresses. The sender peels off a small number of bitcoins to one recipient and sends the remaining bitcoins to the other recipient. The latter recipient then follows this pattern and conducts the next peeling chain transaction.
- *Locktime transaction*: The transaction uses the optional field *Locktime* to preset its effective time, i.e., to take effect at a specific block height or at a specific timestamp. Generally, Bitcoin users have their own setting preferences.

2.2   Address Association in Bitcoin

In practice, many Bitcoin users often reuse their addresses in multiple transactions for convenience, which may expose the potential address association. Since only the sender can use the private key to unlock the balance in the addresses, all input addresses of the transaction should belong to the same sender. Once the sender reuses these input addresses in other transactions, the reused addresses will serve as bridges to associate other addresses together. In addition, the study [5] states that the transaction preferences of Bitcoin users can reflect the relationship between addresses and their owners. In other words, personal behaviors in transactions, particularly the usage of change addresses, may become an important entry point for address association detection.

Based on the above observations, we consider the effect of special transaction patterns when performing address clustering in Sect. 4.1. In particular, we aim to improve the association of addresses involved in two transaction patterns: peeling chain and locktime, which are often ignored in previous studies.

2.3   Industries in Bitcoin

Referring to the classification of activities in macroeconomics [2], we define the concept of the Bitcoin industry as follows: a Bitcoin industry consists of activities that provide goods or services for similar purposes. Specifically, we divide activities into five industries: (1) Darknet, where trading smuggling or illegal service through bitcoins, e.g., SilkRoad. (2) Exchange, where conducting exchanges between bitcoin and other currencies, e.g., Mt. Gox. (3) Gambling, where gambling with bitcoins, e.g., SatoshiDice. (4) Investment, where offering the services of bitcoin returns and management, including bitcoin lending (e.g., Nexo), bitcoin faucet (e.g., Cointiply) and wallet management (e.g., Trezor). (5) Miner, where generating new blocks and distributing rewards to miners, e.g., F2Pool.

Based on the activity purposes and patterns of Bitcoin users in the industries, we describe industry members in two roles: *organizer* and *participant*. As organizers, Bitcoin users provide goods or services to participants in their activities, such as drug traffickers. This paper describes industry organizers as darknet vendors, exchange sites, gambling bankers, investment merchants, and miner pools, respectively. Their corresponding participants are darknet customers, exchange buyers, gamblers, individual investors, and individual miners. These industry roles are treated as class labels for industry identification in Sect. 4.2.

3   Datasets

We collect Bitcoin transaction data and entity labels of addresses as datasets for our work. The dataset *Transactions* records all historical transaction data of Bitcoin users. The dataset *Entity Identities* stores the addresses of well-known entities, mapping anonymous addresses to their real-world identities. Below, we detail the collection and preparation of each dataset.

(1) *Transactions*: We download raw Bitcoin transaction data from the genesis block to 12/31/2020, parse the data into address-based transactions. In total, we obtain 601,452,574 transactions and 759,091,687 addresses.

(2) *Entity Identities*: We collect entity labels of addresses from website *Wallet-Explorer* [6] and *Ethonym* [7], where the former has been used as ground truth in the study [8]. In the preparation step, we perform data cleansing of addresses and classify them into industry roles. We first exclude addresses

that are duplicated or failed in validation checks. Based on the service rules of different activities, we then classify these addresses into industry organizers and participants. We treat the addresses of wallet management as participants and classify the remaining addresses as organizers. Moreover, we identify other participants from organizer-related transactions and coinbase transactions to enrich the dataset.

Consequently, this dataset covers 382 entities, including 21,057,772 organizers and 130,145,529 participants, accounting for 2.77% and 17.14% of the total addresses. Table 1 details the number of addresses in different industries. In particular, the relationship between entities and their containing addresses helps to evaluate the address clustering method in Sect. 4.1; the labels of organizers and participants are used to train an industry identifier classifier in Sect. 4.2.

Table 1. The number of addresses in five Bitcoin industries.

Industry	# of Organizers	# of Participants
Darknet	2, 332, 854	5, 657, 783
Exchange	9, 967, 932	87, 932, 289
Gambling	3, 098, 500	14, 451, 596
Investment	5, 619, 822	21, 420, 157
Miner	38, 664	683, 704

4   Industry Identification

In this section, we introduce an industry identification approach for Bitcoin users. This approach consists of three steps: address clustering, multi-industry identifier classification, and major industry identifier detection.

To break the protection of anonymous payment mechanism, Sect. 4.1 proposes an address clustering method to capture the hidden associations among Bitcoin addresses and cluster them as users. After that, Sect. 4.2 takes these users as the basic units and designs a multi-label classification model to master dynamic industry identifiers of users within certain periods. To understand the major activity purposes of multi-identifier users, Sect. 4.3 devises a quantitative method to determine their major industry identifier.

4.1   Bitcoin Address Clustering

Protected by anonymous transactions, it is hard to figure out the whole activity intent of Bitcoin users if we just analyze their transactions based on individual addresses. Therefore, we develop an address clustering method to mine address association before capturing multiple industry identifiers of Bitcoin users.

Discussion of Existing Methods. Several heuristic rules are widely used in existing address clustering methods. (1) *MI* (Multiple Input) [9]: all input addresses of a transaction belong to one user; (2) *MX* [5,10]: excluding mixing transactions before applying method *MI*, where *X* denotes the mixing transactions; (3) *NA* (New Address) [9,11]: an address which first appears as an output address belongs to the change address of the sender; (4) *DP* (Decimal Points) [10]: in a two-output transaction, an output address which has three more decimal points than the other output value belongs to the change address of the sender; (5) *SP* (SPecial) [5]: the addresses in two consecutive transactions with the same transaction pattern belong to one user.

However, indiscriminately applying these coarse-grained heuristic rules to different transaction patterns may lead to the over-merging of clusters.

Transaction Pattern Observation. To mitigate the problem of over-merging, we observe the features of two special transaction patterns: peeling chain and locktime. (1) Peeling chain pattern is a typical pattern, with 43.11% of transactions matching this pattern. Moreover, 83.82% of the output addresses are used for one-time bitcoin transfers. Combined with the peeling off behaviors of bitcoin transfers, we argue that the features of the new addresses and the number of received bitcoins can help mine address association in this pattern. (2) For locktime transactions, Bitcoin users usually generate them under the same type of effective condition, i.e., at a specific block height or timestamp. Also, 89.19% of these transactions have spent all output bitcoins for subsequent payments. These preferences can help mine address association in locktime transactions.

Based on these observations, we design a series of experiments to develop a fine-grained address clustering method with high precision and recall.

Our Method. The address clustering method consists of three heuristic rules. We apply *MX* as a basic rule[1] to eliminate the interference of mixing transaction JoinMarket [5] and CoinJoinMess [12]. The other two heuristic rules as follows.

- *Heuristic rule 1:* The output address of a peeling chain transaction is the change address of the sender if it meets three features: (1) the address is a new address, (2) the address receives a larger number of bitcoins, and (3) the number of bitcoins received in this address has three more decimal points than that in the other output address.
- *Heuristic rule 2:* The input addresses of two consecutive locktime transactions belong to the same user if each transaction meets two features: (1) all the outputs of the transaction have been spent, and (2) the transaction specifies the effective time in the same way, i.e., a specific block number or a specific timestamp.

---

[1] Addresses excluded in mixing transactions can be associated with addresses through other normal transactions or recorded as isolated users.

Evaluation. We use three existing address clustering methods [5,9,10] as baselines to evaluate the quality of our method. We take the address association of entities in *Entity Identities* as the evaluation dataset and measure the clusters in two aspects. First, we evaluate the number of identified entities, including the number of entities successfully identified (indicator N) and the number of entities incorrectly identified into one cluster (indicator E). Second, we use four indicators to evaluate the quality of the clusters, including *Precise* (P), *Recall* (R), *Weighted Precise* (*WP*) and *Weighted Recall* (*WR*). The first two indicators have been used in the study [13]. Considering that clusters with a larger number of addresses usually contain more information, we further take the number of addresses per cluster as weight and propose the latter two indicators.

$$WP = \frac{1}{m} \sum_{i=1}^{m} \sum_{j=1}^{n} w_{ij} \frac{|o_{ij}|}{|S_i|} \tag{1}$$

$$WR = \frac{1}{m} \sum_{i=1}^{m} \sum_{j=1}^{n} w_{ij} \frac{|o_{ij}|}{|E_i|} \tag{2}$$

Equation 1 and Eq. 2 introduce the indicators *WP* and *WR*, where E_i is the ith entity and S_i is the group of identified clusters mapping to E_i. The number of entities and the number of clusters in S_i are denoted by m and n. In addition, s_{ij} is the jth cluster of S_i, o_{ij} is the overlap between E_i and s_{ij}, and w_{ij} is the proportion of the number of addresses in s_{ij} to that in S_i.

Table 2. Evaluation of several address clustering methods.

Method	N	E	P	R	WP	WR
MI + NA	336	154	0.15	0.02	0.07	0.03
MX + NA + DP	339	96	0.43	0.09	0.18	0.13
MX + SP	355	37	0.80	0.60	0.28	0.20
Our method	**366**	**17**	**0.94**	**0.96**	**0.31**	**0.31**

Table 2 presents the evaluation results. We observe that our method can cluster more (95.81% of the total) entities and reduce the over-merging of entities by 20.59% on average. Moreover, the evaluation results of indicators P and R both exceed 0.90 in our method. Compared to the best values of the baselines, indicators P, R, *WP* and *WR* have increased by 0.18, 0.60, 0.11 and 0.55, respectively. These improvements show that our fine-grained method can mitigate the problem of over-merging and provide clusters with high precision and recall.

Results Analysis. Since the clusters can well reflect the transaction behaviors of Bitcoin users, we call them *users*. As a result, we generate a total of 337,158,548 users, of which 81.67% have one address (called *isolated users*),

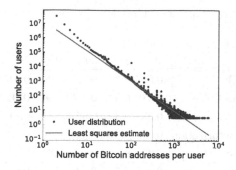

Fig. 1. User distribution follows Zipf's law.

17.66% have 2–10 addresses, and 0.04% have more than 100 addresses. Figure 1 describes the distribution between users and addresses[2] and further performs a linear regression on this distribution. The coefficient of determination R^2 is 0.95, which indicates this distribution largely follows Zipf's law [14]. In the next step, we use these users as the basic unit to classify industry identifiers.

4.2   Multi-industry Identifier Classification

Similar to social network users [4], Bitcoin users can change their current activities and engage in activities of other industries (i.e., activity migrations), or perform various activities across multiple industries (i.e., activity overlaps). In a short period, a Bitcoin user tends to concentrate on specific industries and exhibits a stable activity pattern, which allows us to identify his dynamically changing industry identifiers within a certain period (e.g., one week).

Based on temporal networks, we design a multi-label classification model to identify the dynamic industry identifiers of users. We construct a transaction graph to describe user interactions, extract temporal activity patterns of users, and train an industry identifier classifier for industry identification.

Graph Construction. We construct a directed graph *User-Transaction*, where each node represents a user and each edge represents the transaction interaction from a sender to a recipient. In addition, we record the timestamp and the number of bitcoins received by the recipients as edge annotations.

Feature Extraction. Since some special Bitcoin events may lead to imbalances among different industries in training data, we extract features from the temporal networks of several Bitcoin events to improve the robustness of the model. Based on the search popularity in Google Trends [15], we select five events related to the industries, including SatoshiDice game released in Gambling, Liberty Reserve

---

[2] We group users by the number of addresses they hold and filter out the group with less than three users.

Table 3. Comparison of graph embedding algorithms in multi-label classification.

Algorithm	Macro-F1			Micro-F1		
	10%	20%	30%	10%	20%	30%
DeepWalk	0.62	0.72	0.76	0.90	0.91	0.92
GraphSAGE	**0.70**	**0.75**	**0.77**	**0.90**	**0.91**	**0.93**
LINE	0.33	0.35	0.35	0.81	0.81	0.81
Matrix factorization	0.30	0.33	0.42	0.80	0.80	0.82
Node2Vec	0.47	0.52	0.62	0.84	0.87	0.88
SDNE	0.46	0.54	0.54	0.79	0.81	0.81

unsealed in Investment, SilkRoad shut down in Darkent, Mt. Gox disappeared in Exchange and BTC Guild announced to shut down in Miner. We then extract sub-graphs of *User-Transaction* before and after the events as temporal networks.

In each temporal network, the proportion of known industry identifier labels is rather limited, accounting for 10%–30% of the total users. To ensure the quality of the features extracted at such proportions of recognized labels, we test the performance of six graph embedding algorithms listed in the study [16], i.e., *DeepWalk, GraphSAGE, LINE, Matrix Factorization, Node2Vec* and *SDNE*. We apply one-vs-rest logistic regression to evaluate the performance of these graph embedding algorithms. Specifically, we randomly sample 10%, 20% and 30% of labeled users as training data and the rest of labeled users as the testing data. To eliminate the contingency, we repeat this process ten times and record the average results in Table 3. The results indicate that *GraphSAGE* [17] performs better accuracy and stability, so we choose it to extract the features of users.

Model Training and Evaluation. We apply MLP model [18] to build the classification model. We first filter out labeled users involved in less than three transactions to ensure the quality of training data. After that, we define the size of the training data as 0.67 and adopt 3-fold cross-validation to train the model. Based on the selected event of each industry, we evaluate the performance of the model in different temporal networks (see Table 4). We observe that our model presents high accuracy with an average of 0.92, which can well identify multiple industry identifiers of users in a certain period.

4.3 Major Industry Identifier Detection

We observe that 23.35% of users engage in multiple industries during a week and call them multi-industry users. Such a non-negligible proportion further motivates us to detect the industry where they are mostly engaged, i.e., to detect their major industry identifier. Being an industry member, the user is active inside the industry and rarely participates in other activities outside the industry. If a user devotes more participation frequency and bitcoin traffic to a specific industry, we determine this industry identifier as his major industry identifier.

Table 4. Evaluations for temporal networks in five events.

Industry	Network time span	Accuracy	Macro-F1	Micro-F1
Gambling	04/01/2012–04/07/2012	0.92	0.88	0.94
	05/22/2012–05/28/2012	0.96	0.89	0.97
Investment	04/04/2013–04/10/2013	0.92	0.90	0.94
	05/28/2013–06/03/2013	0.91	0.88	0.94
Darknet	09/18/2013–09/24/2013	0.89	0.87	0.93
	10/04/2013–10/10/2013	0.90	0.89	0.93
Exchange	01/02/2014–01/08/2014	0.92	0.85	0.94
	02/12/2014–02/18/2014	0.94	0.87	0.95
Miner	03/02/2015–03/08/2015	0.93	0.87	0.94
	03/24/2015–03/30/2015	0.91	0.88	0.94

Based on these observations, we define the indicators of participation frequency and bitcoin traffic, determine their weights, and calculate active scores of users in different industries to detect the major industry identifier.

Indicator Extraction. For multi-industry users, we treat the transactions they perform within a single industry as internal transactions and extract indicator values from these transactions. In each internal transaction, the participation frequency (f) is the reciprocal of the time difference between the current transaction and the previous internal transaction conducted in the same industry. The bitcoin traffic (v) is the number of bitcoins transferred to the industry. When both parties of a transaction are multi-industry users, if the senders and recipients have at least one same industry identifier, we treat their interaction in the transaction branch as an internal transaction of this industry. Based on the above extraction rules, we obtain the indicator sequences F and V.

Weight Calculation. In general, sequences with higher entropy contain richer information and should be given more weight to determine the major industry identifier. Therefore, we apply entropy weight method (EWM) [19] to calculate the weights of these indicators. Specifically, we normalize the sequences, compute their entropy values (e_F and e_V) and obtain the weights through Eq. 3.

$$w_i = \frac{1 - e_i}{\sum_{j \in \{F,V\}}(1 - e_j)}, \; i \in \{F, V\} \tag{3}$$

Active Score Calculation. We use Eq. 4 to calculate the active scores of users in different industries. For industry i, we calculate its active score S_i based on the behaviors of internal transactions (A_i) and the prediction probability of the industry identifier (P_i). Among them, A_i is calculated from the average time of participation frequency (t_{iF}) and the total sum of bitcoin traffic (t_{iV}).

$$S_i = P_i * A_i = P_i * (t_{iF} * w_F + t_{iV} * w_V) \tag{4}$$

Finally, we rank the active score of each industry identifier and determine the industry identifier with the highest score as the major industry identifier.

4.4 Summary

In short, our approach clusters addresses into users with high accuracy, identifies dynamic industry identifiers of users, and detects major industry identifier to reproduce the major activity trajectories of users across the industries.

5 Related Work

In this section, we introduce studies that are closely related to address clustering and activity identifier classification in Bitcoin.

Address Clustering. As we discussed in Sect. 4.1, many heuristic rules are proposed to mine address association in Bitcoin. Some studies focus on the association of input addresses. Interfered by mixing transactions, the original method *MI* generates users with relatively low recall [13]. On this basis, an improved method *MX* is proposed to filter out mixing transactions before applying the method *MI*, which has been widely used for address clustering. However, the exclusion of addresses involved in mixing transactions somewhat reduces the recall of clustering results. Other studies mine the association of output addresses through several patterns, such as method *NA* and method *DP*. Currently, many of these methods have been extended to detect associated addresses in other cryptocurrencies, such as Zcash [20]. In practice, some transactions may mismatch the patterns, resulting in incorrect address association. For example, in the ransomware activity Locky, criminals use the new output address of the ransom payment transaction to receive the ransoms [21]. However, the method *NA* would treat this new output address as the change address of the victim.

To mitigate these problems, we develop several fine-grained heuristic rules and further mine the association of addresses involved in mixing transactions.

Activity Identifier Classification. Classifying the activity identifiers of Bitcoin users is essential to explore their behavior purposes across various activities. At present, many studies apply supervised machine learning techniques to detect the addresses of the activities. Usually, researchers extract features from the transaction behaviors of the addresses, such as the number of bitcoins transferred in a transaction. For instance, Toyoda et al. [22] analyze the transfer features of addresses in high yield investment programs (HYIP) and design a classifier with an accuracy of 0.94. Moreover, a few studies introduce features of different dimensions to improve the quality of identification. Li et al. [23] extract features from three dimensions to identify addresses involved in illegal activities, including transaction, topology and time. Besides, other studies exploit graph techniques to detect anomalous addresses. For example, Chen et al. [24] build the transaction graphs of the exchange site Mt.Gox and calculate singular value decomposition to identify abnormal accounts related to market manipulation.

Most studies assume that Bitcoin users are only active in a single activity and ignore to classify users with multiple activity identifiers. In this paper, we train a multi-label classification model from an industry perspective, which can accurately describe the whole behaviors of Bitcoin users across various activities.

6 Conclusion and Future Work

In this paper, we have proposed a practical approach for identifying dynamic industry identifiers of Bitcoin users based on temporal networks. First, we developed a fine-grained address clustering method to mitigate the problem of over-merging, which improved over existing methods 0.18 in precision and 0.60 in recall. We then trained an industry identifier classification model to identify dynamic industry identifiers of users with an average accuracy of 0.92. For multi-industry users, we further calculated the active scores in different industries to detect their major industry identifier. Based on this approach, we captured the major activity trajectories of users across the industries. In the future, we will study more transaction patterns in address clustering and apply our approach for analyzing the interactions and migrations of users across the industries.

Acknowledgement. This paper has been supported by the National Key R&D Program of China (2018YFC0830900), Natural Science Foundation of China (U1836207), and China Postdoctoral Science Foundation (2020M670998).

References

1. Phillips, D.: Bitcoin is now the 5th largest world currency (2021). https://decrypt. co/39425/bitcoin-is-now-the-5th-largest-world-currency
2. Syverson, C.: Macroeconomics and market power: context, implications, and open questions. J. Econ. Perspect. **33**(3), 23–43 (2019)
3. Quiles, M.G., Macau, E.E., Rubido, N.: Dynamical detection of network communities. Sci. Rep. **6**, 25570 (2016)
4. Newell, E., et al.: User migration in online social networks: a case study on reddit during a period of community unrest. In: Proceedings of the 10th International Conference on Web and Social Media, pp. 279–288 (2016)
5. Kalodner, H.A., et al.: BlockSci: design and applications of a blockchain analysis platform. In: Proceedings of the 29th USENIX Conference on Security Symposium, pp. 2721–2738 (2020)
6. Walletexplorer (2021). https://www.walletexplorer.com
7. Ethonym (2021). https://ethonym.com
8. Foley, S., Karlsen, J.R., Putniņš, T.J.: Sex, drugs, and bitcoin: How much illegal activity is financed through cryptocurrencies? Rev. Fin. Stud. **32**(5), 1798–1853 (2019)

9. Spagnuolo, M., Maggi, F., Zanero, S.: BitIodine: extracting intelligence from the bitcoin network. In: Christin, N., Safavi-Naini, R. (eds.) FC 2014. LNCS, vol. 8437, pp. 457–468. Springer, Heidelberg (2014). https://doi.org/10.1007/978-3-662-45472-5_29

10. Athey, S., Parashkevov, I., Sarukkai, V., Xia, J.: Bitcoin pricing, adoption, and usage: theory and evidence, vol. 13, no. 4, pp. 675–746. Stanford Institute for Economic Policy Research (2016)

11. Meiklejohn, S., Pomarole, M., Jordan, G., Levchenko, K., Savage, S.: A fistful of bitcoins: characterizing payments among men with no names. In: Proceedings of the 13th Conference on Internet Measurement, pp. 127–140 (2013)

12. Coinjoinmess (2021). https://www.walletexplorer.com/wallet/CoinJoinMess

13. Remy, C., Rym, B., Matthieu, L.: Tracking bitcoin users activity using community detection on a network of weak signals. In: Cherifi, C., Cherifi, H., Karsai, M., Musolesi, M. (eds.) COMPLEX NETWORKS 2017 2017. SCI, vol. 689, pp. 166–177. Springer, Cham (2018). https://doi.org/10.1007/978-3-319-72150-7_14

14. Newman, M.E.: Power laws, pareto distributions and Zipf's law. Contemp. Phys. **46**(5), 323–351 (2005)

15. Google trends (2021). https://trends.google.com

16. Cai, H., Zheng, V.W., Chang, K.C.C.: A comprehensive survey of graph embedding: problems, techniques, and applications. IEEE Trans. Knowl. Data Eng. **30**(9), 1616–1637 (2018)

17. Hamilton, W., Ying, Z., Leskovec, J.: Inductive representation learning on large graphs. In: Proceedings of the 31st Conference on Neural Information Processing Systems, pp. 1024–1034 (2017)

18. Bishop, C.M., et al.: Neural Networks for Pattern Recognition. Oxford University Press, Oxford (1995)

19. Cheng, Q.: Structure entropy weight method to confirm the weight of evaluating index. Syst. Eng. Theor. Pract. **30**(7), 1225–1228 (2010)

20. Kappos, G., Yousaf, H., Maller, M., Meiklejohn, S.: An empirical analysis of anonymity in Zcash. In: Proceedings of the 27th USENIX Conference on Security Symposium, pp. 463–477 (2018)

21. Huang, D.Y., et al.: Tracking ransomware end-to-end. In: Proceedings of the 39th IEEE Symposium on Security and Privacy, pp. 618–631 (2018)

22. Toyoda, K., Mathiopoulos, P.T., Ohtsuki, T.: A novel methodology for HYIP operators' bitcoin addresses identification. IEEE Access **7**, 74835–74848 (2019)

23. Li, Y., Cai, Y., Tian, H., Xue, G., Zheng, Z.: Identifying illicit addresses in bitcoin network. In: Proceedings of the 2nd Conference on Blockchain and Trustworthy Systems, pp. 99–111 (2020)

24. Chen, W., Wu, J., Zheng, Z., Chen, C., Zhou, Y.: Market manipulation of bitcoin: evidence from mining the Mt. Gox transaction network. In: Proceedings of the 38th IEEE Conference on Computer Communications (2019)

Blockchain-Based Data Ownership Confirmation Scheme in Industrial Internet of Things

Guanglin Zhou[1], Biwei Yan[1], Guijuan Wang[1(✉)], and Jiguo Yu[1,2]

[1] School of Computer Science and Technology, Qilu University of Technology
(Shandong Academy of Sciences), Jinan 250353, China
jiguoyu@sina.com
[2] Shandong Laboratory of Computer Networks, Jinan 250014, China

Abstract. With the development of blockchain and Industrial Internet of Things (IIoT), there have been many problems in the combination of them. Due to the complexity and huge amount of data, it will face the problems of privacy leakage and circulation difficulties. Especially in the ownership confirmation, the current research mostly considers how to confirm, but ignores how to transfer safely and efficiently, and does not fully consider how to adapt to the IIoT environment. This paper proposes a data ownership confirmation scheme. We have verified the feasibility and rationality of the proposed scheme through a large number of experiments, and the results show that our scheme is more suitable for IIoT scenarios.

Keywords: Permissioned consortium blockchain · Data ownership confirmation · IIoT

1 Introduction

The information age has changed our traditional way of life and production. The Internet of Things (IoT) [3] is reshaping existing industries into smart industries featuring data-driven decision-making. However, the inherent characteristics of the IoT have led to many challenges, such as decentralization, poor interoperability, privacy leakage, and security vulnerabilities. This paper proposed an Industrial Internet of Things (IIoT) architecture based on the permissioned consortium blockchain to adapt to the needs of the actual production environment of IIoT. In general, the main contributions of this article are as follows.

This work was supported in part by National Key R&D Program of China with grant No.2019YFB2102600, and the NSF of China under Grants 61832012 and 61771289, and the Key Research and Development Program of Shandong Province under Grant 2019JZZY020124, and the Pilot Project for Integrated Innovation of Science, Education and Industry of Qilu University of Technology (Shandong Academy of Sciences) under Grant 2020KJC-ZD02.

Z. Liu et al. (Eds.): WASA 2021, LNCS 12937, pp. 121–132, 2021.
https://doi.org/10.1007/978-3-030-85928-2_10

1) For architecture, the combination of blockchain and traditional 5 layers architecture of the Internet of Things, which includes node grading and classification strategies, a modular consensus mechanism and hash algorithm to achieve more efficient and flexible goals.
2) For data, a new data ownership verification model is designed, which manages data sets like Token, which is not only safe and auditable, but also enables more efficient data circulation. In particular, the concept of data identity is introduced, which can better isolate other businesses.
3) The entire data transfer process is demonstrated, and the way of ownership confirmation is elaborated in detail.

The rest of this article is organized as follows. Section 2 reviewed the related research to solve the problem. Section 3 proposed a blockchain-based IIoT architecture and architecture analysis. Section 4 elaborated on the proposed data confirmation scheme in detail. Section 5 introduced a critical data interaction process. Section 6 is related to experimental analysis and performance evaluation. In Sect. 7, we summarized and looked forward to future work.

2   Related Work

At present, there have been many studies combining blockchain technology to solve related problems in IIoT, including data security, data privacy protection, data auditing and right confirmation. Cai et al. [1] proposed a framework for generating approximate counting results based on sampling method, which is not affected by arbitration attack. Liu et al. [8] proposed a lightweight blockchain system called LightChain, and a lightweight data structure called LightBlock to simplify the broadcast content. A security and privacy model is introduced to help reshape the traditional IIoT architecture [10].

Yan et al. [13] proposed a blockchain-based service recommendation scheme (BPDS SR) which can achieve a higher accuracy and lower cost with more profits. Yu et al. [14] proposed LH-ABSC, a lightweight ABSC scheme which adopts ciphertext-policy encryption (CPABE) and key-policy attribute-based signature (KPABS). Liu et al. [7] proposed a blockchain-aided searchable attribute-based encryption (BC-SABE) with efficient revocation and decryption. Cai et al. [2] put forward a new data uploading mechanism, which considers energy saving and privacy protection at the same time. Wang et al. [11] construct a decentralized distributed edge node network based on blockchian, which guarantees the information sharing among the edge nodes as well as processing the data efficiently. Li et al. [6], discussed the problem of blockchain storage and protection of large-scale Internet of Things data. Gao et al. [4] proposed a data permission confirmation mechanism based on blockchain and local sensitive hashing. A distributed scheme that eliminates the requirement for a central node that holds users' biometric templates is presented [9,12]. Gong et al. [5] proposed to establish fine-grained digital resource rights, which are divided into ownership and usufruct. Xu et al. [15] put forward a privacy protection data sharing framework for IIoT, which allows data contributors to share their content on request.

3   Blockchain-Based IIoT Data Ownership Confirmation Architecture

We combined blockchain in the classic IoT architecture, as shown in Fig. 1. The architecture is divided into 5 layers, namely Device Sensing Layer, Data Preprocessing layer, Transport Gateway Layer, Data Storage Layer, Application Layer. The device sensing layer mainly includes related equipment in industrial production, such as robotic arms and automatic assembly robots. There will be data input for the device, and some data will be generated at the same time, and then the data will flow to the data pre-processing layer for processing. In the data pre-processing stage, relevant data will be desensitized, encrypted, and classified, and aggregated to a certain extent. The next stage is to send data to the data storage layer through the transport gateway layer and use a combination of distributed cloud storage and enterprise local storage for data storage to achieve more flexibility, security, and efficiency. Finally, there is the application layer, which contains more content. Enterprises can develop their businesses and cooperation.

As can be seen from Fig. 1, the data pre-processing layer and data storage layer are combined with blockchain. This is because if you want to ensure that the source of the data is credible and authentic, you must have relevant data on the chain from the source so that it can be better.

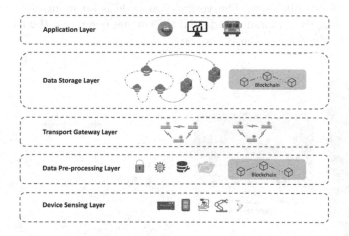

Fig. 1. Blockchain-based IIoT architecture

3.1   Permissioned Consortium Blockchain Design

In IIoT scenario, it is more suitable to choose the architecture based on the permissioned consortium blockchain, improving operation efficiency. The schematic diagram of the overall design of the architecture we proposed is shown in Fig. 2.

Node Level Design. The blockchain network is maintained by multiple nodes. Here we have designed a node grading strategy for the special scenarios of IIoT. Most IIoT devices are resource-constrained, so we divide all participating nodes into three levels. The first is the Level 1 node, which stores all the ledger data. The second is the Level 2 node, which does not store all the ledger data, but only stores the block header and part of the data summary. There are Level 3 nodes. This type of node further reduces storage pressure. It only needs to store the hash of the block header, which is suitable for direct deployment to IIoT devices. Through the design of three levels of nodes, the scalability of the proposed blockchain architecture and the security of the entire ecosystem can be effectively enhanced. Besides, we also divide the nodes of the same level into different identities to further improve their efficiency. The division of node identities is mainly carried out in the Level 1 node and the Level 2 node. The work of the node mainly includes receiving transaction proposals, sorting transactions, packaging blocks, distributing blocks, verifying block transactions, and synchronizing ledgers. We set up a type of node called endorsement nodes, which receive transaction proposals and pre-execute transactions through smart contracts. The endorsement nodes are designated by users, and different partners can customize them according to their own cooperation needs. There is also a type of nodes called ordering nodes, which are responsible for the transactions pre-executed by the endorsing node are sorted, then packaged into blocks, and then distributed to all nodes for verification. The verification node is an identity owned by all nodes, including the endorsing node and the sorting node, and the ledger can be updated after the transaction is verified.

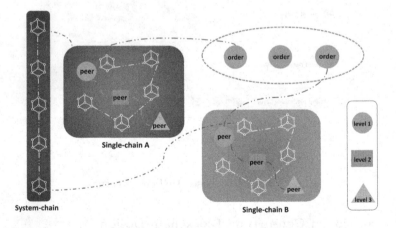

Fig. 2. Permissioned consortium blockchain network figure

Single-Chain. The permission consortium chain is a multi-chain structure, and the services of each chain are isolated from each other, but the same node can be added to multiple chains for interworking business needs. In the permissioned consortium chain, the establishment of a single chain is relatively flexible. When multiple parties have cooperation needs, they can create a single chain that only allows partners to participate. The permissions are controlled by certificates and keys, and then according to specific business needs develop smart contracts. Smart contracts are the bridge for operating the ledger. The designation of endorsement methods and the selection of consensus algorithms can be individually designated. Each single-chain has a ledger, which makes the business form more refined, and the node does not maintain a ledger unrelated to it and improves performance in a safer way.

System-Chain. With each single-chain, there is also a need for a system-chain to link them together to form the entire permissioned consortium blockchain system. System-chain mainly stores the genesis block of each single-chain, and stores some related configuration information.

4   Data Ownership Confirmation Model

If the data ownership confirmation work is done well, there will be better solutions to problems such as leakage and loss in the subsequent data circulation process. We proposed a blockchain-based data ownership confirmation model.

Algorithm 1. DID Generation

Input: pk, cert;
  1: hash1 = hash(hash(pk) + hash(cert))
  2: hash2 = stamp + hash1[0:26]
  3: check = hash(hash(hash2))[0:5]
  4: ID_bytes = hash2 + check
  5: DID = Base58(ID_bytes)
Output: DID

4.1   Identity

Classification

Owner. The data owner can flexibly choose the encryption attributes according to the different confidentiality levels of the data, and it has the management authority of the "super administrator" for the data.

Users. Members in the same single-chain can become data users, and data users can apply for data usage rights from the data owner. Data circulation records need to be stored on the chain, and the detailed information will be reflected in the Token.

Illegal Member. As long as it is a party without the consent of the data owner, obtaining data, using data, and performing any operation on the data are considered illegal.

Generation. This identity is for data ownership. It generates a data identity DID (Data ID) based on the certificate and key participating in the permissioned consortium blockchain, which is mainly used during data transfer. For the generation process of DID, Algorithm 1 is given.

4.2   Token

We generate the corresponding Token to manage the related data. A Token corresponds to the only data. The related information of the data is recorded by the Token. Only the data owner can have all rights to it, but the circulation record will not be deleted. It mainly consists of the following three stages.

Generation. The data set will be generated by the data owner according to their needs by selecting different attributes to generate the Token. The generation of the Token is completed by the structure of the Merkle Tree. Firstly, the data owner selects different parameters for the security requirements of the data. Then selects the hash algorithm to be used in the Merkle Tree that generates the data attributes according to the encryption level E specified by the user. Then use the selected parameters as leaf nodes to generate the Merkle Tree, take the root hash and the encrypted data to generate a hash to generate the *token*. Finally, the Token$\langle token, E, State, From, To, key \rangle$ is generated. Token is a six-tuple and needs to be uploaded to the blockchain, where *token* represents the unique corresponding value of the data; E represents the encryption level, e1 represents the high encryption level, the sha256 algorithm is used, and e2 represents the low encryption level, and Hash-1 is selected; *State* represents the state of the Token, valid can be used for access, invalid, that is, the data is inaccessible and unavailable, and only the data owner can manipulate the data at this time; *From* has two attributes, namely *from*, which means data owner's DID and *num* of the data owner are the distributed number; *To* also has two attributes, one is *to*, which is the DID of all data applicants and the total number; the *key* records all the Keys that have been distributed and their usage, as a list of data record, each record includes to (mark user), *time* (start and end date of the expiration date), *permission* (currently the owner of the data is super, which means that it can be accessed and updated, and the users only supports read). The specific process of Token generation is shown in Fig. 3.

Distribution

Owner. When generating the Token, a Key will be distributed to the data owner. Especially, the permission of the rule is super, the time is permanent, and from and to are their own DID.

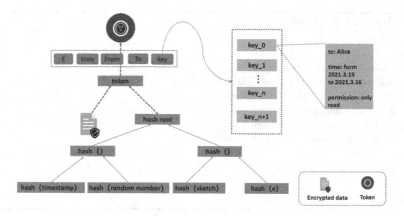

Fig. 3. Token generation process

User. When the participants in the cooperative relationship have data interaction requirements, they send their own DID and data requirements to the data owner. The data owner first verifies whether the DID is legal, as in Algorithm 2. When the identity verification is passed, the data owner generates a Key$\langle Token\_key, State, rule \rangle$ and returns it to the user. The Key is a triple, where *Token_key* is used to find the unique corresponding value of the corresponding Token; The *State* is consistent with the state in the Token; The *rule* represents the applicant relevant rules for data operations include *from* (mark the owner of the data), *time* (start and end date of the expiration date), *permission* (operate on the data, only read).

Ownership Verification. With Token, we can anchor to unique data. When verifying the Key, verify whether the Token is in a valid state, that is, whether multiple *from* is consistent; Then verify whether the number of *from* and *to* is valid, that is, $to = from$ is normal, and $to \neq from$ prove that the Token may be forged or illegal forwarding; Finally, compare and verify whether the rule attributed in the Key and the key in the Token are consistent to prove permission to the data. Only the data owner has read and write permissions, and the rest are only read permissions. We show the verification process in the form of Algorithm 3.

Token-related circulation information is deposited and linked by the chain. When there is a problem of ownership authentication, both the data owner and data user can provide evidence through the Key, and automatically verify with the Token through the smart contract. Data-related work has taken a crucial step. Generally, data is circulated in the blockchain in the form of Token, and users use Key to prove their ownership.

Algorithm 2. DID Verification

Input: DID;
 1: result = Failed
 2: DIDBytes = Base58Decode(DID)
 3: CheckBytes = DIDBytes[len(DIDBytes)-5:last]
 4: hash2 = DIDBytes[0:len(DIDBytes)-5]
 5: check = hash(hash(hash2))[0:5]
 6: **if** CheckBytes == check **then**
 7:     result = Success
 8: **else**
 9:     result = DID error
10: **end if**
Output: result

5 Data Interaction Process

Algorithm 3. Ownership Verification

Input: Key, DID = user's DID;
 1: result = Failed
 2: **for** key in Token.key **do**
 3:     **if** key.to == DID **then**
 4:         **if** key.time == Key.rule.time **then**
 5:             **if** key.permission == Key.rule.permission **then**
 6:                 result = Succeed
 7:             **else**
 8:                 result = permission is error
 9:             **end if**
10:         **else**
11:             result = time is error
12:         **end if**
13:     **else**
14:         result = DID is error
15:     **end if**
16: **end for**
Output: result

There is a critical data interaction process that occurs when a data applicant applies for access to related data. The process is shown in Algorithm 4. Firstly, the user will send a data access application to the owner according to its own needs, including its own DID and requirements. After receiving the request, the owner will verify whether the user's identity is legal. For the specific algorithm, see the DID authentication stage. After the verification is passed, the Key will be generated according to the demand and returned to the user; then the user sends the Key to the distributed cloud database to apply for data. When the cloud database is verified, the target data is returned to the user, and the relevant records are uploaded to the blockchain and synchronized to the owner.

Algorithm 4. Interaction Verification

Input: Key, DID = user's DID;
 1: result = Failed
 2: Token = get Token by Key.Token-hash
 3: **if** Token.State *is* valid **then**
 4:     **if** len(Token.From) == len(Token.To) **then**
 5:         **if** are all the From.from is same **then**
 6:             execution Key verification
 7:         **else**
 8:             result = from error
 9:             return
10:         **end if**
11:     **else**
12:         result = From and To error
13:         return
14:     **end if**
15: **else**
16:     result = Token's state invalid
17:     return
18: **end if**
19: Key verification
20: **if** Key verification succeed **then**
21:     result = Succeed
22: **else**
23:     result = Error
24: **end if**
Output: result

---

6   Experiment and Analysis

In this section, we conduct experimental simulation tests on the proposed scheme and analyze the results to demonstrate the feasibility of our scheme. We use the Linux operating system as the basis, select Hyperledger Fabric version 1.4 as the blockchain platform, and develop smart contracts that meet our plan for testing.

6.1   Data Set Selection

We choose the data set used in Detecting Anomalies in Wafer Manufacturing on Kaggle as the data set used in this experiment. This data set is used for the prediction of semiconductor anomalies and comes from one of the leading wafer (semiconductor) manufacturers in India. It is a real data collection in the IIoT scenario.

6.2   DID Generation and Verification

We write the generation and verification of DID into smart contracts, tested 100 times, and took the odd number of them to show the result distribution more clearly, and the experimental results are shown in the Fig. 4(a). It can be seen from the figure that the verification time is more stable than the generation time, but the fluctuation range of the generation time is only within 600 μs, which is an acceptable range.

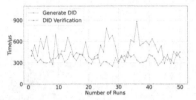

(a) DID Generation and Verification.

(b) Token and Owner's Key Generation and Verification.

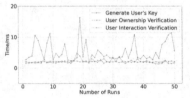

(c) User's Key Generation and Verification.

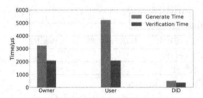

(d) Average Time Consumption.

Fig. 4. Experiment result.

6.3   Token Generation, Owner's Key Generation and Verification

The generation of Token and Owner's Key and the test of ownership verification and interaction verification are also carried out through smart contracts. Here, we have tested 100 times and the experimental results are shown in the Fig. 4(b). In general, the time consumption of the three is relatively close, and there are individual fluctuations only in the generation stage, and the impact is not large.

6.4   User's Key Generation and Verification

We did the same test on the User's Key as the owner's Key and the experimental results are shown in the Fig. 4(c). It can be seen that the time of ownership verification and interaction verification is relatively stable and close. There are also some fluctuations in the generation stage, but they are about 10 ms, which is also within the controllable range.

6.5   Average Time Analysis

Based on the above analysis, we put together the average time of the owner's Key, user's Key, and DID generation and verification the experimental results shown in the Fig. 4(d). From the figure, we can see that the average time consumption is in milliseconds, and DID even reaches the microseconds level.

6.6   Comparison with Existing Methods

We also made a comparative analysis with the existing weight confirmation schemes. As shown in Table 1, it can be seen that our scheme is superior.

Table 1. Comparison with existing methods.

Method	Blockchain category	Resource consumption	Data mobility
[5]	Public blockchain	High	Middle
[4]	Permissioned consortium blockchain	Middle	Low
[9]	Unkonw	High	High
This paper	Permissioned consortium blockchain	Low	High

6.7   Safety Analysis

In this section, we will analyze the security of the scheme. The scheme we propose is based on the permissioned consortium blockchain, which has the function of identity authentication, and controls related permissions through keys and certificates. Only the partner have the right to participate in the blockchain network, which excludes criminals to a large extent. We also designed DID to further isolate data and improve circulation efficiency. The DID can further restrict identities. It also improves the reliability of the network. In addition, the data exists in the form of ciphertext during circulation, and the Token is generated by the sha256 algorithm, which is irreversible and unbreakable. When applying for data, it is necessary to verify the DID and Token at the same time, providing security double insurance. We also show the time spent on its generation and verification in Fig. 4.

7   Conclusion

This paper proposed a mechanism for confirming IIoT data rights based on the permissioned consortium blockchain. We also proposed a blockchain architecture of node classification strategies for the resource-constrained scenarios of IIoT to better apply them in actual scenarios. Different from some existing data verification schemes, we proposed a data-based identity authentication method to better control data flow issues and isolate them from other businesses. We also consider the issue of efficient data flow, and Token anchoring can not only do a good job in confirming the right, but also make the data play more valuable.

References

1. Cai, Z., He, Z.: Trading private range counting over big IoT data, pp. 144–153 (2019)
2. Cai, Z., Zheng, X.: A private and efficient mechanism for data uploading in smart cyber-physical systems. IEEE Trans. Netw. Sci. Eng. **7**(2), 766–775 (2020)
3. Dai, H.N., Zheng, Z., Zhang, Y.: Blockchain for internet of things: a survey. IEEE Internet Things J. **6**(5), 8076–8094 (2019)
4. Gao, Z., Cao, L., Du, X.: Data right confirmation mechanism based on blockchain and locality sensitive hashing. In: 2020 3rd International Conference on Hot Information-centric Networking (HotICN), pp. 1–7 (2020)
5. Gong, J., Lin, S., Li, J.: Research on personal health data provenance and right confirmation with smart contract. In: 2019 IEEE 4th Advanced Information Technology, Electronic and Automation Control Conference (IAEAC), vol. 1, pp. 1211–1216 (2019)
6. Li, R., Song, T., Mei, B., Li, H., Cheng, X., Sun, L.: Blockchain for large-scale internet of things data storage and protection. IEEE Trans. Serv. Comput. **12**(5), 762–771 (2019)
7. Liu, S., Yu, J., Xiao, Y., Wan, Z., Wang, S., Yan, B.: BC-SABE: blockchain-aided searchable attribute-based encryption for cloud-IoT. IEEE Internet Things J. **7**(9), 7851–7867 (2020)
8. Liu, Y., Wang, K., Yun, L., Xu, W.: LightChain: a lightweight blockchain system for industrial internet of things. IEEE Trans. Ind. Inform. **15**(6), 3571–3581 (2019)
9. Qian, P., Liu, Z., Wang, X., Chen, J., Zimmermann, R.: Digital resource rights confirmation and infringement tracking based on smart contracts. In: 2019 IEEE 6th International Conference on Cloud Computing and Intelligence Systems (CCIS) (2019)
10. Wan, J., Li, J., Imran, M., Li, D., Fazal-e-Amin: A blockchain-based solution for enhancing security and privacy in smart factory. IEEE Trans. Ind. Inform. **15**(6), 3652–3660 (2019)
11. Wang, Y., Yu, J., Yan, B., Wang, G., Shan, Z.: BSV-PAGS: blockchain-based special vehicles priority access guarantee scheme. Comput. Commun. **161**, 28–40 (2020)
12. Xu, Y., Ren, J., Zhang, Y., Zhang, C., Shen, B., Zhang, Y.: Blockchain empowered arbitrable data auditing scheme for network storage as a service. IEEE Trans. Serv. Comput. **13**(2), 289–300 (2020)
13. Yan, B., Yu, J., Wang, Y., Guo, Q., Chai, B., Liu, S.: Blockchain-based service recommendation supporting data sharing. In: Yu, D., Dressler, F., Yu, J. (eds.) WASA 2020. LNCS, vol. 12384, pp. 580–589. Springer, Cham (2020). https://doi.org/10.1007/978-3-030-59016-1_48
14. Yu, J., Liu, S., Wang, S., Xiao, Y., Yan, B.: LH-ABSC: a lightweight hybrid attribute-based signcryption scheme for cloud-fog-assisted IoT. IEEE Internet Things J. **7**(9), 7949–7966 (2020)
15. Zheng, X., Cai, Z.: Privacy-preserved data sharing towards multiple parties in industrial IoTs. IEEE J. Sel. Areas Commun. **38**(5), 968–979 (2020)

Fault-Tolerant Consensus in Wireless Blockchain System

Yifei Zou, Yufan Li, Dongxiao Yu, Feng Li, Yanwei Zheng[✉], and Yan Zhang

Institute of Intelligent Computing, School of Computer Science and Technology, Shandong University, Qingdao 266237, People's Republic of China
{yfzou,dxyu,fli,zhengyw}@sdu.edu.cn

Abstract. In recent years, the blockchain system on multi-agents has drawn much attention from both of the broad academic research and industries due to its popular applications, such as Bitcoin [15]. Meanwhile, it is also an important part in city/industrial Internet-of-Things and artificial intelligence areas. In this paper, we investigate the fault-tolerant consensus problem in wireless blockchain system. Considering that the multi-agents in reality are inevitable to break down or send wrong messages because of some uncertain errors, in this paper, we propose a fault-tolerant consensus protocol, which can achieve consensus over multi-agents in wireless blockchain network within $O((f + 1) \log n)$ time steps with high probability. f is the upper bound of invalid agents, and n is the number of agents in the blockchain system. Rigorous theoretical analysis and extensive simulations are given to show the efficiency of our algorithm.

Keywords: Consensus in multi-agents · Wireless blockchain system · Fault-tolerant · Internet-of-Things

1 Introduction

In the past decades, with an enormous demand on the safety and convenience in distributed systems, it is highly possible for blockchain technology to become ubiquitous in cities and industries. Blockchain technique is envisioned as the core mechanism of publicized cryptocurrencies, and it can be used in a variety of applications, such as the Internet of Things (IoT), which allows direct communication and interaction among multi-agents via the Internet. As the number of multi-agents keeps increasing, traditional IoT applications no longer suit well for the data integrity, security, and robustness. Fortunately, blockchain provides

This work was partially supported by National Key R&D Program of China under Grant 2020YFB1005900, the Blockchain Core Technology Strategic Research Program of Ministry of Education of China (No. 2020KJ010301), and NSFC (No. 61971269, No. 620722278, No. 61832012).

Z. Liu et al. (Eds.): WASA 2021, LNCS 12937, pp. 133–146, 2021.
https://doi.org/10.1007/978-3-030-85928-2_11

a practical solution to overcome the limitations of traditional IoT applications. Briefly, the blockchain technologies consist of P2P network protocol, distributed consensus protocol, cryptography technology, account and storage model. Among all technologies above, the distributed consensus protocol is the cornerstone of blockchain. Agents in the blockchain network exchange their messages and make local decisions by executing distributed consensus protocol, which guarantee the consistency of distributed ledger. And the distributed consensus protocol enables blockchains decentralization indeed. Moreover, the blockchain consensus protocol has great influences on the performance of a blockchain system, including throughput, scalability, and fault tolerance. Therefore, an efficient and effective fault-tolerant consensus protocol is of great significance.

Generally, there are two kinds of consensus protocols widely used in blockchains: the Proof-of-X (PoX) consensus protocols (e.g., Proof-of-Work (PoW), Proof-of-Stake (PoS) [2]), and the Byzantine Fault Tolerant (BFT)-based consensus protocols (e.g., Practical Byzantine Fault Tolerance (PBFT) [4] and HotStuff [21]). Nodes in the blockchain who execute PoX consensus protocols need to prove that they are more competent for appending work than other nodes. Nodes in the blockchain network who execute BFT-based consensus protocols need to exchange the results of verifying a new block before voting on the final decision. However, each of them has its pros and cons. Most of PoX consensus protocols have high scalability but low efficiency, which are more suitable in public blockchain. Whereas, BFT-based consensus protocols have high efficiency but are not scalable, which are mainly used in consortium and private blockchain.

Main Challenges. Considering both the IoT environment and multi-agents constraints, there are four mainly challenges to design an efficient fault-tolerant consensus protocol in blockchain system. Firstly, in order to meet the requirements of low-power multi-agents in the IoT, it is necessary for the consensus protocol to have the characteristics of high throughput, high energy efficiency and insensitive to device mobility. Secondly, multi-agents can access the same wireless channel, so the transmission between nodes can affect each other. One is that the success rate of transmission is uncertain, and the other is that the channel is unstable, i.e., it is difficult to guarantee the long-term effective transmission of information. Both of them make it difficult to achieve a consensus in a wireless environment. Thirdly, the severe state fork problem which occurs when there are multiple valid blocks appearing at the same time is also a challenge for the design of the fault-tolerant consensus protocol. The last challenge is that there are some fault nodes in the wireless blockchain system which may cause the whole system to fail to work or write invalid blocks in the blockchain. As a result, these fault nodes may prevent nodes from achieving a consensus.

To tackle the above challenges, we propose a fault-tolerant Proof-of-Communication (FTPoC) consensus protocol in wireless blockchain network in this paper. Specifically, all of miners, i.e., multi-agents of IoT participate in multiple leader competition process via communication. Each time a leader is elected, this leader will propose a new block, broadcast and record it, and other miners will record the block and count the number of times the block has been received until $f + 1$ the same blocks are recorded. We adopt an efficient leader competition scheme, which makes full use of the signals received in the wireless channel to elect multiple leaders so as to meet the requirements of the multi-agents and environment of IoT and reduce the influence of nodes on each other. We adopt voting mechanism which guarantees that one and only one valid block is written in the blockchain in order to solve the fork problem and the device failure problem.

Our Contributions. In this paper, we present an efficient fault-tolerant consensus protocol for the multi-agents in wireless blockchain system. All multi-agents can achieve a consensus within $O((f + 1) \log n)$ time steps with high probability[1] by executing our protocol when there are at most f fault agents. The main contributions of our work are summarized as follows:

- We consider the fault-tolerant blockchain consensus protocol in multi-agents wireless networks. Therefore, our wireless blockchain consensus protocol is closer to reality and makes the wireless research in blockchain system more completed.
- Under the faulty assumption in the wireless network, we show how to design a scheme based on fault-tolerant PoC in the context of wireless network to achieve a consensus in blockchain through a wireless competition scheme and voting mechanism, which can provide a completely new perspective for the design of wireless blockchain protocol.

2 Related Work

In 1980, the classical consensus in distributed system was proposed by Pease *et al.* in [17], which theoretically supports the blockchain consensus protocol. Their work mainly considers how non-fault nodes achieve a consensus by point-to-point communication when there are fault nodes involved. In 2008, PoW was the first consensus algorithm in blockchain used by Bitcoin [15]. Nowadays, PoW consensus protocol is also one of the most widely used consensus protocols in public blockchain. However, the mining behavior based on PoW also causes a lot of waste of resources [16]. In addition, one of the reasons for the scalability limitation and energy efficiency of PoW consensus protocol is fork problem. In 2012, Peercoin is released by S. King [12], and the concept of PoS was first proposed to solve the limitations of PoW. In the PoS mechanism, the miners no longer consume a lot of energy to calculate hash function, but mortgage their own assets to become candidates and compete for the power to propose blocks. The miners do not consume any resources [3] (called virtual mining), so PoS does not consume energy and hardware equipment like PoW, which avoids

---

[1] With the probability of $1 - n^{-c}$ for some constant $c > 1$ and w.h.p. for short.

high energy consumption. Although the PoS has its unique advantages, there are still some problems. The system can not guarantee security and fairness well because of centralization risk [10], and weak randomness [11]. In addition, there are other classes of PoX, e.g., Proof-of-Activity [1] and Proof-of-Space [9]. Whereas, they have their own disadvantages, so they are also not suitable for IoT agents. BFT-based consensus protocols are highly efficient and can solve device failure problem. Whereas,because of the communication complexity [18], they are not scalable, which makes them also unsuitable for IoT edge agents. Different from the previous works mentioned above, the consensus problem in our work is considered in the context of wireless network with the faulty assumption, which is more realistic. Besides, the time complexity of our solution on consensus problem is very close to the optimal solution. It is believed that with our work, many problems and applications in reality [5–7,13,14,19,31–34] can get a new solution.

3   Model and Problem Definition

We assume that there is a wireless blockchain network in a two-dimensional Euclidean plane, where each miner can communicate with others by a wireless channel. In each time slot, every miner can listen or transmit but cannot do both. The miners that can work normally are called as the normal miners. In addition, there are some fault miners who may not work or send some wrong messages because of unknown errors, e.g.,calculation error.

In order to get closer to reality, SINR model [22–25,29] is adopted in our model to depict the message reception in this paper. For a miner v, let $Signal(v)$ denote the strength of the signal received by v, and $SINR(u,v)$ denote the SINR ratio of miner v for the transmission from miner u. In this model, we have

$$Signal(v) = \sum_{w \in S} P_w \cdot d(w,v)^{-\alpha} + \mathcal{N},$$

$$SINR(u,v) = \frac{P_u \cdot d(u,v)^{-\alpha}}{\sum_{w \in S \setminus \{u\}} P_w \cdot d(w,v)^{-\alpha} + \mathcal{N}}.$$

In the above two equations, P_w denotes the transmission power of miner w, $d(w,v)$ is the Euclidean distance between miner w and miner v, S denotes the set of miners who transmit in the current slot, $\mathcal{N}$ is the background noise, $\alpha \in (2,6]$ is the path-loss exponent. In this model, a message sent by miner u is successfully decoded by miner v if and only if $SINR(u,v) \geq \beta$, where threshold $\beta > 1$ depends on hardware. We use N to denote a close upper bound of background noise $\mathcal{N}$. They are so close that for any miner the accumulation of background noise and signals from transmissions is larger than N, when there are transmissions in network. Therefore, it indicates that for any listening miner v, as long as the set S is not empty, the strength of the received signal $Signal(v)$ is larger than N. In addition, each miner is equipped with physical carrier sensing, which is part of the IEEE 802.11 standard in the media access control (MAC) layer. The miners adopt synchronous wake-up mode, that is, each miner will wake up at the beginning of the same round. [26–28,30,35–37] are the works who have the similar SINR assumptions with our model in this paper.

Problem Definition. We assume that there are n miners in a 2-dimensional Euclidean plane, all of which wake up synchronously at the beginning and can transmit to each other via the multiple access wireless channel. In addition, we assume that n is sufficiently large and miners only have a rough estimation on n. Among the n miners, there are normal miners and faulty miners, where the number of faulty miners is not larger than f, f is a known number and smaller than $\lceil \frac{n}{2} \rceil$. Normal miners can work normally. However, faulty miners may be out of work (broken down) or send wrong messages (e.g., broadcast an invalid block) because of unknown errors such as the calculation errors, which prevents the normal miners from achieving a consensus. In each interval containing sufficient large slots, the group of miners need to achieve a consensus on a valid block including network transactions that have occurred in the current interval in their local blockchain.

4   FTPoC Consensus Protocol

4.1   Framework of Consensus Protocol

The consensus process in our work is divided into three phases: leader election, block proposal and validation, and chain update. **Leader Election (LE) Phase:** in each phase, one miner will be elected as the leader from the group of miners in network to schedule the following two phases. **Block Proposal and Validation (BPV) Phase:** each time when a leader is elected, it will propose a new block and record it, and other miners will record the block and count the number of times the new block is received. Then, the miners who are not leaders will return to the previous phase until $f+1$ the same blocks are recorded. **Chain Updation (CU) Phase:** all normal miners will write the new block which has been recorded $f + 1$ times into the local blockchain.

In each time of leader election phase, a miner will be elected as the leader w.h.p. After repeating this phase at most $2f+1$ and at least $f+1$ times, at most $2f + 1$ (at least $f + 1$) miners will be elected as leaders, in which $f + 1$ leaders are normal miners and will propose the same blocks. In BPV phase, each leader will propose a block and record it, and other miners will record the block and count the number of times the block is received. The miners who are not leaders will return to the previous phase until $f + 1$ the same blocks are recorded. In the final phase, all miners will write the new block which has been proposed $f + 1$ times in the block.

4.2   Goal of Consensus

Generally, in a distributed system, the consensus is a state that all nodes in system agree on the same data values, which satisfies the following three requirements: termination, validity and agreement [8].

Termination: for each normal miner in blockchain system, a valid transaction/block is written into its local blockchain in finite time. **Validity:** If all normal miners approve the same valid transaction/block, then the transaction/block should be written in their local blockchain. **Agreement:** each valid transaction/block should be written by each normal miners to its local blockchain. For each normal miner, the written block in its local blockchain should be assigned the same sequence number.

In addition to the above basic goals of the consensus protocol design in blockchain network, the efficiency, and security of consensus protocols should be considered comprehensively in our application context. Thus, in Sect. 5, in addition to analyzing the correctness of our fault-tolerant consensus protocol, we also analyze the efficiency and security of it.

4.3   Detail Description for FTPoC Consensus

We divide the execution time into rounds, and each round contains three slots. There are three functions in the protocol: Leader Election ( ), Block Proposal and Validation ( ), and Chain Update ( ). In each round, each miner will execute the above three functions successively. We give the pseudo code in Algorithm 1.

Algorithm 1: FTPoC Consensus Protocol for each miner v

Initialization: $state_v = \mathbb{C}, count_v = 0, C_v = 0, i = 1$;

In each round, each miner v does:
1 Slot 1: Leader Election ( );
2 Slot 2: Block Proposal and Validation ( );
3 Slot 3: Chain Update ( );

We use the following $2f + 3$ states to represent the state of the miners in execution: $\mathbb{C}$ is the candidate state, indicating that the miners are in the leader competition; $\mathbb{S}$ is the silence state, indicating that the miners have given up the leader election; and $\mathbb{L}_i (i = 1, 2..., 2f + 1)$ are the leader states, indicating that the miner succeeded in leader competition and be elected as the i-th leaders.

Initially, each miner is in state $\mathbb{C}$, when it wakes up. Then, it will execute Algorithm 1 in each round. Each miner v is initially in state $\mathbb{C}$ after waking up. Then, it begins to execute the three functions given in Algorithm 1 in each of the following rounds. In each round, all miners execute Algorithm 2 in slot 1.

Algorithm 2: Leader Election ( ) for each miner v

Slot 1:

```
1   if state_v == C then
2       Transmit a message M_v with constant probability p_v or listen
        otherwise;
3       if Received signal is larger than N then
4           state_v = S;
5       else
6           count_v + +;
7           if count_v > k * log n then
8               state_v = L_i;
```

Each miner in state $\mathbb{C}$ transmits with a constant probability. Then, if a miner v listens and the signal it receives has its strength larger than N, miner v becomes in state $\mathbb{S}$, i.e., miner v gives up the leader competition. If miner v keeps in state $\mathbb{C}$ in at least $k * \log n$ rounds, where k is a sufficiently large constant, miner v becomes in state $\mathbb{L}_i$, which indicates that miner v becomes the i-th elected leader. By the action in slot 1, there are multiple miners (at most $2f + 1$ and at least $f + 1$) being elected as the leaders w.h.p, of which $f + 1$ leaders are normal miners, and we will give the proof in the next section.

In slot 2 of each round, each miner execute the function Block Proposal and Validation() which is shown in Algorithm 3. Each time a leader is elected, this leader will propose a new block B_v and disseminate it to all other miners in the wireless blockchain network, and then record the block. If the new block B_v is received by the other miners, they will record the block and count the number of times the block is received. Then, to participate the leader election again, the miners in state $\mathbb{S}$ will move to state $\mathbb{C}$. If a leader is a faulty miner, it may propose an invalid block, but each leader who is a normal miner will propose valid and the same blocks. In particular, this is to make sure that only one valid block is proposed in each time of the consensus process.

In slot 3, each miner execute the function Chain Update() which is given in Algorithm 4. If the new block has been recorded $f + 1$ times by each normal miner in the previous phase, the new block B_v will be written into the local blockchain by each normal miner in the blockchain network.

5   Protocol Analysis

In this section, we first analyze and prove the correctness of the FTPoC consensus protocol, and then analyze the efficiency and security of it.

Algorithm 3: Block Proposal and Validation ( ) for each miner v

---

   Slot 2:

1   **if** $state_v == \mathbb{L}_i$ **then**
2   Broadcast B_v;
3   Record B_v;
4   **if** v *has recorded the same* B_v $f+1$ *times* **then**
         $\lfloor$ $C_v = 1$;

5   **if** $state_v == \mathbb{L}_p(p = 1, 2, ..., i-1)$ *or* $state_v == \mathbb{S}$ **then**
6   Listen ;
7   **if** *receive* B_v **then**
8   Record B_v;
9   **if** v *has recorded the same* B_v $f+1$ *times* **then**
            $\lfloor$ $C_v = 1$;

10   **if** $state_v == \mathbb{S}$ *and* $C_v == 0$ **then**
         $state_v = \mathbb{C}$;
11          $count_v = 0$;

12       $i++$;

Algorithm 4: Chain Update () for each miner v

   Slot 3:

1   **if** $C_v == 1$ **then**
2       $\lfloor$ Use the B_v to update the local Blockchain;
3    $state_v = \mathbb{C}, i = 1, count_v = 0, count_v^a = 0(a = 1, 2, ..., f+1), C_v = 0$;

Theorem 1. *It takes at most $O((f+1)\log n)$ rounds to make all normal miners in blockchain network achieve consensus w.h.p.*

Our proof of Theorem 1 is unfolded in the following three lemmas: Lemma 1, Lemma 3 and Lemma 4. By the three lemmas, we prove that our protocol satisfies termination, validity and agreement respectively.

Lemma 1. *It takes at most $O((f+1)\log n)$ rounds for all miners to terminate the consensus process, w.h.p.*

It is obvious that after $f+1$ normal leaders are elected out, an extra round is enough for miners to make a consensus on the block. Therefore, the termination of our consensus protocol mainly depends on the leader election process, which is analyzed and proved by the following Lemma 2.

Lemma 2. *In each $O(\log n)$ rounds, a leader will be elected out by the function Leader Election ( ) in our algorithm w.h.p.*

Proof. Since all of the miners wake up synchronously and become the candidates for the leader election when they wake up, each time a miner is elected as a leader, the remaining miners in state $\mathbb{S}$ will change to state $\mathbb{C}$ at the same time, and then participate in the next leader election. Then, We take into account the reduction of the candidates in each leader election. According to our algorithm, we just need to prove that after $k * \log n$ rounds, there is only one candidate left in each leader election w.h.p, and it will become the leader.

Let set A denote the collection of the miners who are the candidates for a leader election. In the first leader election, all the miners participate in the leader competition, i.e. $|A| = n$. After each leader election, only those who are not elected will participate in the next leader election, i.e. $|A|$ will decrease by 1. After at least $f + 1$ and at most $2f + 1$ times leader election, all normal miners will record a valid block $f + 1$ times, and then achieve consensus. As for the analysis for candidates' reduction in slot 1, we divided it into following two cases: (1) $|A| = 1$; (2) $|A| > 1$. Obviously, if $|A| = 1$, the miner in set S will become leader. For another case $|A| > 1$, we can see that there are $|A| * p$ miners transmit and $|A| * (1 - p)$ miners listen in expectation in each round. Thus, in expectation, there will be $\min\{1, |A| * p\} * (1 - p) * |A|$ nodes giving up the leader election in each round. By taking a Chernoff bound, we can prove that within $O(\log n)$ rounds, there will be only one leader left in set A and becomes the leader. A detailed and specific proof for the process of Chernoff bound can be found in [20].

According to Lemma 2, one leader will be elected out within $O(\log n)$ rounds in each leader election process w.h.p. Moreover, after at least $f + 1$ and at most $2f + 1$ times leader election, $f + 1$ normal leaders will be elected out. Thus, within $O((f + 1) \log n)$ rounds all miners will get a consensus. Combining the two Lemmas above, we prove that our consensus protocol satisfies the termination requirement and has an efficient time complexity.

Lemma 3. *The protocol satisfies the validity requirement.*

Proof. We divide our analysis into two cases as follows: (1) B_v is invalid, i.e., the leader v who generated B_v is a faulty miner. There are at most f faulty miners in the wireless blockchain network, and only the leader who is a faulty miner may propose and broadcast an invalid block. Therefore, B_v can not be recorded by $f + 1$ times. (2) B_v is valid, i.e., the leader v who generates B_v is a normal miner. Note that any normal leader will propose and broadcast the same valid block, and the invalid blocks from faulty miners can not be recorded by $f + 1$ times. According to Algorithm 3, there must be $f + 1$ normal miners being elected as leaders, and they all propose the same B_v, which indicates that B_v will be recorded by any miner u by $f + 1$ times. Thus, for any u, it will set the value of C_u equal to 1.

Because of the execution of Algorithm 3, if and only if the new block B_v is valid, it will make value $C_u = 1$ for any miner u. Then in the last slot, all of the miners would update their local blockchain with the new block B_v in the current round.

Lemma 4. *The protocol satisfies the agreement requirement.*

Claim. In each consensus process, all normal miners in the blockchain network will update their local blockchain with the same block B_v.

Proof. According to Claim 1, we can draw two conclusions: (1) If the new block B_v is valid, B_v will be recorded by $f + 1$ times, and then all normal miners will update the local blockchain with B_v; (2) On the contrary, if the new block B_v is invalid, B_v can not be recorded by $f + 1$ times, which indicates that normal miners will not update the local blockchain with B_v. Thus, for each normal miner the latest block of its local blockchain is the same.

Claim. For any pair of normal miners u and v in the blockchain network, B_v^i and B_u^i are the same, where B_u^i is the i'th block in local blockchain of u and B_v^i is the i'th block in local blockchain of v.

Proof. If both of the normal miners u and v are leaders. We assume that the i-th valid block B_v^i is generated by v and the i-th valid block B_u^i is generated by u. Because any leader who is a normal miner will propose the same block, B_v^i is the same as B_u^i. From the proof of Claim 1, they will use the same new block to update their local blockchain simultaneously.

If only one of the normal miners u and v is a leader. Without loss of generality, we assume that u is the leader, and the i-th valid block B_v^i is generated by it. From the proof of Claim 1, both v and u will use the block B_v^i to update their local blockchain simultaneously.

If neither u nor v is the leader. Assuming that leader w who is a normal miner propose the i-th valid block B_w^i. From the proof of Claim 1, they will use the block B_w^i to update their local blockchain. Thus, in any case, both B_v^i and B_u^i are the same.

5.1   Discussion for Efficiency and Security

High Throughput and Energy Efficiency. Theorem 1 indicates that the FTPoC consensus protocol has the time complexity of $O((f + 1) \log n)$. In our protocol, each round is divided into 3 slots, and each slot is the minimum time to transmit a packet. Therefore, our protocol has a high throughput. In addition, In the best case, only $f + 1$ leaders need to be elected, and even in the worst case, only at most $2f + 1$ leaders need to be elected. It indicates that only at most $2f + 1$ miners need to propose and broadcast the new block, which avoids the participation of all miners and the sending of a large number of messages. Therefore, it is energy-saving and resource-friendly for the multi-agents in IoT.

Fairness. Because of setting $p_v = p$, each v in slot 1 transmits $\mathcal{M}_v$ with a same constant probability p , which guarantees the fairness of each miner in State $\mathbb{C}$ to compete for leadership. The randomness of leaders can also be guaranteed by the fairness of the leader election, which can guarantee the security of the protocol to a certain extent. It helps prevent the blockchain network from denial-of-service attacks by adversaries who know in advance which leaders will be elected.

State Fork Problem Avoided. In wireless blockchain network, due to the transmission delay and contention in the shared channel, it is difficult to solve the state fork problem. Although there are multiple leaders in our protocol, each leader who is a normal miner propose the same valid block, and only the valid block can be recorded by $f + 1$ times. Therefore, the protocol can ensure that in each time of the consensus process only one valid block is written into the local blockchain of each normal miner eventually, thus avoiding the state fork problem. Meanwhile, it makes our protocol more secure and could prevent the blockchain network from fork attacks by adversary as well.

6 Simulation Result

Parameter Setting. We set that n miners are randomly and uniformly distributed in a wireless blockchain network, of which f are set as faulty miners and the rest are set as normal miners. The background noise upper bound N is normalized as 1.0. The transmission probability p_v is set as 0.2.

Protocol Performance. The efficiency and fault-tolerant rate of our protocol used to achieve the consensus in the wireless blockchain network is given in Fig. 1(a) and Fig. 1(b) in which the x-axes and y-axes represent the fault-tolerant rate (i.e., proportion of faulty miners among all miners) and rounds used to achieve consensus respectively.

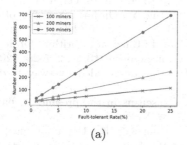
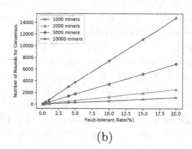

(a)   (b)

Fig. 1. Rounds used for achieving consensus

From Fig. 1(a) and Fig. 1(b), we can see that when the total number of miners is fixed, the higher the proportion of faulty miners in the network, the more rounds it takes to achieve consensus. Figure 1(a) shows the protocol can guarantee both high efficiency and high fault-tolerant rate when the scale of the network is small (e.g., $n = 100, 200, 500$). Even in the case that fault-tolerant rate is more than 20%, which means that proportion of faulty miners among all miners is more than 20%, our protocol can achieve consensus within 800 rounds. Figure 1(b) shows when the scale of the network is large (e.g., $n = 1000, 2000, 5000, 10000$), if we want to ensure high fault-tolerant rate, we need to spend more rounds to achieve consensus.

7 Conclusion

In this paper, for the first time, we consider the fault-tolerant consensus protocol for multi-agents in wireless blockchain system, which is closer to reality compared with the previous consensus protocols in blockchain system, and has an efficient performance on time complexity. Specifically, we propose a fault-tolerant Proof-of-Communication consensus protocol with the time complexity of $O((f+1)\log n)$, which has high energy efficiency and its security guaranteed. In addition, our protocol can provide some new perspectives for the higher-level protocol designs on multi-agents in the blockchain system. Also, byzantine behaviors is a common phenomenon for multi-agents in the blockchain system, and is far more complex. Thus the research in wireless blockchain system to against byzantine will become our direction in the future.

References

1. Bentov, I., Lee, C., Mizrahi, A., Rosenfeld, M.: Proof of activity: extending bitcoin's proof of work via proof of stake [extended abstract]y. SIGMETRICS Perform. Eval. Rev. **42**(3), 34–37 (2014)
2. Bitcoinwiki: Proof of stake (2014). https://en.bitcoin.it/wiki/Proof_of_Stake
3. Bonneau, J., Miller, A., Clark, J., Narayanan, A., Kroll, J.A., Felten, E.W.: SoK: research perspectives and challenges for bitcoin and cryptocurrencies. In: IEEE Symposium on Security and Privacy (2015)
4. Castro, M., Liskov, B.: Practical byzantine fault tolerance. In: OSDI (1999)
5. Chan, W., Chin, F.Y.L., Ye, D., Zhang, G., Zhang, Y.: On-line scheduling of parallel jobs on two machines. J. Discrete Algorithms **6**(1), 3–10 (2008)
6. Chan, W., Zhang, Y., Fung, S.P.Y., Ye, D., Zhu, H.: Efficient algorithms for finding longest common increasing subsequence. J. Comb. Optim. **13**(3), 277–288 (2007)
7. Chin, F.Y.L., et al.: Competitive algorithms for unbounded one-way trading. Theor. Comput. Sci. **607**(1), 35–48 (2015)
8. Dwork, C., Lynch, N.A., Stockmeyer, L.J.: Consensus in the presence of partial synchrony (preliminary version). In: PODC (1984)
9. Dziembowski, S., Faust, S., Kolmogorov, V., Pietrzak, K.: Proofs of space. In: Gennaro, R., Robshaw, M. (eds.) CRYPTO 2015. LNCS, vol. 9216, pp. 585–605. Springer, Heidelberg (2015). https://doi.org/10.1007/978-3-662-48000-7_29
10. Gazi, P., Kiayias, A., Russell, A.: Stake-bleeding attacks on proof-of-stake blockchains. In: CVCBT (2018)
11. Kiayias, A., Russell, A., David, B., Oliynykov, R.: Ouroboros: a provably secure proof-of-stake blockchain protocol. In: Katz, J., Shacham, H. (eds.) CRYPTO 2017. LNCS, vol. 10401, pp. 357–388. Springer, Cham (2017). https://doi.org/10.1007/978-3-319-63688-7_12
12. King, S., Nadal, S.: PPcoin: peer-to-peer crypto-currency with proof-of-stake (2012). https://peercoin.net/assets/paper/peercoin-paper.pdf
13. Li, F., Luo, J., Shi, G., He, Y.: ART: Adaptive fRequency-Temporal co-existing of ZigBee and WiFi. IEEE Trans. Mobile Comput. **16**(3), 662–674 (2017)
14. Li, F., Yu, D., Yang, H., Yu, J., Karl, H., Cheng, X.: Multi-Armed-Bandit-based spectrum scheduling algorithms in wireless networks: a survey. IEEE Wirel. Commun. **27**(1), 24–30 (2020)

15. Nakamoto, S.: Bitcoin: a peer-to-peer electronic cash system (2008). https://bitcoin.org/bitcoin.pdf
16. O'Dwyer, K.J., Malone, D.: Bitcoin mining and its energy footprint. In: ISSC/CIICT (2014)
17. Pease, M.C., Shostak, R.E., Lamport, L.: Reaching agreement in the presence of faults. J. ACM **27**(2), 228–234 (1980)
18. Vukolić, M.: The quest for scalable blockchain fabric: proof-of-work vs. BFT replication. In: Camenisch, J., Kesdoğan, D. (eds.) iNetSec 2015. LNCS, vol. 9591, pp. 112–125. Springer, Cham (2016). https://doi.org/10.1007/978-3-319-39028-4_9
19. Yu, D., Duan, X., Li, F., Liang, Y., Yang, H., Yu, J.: Distributed scheduling algorithm for optimizing age of information in wireless networks. In: IPCCC (2020)
20. Xu, Q., Zou, Y., Yu, D., Xu, M., Shen, S., Li, F.: Consensus in wireless blockchain system. WASA **1**, 568–579 (2020)
21. Yin, M., Malkhi, D., Reiter, M.K., Golan-Gueta, G., Abraham, I.: HotStuff: BFT consensus with linearity and responsiveness. In: PODC (2019)
22. Yu, D., Ning, L., Zou, Y., Yu, J., Cheng, X., Lau, F.C.M.: Distributed spanner construction with physical interference: constant stretch and linear sparseness. IEEE/ACM Trans. Netw. **25**(4), 2138–2151 (2017)
23. Yu, D., Wang, Y., Halldórsson, M.M., Tonoyan, T.: Dynamic adaptation in wireless networks under comprehensive interference via carrier sense. In: IPDPS (2017)
24. Yu, D., Zhang, Y., Huang, Y., Jin, H., Yu, J., Hua, Q.: Exact implementation of abstract MAC layer via carrier sensing. In: INFOCOM (2018)
25. Yu, D., et al.: Stable local broadcast in multihop wireless networks under SINR. IEEE/ACM Trans. Netw. **26**(3), 1278–1291 (2018)
26. Yu, D., Zou, Y., Wang, Y., Yu, J., Cheng, X., Lau, F.C.M.: Implementing the abstract MAC layer via inductive coloring under the Rayleigh-fading model. IEEE Trans. Wirel. Commun. https://doi.org/10.1109/TWC.2021.3072236
27. Yu, D., et al.: Competitive age of information in dynamic IoT networks. IEEE Internet Things J. (2020). https://doi.org/10.1109/JIOT.2020.3038595
28. Yu, D., et al.: Implementing the abstract MAC layer in dynamic networks. IEEE Trans. Mob. Comput. **20**(5), 1832–1845 (2021)
29. Yu, D., et al.: Distributed dominating set and connected dominating set construction under the dynamic SINR model. In: IPDPS (2019)
30. ?ibitemch112704 Yu, D., Zou, Y., Zhang, Y., Sheng, H., Lv, W., Cheng, X.: An exact implementation of the abstract MAC layer via carrier sensing in dynamic networks. IEEE/ACM Trans. Netw. (2021) https://doi.org/10.1109/TNET.2021.3057890
31. Zheng, X., Cai, Z.: Privacy-preserved data sharing towards multiple parties in industrial IoTs. IEEE J. Sel. Areas Commun. **38**(5), 968–979 (2020)
32. Zhu, S., Cai, Z., Hu, H., Li, Y., Li, W.: zkCrowd: a hybrid blockchain-based crowdsourcing platform. IEEE Trans. Ind. Inform. **16**(6), 4196–4205 (2020)
33. Zhang, Y., Chen, J., Chin, F.Y.L., Han, X., Ting, H.-F., Tsin, Y.H.: Improved online algorithms for 1-space bounded 2-dimensional bin packing. In: Cheong, O., Chwa, K.-Y., Park, K. (eds.) ISAAC 2010. LNCS, vol. 6507, pp. 242–253. Springer, Heidelberg (2010). https://doi.org/10.1007/978-3-642-17514-5_21
34. Zhu, S., Li, W., Li, H., Tian, L., Luo, G., Cai, Z.: Coin hopping attack in blockchain-based IoT. IEEE Internet Things J. **6**(3), 4614–4626 (2019)
35. Zou, Y., Xu, M., Sheng, H., Xing, X., Xu, Y., Zhang, Y.: Crowd density computation and diffusion via Internet of Things. IEEE Internet Things J. **7**(9), 8111–8121 (2020)

36. Zou, Y., et al.: Fast distributed backbone construction despite strong adversarial jamming. In: INFOCOM (2019)
37. Zou, Y., Yu, D., Yu, J., Zhang, Y., Dressler, F., Cheng, X.: Distributed Byzantine-Resilient multiple-message dissemination in wireless networks. In: IEEE/ACM Trans. Netw. (2021). https://doi.org/10.1109/TNET.2021.3069324

An Efficient and Secure Power Data Trading Scheme Based on Blockchain

Yang Shi[1], Zewei Liu[2(✉)], Chunqiang Hu[2], Bin Cai[2], and Binling Xie[1]

[1] Meizhou Power Supply Bureau, Meizhou 514021, Guangdong, China
[2] School of Big Data and Software Engineering, Chongqing University,
Chongqing 400044, China
{zwliu,chu,caibin}@cqu.edu.cn

Abstract. The traditional mode of power data transaction is mediated by web pages, which cannot be employed to data explosion as the power trading reform. It is a challenge issue to improve efficiency and privacy under the premise of transaction security and data reliability in power data trading. In this paper, we propose a novelty efficient and secure power data trading scheme (PDTS) based on blockchain and trusted execution environment platform (PDTP). PDTS makes full use of the dispersibility and immutability of blockchain to ensure the reliability of data transaction. It is noteworthy that the power data processing tasks take the form of smart contracts to ensure the efficiency of the transaction process. Meanwhile, trusted execution environment (TEE) is employed to ensure the security of power data processing. Finally, we analyze the security of the scheme and prove that the scheme can resist single point attack, external attack and internal attack. Moreover, the experimental results prove the feasibility and efficiency of the proposed scheme.

Keywords: Power data trading · Blockchain · Consensus · TEE

1 Introduction

In the traditional power data trading model, the data exchange between grid company and market members is mainly achieved through web pages. Market members analyze and process the source data by logging into the power trading system to view or report the data [1]. With the continuous expansion of market power data and the continuous improvement of market transaction frequency, the original transaction mode can not meet the demand of modern power analysis [2,3]. Moreover, power data involves the national basic energy support system and the information of many power customers, and their privacy security is extremely important [4,5]. However, the power data itself is directly taken as

Supported by National Key Research and Development Project under Grant 2018AA A0101800, the National Natural Science Foundation of China under grant 62072065, Science and Technology Projects of China Southern Power Grid (031400KK52190059 (GDKJXM20198151)).

Z. Liu et al. (Eds.): WASA 2021, LNCS 12937, pp. 147–158, 2021.
https://doi.org/10.1007/978-3-030-85928-2_12

the transaction object without screening, anonymization and desensitization in traditional model. Based on it, malicious adversaries may infer the living habits of power customers through their consumption records, resulting in a serious threat to the privacy of customers, or even an irreparable situation [6].

Consequently, in the conventional power data trading system, the following key problems need to be effectively solved:

- Market members can try to figure out the privacy of power customers from power source data or processed statistics, resulting in information disclosure.
- Due to the increase of power data volume, the efficiency of the trading system needs to be improved in order to cope with the demand of power analysis.

Based on the above ideas and problems to be solved, in this paper, we propose an efficient and secure power data trading scheme based on data processing-as-a-service mode. The contributions of our PDTS can be summarized as follows:

- Firstly, blockchain and smart contract are utilized to guarantee the tamper-resistant of data and provide automated transactions.
- Secondly, the power data processing tasks are carried out in the form of smart contract to improve the enforcement efficiency of the PDTS.
- Thirdly, in order to provide a secure and reliable environment for the power data processing, we adopt the trusted execution environment, that is, to protect the operation involving source data by means of hardware isolation.
- Finally, a comprehensive safety analysis and experiment are carried out on PDTS. From the aspect of security, the scheme can resist many kinds of attacks. The experimental results show that the scheme is effective and brings low computation cost for both parties of power data transaction.

The remainder of this paper is organized as follows. Section 2 introduces related works. Section 3 briefly describes related preliminaries contained in our scheme. Section 4 presents the system model and design goals. Section 5 shows the overall detailed flow of PDTS. Sections 6 and 7 present the security and performance analyses, respectively. Finally, conclusions are drawn in Sect. 8.

2   Related Works

In this section, we will compare the existing work based on the features in our system [7]. The PoweePeers platform, developed by Vattenfall Company in the Netherlands, makes full use of the blockchain technology and constructs the corresponding website platform, which is committed to solving the distributed application characteristics of power consumption effectively [8]. Residential users on the platform will be able to buy and sell energy to their neighbors via the blockchain, although the number of nodes in the microgrid is relatively small [9]. Filament [10], an American company, builts a series of TAPS detection devices based on Australia's power grid nodes, and uses blockchain technology to build a complete communication mechanism. Aitzhan et al. [11] proposes a scheme that does not rely on third parties, uses multi-signature and anonymous encrypted message flow to spread energy transaction information and ensure the security of energy transaction. Wu et al. [12] proposes a smart grid data security storage system, which enables the perceived data to be safely stored in a decentralized way and solves the security risks of centralized data storage.

Still, there has been little research on the trading of power data itself. Power data is the core asset and has great application value. It can optimize the management mode internally and enrich the value-added services externally. Therefore, it is an inevitable trend to build a safe trading platform for power data.

3   Preliminaries

In this section, we will introduce blockchain, TEE with Intel SGX, and explain some of the important features on which our scheme relies.

3.1   Blockchain and Smart Contract

Blockchain is a decentralized distributed ledger composed of immutable data packets, also known as "blocks". Each block is linked together to form a "blockchain" [13]. It is a technical solution to collectively maintain a reliable database in a decentralized and trustless way. Smart contracts were first proposed in 1996 by Nick Szabo in his article "Smart contracts: building blocks for digital markets" [14]. Its existence enables transactions to be conducted automatically after the initial conditions are met without the supervision of third-party entities (such as courts, health authorities or banks), which promotes safe and convenient business activities and expands the application scenarios [15].

3.2   TEE with Intel SGX

Trusted execution environment, or TEE for short, can refer to be a region on the CPU. The purpose of this area is to provide a more secure space for the execution of data and code, and to ensure their confidentiality and integrity [16]. Intel software guard extensions (SGX) is a feature of modern Intel processors that allows applications to create enclaves, which can be understood as a secure environment where data is running. SGX's protection of software is not to identify or isolate malicious software in the system, but to encapsulate the operations of legitimate software for sensitive data (such as encryption keys, passwords, user data, etc.) in a "small black box", making it impossible for malicious software to access these data [17]. Of course, Intel provides a authentication mechanism to verify that a piece of code is running on the Intel SGX platform [18].

4   System Model, Security Requirements, and Design Goals

In this section, we mainly formalize system model, analyze attacker model and design goals.

4.1 System Model

In PDTS, there are mainly four entities, including trusted authority (TA), grid company (GC), research institution (RI) as representative of market members and power data trading platform (PDTP). This model is shown as Fig. 1.

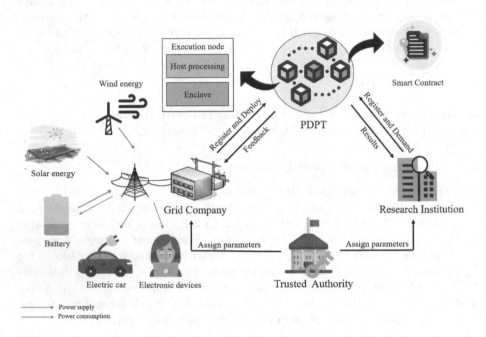

Fig. 1. PDTS model

- *TA*: TA is a fully trusted entity responsible for registering other entities. In addition, it generates the necessary public and private parameters, including the communication key for the registered entity.
- *GC*: GC is the owner of power data, which collects privacy data about customers' power consumption through smart devices. At the same time, GC is responsible for optimizing the layout of the power dispatching plan.
- *RI*: RI is an honest but curious market member which hopes to gain mass of information about consumers' power data to support their research. Merely, RI may also try to reveal consumers' privacy information from data.
- *BDPT*: It is a platform responsible for power data processing and consensus. The BDPT is composed of execution node (with TEE) and participating nodes. The internal structure of the execution node is shown in Fig. 2. The functions of execution nodes are described in detail in Sect. 5.

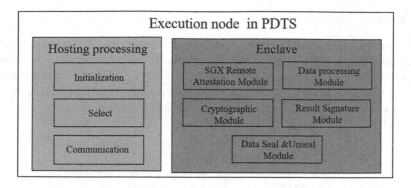

Fig. 2. The structure of the execution node

4.2 Attacker Model

Single Point Attack. In PDTP, some nodes are attacked by malicious opponents or are forced to stop working, which leads to the leakage of power customers' source data or the collapse of the whole scheme.

External Attack. There is the possibility of communication attack between any entity in the scheme, such as tampering with communication content.

Internal Attack. Since RI is honest and curious, they want to extrapolate private information about power customers from the analysis data they obtain.

4.3 Design Goals

Based on the above threat model, our system design goals are listed as follows:

- **Data confidentiality:** Under the above attack model, neither party can obtain or infer the source data information.
- **Data integrity:** Data integrity should be provided in the communication.
- **Authentication:** The data received on the BDPT shall be guaranteed to be valid and the sender of the data shall be from a legal entity.
- **Low computing cost:** As the demand of analyzing power data increases, the efficiency of processing data should be improved while minimizing the local computational time spent on both sides of the transaction.

5 Our Schemes

To achieve the four key security features discussed in the preceding section, we will now present the hierarchical design of PDTS.

5.1   Module Design

PDTS contains four important function requirements, namely: contract register, demand for matching, process task execution and financial management,
which are presented as demand task broadcast contract (DTBC), data management and reward contract (DMRC) and execution node separately. Here, we will
expound the design of those function modules first - see also Fig. 3.

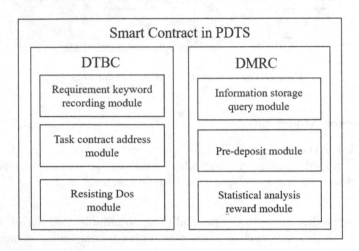

Fig. 3. Deployment of the contract

- **DTBC**: DTBC records RI's keywords of processing tasks through requirement keyword recording module. Task contract address module is mainly
  responsible for the storage of the processing task contract address. Finally,
  the main function of the resisting denial-of-service (Dos) module is that RI
  should provide some fee to avoid Dos attacks.
- **DMRC**: Information storage query module records the necessary information
  about the transaction and provides a reward query function for execution
  node and GC. Pre-deposit module requires RI to deposit some fee to pay for
  GC and execution nodes after execution. Finally, statistical analysis reward
  module is used to analyze the result data, and the corresponding reward is
  allocated according to the result.
- **Execution node**: It consists of an untrusted hosting processing and a trusted
  Enclave. The former is mainly responsible for the initialization of Enclave,
  selection of trading parties and communication with other nodes. The latter
  can be divided into several submodules. SGX remote attestation module is
  employed to authenticate nodes' SGX environment remotely and establish
  a secure channel for data interaction. Data processing module deals with
  GC's data by using RI's processing task contract. Cryptographic module is
  used to decrypt the source data from GC. Also, it encrypts result data from

execution node. In order to prevent the node from falsifying the result, the result signature module is designed. The data seal and unseal module can store data safely and secretly outside or read the sealed data into Enclave.

5.2 Summary of Notations

Table 1 provides a summary of the symbols used in our PDTS.

Table 1. Summary of notation

Notations	Description
$IP_{Node}, IP_{GC}, IP_{RI}$	The IP address of execution node, GC and RI
SN	$SN = Hash(PK_{RI} + IP_{RI})$, an identifier for a transaction
PK_{GC}, PK_{RI}	An RSA-256 public key, TA created
mk_{GC}, mk_{RI}	An RSA-256 private key, TA created
$Pub_{enclave}$	An RSA-256 public key, Enclave created
M_{data}	Source data provided by GC
C_{task}	Power data processing task contract
M_{res}	Output result of C_{task}
F_{Node}, F_{GC}	The fee of executing C_{task}

5.3 Join the PDPT Phase

Several entities including RI, GC and execution node that participate in the blockchain should be registered. Meantime, TA is also responsible for entities authentication and distribution of associated public and private keys.

5.4 Contract Deployment Phase

The deploy process of C_{task} is the same as the traditional Ethereum deployment process. The address obtained after deploying the C_{task} is the $R_{Contract}$.

5.5 Demand Matching Phase

At this phase, GC needs to select RI based on the published keywords and C_{task}. Meanwhile, RI needs to choose execution nodes to execute the C_{task}. We define this process as demand matching and the detailed process is as follows.

Step 1: RI posts its task keywords and $R_{Contract}$ on DTBC and broadcasts them out. Simultaneously, in order to avoid RI sending task keywords without taking the next step, it needs to pay some fee to DTBC.

Step 2: GC and execution node judge whether they can accept the transaction according to the keywords of RI and the contents of the C_{task}. If matched, then send own IP address to RI.

Step 3: The first n execution nodes which have send address will be selected by RI to execute authentication and establish a secure communication channel.

Step 4: RI will send $SN, PK_{RI}, R_{Contract}$ to the selected node's Enclave through the secure channel, and $< SN, IP_{RI}, PK_{RI}, R_{Contract} >$ will use SGX seal method to store outside of Enclave securely.

5.6 C_{task} Execution Preparation Phase

Before executing $R_{Contract}$, RI needs to record some information on DMRC. At the same time, the GC should also carry out remote authentication with the execution node and establish a secure channel. The process is as follows.

Step 1: RI stores $SN, IP_{node}, IP_{GC}, F_{node}, F_{GC}, Pub_{enclave}$ into information storage query module of DMRC. It's worth noting that SN is unique identifier of the transaction. F_{node} and F_{GC} is the corresponding amount of expenses for execution node and GC. $Pub_{enclave}$ is used to verify that the result data sent from the execution node is generated in Enclave to prevent the node from deliberately tampering with the data in return.

Step 2: RI sends SN to GC and execution nodes. They can view transaction information, including the fees received, through SN values.

Step 3: Through the information obtained from DMRC, GC and execution node conduct authentication and establish a secure channel.

Step 4: GC sends SN, PK_{GC} to the execution node in Enclave via the established secure channel. After receiving the information, Enclave saves $< SN, PK_{GC} >$ outside of Enclave by seal method.

5.7 C_{task} Execution Phase

After the preparation phase is complete, the execution node can perform the C_{task} of the RI. The whole process is as follows.

Step 1: GC sends $SN, mk_{GC}(M_{data})$ to the execution nodes. The nodes use SN to obtain $R_{Contract}, PK_{GC}$ by unseal method and place them in the Enclave.

Step 2: After that read the encrypted raw data $mk_{GC}(M_{data})$ into the Enclave and decrypt it with PK_{GC}. Then data processing module in Enclave can use $R_{Contract}$ to process the GC's power data.

Step 3: Cryptographic module in Enclave use RI's PK_{RI} to encrypt the results of the computation $PK_{RI}(M_{res})$. Then, result signature module uses the signature algorithm to generate the signature $Sig = pri_{enclave}(PK_{RI}(M_{res}))$. Finally, the nodes output SN, Sig and $PK_{RI}(M_{res})$ to DMRC for consensus.

Step 4: Statistic analysis reward module performs signature authentication to judge whether the result comes from the selected node and whether it is tampered with. When checked correctly, the qualified $PK_{RI}(M_{res})$ will be counted, and the result with the highest number of votes will be the final result.

Step 5: According to the final result, DMRC will send the fee to the specified node and GC via the address. The result $PK_{RI}(M_{res})$ will also be sent from DMRC to RI. Finally, RI can get the final plaintext result data through decryption key mk_{RI}.

Step 6: The trade information $< SN, IP_{Node}, IP_{GC}, R_{Contract} >$ is recorded on the blockchain for the necessary queries.

6   Security Analysis

6.1   Single Point Attack

Because the PDTS uses a consensus algorithm, the entire platform will not collapse because of the failure of one node. Secondly, even if individual nodes fail, there is no risk of power data loss. Because the raw data is stored directly in Enclave on the execution node, the data in Enclave is protected by hardware.

6.2   External Attack

Grid company's source data is encrypted via the public key and the result data is also encrypted. Based on this, an external attacker without a corresponding private key cannot decrypt the transmitted data. So the nodes in PDTS or other attackers cannot deduce any information about the content of any ciphertext.

6.3   Internal Attack

The decryption and calculation of the data are all performed in Enclave, so the malicious nodes have no chance to get the plaintext of the data. To ensure that the execution results received by DMRC are not tampered with malicious nodes, $pri_{enclave}$ is used to sign execution information in Enclave. Based on this, it is impossible for a node to falsify the execution results.

7   Performance Evaluation

In this section, we will evaluate the computation overhead of PDTS.

7.1   Experimental Setup

One of the design objectives of this scheme is to reduce the local computing cost of both parties in the power data trading market. Therefore, it evaluates whether the system meets the target of lower local computing cost by calculating the major local time-consuming processes on both sides of the transaction.

7.2   Experimental Results

First, we study the used encryption and decryption algorithm on 32 bytes data. The encryption and decryption algorithm in this scheme adopts RSA algorithm. Previous experiments have shown that a RSA with 256 bit key whose encryption operation E_R and decryption operation D_R cost about 0.17 ms and 3.8 ms.

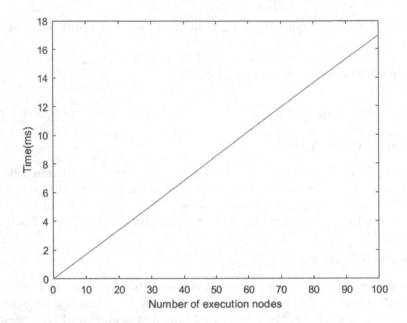

Fig. 4. Local time variation of GC

Through the transaction process, it can be found that the local end of GC mainly spends time on the encryption of the source data. Therefore, the number of nodes is taken as the independent variable to analyze the time change. The experimental results are shown in Fig. 4.

As we can see from the figure, time consuming of GC increases as the number of nodes increases. Nevertheless, the local time is within the acceptable range.

Finally, RI is taken as the research object to observe its main time consuming at the local end. From the analysis of the whole transaction process, the local time of RI is mainly consumed in the decryption of the result data. Therefore, the local time of RI is observed through experiments. The experimental results are shown in Fig. 5.

It can be seen that there is no obvious relationship between the change of the number of nodes and the local time consumption in RI. Of course, it can also be analyzed theoretically, because the result data needs to be agreed by the nodes, and the final processing is done by the DMRC. Therefore, the time required to decrypt is not directly related to the number of the nodes.

In short, through the above experimental results, it can be concluded that this scheme consumes less time locally on both sides of the power trading scheme, which can effectively improve the performance of the scheme.

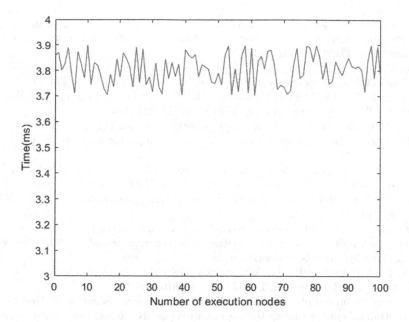

Fig. 5. Local time variation of RI

8 Conclusion

In this paper, we propose an efficient and privacy preserving power data trading scheme. In this scheme, grid companies exploit the value of power data to a large extent without the risk of source data leakage. Under the protection of Intel SGX, market members such as research institution get the processing results of power data in the form of smart contracts and carry out the next step of research. In addition, for the sake of preventing the attack of external or internal opponents, all the key information in the transaction is transmitted in the form of ciphertext to achieve the purpose of privacy protection. When the transaction is completed, the immutability of the blockchain is used to record the important information of the transaction on the chain for query.

References

1. Ye, F., et al.: Research on data exchange mechanism of power trading. In: 2018 IEEE 4th Information Technology and Mechatronics Engineering Conference (ITOEC), pp. 874–878 (2018)
2. Xianghui Cao, L., Cheng, L.Y., Shen, X.: Towards energy-efficient wireless networking in the big data era: a survey. IEEE Commun. Surv. Tutor. **20**(1), 303–332 (2018)
3. Cai, Z., Zheng, X.: A private and efficient mechanism for data uploading in smart cyber-physical systems. IEEE Trans. Netw. Sci. Eng. **7**(2), 766–775 (2020)

4. Shi, L., Shao, P., Zhang, X., Huang, L., Ye, F.: Discussion on architecture of new-generation electricity trading platform. Dianli Xitong Zidonghua/Autom. Electr. Power Syst. **41**(24), 67–76 (2017)
5. Hu, C., Cheng, X., Tian, Z., Yu, J., Lv, W.: Achieving privacy preservation and billing via delayed information release. IEEE/ACM Trans. Netw. (2021)
6. Zhu, S., Li, W., Li, H., Tian, L., Luo, G., Cai, Z.: Coin hopping attack in blockchain-based IoT. IEEE Internet Things J. **6**(3), 4614–4626 (2019)
7. Cai, Z., He, Z.: Trading private range counting over big IoT data. In: 2019 IEEE 39th International Conference on Distributed Computing Systems (ICDCS), pp. 144–153 (2019)
8. Danzi, P., Angjelichinoski, M., Stefanović, Č., Popovski, P.: Distributed proportional-fairness control in microgrids via blockchain smart contracts. In: 2017 IEEE International Conference on Smart Grid Communications (SmartGrid-Comm), pp. 45–51 (2017)
9. An indie, off-the-grid, blockchain-traded solar power market comes to brooklyn. http://motherboard.vice.com/read/the-plan-to-power-Brooklyn-with-a-block-chain-basedmicrogrid-transactive-solar
10. Lee, L.: New kids on the blockchain: how bitcoin's technology could reinvent the stock market. Hastings Bus. Law J. **12**, 81 (2016)
11. Nurzhan Zhumabekuly Aitzhan and Davor Svetinovic: Security and privacy in decentralized energy trading through multi-signatures, blockchain and anonymous messaging streams. IEEE Trans. Dependable Secure Comput. **15**(5), 840–852 (2018)
12. Zhenquan, W.U., Liang, Y., Kang, J., Rong, Y.U., Zhaoshui, H.E., Automation, F.O.: Secure data storage and sharing system based on consortium blockchain in smart grid. J. Comput. Appl. (2017)
13. Sun, Z., Wang, Y., Cai, Z., Liu, T., Tong, X., Jiang, N.: A two-stage privacy protection mechanism based on blockchain in mobile crowdsourcing. Int. J. Intell. Syst. **36**(5), 2058–2080 (2021)
14. Szabo, N.: Smart contracts: building blocks for digital markets. Extropy J. Trans-shuman Thought (1996)
15. Wang, X., He, J., Xie, Z., Zhao, G., Cheung, S.-C.: ContractGuard: defend ethereum smart contracts with embedded intrusion detection. IEEE Trans. Serv. Comput. **13**(2), 314–328 (2020)
16. Costan, V., Lebedev, I., Devadas, S.: Sanctum: minimal hardware extensions for strong software isolation (2016)
17. Kim, S., Han, J., Ha, J., Kim, T., Han, D.: SGX-Tor: a secure and practical tor anonymity network with SGX enclaves. IEEE/ACM Trans. Netw. **26**(5), 2174–2187 (2018)
18. Li, S., Xue, K., Wei, D.S.L., Yue, H., Yu, N., Hong, P.: SecGrid: a secure and efficient SGX-enabled smart grid system with rich functionalities. IEEE Trans. Inf. Forensics Secur. **15**, 1318–1330 (2020)

Fully Discover the Balance of Lightning Network Payment Channels

Zhixin Zhao[1], Chunpeng Ge[1], Lu Zhou[1(✉)], and Huaqun Wang[2]

[1] Nanjing University of Aeronautics and Astronautics, Nanjing, China
`{zhaozx,gecp}@nuaa.edu.cn`
[2] Nanjing University of Posts and Telecommunications, Nanjing, China
`wanghuaqun@aliyun.com`

Abstract. The Lightning Network is a payment channel network that runs on top of Bitcoin. It is an open network, in which anyone with a computing device capable of connecting to the Internet can participate. Every participant is referred as a node. The direct link between two nodes is called a payment channel. Two nodes connected by the payment channel can conduct transactions, even in parallel. If two nodes without connecting directly a payment channel want to trade, the sender needs to start the route discovery algorithm to find a payment path connecting the sender and the receiver. The route discovery algorithm is based on the channel capacity, and the ip address of the node is public. To protect the privacy of users, the specific distribution of balances in the channel is confidential. The channel capacity is public and has been determined at the beginning of the channel establishment. The balance is private and has been dynamically changing, which brings challenges to the routing discovery algorithm. A channel balance disclosure attack was proposed to reveal the channel balance of most channels in the network. In this paper, we propose an enhanced channel balance disclosure attack that can reveal the balance of any channel in the network. We utilize a payment channel that can contain multiple outstanding parallel transactions at the same time to break the limit of the maximum value of a single transaction, thereby revealing the user's precise balance. We explore countermeasures against enhanced balance disclosure attacks.

Keywords: Lightning Network · Privacy · Balance

1 Introduction

Bitcoin [4,8] is by far the most successful encrypted digital currency and the most successful application of the public chain. However, due to its low transaction

Supported by the National Key R&D Program of China (Grant No. 2020YFB1005900), the National Natural Science Foundation of China (Grant No. 62032025, 62071222, U20A201092), and the Natural Science Foundation of Jiangsu Province (Grant No. BK20200418), the Natural Science Foundation of Guangdong Province (Grant No. 2021A1515012650), and the Natural Science Foundation of Jiangsu Province (Grant No. BE2020106).

Z. Liu et al. (Eds.): WASA 2021, LNCS 12937, pp. 159–173, 2021.
https://doi.org/10.1007/978-3-030-85928-2_13

processing speed, almost no one regards Bitcoin as a daily transaction currency. Most people regard Bitcoin as a product of investment and financial management, while ignoring the currency properties of Bitcoin. Two ways to improve the scalability of the Bitcoin have been proposed. One of them is to increase the size of the block. But this will lead to a hard fork, and ordinary individuals cannot afford the data volume of the entire blockchain. Another method is to build a second-layer payment channel network on top of the Bitcoin blockchain. The Lightning Network is one of the most successful applications in the payment channel network, and it is also considered the most promising solution to the scalability problem of Bitcoin.

The Lightning Network consists of payment channels and nodes. A user can choose to use a client to join the Lightning Network as a node. Both parties who have opened the channel can conduct any number of off-chain transactions without interacting with the blockchain. A payment channel is opened by depositing a certain amount of funds (called *channel capacity*) by two nodes. The channel capacity and the node's ip address are allowed to be observed by other nodes in the network. With this information, each node maintains a local view of the network. When two nodes that are not connected by a direct channel execute a transaction, the sender first starts a route discovery algorithm based on the local view of the network to find a payment path that connects the sender and receiver. The channel capacity of all payment channels in the payment path is larger than the transaction amount. The transaction is sent from the sender to the receiver by means of onion routing, which means that the intermediate node cannot know the information of other nodes on the payment path except the previous hop node and the next hop node. Multiple transactions can be carried out simultaneously on the same payment path. These allow the Lightning Network to provide better privacy and flexibility.

However, transactions routed through a payment path may still fail, because the specific distribution of the balance in the payment channel is private. When a transaction fails, the sender will receive an error message, and then the sender will re-select the payment path or cancel the payment based on the error message [10]. A balance disclosure attack was proposed to reveal the channel balance of the payment channel whose channel capacity is lower the maximum amount to pay in one single payment. The attacker sends a fake transaction to the channel counterparty of the victim's node, and adjusts the transaction amount according to the returned error message, thereby continuously approaching the victim's channel balance. According to the sum of the balances of both parties equal to the channel capacity, the attacker can obtain the channel balance of the counterparty.

In this paper, we propose an enhanced balance disclosure attack that can reveal the balance of any channel in the network. We set the node we control as the receiver and the channel to be probed as the payment path. The receiver delays the settlement of the transaction so that the sender can send multiple parallel transactions to probe the balance.

2   Background

In essence, the Lightning Network [9] is a way for Bitcoin users to exchange currency from the Bitcoin blockchain. This is achieved through some complex scripts that interact with the Bitcoin blockchain, and it allows micropayments to be completed quickly with negligible transaction fees. Both parties connected to the payment channel can conduct multiple instantaneous confirmation micropayments. Consider that the two parties do not have a direct peer-to-peer payment channel, as long as a payment path that comprises of multiple payment channels and connects the two parties exists in the network, the Lightning Network can also utilize this payment path to reliably transfer the funds of both parties.

The excellence of the Lightning Network is that users can conduct real-time, massive transactions without trusting counterparty and third parties. The Lightning Network realizes instant peer-to-peer off-chain micropayments, overcomes the obstacles in transaction processing capability, and provides more privacy than Bitcoin blockchain. The Lightning Network creatively designs two types of transaction contracts: Revocable Sequence Maturity Contract (RSMC) and Hashed Timelock Contract (HTLC). RSMC solves the problem of the one-way flow of currency in a payment channel and protects the security of off-chain transactions in a payment channel. HTLC solves the problem of currency transfer across nodes and protects the security of transactions on a payment path composed of multiple payment channels. We introduce the technical details of the Lightning Network and how the balance disclosure attack is carried out as following.

2.1   Payment Channels

Both parties utilize the payment channel [3] to conduct off-chain transactions without waiting for confirmation from the blockchain. A payment channel consists of three stages: creation, execution and closure. Two parties establish a payment channel by depositing funds in a 2-of-2 multi-signature address and broadcasting the transaction, called Funding Transaction, to the blockchain. The amount of both parties deposited bitcoins are called *channel capacity*. The amount of funds deposited by one party is its balance in the channel.

During the execution phase, both parties conduct high-frequency, instant off-chain transactions, called Commitment Transaction, which adjust the distribution of the deposit in the payment channel. A valid transaction needs to be signed by both parties of the payment channel without confirmation from the blockchain, thus increasing the transaction rate.

Either user can broadcast the latest Commitment Transaction to the blockchain to close the payment channel. A cooperating counterparty can speed up the process of closure. The transaction used to close the payment channel is known as the Settlement Transaction.

However, malicious users prefer to broadcast the more lucrative Committed Transaction to close the payment channel than the last Committed Transaction.

RSMC can prevent this malicious behavior. When a new commitment transaction is signed, penalty transactions are created for the previous commitment transaction. At the same time, both parties exchange keys for penalty transactions. The function of the penalty transaction is to transfer all the funds in the payment channel to the counterparty. When a user broadcasts a settlement transaction to the blockchain to close the payment channel, the counterparty checks whether the settlement transaction is the latest within a period of time. Once the settlement transaction is found to be stale, the counterparty can use the previously obtained key of the penalty transaction to gain all the funds of the payment channel, so that the malicious user loses his funds in the payment channel. It is worth noting that users must report malicious behavior within a certain period of time, and the funds will not be recovered after timeout.

2.2 Payments via Third Parties

The Lightning Network consists of payment channels and nodes that issue and relay payments. According to 1ML, there are about 17,000 nodes and 38,000 payment channels in the Lightning Network. It can be seen that there is no direct payment channel connection between most of the nodes in the Lightning Network. Therefore, further extensions are required to enable any two nodes in the Lightning Network to perform transactions. In the Lightning Network, the payment channel can be extended by Hash Timelock Contract into a payment path consisting of multiple payment channels in series, on which users can create conditional fund payments. This allows $user_1$ to pay $user_2$, even if there is no direct connection between them.

Firstly, $user_1$ finds a payment path $i_1, ..., i_n$ to connect to $user_2$ based on the local network view. $user_1$ then sends a transaction with HTLC to i_1. i_1 needs to provide $user_1$ with a secret R within a certain time T to obtain the funds in the HTLC. If i_1 fails to provide secret R within time T, then $user_1$ will withdraw the funds. The secret R is generated by the receiver using the pseudo random number generator. The receiver uses a one-way hash function to calculate $h(R)$ and send $h(R)$ to the sender via a secure secret communication channel. Only users who know the Hash preimage R can obtain funds. If the receiver $user_2$ does not disclose the secret R, no one can get funds from the HTLC transaction. Then i_1 sends an HTLC transaction to i_2, ... i_n sends an HTLC transaction to $user_2$. There is a scenario where $user_1$ withdraws funds from i_1 due to time T_1 overrun, but i_2 pulls funds from i_1 within time T_2. This is due to the fact that subsequent HTLC transactions have longer expiration times than the previous. Therefore, the expiration time T of these HTLC transactions is decreasing. After receiving the HTLC transaction, the receiver reveals the secret R to i_n to pull funds. Similarly, i_n continues to reveal the secret R until i_1 reveals the secret R to $user_1$ to pull the funds.

The whole process is carried out in the form of ciphertext. The original ciphertext is encrypted layer by layer from the receiver's public key to i_1's public key. Each node can only decrypt the outermost layer with its own key to obtain the identity information of the next hop node. As a result, each node cannot learn information on the payment path other than the previous and next hop nodes. Compared to the Bitcoin blockchain, the Lightning Network enhances privacy.

When a user sends a payment to another user through HTLC, usually the receiver immediately reveals the secret R to the previous hop node to pull funds. However, when the recipient is not online, it cannot respond to HTLC payments in real time. This will cause HTLC payments in the channel to be outstanding. Offline or inactive users can still receive HTLC transactions, and these outstanding HTLCs can also temporarily consume a user's channel balance. The channel balance has been occupied by HTLCs until the lock time expires. The lock time is usually set to a few days, and the maximum can be set to 2 weeks. Sufficient lock time makes it easier for attackers to detect channel balances.

2.3 Channel Balance Disclosure Attack

The channel balance disclosure attack [5] continuously sends a fake HTLC transaction to the victim's counterparty, and adjusts the transaction amount based on the returned error information to obtain the victim's channel balance. An HTLC transaction can be faked by replacing the hash $h(R)$ with $h(R')$. When the receiver receives the faked HTLC transaction, the corresponding secret R' cannot be retrieved, so an error message of unknown payment will be returned. However, only when the channel balance is greater than or equal to the payment amount, the receiver can return an error message of unknown payment. When the channel balance of the intermediary is insufficient, the payment cannot be transferred to the receiver, and the invalid payment can only be determined by the receiver instead of the intermediary, so the intermediary only returns the error message of insufficient balance.

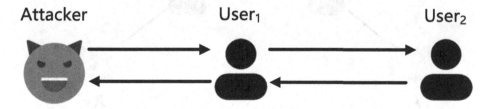

Fig. 1. Example of the channel balance disclosure attack.

As shown in Fig. 1, an attacker who wants to probe the channel balance of $user_1$ first needs to establish a payment channel with $user_1$. The attacker then constructs an invalid HTLC payment. Since the channel balance must not exceed the channel capacity, the payment amount must range from 0 to the channel capacity of the channel between $user_1$ and $user_2$. To efficiently probe the channel, the initial value of the payment amount is set to the middle value of the payment value range, that is, half of the channel capacity.

The attacker receives the error message of insufficient funds, indicating that $user_1$ successfully relays the transaction to $user_2$, and the channel balance of $user_1$ is greater than the payment amount. Then, the payment amount ranges from the original 0 to the channel capacity (half of the channel capacity) to the current payment value to the channel capacity. The attacker receives the error message of insufficient funds, indicating that $user_1$ can not relay the transaction and the channel balance was less than the payment amount. Then, adjust the payment amount range from the minimum value to the current payment amount. When receiving the error message of insufficient funds, the upper bound is reduced to the current payment amount, and when the unknown payment error message is received, the lower bound is increased to the current payment amount. Repeat this process until the difference between the upper bound and the lower bound is less than the preset accuracy. It can be considered that the current payment amount is the channel balance of $user_1$. According to the sum of the channel balance of $user_1$ and $user_2$ equal to the channel capacity, the channel balance of $user_2$ can be calculated.

3   Design

In order to better describe our scheme, we denote the nodes controlled by the attacker as A_1 and A_2, and the victim nodes as U_1 and U_2. The channel capacity between U_1 and U_2 is recorded as $C_{u_1 u_2}$, and the channel balance of U_1 and U_2 is recorded as B_{u_1} and B_{u_2}, respectively (Fig. 2).

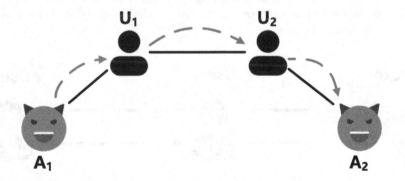

Fig. 2. Illustrative example of the enhanced channel balance disclosure attack. The black solid line represents the bidirectional payment channel connecting the two parties. The blue dashed line only indicates the direction of the transaction flow in the attack scenario. In practice, transactions can flow in both directions in the channel. (Color figure online)

First, A_1 and A_2 establish channels with both ends of the channel to be probed. After establishing channels, A_1 sets up a route through U_1 and U_2 to reach A_2. At the beginning of the balance detection process, A_1 can initially perform a single balance upper limit detection that the transaction amount is set to the maximum amount allowed in a single transaction.

A_1 sends the transaction with the maximum amount to A_2 according to a pre-defined route. If the transaction does not arrive successfully at A_2 and an error message is returned from A_1 that the transaction amount is insufficient, the balance of A_1 is less than the current payment amount. This shows that the balance of the channel is within the capabilities of the channel balance disclosure attack, so the disclosure attack can be used to probe the channel balance of A_1. If the transaction reaches A_2 successfully, it means that the channel balance of A_1 exceeds the amount of the current transaction. At this time, the channel balance disclosure attack cannot probe the specific balance of A_1.

As we introduced in Sect. 2.2, payments across multiple channels require utilizing HTLC, which allows participants to route payments through untrusted intermediate nodes. When A_2 receives the HTLC from A_1, A_2 is supposed to accept the transaction by sending back a pre-image of the hash value. But A_2 avoids doing so for two reasons. One is that A_2 needs to continue to wait for payments from A_1, and the other is that A_2 should not complete the payment, which will cause the attacker to lose the transaction fee paid for routing in the network. A_2 refuses to accept all outstanding payments before HTLCs expired, so payments are not completed.

3.1 Enhanced Balance Disclosure Attack

The main idea behind our scheme is to make multiple outstanding transactions stay in the payment channel and consume the channel's balance by delaying the settlement of the payment on the last hop. The attack degenerates into the balance disclosure attack when the victim node is unable to relay a transaction with the maximum limit amount in a single payment. We establish payment channels with both ends of the channel to be probed, setting up the ends of the channel as intermediate nodes for routing multiple payments to another node that we control. Before the payment times out, we cancel all transactions on the last hop to avoid transaction fees. As shown in Fig. 3, our scheme can easily be extended to target multiple payment channels.

3.2 Probing Algorithm

We describe our probe process in Algorithm 1. The inputs to Algorithm 1 are the route to A_2, the maximum amount allowed for the payment, the target node A_2, the destination node U_{i_2}, the probed node U_{i_1}, the range of the payment amount UpperValue and LowerValue, and the accuracy of the balance. Algorithm 1 returns a range of node balance.

First the attacker has to establish a connection with the nodes at both ends of the channel, followed by the establishment of the payment channel. It should be noted that when establishing a channel with a counterparty to the node to be probed, it is necessary to request the counterparty to fund the same amount

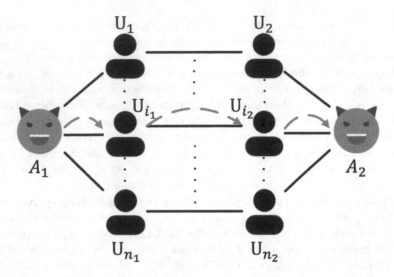

Fig. 3. Illustrative example of the enhanced channel balance disclosure attack against multiple payment channels. For the sake of brevity of the picture, we have not drawn the direction of payment flow on each payment path, only on the i-th payment path. The payment flow direction on each of n payment paths is the same as the i-th one.

of currency into the channel. The amount deposited in the channel is the maximum amount with which to put into a channel. After the channels have been established, A_1 sets the payment route to A_2 to go through U_{i_1} and U_{i_2} and sets the payment amount to the maximum allowed for a single payment. Continue the process of sending the maximum amount of payment until U_{i_1} does not have enough funds to forward the payment. During this process, A_2 chooses to delay finishing transactions from A_1 until the entire balance disclosure process is completed before failing all outstanding transactions. And for each transaction relayed by the node, the maximum payment amount allowed for a single payment is added to the *currBalance*.

When the loop in Line 16–22 is broken, the node's channel balance is already less than the maximum allowed payment and the process of balance disclosure degenerates to that described in [5]. A_1 continuously sends a faked payment to the node's counterparty, which can only be penetrated by the destination node but not by the intermediate nodes, and adjusts the amount of the payment based on the error message returned.

The initial upper and lower bounds for the payment amount are generally set at 0 and the channel capacity of U_{i_1} and U_{i_2}. When an InsufficientFunds error message is returned indicating that the current payment amount is greater than the node's channel balance, the upper limit is reduced to the current payment amount. When an UnknownPayment error message is returned, indicating that the current payment amount is less than the node's channel balance, the lower limit is raised to the current payment amount. The payment amount changes in

Algorithm 1. Multi-payment Probing

Input: Route, MaxPaymentAllowed, TargetA, TargetB, node, UpperValue, Lower-Value, Accuracy

Output: the range of node channel balance

1: connected = false;
2: connectedA = false;
3: **while** connected = false **do**
4:     connected := Connection(node.publicKey@node.externalIP);
5: **while** connectedA = false **do**
6:     connectedA := Connection(TargetA.publicKey@TargetA.externalIP);
7: fundingNode := openChannel(node.publicKey, 2^{24});
8: fundingA := 0;
9: **while** fundingA.Capacity $<2^{25}$ **do**
10:     fundingA := openChannel(TargetA.publicKey, 2^{24});
11: currBalance := 0;
12: smallBalance := True;
13: paymentValue := MaxPaymentAllowed;
14: maxValue = UpperValue;
15: minValue = LowerValue;
16: **while** smallBalance **do**
17:     response := sendToRoute(route = [Route, TargetA], paymentValue);
18:     **if** response = InsufficientFunds **then**
19:         smallBalance := False;
20:     **else**
21:         currBalance := currBalance + paymentValue;
22:         Wait for payment to be completed;
23: **while** maxValue - minValue > Accuracy **do**
24:     currValue := (maxValue + minValue)/2;
25:     response := sendFakePayment(route = [Route, TargetB], h(x), currValue);
26:     **if** response = InsufficientFunds **then**
27:         **if** maxValue > currValue **then**
28:             maxValue := currValue;
29:     **else if** response = UnknownPaymentHash **then**
30:         **if** minValue < currValue **then**
31:             minValue := currValue;
32: Balance$_{min}$:= currBalance + minValue;
33: Balance$_{max}$:= currBalance + maxValue;
34: **return** Balance;

---

a binary search mode. Exit the loop when the difference between the upper and lower bounds of the payment amount is less than the accuracy of the input. The previously recorded currBalance is added to the upper and lower bounds and the result is the range of the balance of the node. Finally, A_2 fails all outstanding transactions to avoid transaction fees.

4 Results

We launched an attack on the Bitcoin testnet to verify the feasibility and performance of our scheme. On the Bitcoin mainnet, we analyzed the improvement of de-anonymization for high-capacity channels.

4.1 Bitcoin Testnet Evaluation

We connected the 10 top capacity nodes in the Lightning Network testnet and established payment channels with them. The channel capacity of 10 nodes accounts for 58.7% of the entire Lightning Network testnet. The reason why we choose high-capacity node connections is that high-capacity nodes have more high-capacity channels. A total of 2,520 payment channels were opened in the six active nodes.

Many of the nodes in the test network are intended for testing purposes and usually choose to go offline afterwards. Of the 10 nodes we connected, only 6 are active and they connect only 11.18% of all connected nodes that are active. However, payments in the Lightning Network require both parties to the payment to be online, so the low number of active nodes is an obstacle to performing tests on the Lightning Network testnet.

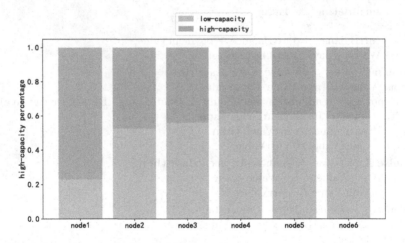

Fig. 4. Percentage of high capacity channels in the payment channels.

When the channel capacity is less than the maximum amount allowed for a single payment, our algorithm degrades to the balance disclosure attack, so we only focus on payment channels where the channel capacity is greater than the maximum amount allowed for a single payment. We define a channel with a channel capacity greater than the maximum amount allowed for a single payment as a high-capacity channel. Figure 4 shows the percentage of high-capacity channels among those opened by each node.

For high-capacity channels, we perform the enhanced balance disclosure attack. Since the balance disclosure attack cannot disclose channels with a capacity exceeding the maximum payment amount allowed for a single payment, we default the execution time of the balance disclosure attack for high-capacity channels to be equal to the execution time of the balance disclosure attack for channels with the maximum payment amount allowed for a single payment. Figure 5 illustrates the execution time comparison between the enhanced balance disclosure attack and the balance disclosure attack.

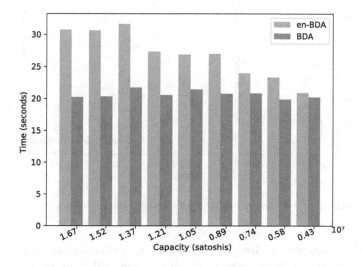

Fig. 5. Percentage of high capacity channels in the payment channels.

4.2 Impact on Bitcoin Mainnet

We take a snapshot of the Lightning Network mainnet on January 24, 2021. A total of 16,563 nodes and 38,321 payment channels.

In [5], each balance disclosure is completed by sending a single transaction, so the ability of balance disclosure is limited by the maximum payment amount allowed by a single transaction. When the capacity of a payment channel is greater than the maximum payment amount, the funds may be unevenly distributed in the channel, leaving a balance at one end in excess of the maximum payment amount. This causes the balance disclosure attack to be ineffective for high-capacity channels. It is introduced in BOLT [1] that the current Lightning Network has options to support large payment channels when opening channels, which will allow the capacity of payment channels to break the upper limit of channel capacity (2^{24} satoshi).

The Lightning Network supports large channels increasing the number of high-capacity channels. This new feature leads to a loss of de-anonymity for balance disclosure attacks. Balance disclosure attacks should be improved if better de-anonymity is to be achieved.

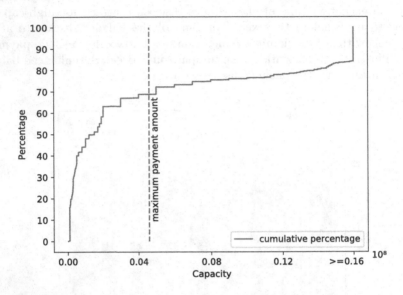

Fig. 6. Cumulative percentage of payment channels in the Lightning Network mainnet.

Figure 6 illustrates the distribution of payment channel capacity across the Lightning Network mainnet. We count all channels with the channel capacity greater than 1.6×10^7 satoshis together. It can be concluded from the graph that 68.66% of the payment channels have a capacity lower than the maximum amount allowed for a single payment. As a result, our scheme can improve the ability to disclose channel balances by 31.34%.

5   Discussion

We explore several countermeasures to mitigate enhanced balance disclosure attacks.

5.1   Precaution

As we described in Sect. 3, a prerequisite for balance disclosure for high-capacity channels is the establishment of a large payment channel with the node. When a node receives a request to establish a large payment channel, it should treat the request with more caution. In the process of establishing a channel, the node requests the establishment of a large payment channel by using the *option_support_large_channel* parameter. When a node receives the request, it should ensure that there is an actual need for a large transaction with the requesting party.

When there is a need for a large payment, we recommend that the transaction is done through on-chain to ensure the security of the payment.

5.2 Avoiding

It is also worth noting that multiple outstanding payments with large payment amount existing simultaneously in one payment channel can make balance disclosure easier. Therefore, when a node notices a large number of outstanding large transactions in a payment channel, it should close that payment channel.

Our scheme utilizes the error message returned when a payment fails. Therefore, an intuitive approach is not to classify the error message so that the sender does not know the reason for the payment failure. However, this also leads to a new problem, routing payments becomes less efficient. An honest node routing a payment has no way of knowing the exact reason why the payment failed and cannot take action against the failed payment.

5.3 Relieving

When a balance has been probed by a malicious node and the user is conscious of the privacy of his channel balance, the user can use the channel rebalancing algorithm [2] as a remedy. Channel rebalancing also benefits channels where funds are significantly unevenly distributed between both ends of the channel. It also improves the efficiency of route discovery for payments.

6 Related Work

The privacy notions of the Lightning Network were first formalized in [6]. The off-chain nature of Lightning Network transactions and onion routing makes it more private than the Bitcoin platform, however, it does not mean that privacy is fully protected in the Lightning Network.

The channel balance privacy was first proposed in [5] and a channel balance probing attack was shown to be effective in the Lightning Network. Improvements [11,12] to its disclosure process have subsequently been proposed. When the balance at one end of the channel exceeds the capacity of a single probe, an attacker can perform a balance disclosure from the counterparty [12]. The channel balance at the other end can be obtained by using the sum of the balances on both sides of the channel to equal the channel capacity.

An HTLC payment routed through multiple payment channels allows for balance probe for all channels on the path [11]. This allows fewer transactions to cover more payment channels, improving the efficiency of disclosure.

Ayelet Mizrahi et al. [7] explored the hazards posed by deliberately delaying settlement of HTLC payments to the security of the Lightning Network. As described in our paper, this can likewise harm privacy of the Lightning Network.

7 Conclusion

In this paper, we propose an enhanced balance disclosure attack. Our scheme breaks the limitations of the original balance disclosure attack and can disclose the balance of nodes in high capacity channels. We utilize the fact that outstanding payments occupy the channel balance by constantly sending HTLC payments. Consuming the balance of high capacity nodes in the channel allows the probing process to degenerate into the balance disclosure process. We show the efficiency of enhanced balance disclosure attacks. Our scheme is slightly less efficient than the balance disclosure attack scheme due to the need to send several rounds of pending HTLC payments. Due to the support of large channels, the number of high-capacity channels in the Lightning Network has increased, which also makes our scheme more significant.

We consider that the disclosure of payment channel balance is beneficial to discover payment routes. We will explore a balance between privacy and efficiency in the future.

References

1. Bolt # 2: Peer protocol for channel management. https://github.com/lightning network/lightning-rfc/blob/master/02-peer-protocol.md
2. Conoscenti, M., Vetrò, A., Martin, J.C.D.: Hubs, rebalancing and service providers in the lightning network. IEEE Access **7**, 132828–132840 (2019)
3. Decker, C., Wattenhofer, R.: A fast and scalable payment network with bitcoin duplex micropayment channels. In: Pelc, A., Schwarzmann, A.A. (eds.) SSS 2015. LNCS, vol. 9212, pp. 3–18. Springer, Cham (2015). https://doi.org/10.1007/978-3-319-21741-3_1
4. Donet Donet, J.A., Pérez-Solà, C., Herrera-Joancomartí, J.: The bitcoin P2P network. In: Böhme, R., Brenner, M., Moore, T., Smith, M. (eds.) FC 2014. LNCS, vol. 8438, pp. 87–102. Springer, Heidelberg (2014). https://doi.org/10.1007/978-3-662-44774-1_7
5. Herrera-Joancomartí, J., Navarro-Arribas, G., Ranchal-Pedrosa, A., Pérez-Solà, C., Garcia-Alfaro, J.: On the difficulty of hiding the balance of lightning network channels. In: Proceedings of the 2019 ACM Asia Conference on Computer and Communications Security, pp. 602–612 (2019)
6. Malavolta, G., Moreno-Sanchez, P., Kate, A., Maffei, M., Ravi, S.: Concurrency and privacy with payment-channel networks. In: Proceedings of the 2017 ACM SIGSAC Conference on Computer and Communications Security, pp. 455–471 (2017)
7. Mizrahi, A., Zohar, A.: Congestion attacks in payment channel networks. arXiv preprint arXiv:2002.06564 (2020)
8. Nakamoto, S.: Bitcoin: a peer-to-peer electronic cash system. Technical report, Manubot (2019)
9. Poon, J., Dryja, T.: The bitcoin lightning network: scalable off-chain instant payments (2016)
10. Prihodko, P., Zhigulin, S., Sahno, M., Ostrovskiy, A., Osuntokun, O.: Flare: an approach to routing in lightning network. White Paper (2016)

11. Tikhomirov, S., Pickhardt, R., Biryukov, A., Nowostawski, M.: Probing channel balances in the lightning network. arXiv preprint arXiv:2004.00333 (2020)
12. van Dam, G., Kadir, R.A., Nohuddin, P.N.E., Zaman, H.B.: Improvements of the balance discovery attack on lightning network payment channels. In: Hölbl, M., Rannenberg, K., Welzer, T. (eds.) SEC 2020. IAICT, vol. 580, pp. 313–323. Springer, Cham (2020). https://doi.org/10.1007/978-3-030-58201-2_21

Algorithms

IoT-Based Non-intrusive Energy Wastage Monitoring in Modern Building Units

Muhammad Waqas Isa and Xiangmao Chang[✉]

School of Computer Science and Engineering, Nanjing University of Aeronautics
and Astronautics, Nanjing, China
{waqas.isa,xiangmaoch}@nuaa.edu.cn

Abstract. Energy wastage is common in commercial buildings. There
are many occasions that lighting, heating/cooling, and ventilation systems remain ON even when the area is unoccupied. However, conserving
energy while having no effect on the occupants' activities for different
rooms in a building is a challenging objective. In this paper, we propose
an Internet-of-Things (IoT)-based non-intrusive energy wastage monitoring system for efficient energy wastage monitoring in modern building
units. The human presence in a room is monitored by using low-cost
low-resolution Passive InfraRed (PIR) and thermal sensors. The operating states of Lighting and Heating/Cooling systems are detected by
multi-sensor fusion and non-intrusive state monitoring. The sensor data
is transmitted to the server by Narrowband IoT (NB-IoT) and the energy
wastage event can be detected within a short period on the server. We
implement an energy efficient operational algorithm along with several
power optimizations. We also provide a complete power profile of the
node to demonstrate energy efficiency. Experimental results show that
the detection accuracy of an electricity wastage event is more than 94%.

Keywords: Efficient energy monitoring · Energy wastage alert ·
Human-detection · Non-intusive state monitoring · NB-IoT

1 Introduction

A building unit has emerged as a major consumer of energy in the modern ecosystem. In the US, general commercial buildings account for 35% of all electricity
consumed [1]. Nowadays, with fast-paced urbanization and the ever-expanding
infrastructure of contemporary commercial buildings, the amount of energy consumption has increased many folds [2]. Electricity represents a major chunk of
energy consumed in commercial buildings i.e. 61%, followed by natural gas that
represents 32% [3]. The two major consumers of electrical energy in a commercial building are heating/cooling systems (HVAC) 33% and lighting 17% [3].
Conserving energy by avoiding electricity wastage is essential for buildings.

This work was supported by the National Key Research and Development Program of
China under grant No. 2019YFB2102200.

Z. Liu et al. (Eds.): WASA 2021, LNCS 12937, pp. 177–189, 2021.
https://doi.org/10.1007/978-3-030-85928-2_14

The energy wastage is largely related to the scenarios of energy usage. The two major consumers of electricity (HVAC and lighting) are needed when the building is occupied. But the wastage of energy takes place when the lighting and heating/cooling system are left operating even after the building is unoccupied and no human is present, which can be observed quite commonly in commercial buildings due to negligence or maybe carelessness.

Many methods have been proposed for human occupancy detection, including methods based on videos/images from various cameras [4], sensors-based approaches [5,6] and Machine Learning algorithms [7]. These methods rely on specific environmental settings and careful parameters tuning, moreover, they present varied drawbacks such as security/privacy concerns of the user (e.g. solutions utilizing camera). The methods employing machine learning usually bring high computational costs which require offline processing or cause high communication costs with the clouds, thus they are not suitable for embedded terminals which have limited capability of computation and communication.

As for state monitoring of electric appliances, there are mainly two kinds of approaches in the literature. One is direct sensing, which places the sensor in the direct path of electricity to monitor power [8]. The other is indirect sensing making use of smart meter data [9,10]. As altering the electrical wiring of building for direct sensing and modifying electrical panel for the provision of smart meters would cause high installation cost, both these approaches are hard to be popularized. In SUPERO [11], the author had made use of environmental information to detect appliance operational state. But it needs to sample the light intensity with a relatively high frequency (4 Hz) which corresponds to low battery life (a week).

A commercially feasible energy wastage monitoring solution should be non-intrusive with long battery life. Designing such solution faces the following three challenging design rules: (i) low-cost development/communication platform and sensors should be adopted for the economy of scale deployment, (ii) low power methodology should be implemented due to battery life constraints, (iii) The terminal nodes can be easily installed, without changing any deployment of the building unit.

In this work, we propose a human occupancy-based non-intrusive energy monitoring system based on a NB-IoT communication architecture. The proposed system has the following properties: (i) detects the occupancy of the subject area, (ii) monitors operational state of electric systems (our main interest is in heating/cooling and lighting systems), and (iii) relay the information to the central server. Experimental results show that the designed system is power efficient and the detection accuracy is more than 94%. With such a system, the management of the building can be alerted when the heating/cooling or lighting system is found operating unattended.

The rest of the paper is organized as follows. The system design is detailed in Sect. 2. The system implementation and performance evaluation are described in Sect. 3. At last, conclusion are stated in Sect. 4.

2   The Proposed Solution

In this section, we introduce our system architecture and workflow, along-with a detailed hardware description of our node. We also describe the methods of achieving human occupancy detection and non-intrusive state monitoring of heating/cooling and lighting systems.

2.1   System Architecture

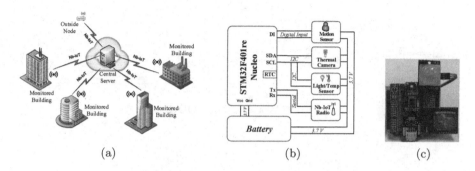

(a)   (b)   (c)

Fig. 1. System design (a) architecture, (b) hardware design, and (c) developed node.

Our proposed solution is to design a system that is able to detect energy being wasted, when lighting and cooling systems are left operating without any human presence. Our system architecture is composed of several sensors placed inside rooms of multiple buildings in an area, as shown in Fig. 1a. All sensors are connected to the central server via NB-IoT link, as it can support massive sensor deployment. One sensor is placed outside to provide ambient light intensity and temperature readings for reference. All the sensors inside the rooms update the central server with their occupancy state along with light intensity and temperature readings. Based on these information, the central server monitors for any energy wastage event. When energy wastage is detected, the central server promptly generates an alert to building management station.

2.2   Hardware

Our system is based on the COTS development platform of STM32F401re NUCLEO board. The board has an STM32F401RE microcontroller device with multiple peripherals, 512 Kbytes Flash, 96 Kbytes SRAM and an on-chip real time clock (RTC). This makes it a robust solution to incorporate a variety of sensors. Moreover, it incorporates a set of efficient power-saving modes which allows the low-power mode operations suitable for embedded applications.

We have leveraged a combination of Infrared Motion sensor with the low cost and low power AMG8833 Grid-Eye thermal sensor by Panasonic. The Microcontroller Unit (MCU) is connected with the Grid-Eye over the I2C line. We have also used the I2C peripheral line to integrate the VEML7700 high accuracy ambient Light sensor and Si7021 temperature sensor. While the PIR motion sensor is connected via the Digital Input line. For communication, we have used BC35-G which is a high-performance NB-IoT module, integrated over serial line with MCU. The whole Node is powered using 3.3 V Li-ion battery. The hardware design and the developed node are as shown in Fig. 1b and Fig. 1c.

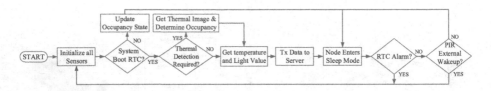

Fig. 2. Work flow of NODE

2.3   Node Work Flow

We have created a workflow in which the node remains in sleep mode for most of the time, thus consuming minimal power. The node can be made to wake up at any detected motion by PIR or periodically after every 15 min by an RTC alarm wake up. We have used the Standby mode of STM32F4 for the lowest possible power consumption. The controller basically reboots on every wakeup. Once the process of boot-up is triggered, the controller first investigates the reason for boot-up. If it is due to an external interrupt bythe PIR sensor, then the node updates the PIR state variable stored in SRAM and then goes back to sleep. Whereas, if the reboot is due to RTC alarm wake up, then the node checks the PIR state variable firstly. If the PIR interrupt is detected during two RTC wake up cycles, then thermal camera is turned ON to check for occupancy as the PIR interrupt may be due to someone entering or exiting the room. The occupancy state is updated accordingly. Else, if the room was occupied on the previous wake up but there is no PIR interrupt detected during two RTC cycles, then the node once again turns on the thermal camera to scan the area for any stationary human presence and updates the occupancy state variable accordingly. Lastly if the room was unoccupied in the previous wake up cycle and there is no PIR interrupts available the thermal camera remains off and no occupancy is determined. Now after determining the occupancy state the node powers up the light and temperature sensor. It then transmits the current values of occupancy status, light intensity and temperature to the server and enters sleep mode. The detailed workflow is as shown in Fig. 2.

2.4   Human Object Detection

Our first task is to detect the presence or absence of a human subject within an area. For that, we have used a combination of PIR motion and thermal Sensor. We have two reasons for selecting this combination. Firstly, PIR sensors are very good at detecting human motion, utilizing a difference of thermal signature in its field of view. But it cannot detect the presence of human subject when there is not enough motion in field of view of PIR sensor. This deficiency arises due to the human subject being stationary. To overcome this, we make use of the low-resolution thermal array sensor. Secondly, while adopting a PIR motion sensor ahead of the thermal sensor for human detection, we save energy by avoiding the thermal sensor and associated MCU turned ON unnecessarily. Therefore, we first detect the motion using PIR motion sensor while the rest of the system is in sleep mode. At a periodic cycle (15 min in our experiment setting), RTC wakes up the node. The thermal sensor is powered as per the defined work flow to make sure the presence or absense of human in the subject area. We employ a four-step methodology to extract human presence information. This multi-layer approach allows us a robust algorithm taking in account multiple dimensions of a thermal image.

Noise Removal from Thermal Image. Since we are using low-resolution thermal image, the effect of noise shall have a great effect on the thermal image. Therefore, we employ Kalman Filtering for noise removal. We have used an error margin of 2.5 °C as given in the datasheet of AMG8833 [12]. We construct the image by taking data at 1 s intervals for 10 s and updating the image readings using the following Kalman Filter equation

$$KG = E_{est}/(E_{est} + E) \tag{1}$$

$$E_{est(t)} = E_{est(t-1)} + KG[E_{mea} - E_{est(t-1)}] \tag{2}$$

where KG is the Kalman gain, E_{est} is the error in estimate, E_{mea} is the error in measurement, $E_{est}(t)$ is the current estimated value and $E_{est(t-1)}$ is the previous estimated value.

Temperature Gradients. After filtering noise and obtaining a stable low-resolution thermal image, we collect three images with fifteen seconds intervals, so that we are able to calculate the rate of change (RoC) of temperature i.e. temperature gradient of each pixel as given by the following equation:

$$RoC = (Currentl - Previous)/Previous \tag{3}$$

A disparity between the amount of metabolic heat generated by the body and accumulative body heat loss results in a change in body temperature. It is the property of all humans to be able to regulate their body temperature by regulating the body metabolic processes. The human body can regulate its body temperature within a range of about 1 °C [13], despite large variations in the surrounding temperature. Thus, any pixel in the image showing a change in temperature greater than 1 °C within the three images is denoted as non-Human and removed from further processing. Since our scene is static as we have no movement on the PIR sensor, we take the pixel with the least stable temperature value as the background temperature.

Temperature Spread. We now perform statistical analysis of the temperature spread in the image by calculating variance, denoted by α_{th}, over the pixels of interest. The variance in the spread of temperature values over a scene is an important feature in pointing towards the presence of a human within the scene. A uniform spread depicts the absence of thermal disturbance which can be classified as an absence of a human subject. Whereas a large variance denotes the presence of thermal disturbance which can be investigated for human presence. The threshold variance α_{th} is determined by experiments as detailed in the experiments section.

Temperature Thresholding. To get a more robust human detection algorithm we have also applied temperature thresholding to our pixels of interest. We have implemented two temperature thresholds: human temperature threshold denoted by β_{th} and temperature difference threshold denoted by γ_{th}.

In line with the several studies [14] and our experiments conducted, the human body temperature lies within the range of 29 °C–32 °C when detected by the thermal camera. We have used this range to mark any pixel with an apparent human presence.

Next, we have made use of the fact that the human body temperature is greater than the background temperature. We use the γ_{th} threshold, i.e. the maximum difference in temperature between each pixel of interest with background temperature, to help us in determining human presence. The value of γ_{th} is selected after robust experiments performed, as detailed in the experiments.

2.5   Non-intrusive State Monitoring

Heating/cooling and lighting systems are two major power consumers in a building unit. Therefore, we focus on state monitoring of lighting and heating/cooling systems in our work.

Heating/Cooling Systems. To detect the operation state of heating/cooling systems without employing any intrusion, we investigate the variations in room temperature as a feature metric. In order to gauge natural temperature variations, we conducted our study over several days collecting variations in outside and room temperature with 15 min sampling period. We also observed the yearly data set of multiple weather centers at different demographic locations, made available by NCIE, USA [15]. It was observed that the ambient outside temperature tends to vary gradually within the range of less than 1 °C during a 15-min interval, as shown in Fig. 3a. These variations even if greater than

1 °C within this short period has a negligible effect on the room temperature variations within this short time. Whereas with sufficient heating/cooling capacity installed, the change in room temperature due to artificially assisted heating/cooling is much more rapid as evident from Fig. 3a. Therefore, we selected change in room temperature ΔT as our feature for heating/cooling system operation detection. We evaluated different values of ΔT to determine the optimized threshold for the detection of heating/cooling system ON/OFF event as detailed in experiments section.

We have placed one sensor outside to get the ambient temperature, while our room sensor shall provide us the temperature reading inside the room. We then progressively take temperature readings by both outside sensor and inside sensor with fifteen minutes intervals. We can now detect the ON/OFF event of heating/cooling system if the temperature inside the room increases or decreases greater than the threshold ΔT as compared with the outside temperature. For example, We can estimate that the artificial heating/cooling system has turned on at 21:07 as shown in Fig. 3a. Moreover, once the system is turned off, the room temperature tends to achieve the same equilibrium state as before the artificial heating/cooling system was operated. This also shows an increase/decrease in temperature steeper than equilibrium state, i.e., in excess of ΔT, as can be seen at 22:33 in Fig. 3a.

Additionally, in order to cater to the effect of room isolation, we also consider the change relative to two previous 15-min readings. For example, there may be a case where the temperature change is not evident in 15-min so we consider the change with respect to previous readings as well. So that any variations within 30-min period may also be detected and considered against the established threshold. This improves our ability to cater the rooms where there is excessive isolation or not much isolation from the surroundings.

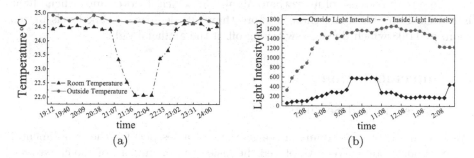

Fig. 3. Non intrusive state monitoring method (a) heating cooling system, (b) lighting system.

Lighting Systems. According to [16], the recommended lighting level per square meter i.e. lux for different office premises is around 300–500 lux. Thus, for a properly lit workplace room, the artificial light illumination should be greater than 300 lux at the working plane. This is to ensure sufficient lighting even at night.

However, the lux level in a room is also affected by the amount of natural light. This effect of the ambient natural light outside over the light intensity inside a room depends on the daylight factor (DF) of the room. According to established standards for construction [16], the daylight factor of a room is recommended to be around 5%. From experiments, we found that in a relatively short interval of 15 min, the change in outside light intensity is around 500 lux as can be observed in the Fig. 3b. This can be accounted as the variations due to the rotation of the earth at different times of the day or due to some natural weather conditions like cloud coverings. Altogether, the overall effect of daylight factor on illumination inside the room is observed to be minimal as compared to the change in lux due to artificial light, as shown in Fig. 3b.

Thus, we use the change in lux ΔL as the parameter to establish the lighting system operational state. Here we have also adopted a multi-sensor correlation approach. We placed a sensor outside to get the ambient light intensity outside, while another sensor is placed inside the room to get the current light intensity level in the room. We have adopted a low sampling rate of 15 min. We use the value from the outside sensor along with the average daylight factor to get the effect of outside light illumination inside the room. While the sensor inside the room gives us the change in lux levels inside the room. Altogether, we use the data from both the sensors to first remove the effect due to outside light change and then extract the actual change in light level inside the room. Therefore, if the change in lux levels inside the room is greater than threshold ΔL (valuated after experiments in the subsequent section), we characterize this event as the operation of artificial light in the room. As Fig. 3b shows, the actual change inside the room is an increase of more than ΔL at 9:38 which denotes an artificial light is switched on. Whereas, there is more than ΔL decrease in lux levels of the room at 11:08 which denotes switching off of the artificial light.

3 Implementation

3.1 Experimental Settings

We have used the classrooms of our campus as a testbed for the experimental study of our system. We have placed the inside sensor in front of the classroom, at a height of 3 m, with two windows and two doors. This position provides the proper view of the sitting area and covers the maximum area of the room. It also allows adequate light illumination for the sensor. There is no artificial source blocking the path of light to the sensor. The outside sensor is placed on the outside wall of the room such that it is away from direct sunlight, getting us ambient light and temperature without any direct influence of the sun.

3.2   Experiment

We performed separate evaluation for all the three detections we proposed.

Heating/Cooling System Detection. We evaluated different values of the temperature change threshold, ΔT. The accuracy and false alarm rate of the different values of threshold ΔT are shown in the Fig. 5a. We observed that the threshold value of 1 °C has the most accurate result in heating/cooling system ON/OFF event detection.

A sample data from the operation of the node and prediction for one week is as shown in the Fig. 4a. The node is mostly able to detect the operating state of the heating/cooling system by the variations in temperature. There is a latency in the detected state which arises as a trade-off due to a low sampling rate. Very rarely, when temperature variations are subtle and the heating/cooling system is operated for a small amount of time, our system may not trigger. Overall, over a period of several days, we found out the accuracy of heating/cooling state detection to be around 92.5% with such a low sampling rate.

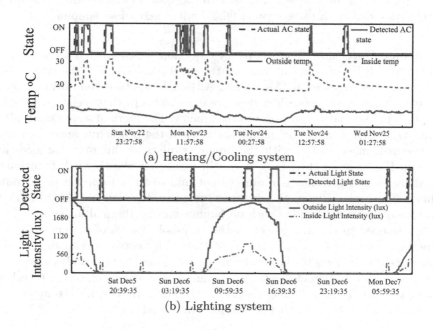

(a) Heating/Cooling system

(b) Lighting system

Fig. 4. Non intrusive state monitoring experiment

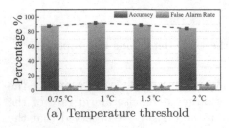
(a) Temperature threshold

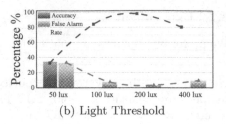
(b) Light Threshold

Fig. 5. Threshold experiment

Lighting System Detection. We conducted our experiments over several days in different light conditions. We evaluated different threshold values of light intensity change ΔL. The accuracy and false alarm rate of the various values of threshold ΔL are as shown in Fig. 5b. It was observed that the threshold value of 200 lux has the most accurate result. Therefore, the ΔL value of 200 lux has been selected as our threshold light intensity parameter.

A sample of the observed data and system predicted results are as shown in Fig. 4b. Overall, over a period of several days, we found out the accuracy of lighting state detection to be around 96.3% with such a low sampling rate.

Occupancy Detection. For occupancy detection, we conducted several experiments with different ambient temperature settings. The PIR motion sensor gives stable readings within 15 ft radius. Although due to its limitation, it cannot detect human subjects when they are stationary. In that scenario, we have employed the thermal sensor to detect occupancy. The thermal sensor has limited range, its accuracy tapers off significantly when the object distance increases. The thermal images taken with the human subject at different distances are shown in Fig. 6. From the Fig. 6, it can be seen that the thermal disturbance caused by human presence is quite evident and distinct from the background within a 3-m range. But as the distance increases, the thermal spread is more diluted and starts overlapping with no human present thermal image.

As discussed in the above section the threshold values of variance α_{th} and temperature difference γ_{th} need to be ascertained for correct occupancy classification. The Fig. 7 shows the variations in values of variance α_{th} and temperature difference γ_{th} with different measuring distances. We have selected the threshold values that give the most distinct results. We have determined 3.5 as temperature difference threshold γ_{th} and 0.4 as variance threshold α_{th}.

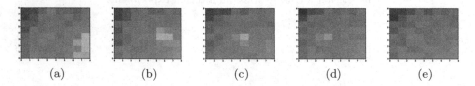
(a)   (b)   (c)   (d)   (e)

Fig. 6. Variations of thermal sensor readings with distance. Distance (a) 1 m (b) 2 m (c) 3 m (d) 4 m (e) No human

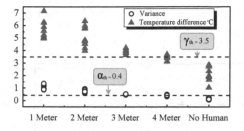

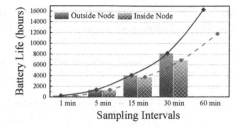

Fig. 7. Variance and temp difference in thermal image with distance

Fig. 8. Battery life of node with sampling intervals

Power Profile. We performed extensive experiments analyzing the power consumption of our nodes in various operating modes. Our outside node wakes up after every 15 min, powers up the temperature and light sensor, and takes the reading. It then transmits the values via Nb-IoT radio to the server. Then the node goes back to sleep, as shown in the Fig. 9a. Whereas the inside node, apart from having 15 min wake-up cycle, can also be interrupted by detected motion on the PIR sensor. Furthermore, thermal sensor maybe powered up as per node work flow at 15 min RTC cycle. The power profile of the outside node is shown in the Fig. 9b. Based on the power profile the calculated battery life with different sampling intervals is shown in Fig. 8.

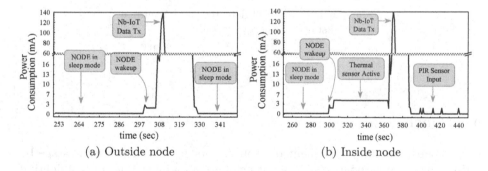

(a) Outside node   (b) Inside node

Fig. 9. Node power profile

Cumulative Prediction. Finally, we can combine the overall detection of these events and predict energy wastage, as shown in the Fig. 10. At around 9:43 am, our system detected a cooling system ON event due to a change in temperature of more than 1 °C. Furthermore, at 10:08 AM a light ON event is reported by a change in light intensity of more than 200 lux. Therefore, when our system detects an unoccupied room at 10:15 AM, our system reports that the room is unoccupied, with energy being wasted and generates an alarm. The Accuracy of the system after test is presented in Table 1.

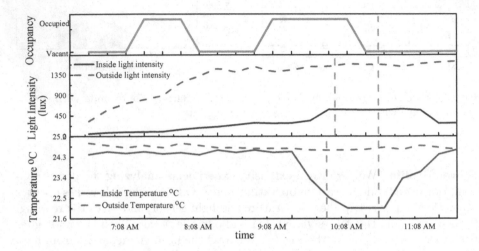

Fig. 10. Experiment to detect energy wastage

Table 1. Experimental results energy wastage detection

# of actual energy wastage	# of detected energy wastage	Accuracy
75	71	94.6%

4   Conclusion

In this paper, we have implemented a solution for predicting energy wastage by estimating room occupancy and operating state of peripheral systems of lighting and cooling. As a future enhancement, we are working on displaying the accumulated data with geographical tag and add supervisory control in our architecture. That can enable the management to control the lighting and AC state remotely based on the current data and generated alarms. This shall add human intelligence to the system which shall improve the utility of the solution.

References

1. Energy Information Administration: U.S. Energy-Related Carbon Dioxide Emissions. U.S. Department of Energy (23 November 2015)

2. Energy Information Administration: Annual Energy Outlook 2020 Commercial Sector Key Indicators and Consumption. U.S. Department of Energy (2020)
3. Energy Information Administration: Commercial Building Energy Consumption Survey. U.S. Department of Energy (2012)
4. Sgouropoulos, D., Spyrou, E., Siantikos, G.: Counting and tracking people in a smart room: an IoT approach. In: 10th International Workshop on Semantic and Social Media Adaptation and Personalization (SMAP). IEEE, Trento (November 2015)
5. Choi, J.W., Yim, D.H., Cho, S.H.: People counting based on an IR-UWB radar sensor. IEEE Sens. J. **17**, 5717–5727 (2017)
6. Yuan, Y., Zhao, J., Qiu, C., Xi, W.: Estimating crowd density in an RF-based dynamic environment. IEEE Sens. J. **13**(10), 3837–3845 (2013)
7. Vela, A., Alvarado-Uribe, J., Davila, M., Hernandez-Gress, N., Ceballos, H.G.: Estimating occupancy levels in enclosed spaces using environmental variables: a fitness gym and living room as evaluation scenarios. Sensors **20**, 6579 (2020)
8. Jiang, X., Dawson-Haggerty, S., Dutta, P., Culler, D.: Design and implementation of a high-fidelity AC metering network. In: 8th International Conference on Information Processing in Sensor Networks, pp. 253–264. IEEE Computer Society, USA (2009)
9. Hart, G.W.: Nonintrusive appliance state monitoring. Proc. IEEE **80**(12), 1870–1891 (1992)
10. Patel, S.N., Robertson, T., Kientz, J.A., Reynolds, M.S., Abowd, G.D.: At the flick of a switch: detecting and classifying unique electrical events on the residential power line (nominated for the best paper award). In: Krumm, J., Abowd, G.D., Seneviratne, A., Strang, T. (eds.) UbiComp 2007. LNCS, vol. 4717, pp. 271–288. Springer, Heidelberg (2007). https://doi.org/10.1007/978-3-540-74853-3_16
11. Tan, R., Phillips, D.E., Moazzami, M.-M., Xing, G., Chen, J.: Unsupervised residential power usage monitoring using a wireless sensor network. ACM Trans. Sens. Netw. **13**, 1–28 (2017)
12. Built-in Sensors Catalog: Panasonic Industry (2020). https://industrial.panasonic.com/cdbs/www-data/pdf/ADI8000/ADI8000COL13.pdf. Accessed 31 Mar 2021
13. Heat Balance in the Human Body. https://c21.phas.ubc.ca/article/heat-balance-in-the-human-body-2/. Accessed 31 Mar 2021
14. Singh, S., Aksanli, B.: Non-intrusive presence detection and position tracking for multiple people using low-resolution thermal sensors. J. Sens. Actuator Netw. **8**, 40 (2019)
15. Diamond, H.J., Kar, T.R., et al.: U.S. climate reference network after one decade of operations: status and assessment. Bull. Am. Meteorol. Soc. **94**, 489–498 (2013). https://doi.org/10.1175/BAMS-D-12-00170.1
16. Rea, M.S., Illuminating Engineering Society of North America: The IESNA lighting handbook: Reference & application. 9th edn. Illuminating Engineering Society of North America, New York (2000)

A Robust IoT Device Identification Method with Unknown Traffic Detection

Xiao Hu[1,2], Hong Li[1,2], Zhiqiang Shi[1,2], Nan Yu[2(✉)], Hongsong Zhu[1,2], and Limin Sun[1,2]

[1] School of Cyber Security, University of Chinese Academy of Sciences, Beijing, China
{huxiao,lihong,shizhiqiang,zhuhongsong,sunlimin}@iie.ac.cn
[2] Institute of Information Engineering, Chinese Academy of Sciences, Beijing, China
yunan@iie.ac.cn

Abstract. Internet of Things (IoT) device identification plays a basic and essential role in network management and cyberspace security. Previous device identification methods perform poorly in real-world networks where much unknown traffic exists, since they only focus on improving performance on closed datasets and rely on manual features that are difficult to generalize. To achieve robust IoT device identification, we propose a new approach with unknown traffic detection, which consists of general training and novel inference stage. In the first stage, a simple neural network is trained to extract spatial-temporal features automatically and explicitly form tight clusters of known devices through multi-task learning. Furthermore, we use extreme value theory (EVT) to model the boundary of each cluster in the feature space. Then the probability of unknown traffic is recalibrated in the inference stage. Experiments on a public IoT traffic dataset show that the accuracy and f1 score of our method are both over 92%, which significantly outperforms all compared methods under diverse experimental settings. In addition, the visualization of intermediate results illustrates the interpretability of our method.

Keywords: IoT · Device identification · Unknown network traffic detection · Deep learning · EVT

1 Introduction

Forecasts by Statista Research Department suggest that by 2030 around 50 billion IoT devices will be in use around the world. The wide variety of IoT devices providing diverse services bring convenience to our daily lives [1]. However, IoT devices also introduce numerous security risks such as network management [2,3] and privacy disclosure [4]. To address such challenges, identifying which IoT devices are connected to the network is significant. Generally, there are two kinds of methods to identify devices: 1) actively detecting and 2) passively monitoring network traffic. The former usually takes up network resources, while the latter just collects traffic at the router or gateway. In addition, traffic contains a wealth of information about the corresponding device, which is sufficient to

© Springer Nature Switzerland AG 2021
Z. Liu et al. (Eds.): WASA 2021, LNCS 12937, pp. 190–202, 2021.
https://doi.org/10.1007/978-3-030-85928-2_15

identify the device itself, vendor and version, etc. [5]. Accordingly, identifying IoT devices from the traffic is low-cost and effective.

Existing methods using network traffic are able to identify known devices with high accuracy [6–8]. However, these methods do not consider how to handle new or unseen traffic outside the dataset, which forces unknown traffic to be misclassified into one of the predefined known classes. Besides, they typically design many manual traffic features in a closed dataset, which requires domain expertise and is hard to generalize.

To address these challenges, we propose a robust IoT device identification approach with unknown traffic detection. We represent the traffic rationally and take advantage of deep neural networks to extract features automatically. Furthermore, we introduce a multi-task loss which ensures classification performance and explicitly trains known device traffic to form tight clusters in the feature space. Then the likelihood of traffic being classified as unknown class is estimated based on EVT. Finally, test traffic is identified as one of the $N + 1$ classes (N known devices and 1 *Unknown*). In summary, the contributions of this paper are as follows:

- We design a robust method to identify known devices and detect unknown traffic simultaneously based on multi-task learning and EVT.
- We properly represent the traffic by inspecting the IoT traffic and subsequently extracting spatial-temporal features automatically with deep neural networks to avoid the drawbacks of manual features.
- We evaluate our approach on a public dataset [6]. The experimental results show that our method achieves best performance against all baselines under diverse settings.

The rest of this paper is organized as follows: Sect. 2 discusses relevant prior work. We illustrate the framework of the proposed method in Sect. 3. In Sect. 4, we describe the experimental setup in detail and discuss the results. Finally, this paper is concluded in Sect. 5.

2   Related Work

In recent years, more and more researchers focus on IoT traffic analysis. Sivanathan et al. [9] extract header fields and statistical attributes to classify IoT device by random forest algorithm. In their subsequent work [6], they propose a multi-stage machine learning based classification algorithm that achieves high classification accuracy. Santos et al. [10] present a feasible approach, which combines random forest and content packet detection techniques to improve the performance. In [11], the authors propose an automatic cross-device classification method by identifying the semantic type of a device. The model learns the similarity between devices of the same category but cannot determine device traffic specifically.

Many novel technologies have also been applied to the IoT device classification. Yao et al. [12] propose an end-to-end device identification method which

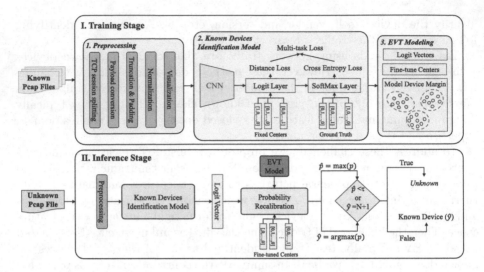

Fig. 1. The framework of the proposed method.

applies a capsule network to the device identification task for the first time. To reduce the cost of labeling IoT traffic, Fan et al. [8] present a semi-supervised learning based device identification method. They manually extract more than 200 features and use multi-task learning for training.

Although the above approaches investigate various aspects such as feature extraction, model design, labeling cost, and even classification confidence, they still cannot handle traffic beyond the labeled dataset.

3   Proposed Method

Figure 1 shows the framework of our method. It consists of the general training stage and novel inference stage. In the training stage, we aim to accurately classify all known devices using multi-task loss and build an EVT model for each device. In the next inference stage, we use the built EVT model to recalibrate the probabilities of $N + 1$ classes.

3.1   Training Stage

Raw Traffic Data Preprocessing. When an IoT device is deployed successfully, it generates traffic according to its services. Usually, we can install traffic analysis tools such as tcpdump on the gateway or router to capture the incoming and outgoing traffic. When inspecting IoT device traffic, we found that many devices generate similar UDP based traffic such as NTP and DNS traffic. However, it is difficult to distinguish different IoT devices with such traffic. Hence we consider using the payload of TCP session to represent traffic [5] as the payload carries the content of the communication with the server, which contains

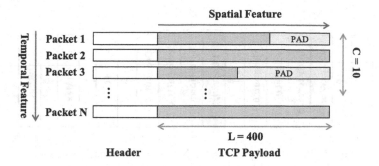

Fig. 2. Traffic is represented as a 400 × 10 two-dimensional matrix, where the horizontal and vertical axes represent the spatial and temporal characteristics, respectively. The gray "PAD" means that the packet is pad with 0.

device-specific information even though it may be encrypted. Besides, dropping the header prevents the model from over-fitting IP and MAC addresses. In particular, a TCP session composes of two unidirectional TCP flows with opposite 5-tuples (i.e., source IP, source port, protocol, destination IP, destination port) in temporal order. Since neural networks need fixed shape inputs, we transform the payload to a two-dimensional matrix. The traffic is first converted from binary to decimal in bytes then truncated and padded according to the empirical distribution of the number of payload packets and the load length. Figure 2 shows the representation of each TCP session. All duplicate data will be dropped and the converted decimal data will be normalized before being input into the model. We will display and discuss the visualization outcomes of the preprocessed traffic in Sect. 4.4.

Device Identification Model Training. To classify known devices, we introduce multi-task learning to train our model. In particular, there are two tasks: 1) classifying known devices with a labeled dataset, which ensures that the model distinguish observed devices accurately, and 2) making the cluster of the same device traffic in the feature space as tight as possible, which makes it easier to distinguish known and unknown inputs during subsequent inference stage 3.2. We choose the penultimate layer [14], which is generally called the logit layer, as the feature space.

Given the preprocessed traffic in a batch $X = \{x_1, x_2, ..., x_M\}$, and the corresponding device label $Y = \{y_1, y_2, ..., y_M\}$, $\forall y_i \in \{1, 2, ..., N\}$. Here, M is the batch size and N is the number of known device classes. We define a deep neural network f which projects traffic into the logit space to obtain a feature vector $l = f(x_i) = (l_1, l_2, ..., l_N)$. Figure 3 demonstrates the structure of our neural network. The neural network consists of only four 2D-CNN layers, each followed by a batch normalization (BN) and a LeakyReLu activation function. Each two CNN layers are connected with a dropout layer. The model is trained using the following cross entropy loss for the first task:

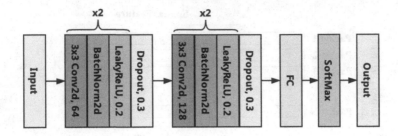

Fig. 3. The architecture of CNN based identification model.

$$\mathcal{L}_{ce}(X,Y) = -\frac{1}{M}\sum_{i=1}^{M}\sum_{j=1}^{N} I_{y_i}(j) \log p_i(j) \tag{1}$$

where $I_{y_i}(j) = 1$ if $y_i = j$ and 0 otherwise. $p_i(j)$ is a softmax function that represents the probability the ith traffic being classified into the jth class.

To build tight clusters explicitly, we set fixed class centers for each known device which are defined as:

$$C = \alpha \times (c_1, c_2, ..., c_N) \tag{2}$$

$$c_1 = (1, 0, ..., 0), c_N = (0, 0, ..., 1) \tag{3}$$

where α is a hyperparameter for scaling standard basis vector c_i. We introduce a distance loss to ensure that the absolute distance from the input to its correct class center is forced to decrease. The distance loss is used to optimize the model on task 2, which is formulated as:

$$\mathcal{L}_{dis}(X,Y) = \frac{1}{M}\sum_{i=1}^{M} \|f(x_i) - c_{y_i}\| \tag{4}$$

We combine the cross-entropy loss and the distance loss to obtain the final loss function:

$$\mathcal{L}(X,Y) = \lambda\mathcal{L}_{ce}(X,Y) + (1-\lambda)\mathcal{L}_{dis}(X,Y) \tag{5}$$

where $\lambda \in (0,1)$ is a hyperparameter to adjust the proportion of the two losses.

By minimizing the final loss function, our model is trained to accurately identify known devices and form tight cluster of the same device traffic.

EVT Modeling. Extreme value theory [15] describes the probability distribution of extreme values, which is an effective tool for modeling post-training scores. Previous work analyzed the distribution of the final scores and found that these distributions followed the Weibull distribution. The Weibull cumulative distribution function (CDF) models the probability of an input falling into the extreme value region, which means that if the output probability is higher, then the less likely the input belongs to the corresponding class. The CDFs of known devices are formulated as:

$$\Phi = \{\phi_1, \phi_2, ..., \phi_N\} \tag{6}$$

$$\phi_i(x; \tau_i, \lambda_i, \kappa_i) = 1 - e^{-(\frac{\|x-\tau_i\|}{\lambda_i})^{\kappa_i}} \tag{7}$$

where x is the distance from the logit vector to one of the centers. τ_i, λ_i, κ_i are shift, scale and shape parameter, respectively. To estimate these parameters, a hyperparameter η called tail size is introduced. It indicates the number of samples that are top η far from the corresponding class center.

Given the logit space vectors of all the correctly classified samples during training: $L = \{L_1 \cup L_2 \cup ... \cup L_N\}$, $L_i = \{l_{i1}, l_{i2}, ..., l_{iK}\}$. We fine-tune the original fixed center by calculating the mean of the same class vectors. With the above preparations, we fit the Weibull CDF distribution for each known device. Algorithm 1 summarizes overall EVT modeling process.

Algorithm 1. EVT Modeling

Input: All the logit vectors being classified correctly L
Input: Tail size η, number of known devices N
Output: EVT models Φ and fine-tuned centers $\hat{C}$
1: Let $\Phi = \emptyset$, $\hat{C} = \emptyset$
2: **for** $i = 1$ **to** N **do**
3:    Adjust original fixed center: $\hat{c}_i = Mean(L_i)$
4:    Save fine-tuned center: $\hat{C} = \hat{C} \cup \{\hat{c}_i\}$
5:    Compute distance of each vector in i^{th} class: $d_i = \|l_{ik} - \hat{c}_i\|$
6:    Select the η farthest distances: $F = top\eta(d_i)$
7:    Fit EVT model: $\phi_i(x; \tau_i, \lambda_i, \kappa_i) = fit(F)$
8:    Save model: $\Phi = \Phi \cup \{\phi_i\}$
9: **end for**

3.2 Inference Stage

Algorithm 2 elaborates the inference procedure. The test traffic is preprocessed following Sect. 3.1 and fed into the trained identification model to obtain its logit vector. Then the distances to each cluster center in logit space are calculated, following by getting output probabilities from each EVT model. Subsequently, we recalibrate the logit vector and assign a score to the unknown class. Finally, we define the maximum probability $\hat{p}$ and its corresponding class id $\hat{y}$. If $\hat{p}$ is lower than ρ or $\hat{y}$ is equal to $N + 1$, the test traffic belongs to the unknown class, otherwise known class with label $\hat{y}$ is returned. Here, ρ is a threshold hyperparameter and will be discussed in Sect. 4.3.

4   Experiments and Results

In this section, we design a large number of experiments to evaluate the proposed method. In the first step, the proposed method is compared with two state-of-the-art IoT device identification methods. Then we simulate the problem of unknown IoT traffic to evaluate the performance under different settings.

Algorithm 2. Device inference

Input: A test traffic T, Number of known devices N
Input: Trained identification model f
Input: EVT models Φ and fine-tuned centers $\hat{C}$
Output: Device class or *Unknown*

1: Preprocess the traffic: $x = preprocess(T)$
2: Get logit vector: $l = f(x)$
3: **for** $i = 1$ **to** N **do**
4:    Compute probability: $w_i = \phi_i(\|x - \hat{c}_i\|)$
5: **end for**
6: Recalibrate logit vector: $\hat{l} = l \circ w$
7: Assigning unknown device score:

$$\hat{l}_{N+1} = \sum_{i=1}^{N}(1 - w_i)\hat{l}$$

8: SoftMax with $N + 1$ classes:

$$P(y = i) = \frac{e^{l_i}}{\sum_{j=1}^{N+1} e^{l_j}}$$

9: Define: $\hat{p} = max(P(y = i))$, $\hat{y} = argmax(P(y = i))$
10: **if** $\hat{p} < \rho$ or $\hat{y} == N + 1$ **then**
11:    Predict T as *Unknown*
12: **else**
13:    Predict T as known device with label $\hat{y}$
14: **end if**

4.1   Experiments Setup

Dataset. To evaluate our proposed approach, we use the publicly available IoT traffic dataset of [6]. The dataset is collected from an instrumented experimental environment including 30 commercial devices (23 IoT devices and 7 non-IoT devices). As described in Sect. 3.1, we extract all the TCP sessions in the traffic and separate them by MAC address since one MAC address corresponds to one device in this dataset. Table 1 shows the number of TCP sessions of all devices.

Implementation Details and Evaluation Metrics. In the proposed method, we use a Stochastic Gradient Descent (SGD) optimizer with a learning rate of 0.0005, and batch size, N = 64. By grid search, the hyperparameter α, λ and η are set equal to 10, 0.1, and 15, respectively. They just affect the performance slightly in the experiment. For another hyperparameter ρ, we will discuss it in Sect. 4.3. The simple Euclidean distance is applied in all $\|\cdot\|$ places.

Two metrics are used to evaluate the performance of our method: accuracy and F1 score. The former is used to measure the accuracy of a classifier on the whole testing data. The latter is the harmonic mean of precision and recall and is used to evaluate the per-class performance.

Table 1. The number of TCP sessions of all device

Device	Count	Device	Count
Belkin wemo motion sensor	38461	Dropcam	40
Samsung SmartCam	9021	Light Bulbs LiFX Smart Bulb	34
Belkin Wemo switch	7031	TP-Link Day Night Cloud camera	31
Withings Smart Baby Monitor	5544	Nest Dropcam	29
Insteon Camera1	3838	Smart Things	26
Withings Aura smart sleep sensor	3583	Withings Smart scale	20
Amazon Echo	3006	Blipcare Blood Pressure meter	4
Netatmo Welcome	2676	Insteon Camera2	1
Netatmo weather station	2338	Samsung Galaxy Tab	12979
PIX-STAR Photo-frame	1118	Laptop	9369
TP-Link Smart plug	232	MacBook	3684
iHome	153	Android Phone2	1552
Triby Speake	142	Android Phone1	252
HP Printer	103	MacBook Iphone	150
NEST Protect smoke alarm	84	IPhone	35

4.2   Experiment I : Known Device Identification

Even though we aim to detect unknown traffic, we should not compromise the performance of identifying known devices. Thus we compare the proposed method with two state-of-the-art IoT device identification approaches. To prevent unbalanced data from degrading model performance, we choose 20 devices (including 14 IoT devices and 6 non-IoT devices) to evaluate the method. We set the number of down-sampling to 3000 and divide the training set and test set at a ratio of 8:2. Tabel 2 shows the average score of 5 runs. The accuracy of our model is higher than [10] and comparable with [6]. Note that their methods excessively use artificial features, making them difficult to generalize. Our method could avoid such problems by learning features automatically. In summary, the proposed method guarantees the classification performance of known classes.

Table 2. The proposed approach provides comparable performance with the state-of-the-art methods that focus only on known device identification.

Method	Accuracy(%)	F1(%)
Santos et al. [10]	98.70	98.70
Sivanathan et al. [6]	99.28	-
Proposed method	99.19 ± 0.02	99.09 ± 0.03

4.3 Experiment II: Unknown Traffic Detection

Since existing studies do not consider addressing device identification and unknown traffic detection simultaneously, we set up rich contrast baselines to evaluate the proposed method.

An intuitive way to distinguish unknown class is setting a confidence threshold. The test traffic is classified as unknown once the output probability is below the threshold. In deep neural networks, a SoftMax function is commonly used in the last layer to generate the probability distribution over N known class labels. Hence, we use SoftMax as one of the baselines to represent the previous approach that uses confidence thresholds. We also set up three ablation baselines. They are described as follows:

1. SoftMax: The SoftMax baseline has the same training process as the proposed method whereas a threshold and the maximum output probability are directly compared in the inference stage.

2. CE: In this model, only cross entropy loss $\mathcal{L}_{ce}$ is applied during the training stage. The inference procedure is the same as the proposed method.

3. CNN: This baseline is identical to our proposed method except that it uses only two CNN layers.

4. CNN-LSTM: This baseline uses two 1D-CNN layers to extract spatial features and feeds them into a two-layer LSTM to capture the temporal features. Both training and inference processes are the same as for the proposed approach.

To simulate unknown traffic, we randomly select 8 IoT devices and 2 non-IoT devices from devices with more than 1000 TCP sessions as known devices and the traffic of other devices as unknown traffic. Then we down-sample the known TCP sessions and split them. The training set is used to optimize the model and all unknown traffic will be added to the test set after being shuffled. The performance is evaluated with accuracy and F1 score in 11 classes (10 known devices and 1 *Unknown*).

Impact of Varying Number of Unknown Traffic. In general, the number of unknown traffic is an important factor affecting the performance of the model. The more unknown traffic makes the detection more difficult. We calculate the metric once for every 1000 added unknown TCP sessions. Figure 4 shows that the unknown traffic, which contains more than 36,000 TCP sessions from 20 different devices, influences the accuracy and the F1 score of all methods to varying degrees. Note that the decline of the F1 score is larger than the accuracy as it is more difficult to classify each class well than the overall accuracy.

The CE baseline, which is trained only with cross entropy loss, has the worst performance. This result illustrates the effectiveness and superiority of distance loss that models class tightness explicitly. The CNN baseline is slightly inferior to the proposed model, which means that the deeper neural network structure helps to capture more advanced features. For the CNN-LSTM model, it is the second-best model because it learns a meaningful representation of the traffic. For SoftMax baseline, the accuracy and F1 scores decline close to 5% and 8%,

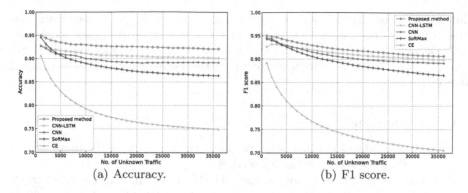

(a) Accuracy.   (b) F1 score.

Fig. 4. Performance against varying number of unknown traffic.

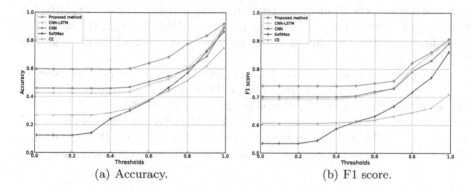

(a) Accuracy.   (b) F1 score.

Fig. 5. Performance against varying thresholds.

respectively, while our method can achieve less than 4% and 5% decreases. Moreover, our method outperforms the SofxMax baseline at all testing steps. the gap between the two broadens as the unknown traffic increases. The results show that the proposed method is more effective in terms of performance and robustness compared to baselines.

Impact of Varying Thresholds. We also investigated the effect of different thresholds. Given a threshold ρ, all methods use the same threshold value to classify all traffic in the test set. Figure 5 reports the performance of all methods. When the threshold is very small, the performance of our method is significantly higher compared to SoftMax (accuracy: more than 40%, F1 score: about 20%). The explanation is the smaller the threshold, the less likely SoftMax will classify the test traffic as unknown traffic. But our method could estimate the probability of unknown traffic through EVT. Compared to other ablation baselines, the proposed method achieves higher performance.

As the threshold value gradually increases, the performance of all methods improves. But our approach consistently surpasses the baselines even when the threshold is close to 1. Notably, the CE model has difficulty in achieving satisfactory scores even with high thresholds as it cannot model class boundaries well without the distance loss. In conclusion, the proposed method effectively detect unknown traffic with less decline in the performance of known device identification.

4.4 Visualization

To provide a graphical interpretation of our work, we visualize the preprocessed traffic and their logit vectors in this section.

Following Sect. 3.1, we convert each TCP session into a grayscale graph. Figure 6 shows the results of three traffic randomly sampled from 4 devices (2 IoT devices and 2 non-IoT devices). Figure 6(a) illustrates IoT devices have a simple task and a relatively fixed traffic pattern, while non-IoT devices Fig. 6(b) have diverse applications and generate multiple forms of traffic. From the perspective of traffic generation, non-IoT devices can be seen as a collection of various IoT devices.

For logit vectors, we visualize them by the t-Distributed Stochastic Neighbor Embedding (t-SNE) [17]. Figure 7 shows the visualization results of the logit vectors obtained from the CE baseline and the proposed method. Each color represents a known device. Compared with Fig. 7(a), the class clusters in Fig. 7(b) are tighter and the boundaries are more clearly. The reason is that the distance loss explicitly models the distance of the traffic to its corresponding class center.

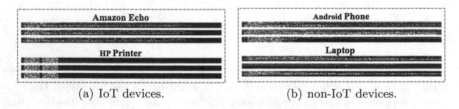

(a) IoT devices.   (b) non-IoT devices.

Fig. 6. The grayscale plots of 3 traffic randomly sampled from 4 devices.

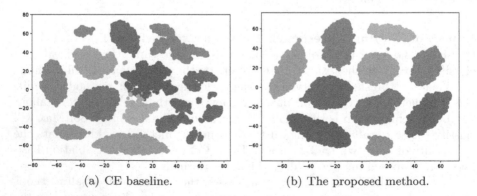

(a) CE baseline.   (b) The proposed method.

Fig. 7. Visualization result of traffic logit vectors by t-SNE.

5 Conclusion and Future Work

To tackle the challenge that unknown traffic leads to degradation of IoT device classification performance in open scenarios, this paper proposes a robust IoT device identification method based on multi-task learning and EVT. The former facilitates the classification of known devices and modeling class clusters explicitly, and the latter supports probabilistic recalibration of unknown traffic.

Experiments on a public IoT device traffic dataset show that the proposed model provides better identification performance, robustness, and interpretability than other baselines.

In future work, we will explore the impact of traffic from all protocols (not just TCP traffic) to fully utilize the dataset. Besides, we will collect more IoT and non-IoT device traffic to evaluate our approach in large-scale scenarios.

Acknowledgements. This work was supported in part by National Key Research and Development Program of China under Grant 2017YFB0802805, 2018YFC0826101.

References

1. Fan, X., et al.: Buildsensys: reusing building sensing data for traffic prediction with cross-domain learning. IEEE Trans. Mob. Comput. **20**(6), 2154–2171 (2020b)
2. Cai, Z., Shi, T.: Distributed query processing in the edge assisted IoT data monitoring system.: IEEE Internet of Things Journal (2020)
3. Zheng, X., Cai, Z., Li, J., Gao, H.: An application-awarescheduling policy for real-time traffic. In: In 2015 IEEE 35th International Conference on Distributed Computing Systems, pp. 421–430. IEEE (2015)
4. Cai, Z., Zheng, X., Yu, J.: A differential-private framework for urban traffic flows estimation via taxi companies. IEEE Trans. Ind. Inform. **15**(12), 6492–6499 (2019)
5. Ortiz, J., Crawford, C., Le, F.: Devicemien: network device behavior modeling for identifying unknown IoT devices. In: Proceedings of the International Conference on Internet of Things Design and Implementation, pp. 106–117 (2019)
6. Sivanathan, A., Gharakheili, H.H., et al.: Classifying IoT devices in smart environments using network traffic characteristics. IEEE Trans. Mob. Comput. **18**(8), 1745–1759 (2018)
7. Hamad, S.A., Zhang, W.E., Sheng, Q.Z., Nepal, S.: IoT device identification via network-flow based finger-printing and learning. In: 2019 18th IEEE International Conference on Trust, Security and Privacy in Computing and Communications/13th IEEE International Conference on Big Data Science and Engineering (Trust-Com/BigDataSE), pp. 103–111. IEEE (2019)
8. Fan, L., Zhang, S., Wu, Y., et al.: An IoT device identification method based on semi-supervised learning. In: 2020 16th International Conference on Network and Service Management(CNSM), pp. 1–7. IEEE (2020a)
9. Sivanathan, A., Sherratt, D., et al.: Characterizing and classifying IoT traffic in smart cities and campuses. In: 2017 IEEE Conference on Computer Communications Workshops (INFOCOM WKSHPS), pp. 559–564. IEEE (2017)
10. Santos, M.R., et al.: An efficient approach for device identification and traffic classification in IoT ecosystems. In: 2018 IEEE Symposium on Computers and Communications (ISCC), pp. 304–309. IEEE (2018)

11. Bai, L., Yao, L., Kanhere, S.S., Wang, X., Yang, Z.: Automatic device classification from network traffic streams of internet of things. In: 2018 IEEE 43rd Conference on Local Computer Networks (LCN), pp. 1–9. IEEE (2018)
12. Yao, H., Gao, P., Wang, J., Zhang, P., Jiang, C., Han, Z.: Capsule network assisted IoT traffic classification mechanism for smart cities. IEEE Internet of Things J. 6(5), 7515–7525 (2019)
13. Wang, W., Zhu, M., et al.: End-to-end encrypted traffic classification with one-dimensional convolution neural networks. In: 2017 IEEE International Conference on Intelligence and Security Informatics (ISI), pp. 43–48. IEEE (2017)
14. Bendale, A., et al.: Towards open set deep networks. In: Proceedings of the IEEE Conference on Computer Vision and Pattern Recognition, pp. 1563–1572 (2016)
15. Kotz, S., Nadarajah, S.: Extreme value distributions: theory and applications. World Scientific (2000)
16. Oza, P., Patel, V.M.: C2ae: class conditioned autoencoder for open-set recognition. In: Proceedings of the IEEE/CVF Conference on Computer Vision and Pattern Recognition, pp. 2307–2316 (2019)
17. Van der Maaten, L., Hinton, G.: Visualizing data using t-sne. Journal of Machine Learning Research, vol. 9, no. 11 (2008)

Temporal Attention-Based Graph Convolution Network for Taxi Demand Prediction in Functional Areas

Yue Wang, Jianbo Li$^{(\boxtimes)}$, Aite Zhao, Zhiqiang Lv$^{(\boxtimes)}$, and Guangquan Lu

College of Computer Science and Technology, Qingdao University, Qingdao 266071, China
lijianbo@qdu.edu.cn

Abstract. Shared travel is increasingly becoming an indispensable way of urban transportation. Accurately calculating the demand for taxis in various regions of the city has become a huge problem. In this paper, we divide the city into multiple lattices of different sizes and propose a graph convolution network based on the temporal attention mechanism for taxi demand prediction in each functional area of the city. The model includes graph convolution network (GCN), temporal convolution network (TCN), and the attention mechanism, which are respectively used to capture the spatial correlation of roads, time dependence, and highlight the characteristics of the time-series data. Extensive experiments on three datasets validate the effectiveness of the proposed method, compared against several state-of-the-art methods. Despite there are amount differences among the three datasets in our experiment, our model still has a high prediction accuracy. Our model code is available at https://github.com/qdu318/TAGCN.

Keywords: Taxi demand prediction · Attention mechanism · Graph convolution network · Temporal convolution network

1 Introduction

In recent years, although domestic private car ownership has increased substantially, due to the rapid development of the sharing economy [1], taxis are playing an increasingly significant role in urban transportation. In 2020, the taxi empty rate in Beijing has risen to nearly 40%, which undoubtedly caused a serious waste of resources and traffic congestion in the city. Therefore, a key aspect of solving the above problem is to accurately predict the demand for taxis in each region.

Traffic forecasting has received extensive attention and research in the past few decades [20, 21]. Traffic prediction models can be divided into non-parametric and parametric models. Among them, the parameters are from the data distribution. Usually, parametric models include the time series model [2], autoregressive integrated moving average model (ARIMA) [3], linear regression model [4], and Kalman filtering model [5]. The parametric models have relatively simple structures and they specify the learning method in the form of a certain function, which strictly depends on the stationary hypothesis and cannot reflect the uncertainty of the traffic state and non-linearity. The

© Springer Nature Switzerland AG 2021
Z. Liu et al. (Eds.): WASA 2021, LNCS 12937, pp. 203–214, 2021.
https://doi.org/10.1007/978-3-030-85928-2_16

data-driven non-parametric models can effectively solve these problems, including traditional machine learning and deep learning approaches. Without prior knowledge, they can still fit multiple functional forms of enough historical data. Traditional machine learning models include k-nearest neighbors [6], decision trees [7] (such as CART and C4.5), naive Bayes [8], support vector machines [9], and neural networks [10]. Since traditional machine learning methods usually require complex feature engineering and are not suitable for processing a large number of datasets, the deep learning algorithm has emerged. Common deep learning models include Auto-encoder [11], generative adversarial networks [12], convolutional neural network (CNN) [13], and recurrent neural network [14]. Although the Recurrent Neural Network (RNN) is designed for dealing with time-series problems, and CNN has the ability to extract spatial correlation, they are only suitable for processing structured data. Especially, CNN divides the traffic network into a two-dimensional regular lattice, which destroys the original structure of the traffic network.

Therefore, we design a temporal attention-based graph convolutional network (TAGCN) for predicting the taxi's demand in the functional area. The model can directly process traffic data on graphics, effectively capture complex spatial-temporal correlations, and more accurately predict local peaks and the values of the start and end points of the data. The main contributions of this paper are summarized as follows:

- We propose a new temporal graph convolutional network model based on the attention mechanism, which embeds Attention to highlight the characteristics of traffic data. The spatial-temporal convolution model includes graph convolutional network (GCN) and temporal convolutional network (TCN) to realize the spatial-temporal correlation of the traffic data.
- After changing the previous lattice division ways, the city is divided into multiple lattices of different sizes according to the function of area, and the spatial location is converted into a graphic structure.
- Three real-world datasets are utilized in the experiment. Compared with 7 state-of-the-art baselines, TAGCN has achieved the best prediction results.

2 Related Work

A large number of methods based on deep learning networks are widely used in traffic prediction problems without artificially synthesizing complex features and cross-domain knowledge sharing. For example, Contextualized Spatial-Temporal Network for Taxi Origin-Destination Demand Prediction (CSTN) [15] uses CNN to learn the dependence of local space and ConvLSTM to analyze the change of taxi demand over time. Deep Multi-View Spatial-Temporal Network for Taxi Demand Prediction (DMVST-Net) [16] uses CNN to capture the spatial proximity and Long Short-Term Memory (LSTM) to model the time series. The short-term time dependence in Revisiting Spatial-Temporal Similarity: A Deep Learning Framework for Traffic Prediction (STDN) [17] is obtained by LSTM, the time periodicity is obtained by Attention for the previous days, and the spatial relationship between adjacent regions is captured by CNN.

Although LSTM performs well on several sequence problems (such as speech/text recognition [18] and machine translation [19]), since the network can only handle one time step at a time, the next step must wait for the previous step to complete the operation. It means that LSTM cannot solve large-scale parallel computing problems. The data processed by LSTM and CNN belongs to the Euclidean space and has a regular structure. However, in real life, there are many irregular data structures, such as social networks, chemical molecular structures, knowledge maps, and other topological structures, which makes the prediction effect of RNN and CNN greatly ineffective. At the same time, the above work divides the region in the form of average size, which cannot well distinguish each functional area.

The non-Euclidean spatial data processing methods include graph convolutional network (GCN) [22], graph neural network (GNN) [23], DeepWalk (Online learning) [24], node2vec [25], etc. The typical model GCN has the same role as CNN as a feature extractor. However, since the spatial relationship of the traffic map is a topological structure, which belongs to non-Euclidean data, GCN can better address the map data and extract the spatial features of the topological map than CNN. The extracted features can be used in graph classification, node classification, link prediction, and graph embedding, which fully proves the ability of GCN to process highly nonlinear data in non-Euclidean space.

Therefore, we select GCN as the internal component to extract the correlation of the input spatial data. For time-series data, the temporal convolutional network (TCN) [28] is utilized to obtain the temporal dependence, meanwhile, the characteristics of the traffic demand data are highlighted by the temporal attention mechanism [34]. In terms of functional areas, we divide the city into multiple lattices of different sizes. This work aims to predict the taxi's demand of each area at the $(t + 1)^{th}$ time interval, given the historical data of the previous t time intervals.

3   Algorithm Design

3.1   Data Design

We extract information about passengers getting on a taxi from the three original datasets, draw a scatter plot based on the extracted data, determine the area with the densest data, and select all the data in that area. To minimize the difference of the data, the final area of the three datasets is about 22.2 km × 9.16 km.

According to the functionality of the region, we divided the cities in the three datasets into four types: school district, recreation area, residential area, and business district. Furthermore, the city is divided into lattices according to the distribution of functional areas, and finally, 60 lattices of different sizes are divided and all lattices are numbered. To determine the scope of each lattice, we extract the boundaries of all lattices one by one and judge the lattice where the starting position of the taxi is as well as the center of each lattice. The calculation of the latitude and longitude of the center point are respectively shown in Eq. (1) and Eq. (2),

$$\varphi = \frac{|\varphi_2 - \varphi_1|}{2} \tag{1}$$

$$\lambda = \frac{|\lambda_2 - \lambda_1|}{2} \tag{2}$$

where φ and λ represent the latitude and longitude of the center point, respectively; φ_2 and φ_1 represent the latitude of the two vertices on the left and right respectively; λ_2 and λ_1 represent the longitude of the two vertices above and below, respectively.

The data should be preprocessed first that can be input into the model, i.e., the A matrix and the V matrix are calculated. The A matrix is an adjacency matrix based on the distance between lattices, used to store the mutual distance between 60 lattices. The V matrix represents the taxi's demand in each lattice. In the calculation of matrix A, we use the distance between the center points of the lattice to represent the distance between each area. The distance between each center point is calculated by Eq. (3).

$$d = 2\pi r \arcsin\left(\sqrt{\sin^2\left(\frac{\varphi_2 - \varphi_1}{2}\right) + \cos(\varphi_1)\cos(\varphi_2)\sin^2\left(\frac{\lambda_2 - \lambda_1}{2}\right)}\right) \qquad (3)$$

where d is the distance between two center points, and r is the radius of the earth.

After the data processing is completed, we use the Z-$score$ data standardization method to standardize the data. The Z-$score$ method is mainly used to process data with too messy distribution and too many singularities. The standard deviation of the data after Z-$score$ processing is 1, and the mean is 0. The calculation of the Z-$score$ is shown in Eq. (4).

$$z = \frac{x - \mu}{\sigma} \qquad (4)$$

where x is the original data, μ and σ are respectively the average and the standard deviation of the overall sample space.

3.2 Model Design

This paper solves the spatial-temporal problem of taxi demand forecast. We use two temporal convolution layers to obtain the long-term dependence of time and a spatial convolution layer to extract the spatial correlation. When the data is input to the first temporal convolutional layer, it is also input to the attention layer to highlight its characteristics, and the output of the attention layer is fed into the first temporal convolutional layer for extracting the low-level feature. The adjacency matrix is mapped from the distance between the lattices. After normalization, the obtained data can be comparable and maintain the relative relationship between the data. The results of the first temporal convolution layer and the adjacency matrix are input to the spatial convolution layer to enhance the spatial relative relationship of features. Enter these results into the second temporal convolution layer to obtain the temporal dependence and high-level feature of the fused data. TCN is composed of dilated convolution, causal convolution, and residual structure. To solve the gradient explosion or disappearance caused by complete convolution networks, we add $BatchNorm2D$ to the data post-processing layer. Finally, to map the learned distributed feature representation to the sample label space, we add a fully connected layer, which retains the complexity of the model. The model structure is shown in Fig. 1.

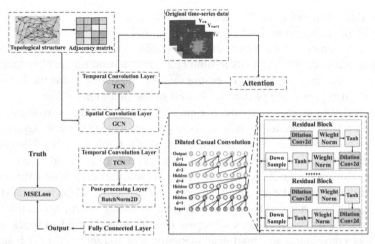

Fig. 1. The model structure. TAGCN is composed of temporal attention mechanism, temporal convolutional layer, spatial convolutional layer, and post-processing layer.

Spatial Convolution Layer. We use GCN to extract spatial correlation based on the distance between lattices. The core of GCN is based on the spectral decomposition of the Laplacian matrix, i.e., the eigenvector of the Laplacian matrix corresponding to the graph is obtained from the eigenfunction e^{-iwt} of the Laplacian operator. Laplacian matrix can make the transfer intensity of the data features in GCN proportional to their state differences. To increase the influence of the original node in the calculation process, we use the modified version of the Laplacian matrix, and the formula is defined as shown in Eq. (5),

$$L = \tilde{D}^{-\frac{1}{2}} \tilde{A} \tilde{D}^{-\frac{1}{2}} \tag{5}$$

where $\tilde{A} = A + I$, I is the identity matrix, $\tilde{D}$ is the degree matrix of $\tilde{A}$, and its formula is $\tilde{D}_{ii=} \sum j \tilde{A}_{ij}$.

However, because the graph convolution kernel is global, the amount of parameters is large, and the calculation process involves high computational complexity feature decomposition, the complexity of the graph convolution operation is extremely high. Using Chebyshev [35] polynomials to fit the convolution kernel can achieve the purpose of reducing computational complexity. The k-th order truncated expansion calculation of Chebyshev polynomial $T_k(x)$ is shown in Eq. (6),

$$g_{\theta'}(\Lambda) \approx \sum_{k=0}^{K} \theta'_k T_k(\tilde{\Lambda}) \tag{6}$$

where $g_{\theta'}(\Lambda)$ is a function expressed by the eigenvalues of the Laplacian matrix, k represents the highest order of the polynomial, $\tilde{\Lambda}$ is the scaled eigenvector matrix, $\tilde{\Lambda} = \frac{2\Lambda}{\lambda_{max}} - I_n$, λ_{max} is the spectral radius of L, and the Chebyshev polynomial is recursively defined as $T_k(x) = 2xT_{k-1}(x) - T_{k-2}(x)$, $T_1(x) = x$, $T_0(x) = 1$.

Temporal Convolution Layer. We use Temporal Convolutional Network (TCN) to obtain the temporal dependence, which is composed of dilated convolution with the same input and output length, causal convolution, and residual structure. Causality means that in the output sequence, the elements at time t can only depend on the elements at time t and before in the input sequence. To ensure that the output tensor has the same length as the input tensor, zeros are padded to the left of the input tensor. For causal convolution, the modeling length of its time is limited by the size of the convolution kernel. To obtain long-term dependence, it is necessary to linearly stack many layers. Therefore, the researchers proposed dilated convolution. When the number of layers of the convolutional network is small, we can obtain a large receptive field after using dilated convolution. However, even if dilated convolution is used, the network structure may still be deep, which will cause the gradient to disappear. The addition of the residual structure can solve it. The reason is that there is a cross-layer connection structure in the residual structure, which transmits messages in a cross-layer manner. A residual block includes two layers of convolution and nonlinear mapping, and *WeightNorm* [27] is added to each layer to regularize the network. To make TCN not just an overly complex linear regression model, we add an activation function *Tanh* to the residual block to introduce nonlinearity.

Attention Mechanism. In the time dimension, there is a correlation between traffic status in different time periods, and the correlation is also different in various actual situation. The addition of the attention mechanism can highlight the correlation between input data and current output data, and obtain the temporal-dependent intensity of time i and time j to improve the accuracy of prediction. By dynamically calculating the current input and learning parameters, we can get the time attention matrix T, as shown in Eqs. (7) and (8). The activation function *sigmoid* is used to normalize the output data, and the range is compressed between [0, 1].

$$T = V_e((X * U_1)U_2(X * U_3) + b_e \tag{7}$$

$$T'_{i,j} = \frac{e^{T_{i,j}}}{\sum_{i=1}^{N} e^{T_{i,j}}} \tag{8}$$

Post-processing Layer. Since the model is composed of complete convolutions, it is easy to cause gradient disappearance and gradient explosion. To solve these problems, we introduce *BatchNorm2D*. *BatchNorm2D* standardizes the output of each layer to make the mean and variance consistent, so as to improve the stability of model training and accelerate the speed of network convergence. We can generally understand it as *BatchNorm2D* pushing the output from the saturated zone to the unsaturated zone. The calculation of *BatchNorm2D* is shown in Eq. (9),

$$y = \frac{x - E(x)}{\sqrt{Var(x)} + \in} \times \gamma + \beta \tag{9}$$

where x is the input data, $E(x)$ and $\sqrt{Var(x)}$ are the mean and variance of x, $\in$ is a variable added to prevent zero from appearing in the denominator, and γ and β are learning parameters of 1 and 0, respectively. In the Adam optimizer, the step size is updated by the mean of the gradient and the square of the gradient. Different adaptive learning rates are calculated by the first-order and the second-order moment estimation of the gradient for different parameters. The role of the fully connected layer is to fuse the learned distributed feature representation together as an output value. Finally, the difference between the predicted value y_i and the actual value x_i is calculated by the mean square loss function MSELoss.

4 Experiment

4.1 Dataset Analysis

Three real-world datasets are used in our experiment, i.e., the taxi order dataset of Chengdu City in August 2014, Chengdu City in November 2016, and Haikou City from May to October 2017 after desensitization [26]. The above datasets all contain the time, longitude, and latitude of the trajectory. We select the start time of the order from 7:00 to 21:00 in all datasets and the latitude and longitude of the pick-up location. For Chengdu City, the longitude range is [103.95, 104.15] and the latitude range is [30.65, 30.75], which is shown in Fig. 2.

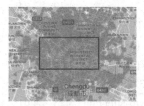

Fig. 2. Parts of Chengdu City, Sichuan Province, China.

4.2 Baselines

In order to specifically judge the performance of our model, we choose seven state-of-the-art models to compare with TAGCN. The baselines are introduced as follows:

- Long Short Term Memory Network (LSTM) [29]: The addition and removal of information can be achieved through the gated structure.
- Gated Recurrent Unit (GRU) [30]: It can realize forgetting and selective memory using one gate.
- Spatial-Temporal Dynamic Network (STDN) [17]: It utilizes CNN, LSTM and attention to obtain spatial-temporal features.
- Graph Convolution Networks (GCN) [22]: It is a generalization of CNN for learning non-grid data in the field of graphs.
- Temporal Graph Convolutional Network (T-GCN) [31]: It combines GCN and GRU to capture the road network topology and the temporal dependence.

- Spatio-Temporal Graph Convolutional Networks (STGCN) [32]: It consists of multiple spatio-temporal convolution modules to capture spatio-temporal correlation.
- Attention Based Spatial-Temporal Graph Convolutional Networks (ASTGCN) [33]: It uses three modules to process three different fragments and the data is processed by two layers of ST blocks.

4.3 Evaluation Index

We use Mean Absolute Error (MAE), Root Mean Square Error (RMSE) and Mean Absolute Percentage Error(MAPE) to evaluate baselines and our model. RMSE is sensitive to the extra-large and extra-small error in the predicted value, so it can well reflect the precision of the model. MAPE is more robust than RMSE. MAE can reflect the real situation of the predicted value error. It can be seen from Table 1 that all the indicators of TAGCN are the smallest.

Table 1. MAE, RMSE and MAPE of each model.

Model	MAE	RMSE	MAPE
LSTM [29]	4.95	7.87	12.43
GRU [30]	4.76	7.61	12.11
GCN [22]	4.39	7.04	11.05
T-GCN [31]	4.21	6.26	9.24
ASTGCN [33]	4.04	5.53	8.01
STDN [17]	3.63	4.79	6.96
STGCN [32]	3.51	4.55	6.37
TAGCN-w/o-attention	3.25	4.01	5.13
TAGCN	**2.96**	**3.75**	**4.56**

4.4 Spatial-Temporal Analysis

Figures 3–6 show the predictions of the taxi's demand in the recreation area, school district, residential area, and business district by eight models. The X-axis represents time, and one unit represents half an hour. The Y-axis represents the demand for taxis. We can see that the prediction results of TAGCN are more accurate than baselines. As can be seen from Fig. 3, 11:00–13:00 and 17:00–20:00 are the peaks for taxi's demand in the recreation area. The reason is that people prepare to leave the area after taking a rest and starting entertainment. It can be seen from Fig. 4 that 11:30–12:30 and 17:00–18:00 are the peaks for taxi's demand in the school district because students leave school during these periods. In Fig. 5, 7:00–8:00 and 12:00–13:00 are the peaks for taxi's demand in the residential area, which are the rush hours before the work time . It can be seen from

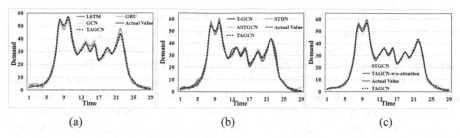

Fig. 3. Demand in recreation area.

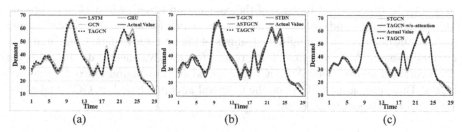

Fig. 4. Demand in school district.

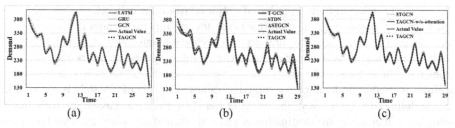

Fig. 5. Demand in residential area.

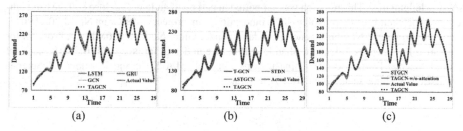

Fig. 6. Demand in business district

Fig. 6 that 11:30–12:00 and 18:00–20:00 are the peaks for taxi's demand in the business district because people knock off work.

The comparisons between TAGCN and LSTM, GRU, and GCN are shown in Figures (a). LSTM and GRU are mainly used to predict sequence information, and they cannot obtain spatial information. GCN can process irregular graph data to obtain spatial characteristics, however, it lacks the capture of temporal characteristics. The comparisons between TAGCN, T-GCN, STDN and ASTGCN are shown in Figures (b). The comparisons of TAGCN with and STGCN and TAGCN-w/o-attention are shown in Figures (c). T-GCN, STDN, ASTGCN, STGCN and TAGCN-w/o-attention can simultaneously obtain spatial and temporal dependence, but it is found that the prediction results of TAGCN for local peaks and edge values are better than baselines. The reason is that traditional neural networks are more difficult to capture long-term dependent information due to the limitation of the size of the convolution kernel, while TCN composed of dilated convolution and casual convolution can extract features across time steps and the temporal attention can highlight the features of the time-series data. Compared with the attention-based ASTGCN model, the reason for the advantage of our model is the TCN mentioned above, while ASTGCN uses standard convolution to extract the time features. Therefore, adding TCN and the temporal attention based on GCN makes the prediction of the model more stable.

5   Conclusion

We proposed a temporal attention-based graph convolution network model, which is used to predict passengers' demand for taxis in each functional area of the city. The model focuses on extracting temporal dependence, spatial information, and highlighting the characteristics of the time-series data. After comparing the indicators and predicted values with some state-of-the-art models, we concluded that TAGCN is superior to the baselines in predicting local peaks and edge values. The role of TAGCN is to assist in the scheduling of taxis to avoid the waste of road resources and passenger time. In the future, we will consider the destination of passengers, and introduce external factors to further improve the accuracy of our model.

Acknowledgments. This research was supported in part by Shandong Province colleges and universities youth innovation technology plan innovation team project under Grant No. 2020KJN011, Shandong Provincial Natural Science Foundation under Grant No. ZR2020MF060, Program for Innovative Postdoctoral Talents in Shandong Province under Grant No. 40618030001, National Natural Science Foundation of China under Grant No. 61802216, and Postdoctoral Science Foundation of China under Grant No.2018M642613.

References

1. Puschmann, T., Alt, R.: Sharing economy. Bus. Inf. Syst. Eng. **58**(1), 93–99 (2016)
2. Hurvich, C.M., Tsai, C.L.: Regression and time series model selection in small samples. Biometrika **76**(2), 297–307 (1989)
3. Saboia, J.L.M.: Autoregressive integrated moving average (ARIMA) models for birth forecasting. J. Am. Stat. Assoc. **72**(358), 264–270 (1977)

4. Maydeu-Olivares, A., Shi, D., Fairchild, A.J.: Estimating causal effects in linear regression models with observational data: the instrumental variables regression model. Psychol. Methods **25**(2), 243 (2020)
5. Patra, A.K.: Adaptive kalman filtering model predictive controller design for stabilizing and trajectory tracking of inverted pendulum. J. Inst. Eng. (India) Ser. B **101**(6), 677–688 (2020)
6. Saadatfar, H., Khosravi, S., Joloudari, J.H.: A new K-nearest neighbors classifier for big data based on efficient data pruning. Mathematics **8**(2), 286 (2020)
7. Yariyan, P., Janizadeh, S., Van Phong, T.: Improvement of best first decision trees using bagging and dagging ensembles for flood probability mapping. Water Resour. Manage. **34**(9), 3037–3053 (2020)
8. Jiang, L., Zhang, L., Yu, L.: Class-specific attribute weighted naive Bayes. Pattern Recogn. **88**, 321–330 (2019)
9. Huang, Y., Zhao, L.: Review on landslide susceptibility mapping using support vector machines. CATENA **165**, 520–529 (2018)
10. Van Gerven, M., Bohte, S.: Artificial neural networks as models of neural information processing. Front. Comput. Neurosci. **11**, 114 (2017)
11. He, Z., Shao, H., Wang, P.: Deep transfer multi-wavelet auto-encoder for intelligent fault diagnosis of gearbox with few target training samples. Knowl. Based Syst. **191**, 105313 (2020)
12. Goodfellow, I.J., et al.: Generative adversarial networks. arXiv preprint arXiv:1406.2661 (2014)
13. Krizhevsky, A., Sutskever, I., Hinton, G.E.: Imagenet classification with deep convolutional neural networks. Adv. Neural. Inf. Process. Syst. **25**, 1097–1105 (2012)
14. Zaremba, W., Sutskever, I., Vinyals, O.: Recurrent neural network regularization. arXiv preprint arXiv:1409.2329 (2014)
15. Liu, L., Qiu, Z., Li, G., Wang, Q., Ouyang, W., Lin, L.: Contextualized spatial–temporal network for taxi origin-destination demand prediction. IEEE Trans. Intell. Transp. Syst. **20**(10), 3875–3887 (2019)
16. Yao, H., et al.: Deep multi-view spatial-temporal network for taxi demand prediction. In: Proceedings of the AAAI Conference on Artificial Intelligence, vol. 32, (2018)
17. Yao, H., Tang, X., Wei, H., Zheng, G., Li, Z.: Revisiting spatial-temporal similarity: A deep learning framework for traffic prediction. In Proceedings of the AAAI Conference on Artificial Intelligence, vol. 33, pp. 5668–5675 (2019)
18. Van Hoai, D.P., Duong, H.-T., Hoang, V.T.: Text recognition for Vietnamese identity card based on deep features network. Int. J. Doc. Anal. Recogn. (IJDAR) **24**(1–2), 123–131 (2021). https://doi.org/10.1007/s10032-021-00363-7
19. Liu, Y., Gu, J., Goyal, N.: Multilingual denoising pre-training for neural machine translation. Trans. Assoc. Comput. Linguist. **8**, 726–742 (2020)
20. Lv, Z., Li, J., Dong, C., Zhao, W.: A deep spatial-temporal network for vehicle trajectory prediction. In: Yu, D., Dressler, F., Yu, J. (eds.) WASA 2020. LNCS, vol. 12384, pp. 359–369. Springer, Cham (2020). https://doi.org/10.1007/978-3-030-59016-1_30
21. Cai, Z., Zheng, X., Yu, J.: A differential-private framework for urban traffic flows estimation via taxi companies. IEEE Trans. Industr. Inf. **15**(12), 6492–6499 (2019)
22. Michaël, D., Xavier, B., Pierre, V.: Convolutional neural networks on graphs with fast localized spectral filtering. Neural Inf. Process. Syst. **3**(1), 1–9 (2016)
23. Scarselli, F., Gori, M., Tsoi, A.C., Hagenbuchner, M., Monfardini, G.: The graph neural network model. IEEE Trans. Neural Netw. **20**(1), 61–80 (2008)
24. Perozzi, B., Al-Rfou, R., Skiena, S.: Deepwalk: Online learning of social representations. In: Proceedings of the 20th ACM SIGKDD International Conference on Knowledge Discovery and Data Mining, pp. 701–710 (2014)

25. Grover, A., Leskovec, J.: Node2vec: scalable feature learning for networks. In: Proceedings of the 22nd ACM SIGKDD International Conference on Knowledge Discovery and Data Mining, pp. 855–864 (2016)
26. Cai, Z., Zheng, X.: A private and efficient mechanism for data uploading in smart cyber-physical systems. IEEE Trans. Netw. Sci. Eng. 7(2), 766–775 (2018)
27. David Cruz-Uribe, S.F.O., Moen, K.: One and two weight norm inequalities for Riesz potentials. Ill. J. Math. 57(1), 295–323 (2013)
28. Bai, S., Kolter, J.Z., Koltun, V.: An empirical evaluation of generic convolutional and recurrent networks for sequence modeling. arXiv preprint arXiv:1803.01271 (2018)
29. Sepp, H., Jürgen, S.: Long short-term memory. Neural Comput. 9(8), 1735–1780 (1997)
30. Chung, J., Gulcehre, C., Cho, K., Bengio, Y.: Empirical evaluation of gated recurrent neural networks on sequence modeling. arXiv preprint arXiv:1412.3555 (2014)
31. Ling, Z., et al.: T-GCN: a temporal graph convolutional network for traffic prediction. IEEE Trans. Intell. Transp. Syst. 21(9), 3848–3858 (2019)
32. Bing, Y., Haoteng, Y., Zhanxing, Z.: Spatiotemporal graph convolutional networks: a deep learning framework for traffic prediction. Int. Jt. Conf. Artif. Intell. Organ. 4(1), 3634–3640 (2017)
33. Guo, S., Lin, Y., Feng, N., Song, C., Wan, H.: Attention based spatial-temporal graph convolutional networks for traffic flow forecasting. In: Proceedings of the AAAI Conference on Artificial Intelligence, vol. 33, no. 01, pp. 922–929 (2019)
34. Qing, G., Zhu, S., Jie, Z., Yinleng, T.: An attentional recurrent neural network for personalized next location recommendation. In: AAAI Conference on Artificial Intelligence (AAAI 34), pp. 83–90 New York (2020)
35. Mason, J.C., Handscomb, D.C.: Chebyshev Polynomials. CRC Press (2002)

MSCNN: Steganographer Detection Based on Multi-Scale Convolutional Neural Networks

Jinglan Yang[1(✉)], Chao Dong[2], Feng Zhang[3], Min Lei[1], and Xu Bai[1]

[1] Information Security Center, Beijing University of Posts and Telecommunications, Beijing 100876, China
{yang_jinglan,leimin}@bupt.edu.cn, 2020140821@bupt.cn
[2] State Information Center, Beijing 100045, China
dongchao@cegn.gov.cn
[3] School of Computer Science and Technology,
Nanjing University of Aeronautics and Astronautics, Nanjing 210016, China

Abstract. Steganographer detection aims to find guilty user who spread images containing secret information among many innocent users. Feature extraction is an important step in steganographer detection. The challenge is that the existing steganalytic feature extraction of steganographer detection is mostly based on manually designed features. A steganographer detection algorithm based on multi-scale convolutional networks (MSCNN_SD) is proposed to automatically extract steganalytic features in the paper. MSCNN_SD introduces the residual maps and quantization truncation idea of classical SRM into deep convolution network. MSCNN_SD uses a set of filters to extract rich residual information and uses a number of quantized truncation combinations are introduced to discretize the residual maps. Finally, two parallel deep learning subnets are used to learn the features of different scale residuals. The simulation results illustrate that the proposed MSCNN_SD method is superior to the state-of-the-art method. MSCNN_SD uses a well-trained model of one steganography payload, which can detect different steganography and payloads used by steganographer. At the same time, MSCNN_SD has a good detection effect when the steganographer uses the hybrid steganography strategy .

Keywords: Steganography · Steganographer detection · Deep learning

1 Introduction

The information encrypted by secret key is often garbled, which is easy to be found by attackers [1]. As an information hiding technology, steganography embeds secret messages [2] into the original carrier to hidden communication without causing human perception, thus reducing the possibility of being attacked [3]. Steganographer detection aims to find guilty user who spread images containing secret information among

This research was supported by CCF-Tencent Open Fund WeBank Special Funding, the National Key R&D Program of China (No. 2017YFB0802803).

Z. Liu et al. (Eds.): WASA 2021, LNCS 12937, pp. 215–226, 2021.
https://doi.org/10.1007/978-3-030-85928-2_17

many innocent users [4]. Research on steganographer detection technology is of great significance for monitoring the communication between illegal organizations.

Initially, Ker et al. [5] transformed the batch steganography problem into steganographer detection, extracted steganalytic features from images, then calculate the Maximum Mean Distance (MMD) of the feature set, and finally use Agglomerative Hierarchical Clustering (AHC) to detect steganographer. Subsequently, Ker et al. [6] converted the steganographer detection task into an outlier detection task. The Local Outlier Factor (LOF) algorithm was used to detect the steganographer.

The framework of steganographer detection can be summarized as three steps: feature extraction, user distance measurement and steganographer detection [7]. Feature extraction is an important step in steganographer detection algorithm [8]. The manual design method is unsuitable for multiple steganography and embedding rate detection.

In order to solve the problem of steganalytic feature design, Zhong et al. [9] first proposed using AlexNet network in steganographer detection. However, the detection target of image recognition is visible, but the difference between cover image and stego image is not visible. Then, the network is not very ideal.

In order to improve the generalization ability of feature extraction network, it can effectively extract the steganalytic features under various steganography and embedding rate. A steganographer detection algorithm based on multi-scale convolutional net-works (MSCNN_SD) is proposed in the paper. Compared with other steganographer detection feature extraction networks, MSCNN_SD introduces the residual extraction and quantized truncation of the classical Spatial Rich Model (SRM) [10] into the deep learning network, using a group of filters to extract rich residual infor-mation from the input images. Based on the extracted multi-dimensional residual maps, multiple groups of quantized truncation combinations are introduced for dis-cretization, and the residual information in different scales is obtained. Finally, two parallel deep learning subnets are used for feature learning of multi-scale residual maps.

The simulation results showed that the accuracy of MSCNN for steganalysis was 80.55%, which was higher than 74.99% in XuNet and 75.61% in YeNet. Trained by WOW with 0.4 bpp, the accuracy of MSCNN_SD in detecting Hugo with 0.1 bpp was 96%, and that in detecting S_UNIWARD with 0.1 bpp is 100%. MSCNN_SD can realize steganographer detection about multiple steganography and payloads.

2 Proposed Method

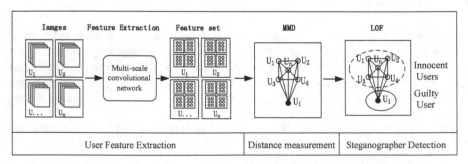

Fig. 1. The steganographer detection algorithm framework of MSCNN_SD.

Figure 1 illustrates the proposed MSCNN_SD framework, which mainly includes three steps. Firstly, a trained MSCNN network is used to extract the features of each image transmitted by users. Then, the MMD distance between users is calculated based on the extracted features as the similarity between users. Finally, the outlier detection LOF algorithm is used to detect the steganographer.

2.1   Multi-scale Convolution Network

Similar to steganalysis, the key to the steganographer detection algorithm is whether it can extract differentiated steganalytic features. Multi-scale convolutional network (MSCNN) is a feature extraction network in MSCNN_SD. Figure 2 shows the structure of MSCNN.

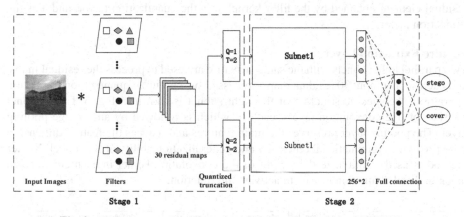

Fig. 2. The steganographer detection algorithm framework of MSCNN.

Pre-processing Layer
MSCNN uses high-pass filter to preprocess the input image in the pre-processing layer. In the SRM model, a total of 78 filters were used to obtain the residual maps, to suppress the image content as much as possible, and to extract the weak steganography noise information. In order to fully reflect the features of pixels in different directions and ranges, control the feature dimension within a reasonable range, and reduce the cost of model training. Inspired by YeNet [11] network, this paper selects 30 filters from SRM filters to extract residual images.

The calculation of residuals can be realized through the convolution, and the input image is convolved as follows:

$$y = I * K \tag{1}$$

Where y is the residual maps obtained after convolution, I denotes the input image, * is the convolution operator, and K is the convolution kernel.

In order to retain the residual elements with strong correlation between adjacent pixels [12], the magnitude of the residual maps is adjusted appropriately through quantization operation, and the residual information is restricted within a certain dynamic range through truncation operation. The quantization truncation operation will increase the degree of discretization of the residuals and improve the detection performance of the model. The processing procedure is to use a predefined quantization step q to quantify each element in the residual characteristic information first, and then use a given threshold T to cut the element. The processing formula is as follows:

$$y_i = f(x_i) = \begin{cases} \min([^{x_i}/_q], T), x_i \geq 0 \\ \max([^{x_i}/_q], -T), x_i < 0 \end{cases} \tag{2}$$

Where y is the residual element after quantization and truncation processing, x is the residual element obtained by the filter kernel, q is the quantization factor, and T is the truncation factor.

Feature Extraction Layer

Two parallel light subnets with the same structure are used to process the residual maps, and each subnet input 30 residual maps processed by a group of quantization truncation operators. The specific structure of the light subnet is shown in Fig. 3. Light subnet consists of five convolution layers, each of which is followed by an average pooling layer. The pooling layer preserves the main features and reduces the feature dimension to improve the computational efficiency and generalization ability of the model. Xavier method is used to initialize the weight of the convolution kernel in each convolution layer, and ReLu function is used to activate the function.

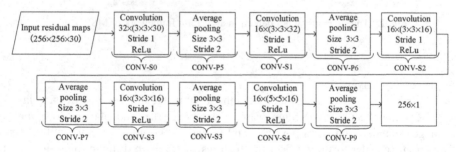

Fig. 3. Light subnet framework for feature extraction.

Classification Layer

MSCNN needs a process of training and learning. Two groups of 256-dimension features are obtained through two parallel subnets, which are combined to obtain a single 512-dimensional features, and then input the features to the classification layer.

Classification layer is composed of three full connection layer and Softmax function, the first full connection layer including 512 neurons, the second full connection layer including 256 neurons, the third full connection layer including 128 neurons, Finally, the Softmax function outputs the prediction probability,

In the process of steganographer detection, Softmax function is removed. The well trained model extracts 128 dimensional features as the steganalytic features of each image, which are directly used in the steganographer detection.

2.2 User Distance Calculation

The steganographer detection task takes the user as the unit and takes all the features of each user obtained from the image of each user through the feature extraction network as a set. In order to measure the distribution distance between users' features, literature [5] proposed to use MMD to measure the distribution distance between two users. MMD is mainly used to measure the distance between two different but related distributions and to measure the similarity of the distribution of feature sets of two users. The smaller the MMD is, the more similar the distribution of two users is.

A set $U = \{U_1, U_2, ..., U_n\}$ composed of n users, each user spreads m images, and the image feature set obtained by each images is $I = \{f_1, f_2, ..., f_{128}\}$, the feature set obtained by each user is $F = \{I_1, I_2, ..., I_m\}$. Assuming that the feature set a_1 extracted by the user U_A is $F_A = \{I_{a0}, I_{a1}, ..., I_{am}\}$, and the feature set b_1 extracted by the user U_B is $F_B = \{I_{b0}, I_{b1}, ..., I_{bm}\}$. Then the MMD between the two users is $MMD(U_A, U_B)$, The calculation formula is:

$$MMD(U_A, U_B) = \sqrt{\frac{1}{m^2}\sum_{i,j=1}^{m} k(I_{a_i}, I_{a_j}) - \frac{2}{m^2}\sum_{i,j=1}^{m} k(I_{a_i}, I_{b_j}) + \frac{1}{m^2}\sum_{i,j=1}^{m} k(I_{b_i}, I_{b_j})} \quad (3)$$

In the formula, k is the kernel function, Gaussian kernel function is used in this article, and the calculation formula is:

$$k(a, b) = \exp(\frac{-||a - b||^2}{\delta}) \quad (4)$$

2.3 Steganographer Detection

LOF is used to detect the steganographer. All the features extracted by n users are taken as a set $U = \{U_1, U_2, ..., U_n\}$, for any two users in the set U_A, U_B, the k-th distance of U_A is defined as $d(U_A, U_O)$, and the distance between U_A and U_B is $d(U_A, U_B)$, then the calculation formula of the k-th reachable distance is $r_k(U_A, U_B) = \max\{d(U_A, U_O), d(U_A, U_B)\}$.

The set U_K is defined as all points within the k-th distance of the U_A. For all points $U_B \subset U_k$, the calculation formula of local reachable density is:

$$lrd_k(U_A) = (\frac{1}{k}\sum_{U_B \in U_K} r_k(U_A, U_B))^{-1} \quad (5)$$

The local outlier factor of U_A is expressed as:

$$lof_k(U_A) = \frac{1}{k}\sum_{U_B \in U_K} \frac{lrd_k(U_A)}{lrd_k(U_B)} \quad (6)$$

The LOF value of each user represents the degree of anomaly, and all user's LOF value in the set are calculated, where the user with the highest LOF value is defined as steganographer.

3   Analysis of Simulation Results

A series of experiments will be carried out on the BOSSbase ver1.01 dataset, including 10000 grayscale cover images with the size of 512×512. The method proposed in [13] is used to crop each image in the dataset into four non-overlapping sub-images with the size of 256×256, and 40000 grayscale cover images are obtained.

In the experiments, the default settings of the proposed method are listed as follows. For the pre-processing network, the values of the two quantization truncation groups are $Q = 1$, $T = 2$ and $Q = 2$, $T = 2$ [14]. The training set includes 16000 cover images and corresponding stego images. The validation set includes 4000 cover images and corresponding stego images. The stego images used in the verification set and training set is steganographed by WOW [15] with a payload of 0.4 bpp. The test set includes 20000 cover images and corresponding stego images. The S-UNIWARD [16], HUGO [17] and WOW are used to steganography the images with the embedding rate of 0.1 bpp, 0.2 bpp, 0.3 bpp and 0.4 bpp, and the corresponding stego images are obtained.

Currently, there are few deep learning networks used for steganographer detection in the existing work. Therefore, the SRMQ1, XuNet [18], and YeNet network are used for comparative experiments in feature extraction. SRMQ1_SD steganographer detection algorithms is composed of feature extraction networks SRMQ1 and LOF algorithm. XuNet_SD steganographer detection algorithms is composed of feature extraction networks XuNet and LOF algorithm. The YeNet network used in this paper removes the knowledge about the selection channels, followed by the LOF algorithm to form the steganographer detection framework YeNet_SD. In the test phase, all the features extracted by the deep learning model come from the previous layer of the network output layer.

In the experiment, 100 users were set up, and each user randomly selected 200 images from the test set [19]. Only one user is selected as guilty user, who will spread stego images generated by steganography algorithm. Other 99 users as innocent users spread cover images without any hidden secret information. All experiments were conducted on a GPU and repeated 100 times, and the number of experiments that can get the correct result is accumulated as p. The final evaluation of accuracy is $ACC = {p}/{100} \times 100\%$. The above is the default setting of the training network and users. More specific details will be given in subsequent experiments.

3.1   The Effectiveness for Steganalysis

The important step and premise of steganographer detection is to extract distinguishing steganalytic features. MSCNN feature extraction network is the main part of the MSCNN_SD proposed in this paper. Before evaluating the performance of steganographer detection, we first verify the effectiveness of the proposed MSCNN network for steganalysis.

MSCNN network introduces multiple groups of quantized truncation. In order to evaluate the effect on the convergence rate and performance of the network, this experiment compares two groups of quantized truncation networks (MSCNN), one group of quantized truncation networks (MSCNN_QT1), and the network without quantized truncation (MSCNN_NQT). Table 1 shows the training accuracy of the three networks when the training epoch is 100.

Table 1. Training accuracy of different quantized truncated when the training epoch is 100.

Models	Accuracy (%)
MSCNN	73.17%
MSCNN_QT1	70.72%
MSCNN_NQT	68.55%

It can be seen from Table 1 that for the same training epoch, the accuracy increases with the increase of quantization truncation groups, indicating that multiple quantization truncation groups can improve the performance of the feature extraction network. At the same time, considering that the more quantization truncation groups, the more subnets are needed. Considering the limitations of hardware equipment, this article only selects two groups quantitative truncation.

In order to analyze the effectiveness of the MSCNN network for steganalysis further, the experiment compares the classic steganalysis algorithm SRMQ1, XuNet, and YeNet. The stego images used in the testing stage are processed by the WOW with the payload of 0.4 bpp.

Table 2. The accuracy of different models in steganalysis of WOW when payload is 0.4 bpp.

Models	Accuracy
SRMQ1	73.21%
XuNet	74.99%
YeNet	75.61%
MSCNN	80.55%
MSCNN_QT1	76.80%
MSCNN_NQT	71.74%

Table 2 shows the accuracy of different networks in steganalysis. Firstly, it can be seen that with the increase of quantitative truncation groups, the accuracy of steganalysis improves, indicating that the quantitative truncation groups are helpful to the network proposed in this article.

Secondly, the accuracy of the proposed method reaches 80.55%, which is higher than 74.99% in XuNet and 75.61% in YeNet. The experimental results show that the accuracy of MSCNN for steganalysis is 80.55%, which is higher than 74.99% in XuNet and 75.61% in YeNet. This shows that the proposed parallel subnet structure of quantized truncation combination improves the effect of steganalysis, and the extracted features are more distinguishable and expressive.

3.2 The Effectiveness for Steganographer Detection

To validate the effectiveness of the MSCNN_SD proposed in this paper for the steganographer detection, this experiment compares the YeNet_SD, XuNet_SD and SRMQ1_SD steganographer detection algorithms. The steganographer uses the WOW steganography algorithm with a payload of 0.4 bpp. In addition, due to the proposed MSCNN_SD algorithm is based on the MMD distance between users. The relationship between MMD distance between users are calculated to study the relationship between user distance and steganographer detection accuracy.

AD1 is defined as the average MMD distance between innocent user and innocent user. AD2 is defined as the average MMD distance between innocent user and guilty user. The smaller the AD1 value is, the more similar the innocent users are. The larger the AD2 value is, the smaller the similarity between the innocent user and the guilty user. The LOF algorithm detects steganographer through the method of local density. Therefore, the larger the value of AD2/AD1, the better the detection effect is. Table 3 shows the distance between users and the accuracy of different steganographer detection algorithms.

Table 3. The detection accuracy of different steganographer detection algorithms on the WOW algorithm with 0.4 bpp.

Models	Dimensions	AD1	AD2	AD2/AD1	ACC (%)
XuNet_SD	128	0.0214	0.2473	11.5560	100
YeNet_SD	144	0.283	0.2624	9.2720	100
SRMQ1_SD	12753	0.0194	0.0201	0.1036	4
MSCNN_SD	128	0.0278	0.8080	29.0647	100

The MSCNN_SD, XuNet_SD and YeNet_SD steganographer detection accuracy are all 100%. However, the AD2/AD1 value of MSCNN_SD is larger than that of XuNet_SD and YeNet_SD, which shows that the steganalytic features of guilty users extracted by the proposed method are more different from those of innocent users.

Meanwhile, the detection accuracy of SRMQ1_SD is only 4%.The accuracy of SRMQ1 for steganalysis is 73.21%, which indicates that the feature extracted from network can distinguish cover images from stego images. However, since steganographer detection is based on MMD distance, the dimension of feature extracted from SRMQ1 network is as high as 12753. High dimensional features may bring dimension disaster, making the difference between AD1 and AD2 small, leading to the failure of SRMQ1_SD method.

3.3 The Effectiveness for Detecting Different Steganography and Payloads

The steganography and payloads used by steganographer may different from the training stage. Therefore, the steganographer detection network needs to have generalization ability, which can detect the strategies of different payloads and steganography used by steganographer.

The experiments were carried out with WOW, HUGO and S_UNIWARD. Each algorithm uses four payloads of 0.1 bpp, 0.2 bpp, 0.3 bpp and 0.4 bpp to generate the stego image. At the same time, the results of the previous experiment show that the SRMQ1_SD method is not suitable for steganographer detection, so the comparison algorithm only uses XuNet_SD and YeNet_SD.

It can be seen from Fig. 4 that when the steganographer uses the WOW and the payload is greater than 0.1 bpp, the accuracy of the three steganographer detection algorithms is 100%, which indicates that the three steganographer detection algorithms are effective for steganographer detection with multiple payloads. When the payload is 0.1 bpp, the detection accuracy of MSCNN_SD and YeNet_SD is also 100%, and the detection accuracy of XuNet_SD is 90%, indicating that the detection effect of MSCNN_SD and YeNet_SD for multiple steganography is better than XuNet_SD.

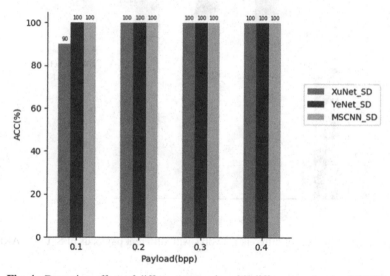

Fig. 4. Detection effect of different networks with different payloads of WOW.

It can be seen from Fig. 5 and Fig. 6, when the payload is 0.1 bpp, the accuracy of XuNet_SD and YeNet_SD for HUGO and S_UNIWARD is severely reduced. The accuracy of MSCNN_SD is 96% for Hugo and 100% S_UNIWARD. It shows that MSCNN_SD is far more effective in steganographer detection in the case of multiple steganography and multiple payloads, especially for low payloads, MSCNN_SD is far better than XuNet_SD and YeNet_SD.

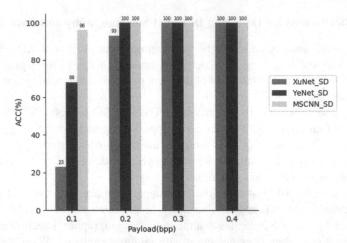

Fig. 5. Detection effect of different networks with different payloads of HUGO.

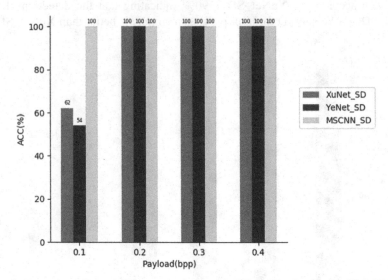

Fig. 6. Detection effect of different networks with different payloads of S_UNIWARD.

3.4 The Effectiveness for Detecting the Hybrid Steganography

In order to test the MSCNN_SD algorithm when the steganographer uses the hybrid steganography strategy. The images transmitted by steganographers were divided into three groups, each group was generated by one steganography with the same embedding rate, using HUGO, S-UNIWARD and WOW respectively. When the payload is greater than 0.2 bpp, the detection effect of different feature extraction network achieves better results. Therefore, the payload used in this experiment is 0.1 bpp. The experimental comparison algorithm uses XuNet_SD and YeNet_SD.

Table 4. Performance of different methods when a mixed stegography strategy is used.

Models	AD1	AD2	AD2/AD1	ACC (%)
XuNet_SD	0.0214	0.0515	2.1369	100
YeNet_SD	0.0254	0.0661	2.6023	100
MSCNN_SD	0.0182	0.0887	4.8736	100

It can be seen from Table 4 that the detection effect of different steganographer algorithms is 100% when using hybrid steganography strategy. In experiment 3.3, the detection effect of XuNet_SD and YeNet_SD are not as good as that of hybrid steganography strategy when only using Hugo or S_UNIWARD steganography under 0.1 bpp payload. The reason is that when the stegangrapher uses the strategy of mixed steganography, the feature set contains a variety of steganalytic features of steganography. Using MMD distance to calculate the feature distance with other innocent users, the feature differences are accumulated, which is helpful for steganographer detection.

In addition, in steganalysis, when the training payload and detection payload is different, the detection effect of steganalysis will drop sharply. It is difficult to achieve the ideal effect when using the hybrid steganography strategy. But if the steganographer detection algorithm is used, it can help the steganographer detection process, which also shows the importance of steganographer detection.

4 Conclusion

The accuracy of WOW detection by the MSCNN network was 80.55%, indicating that the features extracted by MSCNN can be used to distinguish between guilty user and innocent users. In addition, compared with the application of other steganalysis networks in steganographer detection, the MSCNN_SD algorithm shows better performance in the multiple steganography and multiple payloads steganographer detection. In the hybrid steganography strategy detection, even at a low payload of 0.1 bpp, the steganographer detection accuracy of MSCNN_SD is 100%. Although the algorithm proposed in this article is effective, it still has shortcomings. For example, the pre-processing layer of the feature extraction of MSCNN_SD uses the spatial residual filter, which can only detect gray images, but cannot extract the steganalytic features of color images. Future research may be able to design a universal steganalytic feature extraction model for both of color images and gray images.

References

1. Ge, C., Susilo, W., Wang, J., et al.: A key-policy attribute-based proxy re-encryption without random oracles. Comput. J. **59**(7), 970–982 (2016)
2. Wang, G, Liu, H, Wang, C, et al.: Revocable attribute based encryption in cloud storage. IEEE Trans. Dependable Secure Comput. (2021)
3. Fang, L., Susilo, W., Ge, C., et al.: Public key encryption with keyword search secure against keyword guessing attacks without random oracle. Inf. Sci. **238**, 221–241 (2013)

4. Li, F., Wen, M., Lei, J., Ren, Y.: Efficient steganographer detection over social networks with sampling reconstruction. Peer-to-Peer Netw. Appl. **11**(5), 924–939 (2017). https://doi.org/10. 1007/s12083-017-0603-3

5. Ker, A.D., Pevny, T., et al.: A new paradigm for steganalysis via clustering. In: Proceedings of the Conference on Media Watermarking, Secruity, and Forensics III, pp. 78800U-1–78800U-13 (2011)

6. Ker, A.D, Pevny, T., et al.: The steganographer is the outlier: realistic large-scale steganalysis. IEEE Trans. Inf. Forensics Secur. **9**, 424–1435 (2014)

7. Zheng, M, Zhang, S.H., Wu, S., et al.: Steganographer detection via deep residual network. In: Proceedings of the IEEE International Conference on Multimedia & Expo, pp. 235–240. IEEE Computer Society, ICME, Buet (2017)

8. Qian, Y., Dong, J., Wang, W., Tan, T.: Feature learning for steganalysis using convolutional neural networks. Multimedia Tools Appl. **77**(15), 19633–19657 (2017). https://doi.org/10. 1007/s11042-017-5326-1

9. Zhong, S.H., Wang, Y.T., Ren, T.W., et al.: Steganographer detection via multi-scale embedding probability estimation. ACM Trans. Multimedia Comput. Commun. Appl. (TOMM) (2019)

10. Fridrich, J., Kodovsky, J.: Rich models for steganalysis of digital images. IEEE Trans. Inf. Forensics Secur. **7**(3), 868–882 (2012)

11. Ye, J., Ni, J., Yi, Y.: Deep learning hierarchical representations for image steganalysis. IEEE Trans. Inf. Forensics Secur. **12**(11), 2545–2557 (2017)

12. Tang, W.X., Tan, S.Q., Li, B., et al.: Automatic steganographic distortion learning using a generative adversarial network. IEEE Signal Process. Lett. **24**(99), 1547–1551 (2017)

13. Zheng, M.J., Zhong, S.H., Wu, S.T., et al.: Steganographer detection based on multi-class dilated residual networks. In: Proceedings of the ACM International Conference on Multimedia Retrieval, pp. 300–308. ACM Multimedia, Yokohama (2018)

14. Zeng, J.S., Tan, S.Q., Li, B., et al.: Pre-training via fitting deep neural network to rich-model features extraction procedure and its effect on deep learning for steganalysis. Electron. Imaging **2017**(7), 44–49 (2017)

15. Pevný, T., Filler, T., Bas, P.: Using high-dimensional image models to perform highly undetectable steganography. In: Böhme, R., Fong, P.W.L., Safavi-Naini, R. (eds.) IH 2010. LNCS, vol. 6387, pp. 161–177. Springer, Heidelberg (2010). https://doi.org/10.1007/978-3-642-16435-4_13

16. Holub, V., Fridrich, J., et al.: Designing steganographic distortion using directional filters. In: IEEE Workshop on Information Forensic and Security. pp. 234–239. IEEE, Tenerife (2012)

17. Holub, V., Fridrich, J., et al.: Digital image steganography using universal distortion. In: Proceedings of the First ACM Workshop on Information Hiding and Multimedia Security, pp.59–68. IH&MMSEC, Montpellier (2013)

18. Xu, G., Wu, H.Z., Shi, Y.Q., et al.: Structural design of convolutional neural networks for steganalysis. IEEE Signal Process. Lett. **23**(5), 708–712 (2016)

19. Zheng, M.J., Zhong, S.H., Wu, S.T., et al.: Steganographer detection based on multi-class dilated residual networks. In: Proceedings of the ACM International Conference on Multimedia Retrieval, pp. 300–308. .ICMR, Yokohama (2018)

MFAGCN: Multi-Feature Based Attention Graph Convolutional Network for Traffic Prediction

Haoran Li, Jianbo Li$^{(\boxtimes)}$, Zhiqiang Lv$^{(\boxtimes)}$, and Zhihao Xu

College of Computer Science and Technology, Qingdao University, Qingdao 266071, China
lijianbo@qdu.edu.cn

Abstract. Large-scale traffic data mining provides a new solution to alleviate traffic congestion and improves traffic service. As an important part of traffic data analysis, traffic multi-feature prediction is widely concerned, and several machine learning algorithms are also applied in this field. However, this is very challenging, because each traffic feature has a highly nonlinear and complex pattern, and there are great differences between multiple features. A large number of the existing traffic feature prediction methods focus on extracting a single traffic feature and lack the ability of analyzing multiple features. This paper proposes a new multi-feature based attention graph convolutional network (MFAGCN) to solve the problem of the prediction of multiple features in traffic, the proposed method has 4.53% improved to the conventional methods. The three features predicted by MFAGCN are traffic flow, occupancy rate, and vehicle speed. Each feature is modeled with three temporal attributes, namely weekly period, daily period, and nearest period. In this paper, multi-feature prediction mainly includes two parts: (1) Establish a spatiotemporal attention mechanism for capturing the dynamic spatiotemporal correlation of multiple features. (2) Different convolutional kernels and activation functions are used for each feature after splitting. The experimental results on real traffic datasets have verified the effectiveness of the MFAGCN .

Keywords: Multi-feature prediction · Spatiotemporal attention mechanism · Graph convolutional network

1 Introduction

In recent years, many countries have been vigorously developing intelligent transportation, which helps to achieve efficient traffic management, and traffic prediction is an indispensable part. A large number of diverse traffic data with geographic and time information can be obtained, which provides data support for realizing simultaneous prediction of multiple traffic features.

Nowadays, researchers have designed several time-series-based models to predict traffic. Adopting graph convolutional networks (GCN) [14], researchers have begun to integrate the spatial feature of the traffic data, and propose temporal graph convolutional network (TGCN) for traffic prediction methods. However, TGCN [3] has obtained relatively fewer spatial attributes, which limits the prediction ability of TGCN's prediction

© Springer Nature Switzerland AG 2021
Z. Liu et al. (Eds.): WASA 2021, LNCS 12937, pp. 227–239, 2021.
https://doi.org/10.1007/978-3-030-85928-2_18

ability to some extent. For instance, Yu et al. proposed a spatiotemporal graph convolutional network (STGCN) [2] for traffic prediction methods which combined convolutional layers and convolutional sequence learning layers to simulate spatial and temporal correlations. Guo et al. proposed a graph convolutional neural network based on spatiotemporal attention (ASTGCN) [1], which highlighted the spatiotemporal features of the traffic data by acquiring temporal and spatial attention of traffic information. However, the above neural networks only predict one certain type of traffic data, ignoring the dynamic correlation between various traffic data [31]. To predict traffic conditions more accurately, a variety of traffic data needs to be analyzed and compared for achieving high-precision traffic prediction methods. Explore multiple traffic features in different value ranges, discover its inherent temporal and spatial patterns, and make accurate simultaneous predictions of multiple features are challenging problems.

To solve the above problems, we propose a new deep learning model: multi-feature based attention Graph Convolutional Network (MFAGCN).

The contributions of this work are summarized as follow:

- We propose a multi-feature based attention graph convolutional network for traffic prediction (MFAGCN). The attention mechanism is used to highlight the temporal and spatial features, and GCN is used to extract the spatial feature of the traffic data, and then the original traffic data is combined with the temporal and spatial features to highlight the temporal and spatial correlation of the traffic data.
- Most existing models can only predict a single feature, while our model can jointly predict multiple features in traffic data, i.e., average traffic volume, road occupancy rate, and average vehicle speed.
- The MFAGCN is evaluated on two real traffic datasets. Experiments show that our model is better than the existing baselines.

2 Related Work

Compared with traditional models, the deep learning model can capture nonlinear features and has achieved good results in computer vision and natural language processing. Zhang et al. [37] proposed the spatiotemporal residual networks (ST-ResNet) based on residual convolutional unit, which can predict the crowd flow, the spatiotemporal dynamic network for taxi demand prediction proposed by Yao et al. [18] can dynamically learn the similarity between locations. However, these methods cannot fit spatial feature well leading to low accuracy. Benefiting from the GCN, researchers can obtain spatial feature between traffic data through graph convolution. GCN-based models, like TGCN and STGCN, failed to extract the spatiotemporal features of traffic data well. Liang et al. [18] proposed a multi-level attention network that adaptively adjusts the correlation of time series in 2018, and achieved remarkable results in time series prediction. Guo et al. [1] proposed a spatiotemporal attention-based graph convolutional network (ASTGCN), which used the attention mechanism to highlight the spatiotemporal features of the traffic data, and then adopted the graph convolutional neural network to extract the spatiotemporal features. Although good results have been achieved in traffic flow prediction [15], only considering a single traffic feature will cause lots of errors when judging the road condition.

Driven by the above studies, a new neural network is proposed here, which can capture the complex temporal and spatial feature of the traffic data, and complete the task of prediction of much traffic data.

3 Model Design

3.1 Data Partition

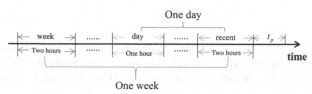

Fig. 1. An example of the input data for constructing traffic prediction method. (Color figure online)

(1) Recent segment: the recent value selects the data X_h of two hours before the predicted period t_p, then $X_h = (X_{t_p-24}, X_{t_p-23}, \ldots, X_{t_p}) \in R^{N \times F \times T_h}$, as shown in the green area in Fig. 1, because the traffic conditions gradually change over time. Therefore, the future traffic conditions will be affected by the traffic conditions in the first two hours.

(2) Daily-periodic segment: the daily cycle selects the previous hour data in the same period of the previous day, t_p, then the input data is defined as, $X_d = (X_{t_p-24*12-12}, X_{t_p-24*12-11}, \ldots, X_{t_p-24*12}) \in R^{N \times F \times T_d}$, as shown in the yellow area in Fig. 1, due to the regularity of human lives, the daily similar rules exist in traffic data. The daily cycle highlights the regularity of traffic data and plays an important role in the accurate prediction of the traffic data.

(3) Weekly-periodic segment: the weekly period selects the first two hours of the same period in the previous week, then $X_w = (X_{t_p-7*24*12-24}, X_{t_p-7*24*12-23}, \ldots, X_{t_p-7*24*12}) \in R^{N \times F \times T_w}$, as shown in the red area in Fig. 1, the historical data of the weekly period is the same as the predicted traffic data. Therefore, weekly cycled data is mainly used to capture the weekly cycled features in traffic data.

The MFAGCN network structure is shown in Fig. 2. For the input data of the three different periods, three components are designed for data processing respectively. Each component embeds attention mechanism to highlight the spatiotemporal features of the input traffic data and uses GCN to extract the spatiotemporal features of the traffic data. After feature extraction, the traffic data is spliced together, and the fused outputs from different components are obtained through a fully connected layer. The output of the predicted data and the real data are respectively trained to reduce the loss [37], which is

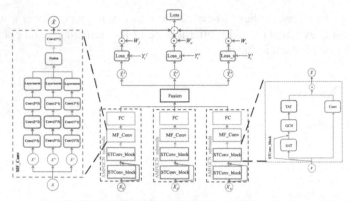

Fig. 2. The structure of MFAGCN. STConv_block is a spatiotemporal convolutional module including attention mechanism; MF_Conv is a multi-feature convolutional module; FC is a fully connected layer; SAT is a spatial attention mechanism; TAT is a temporal attention mechanism.

multiplied by a learnable parameter and added together to generate a total loss. In Fig. 2, W_1, W_2, $W_3 \in R$ are learnable parameters. During the optimization process, affected by the learnable parameters W_1, W_2, $W_3 \in R$, the optimizer will automatically adjust the weights of the three traffic data to achieve the effect of simultaneously optimizing multiple features with one optimizer.

3.2 Spatiotemporal Convolution

To capture the temporal and spatial features of the traffic data, this paper proposes a new spatiotemporal attention mechanism, which includes spatial and temporal attention [29].

Spatial Attention. Generally, the traffic conditions between two adjacent points will affect each other, so the traffic data presents a strong spatial correlation. In this work, the spatial attention mechanism is chosen to capture the dynamic correlation of the space [33].

Take the spatial attention mechanism in the weekly-periodic segment component as an example [35]:

$$S = V_S \cdot relu((X_w W_1) W_2(X_w) + b_S) \tag{1}$$

$$S'_{i,j} = \frac{e^{S^{i,j}}}{\sum_{i=1}^{N} e^{S^{i,j}}} \tag{2}$$

where $X_w = (X_1, X_2, \ldots, X_r) \in R^{N \times F \times r}$ represents all the features of all traffic nodes with r time-series length. $W_1 \in R^r$, $W_2 \in R^{F \times r}$, $W_3 \in R^F$, $V_S \in R^{N \times N}$, $b_S \in R^{1 \times N \times N}$, are all learnable parameters, *relu* is the activation function, $relu = max(0, x)$, compared with the sigmoid activation function used in ASTGCN [1], *relu* can reduce the amount of calculation, accelerate the training speed, avoid the disappearance of the gradient during the training process, and thus solve the convergence problem of the deep network. In graph convolution, the adjoint matrix and the spatial attention. The weight matrix is combined to extract the spatial feature of the traffic data [10].

Temporal Attention. In the time dimension, different periods of the same node have mutual influence, and the degree of mutual influence is different in various situations [38]. In this work, the attention mechanism is used to highlight the temporal feature in traffic data.

Take the temporal attention mechanism in the weekly-periodic segment component as an example:

$$T = V_T \cdot relu((X_w U_1)U_2(X_w U_3) + b_T) \tag{3}$$

$$T'_{i,j} = \frac{e^{T^{i,j}}}{\sum_{i=1}^{N} e^{T^{i,j}}} \tag{4}$$

$U_1 \in R^N$, $U_2 \in R^{F \times N}$, $U_3 \in R^F$, $b_T \in R^{1 \times N \times N}$, $V_T \in R^{r \times r}$ are all learnable parameters, the temporal attention matrix T is dynamically calculated according to the current input traffic data and learnable parameters [12]. $T^{i,j}$ represents the strength of the dynamic correlation between period i and period j. Then use the *softmax* function to normalize the temporal attention matrix to obtain a weight matrix with a value range of (0, 1). Finally, the temporal attention weight matrix is multiplied by the input X, which is $\hat{X} = XT'$, to highlight the temporal feature of the traffic data [21].

The spatiotemporal attention mechanism highlights the spatiotemporal features of the traffic data and then uses the spatiotemporal convolutional module to extract the features of the input data [33]. The spatiotemporal convolution is composed of graph convolution in the spatial and temporal dimensions, which captures the traffic features separately. The spatial and temporal features extraction process of the data is shown in Fig. 3.

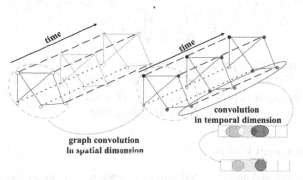

Fig. 3. The process of spatiotemporal convolution in MFAGCN.

Spatial Convolution. The traffic network can be understood as a graph structure, and the traffic data is the signal of the nodes in the graph. The spectrogram theory extends the convolutional operation based on network data to the convolutional operation based on graph structure data [27]. In spatial convolution, all the nodes on each time slice are regarded as a graph, and graph convolution is used to extract spatial feature. For the graph $G = (V, E)$, its Laplacian matrix is defined as $L = D–A$. L is the Laplacian matrix; D is the degree matrix, and the element on the diagonal is the degree of the vertex, the number of elements linked by the element; A is the Adjacency matrix, indicating the adjacency relationship between any two vertices, adjacent is 1 and non-adjacent is 0.

The graph and the convolutional kernel are first Fourier transformed and then multiplied, and then the inverse Fourier transform is returned to obtain the results of the graph convolution [28].

Temporal Convolution. After the graph convolution, the spatial feature of the traffic data are extracted [18], and then the standard convolutional operation is used to convolve the traffic data to extract the temporal feature to obtain the information of adjacent time slices to update the node signal [20], as shown in Fig. 3.

Among them, the symbol * represents the standard convolutional operation, Φ is the convolutional kernel of the time convolutional operation and relu as the activation function [35].

3.3 Multi-Feature Convolution

After obtaining the output of the attention-based spatiotemporal convolution module, the output traffic data is passed to the multi-feature convolutional module for operation [16]. Because the traffic data have different value ranges and convergence domains, it is necessary to split the traffic data according to different types, and select different convolutional kernels for different traffic data to perform standard convolution [21], and extract different types of traffic data. After the convolutional operation of each traffic data is completed, the LayerNorm function is used to normalize the traffic data, which is shown as follows:

$$y = \frac{x - E[x]}{\sqrt{Var[x] + \varnothing}} * \gamma + \beta \tag{5}$$

After the normalization process, different types of data are fused together, and the final output result is obtained by standard convolutional operation of convolutional kernel size (1×1). The output is processed by the all connect layer to obtain the prediction result of multi-feature traffic data under one component.

3.4 Multi-Component Fusion

In this work, the traffic data is divided into three components in terms of recent, daily, and weekly cycles, and the data in the three components are trained separately. After training, the data of the three components need to be fused to obtain the final prediction result [23]. Because the traffic data present strong dynamics, periodic features have different effects on locations [11]. For example, in the morning rush hour at 8:00 from Monday to Friday in the business district, there is a strong traffic regularity. At this time, the weekly and daily cycles have greater influence. Sometimes, the traffic data does not have an obvious cycle pattern [30]. At this time, the influence of the weekly-periodic and the daily-periodic segments is relatively small, and the recent influence is relatively large [23]. Therefore, when fusing the outputs of the three components, it is necessary to adjust the weights of different components so that the data is dynamically fused. The final fusion result is:

$$\hat{Y} = \hat{Y}_w W_1 + \hat{Y}_d W_2 + \hat{Y}_h W_3 \tag{6}$$

where $\hat{Y}_w$, $\hat{Y}_d$, $\hat{Y}_w \in R^{N \times T \times F}$ are the prediction results output by the weekly, daily, and recent components respectively. The W_1, W_2, W_3 are learnable parameters and weights of the three components for obtaining final prediction results.

4 Experiments

4.1 Datasets

The dataset used in this paper is the traffic data on the PeMSD04 and PeMSD08 highways in California, USA, which include average traffic volume, average occupancy rate, and average vehicle speed. 7769 continuous-time slices in the PeMSD04 dataset are selected as the training set, 2590 continuous-time slices are the testing set. In the PeMSD08 dataset, 9794 continuous-time slices were selected as the training set, and 3166 continuous-time slices were taken as the testing set.

4.2 Evaluation Metric and Baselines

This work uses three indicators to evaluate the performance of different models, including Mean Absolute Errors (MAE), Root Mean Squared Errors (RMSE), and Mean Absolute Percentage Errors (MAPE).

In this paper, the model MFAGCN is compared with the following 6 baselines:

- LSTM: Long Short-Term Memory network, a special RNN model.
- GCN: Graph Convolutional Network, a special CNN model.
- GRU: Gated Recurrent Unit network, a special RNN model.
- TGCN: A Temporal Graph Convolutional Network for Traffic Prediction.
- STGCN: Spatiotemporal Graph Convolutional Networks, a deep learning framework for traffic prediction.
- STDN: It is a deep learning framework for traffic prediction revisiting spatiotemporal similarity.

4.3 Comparison and Results

Table 1 shows the three predictions of average traffic flow, average occupancy rate and average vehicle speed for the results of the evaluation indicators. It can be seen from the results of the evaluation indicators that MFAGCN is more accurate than the other six baselines in the prediction results of the three traffic data. It can be seen from the experimental results that the traditional LSTM model [21] lacks the analysis of the temporal and spatial dimensions of the traffic data, and cannot accurately extract the temporal and spatial features of the traffic data, showing the disadvantage of modeling the nonlinear and complex traffic data. TGCN adds feature extraction in the temporal dimension, and the prediction results are superior to that of the GCN and GRU models, which only consider the spatial correlation. By evaluating the parameters, it can be seen that STGCN and STDN outperform GCN and GRU, indicating that it is effective to add a new spatial feature extraction approach based on temporal feature extraction and graph convolution. The MFAGCN model takes advantages of the above models, and develops a spatiotemporal attention mechanism to highlight spatiotemporal features. It not only completes multi-feature prediction, but also has a more accurate prediction effect than the six baselines, which further reduces the prediction error.

Table 1. Comparison of the performance of different models for predicting the average traffic flow, road occupancy and speed in the PeMSD04 dataset.

Epochs	Flow			Occupancy			Speed		
LSTM	53.31	75.12	66.08	3.42	5.13	74.18	8.04	11.18	16.84
GCN	41.9	59.74	41.59	2.38	4.23	40.14	4.79	8.1	11.38
GRU	32.88	47.01	32.91	2.29	4.14	38.29	4.73	7.98	11.22
STDN	30.89	46.6	26.03	1.32	4.05	35.92	4.68	7.89	8.02
TGCN	26.16	42.93	22.62	1.30	2.76	35.74	3.01	5.37	6.56
STGCN	26.05	41.59	20.96	1.20	2.68	34.23	2.24	4.62	6.33
MFAGCN	**25.15**	**40.09**	**18.09**	**1.10**	**2.52**	**33.54**	**2.16**	**4.51**	**4.65**

To conveniently show the prediction effect of different models on traffic features, this work compares the prediction results of each model. The comparison of the prediction results of average traffic flow is shown in Fig. 4. The prediction results of the average occupancy rate of aeveral advanced models are shown in Fig. 5. The prediction results of the average speed of each model are shown in Fig. 6. Among them, Figs. 5(a), 6(a), and 7(a) show the comparison between the neural networks without considering the temporal and spatial features of the traffic data, while Figs. 5(b), 6(b), and 7(b) show the comparison between the neural networks considering the temporal and spatial features of traffic data and MFAGCN.

Since the average traffic flow is the largest of the three kinds of traffic data, the prediction of other traffic data in the training process will be affected by the average traffic flow data. In Fig. 4, the prediction results of all models are close to the real value. But in Figs. 6 and 7, it can be seen that due to the influence of large-scale data, the predicted results of models are quite different from the real values. To avoid the small average occupancy rate leads to the inaccurate prediction, the average occupancy rate is increased by 100 time slices after obtaining the average occupancy rate. As can be seen from Table. 1 and Fig. 4(a), due to the large range of average traffic flow, although the prediction effect of each model in Fig. 4 on average traffic flow is similar, the evaluation

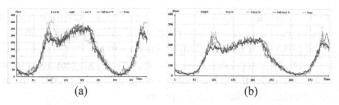

Fig. 4. The prediction results of the average traffic flow.

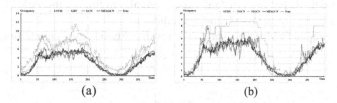

Fig. 5. The prediction results of the average occupancy rate.

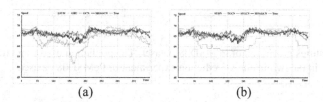

Fig. 6. The prediction results of the average speed.

indexes are quite different. It can be seen from Fig. 5(a) and Fig. 6(a) that the traditional deep learning model has a smaller prediction error for one feature and a larger prediction error for the other features. This is because the traditional deep learning model aims at a single feature. The model may ignore the training data with small values. Therefore, MFAGCN not only achieves a more accurate prediction effect in the direction of traffic data prediction but also integrates multi-feature prediction.

To make the experiment more sufficient, the two features prediction is carried out in the PeMSD04 dataset, which is average traffic flow and average occupancy rate. Then the MFAGCN model has trained again, and the experimental results are shown in Fig. 7.

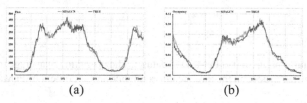

Fig. 7. Two features prediction of PeMSD04 dataset. MFAGCN model is used to predict the average traffic flow and road occupancy in the two features prediction experiment of PeMSD04 dataset.

It can be seen from Fig. 7 that the MFAGCN model has high accuracy for the prediction results of two features. In the process of model training, the loss value of two features in the process of data training decreases faster than that of three features, and after the training, the three evaluation parameters of two features are smaller than those of three features, under the same training conditions, the prediction results of two features is more accurate than that of three features.

To explore the influence of the number of nodes on the experimental results, we use the PeMSD08 dataset which contains 170 nodes to further verify the validity of the MFAGCN model. Based on constant experimental conditions, the PeMSD08 dataset was trained to complete the two features prediction.

After training the PeMSD08 dataset, the results of two features prediction are shown in Fig. 8.

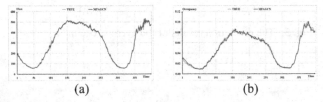

(a)   (b)

Fig. 8. Two features prediction of PeMSD08 dataset. The prediction of average traffic flow and road occupancy in the two features prediction experiment of PeMSD08 dataset.

By comparing the experimental results of two features prediction under PeMSD04 and PeMSD08 datasets, it can be found that the prediction result of average traffic flow and average occupancy under the PeMSD08 dataset is more accurate and has a better fitting performance. Due to the small number of nodes in the PeMSD08 dataset, the corresponding graph is simpler and easier for feature extraction. Under the same experimental conditions, the prediction results of the datasets with fewer nodes are more accurate.

After the realization of two features prediction for the PeMSD08 dataset, this paper conducts three features prediction experiments on the PeMSD08 dataset, and the experimental results are shown in Fig. 9.

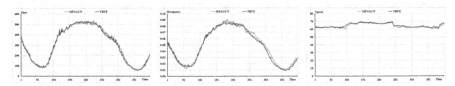

Fig. 9. Three features prediction of PeMSD08 dataset. The prediction of average traffic flow, road occupancy, and average speed in the three features prediction experiment of PeMSD08 dataset.

By comparing Figs. 8 and 9, it can be seen that adding new feature data will reduce the prediction accuracy of the model for all features under the same training conditions.

This is due to the addition of new features, the amount of data processed by the model will increase, and different features convergence regions will increase the difficulty of data training. Although adding a new feature will lead to the decline of the prediction accuracy of the model for each feature, the MFAGCN model still has a high accuracy after adding a new feature, which is slightly different from the double feature prediction effect and better than baselines.

5 Conclusion

We propose a multi-feature prediction network based on an attention mechanism (MFAGCN), which can predict multiple features of the traffic data. MFAGCN uses a spatiotemporal attention mechanism to highlight the spatiotemporal characteristics of traffic data, and uses different convolutions on the spatial and temporal dimensions of traffic data to extract spatiotemporal features respectively. Experiments on two real traffic datasets demonstrate that our model's prediction accuracy outperforms other existing models. Evidence shows that MFAGCN can deal with unstructured data and has strong portability, which can be applied to other fields of graph-structured prediction, such as urban area division, traffic flow forecasting at bus stations, etc.

However, multiple traffic data is affected by many external factors, e.g., holidays and traffic accidents. In the future, we will consider more external factors when building the model to further improve the accuracy of the prediction.

Acknowledgments. This research was supported in part by Shandong Province colleges and universities youth innovation technology plan innovation team project under Grant No. 2020KJN011, Shandong Provincial Natural Science Foundation under Grant No. ZR2020MF060, Program for Innovative Postdoctoral Talents in Shandong Province under Grant No. 40618030001, National Natural Science Foundation of China under Grant No. 61802216, and Postdoctoral Science Foundation of China under Grant No.2018M642613.

References

1. Shengnan, G., Youfang, L., Ning, F., Chao, S., Huaiyu, W.: Attention based spatial-temporal graph convolutional networks for traffic flow prediction. AAAI Conf. Artif. Intell. **33**(1), 922–929 (2019)
2. Bing, Y., Haoteng, Y., Zhanxing, Z.: Spatio-temporal graph convolutional networks: a deep learning framework for traffic prediction. In: International Joint Conferences on Artificial Intelligence Organization, pp. 3634–3640 (2017)
3. Ling, Z., et al.: T-GCN: a temporal graph convolutional network for traffic prediction. IEEE Trans. Intell. Transp. Syst. **21**(9), 3848–3858 (2019)
4. Huaxiu, Y., Xianfeng, T., Hua, W., Guanjie, Z., Zhenhui, L.: Revisiting spatial-temporal similarity: a deep learning framework for traffic prediction. AAAI Conf. Artif. Intell. **33**(1), 5668–5675 (2019)
5. Chuanpan, Z., Xiaoliang, F., Cheng, W., Jianzhong, Q.: GMAN: a graph multi-attention network for traffic prediction. AAAI Conf. Artif. Intell. **34**(1), 1234–1241 (2020)
6. Yaguang, L., Rose, Y., Cyrus, S., Yan, L.: Diffusion convolutional recurrent neural network: data-driven traffic prediction, pp. 1–16 (2018)

7. Jiabin, Q., Xinyu, G., Lin, Z.: Improved UGRNN for short-term traffic flow prediction with multi-feature sequence inputs. In: 2018 International Conference on Information Networking (ICOIN), Chiang Mai, pp. 13–17 (2018)

8. Di, Y., Songjiang, L., Zhou, P., Peng, W., Junhui, W., Huamin, Y.: MF-CNN: traffic flow prediction using convolutional neural network and multi-features fusion. IEICE Trans. Inf. Syst. **102**(8), 1526–1536 (2019)

9. Lin, Y., Wang, R., Zhu, R., Li, T., Wang, Z., Chen, M.: The short-term exit traffic prediction of a toll station based on LSTM. In: Li, G., Shen, H.T., Yuan, Ye., Wang, X., Liu, H., Zhao, X. (eds.) KSEM 2020. LNCS (LNAI), vol. 12275, pp. 462–471. Springer, Cham (2020). https://doi.org/10.1007/978-3-030-55393-7_41

10. Eunjoon, C., Seth, A.M., Jure, L.: Friendship and mobility: user movement in location-based social networks. In: 17th ACM SIGKDD International Conference on Knowledge Discovery and Data Mining (KDD 2004), San Diego, pp. 1082–1090 (2011)

11. Zheng, Z., Weihai, C., Xingming, W., Peter, C.Y.C., Jingmeng, L.: LSTM network: a deep learning approach for short-term traffic prediction. IET Digit. Libr. **11**(2), 68–75 (2017)

12. Qing, G., Zhu, S., Jie, Z., Yinleng, T.: An attentional recurrent neural network for personalized next location recommendation. In: AAAI Conference on Artificial Intelligence, New York, vol. 34, pp. 83–90 (2020)

13. Michaël, D., Xavier, B., Pierre, V.: Convolutional neural networks on graphs with fast localized spectral filtering. In: Neural Information Processing Systems, pp. 1–9 (2016)

14. Hussein, D.: An object-oriented neural network approach to short-term traffic prediction. Eur. J. Oper. Res. **131**(2), 253–261 (2001)

15. Paulo, C., Miguel, R., Miguel, R., Pedro, S.: Multi-scale Internet traffic prediction using neural networks and time series methods. Expert. Syst. **29**(2), 143–155 (2010)

16. Alireza, E., David, L.: Spatiotemporal traffic prediction: review and proposed directions. Transp. Rev. **38**(6), 786–814 (2017)

17. Yuxuan, L., Songyu, K., Junbo, Z., Xiuwen, Y., Yu, Z.: GeoMAN: multi-level attention networks for geo-sensory time series prediction. In: International Joint Conferences on Artificial Intelligence Organization, pp. 3428–3434 (2018)

18. Filmon, G.H., Mecit, C.: Short-term traffic flow rate prediction based on identifying similar traffic patterns. Transp. Res. Part C Emerg. Technol. **66**, 61–78 (2016)

19. AbuShaaban, M., Brazil, T.J., Scanlan, J.O.: Recursive causal convolution [passive distributed circuits]. In: IEEE MTT-S International Microwave Symposium Digest, Denver, pp. 8–13 (1997)

20. Sepp, H., Jürgen, S.: Long short-term memory. Neural Comput. **9**(8), 1735–1780 (1997)

21. Zhao, A., Li, J., Ahmed, M.: SpiderNet: a spiderweb graph neural network for multi-view gait recognition. Knowl. Based Syst. **206**, 106273 (2020)

22. Shifen, C., Feng, L., Peng, P., Sheng, W.: Short-term traffic prediction: an adaptive ST-KNN model that considers spatial heterogeneity. Comput. Environ. Urban Syst. **71**, 186–198 (2018)

23. Weiqi, C., Ling, C., Yu, X., Wei, C., Yusong, G., Xiaojie, F.: Multi-range attentive bicomponent graph convolutional network for traffic prediction. In: AAAI Conference on Artificial Intelligence, New York, pp. 3529–3536 (2020)

24. Yang, Y.: Spatiotemporal traffic-flow dependency and short-term traffic prediction. Environ. Plan. B Urban Anal. City Sci. **35**(5), 762–771 (2008)

25. Bin, S., Wei, C., Prashant, G., Guohua, B.: Short-term traffic prediction using self-adjusting k-nearest neighbours. IET Digit. Libr. **12**(1), 41–48 (2018)

26. Zhao, A., Li, J., Dong, J.: Multimodal gait recognition for neurodegenerative diseases, pp. 1–15 (2021)

27. Michael, G., Konrad, D., Ulrich, B., André, G., Bernhard, S.: Pedestrian's trajectory prediction in public traffic with artificial neural networks. In: 22nd International Conference on Pattern Recognition, Stockholm, pp. 4110–4115 (2014)

28. Huakang, L., Dongmin, H., Youyi, S., Dazhi, J., Teng, Z., Jing, Q.: ST-TrafficNet: a spatial-temporal deep learning network for traffic prediction. Electronics **9**(9), 1–17 (2020)
29. Weiwei, J., Lin, Z.: Geospatial data to images: a deep-learning framework for traffic prediction. TUP **24**(1), 52–64 (2018)
30. Haider, K.J., Rafiqul, Z.K.: Methods to avoid over-fitting and under-fitting in supervised machine learning (comparative study). In: Communication and Instrumentation Devices, Aligarh, pp. 163–172 (2015)
31. Zulong, D., Xin, W., Dafang, Z., Yingru, L., Kun, X., Shaoyao, H.: Dynamic spatial-temporal graph convolutional neural networks for traffic prediction. In: AAAI Conference on Artificial Intelligence, California, pp. 890–897 (2019)
32. Toon, B., Antonio, D.M., Juan, S.A., Enrique, O., Peter, H.: A graph CNN-LSTM neural network for short and long-term traffic prediction based on trajectory data. Transp. Res. Part C Emerg. Technol. **112**, 62–77 (2020)
33. Zhao, A., Dong, J., Li. J.: Associated spatio-temporal capsule network for gait recognition, pp. 1–14 (2021)
34. Jiawei, Z., Yujiao, S., Ling, Z., Haifeng, L.: A3T-GCN: attention temporal graph convolutional network for traffic prediction, pp. 1–9 (2020)
35. Leung, F.H.F., Lam, H.K., Ling, S.H., Tam, P.K.S.: Tuning of the structure and parameters of a neural network using an improved genetic algorithm. IEEE Trans. Neural Netw. **14**(1), 79–88 (2003)
36. Florin, S., Xuan, V.N., James, B., Chris, L., Hai, V., Rao, K.: Traffic prediction in complex urban networks: Leveraging big data and machine learning. In: 2015 IEEE International Conference on Big Data, Santa Clara, pp. 1019–1024 (2015)
37. Chenhan, Z., James, J.Q.Y., Yi, L.: Spatial-temporal graph attention networks: a deep learning approach for traffic prediction. Artifi. Intell. (AI)-Empowered Intell. Transp. Syst. **7**, 166246–166256 (2019)
38. Zhiqiang, L., Jianbo, L., Chuanhao, D., Wei, Z.: A deep spatial-temporal network for vehicle trajectory prediction. In: International Conference on Wireless Algorithms, Systems, and Applications, Qingdao, pp. 359–369 (2020)

Judicial Case Determination Methods Based on Event Tuple

Guozi Sun[1,2], Zhi Li[1], Huakang Li[2,3]([✉]), and Xiangyu Tang[1]

[1] School of Computer Science, Nanjing University of Posts and Telecommunications, Nanjing 210023, Jiangsu, China
[2] Key Laboratory of Urban Land Resources Monitoring and Simulation, MNR, Shenzhen 518000, Guangdong, China
[3] Institute of Artificial Intelligence and Advanced Computing, Xi'an Jiaotong-Lliverpool University, Suzhou 215123, Jiangsu, China

Abstract. Judges have to consider the motives of the defendant's side and the sequence of actions of all judicial subjects in the process of sentencing. Text analysis methods based on word vectors and deep neural networks, although they give statistically better classification results, cannot explain the causality of the actions of various subjects in the case logic. In this paper, we propose an event semantic mining algorithm that attempts to make judicial decisions from the causal logic. The method identifies the behavioral subjects in judicial documents through an entity extraction algorithm and extracts the subjects' core behavior and motivation to achieve the construction of the underlying event tuple. By calculating the event tuple weights between different categories of cases, combined with a heap sorting algorithm, an event semantic tree is constructed for each case. Finally, a set of event tuple coding algorithm is designed to input the event semantic tree into the deep forest algorithm for inference. The experimental results show that the proposed event semantic tree construction method and event tuple coding method not only have a good case decision accuracy. It also has a good logical explanation.

Keywords: Judicial text · Case logic · Event tuple · Semantic tree · Deep forest

1 Introduction

In 2017, courts nationwide comprehensively announced the real-time situation of court trials and execution work through four major platforms: the China Judgment Process Information Open Network, the China Judgment Documents Network, the China Execution Information Open Network and the China Court Trial Open Network, enhancing judicial transparency and social supervision. As of January 25, 2021, the total number of visits to the China Judgment Documents Website exceeded 55.3 billion, with the total number of documents exceeding 100 million and the number of new visits exceeding 20,000 on a single day. The huge volume of judicial documents has made intelligent case judgments a new research hotspot in the field of natural language understanding.

In terms of content, court judgement documents contain information such as the time of the hearing, the identity of the prosecutor, the identity of the defendant, the cause

Z. Liu et al. (Eds.): WASA 2021, LNCS 12937, pp. 240–252, 2021.
https://doi.org/10.1007/978-3-030-85928-2_19

of the case, the statement of legal facts and the judgement result [1]. The traditional keyword retrieval algorithm [2] can achieve simple case screening and discrimination through the similarity calculation of the case statement content. The use of machine learning algorithms such as SVM [3] or Bayes models gives good results in terms of statistical results [4]. However, the final verdict, especially in sentencing, requires in-depth comparative analysis of the differences between cases by judges and lawyers [5].

The research attempts to mine the behavioural relationships between subjects in the case document descriptions, discover their behavioural sequences and motivations, and discriminate the cases interpretatively from the perspective of event semantic analysis. Firstly, the actor subjects and core actions of the event tuple are extracted through entity extraction algorithm and dependency parsing algorithm. Secondly, the complete event semantic tree of the case is constructed using the sequence of weights of the event tuples. Finally, the event tree is vector coded and embedded into a deep forest algorithm to implement logical inference. The experimental results show that the proposed event semantic mining algorithm not only has a good case decision accuracy but also a good logical interpretation.

2 Related Work

The logical content of acts of justice can be interpreted in processing as behavioural relations between actors, and the extraction and analysis of associative relations between entities is one of the tasks at the heart of long-term research in the field of natural language processing [6]. There are currently two main popular frameworks for relationship extraction between entities [7]. One is an approach that uses pre-trained models for classifying relations between entities, and the other is an approach that performs entity relation extraction through the syntax itself.

The method of extracting relationships between entities using pre-trained models can be split into two separate tasks, named entity recognition (NER) and relationship classification. In recent years, several neural network structures by Chiu [8], Huang [9], Lample [10] and others have been successfully applied to NER to process the named entity recognition task into a sequence labeling task. Currently, relational classification methods also mainly use training learning methods of neural networks. Although pre-trained models are simple and effective for entity relationship extraction, they require a large amount of labelled data as a prerequisite and are labour-intensive.

The extraction of relations between entity relations through the syntax itself, as a semantic analysis technique approach maps sentences into syntactic trees and achieves the extraction of relations between entities through the analysis of syntactic trees. Geng [11] proposes an end-to-end model of a bidirectional tree structure LSTM based on a dependency relation tree, He [12] uses a tree-based model structure for learning syntax-aware entity representations for neural relations extraction, Jiang [13] selected syntactic features through component analysis trees to automatically extract entities and construct graphs of node representation relations.

The analysis of case to case comparison, on the other hand, can be seen as the structural information of the event refers to the intrinsic connection between data from the perspective of textual analysis, and the association relationship between events and events can be represented as both graph and tree structures. By comparing two different graph structures or tree structures, it is possible to know whether two text events are similar to each other in terms of intrinsic structure. Simrank [14] proposed by Jeh G is a model based on graph structural similarity, and Struc2vec [15] proposed by Ribeiro L F R is a model based on semantic and graph structural similarity. Deep forest proposed by Zhou Z H [16] is a model based on semantic and tree structure similarity.

3   Construction Judical Tree(CJTE)

Assuming that each judicial case Doc_i can be extracted into a separate and complete event tree ET_i, the following definition is given.

Definition 1. The i-th judicial decision document Doc_i is given an event tree ET_i by the event tree algorithm $CE(Doc_i)$, i.e. $ET_i = CE(Doc_i)$.

Definition 2. Judicial decision document Doc_i can get n_i sentences by cutting algorithm, which contains m_i event tuples se, i.e. $Doc_i = \{Sent_0, Sent_1, ..., Sent_n\} \rightarrow ET_i = \{se_0, se_1, ..., se_m\}$, where n >= m. The following describes the process of building the event tree in detail.

3.1   Event Tuple Extraction

In a judicial decision, the actions between the actors are the central element in the discrimination of the case. It is therefore assumed that the sentences as $Sent_j$ of a certain judicial decision document can be extracted into the triad <Subject,Predicate,Object> as <NP,IP,VP> of the semantic description of natural language, i.e. an event tuple se_j is obta.ned, as in Eq. (1).

$$\forall se_j, \exists \langle NP_j, IP_j, VP_j \rangle \in Sent_j, \tag{1}$$

Considering the completeness of the text description and the missingness problems that may arise in cutting, one or more of NP_j, IP_j and VP_j may be empty. Assuming that the core of the description of an event is a verb, the following treatment is given in this paper.

1) No event tuple exists when there is no predicate verb and $IP_j = \emptyset$, i.e. $se_j = \emptyset$.
2) When a predicate verb is present and subject is missing, the missing word of the subject is made up to 0, i.e. $se_j = \langle 0, IP_j, VP_j \rangle$.
3) When a predicate verb is present and the object are missing, the missing words of the object are filled with 0, i.e. $se_j = <NP_j, IP_j, 0>$;
4) When a predicate verb is present and the subject and object are missing, the missing words of the subject and object are filled with 0, i.e. $se_j = <0, IP_j, 0>$;
5) When subject, predicate and object are all present, i.e. $se_j = <NP_j, IP_j, VP_j>$;

In this paper, dependency syntactic parsing is used to implement the extraction of minimal event tuple triples. Figure 1 shows a concrete example of dependency syntactic parsing.

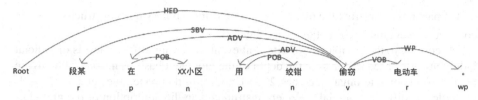

Fig. 1. An example of dependent parsing

1) Pre-processing the sentence by splitting words and deleting stop words to obtain the Chinese core words of the sentence, e.g. "段某".
2) The POS Tagger is used to label the result of splitting words, e.g. the lexical nature of "段某" is "r(pronoun)".
3) Finding the core verb of a sentence, e.g. "偷窃", through the core relation (HED) of dependency syntactic parsing.
4) Finding the subject of a sentence, e.g. "段某", by means of the subject-predicate relationship (SBV) of dependency syntactic parsing.
5) Find the object of a sentence by using the verb-object relationship (VOB) of dependency syntactic parsing, e.g. "电动车".

3.2 Core Event Tuple Filtering

In the process of judicial case adjudication, the core actions generated by both parties will be the main basis for the judge's final decision, such as "杀害", "伤害" and "借款". Therefore, in this paper, we use the TF-IDF algorithm to filter the tuple of core events for the classification of judicial decision documents. The specific steps are shown in Algorithm 1.

Algorithm 1. TF-IDF picking event tuple algorithm:
Step1: Import of all event tuples drawn from Doc_i of a particular judicial decision file set;
Step2: Split the event tuple to get the set of all core predicates $IP_0, IP_1, ..., IP_m$;
Step3: Calculation of word frequency IF and inverse text frequency IDF for the core predicate IP_j;
Step4: Calculate IF-IDF = TF*IDF for each core predicate IP_j;
Step5: Sort all core predicates in order of highest to lowest IF-IDF value;
Step6: Select the top-k core predicates with higher weights to obtain the weight matrix $\vec{IP_i} = \{\vec{IP_0}, \vec{IP_1}, ..., \vec{IP_k}\}$;
Step7: The corresponding set of core event metasets $\vec{SE} = \{\vec{se_0}, \vec{se_1}, ..., \vec{se_k}\}$ is obtained by ordering the core predicates

3.3 Event Tree Construction

In order to be able to better justify the judicial decision document in terms of logical semantics and to interface with the deep forest algorithm oriented to structure mining, in this paper, we construct the overall event tree using a binary tree construction for the core set of event tuples $\overrightarrow{SE}$ obtained by filtering.

According to the complexity of different events, defining different levels of judicial judgment cases need to consider the depth of the judgment basis as h. According to the height of h complete binary tree has $2^h - 1$ nodes, in this paper, we set $k = 2^h - 1$. Considering different judicial judgment instruments in the description of the granularity of the process of detailed inconsistency, the accuracy of the event tuple extraction algorithm and other issues, we give the following treatment.

1) If the top-k core event tuples that can be extracted from a judgement instrument of case complexity h are used directly to construct a Complete Binary Tree using the top-k event tuples.
2) If the top-k core event tuples that could not be extracted from the judgment instrument with case complexity h are used, the empty event tuples are used to complement to the k event tuples.

4   Deep Forest Learning

4.1   Event Tree Embedding

We use word vectors to Embedding representations of event tuples in event trees, representing the semantic information between words through the Word2vec [17–19] word vector tool.

In this paper, the event tuples extracted from the massive judicial documents are disassembled to obtain the $\overrightarrow{NP}$ set, $\overrightarrow{IP}$ set, and $\overrightarrow{VP}$ set. The $\overrightarrow{NP}$ set, $\overrightarrow{IP}$ set, and $\overrightarrow{VP}$ set were then trained by Word2vec to obtain the Pre-training Word2vec_NP model, the Pre-training Word2vec_IP model, Pre-training Word2vec_VP model three pre-training models corresponding to the event tuples.

As shown in Fig. 2, the event tuple se_i for each node in the event tree is obtained by Breadth First Search of the tree. The $<NP_j, IP_j, VP_j>$ in se_i are Embedding by the corresponding Word2vec pre-training model to obtain the vectorised tree nodes $\overrightarrow{se_j} = <\overrightarrow{NP_j}, \overrightarrow{IP_j}, \overrightarrow{VP_j}>$. where $\overrightarrow{NP_j}, \overrightarrow{IP_j} and \overrightarrow{VP_j}$ denote the numerical vectors respectively. The vector dimensions of $\overrightarrow{NP_j}, \overrightarrow{IP_j} and \overrightarrow{VP_j}$ are determined by the parameters used during Word2vec training. Because the tree nodes are vectorised using Breadth First Search, the structure of the entire event tree after Embedding remains the same as the event tree structure before Embedding. The vectorised event tree can then be embedded in Deep Forest for event tree similarity calculation.

4.2   Deep Forest Based on Tree Structures

Decision Tree. In this paper, decision tree is used to implement split-tree nodes of event tree for segmented object feature extraction. The classification evaluation metric of the decision tree can be measured using the Gini index or the Kullback–Leibler divergence.

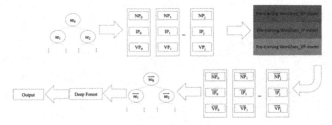

Fig. 2. Event tree embedding into deep forest

To obtain the maximum Kullback–Leibler divergence for each decision, the objective function of the decision tree is defined as Eq. (2).

$$IG(D_p, f) = I(D_p) - \sum_{j=1}^{m} \frac{N_j}{N_p} I(D_j)j, \tag{2}$$

where f is the feature of the tree node, D_p and D_j are the parent and j-th child node respectively, I is the impurity measure, N_p is the total number of samples of the parent node and N_j is the total number of samples of the j-th child node. In general, the decision tree uses a binary tree, which is consistent with the event tree structure built in this paper. At this point the two child nodes of the parent node classification are D_{left} and D_{right}, respectively, brought to formula (2), the objective function of the binary decision tree is obtained as formula (3).

$$IG(D_p, a) = I(D_p) - \frac{N_{left}}{N_{right}} I(D_{left}) - \frac{N_{right}}{N_p} I(D_{right}), \tag{3}$$

where $I(D_{left})$ and $I(D_{right})$ are the amount of impurity of the left and right nodes of the event tree, N_{left} and N_{right} are the number of left and right nodes of the event tree, and N_p is the number of all tree nodes of the event tree. The nodal Kullback–Leibler divergence assessment uses the amount of impurity as a parameter and is derived from the information entropy function as Eq. (4).

$$I_H(t) = - \sum_{i=1}^{n} p(i|t) \log_2 p(i|t), \tag{4}$$

where p(i|t) denotes the probability that tree node t belongs to the n-class event tree.

Random Forest. In the process of ensemble learning, the different categories are counted to obtain the proportions of each category, and then the probability distribution of the whole forest is generated by averaging the proportions of all the trees. Ensemble learning classification algorithms are combined in two ways: Bagging and Boost Bagging. Random Forest is a Bagging approach to ensemble learning. It generates multiple decision trees to obtain different classification strategies by Bagging. As shown in Fig. 3, this is a simplified forest for the binary classification problem, where each sample finds a path to its corresponding leaf node in each decision tree, and the training data in this same leaf node is likely to have different classes.

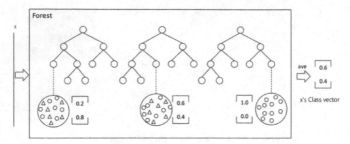

Fig. 3. Random forest policy decision

Deep Forest. Deep forest is a tree-based ensemble method [20] that learns semantic and structural information about trees, and achieves representation learning by integrating and stringing a forest of trees back and forth [21]. The test set is estimated by K-fold cross-validation and the training is terminated when the accuracy saturates, allowing the number of layers in series to be determined adaptively.

The basic structure is shown in Fig. 4, where each layer consists of a forest of decision tree, i.e. each layer is an "ensemble of ensembles". It is worth noting that each layer is made up of two different forests.

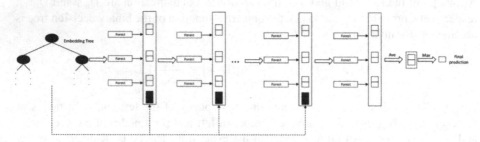

Fig. 4. Cascade forest structure

5 Experiments and Analysis of Results

5.1 Evaluation Indicators

In the traditional classification system, when the prediction result is positive class, it is noted as TP, and when the prediction result is negative class, it is noted as FN. In the negative class prediction, the positive class result is noted as FP, and the negative class result is noted as TN. In the fields of natural language processing and information retrieval, P, R and F1 are commonly used as evaluation metrics. However, the data set used in this paper has data imbalance, and the number of samples of large classes on the imbalanced data set accounts for a large proportion, so in this paper, we use P, R and F1 for evaluation, and also use macroF1 and microF1 metrics, which are more suitable for the imbalanced data set, for algorithm performance evaluation. macroF1 and microF1 are defined in Eqs. (5) and Eq. (6) are shown.

$$macroF1 = \frac{2 \times macroP \times macroR}{macroP + macroR}, \tag{5}$$

$$microF1 = \frac{2 \times microP \times microR}{microP + microR}, \tag{6}$$

where $macroP = \frac{1}{n}\sum_1^n P_i$, $macroR = \frac{1}{n}\sum_1^n R_i$, $microP = \frac{TP}{TP \times FP}$, $microR = \frac{TP}{TP \times FN}$.

5.2 Data Set

In this paper, we use the CAIL2018 publicly available judicial instruments dataset [22], which contains a total of 134,592 judicial decision instruments for training and 30,000 for testing, all of which are classified into 202 different offence categories.

To illustrate the severe asymmetry in this dataset, the left half of Fig. 5 shows the distribution of the 134592 data items in the training set. It is clear that the largest category 1 has 33,705 training data, while category 189 has only 2,278 data and the smallest category 110 has only 8 data. And the right half of Fig. 5 shows the distribution of the test data categories. Combining the figure shows that the data distribution of the test data is similar to that of the training data, which justifies the use of macroF1 and microF1 for evaluation.

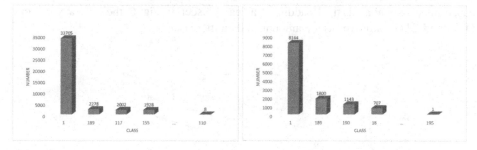

Fig. 5. Train data class-number (left) and test data class-number (right)

5.3 Parameter Setting

In this paper, we compare the deep neural networks (DNN) approach in deep learning to validate the model. In this paper, the word vector is generated by Word2vec. The dimension of the word vector is 256, the hidden layer dimension of the DNN is set to 300, the learning rate is 0.01, the maximum number of CJTE layers is 30, and each layer consists of 4 ExtraTreesClassifier and 4 RandomForestClassifier. There is no limit to the depth of the tree in each layer.

For DNN, the text data is split and has its stop words removed. Then the data is vectorised by basic natural language pre-processing, and then the model is trained.

For CJTE, the event tree was embedded into a deep forest for training using the event tree construction and Embedding methods in the paper. For better comparison of the experimental results, three different random samples were taken from the CAIL2018 dataset in this paper, 40,000, 80,000 and 120,000 items as training and 10,000, 20,000 and 30,000 as testing. Their training and testing data comparison amounts are shown in Table 1.

Table 1. Comparison of training set and testing set data volume

Train	40000	80000	120000
Test	10000	20000	30000

5.4 Analysis of Results

As given in Fig. 6, the class discrimination accuracy results of CJTE and DNN on different data subsets of CAIL2018 are presented. It can be seen that the method in this paper outperforms DNN in terms of accuracy scores on the 40,000, 80,000 and 120,000 datasets, and the accuracy rates are all improved by about 3%. The experimental results prove the effectiveness of this paper's method and illustrate that models based on event semantics and event structure have better results and are more interpretable than those based on statistical analysis. In addition, as can be seen in Fig. 6, the accuracy of both DNN and CJTE improves as the amount of data increases.

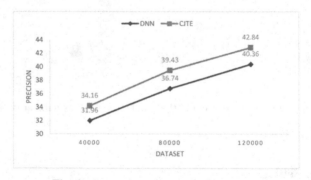

Fig. 6. Comparison of experimental results

Due to the unbalanced nature of the dataset, in this paper, the models obtained from the training of CJTE and DNN on the 120,000 dataset are expanded by ranking the test evaluation reports for each category by F1 values when testing the prediction of multiple categories of the data. As can be seen from Table 2, on small category data, such as categories 33, 108, 132 and 194 in the table, the accuracy of CJTE's prediction for these categories is much higher than that of DNN. The semantics and structure of small category data are largely similar, so the CJTE model based on semantic and structural similarity can identify these features well, while the DNN model based on statistical analysis selectively ignores the features of small category features of the data, resulting in low accuracy in prediction on small categories. Analysis of Table 3 shows that CJTE does not predict as well as DNN for category 1 (the largest proportion of both the training and test sets). The reason for this is the opposite of small category data, where the common large category data contains more semantic and structural features and requires more samples to be learned when using the semantic and structural model CJTE, whereas the statistical model based DNN is able to determine the outcome of the category based on a few frequency words in these samples. So with insufficient data, CJTE is not sufficient to learn more structural features, resulting in its prediction results for the largest class not being as good as DNN.

Table 2. CJTE/DNN multi-classification assessment report top5

CJTE					DNN				
Class	Precision	Recall	F1-score	Support	Class	Precision	Recall	F1-score	Support
194	0.794	0.812	0.803	356	132	0.684	0.765	0.722	17
110	**1**	**0.667**	**0.8**	**3**	194	0.656	0.713	0.684	356
108	0.778	0.763	0.771	350	33	0.8	0.545	0.649	22
132	0.765	0.765	0.765	17	108	0.636	0.603	0.619	350
33	0.875	0.636	0.737	22	**1**	**0.599**	**0.618**	**0.608**	**8144**

Table 3. CJTE/DNN multi-classification assessment report between 36 and 40

CJTE					DNN				
Class	Precision	Rrecall	F1-score	Support	Class	Precision	Recall	F1-score	Support
100	0.542	0.475	0.506	343	135	0.448	0.404	0.425	317
149	0.537	0.477	0.506	311	148	0.529	0.346	0.419	26
1	**0.436**	**0.58**	**0.498**	**8144**	163	0.281	0.818	0.419	11
70	0.491	0.503	0.497	322	14	0.352	0.5	0.413	100
58	0.619	0.401	0.486	292	155	0.415	0.407	0.411	334

Table 4 shows that the microF1 values of CJTE are higher than those of DNN on the 40,000, 80,000 and 120,000 data sets. Again, it is verified that although CJTE does not predict the largest category as well as DNN, CJTE predicts better than DNN in other large categories of data relative to the largest category. At the same time, the macroF1 values of CJTE have been stable relative to their own microF1 values on the 40,000, 80,000 and 120,000 data sets, while the macroF1 values of DNN have been very different relative to their own microF1 values, thus illustrating that the CJTE model based on semantic and structural similarity is more predictive for small categories compared to DNN accurate, while the DNN based on statistical analysis is somewhat weak in predicting small categories.

Table 4. Comparison of model experiment results

Dataset	macroF1		microF1	
	CJTE	DNN	CJTE	DNN
40000	29.38	19.17	32.24	29.32
80000	36.32	25.49	38.46	35.17
120000	**39.40**	30.70	**41.60**	39.50

Combining all the experimental results, it can be seen that the DNN based on statistical models produced overfitting in the data categories that accounted for a relatively large proportion of the data, and tended to perform poorly and the model was not stable enough for the prediction of a small proportion of the data. In contrast, the CJTE based on semantic and structural similarity was able to perform well in predicting both large and small categories, and the model was relatively stable.

6 Conclusion

In this paper, we introduce a method for building event trees for judicial judgment instruments, embedding the constructed event trees into a deep forest of tree models for event tree similarity comparison, and realizing semantic logical judgments for judicial judgment instruments. The results show that the proposed method solves the phenomenon of large class overfitting of deep neural networks in asymmetric data classification, and has better semantic description of events and logical judgments. However, in terms of the overall classification results of judicial judgement instruments, it has not yet reached the stage of practical usability, and therefore this paper will explore future work in the following directions.

1) The event tuple extraction process in this paper is still relatively shallow and does not implement the most fine-grained event tuple extraction algorithm.
2) During judicial decisions, reversals of subject and object entities may occur in different scenarios. How NP and VP can be abstracted will also be a new research.
3) The event tree construction process still has room to improve, and factors such as the sentiment and degree of the event tuple will also be the subject of our future research.

Acknowledgments. This work is supported by National Natural Science Foundation of China with Grant (NO. 61906099), Open fund project of Key Laboratory of urban natural resources monitoring and simulation, Ministry of natural resources (NO. KF-2019–04-011) and Suzhou Gusu Technology Venture Angel Program Project (NO. CYTS2018233).

References

1. Liu, C.-L., Hsieh, C.-D.: Exploring phrase-based classification of judicial documents for criminal charges in chinese. In: Esposito, F., Raś, Z.W., Malerba, D., Semeraro, G. (eds.) ISMIS 2006. LNCS (LNAI), vol. 4203, pp. 681–690. Springer, Heidelberg (2006). https://doi.org/10.1007/11875604_75
2. Khan, A., Baharudin, B., Lee, L.H., et al.: A review of machine learning algorithms for text-documents classification. J. Adv. Inf. Technol. 1(1), 4–20 (2010)
3. Lin, W., Guo, Z., Zhang, D., et al.: Marking, case classification and sentence prediction in chinese legal documents using machine learning. Chin. J. Comput. Linguist. 17(4), 49–67 (2012)
4. Luo, B., Feng, Y., Xu, J., et al.: Learning to predict charges for criminal cases with legal basis. arXiv preprint arXiv:1707.09168 (2017)
5. Zhong, H., Zhipeng, G., Tu, C., et al.: Legal judgment prediction via topological learning. In: Proceedings of the 2018 Conference on Empirical Methods in Natural Language Processing, pp. 3540–3549 (2018)
6. Ren, X., Wu, Z., He, W., et al.: Cotype: joint extraction of typed entities and relations with knowledge bases. In: Proceedings of the 26th International Conference on World Wide Web. International World Wide Web Conferences Steering Committee, pp. 1015–1024 (2017)
7. Augenstein, I., Vlachos, A., Maynard, D.: Extracting relations between non-standard entities using distant supervision and imitation learning. In: Proceedings of the 2015 Conference on Empirical Methods in Natural Language Processing, Association for Computational Linguistics, pp. 747–757 (2015)
8. Chiu, J.P.C., Nichols, E.: Named entity recognition with bidirectional LSTM-CNNs. Trans. Assoc. Comput. Linguis. 4, 357–370 (2016)
9. Huang, Z., Xu, W., Yu, K.: Bidirectional LSTM-CRF models for sequence tagging. arXiv preprint arXiv:1508.01991 (2015)
10. Lample, G., Ballesteros, M., Subramanian, S., et al.: Neural architectures for named entity recognition. arXiv preprint arXiv:1603.01360 (2016)
11. Geng, Z.Q., Chen, G.F., Han, Y.M., et al.: Semantic relation extraction using sequential and tree-structured LSTM with attention. Inf. Sci. 509, 183–192 (2020)
12. He, Z., Chen, W., Li, Z., et al.: Syntax-aware entity representations for neural relation extraction. Artif. Intell. 275, 602–617 (2019)
13. Jiang, M., Diesner, J.: A constituency parsing tree based method for relation extraction from abstracts of scholarly publications. In: Proceedings of the Thirteenth Workshop on Graph-Based Methods for Natural Language Processing (TextGraphs-13), Association for Computational Linguistics, pp. 186–191 (2019)
14. Jeh, G., Widom, J.: A measure of structural-context similarity. In: Proceedings of the 8th ACM SIGKDD, pp. 538–543
15. Ribeiro, L.F.R., Saverese, P.H.P., Figueiredo, D.R.: struc2vec: Learning node representations from structural identity. In: Proceedings of the 23rd ACM SIGKDD International Conference on Knowledge Discovery and Data Mining, pp. 385–394 (2017)
16. Yang, L., Wu, X.Z., Jiang, Y., et al.: Multi-label learning with deep forest. arXiv preprint arXiv:1911.06557 (2019)
17. Mikolov, T., Chen, K., Corrado, G., et al.: Efficient estimation of word representations in vector space. arXiv preprint arXiv:1301.3781 (2013)
18. Le, Q., Mikolov, T.: Distributed representations of sentences and documents. In: International Conference on Machine Learning, pp. 1188–1196 (2014)
19. Bojanowski, P., Grave, E., Joulin, A., et al.: Enriching word vectors with subword information. Trans. Associ. Comput. Linguis. 5, 135–146 (2017)

20. Zhou, Z.H., Feng, J.: Deep forest. arXiv preprint arXiv:1702.08835 (2017)
21. Kim, S., Jeong, M., Ko, B.C.: Interpretation and simplification of deep forest. arXiv preprint arXiv:2001.04721 (2020)
22. Xiao, C., Zhong, H., Guo, Z., et al.: Cail2018: a large-scale legal dataset for judgment prediction. arXiv preprint arXiv:1807.02478 (2018)

A Construction for Constant Dimension Codes from the Known Codes

Kunxiao Zhou[1], Yindong Chen[2], Zusheng Zhang[1], Feng Shi[1],
and Xianmang He[1(✉)] (iD)

[1] Dongguan University of Technology, Dongguan, China
{zhoukx,zhangzs,hexm}@dgut.edu.cn
[2] Shantou University, Shantou, China
ydchen@stu.edu.cn

Abstract. One of the most fundamental topics in subspace coding is to explore the maximal possible value $\mathbf{A}_q(n, d, k)$ of a set of k-dimensional subspaces in $\mathbb{F}_q^n$ such that the subspace distance satisfies $d_S(U, V) = \dim(U + V) - \dim(U \cap V) \geq d$ for any two different k-dimensional subspaces U and V in this set. In this paper, we propose a construction for constant dimension subspace codes from the existing results. This construction is done by merging two existing constructions, which exceeds the latest improvements including the cases: $A_2(8, 4, 3) \geq 1331$ and $A_2(8, 4, 4) \geq 4802$.

Keywords: Subspace coding · Constant dimension codes · Lifted MRD code

1 Introduction

In traditional communication networks, it is generally believed that processing the data of intermediate routing nodes will not get any benefits. However, the network coding theory proposed by R. Ahlswede [1] completely overturned this traditional view. Taking the butterfly network as an example to illustrate that network coding can enable network information flow to be compressed. Therefore, the classic conclusion is overturned, that is, "independent bits can no longer be compressed." Subsequent research results slowly established the basic framework for network coding. In 2003, Li Shuoyan and Yang Weihao et al. proved in their famous paper [28] that as long as the number of the network node is large enough, the linear random network coding can reach the multi-cast capacity. Since then, the linear random network coding became one of the most important topics in the network.

In practical applications, how to ensure the error correction capability of the communication network is a very important issue. The interest in subspace coding was originally proposed in [22] by R. Köetter and F. R. Kschischang. This is due to the findings that codes in the projection space can be applied for error control in random linear network coding. Let q be prime powers, and $\mathbb{F}_q$

© Springer Nature Switzerland AG 2021
Z. Liu et al. (Eds.): WASA 2021, LNCS 12937, pp. 253–262, 2021.
https://doi.org/10.1007/978-3-030-85928-2_20

be the finite field with q elements. The set of all subspaces of $\mathbb{F}_q^n$ is denoted by $\mathcal{P}_q(n)$. It holds that $\mathcal{P}_q(n) = \bigcup_{k=0}^n \mathcal{G}_q(k, n)$, where $\mathcal{G}_q(k, n)$ denotes the set of all k-dimensional subspaces of $\mathbb{F}_q^n$ forms the Grassmannian over $\mathbb{F}_q$. Without loss of generality, we assume that $n \geq k$. Let

$$\binom{n}{k}_q = \prod_{i=0}^{k-1} \frac{q^{n-i} - 1}{q^{k-i} - 1}$$

be the q-ary Gauss binomial coefficient, which is the number of k-dimensional subspaces in $\mathbb{F}_q^n$. All subspaces forms a metric space with respect to the *subspace distance* characterized by

$$d_s(U, W) = \dim(U + W) - \dim(U \cap W), \ \forall U, W \in \mathcal{P}_q(n).$$

A subspace code $\mathcal{C}$ is a subset of the subspaces in $\mathbb{F}_q^n$. Its *minimum distance* of $\mathcal{C}$ is bounded by $d = \min\{d_s(U, W) \mid U, W \in \mathcal{C}, U \neq W\}$. If all subspace in $\mathcal{C}$ have the same dimension k, we use the notation $(n, \#\mathcal{C}, d, k)_q$ and call $\mathcal{C}$ a *constant dimension code (abbreviated with CDC)*. Often than not, the maximum possible value of an $(n, \#\mathcal{C}, d, k)_q$ CDC is usually denoted by $A_q(n, d, k)$.

In the past few years, a lot of new lower bounds from various constructions have been developed extensively in [5,6,16,17,24,26,32]. It is becoming more and more difficult to construct constant dimension subspace codes. However, there are still big gaps between presently best upper bounds and lower bounds for small parameters $n \leq 19$ and $q \leq 9$ in [18]. In this paper, we propose a method to improve the lower bounds for the CDCs' construction through Hungarian algorithm. Specifically, the codewords constructed by two different construction methods can be regarded as the two parts in the bipartite graph, and then the Hungarian algorithm can be used to calculate how many codewords when the two methods are combined together, and in the meanwhile the distance can be preserved.

The rest of the paper is organized as follows. In Sect. 2, we describe the previous known results about the construction of constant dimension code. The Hungarian algorithm is depicted in Sect. 3. Then, in Sect. 4, we present our main result. Section 5 gives some condition for the better results. Finally, the paper is concluded in Sect. 6.

2   Previous Known Results

There are a variety of lower bounds and upper bounds for constant dimension codes. The research team in University of Bayreuth has launched a website with tables for the presently best known upper and lower bounds for subspace coding. We refer to [18] and the website http://subspacecodes.uni-bayreuth.de. Even when the parameters are relatively small, the exact calculation of $A_q(n, d, k)$ is a difficult problem both algorithmically and theoretically generally.

The key element of the construction is the lifted maximum rank distance (MRD for short) code. It is of great interest to provide constructions of CDCs to improve its lower bound. An excellent work with this regard was done by the Echelon-Ferrers construction in the year of 2009 [12]. This construction generalizes the lifted MRD codes by introducing a new class of rank-metric codes having a given shape of their codewords. Later, the idea of the echelon-Ferrers construction was widely used, including coset construction [19], parallel construction [16,32], parallel linkage construction [5], combining method [6], pending dot [31], etc. The most powerful construction is the linkage construction [13] and its improved construction [20]. Since 2018, the linkage construction is improved by these new works [6,16,17,27].

A plethora of improvements for echelon-Ferrers construction by greedy algorithmic are given in [11,25]. X. He [15] etc. improved the linkage construction with the echelon-Ferrers. Authors of [23] modified a method of Braun, Kerber and Laue [3] to construct CDCs with a prescribed minimum distance. They also handled larger cases which have a prescribed group of automorphism. With a stochastic maximum weight clique algorithm and a systematic consideration of groups of automorphism, new lower bounds for $8 \leq n \leq 11$ are obtained in [2]. In [14], authors designed and implemented a series of algorithms using the GAP System for Computational Discrete Algebra and Wolfram Mathematica software, and presented a new method for the construction of cyclic Grassmannian codes.

All in all, it is more difficult to improve this bound at present, the gap between the upper and lower bounds of the constant dimension code is still very large, therefore, new construction methods are needed to reduce this gap.

3   Hungarian Algorithm

From the point of view of algorithm, given a large graph, it is not realistic to explore the largest complete subgraph. Silberstein et al. [30] gave the enumeration method of Grassmannian space $\mathcal{G}_q(k, n)$, that is, given parameters n, q, k, all of its k-dimensional subspaces can be represented by matrices, and the number of subspaces is $\begin{bmatrix} n \\ k \end{bmatrix}_q = \prod_{i=0}^{k-1} \frac{q^n - 1}{q^k - 1}$. As an example, we consider a simple case: $n = 6, d = 4, k = 3, q = 2$, then $\begin{bmatrix} 6 \\ 3 \end{bmatrix}_2 = 1275$, indicating that the running time of the largest complete subgraph algorithm is unacceptable. Consider this, we need other methods to solve this problem. For bipartite graphs, it is possible to find the largest complete subgraph by Hungarian algorithm.

3.1   Bipartite Graph

For the following results about bipartite graph, please refer to book graph theory [9,10]. Bipartite graph is a special model in graph theory. Let $G = (V, E)$ be an undirected graph. If the vertex set V can be divided into two disjoint subsets X and Y, and one of the two vertices connected by each edge of the graph is in X while the other is in Y, then the graph G is called a bipartite graph.

Throughout, we focus on problems of bipartite graphs $G = (V, E)$. In the following text, several basic concepts are described.

Definition 1 (match). *Given a bipartite graph G, a match is a set of edges, where any two edges have no common vertices.*

Definition 2 (maximum match). *Among all matches in a graph, the match with the most matching edges is called the maximum match of this graph.*

Given a bipartite graph, the maximum matching problem is solved by the Hungarian algorithm.

Definition 3 (point cover). *Given a graphs $G = (V, E)$, the point cover is a subset of V such that relative to all the edges.*

Definition 4 (minimum point cover). *Among all point covers in a graph, the one with the least points is called the minimum point cover of this graph.*

3.2 Hungarian Algorithm

Before we can describe the Hungarian algorithm, we need two following basic concepts.

Definition 5 (alternate path). *Starting from an unmatched point, the path formed by successively passing through non-matching edges, matching edges, non-matching edges... is called an alternate path.*

Definition 6 (augmentation path). *Let M be the set of matched edges in the bipartite graph G, if P is a path connecting two unmatched vertices in the graph G (the starting point of P is in the X part, the end point is in the Y part, and vice versa), and the edges belonging to M and edges not belonging to M (that is, the matched and waiting edges) alternately appear on P, then P is called an augmentation path relative to M.*

Now, we are ready to depict the Hungry algorithm. The framework of the algorithm is demonstrated in Algorithm 1.

The augmentation path is a "staggered track". In other words, its first edge has not participated in the matching yet, the second edge has participated in the matching, the third edge has not participated in the matching, ... It is staggered in this way, and the last edge has not participated in the matching. Thus the starting point and the ending point have not yet been matched.

Obviously, P has an odd number of edges, and the number of unmatched edges is exactly one more than that of the matching edges. According to the idea of "inverting", change the matching edges to unmatched, and unmatched to matching. Therefore a larger match is found. Repeat the previous steps until there is no more augmentation path, then a maximum match comes to be. This is the Hungarian algorithm, also called Kuhn-Munkres algorithm [21,29]. It is an $O(|V|^3)$ algorithm to find maximum matchings in bipartite graphs.

We can use Depth-First-Search (DFS) to find an augmentation path P starting from an unmatched vertex u in part X: Find an unvisited adjacent point v of u (v must be a Y vertex). If v is unmatched, an augmentation road u-v has been found. If v has been matched, then take out the matching vertex w of v (w must be an X vertex). Recursively, suppose P' is an augmentation path starting from w, then u-v-P' is an augmentation path starting from u. The outline of finding an augmentation path is illustrated in the Algorithm 2.

Algorithm 1. Hungarian Algorithm

Require: G, X, Y
Ensure: Maximum match M
1: Set M to be empty
2: do
3:      find an augmentation path P starting from unmatched vertex
4:      obtain a larger matching M' instead of M
5: until no augmentation path can be found

Algorithm 2. Augmentation-Path(G, X, Y, u)

Require: G, X, Y, a vertex $u \in X$
Ensure: an augmentation path starting from u
1: For each unvisited adjacent point v of u
2:      If v does not matched
3:          Return u-v
4:      Else
5:          take out the matching vertex w of v
6:          $P' = $ Augmentation-Path$(G-\{u,v\}, X-\{u\}, Y-\{v\}, w)$
7:          Return u-v-P'
8: End for

3.3 Minimum Point Cover for Bipartite Graph

Based the maximum match M, the minimum point cover C is easy to find (illustrated in Algorithm 3), according to the bipartite graph theory [10].

Algorithm 3. Minimum-Point-Covering (from maximum-match)

Require: G, X, Y, maximum-match M
Ensure: Minimum Point Cover C
1: Let M_X be the point set both in M and X
2: Set $C \leftarrow M_X$
3: For each point $x \in X - M_X$
4:      find an alternate path P starting from x
5:      Let X', Y' be the point sets of P such that relative to X, Y, respectively
6:      $C \leftarrow C \cup Y' - X'$
7: End for
8: Output C as the minimum point cover

---

4 Our Construction

In this section, we give our construction on how to improve the lower bounds through Hungarian algorithm.

4.1   Lifted MRD Code

In this subsection, we give the definition of lifted MRD code, which will be used as a building block in our construction.

A theory of matrix codes with the rank-distance has been widely used to construct CDC. Let $A, B \in \mathbb{F}_q^{n \times k}$ of size $n \times k$ matrices over $\mathbb{F}_q$, and the rank-distance is defined as

$$d_r(\mathbf{M}) = \min_{A \neq B} \{ d_r(A, B) : A, B \in \mathbf{M} \},$$

where $d_r(A, B) = \text{rank}(A - B)$ is the rank-distance of A and B. An $[n \times k, \varrho, d]$ rank-metric code C is a linear code, whose codewords are $n \times k$ matrices over $\mathbb{F}_q$. These matrices form a linear subspace of dimension ϱ of $\mathbb{F}_q^{n \times k}$, and for each two distinct codewords A and B we have $d_r(A, B) \geq d$. For an $[n \times k, \varrho, d]$ rank-metric code C, it was proved in [7,8] that

$$\varrho \leq \min \{ n(k-d+1), \ k(n-d+1) \}.$$

For any given MRD code $Q_q(n, k, d)$ with rank-distance d, we have an $(n + k, q^{n(k-d+1)}, 2d, k)_q$ CDC, consisting of $q^{n(k-d+1)}$ subspaces of dimension k in $\mathbb{F}_q^{n+k}$, defined as $\text{lift}(U_A) = \{ \text{rowspace}[I_k, A] \}$, and spanned by rows of (I_k, A). Here I_k is the $k \times k$ identity matrix. For any A and B, the subspaces U_A and U_B, spanned by rows of (I_k, A) and (I_k, B) respectively, are the same if and only if $A = B$. The intersection $U_A \cap U_B$ is the set $\{ (\alpha, \alpha A) : \alpha A = \alpha B, \alpha \in \mathbb{F}_q^k \}$. Thus $\dim(U_A \cap U_B) = k - \text{rank}(A-B) \leq k - d$. We can easily check that the distance of this CDC is $2d$. This construction is often called a lifted MRD code.

4.2   Our Method

In this subsection, we depict our method on how to improve the lower bounds by Hungarian algorithm. In the website http://subspacecodes.uni-bayreuth.de/, there exists a plethora of constructions. Any two constructions can be regarded as parts X and Y in a bipartite graph, respectively. Then the Hungarian algorithm can be applied to calculate the size of $X \cup Y$. Towards this, the distance d_s should be preserved. More generally, we need the following Algorithm 4 to get our final result:

At the beginning, we choose two constructions from the existing results. These two sets of codewords are regarded as X and Y in the bipartite G. Each codeword is treated as a node in G. Then we need to decide the edge sets E. For this, we compute the distance between any pair $d_s(x_i, y_j), x_i \in X, y_j \in Y$. There is a edge $e \in E$ between x_i and y_j if $d_s(x_i, y_j) < d$. Otherwise, no edge between nodes x_i and y_j. Later, we apply Hungarian algorithm to get a maximum match set M, based on which, the minimum point cover C is gotten by Algorithm 3.

In the final step, we output the final results, i.e., the maximum independent set: $X \cup Y - C$. We notice that for any two nodes v_1, v_2 in the maximum

---

Algorithm 4. Apply for CDCs' Construction

Require: G, X, Y, d
Ensure:
 1: pick codewords from two constructions as X and Y, respectively
 2: compute the distance between each pair $d_s(x_i, y_j), x_i \in X, y_j \in Y$
 3: If $d_s(x_i, y_j) < d$,
 4:       then there is a edge $e \in E$ between x_i and y_j
 5: else
 6:       no edge between nodes x_i and y_j
 7: apply the Hungarian algorithm to the maximum match set M
 8: apply Algorithm 3 to get the minimum point cover C
 9: output the maximum independent set: $I = X \cup Y - C$

---

independent set, there's no edge between them, meaning they have a distance $d_s(v_1, v_2) \geq d$. This induces the following Theorem 1. In addiction, the overall cost is bounded by $O(|V|^3)$, where V is the size of the graph.

Theorem 1. *The code produced by Algorithm 4 is a constant dimension code.*

Proof. First, all nodes in the set $X \cup Y - C$ are k-dimensional subspaces. Notice that the set $X \cup Y - C$ is a maximum independent set, then for any nodes $v_1, v_2 \in X \cup Y - C$, then $d_s(v_1, v_2) \geq d$, therefore, the set $X \cup Y - C$ is a constant dimension code.

4.3 Examples

In this subsection, we give some examples to illustrate our construction. The lifted MRD codes play a role as the X part in the bipartite.

Example 1. Let $n = 8, k = 4, d = 4$, X is the lifted MRD code rowspace$[Q_2(4,4,2), I_4]$, with the size 4096; Y is the code from the paper [4] with the size 4801. Apply the Hungarian algorithm to get the set I with the size 4802.

The current best bound for $A_2(8,4,4)$ is 4801, which is adopted from the paper [4]. This lower bound is the result of the algorithm, while theoretically the result of using various methods is 4799.

Example 2. Let $n = 8, k = 3, d = 4$, X is the lifted MRD code rowspace$[Q_2(5,2,3), I_3]$, with the size 1024; Y is the code from the paper [4] with the size 1326. Apply the Hungarian algorithm to get the set I with the size 1331.

The current best bound for $A_2(8,4,3)$ is 1326, which is adopted from the paper [4]. This lower bound is also the result of the algorithm, while theoretically the result of using various methods is 1179. This shows that the algorithm is very effective in some cases.

Example 3. Let $n = 7, d = 4, k = 3$, X is the lifted MRD code rowspace$[Q_2(4, 2, 3), I_3]$, with the size 256; Y is the code from the paper [4] with the size 333. Apply the Hungarian algorithm to get the set I with the size 333.

Remark: In brief, the main idea behind our improvement is exploiting the fact that the Hungarian algorithm can produces larger codes, at least not less than the original construction.

5   Conditions for Better Result

From Example 3, we found that the Hungarian algorithm does not always produce better results. Actually, this is the most cases. Therefore, we are wondering whether there exists some cases that $|I|$ is strictly larger than $\max\{|X|, |Y|\}$? We can answer this question in the following theorem. Without loss of generality, assume that $|X| \geq |Y|$.

Theorem 2. $|I| > |X|$ *if and only if the vertices in the Y part are not fully matched.*

Proof. (1) If $|I| > |X|$, then the vertices in the Y part are not fully matched, otherwise, the Y part are fully matched, then $|I| = |X|$. This is a contradiction.

(2) If the vertices in the Y part are not fully matched, then the size of the maximum match is less than $|Y|$. It is clear that $I = |X| + |Y| - |M| > |X|$.

In order to determine whether a complete matching exists, we turn to Hall's marriage theorem. Let $N(A)$ be the set of nodes adjacent to node $v \in A$.

Theorem 3. *[Hall's Marriage Theorem] The bipartite graph $G = (V, E)$ with bipartition (X, Y) has a full matching from X to Y if and only if $|N(A)| \geq |A|$ for all subset A of X.*

Combining Theorem 2 and Theorem 3, the following theorem is obvious.

Theorem 4. $|I| > |X|$ *if and only if $\exists A \subseteq Y$ such that $|N(A)| < |A|$.*

6   Conclusion

In the paper, we apply the Hungarian algorithm to improve the lower bounds for the constant dimension codes. Some improvements are given in the examples. This construction allows us to calculate the union of any two constructions, which helps us to explore the new bounds for constant dimension codes construction. This method can be used to do more examples. We need to find two different sets as $\{X, Y\}$ parts in a bipartite graph, then there may be further improvements in the future.

Acknowledgement. The work is supported by the Science and Technology Planning Project of Guangdong Province (No. 190827105555406, 2019B010116001), the Natural Science Foundation of Guangdong Province (No. 2020A1515010899), the Key Scientific Research Project of Universities in Guangdong Province (No. 2020ZDZX3028), the innovation strong school project of Guangdong Province (No. 2020K2D2X1201) and the Natural Science Foundation of China (NO.61672303,61872083,61872081).

References

1. Ahlswede, R., Ning Cai, Li, S.R., Yeung, R.W.: Network information flow. IEEE Trans. Inf. Theory **46**(4), 1204–1216 (2000)
2. Braun, M.J., Ostergrad, P.R., Wassermann, A.: New lower bounds for binary constant-dimension subspace codes. Exp. Math. **27**(2), 179–183 (2018). https://doi.org/10.1080/10586458.2016.1239145
3. Braun, M., Kerber, A., Laue, R.: Systematic construction OFQ-analogs of (v, k,)-designs. Des. Codes Crypt. **34**(1), 55–70 (2005)
4. Braun, M., Ostergard, P.R.J., Wassermann, A.: New lower bounds for binary constant-dimension subspace codes. Exp. Math. **27**(2), 179–183 (2016). https://doi.org/10.1080/10586458.2016.1239145
5. Chen, H., He, X., Weng, J., Xu, L.: New constructions of subspace codes using subsets of MRD codes in several blocks. IEEE Trans. Inf. Theory **66**(9), 5317–5321 (2020). http://arxiv.org/abs/1908.03804
6. Cossidente, A., Kurz, S., Marino, G., Pavese, F.: Combining subspace codes. CoRR abs/1911.03387 (2019)
7. Cruz, J.D.L., Gorla, E., Lopez, H.H., Ravagnani, A.: Rank distribution of Delsarte codes. Mathematics (2015)
8. Delsarte, P.: Bilinear forms over a finite field, with applications to coding theory. J. Comb. Theory **25**(3), 226–241 (1978)
9. Diestel, R.: Graph theory. Math. Gazette **173**(502), 67–128 (2000)
10. Duo, L.: Discrete Mathematics and Applications. Tsinghua University Press (2013). (in Chinese)
11. He, X.: A hierarchical-based greedy algorithm for Echelon-Ferrers construction. arXiv (2019)
12. Etzion, T., Silberstein, N.: Error-correcting codes in projective spaces via rank-metric codes and Ferrers diagrams. IEEE Trans. Inf. Theory **55**(7), 2909–2919 (2009)
13. Gluesing-Luerssen, H., Troha, C.: Construction of subspace codes through linkage. Adv. Math. Commun. **10**(3), 525–540 (2016)
14. Gutirrez-Garca, I., Naizir, I.M.: Finding cliques in projective space: a method for construction of cyclic Grassmannian codes. IEEE Access **8**, 51333–51339 (2020). https://doi.org/10.1109/ACCESS.2020.2980670
15. He, X., Chen, Y., Zhang, Z.: Improving the linkage construction with Echelon-Ferrers for constant-dimension codes. IEEE Commun. Lett. **24**, 1875–1879 (2020)
16. He, X.: Construction of constant dimension code from two parallel versions of linkage construction. IEEE Commun. Lett. **24**(11), 2392–2395 (2020)
17. Heinlein, D.: Generalized linkage construction for constant-dimension codes. arxiv.org (2019)
18. Heinlein, D., Kiermaier, M., Kurz, S., Wassermann, A.: Tables of subspace codes. arxiv.org (2016)
19. Heinlein, D., Kurz, S.: COSET construction for subspace codes. IEEE Trans. Inf. Theory **PP**(99), 1 (2015)
20. Heinlein, D., Kurz, S.: Asymptotic bounds for the sizes of constant dimension codes and an improved lower bound. In: Coding Theory and Applications, ICMCTA 2017 (2017)
21. Kuhn, H.W.: The Hungarian method for the assignment problem. Naval Res. Logist. Quart. **2**, 83–97 (1955)

22. Koetter, R., Kschischang, F.R.: Coding for errors and erasures in random network coding. IEEE Trans. Inf. Theory **54**(8), 3579–3591 (2008)
23. Kohnert, A., Kurz, S.: Construction of large constant dimension codes with a prescribed minimum distance. In: Calmet, J., Geiselmann, W., Müller-Quade, J. (eds.) Mathematical Methods in Computer Science. LNCS, vol. 5393, pp. 31–42. Springer, Heidelberg (2008). https://doi.org/10.1007/978-3-540-89994-5_4
24. Kurz, S.: A note on the linkage construction for constant dimension codes. arXiv:1906.09780, https://arxiv.org/abs/1906.09780 (2019)
25. Kurz, S.: Lifted codes and the multilevel construction for constant dimension codes. arXiv:2004.14241 (2020)
26. Lao, H., Chen, H., Weng, J., Tan, X.: Parameter-controlled inserting constructions of constant dimension subspace codes. arxiv.org (2020)
27. Li, F.: Construction of constant dimension subspace codes by modifying linkage construction. IEEE Trans. Inf. Theory **66**(5), 2760–2764 (2020)
28. Li, S., Yeung, R., Cai, N.: Linear network coding. IEEE Trans. Inf. Theory **49**(2), 371–381 (2003)
29. Munkres, J.: Algorithms for the assignment and transportation problems. SIAM. J **10**, 196–210 (1962)
30. Silberstein, N., Etzion, T.: Enumerative coding for Grassmannian space. IEEE Trans. Inf. Theory **57**(1), 365–374 (2011)
31. Silberstein, N., Trautmann, A.L.: Subspace codes based on graph matchings, Ferrers diagrams, and pending blocks. IEEE Trans. Inf. Theory **61**(7), 3937–3953 (2015)
32. Xu, L., Chen, H.: New constant-dimension subspace codes from maximum rank-distance codes. IEEE Trans. Inf. Theory **64**(9), 6315–6319 (2018)

CSI-Based Calibration Free Localization with Rotating Antenna for Coal Mine

Tieyang Zhang, Kuiyuan Zhang, Dongjingdian Liu, and Pengpeng Chen[✉]

China University of Mining and Technology, Xuzhou, China
{zhangty,chenp}@cumt.edu.cn

Abstract. Accurate mine localization has always been an urgent demand. With the widespread emergence of cheap wireless devices in our life, channel state information (CSI) based indoor localization has attracted people's attention. In the existing CSI-based localization methods, fingerprint-based localization needs to build a huge database with poor robustness, and the methods based on angle of arrival (AOA) need specific antenna arrays and complex phase calibration. Because mobile devices such as smartphones only have one or two antennas, and the antennas inside the devices cannot form a receiving array, the conventional AOA estimation system cannot be deployed on such mobile devices. Therefore, we propose an AOA estimation method using rotating AP antennas. This method only needs one antenna at the receiving end to work and does not need to calibrate the phase. Firstly, the CSI phase of the rotating antenna is collected and the phase difference is calculated. Then, empirical mode decomposition (EMD) algorithm based on mutual information is used to remove the noise, and subcarrier selection is used to reduce the multipath effect in the data processing part. Finally, the AOA is estimated according to the relative position of the antenna. We conduct extensive experiments in mine and laboratory scenarios, and the median localization errors in mine and laboratory are $0.4\,\mathrm{m}$ and $0.6\,\mathrm{m}$, the median angle errors are $4.2°$ and $5.2°$ respectively.

Keywords: Indoor localization · Channel state information · Smartphone

1 Introduction

Accurate mine localization has always been an urgent demand. Among the existing localization methods, the Global Positioning System (GPS) has a perfect practical application, which can have a good localization and tracking effect outdoors. However, in closed environments, such as mines and indoors, the precision of GPS is limited. ZigBee [2] and UWB [4] have high accuracy, but they both need additional relatively expensive hardware facilities. In recent years,

This work was supported by Chinese National Natural Science Foundation (51774282) and Fundamental Research Funds for the Central Universities (2020ZDPY0305).

© Springer Nature Switzerland AG 2021
Z. Liu et al. (Eds.): WASA 2021, LNCS 12937, pp. 263–274, 2021.
https://doi.org/10.1007/978-3-030-85928-2_21

wireless devices appear widely in people's lives. Due to the low complexity and low cost of wireless WiFi equipment deployment, it has become a new choice for indoor localization.

In the early days, people used RSSI [3] for localization. After CSI, which is more fine-grained than RSSI, can be extracted from hardware [8], it becomes a trend to use CSI for localization. In the existing work, fingerprint-based localization [11,17,18,23] focuses on extracting the characteristics of CSI in different locations to construct a fingerprint database and designing a matching algorithm. Nevertheless, this is a labor-intensive method, the location accuracy is related to the fingerprint database, and once the environment changes, it needs to update the fingerprint database, which has poor robustness. AOA-based localization [10,13,14,22] reduces labor. However, while commercial WiFi is cheap and easy to deploy, it is different from the special wireless module in that it introduces various phase offsets due to its uncalibrated signal. Although researchers have proposed many methods [12,16,22] to correct the error, these methods can not completely eliminate the phase offset. Most importantly, these methods require a specific number and layout of antennas. In the real home environment, some routers only have two transmit antennas at 2.4 GHz or 5 GHz, mobile devices such as mobile phones often have only one or two antennas, and different devices have different antenna layouts, which also limits the actual deployment of CSI based localization system.

In this paper, we propose an AOA estimation method based on rotating antennas. In this method, two antennas are rotated at the transmitting end, and one antenna of the mobile device is used for acquisition. The position of the mobile device relative to AP is estimated by unwrapping of phase difference, empirical mode decomposition (EMD) denoising based on mutual information, selection of subcarrier and determination of extreme point of phase difference. The main contributions of this paper are as follows:

- We propose a rotating AP localization method, which is suitable for equipment with only one antenna. And it doesn't need complex phase correction, and it doesn't need to build a fingerprint database.
- In view of the characteristics of the phase difference of rotation signal, EMD algorithm based on mutual information is used for denoising. In addition, a subcarrier selection algorithm is proposed to reduce environmental interference.
- We conduct experiments in two scenarios, and the results show that this method has good performance.

2   Preliminaries

CSI can represent the state properties of a communication link between a sender and a receiver. The CSI obtained by modifying the firmware is in the form of channel frequency response (CFR). CFR can be expressed as:

$$H(f_i) = |H(f_i)|e^{j(\angle H(f_i))} \tag{1}$$

where $|H(f_i)|$ represents the amplitude, $\angle H(f_i)$ represents the phase, and f_i represents the frequency of the ith subcarrier. There are several types of CSI information that can be used for location.

CSI Amplitude: In early studies, the amplitude of CSI was often used for distance estimation [20] and fingerprint construction. However, in later studies [5,15], it was found that CSI amplitude was stable at different distances, and CSI amplitude could not directly reflect the distance relationship between transmitter and receiver. It is because that WIFI is designed for communication, automatic gain control (AGC) can dynamically adjust the gain of the amplifier to maintain an appropriate signal amplitude at the output, regardless of how the signal amplitude (RSSI) changes at the input. Therefore, CSI amplitude is difficult to be used for localization. Many fingerprint localization methods using CSI amplitude make more use of the multipath effect reflected in CSI amplitude.

CSI Phase: Because the CSI phase in commercial wireless devices is affected by carrier frequency offset (CFO) [6], sampling frequency offset (SFO) [21], packet boundary delay detection (PBD) [9] and etc., Consequently, the CSI phase is instable even at a fixed position. Many studies have proposed methods to calibrate CSI phase, such as Using Channel Reciprocity [16], Using Wired Communication to calibrate the offset [22], etc. All of these methods can reduce the CSI phase offset, but some of them are limited by equipment and other factors. The wired method must stop communication and calibrate offline. Channel reciprocity requires complex calculations, etc. And these methods can not completely eliminate the phase offset of CSI.

CSI Phase Difference: Many existing CSI systems use phase differences [19] to remove phase offsets. In addition to channel noise, there are three offsets in the original phase of CSI :CFO, SFO, and PBD. On the original CSI data, these offsets result in a uniform phase distribution at $[-\pi, \pi]$. The acquired CSI phase can be expressed as

$$\angle \overline{CSI}_i = \angle CSI_i + (\lambda_p + \lambda_s)m_i + \lambda_c + \beta + N \qquad (2)$$

Where $\angle CSI_I$ is the true phase value, m_i is the subcarrier index of subcarrier i, β is the initial phase offset caused by phase-locked loop (PLL), N is the measurement noise, λ_p, λ_s and λ_c are PBD, SFO and CFO respectively. Because the antennas of the NIC use the same clock and the same down-conversion frequency. Therefore, the phase of the measured subcarrier i in the two antennas has the same packet detection delay, sampling period, and frequency difference. Thus, the phase difference measured by subcarrier i between the two antennas can be approximated as:

$$\Delta \angle \overline{CSI}_i = \Delta \angle CSI_I + \Delta \beta + \Delta N \qquad (3)$$

Where $\Delta \angle CSI_i$ is the true phase difference of the subcarrier, $\Delta \beta$ is a constant phase offset [6], and ΔN is the noise with the variance of σ^2. So the phase difference can reflect the change of the real phase difference.

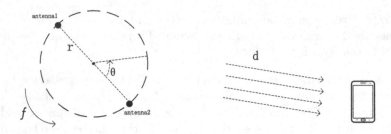

Fig. 1. Rotation model

3   Antenna Rotation Model

3.1   Rotating Signal

In this paper, we rotate the router and receive the phase of the two antennas at the transmitter respectively at the receiver end, as shown in the Fig. 1. The phase collected by the receiver can be written as:

$$\angle CSI_i = (\frac{2\pi}{\lambda_i}D + C + N) \bmod 2\pi \qquad (4)$$

Where i is the subcarrier number, λ_i is the wavelength, D is the distance between the antenna of the transmitter and the receiver, C is the SFO, CFO, PBD caused by the equipment, and N is the noise. When the antenna rotates, the CSI phase collected is:

$$\angle CSI_i = (\frac{2\pi}{\lambda_i}(d + r\cos(2\pi f_s t + \theta)) + C + N) \bmod 2\pi \qquad (5)$$

Where d is the distance from the rotation center to the antenna at the receiving end, r is the rotation radius, f_s is the rotation speed, t is the time, and θ is the angle at the initial moment. Similarly, we can write the acquisition phase of another antenna:

$$\angle CSI_i = (\frac{2\pi}{\lambda_i}(d - r\cos(2\pi f_s t + \theta)) + C + N) \bmod 2\pi \qquad (6)$$

According to the phase difference theory in the previous section, we can use phase difference to eliminate partial phase shift. So the phase difference can be written as:

$$\Delta\angle CSI_i = (\frac{4\pi}{\lambda_i}r\cos(2\pi f_s t + \theta) + \Delta\beta + \Delta N) \bmod 2\pi \qquad (7)$$

From the formula 7, It can be seen that the phase difference of the rotating antenna is related to the distance of the antenna, the speed of rotation, the wavelength of the subcarrier, the initial position, and the initial phase distortion. Since the initial phase distortion does not change with time, for a rotating AP

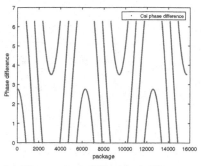

(a) Theoretical CSI phase difference

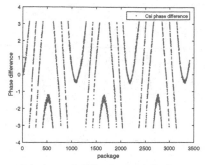

(b) Actual CSI phase difference

Fig. 2. When the antenna distance is 18 cm, the theoretical CSI phase difference and the actual CSI phase difference

with a certain antenna spacing, the phase difference of the same subcarrier is a cosine function.

Since the collected data is obtained by taking the remainder of the real data, the phase jump will occur at $-\pi$ and π. By the property of the cosine function, when $COS(2\pi f_s t + \theta)$ is -1 or 1, CSI phase difference should be the extreme point. From an experimental point of view, the distance between the two antennas of the router and the antenna on the smartphone is greatest when they are in a straight line, and the phase difference is an extremum. This phenomenon can be observed in an empty laboratory with LOS, as shown in the Fig. 2.

However, the indoor environment is very complex. The signal from the transmitter to the receiver will often travel through the light of sight (LOS) and multiple reflection paths (such as human body, wall, furniture reflection). Therefore, the CSI actually collected can be written as the superposition of multiple paths. Therefore, the router rotation model mentioned above can be written as:

$$\Delta \angle CSI_i = [\sum_{k=1}^{m} \frac{4\pi}{\lambda_i} r \cos(2\pi f_s t + \theta_k) + \Delta \beta_k + \Delta N_k] \bmod 2\pi \qquad (8)$$

It can be seen from the formula 8 that the collected CSI phase difference data is the superposition of k path signals, and its value is still related to the rotation of the antenna. However, due to the influence of the multipath effect, when the phase difference is at the maximum or minimum value, the two rotating antennas and the receiving antenna are not necessarily in a straight line.

In order to observe the influence of multipath reflection, we place the transmitter and receiver 0.1 m above the ground with an interval of 2 m. Move a cabinet that is 1 m high, 0.6 m long, and 0.4 m wide into the LOS between the transceiver antennas. As shown in the Fig. 3 (the data is partially processed in the next section), it can be observed that when the LOS is not occluded, the reflection caused by the cabinet has little effect on the CSI phase difference. When the LOS is occluded by the cabinet, the phase difference of CSI changes

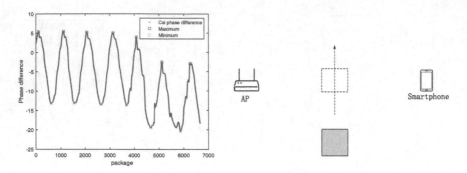

Fig. 3. Move the cabinet from outside LOS to inside LOS, the phase difference of subcarrier 1

greatly, but the rotation characteristic can still be observed. Therefore, to accurately locate the location of the receiving device, it is necessary to process the data to weaken the influence of multipath on the phase difference of CSI.

3.2   Data Processing

Unwrapped CSI Phase Difference. Since the CSI data collected by the device is in the range of $[-\pi, \pi]$ after the mod operation, there will be a phase jump at $-\pi$ and π. First of all, we need to unwrap the CSI phase difference data collected (see in Fig. 5(a)).

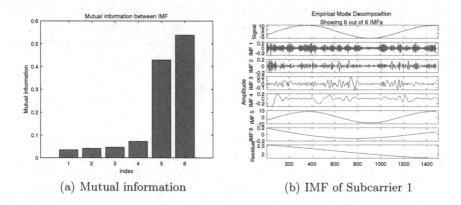

(a) Mutual information   (b) IMF of Subcarrier 1

Fig. 4. Noise Removal based on mutual information and EMD

Noise Removal Based on Mutual Information and EMD. According to the conclusion in the previous section, when the phase difference of CSI is between maximum and minimum, the two antennas of the router and the antenna at the receiving end are in a straight line. As there are many noises during data collection, there will be many "fake peaks", (see Fig. 5(b)) which affect the determination of the extreme point. In this paper, empirical mode decomposition (EMD) is used to remove noise. Compared with traditional denoising methods, EMD-based filtering is completely data-driven and can dynamically filter non-signal components according to the characteristics of the signal itself rather than the fixed cutoff frequency. EMD decomposes CSI phase difference $H_i(t)$ into a series of the intrinsic mode functions $IMF(t)$ and a residual $r(t)$.

$$H_i(t) = r(t) + \sum_{n=1}^{m} IMF_n(t) \tag{9}$$

As can be seen from Formula 8, for a rotating AP, the CSI change caused by its rotation is related to rotation speed and antenna spacing.

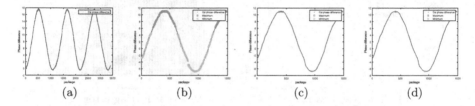

(a)   (b)   (c)   (d)

Fig. 5. (a) Unwrapped CSI phase difference. (b) Before denoising. (c) After the EMD filter. (d) After threshold filtering.

Therefore, the mutual information between IMF is calculated first, and the IMF with low mutual information is deleted. After that, the rest IMF and residual were reorganized to filter out the ambient noise unrelated to rotation. As shown in the Fig. 4(a), each bar in the figure represents the mutual information between the ith IMF and the i+1th IMF. It can be seen that from the fifth IMF, the degree of correlation between the IMF was significantly increased, so the first four IMF were deleted, and the remaining IMF was reunited with the residual IMF. After processing, it can be seen that the points become smooth, reducing the false peak when looking for the extreme point. After that, thresholds are set according to the sampling rate of CSI collection and the speed of router rotation to filter false peaks.

Subcarrier Selection. In 802.11, each channel consists of multiple subcarriers. Because each subcarrier has a different frequency, its reflection is not the same when propagating in the environment. The study of Zhou [24] shows that the received CSI subcarriers have different performances in AOA calculation.

In the experiment in the previous section, the phase difference of subcarrier 1 and subcarrier 35 is shown in the Fig. 6(a) when the cabinet moves from outside LOS to LOS. It is obvious from the figure that when LOS is not completely blocked by the cabinet, the performance of the two subcarriers is similar, which can reflect the phase difference change with the rotation of the antenna. When LOS is occluded, the performance of subcarrier 1 degrades slightly, while the performance of subcarrier 35 degrades very much, making it difficult to distinguish the rotation changes in the phase difference. Therefore, it is necessary to select the subcarriers that are less affected by the environment to reduce the influence of the multipath effect. In this paper, we consider that the performance of the subcarrier closer to the sin function is better (see Fig. 6(b)), and the best subcarrier is the one with the least fitting error.

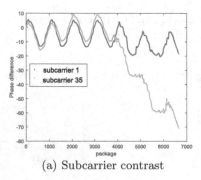
(a) Subcarrier contrast

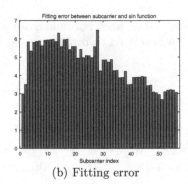
(b) Fitting error

Fig. 6. The change in phase difference of subcarrier 1 and subcarrier 35 when the cabinet moves.

3.3 AoA Estimation

Once the extreme point has been determined, the next step is to estimate the position of the device relative to the rotating router. After data processing, it is considered that when the phase difference of CSI is at the extreme point, the two rotating antennas and the receiving antenna of the device are on the straight line. Therefore, the position of the device's antenna can be determined on a two-dimensional map by knowing the positions of the two rotating antennas so as to obtain the angle of the device relative to the rotating router.

The calculation steps of relative angle are as follows: firstly, the device collects the CSI information of the rotating AP, calculates the CSI phase difference of the rotating antenna, and sends the phase difference data to the server. Then the server processes the phase difference data and calculates the angle of the equipment relative to the antenna according to the position of each rotating antenna. This process requires clock synchronization between the device and the server. The existing clock synchronization protocols [1] have achieved sub-microsecond accuracy, so the angle error caused by clock error can be ignored.

4   Performance Evaluation

4.1   Experimental Scenarios

In the experiment, two TL-wdr 5610 are used as access points, and one nexus 6p with nexmon [7] patch and bcm4358 wifi chip is used as receiver object. TL-wdr 5610 works in 2.4 GHz band, 20 MHz bandwidth, and has two omnidirectional antennas. Eight nokov optical 3D motion capture cameras were used to measure the ground truth. We choose the laboratory and mine for the experiment, and the experimental scene is shown in the Fig. 7.

(a) Laboratory   (b) Mine

Fig. 7. Experimental scenarios

4.2   Experimental Evaluation

Summary: We use spotfi and our method to estimate AOA on nexus 6p. The position of the device is calculated by the AOA of two sets of rotating antennas. Extensive experiments have been carried out in mine and laboratory. It can be seen from Fig. 8 that the median localization errors in mines and laboratories are 0.4 m and 0.6 m, and the median angle errors are 4.2° and 5.2°. The reason for the high localization accuracy of mine is that compared with the table and chair reflection in the laboratory, the mine generally has only LOS and wall reflection. As shown in the Fig. 8(b), (c), the AOA median error of the proposed method is lower than those of spotfi algorithm in both experimental Scenarios. This is because there are only two antennas in the nexus 6p, and the antenna of the mobile phone is built in the body. Compared with the external antenna, it will be interfered with by other components inside the mobile phone. In order to accurately estimate the incident angle of signal, the music algorithm used by spotfi needs more antennas than the number of signal propagation paths. Therefore, when the phase is subject to additional interference, and the number of antennas is insufficient, the performance will be significantly affected. Next, we will further analyze the system performance in the mine.

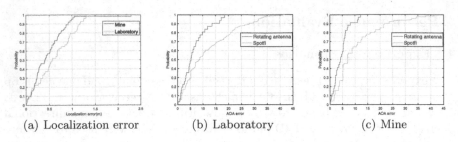

(a) Localization error   (b) Laboratory   (c) Mine

Fig. 8. Performance

Impact of Denoising Methods: Figure 9(a) shows the performance of EMD and savitzky Golay filtering in NLOS. Savitzky Golay filter can smooth the curve and retain the original characteristics of the curve. It can be seen from the figure that the median error of AOA estimation using EMD filter is 5.9° and 80% error is 11.3°, while using savitzky Golay filter is 7.4° and 13.9°. Because CSI has a lot of noise in the acquisition, when the noise is not in the form of outliers, the general denoising method is difficult to remove. Based on the mutual correlation between the IMF and the noise of the system, the maximum degree of correlation between the IMF and the signal can be preserved.

Impact of Subcarriers: Figure 9(b) shows the performance difference of localization using subcarrier 1 and subcarrier 35 in the case of Los. The median error of AOA estimation using subcarrier 1 is 4.2° and 80% error is 6.2°. The median error of AOA estimation using subcarrier 35 is 4.4° and 80% error is 8.5°. It can be seen that even in the same environment, due to different subcarriers, the superposition of multipath effects is different, and the performance gap is huge. Therefore, it is very important to select suitable subcarriers in indoor localization.

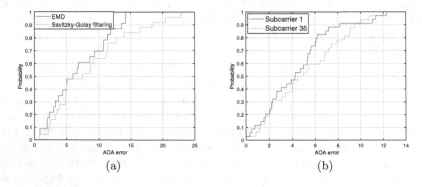

(a)   (b)

Fig. 9. (a) Performance under NLOS. (b) Performance of different subcarriers

5 Conclusion

In this paper, we propose a method of AOA estimation by rotating AP antenna, which is suitable for mobile devices with only one antenna and does not need to calibrate phase. The high-performance AOA estimation can be obtained by simply de-noising and subcarrier selection. In order to test the performance of the system, we conduct extensive experiments in laboratory and mine scenarios, and the median localization errors in mine and laboratory are 0.4 m and 0.6 m, the median angle errors are 4.2° and 5.2°,

References

1. IEEE standard for a precision clock synchronization protocol for networked measurement and control systems. IEEE STD 1588-2019 (Revision of IEEE STD 1588-2008), pp. 1–499 (2020). https://doi.org/10.1109/IEEESTD.2020.9120376
2. Alvarez, Y., Las Heras, F.: ZigBee-based sensor network for indoor location and tracking applications. IEEE Latin Am. Trans. **14**(7), 3208–3214 (2016)
3. Bahl, P., Padmanabhan, V.N.: Radar: an in-building RF-based user location and tracking system. In: Proceedings IEEE INFOCOM 2000. Conference on Computer Communications. Nineteenth Annual Joint Conference of the IEEE Computer and Communications Societies (Cat. No. 00CH37064), vol. 2, pp. 775–784. IEEE (2000)
4. Boston, J.D., Smith, B.J.: Multi-floor and multi-building ultra-wideband (UWB) location device, system, and method, US Patent 10,064,012, 28 August 2018
5. Gao, Z., Gao, Y., Wang, S., Li, D., Xu, Y.: CRISLoc: Reconstructable CSI fingerprinting for indoor smartphone localization. IEEE Internet Things J. **8**(5), 3422–3437 (2020)
6. Gjengset, J., Xiong, J., McPhillips, G., Jamieson, K.: Phaser: enabling phased array signal processing on commodity WiFi access points. In: Proceedings of the 20th Annual International Conference on Mobile Computing and Networking, pp. 153–164 (2014)
7. Gringoli, F., Schulz, M., Link, J., Hollick, M.: Free your CSI: a channel state information extraction platform for modern Wi-Fi chipsets. In: Proceedings of the 13th International Workshop on Wireless Network Testbeds, Experimental Evaluation & Characterization, pp. 21–28 (2019)
8. Halperin, D., Hu, W., Sheth, A., Wetherall, D.: Tool release: gathering 802.11 n traces with channel state information. ACM SIGCOMM Comput. Commun. Rev. **41**(1), 53 (2011)
9. Kandel, L.N., Yu, S.: Indoor localization using commodity Wi-Fi APs: techniques and challenges. In: 2019 International Conference on Computing, Networking and Communications (ICNC), pp. 526–530. IEEE (2019)
10. Kotaru, M., Joshi, K., Bharadia, D., Katti, S.: SpotFi: decimeter level localization using WiFi. In: Proceedings of the 2015 ACM Conference on Special Interest Group on Data Communication, pp. 269–282 (2015)
11. Kui, W., Mao, S., Hei, X., Li, F.: Towards accurate indoor localization using channel state information. In: 2018 IEEE International Conference on Consumer Electronics-Taiwan (ICCE-TW), pp. 1–2. IEEE (2018)
12. Qian, K., Wu, C., Zhang, Y., Zhang, G., Yang, Z., Liu, Y.: Widar2.0: passive human tracking with a single Wi-Fi link. In: Proceedings of the 16th Annual International Conference on Mobile Systems, Applications, and Services, pp. 350–361 (2018)

13. Soltanaghaei, E., Kalyanaraman, A., Whitehouse, K.: Multipath triangulation: decimeter-level WiFi localization and orientation with a single unaided receiver. In: Proceedings of the 16th Annual International Conference on Mobile Systems, Applications, and Services, pp. 376–388 (2018)
14. Tong, X., Li, H., Tian, X., Wang, X.: Triangular antenna layout facilitates deployability of CSI indoor localization systems. In: 2019 16th Annual IEEE International Conference on Sensing, Communication, and Networking (SECON), pp. 1–9. IEEE (2019)
15. Tong, X., Wan, Y., Li, Q., Tian, X., Wang, X.: CSI fingerprinting localization with low human efforts. IEEE/ACM Trans. Netw. 29(1), 372–385 (2020)
16. Vasisht, D., Kumar, S., Katabi, D.: Decimeter-level localization with a single WiFi access point. In: 13th {USENIX} Symposium on Networked Systems Design and Implementation ({NSDI} 2016), pp. 165–178 (2016)
17. Wang, F., Feng, J., Zhao, Y., Zhang, X., Zhang, S., Han, J.: Joint activity recognition and indoor localization with WiFi fingerprints. IEEE Access 7, 80058–80068 (2019)
18. Wang, X., Gao, L., Mao, S., Pandey, S.: CSI-based fingerprinting for indoor localization: a deep learning approach. IEEE Trans. Veh. Technol. 66(1), 763–776 (2016)
19. Wang, X., Yang, C., Mao, S.: Phasebeat: exploiting CSI phase data for vital sign monitoring with commodity WiFi devices. In: 2017 IEEE 37th International Conference on Distributed Computing Systems (ICDCS), pp. 1230–1239. IEEE (2017)
20. Wu, K., Xiao, J., Yi, Y., Chen, D., Luo, X., Ni, L.M.: CSI-based indoor localization. IEEE Trans. Parallel Distrib. Syst. 24(7), 1300–1309 (2012)
21. Xie, Y., Li, Z., Li, M.: Precise power delay profiling with commodity Wi-Fi. IEEE Trans. Mob. Comput. 18(6), 1342–1355 (2018)
22. Xiong, J., Jamieson, K.: Arraytrack: a fine-grained indoor location system. In: 10th {USENIX} Symposium on Networked Systems Design and Implementation ({NSDI} 2013), pp. 71–84 (2013)
23. Zhang, H., Tong, G., Xiong, N.: Fine-grained CSI fingerprinting for indoor localisation using convolutional neural network. IET Commun. 14(18), 3266–3275 (2020)
24. Zhou, Z., Yu, J., Yang, Z., Gong, W.: MobiFi: fast deep-learning based localization using mobile WiFi. In: GLOBECOM 2020-2020 IEEE Global Communications Conference, pp. 1–6. IEEE (2020)

Gray Failures Detection for Shared Bicycles

Hangfan Zhang, Mingchao Zhang, Camtu Nguyen$^{(\boxtimes)}$, Wenzhong Li,
Sheng Zhang, and Xiaoliang Wang$^{(\boxtimes)}$

State Key Laboratory for Novel Software Technology, Nanjing University,
Nanjing, China
{ncamtu,lwz,sheng,waxili}@nju.edu.cn

Abstract. Today bicycle sharing system has been widely deployed around the world to provide a convenient transit connectivity for short trips. However, due to the careless usage or incident, it is inevitable to have some shared bicycles in the bad working condition. Rather than the fail-stop failure, e.g., a broken tire, which can be easily detected by users, the gray failure, i.e., subtle faults, can only be discovered when riding the bike. Such gray failure causes bad user experience and affects the reputation of bicycle sharing system provider. Unfortunately, it is not easy to detect these gray failures. Current solution to this problem mainly relies on users' self-reporting. However, due to the lack of incentive mechanism and the knowledge on bicycle, cyclists may submit inaccurate report or ignore the subtle faults. To provide users the working condition of bicycles in advance and reduce the maintaining cost of system providers, this paper introduces an approach to automatically detect the gray failures of the shared bicycles. To this end, we leverage the smartphone to collect and analyze the data collected from the sensor-equipped bicycle. We extract patterns from sensing signals of broken bikes, and identify the problematic components of shared bicycles. Compared with the conventional user-reporting, the proposed method is cost-effective, automatic, and easy-to-deploy. Extensive experiments based on real bicycle sharing systems show that the proposed method achieves high accuracy in determining gray failures for a variety of scenarios.

Keywords: Bicycle sharing system · Failure detection · Mobile sensing

1 Introduction

Effective failure detection is one of the most important problems in bicycle sharing systems. Due to the careless usage or incidents, it is very common for a shared bike to have problems with its components. Users may be unaware of the gray failures, i.e., subtle faults like rotating handlebars, spongy brakes and bent wheels, etc. Although the bicycles with subtle faults can still be used, they are afflicted by the faults and have bad user experience. Moreover, a few failures such as spongy brakes are dangerous and harmful to the unsuspected users.

Z. Liu et al. (Eds.): WASA 2021, LNCS 12937, pp. 275–287, 2021.
https://doi.org/10.1007/978-3-030-85928-2_22

Currently, failure detection mainly relies on users' report. If a user finds a shared bike with problem, he/she can report the failure to the bicycle sharing system via the corresponding application. Generally, the applications require users to take a photo and demonstrate the failure clearly, which impose high burdens on users. Moreover, user report may be inaccurate (not specific to the actual failure component) or incorrect (refer to the wrong component), which increases the difficulty of failure identification. Specifically, due to the lack of incentive mechanism, users might ignore the gray failure report since it usually takes time to clearly demonstrate the problem.

Recently, multiple public transportation monitoring and evaluation systems have been proposed. With regard to the high energy consumption of GPS [1], sensors in smartphones are used to detect the vehicles driving behavior [2,10] and road condition [7]. For example, SenSpeed [12] is an instant sensing system to estimate vehicle speed in urban area. Tan et al. [8] use mobile crowd sensing [4] to detect and analyze the riding quality of public Transport vehicles. Mobile sensing is able to recognize various bicycling movements and identifying dangerous movements, etc. [5,6,9]. BikeSafe [5] detects cyclist's dangerous behavior during riding. Prior works mainly focus on driving or riding behavior monitoring, but they did not consider the detection of bicycle gray failures.

In this paper, we aim at realizing the automatic gray failures detection for shared bicycles. The smartphone can show the real-time bicycle information collected and processed from the sensing data. The proposed method relies on a smartphone carried by the user and an accelerometer deployed on the bicycle to collect data. Data collected from the smartphone is used to extract user behaviors like pedaling. Data collected from the accelerometer is used to observe the movement of the bicycle, like vibration. Through machine learning algorithms, the system is able to extract the pattern of various gray failures and identify failures in running time. Furthermore, we apply a three-axis accelerometer because the sensor's power consumption is low [11] and the price is cheap, around thirty cents today which is acceptable for shared bikes to reduce maintaining cost.

Our main challenge is how to detect various failures with the minimum number of sensors (low costs) and quantify the signal characteristics of each kind of failures (high accuracy). When a user with a smartphone rides an accelerometer-equipped bicycle, we use the data collected from the accelerometer and the smartphone to form an automatic failure report. Several common gray failures are considered here including bent wheels, leaky tires, spongy brakes, rotating handlebars. We conduct data processing on the raw sensing signal in each pedaling cycle to identify the abnormal behaviors. We use features to describe the data characteristics in each pedaling cycle. For example, to detect bent wheels, we quantify the probability and distribution of peak points. After extracting features for each set of data, the machine learning model will identify gray failures.

We test our system from three bicycle sharing companies: Mo-bikes, Hello-bikes and OfO-bikes. The sensor records the acceleration on three axes 50 times per second. Each set of experiments lasted approximately 20 s, including complete start-up from steady state, riding and braking. The participant cyclists are allowed to have the unusual riding behavior during the experiments. The experiments results have shown that the proposed approach is able to identify five kinds of main failures and distinguish the bicycle with subtle faults from normal bicycles. The accuracy to identify the gray failures can reach to 100%, 93.5% in terms of bent wheel and leaky tire, and 83.3% in terms of other failures.

The contributions of this work are listed as follows:

- We introduce the problem of gray failure detection for the first time on the bicycle sharing system. The identification of gray failures will help users achieve more information about the bicycle to be used, avoid unnecessary payment and the potential hazards.
- We propose a method for bicycle failure detection based on the data collected through an accelerometer attached to the bicycle and a smartphone in the cyclist's pocket. The system is cost effective and easy-to-deploy for current shared bicycle to complete the automatic failure detection. The report can be generated automatically without users' involvement.
- We implement the proposed method on the Android smartphone based prototype and evaluate its performance in practice through three real bicycle sharing systems (Mo-bikes, Hello-bikes and OfO-bikes). The experimental results verify the effectiveness of our gray failures detection.

2   System Design

2.1   Failure Detection Overview

We explain the idea of sensor-based gray failure detection through a well configured micro-benchmark. In order to detect several types of gray failures, we collect sensor data from shared bicycles with a specific failure (bent wheel, leaky tire, spongy brake or rotating handlebar) to see the effect of failure on sensing signal. It is notable that the considered failures of the bicycle are independent, and the probability of each failure is low in practice. According to the law of large number, it is rare that the bicycle has multiple failures at the same time. Hence we only consider the detection of single failure.

The deployment of the sensor needs to be considered in two aspects. On one hand, the sensor rely on the power supply of shared bicycle. It is difficult to deploy sensor on the rotating component of the shared bicycle, such as rim and pedal. On the other hand, the sensor should be deployed on the rigid-body to achieve the vibration signals of the bicycle and the forward speed, etc. Based on above consideration, we place the three-axis accelerometer at the seat stay, which has power supply and senses the vibration of the tube.

Fig. 1. System design

As shown in Fig. 1, We use an accelerometer fixed on the seat stays to provides stable signals other than sensors fixed at pedal, handlerbars or rim. We also collect data from the three-axis accelerometer on smartphone. The accelerometer collects acceleration and linear acceleration on three axes. We calculate the acceleration in the vertical direction and the acceleration in the forward direction from the three-axis acceleration, as well as the lateral acceleration. The bicycles are selected shared bicycles, including normal bicycle and bicycles with only one considered failure listed above. Data is collected by the same cyclist.

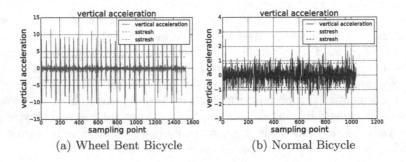

(a) Wheel Bent Bicycle   (b) Normal Bicycle

Fig. 2. Vertical acceleration on seat stays

We first collect vertical acceleration data from a wheel bent bicycle on the plain road. As shown in Fig. 2a, there are periodic bumps (shown as spikes in the collected data) during riding the bicycle. This spike is caused by the bent area of the wheel hitting the ground. The same part of the wheel hits the ground one time per cycle, which means the distance between two spike equals to the perimeter of the wheel. In other words, if we can quantify the distance between the two spikes, we can judge whether the wheel is bent. Figure 2b illustrates the vertical acceleration collected from a normal bicycle. There is no periodic bump in the normal riding process. The absolute vertical acceleration of a normal bicycle is relatively small, and the distribution is uniform. There are no particularly sharp peaks. Therefore, the distribution of spikes and the average of acceleration can also be used to identify abnormal bicycles.

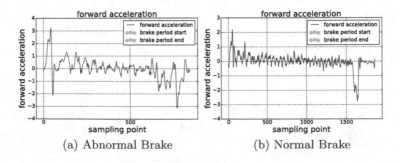

(a) Abnormal Brake   (b) Normal Brake

Fig. 3. Forward acceleration on seat stays

We record the forward acceleration to detect brake failure, which indicates the deceleration process of the bicycle. The forward acceleration from an abnormal braking process is shown in Fig. 3a. Cyclist use feet to stop in time if the brake is spongy. So the bicycle will not slow down in a stable state, and forward acceleration will fluctuate irregularly. And the brake time is longer than a normal bicycle. Figure 3b illustrates the forward acceleration of normal braking process. The deceleration of the bicycle increases after the cyclist tightens the brakes. And the brake period is much shorter than a spongy brake case. Therefore, we can use the characteristics of forward acceleration to judge whether the brake is failed. With regard to a normal braking process, the forward acceleration generally drops to a small value and then becomes zero. The average deceleration of the normal brake is generally large. Although this is related to the cyclist's behavior (for example, the cyclist may not always pinch the brakes), normal brakes usually provide sufficient deceleration.

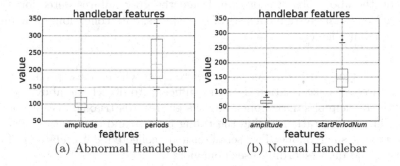

(a) Abnormal Handlebar   (b) Normal Handlebar

Fig. 4. Comparison between normal handlebar and rotating handlebar

The rotating handlebar affects the cyclist and it usually takes the cyclist a long time to get familiar with it. Therefore, a bicycle with an rotating handlebar will experience a longer period of instability during start-up, and the swing amplitude is large. As shown in Fig. 4, it demonstrates the length of unstable periods and amplitude of swing at the beginning of the riding process. We can clearly see that normal bicycles' unstable periods tend to be limited in 250 sampling periods. While in abnormal conditions i.e., rotating handlebars, the bicycles are always unstable because cyclists need more time to get accustomed to the bicycle. Besides, their swing amplitudes also have a big difference.

The flat tire is a common unexpected problem that disables a bicycle. A soft tire slows cyclist down slightly but cyclist may not notice anything unusual until they use the bike for a while. Due to the deterioration of the suspension, the sensing signal is more sensitive to the road condition. The vertical acceleration caused by bumps will be much larger than the average value. As shown in Fig. 5, although the average vertical acceleration of normal bicycles is larger than that of leaky bicycles, their acceleration peaks are almost the same.

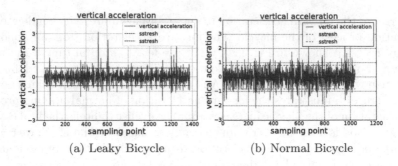

Fig. 5. Comparison between normal bicycle and leaky bicycle

2.2   Architecture

Based on the above observation, we design the gray failures detection system shown in Fig. 1. The system consists of three parts, data collection, data analysis and gray failure detection.

Data Collection: We consider the accelerometer which is cheap (thirty cents) and the three-axis acceleration data are sufficient to detect the above gray failures with the help of smartphone. The system records triaxial acceleration and triaxial linear acceleration during the riding process and automatically submits the data to the smartphone. Two set of data are collected: data related to bicycle movement and data recording user behaviors.

Data Analysis: In this part, the system performs data processing, such as data segmentation, user riding behavior extraction, and eliminating the interference of abnormal riding. In order to clearly quantify the signal characteristics caused by different kinds of failures, we need to extract the key features from the pre-processed signals. Based on the subtle abnormal vibration caused by different gray failures, we can distinguish failures accurately.

Gray Failure Detection: Classification algorithms are applied for gray failure detection. A well-trained machine learning model is used to identify a specific the gray failure.

3   Data Collection

In this section we introduce the data collection process and explain how we use the user's mobile phone and the accelerometer fix at the seat stay to collect data. In order to detect four types of gray failures, we need vertical and forward direction acceleration (for detecting brake faults) as well as lateral acceleration (for detecting handlebar failure). This is achieved by only one accelerometer fixed at the seat stays of the shared bicycle. The applied three-axis accelerometer is cheap (around thirty cents) and the power consumption is low [11], which is acceptable for the shared bikes which acquires for low maintaining cost.

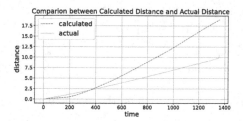

Fig. 6. Accumulated error in distance

We also need the time interval when the wheel passes exactly for one round. If we can measure the value correctly, we can divide the acceleration signal to each pedaling round. For example, if a bicycle has regular spikes in most of the pedaling round, we can judge that the bicycle has a high probability to have a bent wheel. A naive approach is to calculate distance using the product of speed and time. The speed can be estimated by the integration of forwarding acceleration. However, this approach leads to a large deviation due to the accumulation error. Figure 6 compares the deviation between the measured distance(the dash line) and the actual distance(the solid line). We can find that error accumulates quickly with the increase of time. One may wonder whether we can use GPS to locate the bicycle, since the shared bicycles are equipped with the GPS. However, the error of GPS localization (<10 m) is not acceptable with regard to the perimeter of wheel (<1 m). Although sensors on the rim can get the accurate wheel rotation information, it is difficult to deploy sensors on the rotating component of the shared bicycle.

Therefore, we apply the mobile of users to detect the rotation information. In our design, we consider user's mobile phone to detect the pedaling round. Because smartphones today have equipped with many sensors, including the accelerometers. Moreover, Each shared bicycle user needs a mobile phone to unlock the shared bicycle, we can apply the smartphone in our system with no extra expense. When the phone is put in the user's pocket, it moves as the user steps on the pedal. The rotation period of the pedal and the rotation period of the wheel are synchronized when the cyclist pedals to keep or increase speed. Since there is no shifting function for shared bikes, this ratio is bicycle's pedal and wheel gear ratio (PGR). For example, if the pedal gear has 32 teeth, and the wheel gear has 16 teeth, then the wheel will turn two rounds when the pedal turns one round. Therefore, we only need to calculate the cyclist's pedaling round to obtain the period of the wheel.

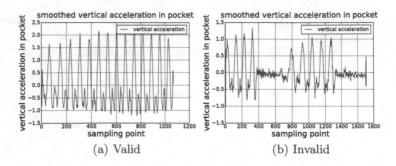

Fig. 7. Vertical acceleration on the mobile phone in pocket.

It is notable that this method to calculate the period of the wheel can be affected by the cyclist behavior. For example, Fig. 7a demonstrates the vertical acceleration of mobile putting in the pocket of the cyclist. From vertical acceleration shown in the figure, it is easy to extract the pedaling round, and then calculate the wheel rotation by the proportion of the number of teeth of the transmission gear. Figure 7b shows vertical acceleration collected when the cyclist lets the bicycle slide. In the period from 400 to 600 and from 1400 to 1600, we can see that the acceleration is very small, and there is no obvious zeropoints. This part of abnormal data needs to be removed to improve the accuracy of the system. The peek appear in the wheel rotating round may have a shift after sliding. However each pedaling contains two wheel rounds, the feature extraction on each pedaling round is not affected.

4   Data Analysis

Table 1. Definition of notations for error analysis

a_x, a_y, a_z (g_x, g_y, g_z)	3-axis acceleration (gravity) of the mobile phone
a_v	Vertical acceleration of the deployed accelerometer
$a_f(a_l)$	Acceleration on the forward (lateral) direction of the bicycle
BP	The set of timestamps in the braking progress. If the braking period starts at $1900th$ sampling point and ends at $2100th$ sampling point, BP = $\{x\|x \in [1900, 2100]\}$
$ST(RD)$	The set of timestamps in the start-up (riding) progress

This section describes how we process and analyze the collected raw data. The corresponding notations used in this section are listed in Table 1

4.1 Pedaling Cycle Extraction

We need the wheel rotation information to judge wheel-related faults. The acceleration data of mobile phone put in the cyclist's pocket is applied to estimate the cyclist's pedaling behavior. Since the accelerometer and gravimeter in the smartphone are coaxial, we can achieve the vertical acceleration as $a_v = a_x \cdot \frac{g_x}{G} + a_y \cdot \frac{g_y}{G} + a_z \cdot \frac{g_z}{G}$, where g_x, g_y, g_z denote the projection of gravimeter on the X, Y, Z axes respectively [8]. Figure 7a demonstrates the vertical acceleration of mobile putting in the pocket of the cyclist. We are able to extract the pedaling cycle by counting the spikes in the time sequence. Notice that the data caused by user's abnormal behavior needs to be removed to improve the accuracy. When people stop pedaling, the amplitude of the vertical acceleration signal decreases. We can remove those signals.

4.2 Data Segmentation

Before feature extraction, we need to identify the periods of starting-up and braking. In the starting-up process, the horizontal acceleration becomes stable and the case of shaking disappears. The braking process starts when the acceleration in the forward direction becomes negative. Based on the signal variation, we can identify the starting-up and the braking phase.

4.3 Feature Extraction

Identify the Rotating Handlebar Issue. According to the observation in Sect. 3, the rotating handlebar affect start-up process. A bicycle with a rotating handlebar tend to swing in the start-up process. We use $amplitude = \overline{|a_{l_i}|}, i \in ST$ to quantify the swing during the start-up of riding.

Identify the Braking Issue. According to the observation in Sect. 3, we can figure out several features which can be applied to effectively characterize the behavior of braking, e.g., the time taken to slow down, average deceleration, and deceleration fluctuations. From Fig. 3b we can see that for the normal brake, the deceleration of the bicycle will rapidly increase, and then rapidly decrease to 0 during braking time. While for the abnormal brake, as shown in Fig. 3a, the acceleration data do not follow the same trend. In order to describe the phenomenon of deceleration fluctuation during braking, we use $\sum_{i \in BP}(index(a_i) - index_{max})$, $|a_i| > a_{max}/2$ to identify the deceleration fluctuation. Here, a_i refers to the acceleration collected at ith sampling point, and $index$ means the timestamp of the corresponding acceleration value. The maximum value is record as $a_{max} = max(|a_f|)$ and record this point's index as $index_{max}$. As discussed before, spongy brakes usually lead to longer brake process as well as smaller acceleration compared to normal brakes. So we also record the average acceleration value during the braking process as $\overline{a_B}$, and we record the time of brake process as $time_{BP}$.

Handle Riding Process. We use four features to represent the characteristics of the acceleration data during riding time: $\overline{|a|}$, R_{avg}, R_{stan}, $S_{|a|}$. $\overline{|a|}$ denotes the average value of acceleration in the vertical direction. R_{avg} denotes the ratio of acceleration whose value exceeds $\overline{|a|}$. R_{stan} denotes the ratio of the absolute value exceeds the standard deviation of the absolute value plus $\overline{|a|}$. $S_{|a|}$ denotes the normalized standard deviation of absolute values of acceleration. $\overline{|a|}$ and $S_{|a|}$ identify the overall acceleration during the riding process. $\overline{|a|}$ shows variation of the signals caused by bumpy road or bent wheel. $S_{|a|}$ relates to the data distribution, indicating abnormal signals on vertical acceleration during the riding. R_{avg} and R_{stan} can identify the frequency of spike signals appear in the data set. R_{stan} is applied for wheel bent bicycles. The standard deviation of acceleration is large for wheel bent bicycles since they have abnormal large peak signals. We introduce the standard deviation plus $\overline{|a|}$ as a threshold to identify these spike signals. $level$ denotes how many valid spikes are included in one pedal cycle. $\overline{level}$ is the average number of spikes in each pedal cycle.

Then we need to measure the periodicity of these spike signals in each pedaling. If the running distance between two valid spikes is equal to the perimeter of the wheel, the two peaks are considered periodic. In order to formalize this characteristic, we define $diff = \frac{D-\delta d}{D}$, where D is the perimeter of the wheel and δd refers to the distance between two spikes which is derived from time interval between spikes and the pedaling round. We use $\overline{diff} = \sum diff / N$ to show the average distribution of spikes where N denotes the number of spike intervals.

5   Evaluation

5.1   Experimental Setup

We collect around 200 sets of data from 50 bicycles belonging to different shared bicycle providers: Mo-bikes, Hello-bikes and Ofo-bikes. These abnormal bicycles reported by users have gray failures such as bent wheel, leaky tire, spongy brake, rotating handlebar. We conducted experiments at both flat roads and bumpy roads. The data collected on flat roads accounts for about 80%. The sampling frequency of acceleration signal is 50 times per second. We tested on both flat roads and bumpy roads. Flat roads are asphalt roads without slopes, and the bumpy road is a road made of bricks with gaps between the bricks.

5.2   Feature Observations

Figure 8 records the features of normal bicycle, wheel bent bicycle and leaky bicycle. The main difference between normal bicycles and leaky bicycles is that $\overline{|a|}$ of normal bicycle is larger than that of leaky bicycles. And $\overline{level}$ of normal bicycle is larger in comparison with leaky bicycles. Since leaky bicycles have poor tire cushioning performance, the sensor fixed on the bicycle is more sensitive to the road condition. The features of wheel bent bicycles shows multiple different characteristics in comparison with normal bicycles and leaky bicycles. According to the discussion in Sect. 4, $S_{|a|}$ and $\overline{|a|}$ of wheel bent bicycles are much larger than that of other failure cases. $\overline{diff}$ of wheel bent bicycle is smaller than that of other bicycles because the distance between continuous spikes is consistent with the perimeter of the wheel. As a result, the value of $\overline{level}$ is small. These features are consistent with the previous discussion, indicating that these feature values reflect the characteristics of gray failures.

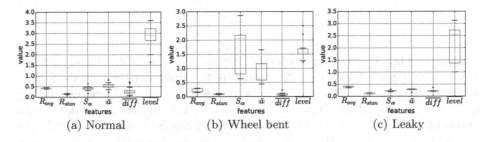

Fig. 8. Confidence interval of different situations.

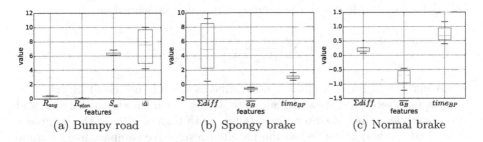

Fig. 9. Confidence interval of different situations.

Figure 9a shows features calculated from bicycles on bumpy road. $S_{|a|}$ and $\overline{|a|}$ of the bicycle on the bumpy road is much higher in comparison with normal bicycles. This is because the bumpy road surface affects the vertical accelera- tion results. Figure 9b and Fig. 9c record features calculated from bicycles with spongy brake and normal brake respectively. Spongy brakes take longer time to stop the bicycle (a large value of $time_{BP}$), and the brake deceleration is low (a small value of $\overline{a_B}$) and causes unstable deceleration (large $\Sigma diff$).

5.3   Failure Classification

Table 2. Comparison of accuracy of different classification algorithms.

	LC	SVM	DT	GTB	KNN	Baseline
A	**98.2%**	94.7%	94.7%	95.6%	93.5%	88.4%
B	**100%**	**100%**	94.3%	**100%**	**100%**	94.4%
C	94.1%	94.4%	**100%**	**100%**	**100%**	94.7%
D	**100%**	94.4%	83.3%	88.9%	83.3%	90.7%
E	86.7%	60%	80%	80%	**100%**	76.9%
F	**78.2%**	73.7%	68.4%	68.4%	73.7%	73.7%

Baseline Algorithm. Our baseline algorithm selects an interval to record features of each kind of failures. It first compute the similarity between the feature of the tested data and the sampling data in practice. Then, the sum of similarity of all the feature values is taken as the similarity between the set of data and a certain failure. The failure with the highest similarity is considered as the failure of the sharing bicycle. Notice that there are some abnormal data in the sensor data, we calculate the confidence interval [3] for each feature of each kind of failure. Confidence interval filters these abnormal data and keeps normal results.

Let the confidence interval corresponding to i-th eigenvalues be (V_{li}, V_{hi}). For a set of data with n features, the similarity function is defined as

$$Sim = \sum_{i=1}^{n} \left(\frac{V_{hi} - V_{li}}{|V_{hi} - V_i| + |V_{li} - V_i|} \right)$$

We calculate Sim for test data to determine failure of the tested bicycle. For example, for a set of test data, we calculate its Sim with wheel bent bicycles and its Sim with leaky bicycle. So we take failure with highest Sim as the judgment result. This method is applied as the baseline result. We compare five machine learning algorithms for failure classification, which are Linear Classifier (LC), Support Vector Machine (SVM), Decision Tree (DT), Gradient Tree Boosting (GTB), and k-Nearest Neighbor (KNN). 30% of data is reserved for test and the rest for training. In Table 2, we compares the accuracy of different machine learning algorithms, where the notation indicates: normal bicycle (A), bent wheel (B), leaky tire (C), bumpy road (D), broken brake (E), rotating handle (F).

Detection of leaky and bent wheel achieves high accuracy, which is higher than 94%. Detection accuracy of normal and bumpy road bicycles is about 90%. Detection accuracy of spongy brake and rotating handlebar are lower than 80%. The brakes and handlebar are more susceptible to the cyclist's behavior. Expert cyclists can adapt handlebar to a right angle quickly, especially when riding with one hand. So abnormal bicycles may be judge as normal. Spongy brake and rotating handlebar have a high possibility misjudge due to the bumpy road. Start-up and brake on a bumpy road tend to be unstable and have similarity with these two failures. For other kinds of failures, the accuracy is high. In general, the macro f1 score reaches 0.86, even when data is imbalanced. The accuracy of machine learning algorithms and the benchmark algorithm are consistent, indicating that the algorithm has less impact on the detection results.

6   Conclusion

In this paper we consider the gray failure issue in the modern bicycle sharing system. To detect the working condition of the shared bicycle and provide users the corresponding information when they start to unlock the bike, we have implemented automatic report generation approach by using a single accelerometer and a smartphone. The system is implemented on Android smartphones and extensive experiments were conducted to evaluate the system performance. The evaluation in real environment has shown that the proposed approach can achieve more than 90% accuracy to detect the common gray failures.

Acknowledgment. This work was partially supported by the National Key R&D Program of China (Grant No. 2018YFB1004704), the National Natural Science Foundation of China (Grant Nos. 61832005, 61832008, 61872174), the Key R&D Program of Jiangsu Province, China (Grant No. BE2017152), the science and technology project from State Grid Corporation of China (Contract No. SGJSXT00XTJS2100049).

References

1. Chen, C.H., Lee, C.A., Lo, C.C.: Vehicle localization and velocity estimation based on mobile phone sensing. IEEE Access **4**, 803–817 (2016)
2. Chen, D., Cho, K.T., Han, S., Jin, Z., Shin, K.G.: Invisible sensing of vehicle steering with smartphones. In: International Conference on Mobile Systems, Applications, and Services, pp. 1–13. New York, NY, USA (2015)
3. CI, A.C.I., Rule, R.O.: Confidence intervals. Lancet **1**, 494–497 (1987)
4. Ganti, R.K., Ye, F., Lei, H.: Mobile crowdsensing: current state and future challenges. IEEE Commun. Mag. **49**(11), 32–39 (2011)
5. Gu, W., Liu, Y., Zhou, Y., Zhou, Z., Spanos, C.J., Zhang, L.: Bikesafe: bicycle behavior monitoring via smartphones. In: ACM Ubicomp (2017)
6. Gu, W., et al.: Bikemate: bike riding behavior monitoring with smartphones. In: ACM MobiQuitous (2017)
7. Takahashi, J., Kobana, Y., Tobe, Y., Lopez, G.: Classification of steps on road surface using acceleration signals. In: MobiQuitous (2015)
8. Tan, S., Wang, X., Maier, G., Li, W.: Riding quality evaluation through mobile crowd sensing. In: IEEE PerCom (2016)
9. Thepvilojanapong, N., Sugo, K., Namiki, Y., Tobe, Y.: Recognizing bicycling states with hmm based on accelerometer and magnetometer data. In: SICE Annual Conference 2011, pp. 831–832. IEEE (2011)
10. Wang, Y., Yang, J., Liu, H., Chen, Y., Gruteser, M., Martin, R.P.: Sensing vehicle dynamics for determining driver phone use. In: MobiSys. ACM (2013)
11. Weinberg, H.: Minimizing power consumption of imems® accelerometers. Analog Devices (2002)
12. Yu, J., et al.: Senspeed: sensing driving conditions to estimate vehicle speed in urban environments. IEEE Trans. Mob. Comput. **15**(1), 202–216 (2016)

Effective Cross-Region Courier-Displacement for Instant Delivery via Reinforcement Learning

Shijie Hu[1], Baoshen Guo[1], Shuai Wang[1], and Xiaolei Zhou[1,2(✉)]

[1] School of Computer Science and Technology, Southeast University, Nanjing, China
{213173028,guobaoshen,shuaiwang}@seu.edu.cn
[2] The Sixty-Third Research Institute, National University of Defense Technology,
Zunyi, China
zhouxiaolei@nudt.edu.cn

Abstract. With the rapid development of mobile phones and the Internet of Things, instant delivery services (e.g., UberEats and MeiTuan) have become a popular choice for people to order foods, fruits, and other groceries online, especially after the impact of COVID-19. In instant delivery services, it is important to dispatch massive orders to limited couriers, especially in rush hours. To meet this need, an efficient courier displacement mechanism not only can balance the demand (picking up orders) and supply (couriers' capacity) but also improve the efficiency of order delivery by reducing idle displacing time. Existing studies on fleet management of rider-sharing or bike rebalancing cannot apply to courier displacement problems in instant delivery due to unique practical factors of instant delivery including region difference and strict delivery time constraints. In this work, we propose an efficient cross-region courier displacement method _Courier Displacement Reinforcement Learning_ (short for _CDRL_), based on multi-agent actor-critic, considering the dynamic demand and supply at the region level and strict time constraints. Specifically, the multi-agent actor-critic reinforcement learning-based courier displacement framework utilizes a policy network to generate displacement decisions considering multiple practical factors and designs a value network to evaluate decisions of the policy network. One month of real-world order records data-set of Shanghai collecting from Eleme (i.e., one of the biggest instant delivery services in China) are utilized in the evaluation and the results show that our method offering up to 36% increase in courier displacement performance and reduce idle ride time by 17%.

Keywords: Courier displacement · Reinforcement learning · Instant delivery

© Springer Nature Switzerland AG 2021
Z. Liu et al. (Eds.): WASA 2021, LNCS 12937, pp. 288–300, 2021.
https://doi.org/10.1007/978-3-030-85928-2_23

1   Introduction

As an alternative and new online to offline service, instant delivery services such as UberEats [17], MeiTuan [13], DoorDash [6], Deliveroo [5], Amazon Prime Now [2], and Eleme [7] have been growing rapidly and spreading worldwide in recent years, especially in big cities, which provide lots of conveniences for people to order food, medicine, and groceries online. In the third quarter of 2019, the number of instant delivery service users in China is 470 million, and the market scale reaches 79.52 billion RMB [1]. Considering the economical and social values of instant delivery services, it is essential to improve the delivery efficiency by leveraging the large volume of delivery demands (orders) and limited supplies (couriers).

To improve delivery efficiency, one of the most critical issues is to balance the demand and supply, i.e., orders of food and couriers' capacity, as the unbalance problem is general in large cities. For example, an enormous number of orders stay in the merchants since either unassigned to a proper courier or waiting for couriers to pick up after the food is prepared. This may lead to a higher overdue rate of orders (i.e., cannot deliver food to users in time as expected), longer waiting time of users, as well as users' complaints. On the other hand, plenty of available couriers cannot be dispatched orders since inadequate orders in specific locations and time slots. The dynamic gap between demand and supply in instant delivery services and corresponding inefficiency issue make it essential to design a courier displacement to balance the demand and supply and reallocate couriers from low demand to high demand ahead of time, to achieve high delivery efficiency and reduce the delivery overdue rate.

A lot of research works have been proposed in recent years to study rebalancing problems such as fleet management in rider-sharing [8,10,14,19] and bike rebalancing in bike-sharing systems [4,11,12,15,18,20]. Particularly, some rebalancing studies in bike-sharing systems [18,20] design the demand prediction module for bike usage demand prediction and rebalance decisions module for relocating bikes. And other studies in rider-sharing focus on fleet management of drivers with the optimization-based methods [19] or reinforcement learning-based methods [10]. However, most existing works cannot be directly applied to solve the courier displacement problems in instant delivery. The behind reasons are (1) as order dispatch and delivery is conducted in the region level, multiple practical factors such as range, demand/supply distribution, delivery types and time constraints make such a problem more complicated. (2) the strict delivery deadline for each order requires reducing the idle ride time when we displace couriers from one region to another.

With the built-in GPS module in smartphones and IoT devices, it is trivial to collect the trajectories of couriers. The courier will report the delivery process and order status as well. Besides, the displacement of couriers in instant delivery can be formulated as a Markov decision process since it is a sequential decision process. Therefore, it is possible to learn the efficient courier displacement decisions from massive historical data.

By incorporating trajectories data of couriers and order-reported process data, we can build a emulator to mimic the courier displacement environment and train a data-drive model with practical factors considered. However, learning order dispatching decision from historical data is not straightforward due to (1) the multiple factors including spatial-temporal demand-supply dynamic and region delivery difference; (2) conflicting objectives (reducing idle ride time for couriers and rebalancing couriers' decisions).

To address the above challenges, we propose a reinforcement learning-based method to conduct the courier displacement in instant delivery services.

Specifically, our main contributions are as follows.

- To the best of our knowledge, we are the first to study cross-region courier displacement problems for instant delivery platforms in the real world. We formally define the courier displacement problem and distinct this problem from other rebalancing problems in rider-sharing or bike-sharing scenarios with practical real-world dataset.
- We design a multi-agent actor-critic reinforcement learning-based courier displacement framework. It consists of (1) a policy network to generate displacement decisions with consideration of multiple practical factors; (2) a value network to evaluate decisions of policy network.
- We conduct extensive experiments based on city-scale real-world order records data-set from Shanghai collecting from Eleme (one of the biggest instant delivery services in China), including one-month order records and couriers' location information. As the experimental results shown, our method greatly outperform four state-of-the-art baselines in terms of idle ride time and rebalancing performances, offering up to a 36% increase in courier displacement performance and reduce idle ride time by 17%.

2   Background and System Overview

2.1   Instant Delivery

In recent years, the rapidly developed instant delivery services are challenged by the delivery efficiency issues. The unbalanced demand and supply result in longer delivery time. Figure 1 shows the spatial distribution of merchants in Shanghai. From Fig. 1, we find that the distribution of merchants is not uniform, and merchants are densely concentrated in the downtown.

Besides, we find that the location of merchants can be clustered into different groups. The instant delivery platforms usually divide different business districts or regions based on the distribution of merchants. Figure 2 shows two peaks of order amount at noon and evening, which are so-called rush hours. The rush hours are from 10 am to 2 pm and 5 pm to 8 pm, respectively. Upon analyzing the merchants' spatial distribution and the number distribution of orders hourly, our key problem is to *conduct the cross-region courier displacement to balance the demand and supply, especially in rush hours efficiently.*

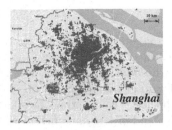

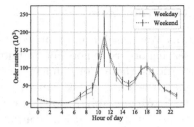

Fig. 1. Merchant location distribution   **Fig. 2.** Number of orders hourly

2.2 System Overview

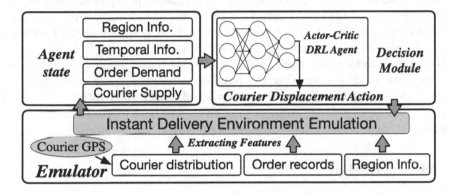

Fig. 3. Actor Critic based Courier Displacement Framework

We present the system overview of the proposed model in Fig. 3, which consists of three modules: (1) a data-driven emulator to emulate couriers rebalancing in instant delivery; (2) an agent state extracting module to integrate the demand (order numbers), supply (couriers), temporal information (current time slot), and the information of different regions into the environmental state at the beginning of each time slot; (3) the decision module utilizes an actor-critic reinforcement learning-based displacement model to make rebalancing actions of couriers.

3 Reinforcement Learning Formulation

3.1 RL Background

Reinforcement learning (RL) is typically used to model sequential decision-making problems. In the Reinforcement Learning setting, an agent takes an action at each timestamp and earns some reward, where the action will change the states of the environment and the agent.

3.2   RL Formulation

- **Agent.** We consider all online couriers in the range as agents, whether they are serving orders or not. For each idle courier, the current grid is used as the start grid of the action, and for the courier who is serving orders, the grid she/he arrived at, at last, is used as the start grid of the action.
- **State S.** We maintain a global state s_t at each time t, considering the spatial distributions of idle couriers, couriers in service and orders and current time. The state of an agent i, s_t^i, is defined as the identification of the grid it located and the shared global state i.e., $s_t^i = [s_t, g_j, t_k] \in R^{N \times 4 + T + T_s}$ where g_j is the one-hot encoding of the grid ID and t_k is the one-hot encoding of couriers serving time (this time of idle couriers is 0).
- **Action $\mathcal{A}$.** Due to the dynamic change of the number of couriers, the total number N_t of actions also changes at each time step. N_t is the sum of the number of idle couriers at t and the number of couriers serving at $t - 1$. The number of actions that each courier can perform is the number of regions, which means to go to each region respectively.
- **Reward function $\mathcal{R}$.** The reward is calculated by taking each region as a unit.For a grid g_j, counting the number of orders o_{r_j} and couriers c_{r_j} in the region r_j which contains the grid g_j, and taking their ratio as a reward $R_t^j = o_{r_j}/c_{r_j}$, to promote couriers to go to regions with more orders but fewer couriers. Then achieve the balance of supply and demand in regions.

4   Model Design

4.1   Model Design

In this section, we show how to solve main problems mentioned above through the deep reinforcement learning-based method. For the cross-region courier displacement problem in this paper, due to a large number of couriers, the number and state of couriers will change dynamically at each time step. Therefore, it is very difficult and costly to model and build a neural network for each courier. In this paper, a centralized network is used to make all couriers share a network to reduce the complexity of the model and the training cost.

The method mainly includes two networks, a value network (i.e., participants, which is used to evaluate the performance of policy network), and a policy network (i.e., actor-network, which is used to output policy). The centralized state-value function is learned by minimizing the following loss function $L(\theta_v)$ which is derived from the Bellman equation.

$$L(\theta_v) = ((V_{\theta_v}(s_t(k))) - V_{tg}(s_{t+1}(k); \theta_v', \pi))^2 \tag{1}$$

And the target value function is shown in Eq. 2.

$$V_{tg}(s_{t+1}; \theta_v', \pi) = \sum_{a_t(k)} \pi(a_t(k)|s_t(k))(r_{t+1}(k) + \gamma V_{\theta_v'}(s_{t+1}(k))) \tag{2}$$

For couriers in the same grid, values are the same, so there are n values $V(s_t, g_i)$ in each time step. Considering the idle time for couriers of distance generation in displacement, although the value and reward of each grid and are fixed, for each action, we need to add the corresponding attenuation.

$$\pi(a_t(k)|s_t(k)) = P(a_t(k)|s_t(k))S(a_t(k), s_t(k))T(a_t(k), s_t(k)) \tag{3}$$

the corresponding action probability should be reduced by calculating the distance length generated by action (i.e., $S(a_t(k), s_t(k))$). The longer the distance, the greater the attenuation. Meanwhile, the algorithm considers both idle couriers and couriers who are in service at each time step. Therefore, the action probability of courier in the service process should decrease with the length of delivery time (i.e., $T(a_t(k), s_t(k))$).

$$[G_{t,g_i}]_k = \begin{cases} 1, & if\ g_j\ next\ to\ g_i \\ 0, & otherwise, \end{cases} \tag{4}$$

$$[C_{t,g_i}]_k = \begin{cases} 1, & if\ V(s_t, g_j)S(a_t(k), s_t(k))T(a_t(k), s_t(k)) >= V(s_t, n_i) \\ 0, & otherwise, \end{cases} \tag{5}$$

$$\pi_{\theta_p}(s_t, a_t) = P(a_t(k)|s_t(k))S(a_t(k), s_t(k))T(a_t(k), s_t(k))G_{t,g_i}C_{t,g_i} \tag{6}$$

In the policy network, the action probability of couriers should also be changed accordingly. Then, by calculating the adjacent relationship between regions, and judging the value of cross-region action and non-move action, the action probability should be selected again.

The gradient is given by Eq. 7.

$$\nabla_{\theta_p}L(\theta_p) = \sum_t \nabla_{\theta_p} \log \pi_{\theta_p}(s_t, a_t)(r_{t+1}(k) + \gamma V_{\theta_v'}(s_{t+1}(k)) - V_{\theta_v}(s_t(k))) \tag{7}$$

4.2   Courier Behavior Modeling

The interactive nature of RL introduces intricate difficulties in training and evaluation, so it provides an RL algorithm training and evaluation environment by building a emulator for the environment. The emulator we build can initialize the courier dist and order dist according to the input data, and simulate the real world to allocate orders and move couriers. This section mainly introduces the behavior pattern of couriers.

There are three types of couriers: offline couriers, idle couriers, and couriers in service. Because of the existence of the "region", couriers usually only move in a fixed region. So the change of the number of couriers in each region is caused by couriers being off-line or online. Therefore, at each time step, the number of couriers changes randomly according to the real data.

Online couriers are all seen as agents. For idle couriers, the action is executed directly in the current time step; for couriers in service, the action is executed after they complete all orders, and do not assign orders to them during the period. Since it is inevitable for couriers to move at a distance in idle after arriving at other regions, only the time before arriving at other regions should be considered. In this way, we can get the $S(a_t(k), s_t(k))$ mentioned in the model.

For the couriers who are still in the current region after action execution, if they are in the "User Grid" (i.e., the grid without merchants), they will automatically go to the "Merchant Grid" (i.e., the grid with merchants) in the current region is random, so that they can obtain orders.

5   Evaluation

5.1   Data Description

We collect one month of real-world data-set of Shanghai from Eleme, include order-reported data and GPS trajectories data. Order information includes start grid, end grid, and duration. And GPS trajectories data shows the location information of couriers in the process of delivery. We extract the characteristics of the location distribution of delivery workers from the data set in time steps. And input them into the emulator together with the real order data, so as to drive the operation of the emulator.

5.2   Experimental Setup

Parameters Setting. In the emulator, orders are sampled from real order data and the order sampling probability is set to 1/28, 1/40,1/50,1/60 and 1/75, to compare the displacement performance under different order numbers. Set the time interval as 10 min. In the model, the value function approximation and policy network in the context algorithm are parameterized by three layers of real with grid sizes of 128, 64, and 32 from the first layer to the third layer. The batch size of all deep learning methods is fixed at 3000. We use Adam optimizer with a learning rate of 1E3. There are 25 rounds. The first 15 rounds are used for model training and the rest for model evaluation.

Baselines

- **Simulation.** There is no displacement between regions for couriers, that is, couriers are fixed in a region.The results of this method can directly reflect the imbalance of supply and demand caused by no scheduling operation.
- **Diffusion** [10]. The couriers in the experimental area are randomly displaced with the same probability without a difference at each time step. Compared with this method, it can reflect the importance of the selection of couriers in displacement.

- **V-G.** V-G is the Value-Greedy method. Give priority to idle couriers and select the most valuable action to execute for each courier who can be displaced. This method can solve the problem of supply and demand balance to some extent.
- **Gap-G.** Gap-G is the Gap-Greedy method. Give priority to idle couriers and select the most ratio of orders and couriers action to execute. The main goal of this method is to eliminate the imbalance of supply and demand among regions.

Metrics

- **Demand and Supply Gap.** The ratio of orders and couriers in each region is calculated respectively. Then the standard deviation of the ratio of each region i.e., the gap is used as one of the Metrics. This metric can directly reflect the overall balance of supply and demand. Our algorithm tries to make it as small as possible.
- **Idle Ride Time.** Idle Ride Time refers to the time that the couriers pass without order service. Idle ride time can reflect the scheduling efficiency of the algorithm. The low idle ride time shows that the algorithm has good scheduling efficiency, that is, couriers can transfer between regions quickly. Reducing the average length of idle ride time is also a focus of this paper.

5.3 Experimental Results

Demand and Supply Gap is shown in Fig. 4 and Idle Ride Time is shown in Fig. 5. It can be seen that CDRL is effective to reduce the gap in regions and it is also helpful for couriers to reduce the average idle ride time. And one of the baselines, Gap-G has a very effective performance of balancing demand and supply, even better than CDRL. But correspondingly, its average idle ride time is much bigger than CDRL's.

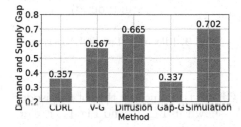

Fig. 4. Average Demand and Supply Gap

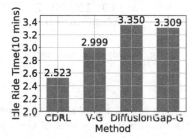

Fig. 5. Average Idle Ride Time

Impacts of Initial Order Numbers on Performances. We evaluate the performance under different initial demand and supply ratio by changing the initial order numbers in the emulator. We evaluated each method under different order quantity by changing the "Probability". And the average of results of each method is as follows. For the same method, the influence of order quantity is shown in Fig. 6 and Fig. 7. The change of order quantity has no effect on the average time of couriers displacement. But for the gap between regions, the less the order quantity, the easier it is to achieve the balance of supply and demand.

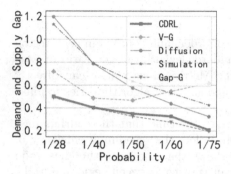

Fig. 6. Gap-Probability

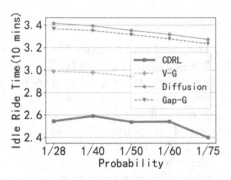

Fig. 7. Idle Ride Time-Probability

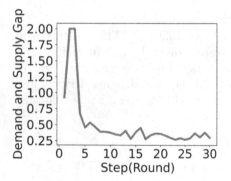

Fig. 8. Gap-CDRL-1/60

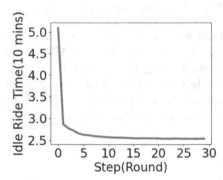

Fig. 9. Idle Ride Time-CDRL-1/60

Figure 8 and Fig. 9 show the metric of CDRL training. Set the total episode to 30 and observe the loss of the model. As shown in Fig. 10 and Fig. 11, it can be seen that the model has reached the convergence state.

6   Insights and Lessons Learned

– **Cross-region Displacement Characteristics.** In instant delivery, courier displacement and order dispatch are conduct at the region level (a region is a sub-area of one city, around 5km × 5km). Each region has its distinct characteristics such as couriers and orders distribution, order number, time constraints due to differences in region level.

– **Impact of Initial Demand and Supply Ratio.** The ratio of demand (orders) and supply (couriers) has a high impact on delivery efficiency and displacement decisions. If we set the initial demand and supply ratio close between regions, that is, every region has a similar demand and supply gap, the performance promotion of displacement decisions is also limited.

7   Related Works

7.1   Heuristic Based Rebalancing Methods

In recent years, online food ordering (OFO) platforms have arisen fast and brought huge convenience to people in daily life. The research of this paper is also based on this scenario. Under the scenario of a realistic OFO platform, to reduce the search space, the OMDP [3] is decomposed into two subproblems, and in the DE-based routing phase, a heuristic considering the urgency of orders is designed to generate the initial population with a certain quality. Considering the uncertainty in the real world online food delivery applications, In [21], the authors address an online order dispatching problem with fuzzy preparation times (FOODP). In the FOA-based search phase, a modified heuristic is used to generate the initial route. In [22], Zhou et al. design two fast heuristics for order dispatching in real-time food delivery. For an O2O food ordering and delivery platform, improving food delivery efficiency, is of paramount importance to reduce the length of time users wait for their food. Thus, Ji et al. [9] propose heuristic algorithms to efficiently obtain effective task grouping results, consisting of a greedy algorithm and a replacement algorithm so as to improve food delivery efficiency.

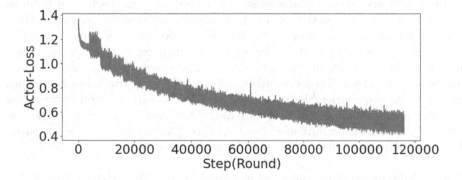

Fig. 10. Actor-Loss observation

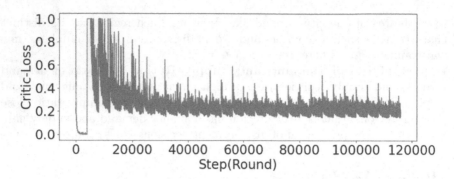

Fig. 11. Critic-Loss observation

7.2 Reinforcement Learning Based Rebalancing Applications

Electric Vehicle (EV) sharing systems have recently experienced unprecedented growth across the world. One of the key challenges in their operation is vehicle rebalancing, i.e., repositioning the EVs across stations to better satisfy future user demand. To tackle these challenges, In [16], authors model the rebalancing task as a Multi-Agent Reinforcement Learning (MARL) problem. Also in [18], to efficiently utilize shared bikes, this paper design eShare to achieve usage efficient sharing. And Lin et al. [10] propose to tackle the large-scale fleet management problem using reinforcement learning and propose a contextual multi-agent reinforcement learning framework.

8   Conclusion

In this paper, we first model the large-scale city-wide courier displacement problem as a sequential decisions problems and formulate it as a Markov decision process. Then, we conduct extensive analysis on order reported data and GPS trajectories data and extract characteristics of these data, and then treat them as new opportunities. Given the courier displacement problem and new opportunities, we propose a novel multi-agent actor-critic reinforcement learning-based displacement framework to conduct efficient courier displacement considering multiple practical factors and idle riding time. we conduct extensive experiments based on a city-scale real-world order record data set from Shanghai including one-month order records and couriers' location information. The experimental results show that our methods outperform four state-of-the-art baselines in terms of idle ride time and rebalancing performances greatly, offering up to a 36% increase in courier displacement performance and reduce idle ride time by 17%.

Acknowledgement. This work was supported in part by National Natural Science Foundation of China under Grant No. 61902066, Natural Science Foundation of Jiangsu Province under Grant No. BK20190336, China National Key R&D Program 2018YFB2100302 and Fundamental Research Funds for the Central Universities under Grant No. 2242021R41068.

References

1. Consulting statistics (2020). http://www.bigdata-research.cn/content/201912/1026.html. Accessed 29 Jan 2020
2. Amazon-Prime-Now: Amazon prime now (2020). https://primenow.amazon.com/. Accessed 20 Apr 2020
3. Chen, J., et al.: A hybrid differential evolution algorithm for the online meal delivery problem. In: 2020 IEEE Congress on Evolutionary Computation (CEC), pp. 1–8 (2020). https://doi.org/10.1109/CEC48606.2020.9185792
4. Contardo, C., Morency, C., Rousseau, L.: Balancing a dynamic public bike-sharing system. CIRRELT (2012)
5. Deliveroo: Deliveroo (2020). https://deliveroo.co.uk. Accessed 20 Apr 2020
6. DoorDash: Doordash (2020). https://www.doordash.com/en-US. Accessed 3 May 2020
7. Ele.me: Ele.me 2008. ele.me website (2020). http://www.ele.me/. Accessed 29 Oct 2020
8. He, S., Shin, K.G.: Spatio-temporal capsule-based reinforcement learning for mobility-on-demand network coordination. In: The World Wide Web Conference, WWW 2019, San Francisco, CA, USA, May 13–17, 2019, pp. 2806–2813 (2019). https://doi.org/10.1145/3308558.3313401
9. Ji, S., Zheng, Y., Wang, Z., Li, T.: Alleviating users' pain of waiting: Effective task grouping for online-to-offline food delivery services, pp. 773–783 (2019)
10. Lin, K., Zhao, R., Xu, Z., Zhou, J.: Efficient large-scale fleet management via multi-agent deep reinforcement learning. In: Proceedings of the 24th ACM SIGKDD International Conference on Knowledge Discovery & #38; Data Mining, pp. 1774–1783. KDD '18, ACM, New York, NY, USA (2018). https://doi.org/10.1145/3219819.3219993
11. Liu, J., Sun, L., Chen, W., Xiong, H.: Rebalancing bike sharing systems: a multi-source data smart optimization. In: Proceedings of the 22nd ACM SIGKDD International Conference on Knowledge Discovery and Data Mining, pp. 1005–1014 (2016)
12. Contardo, C., Morency, C., Rousseau, L.M.: Balancing a dynamic public bike-sharing system. RAIRO - Oper. Res. **45**(1), 37–61 (2011)
13. MeiTuan: Meituan (2021). https://www.meituan.com/
14. Oda, T., Joe-Wong, C.: Movi: a model-free approach to dynamic fleet management. In: IEEE International Conference on Computer Communications, vol. abs/1804.04758, pp. 2708–2716 (2018)
15. Raviv, T., Michal, T., Forma, I.: Static repositioning in a bike-sharing system: models and solution approaches. EURO J. Transp. Logistics **2**(3), 187–229 (2013)
16. Ropke, S., Cordeau, J.F.: Branch and cut and price for the pickup and delivery problem with time windows. Transp. Sci. **43**(3), 267–286 (2009). https://doi.org/10.1287/trsc.1090.0272
17. Ubereats: Ubereats (2020). https://www.ubereats.com/hk. Accessed 20 Apr 2020
18. Wang, S., He, T., Zhang, D., Liu, Y., Son, H.S.: Towards efficient sharing: a usage balancing mechanism for bike sharing systems. In: The World Wide Web Conference, pp. 2011–2021. Association for Computing Machinery, New York, NY, USA (2019). https://doi.org/10.1145/3308558.3313441
19. Xie, X., Zhang, F., Zhang, D.: Privatehunt: multi-source data-driven dispatching in for-hire vehicle systems. Proc. ACM Interact. Mob. Wearable Ubiquitous Technol. **2**, 45:1–45:26 (2018)

20. Yang, Z., Hu, J., Shu, Y., Cheng, P., Chen, J., Moscibroda, T.: Mobility modeling and prediction in bike-sharing systems. In: Proceedings of the 14th Annual International Conference on Mobile Systems, Applications, and Services, pp. 165–178 (2016)
21. Zheng, J., et al.: A two-stage algorithm for fuzzy online order dispatching problem. In: 2020 IEEE Congress on Evolutionary Computation (CEC), pp. 1–8 (2020). https://doi.org/10.1109/CEC48606.2020.9185858
22. Zhou, Q., et al.: Two fast heuristics for online order dispatching. In: 2020 IEEE Congress on Evolutionary Computation (CEC), pp. 1–8 (2020). https://doi.org/10.1109/CEC48606.2020.9185791

A Hybrid Framework
for Class-Imbalanced Classification

Rui Chen[1], Lailong Luo[2(✉)], Yingwen Chen[1(✉)], Junxu Xia[2], and Deke Guo[2]

[1] College of Computer, National University of Defense Technology, Changsha, China
ywch@nudt.edu.cn
[2] Science and Technology on Information Systems Engineering Laboratory,
National University of Defense Technology, Changsha, China
luolailong09@nudt.edu.cn

Abstract. Data classification is a commonly used data processing method in the fields of networks and distributed systems, and it has attracted extensive attention in recent years. Nevertheless, the existing classification algorithms are mainly aimed at relatively balanced datasets, while the data in reality often exhibits imbalanced characteristics. In this paper, we propose a novel Hybrid Resampling-based Ensemble (HRE) model, which aims to solve the classification problem of highly skewed data. The main idea of the HRE is to leverage the resampling approach for tackling class imbalance, and then twelve classifiers are further adopted to construct an ensemble model. Besides, a novel combination of under-sampling and over-sampling is elaborately proposed to balance the heterogeneity among different data categories. We decide the resampling rate in an empirical manner, which provides a practical guideline for the use of sampling methods. We compare the effect of different resampling methods based on the imbalanced network anomaly detection dataset, where few abnormal data need to be distinguished from a large number of common network traffics. The results of extensive experiments show that the HRE model achieves better accuracy performance than the methods without hybrid resampling.

Keywords: Class-imbalanced learning · Resampling · Ensemble model

1 Introduction

In the current era of big data, data mining and analysis take on an increasingly important position for effective decision-making. Among the various data mining techniques, classification analysis [1] is one of the most widely used techniques for various business and engineering problems, such as cancer prediction [2], churn prediction [3], spoofing detection [4], face detection [5], fraud detection [6], and so on. Classification analysis is a kind of supervised classifier learning problem for predicting variables that consist of a finite number of categories called classes [7]. Typically, classifier learning methods are designed to work with reasonably

© Springer Nature Switzerland AG 2021
Z. Liu et al. (Eds.): WASA 2021, LNCS 12937, pp. 301–313, 2021.
https://doi.org/10.1007/978-3-030-85928-2_24

balanced datasets. However, datasets in many real-world situations are often imbalanced.

Class-imbalanced datasets refer to that at least one of their classes is usually outnumbered by the others. For example, a dataset containing two classes with 10 and 1000 data samples is a class-imbalanced dataset. The class imbalance problems have been reported to occur in a wide variety of real-world domains, such as anomaly detection [8], oil spills detection [9], fraudulent credit card transactions identification [10], software defect prediction [11], etc. When addressing imbalanced data problems, people tend to care more about the minority class since the cost of misclassifying minority samples is generally much higher than others [12]. Taking network anomaly detection [13] as an example, the number of abnormal data is much less than the amount of normal data. If the anomaly data is detected as normal data, it may bring network threats and cause security risks.

Currently, there are two mainstream methods to tackle the imbalance classification problem, i.e., oversampling which randomly generates multiple replicas of the existing items to extend the minority classes [14], and undersampling which randomly selects a subset of the existing items to downsize the majority classes. However, we argue that using either the oversampling or the undersampling strategy solely may fall short of mitigating the dataset imbalance problem properly. First, if only the oversampling method is used to increase the number of minority classes, extending the minority classes such that they have the same data volumes as the majority classes is impractical in terms of both time consumption and training cost. Second, if only the under-sampling method is used to downsize the majority classes, an extensive reduction of the datasets may lead to insufficient training results. The generated model may fail to distinguish these classes in the test datasets. Third, there are indeed some works that mention the hybrid sampling method, however, there is not a clear description of such methodology. Consequently, a hybrid sampling method that combines the oversampling with the undersampling strategies together is required by the community.

In this paper, we propose a novel Hybrid Resampling-based Ensemble (HRE) model to classify the highly skewed dataset. Specifically, we apply the proposed model to solve the actual problem in network anomaly detection. The imbalanced network anomaly detection dataset is used to clarify our HRE model. Besides, we propose the combination of resampling methods to reduce the number of majority classes, speeding up the process. We process the imbalanced dataset at the data level and use the resampling technique to transform the dataset into a balanced distribution. Moreover, we build an ensemble model consists of 12 different classifiers, which provide more diverse choices than the five classifiers in previous work. We then use the ensemble model to classify the slightly balanced data obtained after the above processing. We also discuss the setting of the resampling rate in the empirical comparison and get relatively better performance when the sampling ratio is 1:4. The main contributions of our work are summarized as follows:

1. We propose the Hybrid Resampling-based Ensemble (HRE) model for the class-imbalanced problem.
2. We propose a novel combination of under-sampling and over-sampling to balance the heterogeneity among different data categories and speed up the process with less memory overhead.
3. We determine the setting of the resampling rate via empirical comparison, which provides a practical guideline for the use of such sampling methods.

2   Preliminaries and Related Work

In this section, we first introduce the existing methods for solving class-imbalanced problems. These methods could mainly fall into three categories: data-level methods, algorithmic-level methods and ensemble methods [15]. Through the imbalanced data classification methods, the effects caused by the imbalance of data can be reduced. Then, we briefly describe 12 classification algorithms that are commonly used to classify preprocessed data.

2.1   Imbalanced Data Classification Approaches

The purpose of imbalanced learning is to reduce the skewness of the initial data. Thus, the accuracy of classification could be substantially improved compared with traditional classifiers. Hundreds of algorithms have been proposed in the past decades to address imbalanced data classification problems. Those methods can be intuitively divided into three groups: data-level methods, algorithmic-level methods, and ensemble methods. Specifically, we have selected the data-level approaches to carry out our following experiments. The combination of under-sampling and over-sampling methods is adopted to decline the imbalance of data. Another significant benefit of this novel combination is that we can leverage less memory for faster data classification.

Data Level Approaches. Data level approaches focus on resizing the training datasets in order to balance all kinds of classes. A typical method is data resampling. Data resampling can be categorized into three types: over-sampling, under-sampling, and hybrid sampling. The Random Over-Sampling (ROS) method is a simple and basic oversampling method. It carries out random replication on small sample classes to balance the quantitative differences among classes. The famous oversampling algorithm is the Synthetic Minority Oversampling Technique (SMOTE) proposed by Chawla [16]. Its main idea is to form new minority class examples by interpolating between several minority class examples that lie together. In recent years, many over-sampling methods based on SMOTE have been discussed, such as bSMOTE [17] and V-synth [18]. Hybrid methods combine the two previous methods, eliminating the examples of majority class and increasing the instances of minority class at the same time. Compared with over-sampling methods, under-sampling methods re-balance imbalanced class distribution by reducing the number of majority class samples, while hybrid sampling is a combination of the two methods.

Algorithmic Level Approaches. Algorithm-level methods focus on modifying existing classification algorithms to enhance their ability to learn from minority classes. Most algorithms are based on SVM and neural networks. Ando [19] proposed a simple but effective stepwise weighting scheme based on the k-Nearest neighbor density model, called SNN, to solve the class imbalance problem. The cost-sensitive learning technology seeks to minimize the overall misclassification cost and improve classifiers' learning ability by assigning different misclassification costs to the majority class and the minority class. Lopez et al. [20] proposed an algorithm to deal with large-scale imbalanced data using a fuzzy rule and cost-sensitive learning techniques.

Ensemble Approaches. Classifier ensemble has become a popular technique to tackle imbalanced learning problems, mainly due to their ability to improve a single classifier's performance [12]. The ensemble methods can be viewed as building a multiple classifiers system that combines several basic classifiers. For each primary classifier, a data-level method is usually used as a preprocessing. The most widely used MCS is the boosting algorithm proposed by Schapire [21], which has been applied to many well-known ensemble algorithms, such as SMOTEBoost [22], RUSBoost [23], EasyEnsemble [24]. Literature [25] points out that a typical MCS generally contains three processes, that are, resampling, ensemble construction, and fusion rules.

2.2   Classification Algorithms

There are many typical classification algorithms in machine learning. To develop our experimental study, we have selected 12 representative classifiers to achieve data classification, which are summarized in Table 1.

Table 1. The 12 classifiers used in this paper.

Acronym	Classifier
ET	Extra Trees Classifier
RF	Random Forest Classifier
Lightgbm	Light Gradient Boosting Machine
DT	Decision Tree Classifier
Ridge	Ridge Classifier
GBC	Gradient Boosting Classifier
Ada	AdaBoost Classifier
NB	Naive Bayes
LR	Logistic Regression
QDA	Quadratic Discriminant Analysis
KNN	K Neighbors Classifier
SVM	SVM

3 Hybrid Resampling-Based Ensemble Framework

In this section, we present the details of the proposed HRE model framework for imbalanced classification. Consider that using the oversampling strategy to extend the minority classes will increase the training cost, we only specify an ensemble framework with the undersampling strategies. After that, a hybrid ensemble framework that combines both oversampling and undersampling together is proposed to balance the classes in the dataset.

3.1 Undersampling-Based Ensemble Framework

Framework Overview. To solve the class-imbalanced classification problem, we propose an undersampling-based ensemble model. The main idea of this model is to keep the number of minority classes constant, undersample the majority classes proportionally, and then train with a model integrated by 12 classifiers.

The random undersampling method (RUS) is one of the common and simple undersampling techniques. Random undersampling selects samples randomly from the majority class samples until a satisfactory class distribution is obtained. In this way, the number of majority classes is reduced, and relatively fast processing can be achieved with less memory. Also, we can control the proportion of undersampling at will. Therefore, in this model, we use random undersampling as the undersampling method.

The data resampling approach attempts to mitigate the data imbalance problem by removing instances from the majority classes or adding examples to the minority classes. In this model, we use random undersampling to reduce the number of majority classes. It also can obtain faster processing speed with less memory overhead. Besides, compared with a single classifier, multiple classifiers have been proven to be more accurate. Therefore, we have chosen 12 classifiers in the ensemble approach, providing more diverse options than 5 classifiers in the previous work.

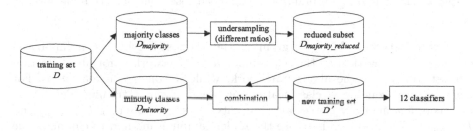

Fig. 1. The steps of the undersampling-based ensemble approach framework.

Figure 1 shows a block diagram of the proposed undersampling-based ensemble framework for the class-imbalanced network anomaly detection dataset. It comprises three steps. For instance, we examine a classification problem, given a training dataset D that contains majority classes and minority classes denoted by $D_{majority}$ and $D_{minority}$. The first step is to use the under-sampling method to eliminate the data samples of majority classes in different ratios and then generate new majority-class datasets (reduced subset), denoted by $D_{majority\_reduced}$. The second step is to combine the reduced subset $(D_{majority\_reduced})$ with the minority dataset to generate a new training dataset (D'). Finally, we use the new dataset (D') to train the ensemble model by 12 classifiers. That is, by different ratios of under-sampling, we analyze the impact on ensemble classification performance for the imbalanced network anomaly detection dataset.

3.2   Hybrid Resampling-Based Ensemble Framework

Overview of the Improved Model. The first model only uses the under-sampling technique for the majority classes, while the small number of minority classes may affect the effectiveness of the classification. Therefore, on the basis of the first model, we further propose an improved Hybrid Resampling-based Ensemble (HRE) model. It further employs the oversampling method to modify the minority classes.

Random oversampling (ROS) is a commonly used oversampling method. It increases the number of minority class samples in some way. It also controls the proportion of sampling. So for the improved model, we choose random oversampling as the sampling technique.

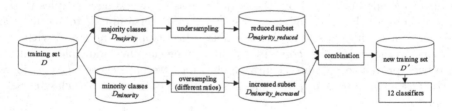

Fig. 2. The steps of the hybrid resampling-based ensemble approach framework.

Figure 2 shows a block diagram of the proposed hybrid sampling-based ensemble framework for the class-imbalanced network anomaly detection dataset. Similar to the above framework, while it consists of four steps. For instance, we examine a classification problem, given a training dataset D that contains majority classes and minority classes denoted by $D_{majority}$ and $D_{minority}$. The first step is to use the under-sampling method to eliminate the data samples of the majority classes and generate a new majority-class dataset (reduced subset), denoted by $D_{majority\_reduced}$. The second step is to employ the over-sampling method to increase the samples of minority classes and generate a new minority-class dataset (increased subset), denoted by $D_{minority\_increased}$. Then, $D_{majority\_reduced}$ is combined with $D_{minority\_increased}$ to produce a new training dataset (D'). Finally, we use the new dataset (D') to train the ensemble model by 12 classifiers. In general, we combine the undersampling with the oversampling method and apply the ensemble model to improve the performance of imbalanced problems.

4 Experiments

4.1 Evaluation Criteria

Model evaluation is one of the crucial processes in machine learning. Performance measures, therefore, are key indicators for both evaluating the effectiveness and guiding the learning of a classifier. Accuracy is the most commonly used evaluation metric for classification [12]. While in the framework of imbalanced datasets, it is not enough to only evaluate the overall accuracy (ACC) because of the bias toward the majority class.

Performance metrics adapted into imbalanced data problems, such as Receiver Operating Characteristics (ROC), G-Mean (GM), and F-measure (FM), are less likely to suffer from imbalanced distributions as they take class distribution into account.

In this paper, regarding the above issue, we choose accuracy (ACC), precision, recall and F-measure (FM) as the measures to evaluate the performance of imbalance learning algorithms. F-measure is the weighted harmonic mean of recall and precision. Using true positive (TP), true negative (TN), false positive (FP), and false negative (FN), these metrics can be calculated as follows:

$$Accuracy = \frac{TP + TN}{TP + TN + FP + FN} \tag{1}$$

$$Recall = \frac{TP}{TP + FN} \tag{2}$$

$$Precision = \frac{TP}{TP + FP} \tag{3}$$

$$F - measure = \frac{2 \times Recall \times Precision}{Recall + Precision} \tag{4}$$

4.2 Network Anomaly Detection Dataset

In this paper, we utilize the network anomaly detection dataset from the Network Anomaly Detection 2021 Challenge (NADC). The anomaly detection dataset contains three days of data on December 3, December 10, and December 16, with a total of more than 9 million samples, and each instance has 22 attributes and one label value.

As shown in Fig. 3, the dataset has five classes, which are Normal, Probing-IP sweep, Probing-Port sweep, DDOS-smurf and Probing-Nmap. The number of instances per class is respectively 8920477, 240524, 77289, 2344 and 829. Obviously, the normal category has the largest number, while the other four types are much less. The network anomaly detection dataset is a typical multi-class imbalanced dataset.

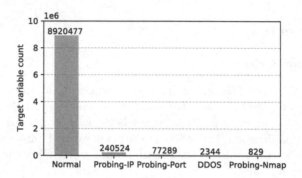

Fig. 3. The network anomaly detection dataset.

4.3 Experimental Settings

The experiments in this paper use the network anomaly detection dataset, and each experiment is carried out using 10-fold cross-validation. The proposed frameworks are implemented using Python.

We conducted two groups of experiments. The first group is based on the undersampling-based ensemble framework. We use the random undersampling method to reduce the samples of the majority classes. To find suitable configurations of sampling rates, we consider different settings for the class ratios: 1:1, 1:2, 1:3, 1:4, 1:5, 1:6 and 1:8 (minority vs majority). Then, the sampling method is combined individually with each of the 12 classifiers. Furthermore, the ensemble model based on undersampling is developed.

For the second group, it is based on the hybrid sampling-based ensemble framework. We use the random undersampling method to reduce the majority samples to a certain number and then oversample the minority samples according to different sampling ratios: 1:4, 2:4, 3:4, 4:4 (minority vs majority). After that, we utilize 12 classifiers to form the ensemble model. Finally, the performance of classifiers is quantified by the metrics.

4.4 Results and Analysis

In this section, we report experimental results and analyses. Firstly, we discuss the effects of different sampling rates on the performance of classifiers. Secondly, we evaluate the effectiveness of our proposed Hybrid Resampling-based Ensemble (HRE) model.

Comparison of Sampling Rates in Under-Sampling Ensemble Model.
In this subsection, we start our investigation by comparing the different sampling
rates. Since we cannot control the exact class ratio when using classifiers.

Firstly, we keep the number of the minority classes (DDOS and Probing-
Nmap) the same as 815, and reduce the number of majority classes (Normal,
Probing-IP, Probing-Port) to 1000, 2000, 3000, 4000, 5000, 6000, 8000 respec-
tively, i.e. the proportion of the minority classes and the majority classes is 1:1,
1:2, 1:3, 1:4, 1:5, 1:6 and 1:8. Part of the sampling data process results is shown in
Fig. 4. Besides, every experiment is repeated five times to eliminate randomness.

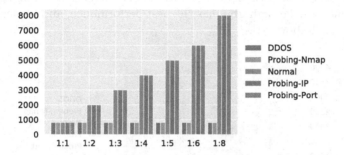

Fig. 4. The ratio between minority classes and majority classes.

We calculate the mean values of each sampling rate across different classifiers.
Table 2 shows the results, where the last row gives the average ranks of the seven
sampling rates in terms of different classifiers on the network anomaly detection
dataset. The best values are shown in bold.

Table 2. The accuracy of classifiers on under-resampling ensemble model (minority:
majority).

Classifier	1:1	1:2	1:3	1:4	1:5	1:6	1:8
RF	0.7773	0.6516	0.5154	**0.7488**	0.5351	0.7453	0.4571
ET	0.4291	0.4733	0.6176	0.4081	0.3919	0.4425	0.3919
Lightgbm	**0.8209**	**0.8221**	**0.8726**	**0.8911**	**0.8726**	**0.8238**	**0.7932**
GBC	0.8225	0.8175	0.7939	**0.8125**	0.7951	0.8159	0.4247
DT	0.7989	0.8047	0.4001	0.4016	0.4332	0.3811	0.3851
NB	0.7689	0.7646	0.7596	**0.7658**	0.7631	0.7596	0.7665
Ridge	0.3705	0.3715	0.3710	**0.7615**	0.3703	0.3695	0.3731
Ada	0.4972	0.4934	0.3726	**0.7453**	0.7801	0.3665	0.2712
LR	0.5682	0.6122	0.6477	**0.6882**	0.7111	0.7152	0.7172
KNN	0.6824	0.6891	0.6952	0.3935	0.7044	0.3896	0.5321
QDA	0.6689	0.3549	0.7646	0.7075	0.3823	0.7654	0.7608
SVM	0.5258	0.3412	0.4699	0.3529	0.3834	0.3688	0.4074
Average	0.6215	0.5793	0.5851	**0.6495**	0.6009	0.5587	0.5116

As to the effect of the sampling rates (imbalance ratio) on classification performance, we observed the following. First, with the number of majority class samples increases gradually, the performance of the ensemble model firstly increases and then decreases when keeping the number of minority classes samples constant. Such experimental results also indicate that the increasing imbalance ratio of the data has effects on the performance of the classifiers. Besides, when the imbalance ratio is slight, the impact on classification performance is not obvious. And when the undersampling ratio is 1:4, the average accuracy reaches relatively higher. If the imbalanced ratio is larger, it will have a negative impact on the performance of the classifier. Furthermore, among these 12 classifiers, the classifier lightgbm has the best performance, and its accuracy has been maintained above 0.8.

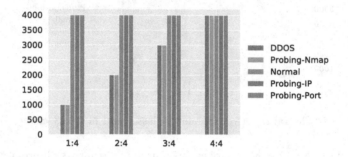

Fig. 5. The ratio between minority classes and majority classes.

Evaluating the Effectiveness of the Hybrid Resampling-Based Ensemble Model.

In this part, we evaluate the performance of the Hybrid Resampling-based Ensemble (HRE) model. First, we undersample the number of the majority classes (Normal, Probing-IP, Probing-Port) to 4000, and then oversample the number of the minority classes (DDOS and Probing-Nmap) to 1000, 2000, 3000, 4000, respectively. That is, the ratio between minority classes and majority classes is 1:4, 2:4, 3:4, 4:4. We gradually decrease the imbalance ratio with hybrid resampling. Part of the sampling data process results is shown in Fig. 5. Each experiment is repeated five times, and the average value is taken to eliminate randomness.

The hybrid resampling is to reduce the number of minority classes to a certain number, and then increase the number of cases in the minority classes so that the number matches the majority classes. We gradually decrease the imbalance ratio with the hybrid resampling. The results are shown in Table 3. It can be seen that as the number of minority samples gradually increases, the accuracy of the classifier lightgbm increases from 0.8393 to 0.8981 as a whole, indicating that the performance of the model is gradually getting better. The experimental results show that when the number of minority classes is small, increasing the number of minority classes and reducing the number of majority classes can improve the accuracy. This also means that the combination of oversampling and undersampling method is effective.

Table 3. The accuracy of classifiers on hybrid-resampling ensemble model (minority: majority).

Classifier	1:4	2:4	3:4	4:4
RF	0.5366	0.5142	0.6296	0.6184
ET	0.4016	0.4147	0.4131	0.4622
Lightgbm	**0.8393**	**0.8644**	**0.8801**	**0.8981**
GBC	0.8155	0.8141	0.8175	0.8182
DT	0.3923	0.7789	0.7773	0.7843
NB	0.7523	0.7601	0.7662	0.7616
Ridge	0.3731	0.3722	0.3731	0.3723
Ada	0.3283	0.6983	0.4328	0.4532
LR	0.6571	0.5725	0.5335	0.5501
KNN	0.5108	0.5343	0.5382	0.3939
QDA	0.6801	0.6712	0.6647	0.6682
SVM	0.3152	0.3422	0.3551	0.3831

5 Conclusion

In this paper, we consider the problem of imbalanced classification in real applications. We propose a new Hybrid Resampling-based Ensemble (HRE) framework, which takes the advantages of both undersampling and oversampling strategies. To this end, 12 typical classifiers are employed in the ensemble model. We evaluate the framework with a typical imbalanced classification scenario, i.e., network anomaly analysis, with real-world traces. The numerical results demonstrate that a recommended size ratio between the minority and majority classes is 1:4 when only the undersampling strategy is adopted. We then execute the oversampling operation to extend the minority classes. The results show that the HRE can significantly increase classification accuracy with reduced computation overhead.

Acknowledgement. The work is supported by the National Key Research and Development Program of China under grant 2018YFB0204301, the National Natural Science Foundation (NSF) under grant 62072306 and 62002378, Tianjin Science and Technology Foundation under Grant No.18ZXJMTG00290, Open Fund of Science and Technology on Parallel and Distributed Processing Laboratory under grant 6142110200407.

References

1. Tsai, C.F., Lin, W.C., Hu, Y.H., Yao, G.T.: Under-sampling class imbalanced datasets by combining clustering analysis and instance selection. Inf. Sci. **477**, 47–54 (2019)
2. Li, H.: A divide and conquer approach for imbalanced multi-class classification and its application to medical decision making. Pak. J. Pharm. Sci. **29** (2016)

3. Mahajan, V., Misra, R., Mahajan, R.: Review of data mining techniques for churn prediction in telecom. J. Inf. Organ. Sci. **39**(2), 183–197 (2015)
4. Liu, Y., Wang, J., Niu, S., Song, H.: Deep learning enabled reliable identity verification and spoofing detection. In: Yu, D., Dressler, F., Yu, J. (eds.) WASA 2020. LNCS, vol. 12384, pp. 333–345. Springer, Cham (2020). https://doi.org/10.1007/978-3-030-59016-1_28
5. Zafeiriou, S., Zhang, C., Zhang, Z.: A survey on face detection in the wild: past, present and future. Comput. Vis. Image Underst. **138**, 1–24 (2015)
6. West, J., Bhattacharya, M.: Intelligent financial fraud detection: a comprehensive review. Comput. Secur. **57**, 47–66 (2016)
7. Kang, S., Cho, S., Kang, P.: Constructing a multi-class classifier using one-against-one approach with different binary classifiers. Neurocomputing **149**, 677–682 (2015)
8. Luo, M., Wang, K., Cai, Z., Liu, A., Li, Y., Cheang, C.F.: Using imbalanced triangle synthetic data for machine learning anomaly detection. Comput. Mater. Continua **58**(1), 15–26 (2019)
9. Kubat, M., Holte, R.C., Matwin, S.: Machine learning for the detection of oil spills in satellite radar images. Mach. Learn. **30**(2), 195–215 (1998)
10. Fawcett, T., Provost, F.: Adaptive fraud detection. Data Min. Knowl. Disc. **1**(3), 291–316 (1997)
11. Pelayo, L., Dick, S.: Applying novel resampling strategies to software defect prediction. In: NAFIPS 2007–2007 Annual Meeting of the North American Fuzzy Information Processing Society, pp. 69–72. IEEE (2007)
12. Yijing, L., Haixiang, G., Xiao, L., Yanan, L., Jinling, L.: Adapted ensemble classification algorithm based on multiple classifier system and feature selection for classifying multi-class imbalanced data. Knowl.-Based Syst. **94**, 88–104 (2016)
13. Tao, X., Peng, Y., Zhao, F., Wang, S.F., Liu, Z.: An improved parallel network traffic anomaly detection method based on bagging and GRU. In: Yu, D., Dressler, F., Yu, J. (eds.) WASA 2020. LNCS, vol. 12384, pp. 420–431. Springer, Cham (2020). https://doi.org/10.1007/978-3-030-59016-1_35
14. Branco, P., Torgo, L., Ribeiro, R.P.: A survey of predictive modeling on imbalanced domains. ACM Comput. Surv. (CSUR) **49**(2), 1–50 (2016)
15. Haixiang, G., Yijing, L., Shang, J., Mingyun, G., Yuanyue, H., Bing, G.: Learning from class-imbalanced data: review of methods and applications. Expert Syst. Appl. **73**, 220–239 (2017)
16. Chawla, N.V., Bowyer, K.W., Hall, L.O., Kegelmeyer, W.P.: Smote: synthetic minority over-sampling technique. J. Artif. Intell. Res. **16**, 321–357 (2002)
17. Han, H., Wang, W.-Y., Mao, B.-H.: Borderline-SMOTE: a new over-sampling method in imbalanced data sets learning. In: Huang, D.-S., Zhang, X.-P., Huang, G.-B. (eds.) ICIC 2005. LNCS, vol. 3644, pp. 878–887. Springer, Heidelberg (2005). https://doi.org/10.1007/11538059_91
18. Young, W.A., Nykl, S.L., Weckman, G.R., Chelberg, D.M.: Using voronoi diagrams to improve classification performances when modeling imbalanced datasets. Neural Comput. Appl. **26**(5), 1041–1054 (2015)
19. Ando, S.: Classifying imbalanced data in distance-based feature space. Knowl. Inf. Syst. **46**(3), 707–730 (2015). https://doi.org/10.1007/s10115-015-0846-3
20. López, V., Del Río, S., Benítez, J.M., Herrera, F.: Cost-sensitive linguistic fuzzy rule based classification systems under the mapreduce framework for imbalanced big data. Fuzzy Sets Syst. **258**, 5–38 (2015)
21. Freund, Y.: Boosting a weak learning algorithm by majority. Inf. Comput. **121**(2), 256–285 (1995)

22. Chawla, N.V., Lazarevic, A., Hall, L.O., Bowyer, K.W.: SMOTEBoost: improving prediction of the minority class in boosting. In: Lavrač, N., Gamberger, D., Todorovski, L., Blockeel, H. (eds.) PKDD 2003. LNCS (LNAI), vol. 2838, pp. 107–119. Springer, Heidelberg (2003). https://doi.org/10.1007/978-3-540-39804-2_12
23. Seiffert, C., Khoshgoftaar, T.M., Van Hulse, J., Napolitano, A.: Rusboost: a hybrid approach to alleviating class imbalance. IEEE Trans. Syst. Man Cybern.-Part A Syst. Hum. **40**(1), 185–197 (2009)
24. Liu, X.Y., Wu, J., Zhou, Z.H.: Exploratory undersampling for class-imbalance learning. IEEE Trans. Syst. Man Cybern. Part B (Cybern.) **39**(2), 539–550 (2008)
25. Nanni, L., Fantozzi, C., Lazzarini, N.: Coupling different methods for overcoming the class imbalance problem. Neurocomputing **158**, 48–61 (2015)

Light Field Super-Resolution Based on Spatial and Angular Attention

Donglin Li[1,2], Da Yang[1,2(✉)], Sizhe Wang[1,2], and Hao Sheng[1,2]

[1] State Key Laboratory of Software Development Environment,
School of Computer Science and Engineering, Beihang University,
Beijing 100191, People's Republic of China
{lidonglincs,da.yang,sizhewang,shenghao}@buaa.edu.cn
[2] Beihang Hangzhou Innovation Institute Yuhang, Beihang University,
Xixi Octagon City, Yuhang District, Hangzhou 310023, People's Republic of China

Abstract. Light field (LF) images captured by LF cameras can store the intensity and direction information of light rays in the scene, which have advantages in many computer vision tasks, such as 3D reconstruction, target tracking and so on. But there is a trade-off between the spatial and angular resolution of LF images due to the fixed resolution of sensor in LF cameras. So LF image super-resolution (SR) is widely explored. Most of the existing methods do not consider the different degree of importance of spatial and angular information provided by other views in LF. So we propose a LF spatial-angular attention module (LFSAA) to adjust the weights of spatial and angular information in spatial and angular domain respectively. Based on this module, a LF image SR network is designed to super-resolve all views in LF simultaneously. And we further combine the LF image SR network with single image SR network to improve the ability to explore spatial information of a single image in LF. Experiments on both synthetic and real-world LF datasets have demonstrated the performance of our method.

Keywords: Light field · Super-resolution · Attention mechanism

1 Introduction

Light field (LF) cameras have attracted a lot of attention in recent years, which can capture both the intensity and direction information of light rays in the scene. So the images acquired by LF cameras, which are called LF images, have unique advantages when used in saliency detection, 3D reconstruction, target tracking and other fields [1]. But there is a trade-off between the spatial and angular resolution of LF images due to the fixed resolution of the sensor in LF cameras. In order to ensure the appropriate angular resolution, the spatial resolution of LF images is much lower than ordinary images captured by traditional cameras. Since LF images with high spatial resolution are needed in LF applications, it is necessary to convert low-resolution LF images into high-resolution counterparts by using light field super-resolution (LFSR).

Z. Liu et al. (Eds.): WASA 2021, LNCS 12937, pp. 314–325, 2021.
https://doi.org/10.1007/978-3-030-85928-2_25

LFSR is similar to single image super-resolution (SISR) to a certain degree. But LFSR needs not only the target low-resolution images of super-resolution, which provide spatial information, but also other views in LF which provide supplementary spatial and angular information. In early LFSR methods [2–5], image prior information was explicitly used to reconstruct high-resolution LF images. However, the performance of these methods is not satisfactory due to limited capability of utilizing image information. Deep learning alleviates this problem, and learning-based methods perform better both visually and quantitatively than above methods. Yoon et al. [6,7] proposed the first CNN-based method (i.e., LFCNN) to reconstruct LF images. In LFCNN, LF images are first super-resolved to the target resolution by convolutional networks, and then fine-tuned according to the angular information provided by adjacent views. Yuan et al. [8] combined the convolutional neural networks (CNNs) with the special structure of LF, and proposed a LFSR network (i.e., LF-DCNN). In the first stage, the sub-aperture images (SAIs) are super-resolved to the target resolution separately. In the second stage, the EPI information is extracted and input into the EPI-enhancement network to reconstruct the results. And other methods [9–14] have also been proposed and achieved the state-of-the-art performance by utilizing the spatial and angular information of LF images. But these methods mainly focus on obtaining more spatial and angular information, ignoring the different importance of the information obtained. In fact, due to the occlusion problems in different views, some information provided by other views is not helpful to super-resolve the target view.

Based on this observation, we propose a LF spatial and angular attention mechanism. It is used in LFSR network to improve the ability to explore the important spatial and angular information. Specifically, an LF spatial-angular attention (LFSAA) module is used to adjust the weights of the key information in spatial and angular domain of LF respectively. Based on this module, an end-to-end LFSR network is proposed, which can super-resolve all images in LF at the same time. Different from most previous methods, our method combines the LFSR network with the SISR network to improve the ability to extract spatial information of a single image in LF. The low-resolution LF images are processed by a SISR network and a LFSR network to learn the feature map of a single image and the one from multi-views in LF respectively. Both the feature are combined to reconstruct the high-resolution LF images. Experiments have demonstrated the effectiveness of our method.

In summary, the contributions of this paper are as follows:

- To distinguish the important spatial and angular information provided by multi-views in LF, a LF spatial and angular attention mechanism is proposed.
- Based on LFSAA module, an end-to-end LFSR network is proposed and realizes the state-of-the-art performance.
- To make full use of the spatial information of a single image in LF, we introduce the SISR network into the LFSR network as the basic network framework.

2 Related Work

In this section, we briefly introduce the major technological achievements of SISR and LFSR.

2.1 Single Image Super-Resolution

Single image super-resolution is the task of converting low-resolution images into high-resolution images, which can be used in repairing images and videos, compressing and uploading data [15–17], etc. Interpolation methods were widely used in early SISR tasks. Due to the excellent performance of deep learning, convolutional neural networks have been the main framework of SISR methods in recent years. This paper mainly introduces the SISR methods based on deep learning.

Dong et al. [19,20] introduced CNNs into the field of SR for the first time, and proposed the first SR convolutional neural network (i.e., SRCNN). SRCNN established the end-to-end SR deep learning framework. The low-resolution images are first sampled directly into the target resolution and then reconstructed into high-resolution images by 3 convolutional layers. Shi et al. [21] used the convolution operation to replace direct interpolation for sampling, and proposed ESPCNN to achieve better reconstruction accuracy. Kim et al. [22] proposed a very deep SR neural network (i.e., VDSR), which increased the depth of SR network to 20 layers. VDSR learns the difference between the input images and output images by using global residual learning strategy. Lim et al. [23] proposed an enhanced deep SR network (i.e., EDSR) after the proposal of Residual Network (i.e., ResNet) [24] which solved the problem of gradient disappearance and explosion, and increased the limit of network depth to more than 100 layers. Zhang et al. [25] proposed a residual channel attention network (i.e., RCAN) combined with the attention mechanism, which has been shown to perform well in other computer vision tasks. RCAN distributes different weights to the channels in the network through attention mechanism, and the channel which gets more high-frequency features acquires higher weights. In addition, generative adversarial networks (GANs) have also achieved good results in SR task [18]. Ledig et al. [26] proposed a SR generative adversarial network (i.e., SRGAN) which can generate high-resolution images close to the original images on the 4× SR task.

Due to the advantage of convolutional networks in the use of spatial information, the reconstruction quality of SISR methods has been greatly improved. At the same time, the depth and complexity of the SR networks are increasing.

2.2 Light Field Super-Resolution

In the early development of LFSR, some SISR methods were also used. But they gradually lost their advantages because they can not use angular information of LF images. Now in the field of LFSR, both methods based on prior information and methods based on deep learning have been widely explored. The general idea of LFSR algorithms is to infer the non-integer offset between different views, and then reconstruct the low-resolution images based on this. The methods based on prior information calculate these offsets explicitly, while methods based on deep learning use neural networks to learn the pixel relationship implicitly and most of them are end-to-end.

Many researchers aim to find different algorithms to make use of image prior information for LFSR. Bishop et al. [2] proposed a two-stage algorithm to super-resolve LF images. Firstly, the scene depth is restored by establishing the corresponding relationship between multi-views. Then, the high-resolution images are estimated by Bayesian deconvolution method. Mitra et al. [3] proposed an algorithm based on Gaussian mixture model (GMM) which can be used in many LF tasks. The parallax of LF is first generated by sub-space projection technology, and then the LF block is modeled as Gaussian random variable based on parallax value. Finally, the GMM model is established for many LF tasks including SR. Wanner et al. [4] calculated the continuous depth map on epipolar plane images (EPIs) by using the structural tensor method, and the LF images based on depth map were super-resolved by using the variational optimization framework. Boominathan et al. [5] proposed a hybrid LF imaging system. The single high-resolution image was captured by the digital single lens reflex camera and a set of low-resolution LF images were captured by the LF camera. Then the image blocks were extracted from the high-resolution image which have the lowest matching cost to the low-resolution LF images. The high-resolution blocks were mixed with the low-resolution LF images based on weighted average value, and finally raised the resolution of LF images.

The methods based on deep learning has been proved to perform better than traditional methods in SISR field. So more and more methods for LFSR focus on neural networks to improve the results inspired by this. Yoon et al. [6,7] first introduced deep learning into LFSR and proposed the first LFSR neural network (i.e., LFCNN). Different from LFCNN, Yuan et al. [8] proposed a LFSR network LF-DCNN, which combines convolutional neural networks with special structure of LF. In order to reduce the dependence of LFSR on accurate prior information such as depth or parallax, Wang et al. [9] proposed an implicitly multi-scale fusion (IMsF) method, which extracts context information from the same image block on multiple scales for LFSR. Zhang et al. [10] designed a residual network ResLF to perform LFSR. The views in LF are divided into four groups according to the angle direction (0°, 45°, 90°, 135°), and input into four different residual network branches to learn the high-frequency details. Yeung et al. [11] proposed to use 4D convolution to make full use of the structure information of LF images in spatial domain and angular domain, and designed an end-to-end deep SR network LFSSR. In order to maintain the parallax relationship of LF images while performing LFSR, Jin et al. [12,13] proposed a novel LFSR network LFSSR-ATO. On the basis of super-resolved LF images by using the complementary information of multi-views, a regularization network trained on the structure perception loss function was added to enforce the correct parallax relationship on the reconstructed images. Wang et al. [14] proposed a spatial-angular interaction network (i.e., InterNet). Specifically, two convolutions (i.e., spatial/angular feature extractor) were designed to extract spatial and angular features from the input LF images respectively, and then the spatial and angular features were interacted and coupled through the interaction block.

Due to the advantages of neural networks in exploring the spatial and angular correlation of images, the performance of LFSR has been greatly improved. But in fact, not all views in LF can provide the necessary information for the target image due to the occlusion problem caused by the small differences between multi-views. Most of the previous methods ignored this problem, and used all images in LF indiscriminately to super-resolve the target LF image, which increased the burden of network to learn the key features.

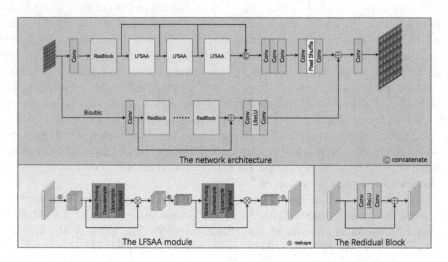

Fig. 1. The architecture of our network

3 The Proposed Method

3.1 Overall Framework

At present, the framework of most learning-based LFSR methods is to use interpolation methods to upsample the low-resolution images directly to the target resolution, and to use neural networks to learn the feature map from low-resolution images to high-resolution counterparts. Then both of them are combined to generate the reconstructed high-resolution images. That is,

$$I^{hr} = H_{CNN}(I^{lr}) + H_{inter}(I^{lr}) \tag{1}$$

where I^{lr} denotes the low-resolution images and I^{hr} is given as the high-resolution images. H_{CNN} refers to the neural networks and H_{inter} represents the interpolation operation.

Interpolation methods are some early SISR methods, which generate new pixels according to the values of adjacent pixels to improve the image resolution. The interpolation methods can only keep the low-frequency information and ignore the high-frequency details which are perceptible in vision. Therefore, almost all the high-frequency information of the reconstructed images comes from the learning of LFSR network. This aggravates the burden of LFSR network, which makes the network must be deep enough to learn the high-frequency information both from the target image and multi-views. It improves the requirements of hardware, and more time is consumed to generate the reconstructed images. So we combine the LFSR network with SISR network to reduce the depth of the network, and use SISR network to learn the spatial information of the target image itself while using LFSR network to learn the spatial and angular information provided by multi-views. The network framework is as follows:

$$I^{hr} = H_{CNN}^{lfsr}(I^{lr}) + H_{CNN}^{sisr}(I^{lr}) \tag{2}$$

where H_{CNN}^{lfsr} denotes a LFSR network and H_{CNN}^{sisr} represents a SISR network. In this framework, the SISR network mines the spatial information of the target view itself, while the LFSR network mines the spatial and angular information provided by other views in LF to the target view. Therefore, the framework gives full play to the capability of neural networks in image information exploration.

3.2   LF Spatial and Angular Attention

As mentioned above, the problem of LFSR is that the current networks focus on improving the ability to explore the spatial and angular information of LF images, but ignore the different degree of importance of spatial and angular information provided by multi-views. Attention mechanism has been proved to be able to find the key information in the feature map in some computer vision tasks. Based on this, we propose a LF spatial and angular attention mechanism and design a module called LF spatial-angular attention module.

As shown in Fig. 1, the input of LFSAA is the feature map from LF SAIs. The feature map is first reshaped into spatial domain, in which the feature maps of SAIs are arranged by channel. Let F denote the input feature map and F_{sd} denote the feature map in spatial domain. So if the size of F is (aH, aW, C), then the size of F_{sd} should be (H, W, a^2C). In spatial domain, the feature map of each channel contains the spatial information provided by other views in LF to the target image. Then an attention mechanism is applied to adjust the weights of channels. Specifically, scale s is calculated

$$s = f(H_{up}(\delta(H_{down}(H_{pooling}(F_{sd,in}))))) \tag{3}$$

where $F_{sd,in}$ denotes the input and $H_{pooling}$ represents the operation of pooling. $f(\cdot)$ and $\delta(\cdot)$ is given as the sigmoid and ReLU function. H_{down} is the operation which downsamples the channels while H_{up} upsamples the channels. And the output of spatial domain is

$$F_{sd,out} = s \cdot F_{sd,in} \tag{4}$$

where $F_{sd,out}$ denotes the output feature map.

The feature map are then resized into angular domain, in which the feature maps of macro pixels are arranged by channel. Let F denote the input feature map and F_{ad} denote the feature map in angular domain. So if the size of F is (aH, aW, C), then the size of F_{ad} should be $(a, a, H \times W \times C)$. In angular domain, the feature map of each channel contains the angular information provided by other views in LF to the target image. Similarly, an attention mechanism is applied to adjust the weights of channels. The details are the same as the one in spatial domain.

Through LF spatial and angular attention mechanism, the weights of spatial and angular information provided by other views are redistributed according to their importance, which enhances the utilization of effective information.

Table 1. LF datasets used in our experiments

Datasets	Type	Training	Test
HCI_new [27]	Synthetic	20	4
HCI_old [28]	Synthetic	10	2
EPFL [29]	Real-world	70	10
INRIA [30]	Real-world	35	5
STFgantry [31]	Real-world	9	2

3.3   Network Architecture

As shown in Fig. 1, our network consists of a SISR sub-network and a LFSR sub-network. In SISR sub-network, the resolution of LF SAIs is first improved to the target resolution by bicubic interpolation. Then the shallow feature F_0^{si} is extracted by a convolutional layer

$$F_0^{si} = H_{Conv,0}^{si}(I_{bicubic}) \tag{5}$$

where $I_{bicubic}$ is the interpolated image which is generated by combing all upsampled views in LF and $H_{Conv,0}^{si}$ denotes the convolution operation. And we use n residual blocks for deep feature extraction, so we have

$$F_n^{si} = H_{Res,n}(F_{n-1}^{si}) \tag{6}$$

where $H_{Res,n}$ denotes the n-th residual block and F_n^{si} represents the output feature of n-th residual block. The final feature F^{sisr} is calculated as:

$$F^{sisr} = H_{Conv,2}^{si}(\delta(H_{Conv,1}^{si}(F_0^{si} + F_n^{si}))) \tag{7}$$

where $H_{Conv,1}^{si}$ and $H_{Conv,2}^{si}$ denote the convolution operation and $\delta(\cdot)$ is the LeakyReLU function.

In LFSR sub-network, the shallow feature of LF SAIs is extracted by a convolutional layer and a residual block

$$F_0^{lf} = H_{Res}(H_{Conv,0}^{lf}(I^{lr})) \tag{8}$$

where $H_{Conv,0}^{lf}$ denotes the convolution operation and H_{Res} represents the residual block. The shallow feature is then input into LF spatial-angular attention module

$$F_d^{lf} = H_{LFSAA,d}(F_{d-1}^{lf}) \tag{9}$$

where F_d^{lf} is given as the output of d-th LFSAA and $H_{LFSAA,d}$ denotes d-th LFSAA. After d LFSAA, the output feature of each module and F_0^{lf} are concatenated in the channel dimension. Then we use 3 convolutional layers to reduce the number of channels gradually. And a reconstruction module is used to upsample the concatenated feature which is composed of 2 convolutional layers and a pixel shuffle layer.

Finally, the reconstructed high-resolution LF images are acquired by

$$I^{hr} = H_{Conv}(F^{sisr} + F^{lfsr}) \tag{10}$$

where H_{Conv} denotes the convolution operation. F^{sisr} and F^{lfsr} are the feature map generated by the SISR sub-network and the LFSR sub-network respectively.

Table 2. PSNR/SSIM values achieved by different methods for 2× and 4×SR

Methods	Scale	HCI_new [27]	HCI_old [28]	EPFL [29]	INRIA [30]	STFgantry [31]
Bicubic	2×	31.55/0.9322	37.33/0.9722	29.28/0.9325	30.98/0.9523	30.58/0.9416
EDSR [23]	2×	34.65/0.9588	40.96/0.9869	32.88/0.9624	34.76/0.9744	36.15/0.9806
RCAN [25]	2×	34.85/0.9598	40.99/0.9870	32.94/0.9629	34.95/0.9751	36.19/0.9816
resLF [10]	2×	36.22/0.9728	42.89/0.9934	32.89/0.9686	34.69/0.9792	36.84/0.9866
LFSSR [11]	2×	36.77/0.9749	43.72/0.9929	33.63/0.9739	35.22/0.9828	38.01/0.9891
LF-ATO [12]	2×	**37.24/0.9771**	43.76/0.9945	34.43/0.9763	36.15/0.9846	**39.03/0.9921**
Ours	2×	37.22/0.9766	**44.68/0.9953**	**34.78/0.9768**	**36.66/0.9847**	38.52/0.9918
Bicubic	4×	27.55/0.8492	32.35/0.9323	24.91/0.8298	26.69/0.8844	25.81/0.8422
EDSR [23]	4×	29.51/0.8868	35.02/0.9522	27.71/0.8842	29.52/0.9239	28.58/0.9061
RCAN [25]	4×	29.56/0.8872	35.09/0.9529	27.76/0.8849	29.61/0.9251	28.69/0.9098
resLF [10]	4×	29.86/0.9002	36.08/0.9639	27.38/0.8889	29.57/0.9331	28.86/0.9202
LFSSR [11]	4×	30.66/0.9118	36.65/0.9686	28.19/0.9069	30.26/0.9439	30.09/0.9374
LF-ATO [12]	4×	**31.03/0.9169**	37.17/0.9711	29.11/0.9166	31.16/0.9503	**30.76/0.9445**
Ours	4×	30.98/0.9163	**37.19/0.9716**	**29.55/0.9171**	**31.69/0.9505**	30.48/0.9417

4 Experiments

4.1 Datasets and Implementation Details

As shown in Table 1, we use 5 LF datasets to evaluate our experiments in training and test stage, which include synthetic LF images from HCI_new [27] and

HCI_old [28], and real-world images from EPFL [29], INRIA [30] and STF-gantry [31]. The LF images are cropped into patches of size 64×64 and used to generate low-resolution patches of size 32×32 and 16×16 by the bicubic downsampling. Data augmentation including random horizontal flipping, vertical flipping and rotation is also used to generate more training data. Note that the images are converted to YCbCr images and trained only on the Y-channel.

By default, we use 4 residual blocks in SISR network and an angular resolution of 5×5 to perform $2 \times$ and $4 \times$ SR. The batch size is set to 8 and the learning rate is initially set to 10^{-4} and decrease by a factor of 0.5 every 30 epochs. The L_1 loss function and the Adam optimization method are used when the model is trained. We implement the network in Pytorch and use two NVidia RTX 3090 GPUs to train it by 150 epochs.

4.2 Experimental Results

We use PSNR and SSIM to evaluate the performance of our method. The bicubic interpolation is used as a baseline. Two state-of-the-art SISR methods (i.e., EDSR [23], and RCAN [25]) and three LFSR methods (i.e., resLF [10], LFSSR [11], and LF-ATO [12]) are compared to our method. We use the same datasets to train these methods for fairness.

The quantitative results are shown in Table 2. Our method achieves the highest PSNR and SSIM on HCI_old, EPFL, INRIA datasets and the second highest results on HCI_new, STFgantry datasets. The qualitative results are shown in Fig. 2 and Fig. 3. Compared with other methods, our method restore the image

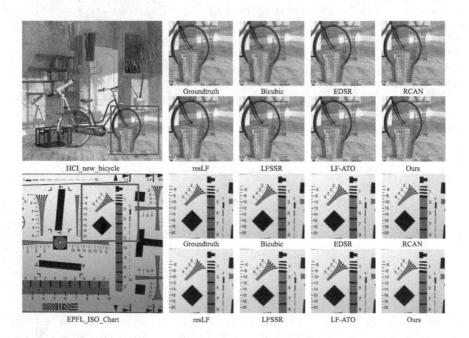

Fig. 2. Visual results of $2 \times$SR

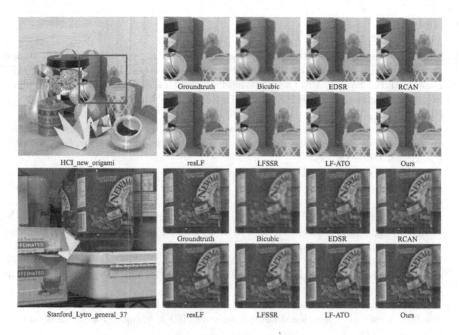

Fig. 3. Visual results of 4×SR

details better. Specifically, for visual results of 2×SR, the reticular structure of the shelf and bin in scene HCI_new_bicycle are reconstructed better than other methods, and the lines in scene EPFL_ISO_Chart are also more similar to the groundtruth. For 4×SR, note that the texture of the wall in scene HCI_new_origami, the reconstruction results of our method is clear and smooth. And the processing results of blurred text is better than other methods in scene Stanford_Lytro_general_37.

5   Conclusion

In this paper, we propose a LF spatial and angular attention mechanism to realize the deep extraction of spatial and angular information provided by multi-views in LF. In addition, we combine the LFSR network with SISR network to improve the learning ability for spatial information of a single image in LF. Based on these, a LFSR network is proposed and achieves state-of-the-art performance on both synthetic and real-world datasets.

Acknowledgement. This study is partially supported by the National Key R&D Program of China (No. 2018YFB2100500), the National Natural Science Foundation of China (No. 61635002), the Science and Technology Development Fund, Macau SAR (File no. 0001/2018/AFJ), the Fundamental Research Funds for the Central Universities and the Open Fund of the State Key Laboratory of Software Development Environment (No. SKLSDE-2021ZX-03). Thank you for the support from HAWKEYE Group.

References

1. Wu, G., Masia, B., Jarabo, A., Zhang, Y., Wang, L., et al.: Light field image processing: an overview. IEEE J. Sel. Top. Signal Process. **11**(7), 926–954 (2017)
2. Bishop, T.E., Favaro, P.: The light field camera: extended depth of field, aliasing, and superresolution. IEEE Trans. Pattern Anal. Mach. Intell. **34**(5), 972–986 (2011)
3. Mitra, K., Veeraraghavan, A.: Light field denoising, light field superresolution and stereo camera based refocussing using a GMM light field patch prior. In: CVPRW, pp. 22–28. IEEE (2012)
4. Wanner, S., Goldluecke, B.: Variational light field analysis for disparity estimation and super-resolution. IEEE Trans. Pattern Anal. Mach. Intell. **36**(3), 606–619 (2013)
5. Boominathan, V., Mitra, K., Veeraraghavan, A.: Improving resolution and depth-of-field of light field cameras using a hybrid imaging system. In: 2014 IEEE International Conference on Computational Photography, pp. 1–10. IEEE (2014)
6. Yoon, Y., Jeon, H.G., Yoo, D., Lee, J.Y., So Kweon, I.: Learning a deep convolutional network for light-field image super-resolution. In: ICCVW, pp. 24–32. IEEE (2015)
7. Yoon, Y., Jeon, H.G., Yoo, D., Lee, J.Y., Kweon, I.S.: Light-field image super-resolution using convolutional neural network. IEEE Signal Process. Lett. **24**(6), 848–852 (2017)
8. Yuan, Y., Cao, Z., Su, L.: Light-field image superresolution using a combined deep CNN based on EPI. IEEE Signal Process. Lett. **25**(9), 1359–1363 (2018)
9. Wang, Y., Liu, F., Zhang, K., Hou, G., Sun, Z., Tan, T.: LFNet: a novel bidirectional recurrent convolutional neural network for light-field image super-resolution. IEEE Trans. Image Process. **27**(9), 4274–4286 (2018)
10. Zhang, S., Lin, Y., Sheng, H.: Residual networks for light field image super-resolution. In: CVPR, pp. 11046–11055. IEEE (2019)
11. Yeung, H.W.F., Hou, J., Chen, X., Chen, J., Chen, Z., Chung, Y.Y.: Light field spatial super-resolution using deep efficient spatial-angular separable convolution. IEEE Trans. Image Process. **28**(5), 2319–2330 (2018)
12. Jin, J., Hou, J., Chen, J., Kwong, S.: Light field spatial super-resolution via deep combinatorial geometry embedding and structural consistency regularization. In: CVPR, pp. 2260–2269. IEEE (2020)
13. Jin, J., Hou, J., Zhu, Z., Chen, J., Kwong, S.: Deep selective combinatorial embedding and consistency regularization for light field super-resolution. arXiv preprint arXiv:2009.12537 (2020)
14. Wang, Y., Wang, L., Yang, J., An, W., Yu, J., Guo, Y.: Spatial-angular interaction for light field image super-resolution. In: Vedaldi, A., Bischof, H., Brox, T., Frahm, J.-M. (eds.) ECCV 2020, Part XXIII. LNCS, vol. 12368, pp. 290–308. Springer, Cham (2020). https://doi.org/10.1007/978-3-030-58592-1_18
15. Cai, Z., Zheng, X.: A private and efficient mechanism for data uploading in smart cyber-physical systems. IEEE Trans. Netw. Sci. Eng. **7**(2), 766–775 (2020)
16. Cai, Z., He, Z.: Trading private range counting over big IoT data. In: 2019 IEEE 39th International Conference on Distributed Computing Systems, pp. 144–153. IEEE (2019)
17. Zheng, X., Cai, Z.: Privacy-preserved data sharing towards multiple parties in industrial IoTs. IEEE J. Sel. Areas Commun. **38**(5), 968–979 (2020)

18. Cai, Z., Xiong, Z., Xu, H., Wang, P., Li, W., Pan, Y.: Generative adversarial networks: a survey towards private and secure applications. ACM **37**(4), 38 (2020)
19. Dong, C., Loy, C.C., He, K., Tang, X.: Image super-resolution using deep convolutional networks. IEEE Trans. Pattern Anal. Mach. Intell. **38**(2), 295–307 (2015)
20. Dong, C., Loy, C.C., He, K., Tang, X.: Learning a deep convolutional network for image super-resolution. In: Fleet, D., Pajdla, T., Schiele, B., Tuytelaars, T. (eds.) ECCV 2014, Part IV. LNCS, vol. 8692, pp. 184–199. Springer, Cham (2014). https://doi.org/10.1007/978-3-319-10593-2_13
21. Shi, W., Caballero, J., Huszár, F., Totz, J., Aitken, A.P., et al.: Real-time single image and video super-resolution using an efficient sub-pixel convolutional neural network. In: CVPR, pp. 1874–1883. IEEE (2016)
22. Kim, J., Lee, J.K., Lee, K.M.: Accurate image super-resolution using very deep convolutional networks. In: CVPR, pp. 1646–1654. IEEE (2016)
23. Lim, B., Son, S., Kim, H., Nah, S., Mu Lee, K.: Enhanced deep residual networks for single image super-resolution. In: CVPRW, pp. 136–144. IEEE (2017)
24. He, K., Zhang, X., Ren, S., Sun, J.: Deep residual learning for image recognition. In: CVPR, pp. 770–778. IEEE (2016)
25. Zhang, Y., Li, K., Li, K., Wang, L., Zhong, B., Fu, Y.: Image super-resolution using very deep residual channel attention networks. In: ECCV, pp. 286–301 (2018)
26. Ledig, C., Theis, L., Huszár, F., Caballero, J., Cunningham, A., Acosta, A., et al.: Photo-realistic single image super-resolution using a generative adversarial network. In: CVPR, pp. 4681–4690. IEEE (2017)
27. Honauer, K., Johannsen, O., Kondermann, D., Goldluecke, B.: A dataset and evaluation methodology for depth estimation on 4D light fields. In: Lai, S.-H., Lepetit, V., Nishino, K., Sato, Y. (eds.) ACCV 2016, Part III. LNCS, vol. 10113, pp. 19–34. Springer, Cham (2017). https://doi.org/10.1007/978-3-319-54187-7_2
28. Wanner, S., Meister, S., Goldluecke, B.: Datasets and benchmarks for densely sampled 4D light fields. In: VMV, pp. 225–226 (2013)
29. Rerabek, M., Ebrahimi, T.: New light field image dataset. In: 8th International Conference on Quality of Multimedia Experience (2016)
30. Le Pendu, M., Jiang, X., Guillemot, C.: Light field inpainting propagation via low rank matrix completion. IEEE Trans. Image Process. **27**(4), 1981–1993 (2018)
31. Vaish, V., Adams, A.: The (new) Stanford light field archive. Comput. Graph. Lab. Stanford Univ. Tech. Rep. **6**(7), 73 (2008)

CamDist: Camera Based Distance Estimation with a Smartphone

Yifan Zhu[1], Xiaojun Zhu[1(✉)], and Cheng Qian[2]

[1] College of Computer Science and Technology, Nanjing University of Aeronautics and Astronautics, Nanjing 211106, China
xzhu@nuaa.edu.cn
[2] Jiangsu Hydraulic Research Institute, Nanjing 210017, China

Abstract. When a user wants to know how far he is away from an object in sight, a typical method is to search the target object in a map application which relies on GPS for distance estimation. This method fails if the target is not listed in the map or GPS signals are not available, such as in a tunnel or in the wild. This paper presents CamDist, a ranging system using the camera of a smartphone. CamDist takes two photos of the target in the direction from the user to the target, and performs distance estimation based on the size difference of the target in the two photos and the moving distance of the smartphone between taking two photos. CamDist has a novel accelerometer based moving distance estimation module that adaptively rotates the smartphone's axis and gives accurate distance estimation. The estimation method applies to other scenarios when the smartphone moves in a direction orthogonal to gravity, and is better than the built-in rotation method of the smartphone. We provide theoretical analysis on the estimation error of CamDist, and show that the working range of CamDist depends on the resolution of the camera as well as the physical size of the remote target. Also, a series of real-world experiments are conducted to verify the effectiveness of CamDist.

Keywords: Distance estimation · Camera-based · Adaptive rotation

1 Introduction

In daily life scenarios, sometimes we see an object and want to know how far it is away. For example, when visiting a new city, one may want to know whether an interesting building is within walking distance. Currently, this is done by searching the target in a map application, which can estimate the distance based on the target and the user's GPS coordinates. This approach fails if the target does not have a well-known name or the user does not know its name, or the user has poor GPS signals when surrounded by tall buildings or in the wild. Though there is specialized ranging equipment such as RADAR or LiDAR, it is not available to most users. We prefer a smartphone-based solution due to its convenience (e.g., [13,18]).

© Springer Nature Switzerland AG 2021
Z. Liu et al. (Eds.): WASA 2021, LNCS 12937, pp. 326–338, 2021.
https://doi.org/10.1007/978-3-030-85928-2_26

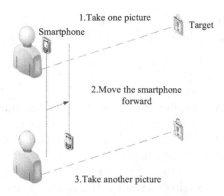

Fig. 1. CamDist estimates distance by taking two photos of the target

In this paper, we consider using a smartphone to estimate the distance by taking photos of the target. The basic idea is that the distance is inversely proportional to the size of the target in the photo, i.e., the further the target is, the smaller it is in the photo. We can have an equation involving the physical size of the target and its pixel size in the photo. Unfortunately, the physical size of the target is usually unknown, e.g., we do not know how tall a remote building is. To address this issue, we propose to take two photos consecutively, along the direction from the user to the target. If the moving distance of the smartphone is known between taking the two photos, we can have a system of equations, removing the target's physical size from the equation.

We propose CamDist, a ranging method shown in Fig. 1, which needs the user to hold up the smartphone to take the first photo, move the smartphone forward, and take the second photo. CamDist estimates the moving distance of the smartphone, compares the target's pixel size in the two photos, and outputs the target's distance. A major challenge of implementing CamDist is to estimate the smartphone's moving distance, which is a multiplicative factor in the final estimated distance. This means that the smartphone's moving distance estimation error directly affects the final error. Estimating smartphone's moving distance is challenging, as a user would slightly rotate the phone during moving, resulting in significant error when integrating acceleration data. We propose a new method to estimate smartphone's moving distance. The key is to rotate the smartphone's axis such that the acceleration along the horizontal direction is estimated accurately. Our method is better than the built-in rotation method of the current Android operating system, and can be applied to other scenarios where the moving direction is orthogonal to gravity.

We make the following contributions. (1) We propose CamDist to estimate the distance to a remote target with a smartphone by taking two photos of the target. The novelty of CamDist is that it has an accurate module to estimate the moving distance of the smartphone. (2) We provide theoretical analysis on the error of CamDist, which helps to understand the ability and limitation of the system. Our analysis shows that the working distance of CamDist depends on the pixel resolution of the camera and the physical size of the remote target. (3) Experiments show the feasibility of CamDist in practice.

2   Related Works

Monocular camera based ranging methods use a single camera (e.g., [10]). Most of them require known object size and camera focal length. The image matching techniques are used for target recognition and the target distance is estimated by the size of the target in the image. These methods have the advantages of lower cost and lower complexity, and have the disadvantage of lower accuracy. Reference [3] consider a ranging method with monocular camera, and prepares a dataset containing the bounding box and actual distance. A network is trained with supervision and the appropriate number of hidden layers and neurons are selected. Its input is the features of the pictures recognized by YOLO and its output is the estimated distance.

Unlike monocular camera, the depth camera can obtain not only the plane image, but also the depth information of the object. It is mainly used for 3D imaging and distance measurement. One implementation technique is stereo vision, such as binocular ranging [1], using parallax between two images. In contrast to using two cameras to take pictures of the target at the same time, reference [16] propose a method to complete binocular ranging with a fixed single camera, taking advantage of the image reflected by plane mirrors. Reference [5] use a flying camera to shoot more than three pictures of a pedestrian for increasing the baseline as far as possible. The structural light in [17] is laser lines produced by a cylindrical lens. It is not suitable for outdoor scenarios. There are some applications of Microsoft Kinect depth sensor [8], which use infrared structured light (i.e., laser speckle) to obtain depth information with three cameras.

There are also non-vision based ranging methods. Ultra Wide Band technology sends and receives very narrow pulse, which has the advantages of strong penetration, low power consumption and accurate positioning accuracy. TOF uses signal arrival time directly, and TDOA [11] uses time difference when multiple base stations receive signals. There is also methods such as [9] that combines two techniques. RSS methods [7,12,20] use the wireless signal strength value or the phase difference of the signal to estimate the distance between nodes through the signal attenuation model. Some works use ultrasonic transmitter and receiver equipment [4,15]. The working distance is roughly ten meters.

3   Overview of CamDist

We first review the mathematical background of imaging with lens, and then introduce the basic idea of CamDist, followed by its key components.

A camera takes photos with a lens following basic mathematical principle as follows. For a target object with height H located distance D away from the lens shown in Fig. 2, the image of the lens is on the opposite side of the lens, with height u and distance v away from the lens satisfying $\frac{H}{u} = \frac{D}{v}$, due to the principle of similar triangles. We are interested in D, but we do not know object height H, image distance v and image height u. Note that v and u are in units of meters, not in pixels. We will remove these three unknowns.

We first remove v. Let the focal length of the lens be f. Due to the principle of lens [14], we have $\frac{1}{f} = \frac{1}{D} + \frac{1}{v}$. Combining the two equations gives $\frac{H}{u} = \frac{D}{f} - 1$.

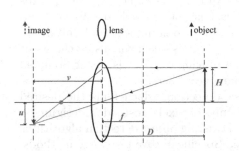

Fig. 2. Imaging principle of a lens

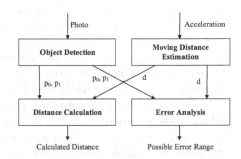

Fig. 3. CamDist modules

3.1 Basic Idea of CamDist

Suppose we take two photos of the object. One is at distance D with image height $p_0 c$ and the other at a closer distance $D - d$ with image height $p_1 c$, where p_0 and p_1 are in units of pixels and c is an unknown constant obtained by dividing image height in meters by its height in pixels. We have two equations: $\frac{H}{p_0 c} = \frac{D}{f} - 1$, and $\frac{H}{p_1 c} = \frac{D-d}{f} - 1$. Eliminating H/c and solving D, we get $D = \frac{p_1}{p_1 - p_0} d + f$. Note that the general idea of taking two photos to eliminate the object's physical size is not new, such as a similar formula appears in [6]. However, previous works do not focus on the smartphone scenario. Though focal length f can be obtained from the manufacture, it is usually several centimeters for smartphones. We can ignore it and get our estimator

$$D = \frac{p_1}{p_1 - p_0} d. \tag{1}$$

Previous works assume the moving distance d is known accurately, and do not analyze the error characteristics. Our work implements the idea in the smartphone, gives a novel method for moving distance estimation and provides in-depth analysis on the error characteristics to help better understand the idea.

3.2 Key Components of CamDist

To estimate the distance based on Eq. (1), CamDist has four modules shown in Fig. 3, including object detection, moving distance estimation, distance calculation and error analysis. The object detection module detects an object in a photo, and outputs the size of the object in units of pixels, i.e., the values of p_0 and p_1. The moving distance estimation module estimates how far the smartphone moves between taking the two photos. It uses acceleration data as input and outputs moving distance d. Finally, the distance calculation module computes distance according to Eq. (1), and the error analysis module outputs the possible error range of the estimation.

It is challenging to estimate d with current techniques and low-cost accelerator sensors in smartphones. Thus, we put requirements on how the two photos are taken in CamDist. In particular, the user is not allowed to walk or bend between taking these two photos. One is required to stand still and only move the arm holding the smartphone. The second photo is taken when stretching out the arm in the object's direction. Thus, the moving distance is upper bounded by one's arm length, which is useful in removing outliers.

A key component of CamDist is object detection, which finds the desired object in the photo and outputs its size in units of pixels. Instead of designing a new object detection method, we try several existing object detection algorithms and select one which is suitable for our task. Specifically, we test three methods, including Canny algorithm, Hough transform and YOLO. After implementation and comparison, YOLO is selected to detect the object due to its high efficiency. Note that YOLO may fail if the target is not in trained categories. When YOLO fails to identify the object in the picture or fails to identify the target the user wants to range, we allow the user to manually delimit the area containing the target.

4   Estimation of Moving Distance

When a user takes the first photo, the smartphone begins to record acceleration data from the built-in accelerometer sensor, and stops recording when the user takes the second photo. The moving distance estimation module estimates the distance of the smartphone between taking the two photos. We first explain why the obvious approach gives significant error, and then propose our novel method.

4.1   Large Error in Straightforward Solution

From the built-in accelerometer sensor, we can get the acceleration of the smartphone along three axes, where the x-axis points to the right of the phone, the y-axis points to the head, and the z-axis is orthogonal to the screen. In Android, we use the 'Linear Acceleration' sensor, which automatically filters out gravity.

By performing integration twice over acceleration, we can get the desired displacement. Let $a(t), v(t), s(t)$ denote the acceleration, velocity and displacement at time t. Observing that $a(t) = 0$, $v(0) = 0$ and $s(0) = 0$, we have $s(t) = \int_0^t v(t)dt = \int_0^t \int_0^t a(t)dtdt$. In practice, acceleration is sampled at discrete time. Summation is used to replace integration. Let the sampled data of accelerometer be $a_0, a_1, a_2, ..., a_n$ at timestamps $t_0, t_1, t_2, ..., t_n$. Then the velocity

v_i and displacement s_i at timestamp t_i are

$$v_i = \sum_{j=1}^{i} a_j(t_j - t_{j-1}), \quad s_i = \sum_{j=1}^{i} v_j(t_j - t_{j-1}). \tag{2}$$

We implement the method and find that it has a significant error. Figure 4(a) shows the velocity along three axes over time, where a user moves the phone ahead as required by CamDist. A disturbing phenomenon is that the velocity at the end of the experiment is not zero, contradicting the fact that the phone is static at that time. In fact, previous research also noticed this problem. Reference [2] propose to subtract velocity proportionally such that the corrected velocity at the end is zero. We implement this approach, and show the corrected velocity in Fig. 4(b). Unfortunately, both approaches have large error in the estimated distance. The distance estimated by the first approach is 0.07 m, and by the second approach is 0.04 m. The ground-truth is 0.27 m, which means the error is 73% and 86%, respectively. Thus, the final system would have large distance error, which is unacceptable for many applications. This problem is also observed in [19], where the solution is to estimate the number of recurring patterns, i.e., the number of walking steps. This solution does not apply to our scenario as a user does not walk when taking the two photos.

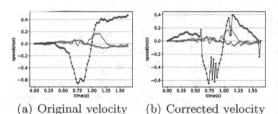

(a) Original velocity   (b) Corrected velocity

Fig. 4. Large error of speed by integrating acceleration

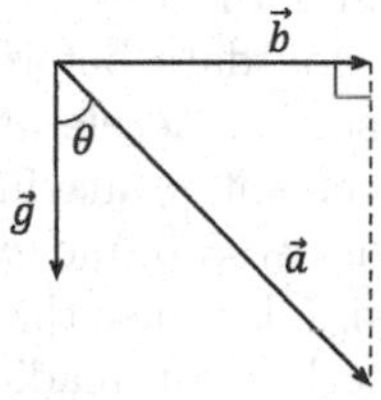

Fig. 5. Acceleration vectors

We believe that the error is caused by the rotation of a user's hand. Because we perform another experiment where the phone is placed on a bracket, which is pushed along a table for approximately 0.5 m. The integrated distance does not show significant error. Consequently, the built-in rotation method does not work well in our application, motivating us to design a new rotation method.

4.2 Projecting Acceleration on Horizontal Plane

Observe that we are only interested in acceleration in horizontal plane, i.e., the plane that is orthogonal to gravity. Thus, instead of using filtered acceleration, we use the raw acceleration data containing the gravity in all readings, and remove gravity by ourselves.

Under the phone's axes, suppose the gravitational acceleration vector is $\vec{g} = (g_x, g_y, g_z)$, and we obtain the overall acceleration vector $\vec{a} = (a_x, a_y, a_z)$. We can compute the projection $\vec{b}$ of $\vec{a}$ on the horizontal plane, the one orthogonal to gravity. The relationship among them is shown in Fig. 5. Note that there might be a vertical acceleration component caused by the moving hand, so $\vec{a}$ might not be equal to $\vec{a} + \vec{b}$. However, in all cases, we can get the magnitude of $\vec{b}$ as $\|\vec{b}\| = \|\vec{v}\| \sin \theta$, where θ is the angle between $\vec{g}$ and $\vec{a}$. We have $\cos \theta = \frac{\vec{g} \cdot \vec{a}}{\|\vec{g}\| \times \|\vec{a}\|}$. Due to $\cos^2 \theta + \sin^2 \theta = 1$, we have $\|\vec{b}\| = \|\vec{v}\| \sqrt{1 - \cos^2 \theta}$.

There are two remaining problems. The first problem is how to get the direction of $\vec{b}$, which is critical in integration. The second problem is how to get gravitational acceleration $\vec{g}$. For the first problem, we base our solution on the following observation. *The smartphone moves along a straight line. Its speed is zero at first, accelerates in the front direction to maximum, then decelerates to zero in the end.* Since the smartphone moves in a straight line, the direction of $\vec{b}$ can only be in two directions, front or back. Based on the speed property, we can safely set the first part of acceleration data as positive, corresponding to acceleration, and the rest part as negative, corresponding to deceleration. The division of the two parts should satisfy that the integrated speed should be zero at timestamp t_n. We can find the division of the two parts as follows.

Let b_i be the magnitude of $\vec{b}$ at timestamp t_i. Let $L_i = \sum\limits_{j=1}^{i} b_j(t_j - t_{j-1})$.

Then, we find the index k such that $L_k = \frac{L_n}{2}$. We then set the direction of all acceleration data before timestamp t_k as positive, and the rest as negative. For the resulting acceleration data, we apply (2) to compute the velocity v_i and displacement s_i at timestamp t_i respectively. One can simply verify that the resulting $v_0 = 0$ and $v_n = 0$. The last problem is how to get gravitational acceleration $\vec{g}$. Because the smartphone is static at timestamp t_0, we can assume that the acceleration reading at t_0 is equal to $\vec{g}$.

We apply the method mentioned above to the data obtained in another experiment. However, we find that the final acceleration value at the last timestamp is not zero shown in Fig. 6(a). Note that non-zero acceleration implies that the speed is not zero either, violating our observation. This phenomenon means that the phone was not moving steadily forward, but was rotating. A single gravitational acceleration vector is not sufficient.

4.3   Projection with Adaptive Gravity Vector

Observing that setting a fixed and uniform value as the acceleration of gravity is not sufficient, we adopt an adaptive approach to find the gravity vector value.

Among all acceleration data points captured during moving, we find all data points whose magnitude is within a small distance from the gravitational acceleration magnitude g, which is defined as the magnitude of acceleration data at time t_0. For all these data points, we treat them as gravitational acceleration. For all other data points, their corresponding gravitational accelerations are linearly interpolated. Finally, we get for each data point a gravitational acceleration vector $\vec{g_i}$. We then use the approach in Subsect. 4.2 to project acceleration readings to the horizontal plane. Figure 6(b) shows the resulting projected acceleration. We can see that the acceleration finally returns to 0.

5   System Error Analysis

This section analyzes the error of CamDist. We first analyze the error caused by pixel size estimation, combine it with moving distance estimation error to give the overall error, and discuss the implication on maximum working distance.

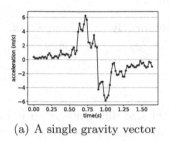
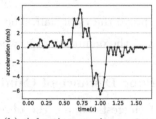

(a) A single gravity vector   (b) Adaptive gravity vectors

Fig. 6. Projected acceleration using a single gravity vector and adaptive gravity vectors

5.1   Quantization Error in Pixel Size Estimation

Pixel sizes of the object can only be integers, causing an inevitable error. The pixel sizes are generally obtained by subtracting two pixel positions. Let $\tilde{p}$ and p be the observed (integral) and ground-truth (fractional) pixel size of the target object. It is obtained by $\tilde{p} = \tilde{y_2} - \tilde{y_1}$, where $\tilde{y_2}$ and $\tilde{y_1}$ are the observed pixel location of the top and bottom of the object. Let y_2 and y_1 be the ground-truth (fractional) pixel locations, i.e., $p = y_2 - y_1$. Due to quantization, we have $y_1 - 0.5 \leq \tilde{y_1} \leq y_1 + 0.5$, and $y_2 - 0.5 \leq \tilde{y_2} \leq y_2 + 0.5$. It follows that

$$\tilde{p} - 1 \leq p \leq \tilde{p} + 1. \tag{3}$$

Lemma 1. *Let p_0, p_1 be the ground-truth pixel sizes of the first and second photos, and $\tilde{p_0}, \tilde{p_1}$ be the observed pixel sizes. We have*

$$\frac{\tilde{p_1} - 1}{\tilde{p_1} - \tilde{p_0} + 2} < \frac{p_1}{p_1 - p_0} \leq \frac{\tilde{p_1} + 1}{\tilde{p_1} - \tilde{p_0} - 2}.$$

Proof. From (3) we have $p_1 \leq \tilde{p_1} + 1$ and $p_1 - p_0 \geq \tilde{p_1} - 1 - (\tilde{p_0} + 1) = \tilde{p_1} - \tilde{p_0} - 2$. Combining them proves the right half. The left half is similar.

5.2   Overall Estimation Error

For moving distance estimation, we say that its error is δ if $(1 - \delta)d \leq \tilde{d} \leq (1 + \delta)d$, where $\tilde{d}$ and d are the estimated and ground-truth moving distance. Then, we have the following theorem regarding the relationship between the ground-truth distance and the observed quantities including pixel sizes and moving distance.

Theorem 1. *Suppose the estimated pixel sizes of the first and second photos are $\tilde{p}_0$ and $\tilde{p}_1$ respectively. Let $\tilde{d}$ be the estimated moving distance with error δ, and D be the ground-truth distance of the remote object. Then,*

$$\frac{\tilde{p}_1 - 1}{\tilde{p}_1 - \tilde{p}_0 + 2} \cdot \frac{\tilde{d}}{1 + \delta} \leq D \leq \frac{\tilde{p}_1 + 1}{\tilde{p}_1 - \tilde{p}_0 - 2} \cdot \frac{\tilde{d}}{1 - \delta} \qquad (4)$$

Proof. We prove the right half. The left is similar. By (1), $D = \frac{p_1}{p_1 - p_0} d$. Due to Lemma 1 and the definition of δ, we have $D \leq \frac{\tilde{p}_1 + 1}{\tilde{p}_1 - \tilde{p}_0 - 2} d \leq \frac{\tilde{p}_1 + 1}{\tilde{p}_1 - \tilde{p}_0 - 2} \cdot \frac{\tilde{d}}{1 - \delta}$,

5.3   Working Distance of CamDist

Theorem 1 suggests that if the observed pixel size difference is no more than 2, then the ground-truth distance may be un-bounded, meaning the ground-truth distance may be arbitrarily long. Intuitively, if there is nearly no difference between these two photos, it may be the case that the object is too far away from the user. This situation is very much like observing a star in the sky.

In particular, when $\tilde{p}_1 - \tilde{p}_0 = 0$, CamDist fails to output any distance according to (1), because the denominator is zero. We can derive a lower bound on D. Observe that $p_1 - p_0 \leq \tilde{p}_1 - \tilde{p}_0 + 2 = 2$, we have

$$D = \frac{p_1}{p_1 - p_0} d \geq \frac{1}{2} p_1 d, \qquad (5)$$

which is the working distance of CamDist. Beyond this distance, the observed object in the two photos may have no change in terms of pixels.

There are several remarks on working distance. First, it increases with the pixel resolution of the camera, when moving distance d and physical object size are fixed. This means a high-quality camera can measure long-distance objects. Second, it increases with the physical size of the object, because p_1 can be larger. Third, it is increasing with respect to moving distance d, meaning that moving a longer distance can help to range a further object. Thus, a user can retry CamDist with a longer distance of movement in case of failure.

6   Experiments

Our experiments are conducted on an Android smartphone with built-in camera and accelerometer. We first evaluate the moving distance estimation module, then evaluate the system in indoor and outdoor scenarios.

6.1   Comparison of Moving Distance Estimation Methods

We implement the following methods:

- SS, which is the straightforward solution using the filtered acceleration of smartphone, i.e., the 'Linear Acceleration' sensor of Android.
- SS+COR, which corrects velocity of SS using the approach in [2].
- PROJ, which uses the unfiltered acceleration of 'Accelerometer' sensor and sets a fixed value as the gravitational acceleration to perform the projection.
- PROJ+ADP, which is our method in Sect. 4.3 that adaptively finds gravity vector for projection.

For comparison, when collecting data, we record the sensor readings of both 'Linear Acceleration' and 'Accelerometer' simultaneously. The real distances of moving are measured by a ruler. We consider the relative error defined as $\frac{\tilde{d}-d}{d}$, where $\tilde{d}$ is the estimated distance and d is the ground-truth.

The CDF of relative error are shown in Fig. 7. It can be seen that our method, PROJ+ADP, achieves the minimum error and performs stably on data samples.

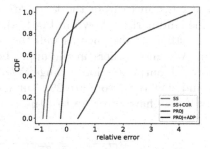

Fig. 7. Relative error of four moving distance estimation methods

(a) Objects   (b) Results

Fig. 8. Distance estimation results for indoor objects

6.2   Ranging for Indoor Short-Range Targets

In the indoor scene, 8 times data are collected for each target object through the procedure shown in Fig. 1. We consider three objects, an air conditioner (AC), cup, and a chair, shown in Fig. 8(a) with real distance ranging from 1 to 2 m. The real distance is measured by a ruler. We use the width of the objects for distance computation, because we find it is more reliable than height. Figure 8(b) shows the estimated distance as well the upper and lower bound by the error analysis component in Sect. 5.

We can see that the range contains the ground-truth value in most cases, suggesting the feasibility of CamDist. Though the error of single experiment can be up to 1 m, the averaged output has small error. We take the average of estimated distance, and find the errors are 0.32 m, 0.32 m and 0.33 m, respectively.

6.3   Ranging for Outdoor Long-Range Targets

For outdoor scenario, a challenge is to get the ground-truth distance. Thus, we consider a landmark building whose GPS location is known so we can use GPS of the smartphone to estimate the ground-truth distance. We stand at two locations with different distances from the landmark and use CamDist to estimate the distance. The landmark is shown in Fig. 9(a).

Figure 9(b) shows the estimated distance as well the possible range by the error analysis component. We find outliers in the upper bounds, meaning that the error analysis component outputs a loose range. We still take average to minimize the error and find that the errors are 29.73 m and 26.22 m, which are acceptable since GPS itself may have error up to 10 m.

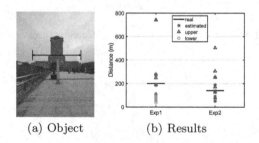

(a) Object   (b) Results

Fig. 9. Ranging results of an outdoor building

We also test the working distance of CamDist for the target in Fig. 9(a). We find that when the ground-truth distance is around 300 m, the object in the two photos do not show any change in pixel size. In this case, CamDist will pop up a warning and suggest a minimum distance calculated by formula (5).

7   Conclusion

In this paper, our method CamDist is proposed to calculate the distance of the object by taking photos. A user first takes a picture of the target to be measured, and then moves the phone forward to take the second picture. The ranging model is obtained by the lens imaging model of the camera jointly. The smartphone's moving distance is calculated by a novel method to rotate the built-in acceleration sensor. For users who want to measure the distance of objects of unlimited categories, shapes and sizes, it provides a smartphone-based ranging method without additional hardware equipment, with low cost consumption, acceptable ranging error, convenient and quick use.

Acknowledgements. This work was supported by the National Natural Science Foundation of China (61972199), Jiangsu Hydraulic Science and Technology Project (No. 2020061) and Hydraulic Research Institute of Jiangsu Province (No. 2020z025).

References

1. Guo, S., Chen, S., Liu, F., Ye, X., Yang, H.: Binocular vision-based underwater ranging methods. In: 2017 IEEE International Conference on Mechatronics and Automation (ICMA), pp. 1058–1063 (2017)
2. Han, H., Yi, S., Li, Q., Shen, G., Liu, Y., Novak, E.: AMIL: localizing neighboring mobile devices through a simple gesture. In: Proceedings of IEEE INFOCOM, pp. 1–9 (2016)
3. Haseeb, M.A., Guan, J., Ristic-Durrant, D., Gräser, A.: DisNet: a novel method for distance estimation from monocular camera. 10th Planning, Perception and Navigation for Intelligent Vehicles (PPNIV18) (2018)
4. Jia, L., et al.: A high-resolution ultrasonic ranging system using laser sensing and a cross-correlation method. Appl. Sci. **9**(7), 1483 (2019)
5. Kim, I., Yow, K.C.: Object location estimation from a single flying camera. In: The Ninth International Conference on Mobile Ubiquitous Computing, Systems, Services and Technologies (2015)
6. Krishnan, J.V.G., Manoharan, N., Rani, B.S.: Estimation of distance to texture surface using complex log mapping. J. Comput. Appl. **3**(3), 16 (2010)
7. Kwon, Y., Kwon, K.: RSS ranging based indoor localization in ultra low power wireless network. AEU-Int. J. Electron. Commun. **104**, 108–118 (2019)
8. Mankoff, K.D., Russo, T.A.: The kinect: a low-cost, high-resolution, short-range 3D camera. Earth Surf. Process. Landf. **38**(9), 926–936 (2013)
9. Mazraani, R., Saez, M., Govoni, L., Knobloch, D.: Experimental results of a combined TDOA/TOF technique for UWB based localization systems. In: 2017 IEEE International Conference on Communications Workshops (ICC Workshops), pp. 1043–1048 (2017)
10. Peyman, A.: Object distance measurement using a single camera for robotic applications. Diss. Laurentian University of Sudbury (2015)
11. Wang, W., Huang, J., Cai, S., Yang, J.: Design and implementation of synchronization-free TDOA localization system based on UWB. Radioengineering **27**(1), 320–330 (2019)

12. Wang, Y., Zhu, X., Xu, L.: Flight path optimization for UAVs to provide location service to ground targets. In: Proceedings of WCNC (2020)
13. Wang, Y., Zhu, X., Han, H.: ChirpMu: Chirp based imperceptible information broadcasting with music. In: Proceedings of IWQoS (2021)
14. Wikipedia: Lens (2021). https://en.wikipedia.org/wiki/Lens
15. Wu, J., Zhu, J., Yang, L., Shen, M., Xue, B., Liu, Z.: A highly accurate ultrasonic ranging method based on onset extraction and phase shift detection. Measurement **47**, 433–441 (2014)
16. Yenamandra, V., Uttama Nambi, A., Padmanabhan, V., Navda, V., Srinivasan, K.: CamMirror: single-camera-based distance estimation for physical analytics applications. In: Proceedings of the 4th International on Workshop on Physical Analytics, pp. 25–30 (2017)
17. Yi, S., Suh, J., Hong, Y., Hwang, D.: Active ranging system based on structured laser light image. In: Proceedings of SICE Annual Conference 2010, pp. 747–752 (2010)
18. Zhang, L., Zhu, X., Wu, X.: No more free riders: sharing WIFI secrets with acoustic signals. In: Proceedings of ICCCN (2019)
19. Zhu, X., Li, Q., Chen, G.: APT: accurate outdoor pedestrian tracking with smartphones. In: Proceedings of IEEE INFOCOM (2013)
20. Zhu, X., Wu, X., Chen, G.: Relative localization for wireless sensor networks with linear topology. Comput. Commun. **36**(15–16), 1581–1591 (2013)

URTracker: Unauthorized Reader Detection and Localization Using COTS RFID

Degang Sun[2], Yue Cui[1,2], Yue Feng[1,2], Jinxing Xie[1,2], Siye Wang[1,2(✉)], and Yanfang Zhang[1,2]

[1] Institute of Information Engineering Chinese Academy of Sciences, Beijing, China
wangsiye@iie.ac.cn
[2] School of Cyber Security, University of Chinese Academy of Sciences, Beijing, China

Abstract. Nowadays, Radio Frequency Identification (RFID) has become one of the most deployed Internet of Things (IoT) technologies. The security threats it facing are gaining more and more attention. In this paper, we focus on the intrusion based on unauthorized (malicious) readers by catching the information of tags and modifying the tags via a standard protocol. We design URTracker to realize the detection and localization of unauthorized readers. This system has two parts: For detection, we analyze the features of reader interference and the RFID signal channel model and propose a throughput-based method. For localization, we use the relationship between throughput and the position as fingerprints, model the localization process into a Markov Decision Process (MDP) for training via deep reinforcement learning (DRL). Experiment results show that URTracker can achieve high accuracy to detect unauthorized readers and low location error for tracking the trajectories.

Keywords: RFID security and privacy · Deep reinforcement learning (DRL) · Intrusion detection · Indoor localization

1 Introduction

With the development of network technology and sensing devices, the Internet of Things (IoT) has taken up an important position in people's daily life. As an important part of IoT technology, Radio Frequency Identification (RFID) technology has become a mainstream technology commonly used in monitoring systems in indoor environments and has been widely used in civil fields, like animal identification [1], supply chain traceability [2], protective equipment verification [3].

EPC Global, ISO, and other standardization organizations have promulgated a series of RFID technology standards [4,5], which regulate the requirements of RFID systems making RFID products from different sources interoperable and greatly promoting the development of the industry. However, the high versatility

© Springer Nature Switzerland AG 2021
Z. Liu et al. (Eds.): WASA 2021, LNCS 12937, pp. 339–350, 2021.
https://doi.org/10.1007/978-3-030-85928-2_27

also leads to the RFID system unable to intercept the unauthorized reader to communicate with the tag (i.e., there is no provision for reader authentication in EPC C1 G2 protocol). The attacker can easily use an unauthorized reader (malicious reader) to intercept the RFID system such as reading and modifying the tag's EPC information and other data stored in the memory bank, conduct the "Kill" command to deactivate the tag due to the tag's promiscuous response to any reader requests [6], so that the RFID system will face serious security threats.

In recent years, many researchers have been working on ensuring the security and privacy of RFID systems. The most common defenses include the use of cryptographic mechanisms [15], proprietary security protocol [16], physical-layer RF equipment [7,8]. However, as mentioned previously, modification of commercial off-the-shelf (COTS) RFID devices' hardware or communication protocol is required if adopting encrypt or protocol method (i.e., in ISO 18000-6C and EPC-C1G2 standard protocol reader and low-cost tags only support simple bit operation, such as XOR operation, cyclic redundancy check, and hash operation). Some studies implement their prototype over Universal Software Radio Peripheral (USRP) platform [7,8].Obviously, the cost of additional monitoring equipment is too high for expansion. In addition, these researches most focus on preventing unauthorized access and are lack of ability to locate and track unauthorized devices.

Therefore, we present URTracker that realize unauthorized reader detection and localization while legitimacy reader normally communicating with tags. The principles of URTracker is that when unauthorized reader shows up in the reading ranges of legitimacy reader and tags, interference in the RFID system will cause that the signals received by legitimacy reader dramatic change. This phenomenon inspires us to deploy some reference tags and choose a proper signal indicator to detect unauthorized readers and we use throughput (TP) [9]. Moreover, in our experiments, we find that the throughput is correlated with the distance of the reader and reference tags. The movement of unauthorized readers in space is a continuous process, and the trajectory formed can be described as a Markov Decision Process (MDP) [10], so it can be located using the DRL method.

Our contributions of this paper are as follows:

1. By analyzing the characteristics of passive RFID system interference, we propose and improve the method of unauthorized reader detection based on throughput, which can complete unauthorized reader detection without additional equipment and modification of existing RFID devices.
2. We model RF signals in space and propose a high-precision reference tags deployment scheme combining relevant factors affecting throughput.
3. We coordinate the localization space, model the trajectory of a unauthorized reader moving in the localization space as an MDP and use throughput to determine the reward function then implement the localization of unauthorized readers using the DRL method. Empirical results show URTracker achieves high accuracy.

2   Background

2.1   Interference in the RFID System

RFID system adopts the backward scattering transmission method, the driving energy that the tag obtains and the reflected backward transmission energy are relatively weak, easy to be interfered by the external RFID device, so it can be discerned whether there is an unauthorized reader through the legitimacy RFID signal changes. There are two main interference types in RFID system:

1. Reader-Tag interference: When the unauthorized reader and the deployed reader try to communicate with the same tag at the same time, will trigger the interference between reader to tag. There appears two readers reading range overlap, the signal of unauthorized reader R1 and signal legitimacy reader R2 may produce the collision at tag T1. In this case, the communication between the tag T1 and the legitimacy reader R2 is disturbed, and the wireless channel state parameter is affected.
2. Reader-Reader interference: The legitimacy reader R1 is located in the working range of the unauthorized reader R2 and the tag T1 is in the reading range of R1. The stronger signal unauthorized reader transmitting meets the weak signal tag replying to the legitimacy reader, causes the interference between the readers. That means the tag reply signal easily gets distorted by the signal from R2.

2.2   RFID Signal Channel Model

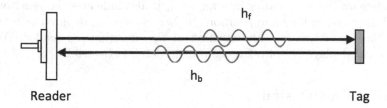

Fig. 1. RFID signal transmission diagram

The signal transmission process between reader and tag in RFID system can be divided into forward data transmission (Reader to Tag), signal propagation model represented by h_f approximated with Ricean model, and backward data transmission (Tag to Reader), signal propagation model represented by h_b approximated with Rayleigh model [11] (Fig. 1).

If the instantaneous signal power received by the receiving antenna of the reader is higher than the recognition of a set threshold P_{set}, the reader identifies the signal of the tag, which means: $P_{T,R} \geq P_{set}$. Then the probability of normal operation of the system is $P_{success} = 1 - Prob(P_{T,R} \geq P_s)$ .We can determine the minimum envelope A_{min} of the received signal according to the minimum power for the normal operation of reader $P_{T,R}$ is given as:

$$P_{success} = 1 - \int_0^{A_{min}} p_h(r)dr \tag{1}$$

We adopt the results in [11]. The results of simulation of Eq. (1) are shown in Fig. 2(a) shows the probability of normal operation of the RFID system when the tag is in each position under the free space condition and Fig. 2(b) shows the probability of normal operation of the RFID system with external interference.

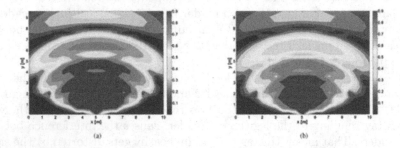

Fig. 2. The probability of reader correctly acquires the data

From the simulation result, we can find that the probability for the RFID system normal operation of one position will change with or without external interference (decreases after interference). It also indicates the sensitivity of external interference for some positions higher. So we can deploy the reference tags at these positions for the detection of the unauthorized reader. We will elaborate the deployment of reference tags in detail in Sect. 3.2.

3   URTracker Design

In this section, we describe the design of URtracker consisting of unauthorized reader detection part and localization part.

3.1   Unauthorized Reader Detection Method Based on Throughput

When the legitimacy RFID system intruded by an unauthorized reader, the legitimacy reader's maximum reading distance will be reduced and the tags in the reading range may not be able to be read anymore [11]; At the same time, the maximum read and write speed will be reduced due to channel conflict interference, etc. As a result, throughput will significantly change. First, we define quaternion series data pattern and normalize the pattern of collected data.

Then form the data in a standard pattern including time, EPC, the number of times the tag_i has been read: $dataflow_{tagi} = <Timestamp, N_{tagi}>$

The throughput of ith tag at j round in this paper is presented as:

$$throughput_j = \frac{N_{tagi}}{Timestamp_t - Timestamp_0} \qquad (2)$$

$Timestamp_t$ is the latest received signal TimeStamp. $Timestamp_0$ is the initial time. The throughput is calculated every set time (window) when $TimeStamp_t - TimaStamp_0 > T_{win}$. Then, update the initial time.

Then, we collect the data when legitimacy RFID system normal working called "stable state data" through deploying the experiment equipment and making the whole system working for a long time without any interference. Therefore, we get the stable state throughput TP_{ss} by average value.

$$Risk_j = \frac{throughput_j - TP_{ss}}{TP_{ss}} \qquad (3)$$

And we use the amount of change in throughput relative to the steady state as an indicator named Risk. If Risk is larger than the threshold θ (via the trial-and-error method), we determine the legitimacy RFID system is intruded which the unauthorized reader is detected.

To reduce the false-positive rate (FPR), we use a voting mechanism: calculate Risk in three consecutive time windows with a 0.5 s overlap, only if all the results are true will we think it's a real alarm.

1. if $sgn(Risk_{(j)} - \theta)\&\&sgn(Risk_{j+1} - \theta)\&\&sgn(Risk_{j+2} - \theta) > 0$ then, true alarm.
2. if $sgn(Risk_{(j)} - \theta)\&\&sgn(Risk_{j+1} - \theta)\&\&sgn(Risk_{j+2} - \theta) \leq 0$ then, false alarm.

Figure 3 shows the results of Risk of one tag in rows from No. 9 to No. 10 and columns from No. 1 to 12. It's obvious that the Risk-based on throughput is relative to the position of the unauthorized reader, which means we can use this indicator as one kind of localization signal (LF).

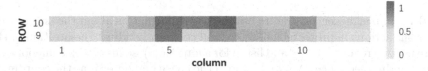

Fig. 3. Heatmap of Risk and position

3.2   Deployment of the Reference Tags for Localization System

The throughput can be affected by many factors, e.g., as previously mentioned, the position of the tags in the reading range. In order to achieve higher accuracy of the localization system, factors and experimental methods we take into consideration are as follows [12]:

1. **the tags position:** as shown in Figure 2, when the tags are deployed in the inference sensitive position, the amount of change in throughput will be more visible. Method: By making the difference between the normal working probabilities of the corresponding positions of the two heat maps, the inference sensitive heat maps of different positions can be obtained.
2. **competing tags:** when multiple signals simultaneously arrive at the reader, preventing the reliable detection of all tags within its interrogation [4]. EPC C1 G2 standard protocol uses the ALOHA as a medium access control mechanism, but multiple tags in the reading range will also lead to the degrading of their communication. Method: We put first tag at set position. Then put second tag at next set position and observe if the throughput of the first tag changes a lot and decide whether we should move the second tag into the neighboring position to avoid competing. Repeat this process until all the reference tags are deployed.
3. **the height of tags:** Since the electromagnetic waves emitted from the machine antenna are scattered in the form of a spherical surface, a single tag is not always successfully detected. This phenomenon may be caused by pass loss of multipath effects or the tags losing their power to backscatter the full response. Method: We performed an experiment that placed one tag at a board and move the board in a serpentine way. Furthermore, at each position, we put the tag from the top of the board to the end with a step of 10 cm. In the end, we find the closer to the bottom the less throughput of tags observed. And when the tag is placed at a height of 95 cm, the system performs best.

3.3   Localization Based on DRL

This section describes the localization of unauthorized reader based on DRL. Once the unauthorized reader is detected, the localization system will start and track the movement of an unauthorized reader as Figure 4 illustrated.

MDP. As an attacker, in order to obtain more information about the tags or take malicious actions in protected space, he will constantly adjust the position of the unauthorized reader (or stay and listen for a long time), so his attack behavior constitutes a time sequence. We can first grid the space and determine the coordinate of each grid, then adopt the Markov decision process (MDP) to model the unauthorized reader movement and furthermore use the DRL approach for localization.

Most approaches used for detecting the near-field condition of the RFID system are based on RSSI or Phase whether passive or active sensing. But in our study, we need to use throughput-based indicators as surrounding localization signals (LFs) for the unauthorized reader. So, we create the fingerprinting

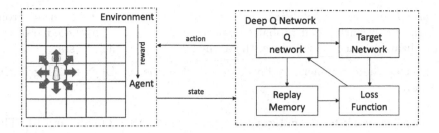

Fig. 4. Architecture of DRL localization

database by gridding the space then collecting Risk at each coordinate. But different from normal fingerprinting methods, we treat the localization task as a continuous localization problem, which is the process that inputs the agent position at time $t-1$ and LF measurement at time t, then outputs the agent position at time t. After getting the position at time t, the agent will take an action at time t, then we continue computing the new position at $t+1$ as previously and repeat this process. In this case, the agent position at each time only depends on the position of the previous time plus the LF of this time step. That's how this process is modeled as a MDP.

An MDP is a discrete-time control process, which has an important characteristic: its current state is only related to the latest state, not to the earlier ones. We need to define the key elements for MDP as fellows:

1. *Agent:* Its task is to interact with the surrounding Environment, receive data and take valid actions. Different actions may lead to different rewards.
2. *States:* $s_t \in S$. We define our state space as S. The state consists of the agent position, Risk as LF, and distance to the target position.
3. *Actions:* $a_t \in A$. It describes the optional operations of the Agent when implementing the state transition. We define the action space as A. In this paper, the action of the agent is to move to neighboring cells or not to move, consisting of west, east, north, south, northwest, northeast, southwest, southeast and staying.
4. *Reward Function:* $r \in R$. It mainly describes the feedback generated by the environment when the agent is in state S, chooses action A, and then arrives at state S' after state transfer. The principle of the reward function is that whenever the agent chooses the right action closer to the target position, it gains more rewards. On the contrary, if the agent is far away from the target (larger than threholdβ), it gains negative rewards. The reward function r_t can be represented as [10]:

$$r_t = \begin{cases} \dfrac{1}{(||P_{agent} - P_{target}||)} & if \quad 0 < ||P_{agent} - P_{target}|| < \beta \\ -||P_{agent} - P_{target}|| & otherwise \end{cases} \quad (4)$$

5. *State Transition Probabilities:* $p(s_{t+1}|s_t, a_t)$. The agent can take actions from A randomly with equal probabilities except the agent is at the edge of the localization space. In this case, the agent has to move back or stay.

After all the components defined, we will describe the DQN training in the next part.

Deep Q-Network for Localization. The key of DQN is Q-learning [13]. The quality of Q function determines the performance of the model. Q function is represented as:

$$Q(S_t, A_t) \leftarrow Q(S_t, A_t) + \alpha[R_{t+1} + \gamma maxQ(S_{t+1}, a) - Q(S_t, A_t)] \tag{5}$$

Where α is the learning rate, $0 < \alpha < 1$, γ is an action factor, indicating the degree of utilization of the value of Q in the next state. Once the Q function is obtained. The main problem is to find a policy $\pi(s)$ maximizing the rewards.

$$\pi(s) = argmaxQ(s, a) \tag{6}$$

In the deep Q-Network method, a deep neural network is used to approximate the optimal action-value function (Q), due to the Q-table in localization situation is difficult to obtain. Thus, we use the DQN architecture in [14].

DQN has two important features. 1. *Experience replay mechanism.* The purpose of the experience replay mechanism is to eliminate correlation between data. The initial state s is obtained at the beginning, and after a certain number of rounds of iterative process, a series of experience tuple $e_t = (s_t, a_t, r_t, s_{t+1})$ can be obtained, which will be deposited into the memory replay dataset D with a certain capacity, and when the amount of data is larger than the upper limit of the memory D, named N_{st}, the memory unit will delete a part of the data according to the time order of deposition, which can update the experience value obtained from the later exploration while preserving the experience of the earlier exploration. After storing the data into the memory D, the current value network will randomly sample a minibatch with length of N_{mb} from the memory D as training data for training. The epsilon-greedy policy is used to select actions.

2. *Dual Network Architecture.* DQN uses two networks (Q-network and the target network Q') for training at the same time. The Q-network generates a result tuple $(s_t, a + t, r_t, s_{t+1})$ during each mapping from the input to the output decision. Then, the result tuple is stored into replay memory D. The target network Q' with parameter θ' is updated from the Q-network every G time steps. The Q-network is trained through the loss of the target network Q' as the following function based on Bellman Equation:

$$L(\theta) = E[(y_j - Q(s, a; \theta_j))^2] \tag{7}$$

where, E represents the expectation value; y_j is the target value defined as:

$$y_j = r_{j+1} + \gamma maxQ'(s_{j+1}, a; \theta') \tag{8}$$

γ is a discount factor, $\gamma \in [0, 1)$

Then, we use stochastic gradient descent (SGD) method to train Q-network.

4   Device Deployment and Experimental Results

In this section, we present the device deployment and experimental results of URTracker.

4.1   Experimental Setup

We implement URTracker in an indoor office environment that has a size of 5 m by 6 m. We set the position of legitimacy reader antenna as the coordinates origin to gird our test area. The 6 reference tags are deployed using the approach described in Sect. 3.2. We choose Impinj R420 to act as the legitimacy reader and select several other readers as unauthorized readers including: another Impinj R420 reader, one Alien Handheld ALH-9001 reader, one Impinj R220 reader. The antenna is Laird S9028PCL. The tags we used are Impinj H47. All the devices are widely used in RFID systems like supply chain, library, or other applications. The legitimacy reader is connected to an MSI laptop that has a processor of Intel(R) Core(TM) i7-8750H CPU @ 2.20 GHz, RAM 16.0GB, RTX 2060. The data processing environment on Python 3.8 with PyTorch 1.8.1.

In this experiment, we grid the area into 750 grids in 30 rows and 25 columns. After coordinating, the test environment is presented as a set of positions labeled by row and column. The unauthorized reader is placed at each position for 10 min. We collect the data as the form described in Sect. 3.1 plus the location label. For training the DRL model, we need to generate a large number of dynamic trajectories. To fulfill that, a grid is selected as the initial point randomly. Then, manufacture an agent and make take actions for 200 times as Sect. 3.3. At last, we generate ten thousand trajectories and separate them into training datasets (9900 trajectories) and testing datasets (100 trajectories).

4.2   Accuracy of Detecting Unauthorized Reader

We first deploy the reference tags and legitimacy reader (one Impinj R420) with antenna and personal computer attached to make them work normally. Then randomly choose 10 locations to deploy one unauthorized reader from mentioned before, each location test for 100 times to simulate the malicious intrusion process. Switch another kind of unauthorized reader and repeat this experiment. The results are shown in Figure 5. The precision (accuracy) reaches 0.96, and the false-negative rates of all readers are lower than about 0.03. Our unauthorized reader detection part achieves high accuracy for detecting the unauthorized reader.

4.3   Evaluation of DRL Localization

We use 100 trajectories from the test dataset to test the trained model. Some of the results are illustrated in Figure 6. On a relatively large scale, the trajectories predicted by testing trained model has a similar trend with the real trajectories. From this outcome, we can recognize the ability of DRL for a long-term

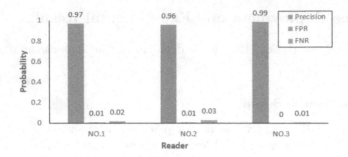

Fig. 5. Overall performance

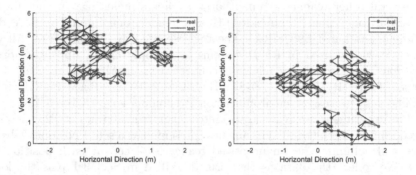

Fig. 6. Example of DRL-based wireless localization solutions

localization. Figure 7 shows the location error statistics compared with unlabeled DRL approach, including mean and root mean square (RMS). The later method trained the model without reference for the achievable localization marker. The location error of labeled DRL is less than the unlabeled one, but unlabeled DRL also reaches a good performance. As we all know, it's a hard job to label all the data in the dataset. The performance of this comparison indicates that we can make a trade-off in the real environment between the labor of labeling and location error.

5   Related Works

There are lots of studies focusing on the security and privacy issues due to the lack of protection method especially for COTS RFID using the standard protocol. However, most works adopt cryptographic authentication protocols. For example, Weis et al. [15] proposed a one-way hash function-based security scheme by giving each tag a temporary ID and in either locked or unlocked state. Tag only responds to requests during locked state. Henrici et al. [16] used one-way hash functions to ensure secure communication between the reader and the server. These works require modification on standard protocol or hardware of tags.

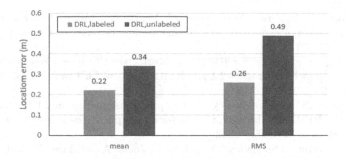

Fig. 7. Statistics of location errors

Some studies are working on physical layer method for RFID system protection. Ding et al. [7]. proposed Arbitrator based on USRP. GenePrint [8] used the similarity of 64-bit precursor sequences in RN16 to resist tag forgery attacks. But these works need expensive USRP device which increases the cost.

DRL impressed the whole world at the performance of AlphaGo beating human top players. In the early stage, DRL algorithms are used for AI in video games. Some navigation methods begin to apply DRL, such as maze navigation [17], camera [18]. For now, localization is a newly application scenario for DRL [10].

6 Conclusion

In this paper, we present the design, deployment, and evaluation results of URTracker, an RFID system for detection and localization of unauthorized reader works in the indoor environment. Our system can apply on COTS RFID devices without the assistance of other equipment or modification on protocol and hardware. The experiment results show that URTracker performs high accuracy for detecting unauthorized readers resilience to the adversary's locations and low location error when predicts the position in the trajectories of unauthorized readers, hence hold full potential for practical environment.

Acknowledgement. This work was supported by the Youth Innovation Promotion Association of Chinese Academy of Sciences, No. Y9YY015104.

References

1. Floyd, R.E.: RFID in animal-tracking applications. IEEE Potentials **34**, 32–33 (2015)
2. Feng, T.: An agri-food supply chain traceability system for China based on RFID and blockchain technology. In: Proceedings of the 13th International Conference on Service Systems and Service Management, Kumming, China, 24–26 June 2016, pp. 1–6 (2016)

3. Barro-Torres, S.J., Fernández-Caramés, T.M., Pérez-Iglesias, H.J., Escudero, C.J.: Real-time personal protective equipment monitoring system. Comput. Commun. **36**, 42–50 (2012)

4. EPCglobal. Specification for RFID air interface. EPC Radio-Frequency Identity Protocols Class-1 Generation-2 UHF RFID Protocol for Communications at, vol. 860, pp. 1–94 (2005)

5. EPCglobal. EPC radio-frequency identity protocols generation-2 UHF RFID; specification for RFID air interface protocol for communications at 860 MHz–960 MHz. EPCglobal Inc., November 2013

6. Heydt-Benjamin, T.S., Bailey, D.V., Fu, K., Juels, A., O'Hare, T.: Vulnerabilities in first-generation RFID-enabled credit cards. In: Dietrich, S., Dhamija, R. (eds.) FC 2007. LNCS, vol. 4886, pp. 2–14. Springer, Heidelberg (2007). https://doi.org/10.1007/978-3-540-77366-5_2

7. Ding, H., Han, J., Zhang, Y., et al.: Preventing unauthorized access on passive tags. In: IEEE INFOCOM 2018-IEEE Conference on Computer Communications, pp. 1115–1123. IEEE (2018)

8. Ding, H., et al.: A platform for free-weight exercise monitoring with RFIDs. IEEE Trans. Mob. Comput. **16**(12), 3279–3293 (2017)

9. Huang, W., Ding, C., Cui, Y., et al.: RFID air port intrusion detection technology based on malicious reader discovery. Acta Sinica Sinica 7 (2018)

10. Mohammadi, M., Al-Fuqaha, A., Guizani, M., Oh, J.-S.: Semisupervised deep reinforcement learning in support of IoT and smart city services. IEEE Internet Thing J. **5**(2), 624–635 (2018)

11. Bekkali, A., Zou, S., Kadri, A., et al.: Performance analysis of passive UHF RFID systems under cascaded fading channels and interference effects. IEEE Trans. Wireless Commun. **14**(3), 1421–1433 (2014)

12. Šolić, P., Maras, J., Radić, J., et al.: Comparing theoretical and experimental results in Gen2 RFID throughput. IEEE Trans. Autom. Sci. Eng. **14**(1), 349–357 (2016)

13. Sutton, R.S., Barto, A.G.: Reinforcement Learning: An Introduction. MIT Press, Cambridge (2018)

14. Hu, X., Liu, S., Chen, R., Wang, W., Wang, C.: A deep reinforcement learning-based framework for dynamic resource allocation in multibeam satellite systems. IEEE Commun. Lett. **22**(8), 1612–1615 (2018)

15. Weis, S.A., Sarma, S.E., Rivest, R.L., Engels, D.W.: Security and privacy aspects of low-cost radio frequency identification systems. In: Hutter, D., Müller, G., Stephan, W., Ullmann, M. (eds.) Security in Pervasive Computing. LNCS, vol. 2802, pp. 201–212. Springer, Heidelberg (2004). https://doi.org/10.1007/978-3-540-39881-3_18

16. Henrici, A., Muller, P.: Hash-based enhancement of location privacy for radio- frequency identification devices using varying identifiers. In: International Workshop on Pervasive Computing and Communication Security PerSec, Orlando, Florida, USA, pp. 149–153 (2004)

17. Dhiman, V., Banerjee, S., Griffin, B., Siskind, J.M., Corso, J.J.: A critical investigation of deep reinforcement learning for navigation, January 2019. https://arxiv.org/abs/1802.02274

18. Zhang, J., Springenberg, J.T., Boedecker, J., Burgard, W.: Deep reinforcement learning with successor features for navigation across similar environments. In: Proceedings of IEEE/RSJ International Conference on Intelligent Robots and Systems, Vancouver, BC, Canada, pp. 2371–2378, September 2017

SDC Error Detection by Exploring the Importance of Instruction Features

Wentao Fang, Jingjing Gu[✉], Zujia Yan, and Qiuhong Wang

Nanjing University of Aeronautics and Astronautics, Nanjing, China
{fangwentao,gujingjing,yanzujia,baoh9491}@nuaa.edu.cn

Abstract. With the continuous improvement of the integration of semiconductor chips, it has brought great challenges to the reliability and safety of the system. Among them, Silent Data Corruption (SDC), as one of the most harmful issues, is difficult to be detected due to its concealment. For the SDC error detection, literatures just focus on fault injection or program analysis, but ignore the relationship of instruction features on the SDC errors. To this end, we propose a SDC error detection model by analyzing the instruction feature importance to the SDC vulnerability (SDIFI) and design the vulnerability prediction method. For the SDC error detection, specifically, we first analyze the correlation between different instruction features and the SDC vulnerability, and characterize the importance of these features. Second, we propose a SDC error detection model based on the SDC vulnerability prediction by an improved Light-GBM model, as well as detecting SDC errors by selective redundancy of high SDC vulnerability instructions. Experimental results on the Mibench benchmarks show that our method has better detection accuracy with low overhead.

Keywords: SDC error · Vulnerability prediction · Instruction feature importance

1 Introduction

With the rapid development of 5G communication, the integration of transistor in chip manufacturing process is increasing [12]. These chips are widely applied in industrial automation, medical services, smart home and other fields. However, the huge size of resources (such as CPU cores and memory) in various devices can be very likely to cause soft errors (e.g. signal or datum error). Among them, Silent Data Corruption (SDC) is more dangerous and hard to be recognized by the system, including the muti-control distributed storage and the public cloud storage. Therefore, it is significant to establish a SDC detection model for enhancing the system reliability and security.

Supported by the National Natural Science Foundation of China under Grant (No. 62072235).

Z. Liu et al. (Eds.): WASA 2021, LNCS 12937, pp. 351–363, 2021.
https://doi.org/10.1007/978-3-030-85928-2_28

In recent years, a number of approaches have been developed for identifying SDC errors accurately and efficiently. Traditionally, fault injection flips the destination operand of instructions randomly and then identifies the wrong result as SDC errors [9,14]. For better evaluating the SDC detection rate, errors are injected into every bit of each instruction, but it can consume more computing resources. Program analysis detects SDC by analyzing historical empirical values of fault propagation [16–18], but its accuracy is lower due to the randomness of dynamic instruction. Machine learning-based SDC detection methods predict instruction SDC vulnerability by building the regression or classification model [2,7,10,11,13,19]. However, these methods can not achieve satisfactory performance because of the huge instruction features scale and the sparse data set.

Therefore, we mainly focus on SDC vulnerability prediction and resources overhead. The main challenges are concluded as follows:

1) It is difficult to characterize the importance of instruction features to SDC vulnerability. Nowadays, instruction feature scale in most programs is enormous. Because instruction features have different impacts on SDC errors, it is difficult to evaluate the relationship of instruction features on SDC vulnerability prediction. As far as we know, there is no previous research characterizing the importance of instruction features to improve the accuracy of SDC vulnerability prediction.

2) It is difficult to integrate the instruction feature importance into SDC vulnerability prediction model. Most SDC detection methods are limited to predict vulnerabilities by extracting instruction features in a program, without considering the impacts of instruction features on the predicted results. Therefore, how to integrate the instruction feature importance into SDC vulnerability prediction model and explore the high SDC vulnerability instruction for protection is of great significance.

To this end, we propose a SDC vulnerability detection model by analyzing the instruction feature importance to SDC vulnerability (SDIFI), and select the instructions with high SDC vulnerability for protection. Specifically, first, we extract the abundant instruction features related to the SDC vulnerability, and analyze the relationship of instruction feature importance to the SDC vulnerability. Second, we build an improved LightGBM model for SDC vulnerability prediction. In order to reduce the memory consumption, we use the histogram algorithm in the LightGBM to discretize the continuous feature vector into the bin value of k-order. In addition, we integrate the instruction feature importance into the Amount of Say (weight of weak learner) of LightGBM sub-decision tree for improving the accuracy of SDC vulnerability prediction. Finally, we design a selective replication SDC detector and perform a series of experimental verification based on LLVM. The main contributions are summarized as follows:

- We propose a model called SDIFI to detect the SDC vulnerability of instructions by analyzing the instruction feature importance, and then excavate high SDC vulnerability instructions for protection.
- We analyze the relationship between different instruction features and the SDC vulnerability and characterize the importance of these features.

- We explore an improved LightGBM by integrating instruction feature importance into the Amount of Say of LightGBM sub-decision tree.
- Experimental results on the Mibench benchmarks show that our method has better prediction accuracy and low time-cost than state-of-the-art algorithms.

2 Related Work

Nowadays, a huge of research works on SDC detection revolves around software-based redundancy technology. They can be divided into three categories: fault injection, program analysis and machine learning.

Fault injection simulates a soft error by flipping one bit of the destination register in the program. However, for SDC detection, massive fault injections bring huge time cost. Li et al. [9] proposed an intelligent fault injection framework to detect SDC errors, which eliminated a lot of invalid fault injections by predicting the fault results. Ma et al. [14] deduced vulnerable SDC instructions based on heuristic methods and error dependency propagation, thereby reducing the number of fault injection instructions.

Program analysis is based on the program's own architecture and behavior model to build a model to predict SDC vulnerability. Sridharan et al. [17] identified the instruction with high SDC vulnerability by analyzing the rule of error propagation in micro architecture and constructing program vulnerability factor. Pattabiraman et al. [16] used symbolic execution to abstract the error state and detect SDC errors. Li et al. [8] analyzed the experience of error propagation in the program, captured error at the static data dependency, control flow, and memory levels, and predicted the SDC vulnerability for the whole and individual instructions without fault injection. Alireza et al. [18] constructed the instruction history result table to judge the matching relationship between the stored value and the current value, and then detected the instruction with SDC.

Machine learning-based predicts SDC vulnerability by extracting instruction features in the program. Laguna et al. [7] used SVM method to predict SDC errors by constructing SOC tags. Wang et al. [2,19] regarded detection of SDC error as a dichotomy problem, which is solved by fitting multiple curve models or constructing convolutional neural networks. Also, several machine learning-based works [4,11,13] predicted the propensity of SDC, such as CART, RF, and SVR. Liu et al. [10] improved the prediction accuracy of instruction SDC vulnerability through cascading regression forest and improved sliding window, which needed a large scale dataset of fault injections.

3 Framework

The overall framework of our method is shown in Fig. 1. It mainly includes three parts: (1) Feature extraction. We extract features by fault injection to collect the training data. (2) Importance analysis. We analyze the importance SI of instruction features to the SDC vulnerability. (3) Vulnerability prediction. We introduce the instruction feature importance into the Amount of Say of

LightGBM sub-tree, and iterate each tree to obtain the final prediction model. Then, we obtain the final results and detect SDC errors by redundancy strategy.

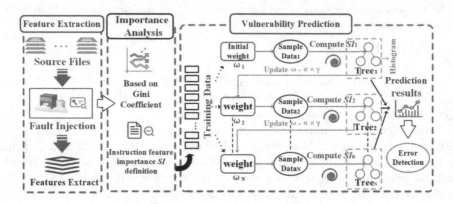

Fig. 1. The overall framework.

4   Methodology

In this section, we define the SDC vulnerability and extract the instruction features. Then we show the characterization of the feature importance. Next, we estimate a lightweight model for SDC vulnerability prediction based on the instruction feature importance. Finally, we design the SDC detector based on selective redundancy strategy.

4.1   SDC Vulnerability

In this paper, we define the following terms:

Definition 1. *Static and Dynamic instructions sets are defined as*

$$\begin{cases} S_{ins} = \{I_1, I_2, \ldots, I_i, \ldots, I_N\}, \\ D_{ins} = \{I_1^1, \ldots, I_1^{d_i}, \ldots, I_i^{d_i}, \ldots, I_N^{d_i}\}, \end{cases} \tag{1}$$

where I_i represents the i_{th} static instruction in the program, and N is the total number of static instructions in the program. $\forall\ I_i \in S_{ins}$, $I_i^{d_i}$ means that the instruction I_i is executed d_i times in a program running process.

Definition 2. *SDC sensitive factor is defined as*

$$factor(I_i) = \ln \frac{1}{\sum_{i=1}^{n} I_i^{d_i}} \times d_i, \tag{2}$$

which represents the ratio of dynamic instruction execution times to the total number of dynamic instruction execution and measures the sensitivity of SDC vulnerability. In this paper, we normalize it for improving calculation efficiency.

Definition 3. *SDC vulnerability is defined as*

$$V_{SDC}(I_i) = P_{SDC}(I_i) \times factor(I_i), \tag{3}$$

$$P_{SDC}(I_i) = \frac{1}{d_i} \times \sum_{I_i^q \in I_i^{d_i}}^{N} \frac{M_i^q}{N_i^q}, \tag{4}$$

which represents the sensitivity of SDC error caused by bit flip in one bit of dynamic instruction operand during program execution. $P_{SDC}(I_i)$ represents the probability of SDC error in dynamic instruction, which is defined as Eq. 4. Here, $I_i^q \in I_i^{d_i}$ represents the q_{th} dynamic instruction of $I_i^{d_i}$, and M_i^q indicates the total number of fault injection to the destination register. N_i^q represents the total number of SDC errors caused by fault injection.

4.2 Instruction Feature Extraction

Instruction features of complex programs are extracted at the Intermediate Representation level. In order to enhance the coverage of the result reliability, we collect about 100 instruction features, including instruction type, basic block, program slice, execution function, etc. In addition, by the error fault propagation, we divide these features into five categories.

$$T = [I_{type}, B_{stru}, L_{level}, P_{oper}, F_{analysis}], \tag{5}$$

where I_{type} represents the instruction type, different instruction types have different damages to fault propagation (e.g. shift instructions, branch instructions). B_{stru} represents the basic block structure, they play a key role in predicting the instruction SDC vulnerability after slicing. L_{level} represents the instruction level, they have fault shielding effect. P_{oper} represents the program operation, including memory read and write. $F_{analysis}$ represents the perform function analysis, they may cause the fault propagation.

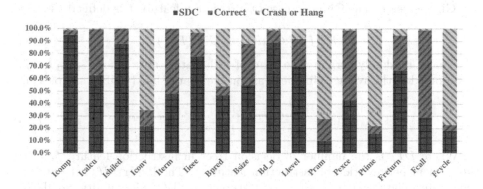

Fig. 2. Impacts of instruction features on fault injection results.

4.3 Instruction Feature Importance

Figure 2 shows the proportion of SDC errors with different instruction features. As we can see in Fig. 2, SDC vulnerability are highly related to the different instruction features. The features of unrelated and redundant may increase computing cost and reduce learning accuracy, on the contrary, some features are positive for model predictions. Therefore, we explore the relationship of different features to the SDC vulnerability by analyzing the instruction feature importance.

Definition 4. *Instruction feature importance*

Let f denote any feature in instruction feature set IF. Instruction feature importance is defined $SI(f)$ to measure the relationship of instruction feature f to the SDC vulnerability.

$$IF = \{f_1, f_2, \ldots, f_k, \ldots, f_m\} \tag{6}$$

SI is an implicit feature importance analysis method based on decision tree [5,20], which is measured by Gini coefficient calculation of node impurity. For given instruction sample $D = \{x_i, V_{SDC}(I_i)\}_{i=1}^{N}$, Gini coefficient is

$$Gini(D) = 1 - \sum_{k=1}^{K} (\frac{|C_k|}{|D|})^2 \tag{7}$$

Assume that the instruction sample D has K categories, the number of the k_{th} category is C_k. In particular, instruction feature f splits the sample D into m sub-samples, $\forall f \in x_i$, $Gini(D, f)$ is as follows

$$Gini(D, f) = \sum_{m=1}^{M} \frac{|D_m|}{|D|} Gini(D_m) \tag{8}$$

Gini coefficient is also called Gini impurity, the smaller the value, the higher the purity. In order to obtain the higher Gini purity, it is necessary to maximize the Gini decrease. The Gini decrease of instruction feature f is defined as

$$GD(f) = Gini(D) - Gini(D, f) \tag{9}$$

Finally, randomly permute the value of each feature after a node split, $SI(f)$ is computed as the average Gini decrease on the "out of bag (OOB)" samples [5]:

$$SI(f) = \frac{\sum_{t \in DT_f} GD_t(f) - GD_t(f')}{DT_f} \tag{10}$$

Where DT_f is the number of decision trees in instruction feature f, f' is the random permutation of instruction feature f. The larger $SI(f)$ it obtains, the greater relationship of instruction feature f on SDC vulnerability. Similarly, $SI(IF)$ represents a set of feature importance scores for a sample x_i.

4.4   Vulnerability Prediction

In this paper, for SDC the vulnerability prediction, we propose an improved LightGBM by combining the LightGBM and the instruction feature importance based on the decision tree. From the proposed improved LightGBM, most of features extracted are Integer, Float and Boolean, which are suitable for the above-mentioned mixed data types. In addition, although scales of data sets are diversity in different benchmarks, the LigthGBM is competent for data sets of different scale [6].

Improved LightGBM. LightGBM consists of k decision trees, its algorithm is to minimize the loss function of each tree to obtain a better tree, is defined as $F_k(x) = \sum_{t=0}^{k-1} \alpha_t f_t(x)$. α represents the Amount of Say of the t_{th} decision tree f_t. Here, Amount of Say represents how much each decision tree says(weights), it is calculated by the total error of the decision tree.

Algorithm 1. The training of improved LigthGBM

Require: Input: Training set $\{(x_i, y_i)\}_{i=1}^N$
Ensure: Output: Final SDC vulnerability prediction model $\hat{y_i}^{(t)}$
  Step 1. First, initialize the first decision tree to a constant.
$$\hat{y_i}^{(0)} = f_0 = 0 \tag{11}$$
  Step 2. Train the next decision tree f_t, and obtain the optimal learning function $f_t(x_i)$ and the original α_t by minimizing the loss function $L(t)$. And calculate the new Amount of Say ω_t of the decision tree f_t.
$$\omega_t f_t(x_i) = \arg\min_{f_t} L(t) + \Omega(f_t) \tag{12}$$
$$L(t) = (y_i - (\hat{y_i}^{(t-1)} + f_t(x_i)))^2 \tag{13}$$
  Step 3. According to the learning function of the previous decision tree, the accumulation model of the t_{th} tree is:
$$\hat{y_i}^{(t)} = \hat{y_i}^{(t-1)} + \omega_t f_t(x_i) \tag{14}$$

  Step 4. Repeat the Step2 and Step 3 until the model reaches the stop condition.
  Step 5. Obtain the final SDC vulnerability prediction model:
$$\hat{y_i}^{(t)} = \sum_{t=0}^{k-1} \omega_t f_t(x_i) \tag{15}$$

In order to improve the prediction accuracy of SDC vulnerability, we improve LightGBM, integrate instruction feature importance into the Amount of Say of each sub-decision tree, and re-decided the new Amount of Say as ω. The SDC vulnerability prediction model is derived from the improved LightGBM.

$$FSI_k(x) = \sum_{t=0}^{k-1} \omega_t f_t(x) = \sum_{t=0}^{k-1} \alpha_t \gamma_t f_t(x) \tag{16}$$

$$\gamma_t = \frac{diag_t(SI(f_1), SI(f_2), ..., SI(f_m))}{|SI(IF)|} \tag{17}$$

Where ω_t represents the Amount of say of the decision tree f_t, which consists of the original α_t and γ_t. And γ is a unitized diagonal matrix, which represents the relationship of instruction features to the SDC vulnerability. In addition, γ is a learning parameter, which is obtained by calculating the instruction feature importance of each decision tree residual, and is updated to reduce the loss function $L(FSI_k(x), y)$.

To clearly illustrate the training process of improved LightGBM, we take a model consisting of k trees as an example described in Algorithm 1.

Here are few explanations of the above process, x_i represents the instruction feature set $T_i = \{I_i, B_i, L_i, P_i, F_i\}$, and y_i represents the SDC vulnerability of instruction I_i. $L(t)$ means the squared loss of SDC vulnerability real and prediction value. $\Omega(f_t)$ represents L2 regularization term to adjust Amount of say ω based on the instruction feature importance.

Based on the above model training steps, by utilizing the histogram algorithm and incorporating the instruction feature importance into the prediction model, our method can effectively improve the prediction accuracy of SDC vulnerability and reduce memory overhead.

4.5 SDC Detection

This paper focuses on the SDC vulnerability prediction of instructions. After the prediction results are obtained, we sort all instructions according to the SDC vulnerability level of the target program and construct the SDC vulnerability sequence table of instructions. We select the high SDC vulnerability instructions of the corresponding granularity, take into account the dependency of the instruction error propagation in the basic block, and establish the instruction copy path $\{i_1, i_2, \ldots, i_k, \ldots, i_n\}$ with the restriction scope within a single basic block. Finally, we perform redundant backup for the selected instruction i_k at LLVM IR.

5 Experiment

In this section, we analyze the validity of SDIFI model by designing fault injection and prediction experiment. First, we verify the accuracy of the SDC vulnerability prediction model and analyze the SDC detection results. Then, we set experiment with parameter selection for our method.

5.1 Experimental Setup

All experiments and evaluations in this section are performed on high-performance machines with a CPU of Intel Xeon E5-2630v4, a running memory of 64G, an operating system of Ubuntu16.04, and a compiler version of LLVM 7.10. We only consider the impact of one bit flip on SDC vulnerability, and focus on failures in data path, control components, and registers in the CPU. We ignore control-flow errors because there are specific detection algorithms to solve it (e.g. CFCSS [15]). In addition, we assume that all operations involving instructions in memory and cache (load, store) are protected by error correction code (ECC) [3].

The experiment randomly selected part of the programs in the Mibench test suite as the training set, and the remaining as the test set. Among them, the data set of each test program will use LLVM to compile the source program into LLVM IR intermediate code, and be extracted by LLVM Pass. And we use the LLFI tool for fault injection to obtain SDC vulnerability for each instruction. The six benchmarks are shown in Table 1.

In addition, we choose four advanced methods as baselines, including SED-SVR [21] for predicting SDC vulnerability by SVR model, SDCPredictor [11] for identifying instructions with SDC vulnerability by Random Forest, XGBoost [1] is an optimized distributed gradient enhancement algorithm, and DFRMR [10] is an improved deep forest regression model, and it has been proved that DFRMR outperforms than most general deep learning-based methods (e.g. RNN, LSTM).

Table 1. Benchmarks used in the experiment

Benchmark	Program size	Description
Dijkstra	525	Shortest path algorithm
BitString	279	Bit pattern of bytes formatted to string
FFT	744	Fast Fourier Transformation
Isqrt	89	Int square root calculations
DFS	161	Depth-first search algorithm
Qsort	184	Quick sorting

The experimental results are comprehensively evaluated by RMSE and R^2 indexes (Eq. 18 and Eq. 19). RMSE is the square root of the average of squared differences between prediction and actual observation, the lower its score, the smaller the error. R^2 is the proportion of the variance in the dependent variable that is predictable from the independent variable(s), the higher its score, the stronger the explanatory power of the regression model. The data split ratio adopted by the test was 8:1:1, in which 80% of the original data was used as the training set, 10% as the verification set for model optimization, and the remaining 10% as the test set to test the forecasting effect of the model.

$$RMSE = \sqrt{\frac{1}{m} \sum_{i=1}^{m} (V_{SDCreal} - V_{SDCpredicted})^2} \qquad (18)$$

$$R^2 = 1 - \frac{\sum_i (V_{SDCpredicted} - V_{SDCreal})^2}{\sum_i (\overline{V_{SDCreal}} - V_{SDCreal})^2} \qquad (19)$$

5.2   SDC Vulnerability Prediction Result Analysis

SDC vulnerability prediction of instruction is the most important part of SDC error detection. We statistically analyze the RMSE and R^2 of each model under different bechmarks, and the detailed results are shown in Table 2. It can be seen from RMSE that SVR and RF have a large error in predicting small sample data sets. Compared with the previous methods, DFRMR performs better but compares poorly with our proposed method. The improved lightweight model SDIFI can obtain the best RMSE in all testing programs and has the best prediction accuracy. Among them, the RMSE of FFT is higher due to the large scale of the program, complex arithmetic operation and more shielding and transfer instructions. Moreover, SDIFI also obtains the best R^2, and XGBoost is closest to it, which shows that the boosting methods have better performance and good interpretability in predicting SDC vulnerability.

Next, we randomly inject 3000 faults into 6 benchmarks, and evaluate the error detection capability of SDIFI model by SDC coverage and time efficacy obtained from the SDC error detection experiment. SDC coverage means the error detection rate of the SDC detector, and time efficacy refers to the ratio of the time spent by the hardened program to the time spent by the un-hardened program. We rank the predicted SDC vulnerability of instructions, select the first 10%, 20% and 30% granularity instruction respectively for redundancy, and compare the obtained SDC coverage and time efficacy with the HotPath [13]. It can be found from Table 3 that under 30% redundancy granularity, our method can achieve higher SDC coverage while ensuring lower time efficacy.

Table 2. The RMSE and R^2 performance of the testing programs

Measure	Benchmark	SED-SVR	SDCPredictor	XGBoost	DFRMR	**SDIFI**
RMSE	*dijkstra*	0.1991	0.1499	0.1243	0.1391	**0.1222**
	bitstring	0.2698	0.2544	0.2213	0.2287	**0.2172**
	fft	0.3495	0.3982	0.3512	0.3432	**0.3018**
	isqrt	0.3087	0.2424	0.2149	0.2127	**0.2033**
	dfs	0.1503	0.0859	0.0695	0.0883	**0.0639**
	qsort	0.2006	0.0925	0.1016	0.1615	**0.0466**
R^2	*dijkstra*	0.2257	0.5611	0.6780	0.6219	**0.7083**
	bitstring	0.5809	0.6272	0.7181	0.6989	**0.7284**
	fft	0.7028	0.6682	0.7352	0.7125	**0.7512**
	isqrt	0.4769	0.6774	0.7463	0.7516	**0.7731**
	dfs	0.4556	0.8223	0.8836	0.8119	**0.9017**
	qsort	0.6242	0.9201	0.9036	0.7564	**0.9798**

Table 3. SDC coverage and time efficiency of different granularities

Granularity	Average SDC coverage	Time efficacy
HotPath	84.2%	50.5%
10%	41.6%	25.1%
20%	71.3%	36.9%
30%	88.4%	47.8%

5.3 Parameter Selection

For better evaluating the algorithm performance, we utilize the classic evaluation index RMSE to select parameters of SED-SVR, SDCPredictor, XGBoost, DFRMR and SDIFI. The smaller the score, the higher the prediction accuracy. Parameters used in all models are tuned by grid search or experiments. In SED-SVR, the punishment coefficient c is 1.0, the kernel type is rbf, and its kernel parameter σ is 0.003. SDCPredictor based on random forest consists of 800 trees. At the max_depth of 8 and the learning_rate of 0.09, XGBoost achieves the best prediction results. In DFRMR, the windows is 5, the tolerance is 0.

In our method, we improve the prediction accuracy by adjusting the parameters num_leaves and learning_rate. In order to speed up training and reduce overfitting, we need to select the appropriate parameters bagging_fraction and bagging_freq. The performance change curve of the above parameters is shown in Fig. 3. It can be found that SDIFI achieves the optimal prediction effect when

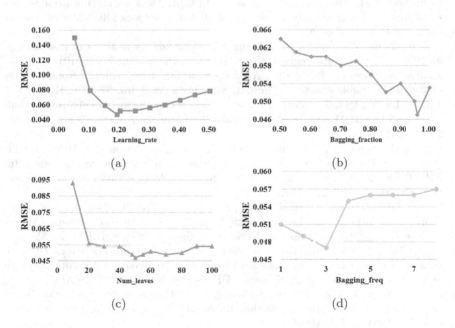

Fig. 3. Parameter selection in SDIFI.

the num_leaves is 50, the learning_rate is 0.19, the bagging_fraction is 0.96 and bagging_freq is 3.

6 Conclusion

In this work, we designed a lightweight SDC detection model SDIFI to solve the huge overhead caused by fault injection and complete instruction redundancy. We first extracted the instruction features, and analyzed the relationship of instruction feature importance to the SDC vulnerability. Then, we integrated the instruction feature importance into the Amount of Say of LightGBM sub-decision tree for improving the SDC prediction model. Finally, we selectively protected the high SDC vulnerability instructions by the SDC detector. Experimental results showed that our method has higher SDC vulnerability prediction accuracy than other methods. The detector obtained higher SDC coverage and lower time overhead with low redundancy granularity, and had better fault tolerance.

References

1. Chen, T., He, T., Benesty, et al.: Xgboost: extreme gradient boosting. R Package Version 0.4-2 **1**(4), 1–4 (2015)
2. Di, S., Cappello, F.: Adaptive impact-driven detection of silent data corruption for HPC applications. IEEE Trans. Parallel Distrib. Syst. **27**(10), 2809–2823 (2016)
3. Earnshaw, A.M., Duggan, J.R., Creasy, T.J.: Code block reordering prior to forward error correction decoding based on predicted code block reliability. US Patent 8,327,234 (4 December 2012)
4. Gu, J., Zheng, W., Zhuang, Y., Zhang, Q.: Vulnerability analysis of instructions for SDC-causing error detection. IEEE Access **7**, 168885–168898 (2019)
5. Janitza, S., Tutz, G., Boulesteix, A.L.: Random forest for ordinal responses: prediction and variable selection. Comput. Stat. Data Anal. **96**, 57–73 (2016)
6. Jin, D., Lu, Y., Qin, J., Cheng, Z.: SwiftIDS: real-time intrusion detection system based on LightGBM and parallel intrusion detection mechanism. Comput. Secur. **97**, 101984 (2020)
7. Laguna, I., Schulz, M., Richards, D.F., Calhoun, J., Olson, L.: IPAS: intelligent protection against silent output corruption in scientific applications. In: 2016 IEEE/ACM International Symposium on Code Generation and Optimization (CGO), pp. 227–238. IEEE (2016)
8. Li, G., Pattabiraman, K., Hari, S.K.S., Sullivan, M., Tsai, T.: Modeling soft-error propagation in programs. In: 2018 48th Annual IEEE/IFIP International Conference on Dependable Systems and Networks (DSN). pp. 27–38. IEEE (2018)
9. Li, J., Tan, Q.: SmartInjector: exploiting intelligent fault injection for SDC rate analysis. In: 2013 IEEE International Symposium on Defect and Fault Tolerance in VLSI and Nanotechnology Systems (DFTS), pp. 236–242. IEEE (2013)
10. Liu, C., Gu, J., Yan, Z., Zhuang, F., Wang, Y.: SDC-causing error detection based on lightweight vulnerability prediction. In: Asian Conference on Machine Learning, pp. 1049–1064. PMLR (2019)

11. Liu, L., Ci, L., Liu, W.: Identifying SDC-causing instructions based on random forests algorithm. KSII Trans. Internet Inf. Syst. **13**(3), 1566–1582 (2019)
12. Liu, X., Jia, M., Zhang, X., Lu, W.: A novel multichannel Internet of Things based on dynamic spectrum sharing in 5G communication. IEEE Internet Things J. **6**, 5962–5970 (2018)
13. Lu, Q., Li, G., Pattabiraman, K., Gupta, M.S., Rivers, J.A.: Configurable detection of SDC-causing errors in programs. ACM Trans. Embed. Comput. Syst. (TECS) **16**, 1–25 (2017)
14. Ma, J., Wang, Y., Zhou, L., Hu, C., Wang, H.: SDCInfer: inference of silent data corruption causing instructions. In: 2015 6th IEEE International Conference on Software Engineering and Service Science (ICSESS), pp. 228–232. IEEE (2015)
15. Oh, N., Shirvani, P.P., McCluskey, E.J.: Control-flow checking by software signatures. IEEE Trans. Reliab. **51**(1), 111–122 (2002)
16. Pattabiraman, K., Nakka, N., Kalbarczyk, Z., Iyer, R.: SymPLFIED: symbolic program-level fault injection and error detection framework. In: 2008 IEEE International Conference on Dependable Systems and Networks With FTCS and DCC (DSN), pp. 472–481. IEEE (2008)
17. Sridharan, V., Kaeli, D.R.: Eliminating microarchitectural dependency from architectural vulnerability. In: 2009 IEEE 15th International Symposium on High Performance Computer Architecture, pp. 117–128. IEEE (2009)
18. Tajary, A., Zarandi, H.R., Bagherzadeh, N.: IRHT: an SDC detection and recovery architecture based on value locality of instruction binary codes. Microprocess. Microsyst. **77**, 103159 (2020)
19. Wang, C., Dryden, N., Cappello, F., Snir, M.: Neural network based silent error detector. In: 2018 IEEE International Conference on Cluster Computing (CLUSTER), pp. 168–178. IEEE (2018)
20. Wei, G., Zhao, J., Feng, Y., He, A., Yu, J.: A novel hybrid feature selection method based on dynamic feature importance. Appl. Soft Comput. **93**, 106337 (2020)
21. Yu, H., Lu, J., Zhang, G.: Continuous support vector regression for nonstationary streaming data. IEEE Trans. Cybern. (2020)

Dual Attention Network Based on Knowledge Graph for News Recommendation

Yang Ren, Xiaoming Wang$^{(\boxtimes)}$, Guangyao Pang, Yaguang Lin, and Pengfei Wan

School of Computer Science, Shaanxi Normal University, Xi'an 710119, China
wangxm@snnu.edu.cn

Abstract. With the continuous development of Internet technology, there are more and more online news readers, and the amount of news is huge and growing explosively. In addition, the news language is highly concentrated and contains a large number of entities. Currently, the commonly used recommendation methods are difficult to make full use of knowledge information and discover the potential interests of users. To solve the above problems, we propose a Dual attention network based on knowledge graph for news recommendation (DAKRec), which takes news titles, the entities contained in them and the contexts as input, and uses knowledge graph to extract news features. In order to better characterize the diversity of users' interests, a dual attention network is constructed to obtain the weight of users' historical news through word-level attention mechanism and item-level attention mechanism (integrating news words, entities, and contexts). Finally, the multi-head attention module is used to connect historical news and candidate news, and the click-through rate is calculated through a fully connected multilayer perceptron after feature fusion. Through a large number of experiments, we prove that our model DAKRec is better than the advanced DKN model and the other comparison models (FM, DMF) in AUC and MSE, further improves the recommendation performance.

Keywords: News recommendation · Knowledge graph · Attention mechanism · Deep neural network

1 Introduction

In the Internet era, people's news reading habits have changed from traditional books and newspapers to online web pages and news information apps. According to the 47th "Statistical Report on the Development of the Internet in China"[1],

---

[1] https://news.znds.com/article/52203.html.

This work was supported by the National Natural Science Foundation of China (Grant No. 61872228), and the Shaanxi Provincial Key R & D Plan of China (Grant No. 2020ZDLGY10-05).

© Springer Nature Switzerland AG 2021
Z. Liu et al. (Eds.): WASA 2021, LNCS 12937, pp. 364–375, 2021.
https://doi.org/10.1007/978-3-030-85928-2_29

the number of Internet users in China has reached 989 million as of December 2020. While the massive amount of information on the Internet brings more convenience to users, it also creates information overload [1]. Different from music and books, the data volume of news is huge, the growth rate is fast, and the content is extensive. Therefore, how to accurately and personalized recommend the content that users are interested in has become a challenge [2].

Traditional recommendation algorithms [3] can be divided into content-based recommendation algorithm [4], collaborative filtering recommendation algorithm [5] and hybrid recommendation algorithm [6]. The content-based recommendation method recommends news similar to the news content that users have browsed. The main disadvantages are that it is impossible to find out the potential interests of users, over-reliance on users themselves. Collaborative filtering recommendation can recommend news browsed by similar users or news that is similar to the news you have browsed. It uses One-Hot coding [7] and has serious data sparsity problem and cold start problem [8]. Hybrid recommendation algorithm refers to the combination of two or more recommendation algorithms. However, the hybrid recommendation algorithm still has shortcomings such as data heterogeneity, data sparsity and cold start problems.

In recent years, the rapid development of deep learning has brought the new trend of artificial intelligence, and the applications of deep learning to recommendation systems have achieved certain results [9]. Common deep learning models include Convolutional Neural Networks (CNN), Recurrent Neural Networks (RNN), Attention Model (AM). The deep learning recommendation technology learns the nonlinear network [10] structure to characterize users and news, and further extracts user interests. It can automatically learn high-level effective features from complex content, which makes up for the shortcomings of traditional recommendation to a certain extent. Traditional deep learning models only use word vectors for feature construction [11], for highly condensed news titles, they do not make good use of the semantic features in the text.

The series of studies on knowledge graph [12,13] provide new ideas for further extracting semantic features in texts. The knowledge graph is a data structure based on the graph [14], which is composed of nodes and edges. Each node represents an entity, and the edges represent the relationship between entities. The recommendation based on knowledge graph extracts features from data to obtain a more fine-grained information representation, so as to make recommendations more accurately. However, the attention mechanism has not been fully applied in the recommendation based on knowledge graph. In view of the above problems in news recommendation and the successful application of knowledge graph and attention mechanism, this paper proposes a Dual attention network based on knowledge graph for news recommendation (DAKRec). The model takes several pieces of historical browsing news of the user and one candidate news as input, and comprehensively considers word-level attention mechanism and item-level attention mechanism through two parallel attention modules, after feature fusion using multi-head attention mechanism, a fully connected multilayer perceptron is used to calculate the probability of the user clicking on the candidate news, so as to judge whether the user will click on the candidate news.

The contributions of this work can be summarized as follows:

- We propose a new dual attention network that combines knowledge representation, which considers word-level attention mechanism and item-level attention mechanism that integrates word, entity, and context of entity comprehensively.
- We construct a new model DAKRec that makes full use of external knowledge for recommendation, extract features through knowledge graph, calculate weights through a dual attention network, use multi-head attention mechanism to connect historical news and candidate news, and use perceptron attention mechanism to calculate the click-through rate.
- Through a large number of experiments on real news data, it is proved that our proposed model DAKRec is better than the current advanced model.

2   Related Works

2.1   Traditional Recommendation Algorithm

The traditional recommendation algorithm is still the mainstream recommendation technology at present. Among them, content-based recommendation algorithm recommends similar content to users based on their historical browsing records. Goossen et al. [15] proposed a news recommendation method combining TF-IDF and a domain ontology, using traditional TF-IDF and CF-IDF to recommend new content to users. In the 1990s, collaborative filtering recommendation was first proposed, using similar users with similar preferences for recommendation. Polatidis et al. [16] constructed a dynamic multi-level collaborative filtering method to improve the recommendation effect. This method is based on the continuous adjustment of both positive and negative sides and can be used in many fields. In the hybrid recommendation method, zhang et al. [17] proposed a hybrid recommendation method that uses user rating data and item metadata to solve the data sparsity problem, and uses sparse implicit feedback data through different types of relationships.

2.2   Recommendation Algorithm Based on Deep Learning

In recent years, with the vigorous development of deep learning, more and more researchers use deep learning for recommendation [18], which solves the problem that traditional recommendation methods rely too much on manual feature extraction. Zheng et al. [19] proposed a deep collaborative neural network (DeepCoNN) model, which uses two parallel neural networks to learn the hidden features of users and items, and improves the recommendation ability. Gabriel et al. [20] proposed a deep learning meta-architecture CHAMELEON for news recommendation, using CNN network to convolve news content at the word-level to generate news embedding representations. CNN is widely used in news recommendation, but it is difficult to capture long-distance word interactions and is not suitable for long-sequence news recommendation tasks. Many researchers use the attention mechanism to expand the neural network to improve the accuracy of text feature extraction. Wu et al. [21] constructed a news recommendation method based on the multi-head self-attention mechanism, which captures the interaction between long-distance words and enhanced the representation of news features.

2.3 Recommendation Algorithm Based on Knowledge Graph

News titles are refined in language, highly concentrated in content, and rich in knowledge and entities. It is difficult to find the potential knowledge-level connections of news when news is represented only from the semantic level. The emergence of knowledge graph effectively solves this problem. Chicaiza et al. [22] made recommendations based on the open link data and combined the characteristics of each user to obtain a recommendation result that is more suitable for the user. Hu et al. [23] designed a three-way neural interaction model that explicitly merges the context based on meta-paths, but it is not suitable for large-scale knowledge graph. Wang et al. [24] proposed a multi-channel knowledge-aware convolutional neural network aligned with word entities, which integrated the semantic layer and knowledge layer representation of news, and introduced attention mechanism into the model, making great progress in recommendation results.

3 Problem Statement

The problem to be solved in this paper is to predict whether users will click on a candidate news that they have never seen before based on their news browsing records. Suppose there are v users $\{u_1, u_2, \cdots, u_v\}$, there are m news $\{t_1, t_2, \cdots, t_m\}$, each news title is composed of multiple words w, namely $t = \{w_1, w_2, \cdots, w_n\}$, The word w is associated with the entity e in the knowledge graph. The news history browsing record of a user u_i is represented as $\{u_{t_1}^i, u_{t_2}^i, \cdots, u_{t_m}^i\}$. Now given a candidate news t_0, it is need to predict whether the user u_i will click this news t_0 (0 means no click, 1 means click).

4 The Proposed Approach

The framework of DAKRec is shown in Fig. 1. Taking user u_i as an example, it takes historical click news $\{u_{t_1}^i, u_{t_2}^i, \cdots, u_{t_m}^i\}$ and candidate news t_0 as input, and aims to output the click rate of candidate news. First connect historical browsing news and candidate nows through word-level attention mechanism, use KCNN to process news titles to generate embedding vectors for each title, and use item-level attention mechanism to match historical click news embedding vectors with candidate news embedding vectors in turn. Then, multi-head attention mechanism is used to obtain the final vector feature representation of the user. After connecting with the candidate news, we use the multilayer perceptron to calculate the probability of the user u_i clicking on the candidate news t_0.

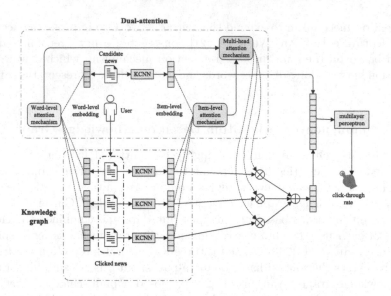

Fig. 1. The framework of the proposed approach DAKRec.

4.1   News Feature Extraction Based on Knowledge Graph

The knowledge graph consists of several triples, namely entity-relation-entity. The process of learning low-dimensional representation vectors for each entity and relationship is called knowledge graph embedding. This paper uses distance-based translation model TransD to learn knowledge graph embedding. TransD uses dynamic mapping matrix to embed, and constructs the projection matrix by multiplying the product of the two projection vectors of the entity relationship pair. The projection matrix is defined as follows:

$$
\begin{aligned}
\mathbf{M}_{rh} &= \mathbf{r}_p \mathbf{h}_p^\top + \mathbf{I}, \\
\mathbf{M}_{rt} &= \mathbf{r}_p \mathbf{t}_p^\top + \mathbf{I}, \\
\mathbf{h}_\perp &= \mathbf{M}_{rh} \mathbf{h}, \\
\mathbf{t}_\perp &= \mathbf{M}_{rt} \mathbf{t}.
\end{aligned}
\tag{1}
$$

$\mathbf{I}$ represents the identity matrix, $\mathbf{M}_{rh}$ and $\mathbf{M}_{rt}$ represent the projection matrix, $\mathbf{h}_\perp$ and $\mathbf{t}_\perp$ are the new vectors obtained by the projection of the head vector and the tail vector. The loss function of TransD is defined as follows:

$$
f_r(h,t) = \| \mathbf{h}_\perp + \mathbf{r} - \mathbf{t}_\perp \|_2^2,
\tag{2}
$$

when the score is lower, it means that the head vector and the tail vector are closely related.

In order to make full use of the rich entity information in news titles, we introduce the KCNN [24]. KCNN is a multi-channel, word entity alignment model, as shown in Fig. 2. The input has three matrices, word embedding, entity embedding, and context embedding. Each word w_i may be associated with an entity

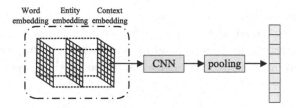

Fig. 2. The architecture of the KCNN model.

e_i in the knowledge graph, and the entity e_i has a corresponding context vector $\bar{e}_i$, it is represented by the average value of context entities, as follows:

$$\bar{e}_i = \frac{1}{|\{e_j| (e_j, r, e_i) \in G \, or \, (e_i, r, e_j) \in G\}|} \sum e_j. \tag{3}$$

Align and superimpose the three input embedding matrices together to get a multi-channel image:

$$\mathbf{W} = [[\mathbf{w}_1, \mathbf{w}_2, \cdots, \mathbf{w}_n], [\mathbf{e}_1, \mathbf{e}_2, \cdots, \mathbf{e}_n], [\bar{\mathbf{e}}_1, \bar{\mathbf{e}}_2, \cdots, \bar{\mathbf{e}}_n]], \tag{4}$$

$\mathbf{W} \in R^{d \times n \times 3}$ is the input of the convolutional neural network, applying multiple filters h with different window sizes to extract news titles:

$$c^{h_i} = f(h_i * \mathbf{W} + b). \tag{5}$$

Then select the most salient features through max pooling:

$$\tilde{c}^{h_i} = \max \left\{ c_1^{h_i}, c_2^{h_i}, \cdots, c_{n-l+1}^{h_i} \right\}, \tag{6}$$

where l is the size of the window, which connects all the most salient features $\tilde{c}^{h_i}$ together to get the final representation of the news headline t, which we call the item-level embedding of the title:

$$\mathbf{e}(t) = [\tilde{c}^{h1} \tilde{c}^{h2}, \cdots, \tilde{c}^{hs}]. \tag{7}$$

4.2 User Interest Extraction Based on Dual Attention Network

Word-Level Attention Mechanism. Users have different interests in different news. Considering users' interest in historical clicked news, we introduce the attention network. Given user u_i, its historical browsing records are represented as $\{u_{t_1}^i, u_{t_2}^i, \cdots, u_{t_m}^i\}$, and the embedding of historical browsing records are $\mathbf{e}(u_{t_1}^i), \mathbf{e}(u_{t_2}^i), \cdots, \mathbf{e}(u_{t_m}^i)$. For each news title, there are multiple different words, $t = [w_1, w_2, \cdots, w_n]$. For a clicked historical news $u_{t_j}^i$, its title can be expressed as $u_{t_j}^i = \left[w_1^{t_j}, w_2^{t_j}, \cdots, w_n^{t_j} \right]$, and the word embedding of its title can be expressed as $\mathbf{u}_{t_j}^i = \left[\mathbf{w}_1^{t_j}, \mathbf{w}_2^{t_j}, \cdots, \mathbf{w}_n^{t_j} \right]$; for a new candidate news t_0, its title can be expressed as $t_0 = \left[w_1^{t_0}, w_2^{t_0}, \cdots, w_n^{t_0} \right]$, and the word embedding of its title can be expressed as $\mathbf{t}_0 = \left[\mathbf{w}_1^{t_0}, \mathbf{w}_2^{t_0}, \cdots, \mathbf{w}_n^{t_0} \right]$. First connect the word-level embedding representation $\mathbf{u}_{t_j}^i$ and $\mathbf{t}_0$, and then use a fully connected layer DNNH as an attention network to calculate the score s^1 between the two news titles:

$$s^1_{u_{t_j}^i, t_0} = H\left(\mathbf{u}_{t_j}^i, \mathbf{t}_0 \right). \tag{8}$$

Item-Level Attention Mechanism. Different from the word-level attention mechanism that only uses word embedding described in the previous section, in order to enrich the title information, item-level embedding combines the word embedding, entity embedding, and context embedding of news titles. For a clicked historical news $u_{t_j}^i$, the item-level embedding of its title can be expressed as $\mathbf{e}\left(u_{t_j}^i \right)$; for a new candidate news t_0, the item-level embedding of its title can be expressed as $\mathbf{e}\left(t_o \right)$. Same as above, and then use a fully connected layer DNNH as the attention network to calculate the weight s^2 between the two news headlines:

$$s^2_{u_{t_j}^i, t_0} = H\left(\mathbf{e}\left(u_{t_j}^i \right), \mathbf{e}\left(t_o \right) \right). \tag{9}$$

Feature Fusion Based on Multi-head Attention Mechanism. Multi-head attention mechanism [25] can be regarded as a multiple linear mapping of query and key value, and then concatenat the mapping results, so that the model can simultaneously pay attention to the information of different representation subspaces. In this paper, multi-head attention mechanism is used to connect word-level attention mechanism and item-level attention mechanism, and normalized by softmax function to obtain the final weight s of user u_i's historical news $u_{t_j}^i$ and candidate news t_0:

$$s_{u_{t_j}^i, t_0} = soft\max\left(concat\left(s^1_{u_{t_j}^i, t_0}, s^2_{u_{t_j}^i, t_0} \right) \right). \tag{10}$$

In the same way, the weight between the remaining pieces of historical browsing news and the candidate news can be calculated. For the candidate news t_0, the historical embedding of user u_i can be calculated by weighting and summing the news titles they have clicked:

$$\mathbf{e}\left(u_i \right) = \sum_{j=1}^{m} s_{u_{t_j}^i, t_0} \mathbf{e}\left(u_{t_j}^i \right). \tag{11}$$

So far, the user's historical embedding $\mathbf{e}\left(u_i \right)$ and candidate news embedding $\mathbf{e}\left(t_o \right)$ have been obtained, and the probability of user u_i click on the candidate news t_0 is calculated through the fully connected multilayer perceptron:

$$p_{u_i, t_0} = v^T \tanh\left(\mathbf{w}_{u_i} \mathbf{e}\left(u_i \right) + \mathbf{w}_{t_o} \mathbf{e}\left(t_o \right) \right). \tag{12}$$

5   Experiments

In this section, we give a detailed introduction to the experiment, including dataset description, baseline model introduction, parameter settings, and corresponding experimental results. We compare with the baseline model to prove that the model proposed in this paper DAKRec has achieved better results.

5.1   Dataset Description

The dataset used in this article is from Microsoft Bing News. The news log data from October 16, 2016 to August 11, 2017 is used as the dataset. The data of the first eight months is used as the training set, and the data of the last two months is used as the test set. Each log mainly includes user ID, news title, and click status. Also, we search for the entity corresponding to the title and its neighbor entities within one hop in the Microsoft Satori knowledge graph to get the entity ID and the name of the entity. The basic information of the dataset is shown in Table 1.

Table 1. Basic statistics of the dataset.

Type	#Users	#News	#Logs	#Entities
Number	141,487	535,145	1,025,192	336,350

5.2   Baselines

FM [26] is a representative model in sparse data scene, using the doc2vec model to encode and calculate news titles.

DMF [27] is a deep matrix factorization model widely used in recommendation systems. It uses multi-layer neural networks to process the input.

DKN [24] proposes a deep knowledge-aware network, which introduces knowledge graph into the recommendation system and predicts click-through rate based on news content.

5.3   Experiment Setup

Our experimental environment is a K40 GPU computing card, python3.6, TensorFlow 1.13 and tensorflow-gpu 1.4, the dimensions of word embedding and entity embedding are both 50, the maximum length of each user's historical news record is 30, and the maximum value of the title is 10. The number of filters is 128, the batch size is 256, the epoch size is 20, and the optimization algorithm is Adam.

Table 2. Comparison of different models.

Models	AUC	MSE
FM	45.81	0.2431
DMF	53.95	0.2589
DKN	58.54	0.2417
DAKRec	**59.67**	**0.2403**

5.4 Experimental Result

We use AUC and MSE as evaluation indicators to evaluate the results of the experiment. The higher the AUC value, the lower the MSE value, indicating that the classification effect of the model is better and the model performance is better. We conducted rich experiments on real dataset, the results are shown in Table 2. DAKRec got the highest AUC value, that was 1.9% better than advanced model DKN. Compared with other baseline models, it was 10%–30% improvement. Also, the lowest MSE value was obtained, the best results were obtained among all the models. Figure 3 and Fig. 4 intuitively describe the AUC value and MSE value of each model. Generally speaking, the traditional recommendation method FM has the worst effect, the recommendation method based on deep learning has a slightly improved effect, and the recommendation method based on knowledge graph DKN has achieved good results, our proposed model DAKRec has the best effect, which proves the performance of the DAKRec is optimal.

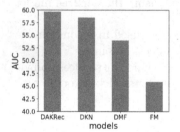

Fig. 3. AUC score of different models.

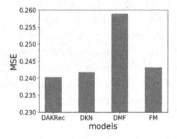

Fig. 4. MSE score of different models.

In addition, in order to better prove the performance of this model, we carried out comparative experiments from the following aspects. As shown in Table 3, the first line of the table is the standard model proposed in this paper. In order to further prove the superiority of the dual attention mechanism that combines word-level attention mechanism and item-level attention mechanism, the second row of the table shows the results when only word-level attention mechanism is

Table 3. Comparison among different components of DAKRec.

Models	AUC
DAKRec	59.67
DAKRec - Item Attention	57.92
DAKRec - Multi-head Attention	58.53
DAKRec with TransE	58.68
DAKRec with TransH	58.71
DAKRec with TransR	59.51

available; to prove the effectiveness of the introduction of multi-head attention, the third row of the table gives the result of Connecting word-level attention mechanism with item-level attention mechanism by addition; different knowledge graph embedding methods get different results, in order to prove the performance of TransD, we carried out TransE, TransH, TransR and TransD, the experiments are shown in rows 4, 5 and 6 of the table. It can be seen that the introduction of knowledge graph and dual-layer attention mechanism in the model has achieved good results and played an important role.

6   Conclusion

This paper proposes a dual attention network based on knowledge graph for news recommendation (DAKRec), which makes full use of the external knowledge information in the news title and further improves the recommendation performance. Firstly, the knowledge graph is used to extract knowledge-level information, which enriches the feature vector representation of news titles; secondly, in order to better characterize user interest, it integrates word-level attention mechanism and item-level attention mechanism, and connects through multi-head attention mechanism to model users' historical preferences for candidate news; finally, the click-through rate of candidate news is calculated by multilayer perceptron. Through a large number of experiments, the recommendation effect of DAKRec has been significantly improved compared with other models, which proves the effectiveness of the model proposed in this paper. In addition, we demonstrate the efficacy of the introduction of knowledge graph and the dual attention model through different comparative experiments. In the future, we will further study the use of knowledge graph and attention mechanism for deep recommendation.

References

1. Wang, X., Wang, X., Min, G., Hao, F., Chen, C.: An efficient feedback control mechanism for positive/negative information spread in online social networks. IEEE Trans. Cybern. (2020). https://doi.org/10.1109/TCYB.2020.2977322

2. Lin, Y., et al.: Dynamic control of fraud information spreading in mobile social networks. IEEE Trans. Syst. Man Cybern. Syst. **51**(6), 3725–3738 (2021)
3. Wang, Y., Yin, G., Cai, Z., Dong, Y., Dong, H.: A trust-based probabilistic recommendation model for social networks. J. Netw. Comput. Appl. **55**, 59–67 (2015)
4. Pang, G., et al.: ACNN-FM: a novel recommender with attention-based convolutional neural network and factorization machines. Knowl.-Based Syst. **181**, 1–13 (2019)
5. Kumar, V., Pujari, A.K., Sahu, S.K., Kagita, V.R., Padmanabhan, V.: Collaborative filtering using multiple binary maximum margin matrix factorizations. Inf. Sci. **380**, 1–11 (2017)
6. Tarus, J.K., Niu, Z., Yousif, A.: A hybrid knowledge-based recommender system for e-learning based on ontology and sequential pattern mining. Futur. Gener. Comput. Syst. **72**, 37–48 (2017)
7. Rodríguez, P., Bautista, M.A., Gonzalez, J., Escalera, S.: Beyond one-hot encoding: lower dimensional target embedding. Image Vis. Comput. **75**, 21–31 (2018)
8. Lin, Y., Cai, Z., Wang, X., Hao, F., Sai, A.: Multi-round incentive mechanism for cold start-enabled mobile crowdsensing. IEEE Trans. Veh. Technol. **70**(1), 993–1007 (2021)
9. Zhang, S., Yao, L., Sun, A., Tay, Y.: Deep learning based recommender system: a survey and new perspectives. ACM Comput. Surv. **52**(1), 1–38 (2019)
10. Cai, Z., Zheng, X.: A private and efficient mechanism for data uploading in smart cyber-physical systems. IEEE Trans. Netw. Sci. Eng. **7**(2), 766–775 (2020)
11. Cai, Z., He, Z.: Trading private range counting over big IoT data. In: 39th International Conference on Distributed Computing Systems, pp. 144–153, July 2019
12. Wang, Q., Mao, Z., Wang, B., Guo, L.: Knowledge graph embedding: a survey of approaches and applications. IEEE Trans. Knowl. Data Eng. **29**(12), 2724–2743 (2017)
13. Wang, X., He, X., Cao, Y., Liu, M., Chua, T.S.: KGAT: knowledge graph attention network for recommendation. In: 25th ACM SIGKDD International Conference on Knowledge Discovery & Data Mining, pp. 950–958, July 2019
14. Li, K., Luo, G., Ye, Y., Li, W., Ji, S., Cai, Z.: Adversarial privacy preserving graph embedding against inference attack. IEEE Internet Things **8**(8), 6904–6915 (2021)
15. Goossen, F., IJntema, W., Frasincar, F., Hogenboom, F., Kaymak, U.: News personalization using the CF-IDF semantic recommender. In: International Conference on Web Intelligence, Mining and Semantics, pp. 1–12, May 2011
16. Polatidis, N., Georgiadis, C.K.: A dynamic multi-level collaborative filtering method for improved recommendations. Comput. Stand. Interfaces **51**, 14–21 (2017)
17. Zhang, H., Ganchev, I., Nikolov, N.S., Ji, Z., O'Droma, M.: Hybrid recommendation for sparse rating matrix: a heterogeneous information network approach. In: 2017 IEEE 2nd Advanced Information Technology, Electronic and Automation Control Conference, pp. 740–744, March 2017
18. Ma, S., Zhu, J.: Self-attention based collaborative neural network for recommendation. In: Biagioni, E.S., Zheng, Y., Cheng, S. (eds.) WASA 2019. LNCS, vol. 11604, pp. 235–246. Springer, Cham (2019). https://doi.org/10.1007/978-3-030-23597-0_19
19. Zheng, L., Noroozi, V., Yu, P.S.: Joint deep modeling of users and items using reviews for recommendation. In: 10th ACM International Conference on Web Search and Data Mining, pp. 425–434, February 2017

20. de Souza Pereira Moreira, G.: CHAMELEON: a deep learning meta-architecture for news recommender systems. In: 12th ACM Conference on Recommender Systems, pp. 578–583, September 2018
21. Wu, C., Wu, F., Ge, S., Qi, T., Huang, Y., Xie, X.: Neural news recommendation with multi-head self-attention. In: 2019 Conference on Empirical Methods in Natural Language Processing and the 9th International Joint Conference on Natural Language Processing, pp. 6390–6395, November 2019
22. Chicaiza, J., Piedra, N., Lopez-Vargas, J., Tovar-Caro, E.: Recommendation of open educational resources. An approach based on linked open data. In: 2017 IEEE Global Engineering Education Conference, pp. 1316–1321, April 2017
23. Hu, B., Shi, C., Zhao, W.X., Yu, P.S.: Leveraging meta-path based context for top-n recommendation with a neural co-attention model. In: 24th ACM SIGKDD International Conference on Knowledge Discovery & Data Mining, pp. 1531–1540, July 2018
24. Wang, H., Zhang, F., Xie, X., Guo, M.: DKN: deep knowledge-aware network for news recommendation. In: 2018 World Wide Web Conference, pp. 1835–1844, April 2018
25. Vaswani, A., et al.: Attention is all you need. In: Advances in Neural Information Processing Systems, pp. 6000–6010, December 2017
26. Rendle, S.: Factorization machines. In: 2010 IEEE International Conference on Data Mining, pp. 995–1000, December 2010
27. Xue, H.J., Dai, X., Zhang, J., Huang, S., Chen, J.: Deep matrix factorization models for recommender systems. In: International Joint Conference on Artificial Intelligence, pp. 3203–3209, August 2017

Social-Based Link Reliability Prediction Model for CR-VANETs

Jing Wang[1], Aoxue Mei[2], Xing Tang[2,3(✉)], and Bing Shi[2]

[1] School of Computer Science, Hubei University of Technology,
Wuhan, People's Republic of China
[2] School of Computer Science and Technology, Wuhan University of Technology, Wuhan,
People's Republic of China
tangxing@whut.edu.cn
[3] Hubei Key Laboratory of Transportation Internet of Things, Wuhan University of Technology,
Wuhan, People's Republic of China

Abstract. Cognitive radio technology can improve the spectrum efficiency, and solve the problem of spectrum scarcity for vehicular communications. Nevertheless, the link reliability of cognitive radio vehicular ad hoc networks (CR-VANETs) is not only related to primary users but also to secondary users, which are acted as vehicles. To address this issue, we propose a social-based link reliability prediction model by jointly considering social characteristics of primary users and secondary users. First, we analyze the probability of the available channel in CR-VANETs based on social characteristics of primary users. Second, we analyze social characteristics of secondary users through the friendliness, the similarity and the centrality. Third, we utilize the social characteristics of primary users and secondary users to propose a link reliability prediction model and to predict the probability of the available link between two neighboring vehicles. Simulation results show that the predicted number of active primary users is consistent with the corresponding value in the real dataset, and the proposed social-based link reliability prediction model is effective.

Keywords: Social characteristic · CR-VANETs · Link reliability

1 Introduction

The US federal communications commission (FCC) has approved 75 MHz of spectrum in 5.9 GHz band for applications of the intelligent transportation system [1]. With an increasing number of vehicular communication requirements, especially in urban environments, the overcrowding of bands and the spectrum scarcity for vehicular communications become a crucial problem [2]. In order to increase the utilization of unused or underused licensed bands, the FCC has opened the licensed bands, such as spectrum bands for TV broadcasting, through the cognitive radio (CR) technology [3]. In cognitive radio vehicular ad hoc networks (CR-VANETs), vehicles (also be referred as secondary users) can opportunistically access the licensed spectrum band without causing any interference to primary users [4]. CR-VANETs offer a reliable vehicular

© Springer Nature Switzerland AG 2021
Z. Liu et al. (Eds.): WASA 2021, LNCS 12937, pp. 376–388, 2021.
https://doi.org/10.1007/978-3-030-85928-2_30

communication network and an efficient utilization of the radio spectrum [5]. Neverthe-less, the primary user activity and the high mobility of the secondary user will cause the link interruption in CR-VANETs.

In CR-VANETs, primary users and secondary users have unique social characteris-tics which can guide us to build effective and accruable models for the link reliability prediction. For one thing, primary users may access and vacate the licensed spectrum based on human social activities [6]. Accurate prediction of primary users' behaviors will facilitate the dynamic spectrum access where secondary users monitor the presence of primary users and opportunistically access the unoccupied licensed bands. For another thing, the mobility of the vehicle (also called the secondary user) in CR-VANETs also relates to human social activities [7]. Actually, the mobility of vehicles is influenced by the behaviors of drivers and their routines [8]. The above considerations motivate us to investigate the social features of both primary users and secondary users and develop a social-based transmission model for urban CR-VANETs.

Some research has been done on the topic of social-based transmission for CR net-works or VANETs. Anna W. et al. present a bio-social inspired paradigm for cognitive radio, and relax the social behavior rules to allow groups to organize into different social structures [9]. Zhaolong N. et al. concentrate on the design of a service access system in social Internet of vehicles, and focus on a reliability assurance strategy and quality optimization method [10]. Dmitri M. et al. conceptualize the socially inspired relaying scenarios and conduct underlying mathematical analysis to facilitate proactive mode selection, and conclude by discussing a practical prototype of a vehicular mmWave plat-form [11]. Peng H. et al. present an integrated approach to deal with the decision-making and motion planning for lane-change maneuvers of autonomous vehicles considering social behaviors of surrounding traffic occupants [12].

However, these works fail to predict the activities of primary users accurately, which is the key factor to ensure the reliability of transmission links in CR-VANETs. Moreover, most of the existing design methods ignore the interactions of them. In this paper, we develop and characterize a link reliability prediction model based on social character-istics of primary users and secondary users. We utilize regular activities of people to deduce activities of primary users and the probability of the available channel in CR-VANETs. Furthermore, we employ the friendliness, the similarity and the centrality to formulate the social characteristics of secondary users. According to the social charac-teristics of primary users and secondary users, we propose a link reliability prediction model for two cases of link interruptions, and analyze the probability of the available link between two neighboring vehicles.

2 System Model

2.1 Urban Street Model

A grid-like urban road layout is shown in Fig. 1(a). The gird is composed of two crossing groups of parallel roads with the number of G. Each line represents a road with a two-lane traffic flow. Each grid side is regarded as a unit with a length e. We assume that the width of the road is less than the interference range of the primary user and the vehicular communication coverage, and meet the requirement $\sqrt{2}\rho_p \leq e \leq 2\rho_p$, where ρ_p is the interference range of primary users. Moreover, the number of crossroads is $O = G^2$, and the number of the road segments is $H = 2G(G + 1)$. The average density of vehicles in each grid is $d = M/H$, where M is the number of secondary users. Here, G and d are used to characterize the scale of the grid. The grid-like urban street models with different values of G and d indicate different scales of urban scenarios from the small town to metropolitan areas.

Figure 1 (b) shows four junctions with the same width of f. In the Fig. 1 vehicles move along the horizontal and vertical directions. The arrival and departure motions of each vehicle include three forms that are straight, left, and right. Each vehicle transmits packages to left, right, or forward node according to a certain probability.

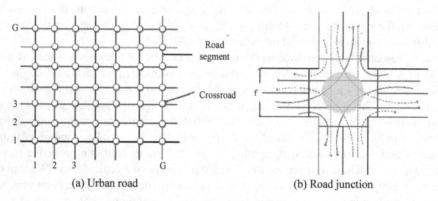

(a) Urban road   (b) Road junction

Fig. 1. A grid-like urban road layout.

2.2 Primary User Network Model

We consider the primary user network as a cellular network, which is composed of several primary users who have granted authorization to the spectrum. The number of each cellular base station is denoted as S_i. The number of primary users is N. The transmission range of the primary user P_i is R_p, and the interference range is ρ_p.

We assume that the spectrum is divided into several authorized channels which are not superposed in the system. The number of authorized channels is C. We denote the set of the channel as Ψ, with element channel $c_i(i \in (1, 2, ..., C))$. Additionally, the common control channel is used to exchange information, and each node can use this channel to exchange control information and routing information, to maintain the network topology structure.

The channel used by the primary users is exclusive, which means that one channel can only be used by one primary user. The occupied situation of the authorized channels can be regarded as a repeated process of mutual transformation between the busy status and the idle status. The busy status indicates that the current authorized channel is being used, and the idle status indicates that there is no primary user using the authorized channel. In each time slot, the primary users are active or inactive. The active time duration and idle time duration of the primary users follow the exponential distribution with parameters λ_{busy} and λ_{idle}, which can be formulated as follows.

$$T_{busy} = \frac{1}{\lambda_{busy}}, T_{idle} = \frac{1}{\lambda_{idle}} \tag{1}$$

2.3 Secondary User Network Model

The secondary network is composed of vehicle nodes with the number of M. Each vehicle has an identification number V_i and moves freely. We assume that each vehicle is equipped with two cognitive transceivers. One is used to transmit and receive data messages, and the other one is used to receive and transmit control messages through the common control channel. The transmission range of each vehicle is R_v and the interference range is ρ_v. Vehicles are densely deployed in an urban environment. We denote the density of the vehicle node as $d_{density}$ and we consider that each vehicle has enough neighbors to transmit data.

Each vehicle is equipped with a GPS device, which can exchange location and distance information with one-hop neighbors. When the Euclidean distance between V_i and V_j is less than R_v, they are considered as neighbor nodes. In the secondary network graph $G = (V, E)$, V is the node set of vehicles $V_i (i \in \{1, 2, ..., M\})$, E is the set of the link e_{ij} between nodes, $N_i = \{V_j | d_{ij} \le R_v, V_i \ne V_j\}$ is the set of neighbor nodes of V_i, and $d_{ij}(t)$ is the Euclidean distance between V_i and V_j in time slot t. We adopt $\theta_{ij}(t)$ to indicate whether there is a link between V_i and V_j in time slot t. When $d_{ij}(t) < R_v$, there is a link between V_i and V_j in the time slot t and $\theta_{ij}(t) = 1$. Otherwise, $\theta_{ij}(t) = 0$.

We assume that when two vehicles are on the same road segment or at the same crossroad, they can communicate with each other. The success or failure of transmission depends on the protocol model defined in [13]. The transmission from V_i to V_j can be successful when the condition is met the following equation.

$$d_{kj}(t) \ge (1 + \Delta)\rho_v \tag{2}$$

where $d_{kj}(t)$ is the Euclidean distance between V_k and V_j in the time slot t, and $\Delta > 0$ is a protective factor. Equation (2) indicates that the transmission between V_i and V_j will not be interfered by the other transmissions of vehicle V_k.

3 Social-Based Link Reliability Prediction Model

In this section, we propose a link reliability prediction model based on social characteristics of primary and secondary users. For primary user social characteristics, we calculate the probability of the available channel by considering active features of primary users. For secondary user social characteristics, we analyze the friendliness, the similarity and the centrality of secondary users. Moreover, we discuss two cases of link interruptions, and analyze the probability of the available link between two neighboring vehicles.

3.1 Primary User Social Characteristics

In CR-VANETs, primary users are people that have regular activities. Accordingly, it can be inferred that the people activities are similar to primary user activities in CR-VANETs. The activity of the primary user follows the normal distribution $N(\mu, \sigma)$ [14], and it can be formulated as a probability density equation:

$$f(x) = \frac{1}{\sigma\sqrt{2\pi}} e^{-\frac{(x-\mu)^2}{2\sigma^2}} \tag{3}$$

where μ is the expectation and σ is the variance. We provide the cumulative density equation as follows.

$$F(x) = \int_{-\infty}^{x} f(t) \cdot dt = \phi(\frac{x-\mu}{\sigma}) \tag{4}$$

We divide time into T timeslots, and each timeslot has a duration τ. We assume that t is one of the timeslots of T, and $t \in (1, 2, ..., T)$. We calculate the active probability of the primary user from t_1 to t_2 as follows.

$$p(t_1, t_2) = \phi(\frac{t_2 - \mu}{\sigma}) - \phi(\frac{t_1 - \mu}{\sigma}) \tag{5}$$

According to Eq. (5), we can calculate the active probability of the primary user in the timeslot t as p^t.

$$p^t = \phi(\frac{t\tau - \mu}{\sigma}) - \phi(\frac{(t-1)\tau - \mu}{\sigma}) \tag{6}$$

Consequently, the probability that there is no available channel can be obtained from t_1 to t_2 can be formulated as follows.

$$q(t_1, t_2) = (p(t_1, t_2))^C \tag{7}$$

where $p(t_1, t_2)$ represents the active probability of the primary user from t_1 to t_2, and C is the number of channels.

3.2 Secondary User Social Characteristics

We utilize the friendliness, the similarity, and the centrality to represent the social characteristics of secondary users. The friendliness indicates the relationship between nodes. The closer the relationship between two nodes, the link of these two nodes is more stable. The similarity measures the degree of separation. When two nodes have the same neighbors or hobbies in the network, they are more probable to establish a link, and the link is more stable. The centrality represents the importance of the nodes in the network. The node in the center of the network is more likely to relay data for other communication flows.

Vehicle Friendliness. According to granovetter's theory [15], depending on the time of encounter and the duration of each encounter, the relationship between vehicles can be divided into four categories. The first category is that the encounter frequency of two vehicles is high, and the duration of the encounter is long. The second category is that the encounter frequency of two vehicles is high, and the duration of the encounter is short. The third category is that the encounter frequency of two vehicles is low, and the duration of the encounter is short. The fourth category is that the encounter frequency of two vehicles is low, and the duration of the encounter is long. We regard the nodes with the first category and the fourth category as friends, and the nodes with the second category and the third category as strangers. We denote $F_\lambda^i (i \in (1, 2, 3, ..., N), \lambda \in (1, 2, 3, ..., K))$ as the friend vehicles of vehicle V_i, and K is the number of friend vehicles.

Vehicle Similarity. The similarity between friend nodes indicates the communication probability and the link stability. We select the node with a higher similarity to establish the link of the data transmission, in order to achieve a higher probability of successful communication between two nodes. We denote the similarity according to the encounter frequency and the encounter time of vehicles as follows.

$$sim(V_i, V_j) = \begin{cases} f_{ij} \cdot t_{ij} & V_i \text{ and } V_j \text{ are friends} \\ 0 & \text{else} \end{cases} \tag{8}$$

where f_{ij} is the encounter frequency between V_i and V_j, and t_{ij} is the encounter duration between V_i and V_j.

Vehicle Centrality. We adopt the degree centrality and the betweenness centrality to measure the centrality of vehicles. Degree centrality mainly refers to the number of direct connections between a node and its neighbors in the network. Betweenness centrality is to evaluate the proportion of the number of shortest paths between all node pairs passing through the current node. The degree centrality of the node is:

$$d(i) = \sum_{j \in V, j \neq i} l_{ij} \tag{9}$$

where l_{ij} is the link between V_i and V_j, and V is the set of vehicle. Friendliness shows that people tend to contact with friends rather than strangers. The links between friends are more stable than the links between strangers. Based on the vehicle similarity, we formulate the vehicle centrality as a subdivided equation.

$$d(i) = \varepsilon \sum_{j \in F_\lambda^i, j \neq i} l_{ij} + \partial \sum_{j \in V, j \notin F_\lambda^i, j \neq i} l_{ij} \tag{10}$$

where $\varepsilon + \partial = 1, \varepsilon > \partial$, l_{ij} is the link between V_i and V_j, F_λ^i is the friends set of V_i. The degree centrality indicates the sum of the number of links between node V_i and its strangers and the number of links between V_i and its friends.

The betweenness centrality of V_i is shown as follows. It represents the proportion between the shortest path passed V_i and all the shortest paths.

where V is the set of vehicles, ω_{jk} is the set of the shortest paths from V_j to V_k, and $\omega_{jk}(i)$ is the number of the shortest paths from V_j to V_k and passed V_i.

$$bc(i) = \sum_{\substack{j \neq i \neq k \\ j,i,k \in V}} \frac{\omega_{jk}(i)}{\omega_{jk}} \tag{11}$$

3.3 Link Reliability Prediction Based on Social Characteristics

According to the causes, interruptions are classified into two cases, which are the physical interruption and the cognitive interruption. When the distance between two vehicles is longer than the transmission distance R_v, we consider this case as the physical interruption. When the channel k used for V_i and V_j communication becomes unavailable, we consider this case as the cognitive interruption.

Based on vehicle friendliness categories, friend vehicles have social features of higher encounter frequency and longer link duration than stranger vehicles. If the duration of the link l_{ij} on the channel k is long enough for data transmission, we consider that there is no physical interruption in the process of communication. Therefore, if V_i and V_j are friends, then $Y_{ij}^k(t) = 1$. If V_i and V_j are not friends, their movements are independent, and there is the possibility of the physical interruption and the cognitive radio interruption. Due to the mobility of vehicles, we provide an approximate algorithm to estimate the value of $Y_{ij}^k(t)$, and formulate the probability that the link l_{ij} will not be physically interrupted in the time period t as follows.

$$Y_{ij}^k(t) = \begin{cases} 1 & V_i \text{ and } V_j \text{ are friends} \\ P\{d_{kj}(t) \geq (1+\Delta)\rho_v | d_{kj}(t) \leq R_v\} & \text{else} \end{cases} \tag{12}$$

As shown in Fig. 2, we assume that the current position of the primary user is fixed at the position P. At the beginning of the time slot, the vehicle V_i is at the position A. At the end of the time slot, the vehicle V_i is at the position B. The primary user is the center of the circle and has the interference range ρ_p. We denote $AP = d$, $BP = d'$, $AB = d_0$, and $AD = d_1$. The angle between AP and AB is ϕ. When any of the following conditions ①, ②, or ③ is satisfied, as shown in Fig. 2 (b) (c) (d), then $I_{iP}^k = 1$, which means the link will not be interrupted. Otherwise, as shown in Fig. 2 (a), $I_{iP}^k = 0$, which indicates the link of the secondary user will be interrupted. We formulate the probability that there is no cognitive interruption as follows.

$$I_{ip}^k = \begin{cases} 1 & \text{condition ①, ②, or ③ is satisfied} \\ 0 & \text{else} \end{cases} \tag{13}$$

where condition ① $\phi \in [\frac{\pi}{2}, \pi]$, ② $\phi \in [0, \frac{\pi}{2}]$, $d \cdot \sin\phi > \rho_p$, and ③ $\phi \in [0, \frac{\pi}{2}]$, $d \cdot \sin\phi \leq \rho_p$, $d_0 < d_1$ and $d_1 = d\cos\phi - \sqrt{(\rho_p)^2 - (d\sin\phi)^2}$.

Accordingly, we formulate the probability that there is no cognitive interruption in time period t as follows.

$$I_{ij}^k(t) = I_{iP}^k \cdot I_{jP}^k \tag{14}$$

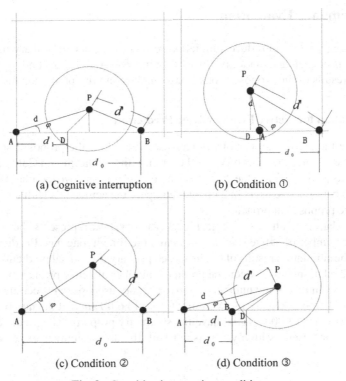

(a) Cognitive interruption   (b) Condition ①

(c) Condition ②   (d) Condition ③

Fig. 2. Cognitive interruption conditions.

where I_{iP}^k indicates the probability that V_i will not be interrupted by the k-th primary user in time period t, and I_{jP}^k means the probability that V_j will not be interrupted by the k-th primary user in time period t. I_{iP}^k and I_{jP}^k have similar deduction processes, we omit the description of I_{iP}^k due to limited pages.

The communication between two vehicles requires the available channel, and also the reliable link. According to the probability of the available link in a certain period of time, and based on the social relationship between secondary users, we formulate the probability that the link between V_i and V_j will not be interrupted as follows.

$$r_{ij}^k(t) = Y_{ij}^k(t) \cdot I_{ij}^k(t) \tag{15}$$

where $Y_{ij}^k(t)$ is the probability that the link between V_i and V_j will not be physically interrupted. $I_{ij}^k(t)$ is the probability that the link between V_i and V_j will not be cognitively interrupted in time period t.

Accordingly, the probability of the available link between two vehicles during time (t_1, t_2) can be formulated as follows. $r_{ij}^k(t)$ is the probability that link l_{ij} is available with channel k in time period t.

$$p_v(t_1, t_2) = (r_{ij}^k(t))^{\left\lfloor \frac{t_2 - t_1}{\tau} \right\rfloor} \tag{16}$$

4 Performance Evaluation

In this section, we first introduce simulation results of the active primary user prediction, which is elementary to the link reliability in CR-VANETs. Second, we introduce simulation results of the proposed social-based link reliability prediction model.

4.1 Simulation for Active Primary User Prediction

We simulate the active number of primary users based on the proposed social-based approach. We adopt the dataset of WLAN user mobility in Dartmouth College collected over five years [16]. We select the data of 100 active users in any two months, calculate the average number of active users in 24 h, and compare the actual data with the simulation results of the proposed approach.

The simulation result is shown in Fig. 3. **RealityData** represents the relationship between the number of active primary users and the time in one day. **PredicationData** represents the simulation results of our proposed primary user social prediction model. It indicates the relationship between the predicted number of active primary users and the time. As shown in Fig. 3, the number of active primary users presents certain regularity. The number of active primary users from 0:00 am to 6:00 am and the number of active primary users from 13:00 to 19:00 have the symmetry property. The predicted number of active primary users is highly consistent with the actual number of active primary users.

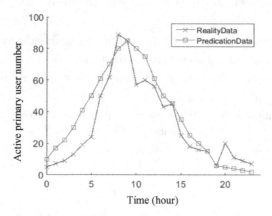

Fig. 3. Predictions of active primary user numbers.

In order to reflect the accuracy of the active primary user prediction, we calculate the error between the simulation result and the actual number of active primary users. We employ E_{error} to represent the error rate as follows.

$$E_{error} = \frac{E_r - E_p}{E_r} \qquad (17)$$

where E_r indicates the actual number of active primary users, and E_p represents the prediction of active primary users.

We calculate the mean value of the error rate in Table 1, the average error rate between prediction results and actual numbers of active primary users is -6.1%. It means that the active primary user prediction is consistent with the reality of the active primary user quantity.

Table 1. The error rate of the active primary user prediction

Time (hour)	0	1	2	3	4	5
$E_{error}(\%)$	−50.0	−41.1	−27.3	−36.7	−41.5	−39.8
Time(hour)	6	7	8	9	10	11
$E_{error}(\%)$	−18.0	−11.4	1.6	0.0	5.8	−25.0
Time (hour)	12	13	14	15	16	17
$E_{error}(\%)$	−25.3	−29.5	−10.0	−28.5	−28.0	20.0
Time (hour)	18	19	20	21	22	23
$E_{error}(\%)$	0.0	0.0	65.0	53.6	56.6	61.4

4.2 Simulation for Social-based Link Reliability Prediction Model

In this subsection, we simulate the social-based link reliability prediction model. We execute the simulation 100 times, and select the mean value of the simulation within 50 s as results. We evaluate the influence of the user social characteristics on the link reliability. If the communication between nodes is not interrupted, we consider the link is reliable. The probability of the link reliability is calculated by the number of reliable links. The simulation parameters are given in Table 2.

Table 2. The simulation parameters

Parameter	Value
The number of vehicles	20
The velocity of vehicles	50km/h
The number of channels	10
The number of roads	5
The length of roads	2km
The transmission range of vehicles	200m
MAC layer protocol	802.11p

Considering the social characteristics of the secondary user, we utilize the similarity, the degree centrality, and the betweenness centrality of vehicles to evaluate and simulate the effect on link reliability. The social characteristics of secondary users can be measured as follows.

$$m(i) = \frac{sim(V_i, V_j) + d(j) + bc(j)}{3} \tag{18}$$

where $sim(V_i, V_j)$ represents the similarity between V_i and its neighbor V_j, V_j, $d(j)$ represents the degree centrality of V_j, and $bc(j)$ represents the betweenness centrality of V_j These parameters can be calculated by Eqs. (8), (10), and (11).

The simulation result is shown in Fig. 4. The abscissa indicates the measurement of secondary user social characteristics, which is formulated in Eq. (18). The ordinate indicates the probability of the link reliability. **Reality** represents the calculated probabilities of the link reliability, which is simulated by the software. **Prediction** represents the simulation results of our proposal. Two curves of **Reality** and **Prediction** have a large degree of consistency, which shows the effectiveness of the social-based link reliability prediction model. With the increase of the value of $m(i)$, the probability of vehicle link reliability is also increased, which indicates the measurement of secondary user social characteristics benefits to the vehicle link reliability. When the measurement increases to a certain value, $m(i) = 0.8$, the prediction of the link reliability has a deviation. However, in real life, the measurement $m(i)$ cannot increase infinitely and it will become stable when it is higher than a threshold value.

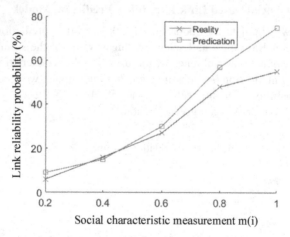

Fig. 4. Link reliability probability with different values of social characteristic measurement.

In order to directly reflect the effectiveness of our social-based link reliability prediction model, we calculate the errors between the simulation results and the actual probabilities of the link reliability.

$$E'_{error} = \frac{E'_r - E'_p}{E'_r} \tag{19}$$

where E'_{error} represents the error rate of link reliability prediction, E'_r represents the actual probability of the link reliability, and E'_p represents the proposed prediction of the link reliability.

We calculate the mean value of the error rate in Table 3. The average error rate of the link reliability prediction model is -7.7%. It means that the social-based prediction result of link reliability is slightly higher than the value of the actual link reliability. The social characteristics of secondary users benefit the link reliability prediction and the proposed social-based link reliability prediction model is effective.

Table 3. The error rate of the link stability prediction

Secondary user measurement	0.2	0.4	0.6	0.8	1.0
$E'_{error}(\%)$	−6.0	2.3	−2.1	−10.5	−22.3

5   Conclusion

In this paper, we proposed a social-based link reliability prediction model for CR-VANETs. We analyzed the social characteristics of both primary users and secondary users. According to the active number of primary users and the friendliness, the similarity, and the centrality of secondary users, we established a link reliability prediction model for CR-VANETs. We compared the proposed model with the real dataset and with theoretical calculations. We showed the correctness and effectiveness of the link reliability prediction model through simulations.

Acknowledgments. This work was supported by the National Natural Science Foundation of China (No. 61170135), the Provincial Natural Science Foundation of Hubei (No. 2020CFB823 and No. 2020CFB749), the Key Research and Development Program of Hubei Province (No. 2020BHB004 and No. 2020BAB012), the Humanity and Social Science Youth Research Foundation of Ministry of Education (No. 19YJC790111) and the Doctoral Scientific Research Project of Hubei University of Technology (No. BSQD2020062).

References

1. Cheng, L., Henty, B., Stancil, D., et al.: Mobile vehicle-to-vehicle narrow-band channel measurement and characterization of the 5.9 GHz dedicated short range communication (DSRC) frequency band. IEEE J. Sel. Areas Commun. **25**(8), 1501–1516 (2007)
2. Xing, T., Junwei, Z., Shengwu, X., et al.: Geographic segmented opportunistic routing in cognitive radio ad hoc networks using network coding. IEEE Access **6**, 62766–62783 (2018)
3. Jing, W., Huyin, Z., Xing, T., et al.: Delay-tolerant routing and message scheduling for CR-VANETs. Future Gener. Comput. Syst. **110**, 291–309 (2020)
4. Wenxuan, D., Xing, T., Junwei, Z., et al.: Load balancing opportunistic routing for cognitive radio ad hoc networks. Wirel. Commun. Mob. Comput. 2018, 9412782 (2018)

5. Jing, W., Huyin, Z., Sheng, H., et al.: An urban expressway forwarding scheme for cognitive Internet of vehicles. Int. J. Distrib. Sensor Netw. **16**(3), 155014772091294 (2020)
6. Husheng, L., Chien, C., Lifeng, L., et al.: Propagation of spectrum preference in cognitive radio networks: a social network approach. In: 2011 IEEE International Conference on Communications (ICC), pp. 1–5. Kyoto, Japan (2011)
7. Anna, M.V., Valeria, L.: A survey on vehicular social networks. IEEE Commun. Surv. Tutorials **17**(4), 2397–2419 (2015)
8. Baoxian, Z., Rui, T., Cheng, L.: Content dissemination and routing for vehicular social networks: a networking perspective. IEEE Wireless Commun. **27**(2), 118–126 (2020)
9. Anna, W., Mohammad, A.S., Bilal, K., et al.: Emergence of pecking order in social cognitive radio societies. In: IEEE INFOCOM 2018 - IEEE Conference on Computer Communications Workshops (INFOCOM WKSHPS), Honolulu, HI, USA, pp. 305–311 (2018)
10. Zhaolong, N., Xiping, H., Zhikui, C., et al.: A cooperative quality-aware service access system for social internet of vehicles. IEEE Internet of Things J. **5**(4), 2506–2517 (2018)
11. Dmitri, M., Roman, K., Mikhail, G., et al.: Socially inspired relaying and proactive mode selection in mmWave vehicular communications. IEEE Internet of Things J. **6**(3), 5172–5183 (2019)
12. Peng, H., Chen, L., Chao, H., et al.: An integrated framework of decision making and motion planning for autonomous vehicles considering social behaviors. IEEE Trans. Veh. Technol. **69**(12), 14458–14469 (2020)
13. Benamar, N., Singh, K.D., Benamar, M., et al.: Routing protocols in vehicular delay tolerant networks: a comprehensive survey. Comput. Commun. **48**(8), 141–158 (2014)
14. Ji, S., Cai, Z., He, J S., et al.: Primary social behavior aware routing and scheduling for cognitive radio networks. In: 2015 12th Annual IEEE International Conference on Sensing, Communication, and Networking (SECON), pp. 417–425. Seattle, WA, USA (2015)
15. Granovetter, M.: The strength of weak ties: a network theory revisited. Sociol Theory **1**(6), 201–233 (1983)
16. Kim, J., Helmy, A.: The evolution of WLAN user mobility and its effect on prediction. In: 2011 7th International Wireless Communications and Mobile Computing Conference, pp. 226–231, Istanbul, Turkey (2011)

IoT and Edge Computing

Parallel Computing of Spatio-Temporal Model Based on Deep Reinforcement Learning

Zhiqiang Lv[1,2], Jianbo Li[1,2(✉)], Zhihao Xu[1], Yue Wang[1], and Haoran Li[1]

[1] College of Computer Science Technology, Qingdao University, Qingdao 266071, China
lijianbo@qdu.edu.cn
[2] Institute of Ubiquitous Networks and Urban Computing, Qingdao 266070, China

Abstract. Deep learning parallel plays an important role in accelerating model training and improving prediction accuracy. In order to fully consider the authenticity of the simulation application scenario of model, the development of deep learning model is becoming more complex and deeper. However, a more complex and deeper model requires a larger amount of computation compared to common spatio-temporal model. In order to speed up the calculation speed and accuracy of the deep learning model, this work optimizes the common spatial-temporal model in deep learning from three aspects: data parallel, model parallel and gradient accumulation algorithm. Firstly, the data parallel slicing algorithm proposed in this work achieves parallel GPUs load balancing. Secondly, this work independently parallelizes the components of the deep spatio-temporal. Finally, this work proposes a gradient accumulation algorithm based on deep reinforcement learning. This work uses two data sets (GeoLife and Chengdu Taxi) to train and evaluate multiple parallel modes. The parallel mode combining data parallel and gradient accumulation algorithm is determined. The experimental effect has been greatly improved compared with the original model.

Keywords: Parallel computing methodologies · Deep learning · Reinforcement learning · Gradient accumulation algorithm

1 Introduction

With the development of deep learning, the design of the calculation model tends to increase the number of network layers or the number of network neurons per layer. Although this design can make the model have higher accuracy, as the number of network layers and network neurons per layer increases, the speed of network convergence during training is greatly reduced. What's more, the total number of parameters of the model will

This research was supported in part by Shandong Province colleges and universities youth innovation technology plan innovation team project under Grant No. 2020KJN011, Shandong Provincial Natural Science Foundation under Grant No. ZR2020MF060, Program for Innovative Postdoctoral Talents in Shandong Province under Grant No. 40618030001, National Natural Science Foundation of China under Grant No. 61802216, and Postdoctoral Science Foundation of China under Grant No.2018M642613.

Z. Liu et al. (Eds.): WASA 2021, LNCS 12937, pp. 391–403, 2021.
https://doi.org/10.1007/978-3-030-85928-2_31

also grow rapidly, which leads to the model being too large. Finally, it causes the model only can't be trained on the GPU unless the model is segmented, which is particularly common in the field of image and big data prediction. The use of high-end hardware resources is the most direct way to increase training speed. For example, the advent of NVIDIA V100 and A100 has greatly promoted the development of deep learning [1], their nanometer scale and large-capacity display memory can finish most model training tasks, but most developers cannot afford the expensive price.

In the field of deep learning research, the parallel computing methods play an important role in improving training speed and accelerating model convergence. Deep learning parallel mainly focuses on data parallel and model parallel [2], as shown in Fig. 1. In the process of data parallel, the model is copied into different GPUs or processes, and then different data are selected for parallel training of the same model. This is the most direct way to increase the speed of model training. However, model parallel is mainly for solving the problem that the model is too large to be loaded into an independent GPU. The same data is loaded into different models for training, and then special methods are used to fuse features that are from the different model.

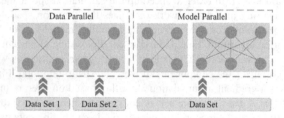

Fig. 1. Data parallel and model parallel.

Deep learning mainly focuses on the perception and expression of the problem, while reinforcement learning mainly focuses on the decision process of the problem, and the optimal behavior decision is obtained by calculating the reward value of the decision. Google's DeepMind [3] team created a deep reinforcement learning model. The team creatively integrated deep learning and reinforcement learning to build a learning system based on model perception and multi-agent decision-making. With the help of DRL's perception and decision-making ability, deep learning parallel computing can determine the decision-making behavior of preset parameters according to the changes of dynamic parameter, thereby improving the dynamic decision-making ability of parallel computing.

In this work, the traffic prediction model DeepTTE [19] is optimized in parallel with multiple modes. In terms of data parallel, we propose a slicing algorithm that can maintain GPU group load balancing. In terms of model parallel, we parallelize the four model components of DeepTTE by segmenting the model and reduced the GPU display memory occupied by the training model. Finally, we propose a gradient accumulation algorithm based on deep reinforcement learning, which can automatically adjust the size of gradient accumulation in deep learning training, and it achieves the task of accelerating training and improving accuracy.

2 Related Work

Data parallel refers to dividing the data into several parts and handing them to different processors for independent calculation. This process is usually run in SPMD [4] mode. In the field of large-scale data research, the distributed deep learning systems have shown more powerful model convergence capabilities and training speed. The parameter server is an important role in the distributed system. It is designed based on the distributed method, and synchronizes the model parameters of different worker nodes of the distributed system through the distributed parameter memory cache mechanism [5], so it can effectively improve the training speed of deep learning. The parameter server generally uses parallel stochastic gradient descent algorithm for gradient update training [6]. The stochastic gradient descent algorithm is mainly divided into two modes: synchronous stochastic gradient descent algorithm (SSGD) and asynchronous stochastic gradient descent algorithm (ASGD). SSGD needs to calculate the data of all nodes, so the node at the end of the queue determines the total calculation time. This calculation mode seriously blocks the parallel process. ASGD uses random data to increase the speed of single-step training, but its randomness makes the model convergence more difficult. The weighted asynchronous parallel protocol (WASP) performs asynchronous parallel training for each process. It redefines the staleness degree of the gradient as the difference between the version number of the current process and the latest version number of the parameter server to fusslgdient weighting. WASP achieves enhanced the speed of asynchronous training while reducing the impact of delay gradient on parameter update [7]. DC-ASGD [8] is realized by Taylor expansion of the gradient function and the Hessian matrix of approximation loss function. The experimental results show that the error rate of DC-ASGD after training the ImageNet dataset with 16 GPU nodes is lower than that of ASGD, reduced by 0.46%.

If the size of the deep learning model is relatively large and cannot be loaded in display memory, we need to segment the model. If it is a linear model, we can segment the model parameters corresponding to different data latitudes into different worker nodes. However, the widely used models are basically nonlinear and complex, which determines that the parallel process of the model must be fully considered the problems of local communication loss and worker node collaboration. The Class-Based RNN [9] optimized the way of RNN data processing. It input multiple sets of data streams in serial and then read part of each set of data streams for parallel calculation. Although this method improves the training speed, it doesn't achieve the purposes of segmenting the model and reducing the size of the model. The work [10] used the improved FlexFlow framework to segment the DNN into three local models. This method increased the training throughput of the two GPU clusters by 3.8 times. In order to complete the task of large model segmentation, the work [11] implemented STRADS composed of ML applications, Topic Modeling, Lasso and Matrix Factorization. Although STRADS didn't focus on the optimization of performance, it proposed a set of algorithms which are suitable for large model segmention in the programming system. With the main idea of reducing communication and storage, Megatron-LM [12] upgraded the traditional single-GPU model training to 8.3 billion parameters on 512 NVIDIA V100 GPUs with 8-way model parallel, and the floating-point operation speed reached 15.1 PetaFLOPs.

Although the distributed system can solve some of the problems of large-scale computing, it has the disadvantages including large communication overhead, complicated data access structure, and difficulty in controlling the security of data. It is not suitable for small-scale computing processes [13]. For small-scale computing, we can consider designing a balanced scale and enhancing adaptive algorithms to achieve parallel. In order to solve the problem that the performance of the average model cannot guarantee the constraints of the local model loss function and the global model loss function in the non-convex neural network model, the work [14] proposed Ensemble-Compression model polymerization algorithm with integration-compression. This algorithm can not only achieve the improvement of performance through integration, but also maintain the scale of the global model in the iterative process of learning. Reinforcement learning has the advantages of getting feedback from the environment and making decisions. The optimization of policy gradients in reinforcement learning is an important aspect of speeding up decision-making. For example, the Istate-GPOMDP algorithm adds a reward baseline that reduces variance, which can improve the convergence efficiency of the learning process under the premise of ensuring the expected value of the gradient estimate [15]. The TD(λ) method is used in the approximation of the value function of the gradient estimation. The eligibility trace in the method can more efficiently propagate the learning experience, which can reduce the variance of the gradient estimation and improve the performance of the algorithm [16]. Combining the reinforcement learning strategy gradient algorithm and deep learning training process, we can perform adaptive control from two aspects: algorithm interference mode and operation steps [17]. Finally, we can implement an adaptive gradient accumulation algorithm based on the maximum value of gradient change [18].

3 Model Architecture

3.1 Data Parallel

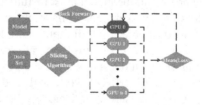

Fig. 2. Data parallel process.

In the process of data parallel, firstly, the network model is copied into the GPU group, and then the data set is divided by the slicing algorithm according to data size. Each GPU performs parallel forward propagation calculation on the data obtained to calculate the average loss. Finally, the calculation of back propagation is used to update the model parameters in each GPU. The above process completes an epoch calculation process, as shown in Fig. 2.

Traditional data parallel copies model into the designated GPU group to ensure that the individuals in the GPU group have the same model structure and it evenly distributes the input data to each individual in the GPU group. Although each individual only calculates feature on the data given, the final feature fusion is performed on the first GPU. The above process leads to the problem of unbalanced load of the GPU group. In order to ensure that the GPU group achieves load balancing during the training process, we use a slicing algorithm that acts on the input data. The algorithm process is as follows:

Input: Dataset X, Devices D.
OutPut: The average value of memory M.

1.Set $M = (X$ size $- \alpha) / ($len $(D) - 1)$
2.If (Devices [0] batch size $< M$):
3. Set *chunk size* $= [D$ [0] batch size] $+ [M] * ($len $(D) - 1)$
4. Set *diff* $= X$ size $-$ sum (*chunk size*)
5. For i in range(*diff*):
6.   *chunk size* $[i+1] +=1$
7. Return *chunk size*
8.Return M

The algorithm separates the first GPU from others. The data size of the first GPU can be freely allocated by the user, while the data size of others is determined by the difference between the total data size and the data size of the first GPU. It is up to the user to freely control the size of GPU group data. Direct calculation of the average will generate floating point numbers due to division, but the size of input data can only be measured as an integer number. This situation will result in data loss. So, when the data size of the first GPU is less than the average value M of the data of others, we use the slicing algorithm to prevent data loss. The *chunk size* is an actual value of each individual data in the GPU group D. The data loss of this calculation is the difference between the data size of the original data X and the sum of the *chunk size*. For the data loss, we average it to give others except the first GPU.

3.2 Model Parallel

The DeepTTE is mainly composed of four components: Attribute, Spatio-Temporal, Entire Estimate, Local Estimate. We segment the four components into four GPUs, as shown in Fig. 3. The purpose of the Attribute component design is that adding the direct and implicit factors that affect the driving process of the vehicle to the feature calculation process. It mainly involves the operation of dimensional transformation and data standardization, so it occupies less display memory during the actual program operation. Attribute component uses the first GPU together with data loading, feature fusion and other processes to achieve the purpose of improving GPU usage. These two Estimate components are to reduce local errors and solve the problem of data sparsity. The feature data from Spatio-Temporal component will be independently calculated in Entire-Estimate component and Local-Estimate component. This independent calculation mode allows us to place two components independently in two GPUs for parallel calculation.

Finally, GPU 0 implements the relevant feature fusion process. This parallel mode not only achieves model segmentation, but also greatly reduces device communication and training time.

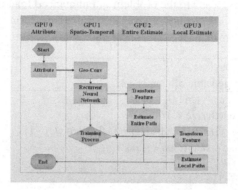

Fig. 3. Model parallel process.

3.3 Gradient Accumulation

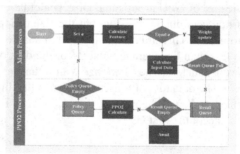

Fig. 4. Main process and PPO2 process.

The degree of convergence of the model is obvious on the whole process, but the change in the results of two adjacent feature calculations is slight. The main idea of the gradient accumulation algorithm is to superimpose a certain size of local features and then update the model weights. It reduces the number of updates to reduce the training time and can reduce local errors. We divide the main process of model training and the reinforcement learning process into two processes and execute them in parallel, as shown in Fig. 4. We first assign an initial value to the accumulation size α, and the weight update is performed after the main process calculation feature number reaches α. The input data required for reinforcement learning is stored in the *result queue*. The PPO2 process calculates when the *result queue* is not empty, otherwise it continues to wait. The PPO2 will obtain the current main process running status according to the input data and calculate the decision on α based on this status. When the *policy queue* is not empty, the main process will modify α. The above process completes an epoch calculation process.

The degree of convergence of the model is obvious on the whole process, but the change in the results of two adjacent feature calculations is slight. The main idea of the gradient accumulation algorithm is to superimpose a certain size of local features and then update the model weights. It reduces the number of updates to reduce the training time and can reduce local errors. We divide the main process of model training and the reinforcement learning process into two processes and execute them in parallel, as shown in Fig. 4. We first assign an initial value to the accumulation size α, and the weight update is performed after the main process calculation feature number reaches α. The input data required for reinforcement learning is stored in the *result queue*. The PPO2 process calculates when the *result queue* is not empty, otherwise it continues to wait. The PPO2 will obtain the current main process running status according to the input data and calculate the decision on α based on this status. When the *policy queue* is not empty, the main process will modify α. The above process completes an epoch calculation process.

In terms of programming, we have done the following extra work:

1. We use Pytorch-Multiprocessing [20] instead of python multiprocessing to solve the flaw of python global lock.
2. The main process and the PPO2 process are friendly. They don't cause conflicts by snatching the global queue.
3. We add a delay mechanism to the PPO2 process. The PPO2 process will modify α after the main process performs some epochs.

During the deep learning model training process, although the overall loss and prediction results change according to the specified trend, the local values are dynamically fluctuating and uncertain. The above reinforcement learning process is based on deep learning local values as input data, so we should focus on how to use the currently available data to take the greatest possible improvement strategy without going too far and accidentally leading to illegal strategies. The biggest innovation of the PPO2 algorithm [21] is the proportional parameters used to describe the differences between the new and old strategies, as shown in Eq. (1), and the loss function Eq. (2) is shown. When A is more than 0, the abscissa is $r_t(\theta)$ and the reward is a positive number. The larger the update range, the better. But the penalty mechanism makes the update range not increase when the abscissa is more than $1 + \varepsilon$. Similarly, when A is less than 0, the abscissa is the update amplitude. If the reward is negative, The smaller the update range, the better. but it cannot be infinitely small.

$$r_t(\theta) = \frac{\pi_\theta(a_t|s_t)}{\pi_{\theta_k}(a_t|s_t)} \tag{1}$$

$$J_{PPO2}^{\theta^k}(\theta) \approx \sum_{st} min\left(r(\theta)A^{\theta^k}(s_t, a_t), clip(r(\theta), 1 - \varepsilon, 1 + \varepsilon)A^{\theta^k}(s_t, a_t)\right) \tag{2}$$

The agent is an important component of reinforcement learning, which determines the content and direction of the decision. It calls the *reset* method periodically to reset the environment to the initial state, return to the next observation action in the *step* method and calculate the *reward*. It periodically calls the *render* method to output the environment's performance. The agent decision algorithm is as follows:

Input: Dataset *Result Queue*.
Output: Environmental weight *env*.

---

1. Get input data from Result Queue.
2. Build the *env*.
3. Set *obs* = *env*.reset()   //Initialize the *env*.
4. for *i* in range(*epoch*):
5.   *action* = ppo2.predict(*obs*)   //Generate the *action*.
6.   obs, rewards, done, info = env.step(action) //Update parameters.
7. *result* = *env*.render()   //Update *env*.
8. Return *env*

We define *Input Data* as five types of data points (initial value, minimum value, maximum value, final value, maximum fluctuation value) of accumulated data. The purpose is that we hope the agent can consider the trend of input data and can make the next better decision. In the agent, we have defined three kinds of decision content: increase, decrease and unchanged. At the same time, we need to use GYM's Box to define an action space with a discrete number of types to represent the size of data that increases or decreases. The *action* decision calculation equation for each step is shown in Eq. (3). N represents the accumulated value of the current agent. Its main function is to record the optimal decision direction for the gradient accumulation size α. It is the minimum value of the current α is multiplied by the input data normalization and the previous value. μ and σ respectively represent the mean and standard deviation of the input data. After deciding the *action*, we need to define the *reward* calculation rules. We set the *reward* as a part of the cumulative size multiplied by the number of time steps so far.

$$N = Min\left\{N, N + \alpha \times \frac{q - \mu}{\sigma}\right\} \tag{3}$$

4 Experiment

4.1 Data Preparation

We use two data sets, including the Chengdu taxi data and the GeoLife data. The Chengdu taxi data contains GPS records of more than 14,000 taxis from August 03 to August 30, 2014. The data set used for training and testing doesn't include daily GPS records between 0 and 6, and we cleared out the repetitive and abnormal data at other times of the day. The data set consists of continuous driving trajectories, and each trajectory includes 10 to 40 GPS position changes, position time changes, distance changes, taxi passenger status changes and other information. The GeoLife data contains 17,621 trajectories with a total distance of 1,251,654 km and a total duration of 48,203 h. 91% of the tracks are recorded in a dense representation, for example every 1 to 5 s or every 5 to 10 m per point.

4.2 Load Balancing

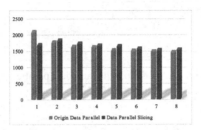

Fig. 5. Display memory usage. The abscissa is the serial number of the GPU. The ordinate is the display memory of GPU during the training process.

The effect of the slicing algorithm in this paper on the actual application of DeepTTE is shown in the Fig. 5. We select 8 Nvidia V100 GPUs for testing. The abscissa is the serial number of GPUs and the ordinate is the actual size of display memory used by each GPU during the training process. In the original data parallel mode, display memory usage decreases in order according to the serial number, especially the display memory usage of the first block is 17.57% more than that of the second block, while the change range of other GPUs memory is only 1.24% ~ 8.09%. We can freely control the memory usage of the first GPU after using the data parallel slicing algorithm. This test sets the batch size to 1024 and the batch size assigned by the first GPU is 70. From the experimental results, we can see that the display memory usage of the first GPU is reduced by 18.63% compared with the original data parallel method and it is lower than the usage of the second GPU. The usage of other GPUs has increased slightly due to the segmentation effect of the slicing algorithm.

4.3 Evaluation Index

The RMSE is the square value of the average squared difference between the predicted value and the real observed value and it can measure the average size of the error. In this experiment, we take RMSE as the main evaluation index and it measures the parallelism and training effect of the model based on the trend of its time-dependent changes during the training process. The experiments were conducted in 8 nvidia V100 GPUs and the results of each experiment are the average value after multiple tests. The Fig. 6 respectively shows the results of the RMSE change during the training process of the DeepTTE original model, the model parallel, and the data parallel on the 4 and 8 V100 GPUs. Compared with the original model, the data parallel realized by 8 GPUs has improved the model convergence speed by 36.71%, but the speed increase of model parallel is not obvious. The communication loss between local models has seriously affected the feature fusion process [22] and it affects the overall training speed. The above experimental results prove that DeepTTE is suitable for data parallel, but not for model parallel.

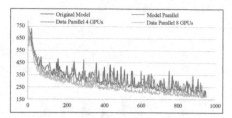

Fig. 6. The results of origin model, model parallel and data parallel. The abscissa is the epoch of training process. The ordinate is the value of RMSE.

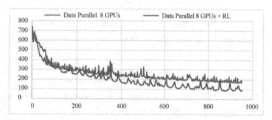

Fig. 7. The results of data parallel and data parallel + RL. The abscissa is the epoch of training process. The ordinate is the value of RMSE.

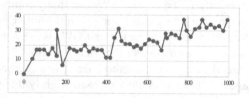

Fig. 8. Accumulation size change. The abscissa is the epoch of training process. The ordinate is the value of accumulation size.

The Fig. 7 and the Fig. 8 show the changes of RMSE in training after the gradient accumulation method is added to deep learning process and the changes of the accumulation size in the whole process. We set the initial accumulation size to 1, which is the same as the ordinary training process. As the loss during training continues to decrease, the cumulative size of gradients also changes continuously. Since the variation degree of the model's convergence becomes smaller and smaller with time, the gradient accumulation size has formed an increasing trend. The continuous increase of the accumulation size allows the gradient update process to calculate more features. Compared with ordinary data parallel training, the convergence speed of the model is increased by 22.55% after adding the reinforcement learning gradient accumulation.

The Table 1 shows the average indicators in the evaluation process of the original DeepTTE model and the four deformation models. The traditional model parallel (Model Parallel and FlexFlow) and data parallel (Data Parallel 4 and Data Parallel 8) methods have not greatly improved the accuracy of the model and the accuracy rate tends to decline in the evaluation of MAPE and MAE. We verify the current and typical gradient descent algorithms. The experimental results show that the stochastic gradient descent algorithm has a certain optimization to the performance of model. However, SSGD needs to calculate the data of all nodes, so the performance of the model is averaged. ASGD uses random data selection operations to increase the speed of single-step training, but its random process makes model convergence more difficult. The WASP performs asynchronous parallel for each process of training, which overcomes the shortcomings of single-step training, but it doesn't avoid the impact of randomness to the accuracy of model. The algorithm of data parallel and reinforcement learning gradient accumulation created in this paper (Data Parallel + RL) not only improves the speed of model convergence, but also greatly improves the accuracy of model prediction. RMSE decreased by 50.12%, MAPE decreased by 62.3%, and MAE decreased by 56.02%.

Table 1. Evaluation results

Model	RMSE	MAPE	MAE
DeepTTE	175.25	8.33%	116.41
Model Parallel	174.44	7.52%	120.32
FlexFlow	174.07	6.53%	110.23
Data Parallel 4	170.67	9.07%	122.96
Data Parallel 8	162.41	6.46%	108.71
Data Parallel + SSGD	156.43	6.21%	102.32
Data Parallel + DC-ASGD	142.23	6.01%	99.23
Data Parallel + Istate-GPOMDP	140.33	5.67%	94.23
Data Parallel + STRADS	134.34	5.34%	90.12
Data Parallel + WASP	132.75	5.27%	89.32
Data Parallel + RL	87.41	3.14%	51.20

5 Conclusion

This article implements three parallel modes for DeepTTE: data parallel, model parallel and gradient accumulation algorithm. The data parallel slicing algorithm effectively avoids the problem of unbalanced load of GPU groups. We verified that DeepTTE is not suitable for model parallel due to frequent communication between the four model components. The gradient accumulation algorithm based on deep reinforcement learning can greatly improve the training speed and prediction accuracy. In the future, our work will focus on parallel acceleration algorithms that are applicable to most models. We will fully exploit the advantages of deep reinforcement learning and set more preset parameters to autonomous learning and dynamic decision-making to further enhance the predictive ability of deep learning.

References

1. Martineau, M., Atkinson, P., McIntosh-Smith, S.: Benchmarking the NVIDIA V100 GPU and Tensor Cores. In: Mencagli, G., B. Heras, D., Cardellini, V., Casalicchio, E., Jeannot, E., Wolf, F., Salis, A., Schifanella, C., Manumachu, R.R., Ricci, L., Beccuti, M., Antonelli, L., Garcia Sanchez, J.D., Scott, S.L. (eds.) Euro-Par 2018. LNCS, vol. 11339, pp. 444–455. Springer, Cham (2019). https://doi.org/10.1007/978-3-030-10549-5_35
2. Zhu, H., Li, P., Jiao, L.: Review of parallel deep neural network. Chin. J. Comput. **41**(8), 1861–1881 (2018)
3. Lui, Q., Zhuo, J., Zhang, Z.: A survey on deep reinforcement learning. Chin. J. Comput. **41**(1), 1–27 (2018)
4. Shu, J., Zheng, W.: Performance analysis for massive problem data parallel computing. J. Softw. **11**(5), 628–633 (2000)
5. Alexander, S.: An architecture for parallel topic models. In: Proceedings of the VLDB Endowment, VLDB, Santa Clara, CA, vol. 3, pp. 703–710 (2010)
6. Wang, S.: Research on parameter-exchanging optimizing mechanism in distributed deep learning. Huazhong University of Science and Technology, pp. 1–64 (2015)
7. Chen, M., Yan, Z., Ye, Y.: Parallel optimization for deep learning based on HPC environment. Comput. Eng. Sci. **40**(8), 133–140 (2019)
8. Zheng, S., Meng, Q., and Wang, T.: Asynchronous stochastic gradient descent with delay compensation. In: 34th International Conference on Machine Learning, ICML, Sydney, Australia, vol. 70, pp. 4120-4129 (2017)
9. Wang, L., Yang, J., Cheng, L.: Parallel optimization of chinese language model based on recurrent neural network. J. Appl. Sci. **33**(3), 253–261 (2015)
10. Jia, Z., Zaharia, M., Aiken, A.: Beyond data and model parallelism for deep neural networks. In: 35th International Conference on Machine Learning, ICML, Stockholm, Sweden, pp. 1-15 (2018)
11. Lee, S., Kim, J.K., Zheng, X.: Primitives for dynamic big model parallelism, 1–22. arXiv (2014)
12. Shoeybi, M., Patwary, M., Puri, R.: Megatron-lm: training multi-billion parameter language models using model parallelism. arXiv, 1–15 (2019)
13. Ding, Y., Liu, B.: Using GPU for high-performance data parallel computing. Programmer **4**(62), 97–99 (2008)
14. Sun, S., Chen, W., Bian, J., Liu, X., Liu, T.-Y.: Ensemble-compression: A new method for parallel training of deep neural networks. In: Ceci, M., Hollmén, J., Todorovski, L., Vens, C., Džeroski, S. (eds.) ECML PKDD 2017. LNCS (LNAI), vol. 10534, pp. 187–202. Springer, Cham (2017). https://doi.org/10.1007/978-3-319-71249-9_12
15. Wang, X., Xv, X., Wu, T.: The optimal reward baseline for policy-gradient reinforcement learning. Chin. J. Comput. Chin. Ed. **28**(6), 1021–1026 (2005)
16. Cheng, S., Gu, R., Cheng, G.: Natural gradient reinforcement learning algorithm with TD(λ). Comput. Sci. **37**(12), 186–189 (2010)
17. Luo, C., Su, R., Wang, X.: Adaptive stochastic parallel gradient descent algorithm and its application in coherent beam combining. Acta Optica Sinica **34**(s1), s1010061–s1010065 (2014)
18. Zhang, L., Sun, H., Guo, H.: Auto focusing algorithm based on largest gray gradient summation. Acta Photonica Sinica **42**(5), 605–610 (2013)
19. Wang, D., Zhang, J., Cao, W.: When will you arrive? Estimating travel time based on deep neural networks. In: Thirty-Second AAAI Conference on Artificial Intelligence, AAAI, vol. 32, pp. 2500-2507, New Orleans, Louisiana, USA (2018)

20. Pérez-García, F., Sparks, R., Ourselin, S.: TorchIO: a python library for efficient loading, preprocessing, augmentation and patch-based sampling of medical images in deep learning, 1–28. arXiv (2020)
21. Bi, B., Wang, Q., Coleman, J.: A novel mutation A212T in chloroplast Protoporphyrinogen oxidase (PPO1) confers resistance to PPO inhibitor Oxadiazon in Eleusine indica. Pest Manag. Sci. **76**(5), 1786–1794 (2019)
22. Sharif, M., Attique, M., Tahir, M.Z.: A machine learning method with threshold based parallel feature fusion and feature selection for automated gait recognition. J. Organ. End User Comput. (JOEUC) **32**(2), 67–92 (2020)

TS-Net: Device-Free Action Recognition with Cross-Modal Learning

Biyun Sheng, Linqing Gui, and Fu Xiao[✉]

School of Computer Science, Nanjing University of Posts and Telecommunications,
Nanjing 210023, China
{biyunsheng,guilq,xiaof}@njupt.edu.cn

Abstract. Internet of Things (IoT) brings opportunities for wireless sensing and device-free action recognition becomes a hot topic for recognizing human activities. Existing works are trying to fuse WiFi and traditional vision modality in a straightforward way for performance improvement. To overcome the problems such as privacy invasion and computational burden, we design an end-to-end cross-modal learning architecture termed teacher-student network (TS-Net) for device-free action recognition. Different from previous methods with both modalities used for the entire process, our model only use WiFi features without any video information involved during the testing phase. More specifically, we construct a cross-modal supervision scheme in which the visual knowledge and robustness capacity of teacher videos can be transferred into the synchronously collected student wireless signals. The experiments show that our TS-Net can efficiently identify human actions at multi-location without environmental constrains of indoor illumination and occlusion.

Keywords: WiFi · Action recognition · Teacher-student network · Cross-modal supervision

1 Introduction

Human action recognition which aims at identifying activity types has played an important role in the sensing field. Because of its potential applications in smart healthcare, safety surveillance and human-computer interaction, researchers have made significant efforts to improve the recognition performance in recent years [1–3]. With the popularization of Internet-of-Things (IoT) systems, device-free such as commercial WiFi based wireless sensing begins to demonstrate the potential in environment and human perception. The WiFi receiver collects the combined signal effects of reflections by different objects in the environment. The principle of WiFi-based action recognition is that signal propagations are affected by human actions and each activity has unique changes.

Although WiFi signals play a critical role in device-free action recognition, it is sensitive to the location variances, leading to significant bias in recognition accuracy. Taking the toy example in Fig. 1 for example, a volunteer operates the

© Springer Nature Switzerland AG 2021
Z. Liu et al. (Eds.): WASA 2021, LNCS 12937, pp. 404–415, 2021.
https://doi.org/10.1007/978-3-030-85928-2_32

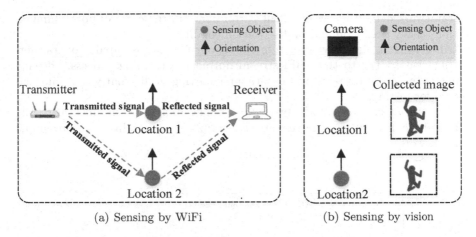

(a) Sensing by WiFi   (b) Sensing by vision

Fig. 1. A toy example of sensing object at different locations by two different modalities. Different sensing locations change the multi-path effects of WiFi propagations but have little effect on collected images.

same action at two different locations, namely Location 1 (L1) and Location 2 (L2). On account of the fact that the received signal strength decreases with the increase of propagation path [4], actions of Fig. 1(a) at the primary path L1 have larger interferences on received signals in comparison to other locations (*e.g.* L2) apart from line-of-sight (LOS) path. In this case, the collected images by camera illustrated in Fig. 1(b) show high robustness because there are only distinctions on the ratio of target to image. Nevertheless, the vision modality involves privacy issues and always fails in application scenarios with extremely dark light or occlusion.

Inspired by knowledge distillation [5], we try to take advantages of video and WiFi signals and transfer the discriminative capacity from the vision domain into the WiFi domain by cross-model supervision learning named teacher-student network (TS-Net) in Fig. 2. During training, we synchronize the camera and commercial off-the-shelf (COTS) WiFi device to obtain visual and wireless data. The entire training process includes training teacher and training student. While traing teacher, a pre-trained C3D deep model [6] on the UCF101 Sports dataset [7] is fine-tuned on our collected videos. The trained vision network predicts are applied as the teacher to supervise a 2D convolutional neural network (CNN) namely the student parameters learning of the wireless stream. Once the model is trained, the performance can be insured with only wireless signals as the input during the test stage. Our proposed method cannot only be efficiently used in scenarios without restrictions of environmental conditions, but also successfully realize the WiFi multi-location sensing problem. The contributions of this investigation can be summarized as follows:

- We propose an unified end-to-end supervised cross-model learning framework termed TS-Net for device-free action recognition. Making full use of the complementarity between the two heterogeneous modalities, our proposed

framework demonstrates excellent performance in the cases of poor illumination, heavy occlusion and multi-location conditions.
– Different from the conventional methods, our network is capable of transferring visual clues to the WiFi stream during the training process, allowing accurate on-the-fly recognition without incurring additional visual information for testing.
– We conduct experiments in two indoor scenes and the experimental results reveal the promise and the desirable generalization capability of our proposed framework.

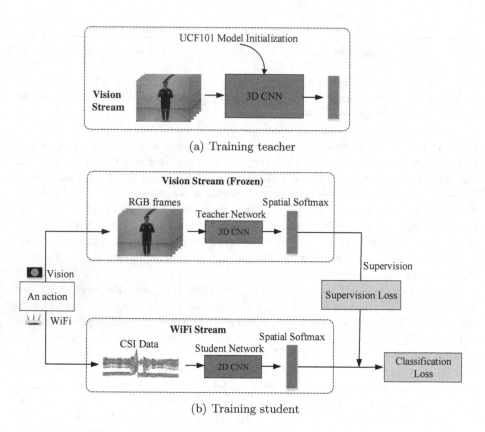

(a) Training teacher

(b) Training student

Fig. 2. The training framework of our proposed TS-Net including training teacher (a) and training student (b). The teacher is fine-tuned with trained UCF101 model as the initialization and then frozen parameters of the trained teacher are attempting to guide the student WiFi stream.

The rest of our paper is organized as follows. Firstly, we review the related work from the aspects of WiFi and multi-model based sensing. Then we further detailedly describe our methodology in Sect. 3. In Sect. 4, we conduct the experiments in two indoor scenes. Finally, Sect. 5 gives the conclusion.

2   Related Work

Inspired by the tremendous success of deep learning in computer vision, researchers begin to establish various deep structures for wireless signals. Wang et al. [8] propose a fine-grained action recognition framework which utilizes the pixel-level semantic segmentation approach to classify every sample in the whole series. Widar 3.0 [9] develops a new type of domain-independent feature named body-coordinate velocity profile (BVP) from which high-level spatial features are further extracted by a deep learning neural network (DNN). WiHF [10] further propose extracting the motion change patterns into a deep learning model for both gesture recognition and user identification tasks. Yao et al. [11] design Short Time Fourier Neural Network (STFNet) which integrates time-frequency analysis into data processing to learn features in the frequency domain. Zou et al. [12] adopt multiple 2D convolutional layers to automatically learn discriminative features from WiFi signals.

In recent years, a good deal of works are concentrated on solving new problems in WiFi perception such as pose estimation and person identification. Zhao et al. [13] present a radio-based system which uses pose results estimated by vision methods to supervise radio frequency (RF) signals, and accurately track the 2D human pose through walls. Korany et al. [14] demonstrate a WiFi-video cross-modal system to identify different persons. Spectrogram features extracted from video and WiFi are compared to indicate whether the person in a video is the same person in a WiFi area. Wang et al. [15] take Joint Heat Maps (JHMs) and Part Affinity Fields (PAFs) learned from vision data as annotations. Then WiFi signals are input into a deep learning framework to obtain human body poses. Jiang et al. [1] utilize VICON motion capture system to generate accurate 3D skeletons which then supervise the deep learning structure.

As for the human activity recognition task, Zou et al. [12] multimodal machine learning at the decision level to sufficiently fuse features of WiFi and vision streams. Xue et al. [16] propose the DeepFusion approach to combine information from heterogeneous sensors. Specifically, three types of data collected from wearable sensing devices are integrated into the unified multi-sensor deep learning with different weights according to the information quality. DeepMV [17] further extracts shared features among different environments to improve the cross-scene accuracy. In spite of its superior performance, the presented multimodel approach simultaneously need two or more modality inputs at the testing stage which leads to computation burden and application scope limitation.

3   Methodology

In this paper, we consider monitoring human activities in indoor application scenarios by only wireless devices without environmental restricts and privacy issues. Vision perception with richer sample property information is usually more robust and superior under ideally environmental conditionals in contrast to WiFi sensing. Once the vision model is trained, the perception accuracy for indoor actions explicitly filmed will be little affected by various locations. If the network with wireless signals has the similar discriminative and anti-interference capacity as vision model, the sensing task to some extent can push the limits of location sensitivity. It is therefore desirable to transfer the knowledge from a vision network that has learned on the video dataset to the WiFi network.

Inspired by knowledge distillation [5] which is originally proposed to compress cumbersome model to a small model, we utilize the class probabilities produced by the vision teacher network as soft labels for training the WiFi student network. In detail, the cross-model teacher-student training framework consists of C3D-based teacher model training and vision-WiFi model training. After simultaneously collecting data of two modalities, we operate the pro-processing and the processed data are further input into our designed network models.

Vision Teacher Network. Video-based human action recognition has achieved tremendous success in recent years. Its performance on deep learning model is always superior due to sufficiently learning abundant information contained in videos. For sake of mining spatial features and temporal dependences between frames, we adopt C3D model as the vision sensing model [6] in Fig. 3. Different from 2D CNN, the output of 3D convolution in each layer is also video volume so that the temporal information can be preserved during the parameter learning process. Three fully connected layers are followed with multiple 3D convolutions to aggregate the former feature maps. The channel number n of final fully connected layer is set as the action types.

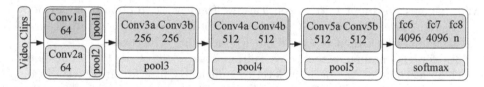

Fig. 3. The C3D model structure. "Conv", "pool", "fc" and "softmax" respectively denote the convolution, pool, fully connected and softmax operations.

Specifically, we sample fixed interval frames from the original videos and processed which are then input into a 15-layer 3D CNN architecture. In order to avoid overfitting, the pre-trained model on UCF 101 is loaded to initialize the C3D network and only the last two fully connected layers are fine-tuned with convolutional parameters fixed. In order to further speed the training process, the fc8 learning rate is set to 10 times as that of the previous fully connected layers. The output of the softmax layer is applied as the supervision information for the following teacher-student model learning.

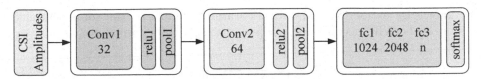

Fig. 4. The 2D CNN model structure. "Conv", "relu", "pool", "fc" and "softmax" respectively denote the convolution, rectified linear unit, pool, fully connected and softmax operations.

WiFi Student Network. Different from 3D image data, CSI streams are 2D time series denoted as $C \subseteq \mathbb{R}^{d \times T}$ where d and T represent channel number and received package number separately. In this work, we only adopt a simple 2D convolutional neural network as the baseline model to learn deep features from the CSI data in Fig. 4. The CNN model consists of two-layer convolutions and three-layer fully connected layers. The last fully connected channel number n equals the action category number. For both teacher and student network, the "dropout" regularization is utilized during the training process to avoid overfitting.

Teacher-Student Network. We denote the synchronously collected video and CSI data as V and C. In the first training stage, the C3D network inputs V and outputs its softmax layer features $T(V) = [t_1, t_2, ..., t_n]$ which represent the confidence score for each class. The formula of softmax function is denoted as:

$$t_i = \frac{e^{z_i}}{\sum_{j=1}^{n} e^{z_j}} \tag{1}$$

where z_i and n are respectively the preceding layer node and total category number.

In contrast to the actual label, the probability distributions $T(V)$ are able to describe more grained action category information. Taking the sample "Box" for example, its softmax outputs may appear relatively stronger response on similar actions (*e.g.* "box") and weaker score on different activities (*e.g.* "jump"). Due to the robustness of vision model, the softmax outputs usually have a superior performance on describing the categorical probability distributions of an action sample.

However, the original softmax function may generate significant discrepancies among predictions which leads to limited knowledge learned from the teacher network. Therefore, we utilized the generalized form of the formula (1):

$$t_i = \frac{e^{z_i/T}}{\sum_{j=1}^{n} e^{z_j/T}} \tag{2}$$

where T is the temperature parameter. It can be easily seen that the Eq. (2) is degraded to (1) with T set as 1 and probability outputs tend to be softer over classes at high temperatures. The softer score distributions are more beneficial for knowledge extraction and network learning. Similarly, the softer softmax output of the WiFi network $S(C) = [s_1, s_2, ..., s_n]$ can be formulated as:

$$s_i = \frac{e^{\tilde{z}_i}/T}{\sum_{j=1}^{n} e^{\tilde{z}_j}/T} \tag{3}$$

where $\tilde{z}_i$ is the fc3 layer node of 2D CNN.

Considering the discriminative power of posterior probability generated by the trained teacher, we attempt to train the $S(C)$ with $T(V)$ and original sample labels $Y(C) = [1, 2, ..., n]$ as supervision information in the second training stage. The training objective of the student network can be formulated as follows:

$$\min_{S} \sum_{V,C} L(T(V), S(C), Y(C)) \tag{4}$$

We utilize the cross entropy loss for all training samples to supervise the student model learning process:

$$\sum_{V,C} L(T, S, Y) = -\sum_i (Y_i' log Y_i + (1 - Y_i') log(1 - Y_i))$$
$$+ \lambda(-\sum_i S_i log T_i + (1 - S_i) log(1 - T_i)) \tag{5}$$

where λ is the balance factor; Y_i' and Y_i are the predictive label by the student network and the actual label; S_i, T_i denote softmax scores from the student and teacher network for the i_{th} sample. The gradient descent method is utilized to update the student model with the trained teacher network parameters fixed.

4 Experiments

In this section, we evaluate the presented TS-Net for WiFi-based action recognition. We first introduce the experimental setups including scenario layout along with dataset and settings. Then quantitative and qualitative analysis is conducted to validate the effectiveness of our approach. Meanwhile, comparative studies are carried out to demonstrate the advantages of our TS-Net against existing frameworks.

4.1 Experimental Setup

We collect activity data from 2 locations of 2 rooms shown in Fig. 5. The distance between the TX-RX device and its height are respectively set as 3m and 1.2m in the sensing area. As shown in Fig. 5, we ask the volunteers to do specified actions at the center of LOS path L1 and 1m distance from the first location L2. The dataset consist of activities in daily life including jump, box, throw, squat and wave. In the two scenes, 5 volunteers are employed to operate each action for 10

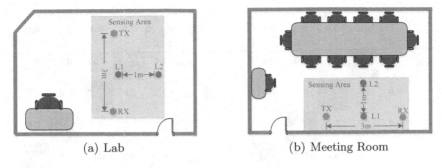

(a) Lab   (b) Meeting Room

Fig. 5. Layouts of the two scenarios.

rounds which leads to 1,000 samples (5 volunteers × 2 positions × 2 scenes × 5 actions × 10 instances) in total.

In our experiments, we capture two kinds of activity data, namely RGB videos and WiFi signals. We use the laptop's own camera to collect vision information. As for the WiFi CSI data, we utilize TP-LINK TL-WDR7660 wireless router as the signal transmitter to send data packages at a transmission rate. The receiver with multiple antennas is connected to a laptop configured with Intel Wireless Link 5300NIC to receive WiFi signals. Specifically, the transmitter broadcasts Wi-Fi packets at a rate of 200 packets per second. The receiver is equipped with three antennas which are placed in a line. With the usage of 1TX-3RX antennas, the total number of the CSI stream sub-carriers is 90. All the networks are implemented by Pytorch. If not specified, the following results are evaluated with the ratio of training and testing data set as 8:2 by random allocation.

4.2 Experimental Results

The Performance of Our Method. As illustrated in Fig. 6, our TS-Net can reach 98% and 94% at lab and meeting L1. In addition, our TS-Net can achieve 92% and 84% recognition accuracy at L2 of both lab and meeting scenes. As we expected, the accuracy is dramatically reduced after transferring the samples from L1 to L2. The location L1 is at the dominant path so that signal influences can be sensitively perceived and captured; however, actions at the deviated location L2 on signal changes are weakened. Besides, the size of meeting is relatively small and crowd which may lead to more strong multi-path effects and poor recognition performance than the lab scene. Especially, the meeting L2 dataset is collected at the place next to a wall. Compared with 88% and 78% at lab and meeting L2 by the original WiFi network, the performance has been improved to some extent (namely 4% and 6% improvement) by TS-Net.

Comparative Studies. In order to investigate the superiority of our approach, we conduct a series of baseline experiments under different sets.

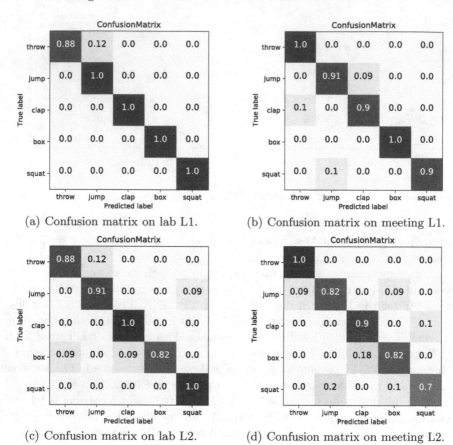

(a) Confusion matrix on lab L1.   (b) Confusion matrix on meeting L1.

(c) Confusion matrix on lab L2.   (d) Confusion matrix on meeting L2.

Fig. 6. Recognition results at L1 and L2 of two scenarios.

- **Vision_only.** The accuracy is obtained by testing RGB videos with the trained C3D model.
- **WiFi_only.** The performance is achieved by the original 2D CNN framework for only CSI streams as the input.
- **WiVi.** As the reference work [12], features of vision and CSI streams are concatenated with deep neural network (DNN) followed for classification.
- **Our TS-Net.** The entire process follows our proposed flowchart in which the softmax layer of C3D vision network in addition to sample labels are used to supervise the CSI wireless network learning.

Specifically, we take the lab data for example and list the experimental results of baselines on sensing objects at multiple locations in Fig. 7(a). As for position L1 of lab scene, both vision_only and WiFi_only can reach satisfactory results 97% and 96% under ideal light conditions. Further, the performance can be improved to nearly 100% by using WiVi or our TS-Net to combine the two

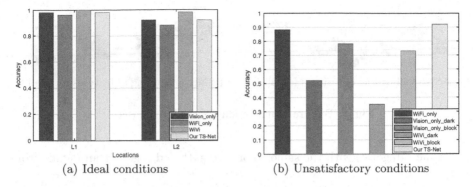

(a) Ideal conditions   (b) Unsatisfactory conditions

Fig. 7. (a) The performances on lab data collected at two locations under ideal conditions. (b) The comparative results at lab L2 under unsatisfactory conditions. "*_dark" and "*_block" are respectively denoted as poor light or occlusion conditions.

modality information. The phenomenon indicates that mining complementary content of vision and WiFi is beneficial for accuracy improvement.

When the sensing object stands at L2 with 1m distance from LOS path, WiFi_only accuracy drops to 88% with little impact on vision_only stream. It mainly because location between sensing objects and devices has a lower influence on vision than WiFi. As for the wireless signals, the fluctuations in CSI amplitudes may be reduced when standing far way from the WiFi receiver. However, the performance can be increased to 92% after using teacher-student model TS-Net. Although our TS-Net accuracy is inferior to WiVi around 100%, it doesn't rely on visual information during the test stage which extends the application scenario and raises the efficiency of the on-the-fly recognition.

Evaluation Under Unsatisfactory Conditions. Further, we simulate the unsatisfactory scenes such as poor illumination and occlusion and evaluate the performances of trained models learned by above baseline methods. As illustrated in Fig. 7(b), the recognition rate of vision modality and WiVi drop dramatically under poor illumination or occlusion conditions. It mainly because the vision flow fails to capture sufficient and effective information in these scenarios. Owning to independence on the vision stream during the test stage, our TS-Net performance is much better than WiVi.

Computation Cost. We conduct the experiments under the Pycharm environment on a machine with GPU GTX1080 Ti. The average consumption time on recognizing a testing sample is separately 0.029 s and 0.012 s by WiVi and TS-Net after loading the trained models of lab L2. With only WiFi inputs, the operation time of TS-Net is reduced by half and computation resources are largely saved.

Visualization. We apply a two dimensional t-SNE embedding to qualitatively visualize lab features learned by our TS-Net. The features are extracted from the fc3 layer of TS-Net supervised by the vision modality. The visualization in Fig. 8 suggests that the learned features can capture some semantic information.

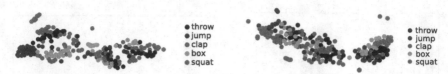

(a) t-SNE embedding of features for lab L1.(b) t-SNE embedding of features for lab L2.

Fig. 8. Feature visualization for the lab dataset.

The same categories with the same colors are gathered together and apart from other classes.

5   Conclusion

In this paper, we propose a unified cross-model supervision structure TS-Net for device-free action recognition. Compared with existing works, we train deep CSI networks by transferring knowledge from the established vision network into WiFi signals. Thus abundant features of teacher RGB videos are delivered to the student wireless stream during the training stage. Meanwhile, the computation efficiency and high accuracy under poor lightness or severe occlusion can be guaranteed due to independence on vision information during test. The experimental evaluations demonstrate the effectiveness and environment adaptation capacity of TS-Net.

Acknowledgement. This work is supported by National Natural Science Foundation of China under Grant No. 61932013, 61803212, 61972201, 61972210, Natural Science Foundation of Jiangsu Province under Grant No. BK20180744, BK20190068, China Postdoctoral Science Foundation under Grant No. 2019M651920, 2020T130315, and NUPTSF Grant No. NY218117.

References

1. Jiang, W., et al.: Towards 3D human pose construction using WiFi. In: Proceedings of Mobile Computing and Networking, pp. 1–14 (2020)
2. Wang, W., Liu, A.X., Shahzad, M., Ling, K., Lu, S.: Understanding and modeling of WiFi signal based human activity recognition. In: Proceedings of Mobile Computing and Networking, pp. 65–76. ACM (2015)
3. Yousefi, S., Narui, H., Dayal, S., Ermon, S., Valaee, S.: A survey on behavior recognition using WiFi channel state information. IEEE Commun. Mag. **55**(10), 98–104 (2017)
4. Yang, Z., Zhou, Z., Liu, Y.: From RSSI to CSI: indoor localization via channel response. ACM Comput. Surv. (CSUR) **46**(2), 1–32 (2013)
5. Hinton, G., Vinyals, O., Dean, J.: Distilling the knowledge in a neural network. In: NIPS Deep Learning and Representation Learning Workshop, pp. 1–9 (2015)
6. Tran, D., Bourdev, L., Fergus, R., Torresani, L., Paluri, M.: Learning spatiotemporal features with 3D convolutional networks. In: Proceedings of the IEEE International Conference on Computer Vision, pp. 4489–4497 (2015)

7. Soomro, K., Zamir, A.R., Shah, M.: UCF101: a dataset of 101 human actions classes from videos in the wild. arXiv preprint arXiv:1212.0402 (2012)

8. Wang, F., Song, Y., Zhang, J., Han, J., Huang, D.: Temporal Unet: sample level human action recognition using WiFi. arXiv preprint arXiv:1904.11953 (2019)

9. Zheng, Y., et al.: Zero-effort cross-domain gesture recognition with Wi-Fi. In: Proceedings of the International Conference on Mobile Systems, Applications, and Services, pp. 313–325 (2019)

10. Li, C., Liu, M., Cao, Z.: WiHF: enable user identified gesture recognition with WiFi. In: IEEE Conference on Computer Communications (INFOCOM), pp. 586–595 (2020)

11. Yao, S., et al.: STFNets: learning sensing signals from the time-frequency perspective with short-time Fourier neural networks. In: The World Wide Web Conference, pp. 2192–2202 (2019)

12. Zou, H., Yang, J., Das, H.P., Liu, H., Zhou, Y., Spanos, C.J.: WiFi and vision multimodal learning for accurate and robust device-free human activity recognition. In: 2019 IEEE/CVF Conference on Computer Vision and Pattern Recognition Workshops (CVPRW), pp. 426–433 (2019)

13. Zhao, M., et al.: Through-wall human pose estimation using radio signals. In: Proceedings of the IEEE Conference on Computer Vision and Pattern Recognition, pp. 7356–7365 (2018)

14. Korany, B., Karanam, C.R., Cai, H., Mostofi, Y.: XMODAL-ID: using WiFi for through-wall person identification from candidate video footage. In: The 25th Annual International Conference on Mobile Computing and Networking, pp. 1–15 (2019)

15. Wang, F., Zhou, S., Panev, S., Han, J., Huang, D.: Person-in-WiFi: fine-grained person perception using WiFi. In: Proceedings of the IEEE International Conference on Computer Vision, pp. 5452–5461 (2019)

16. Xue, H., et al.: DeepFusion: a deep learning framework for the fusion of heterogeneous sensory data. In: Proceedings of the Twentieth ACM International Symposium on Mobile Ad Hoc Networking and Computing, pp. 151–160 (2019)

17. Xue, H., et al.: DeepMV: multi-view deep learning for device-free human activity recognition. Proc. ACM Interact. Mob. Wearable Ubiquitous Technol. 4(1), 1–26 (2020)

18. Chen, Z., Zhang, L., Jiang, C., Cao, Z., Cui, W.: WiFi CSI based passive human activity recognition using attention based BLSTM. IEEE Trans. Mob. Comput. 18(11), 2714–2724 (2018)

19. Halperin, D., Hu, W., Sheth, A., Wetherall, D.: Tool release: gathering 802.11 n traces with channel state information. ACM SIGCOMM Comput. Commun. Rev. 41(1), 53 (2011)

A Priority Task Offloading Scheme Based on Coherent Beamforming and Successive Interference Cancellation for Edge Computing

Zhehao Li, Lei Shi[✉], Xu Ding, Yuqi Fan, and Juan Xu

School of Computer Science and Information Engineering,
Intelligent Interconnected Systems Laboratory of Anhui Procince,
Hefei University of Technology, Hefei 230009, China
shilei@hfut.edu.cn

Abstract. In edge computing environment, edge servers are generally more closer to edge devices which can guarantee time sensitive tasks be completed under their strict requirements. However, with the rapid increase of edge devices and the limited computing resources of edge servers, this guarantee is becoming more and more difficult. In this paper, by using two physical layer techniques, we try to give communication tasks more opportunities for executing under edge computing environment. In specific words, we propose a priority task scheduling scheme based on coherent beamforming (CB) technique and successive interference cancellation(SIC) technique. CB technique give edge devices the chance to be transmitted to distant edge servers, and SIC technique give communication tasks more chance to be received by edge servers. However, these two techniques need some strict conditions for realizing, and if we consider the computing work and the communicating work simultaneously, the problem will become very complex. We first build the system model and analyze it, and show the model a NP-hard problem and cannot be solved directly. Then in our algorithm, we first determine the task transmission of each time slot in turn, and set the fitness threshold so that each task can select the most suitable edge server. After tasks arrive at servers, we insert them into task queues according to their priorities. In simulations, we compare our scheme with other three schemes. Simulation results show that our scheme can improve the task completion rate and reduce completion delay.

Keywords: Edge computing · Task offloading · Coherent beamforming · Successive interference cancellation

Supported by the National Natural Science Foundation of China (Grant No. 61806067), the Anhui Provincial Key R&D Program of China (202004a05020040).

Z. Liu et al. (Eds.): WASA 2021, LNCS 12937, pp. 416–428, 2021.
https://doi.org/10.1007/978-3-030-85928-2_33

1   Introduction

Comparing with the cloud computing [1], in the edge computing structure [2,3], servers are positioned at the edge of the network, which can greatly reduce the distances between edge devices and edge servers [4]. In this way, if edge devices need to unload tasks to servers for computing, there is no need for long-distance transmissions [5]. This will reduce the transmission delay [6] and improve the quality of service [7,8]. However, unlike cloud servers, edge servers usually have limited power. Meanwhile many application tasks are time sensitive and must be completed within specified times [9]. Therefore, when the number of tasks is large, a single edge server may not be able to ensure all tasks completed within the specified time. In this case, the server usually migrates tasks to other edge servers for computing [10,11]. But this will increase the task executing cost, especially for the edge computing environment with 5G techniques [12]. Since the 5G base station has a small coverage compared with the 4G's.

The coherent beamforming (CB) technique is one kind of cooperative communication technologies which are usually used on the transmitters. In [13], authors use distributed coherent communication techniques to enable extended-range communications. In [14], authors proposed a CB technique scheme with minimum transmitting power for multi-input-single-output (MISO) communication with limited rate feedback. In [15], for long-distance communication, the author proposes a distributed optimization solution based on CB technique, which significantly improves the network performance. In [16], authors derive an approximation of the coverage probability of the CB scheme by leveraging two scaling factor. This means that edge devices can directly transmit tasks to distant targets and avoid transmission delay. In this way, we can directly transfer tasks to edge servers with sufficient computing resources.

Unlike the CB technique, the successive interference cancellation (SIC) technique is used on the receivers. Since in the edge computing environment, many edge devices may transmit simultaneously and these may cause lots of interference. By using SIC technique, edge server can accept multiple signals at the same time, and decode the signals in turn according to the signal-to-noise ratio(SINR). In [17], authors propose a heuristic algorithm and use SIC to obtain a bandwidth sensitive high throughput protocol. In [18], authors propose a cross-layer optimization framework for SIC that incorporates variables at physical, link, and network layers, and prove the validity of this framework. In [19], authors proposed a neighbor discovery algorithm based on SIC technique.

In this paper, we combine CB and SIC technique, and apply it to the task offloading in edge computing environment. Because there will be multiple tasks in the server at the same time, the newly arrived task is unlikely executed immediately. These tasks will be stored in the server's task queues [20]. Therefore, it is extremely important to select a suitable position for the task in the queue. Many researchers build task queues based on the order in which tasks arrive at the server, and we will choose the appropriate position of new arrival tasks in the queue according to the task priority. The main work of this paper as follow: (1) In a two-dimensional network with multiple nodes and servers, we use CB technique at transmitter and SIC technique at receiver. We select the appropriate processing server for each task. (2) In edge server, we build the queue according to the actual situation of task. Our goal is try to make all the tasks done within the specified time.

The rest of this paper is organized as follows: In Sect. 2, we build the system model. In Sect. 3, we design a scheduling algorithm according to the model and try to get a feasible solution. In Sect. 4, we give the simulation results in different environments and analyze them. In Sect. 5, we summarize the whole paper.

2   System Model

Consider an edge computing network is consisted with m edge servers and u edge devices in a two-dimensional area(see in Fig. 1). Define D as the set of edge devices and $d_i(d_i \in D, 1 \leqslant i \leqslant u)$ as one edge device. Suppose all devices have the same transmission power P. Define S as the set of edge servers and $s_j(s_j \in S, 1 \leqslant j \leqslant m)$ as one edge server. We divide the whole scheduling time T into h time slots, and denote $t_k(1 \leqslant k \leqslant h)$ as one time slot. Suppose edge devices will generate tasks randomly, and suppose all tasks need to be uploaded for calculating. Define V as the set of tasks and $v_{pi}[k](1 \leqslant p \leqslant n)$ as one task, where p means the task is the p-th task generated in the whole network, i and k indicate that the task is generated by edge device d_i in the time slot t_k.

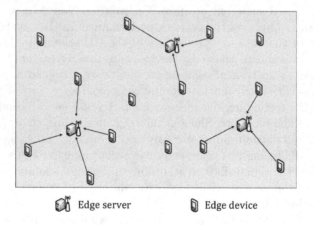

🖥 Edge server   📱 Edge device

Fig. 1. Edge servers, edge devices in the network

Define γ_p as the time of maximum completion delay, which means for each task, it should be completed within γ_p, or we think this task is a failure task. Suppose edge servers are heterogeneous, and they have different calculation capabilities. In this paper, we consider the impact of transmission interference on task offloading. Therefore, in order to reduce the delay of task transmission to the edge server, we use CB and SIC technique. Define T_p as the time consumed by task $v_{pi}[k]$. We have

$$T_p = T_u[p] + T_s[p] + T_c[p], \tag{1}$$

where $T_u[p]$ is the transmission time, $T_s[p]$ is the waiting time in task queue and $T_c[p]$ is the calculation time. In the following we will give these three times in order. We will first give some symbols for preparation, then give the expressions of these times.

Define $e_p(f)$ to indicate whether task $v_{pi}[k]$ is uploaded to a server, i.e.

$$e_p(f) = \begin{cases} 1 : \text{if task } v_{pi}[k] \text{ has been uploaded to server in time slot } t_f; \\ 0 : \text{otherwise.} \end{cases}$$

There are two steps for a transmission when using the CB technique. First, an edge device broadcasts its data to the surrounding devices. Second, multiple devices cooperate to transmit tasks to the server by CB technique. Define $x_p(f)$ and $y_p(f)$ to indicate the transmission states, then we have

$$x_p(f) = \begin{cases} 1 : \text{if the task } v_{pi}[k] \text{ is broadcasting at time slot } t_f; \\ 0 : \text{otherwise.} \end{cases}$$

$$y_p(f) = \begin{cases} 1 : \text{if the task } v_{pi}[k] \text{ is transmitting to an server at time slot } t_f; \\ 0 : \text{otherwise.} \end{cases}$$

Obviously, task $v_{pi}[k]$ can only be in one transmission state in the same time slot. For the convenience of representation, we think $x_i(f) = 0$ when not using CB technique. Therefore, we have

$$x_p(f) + y_p(f) \leqslant 1 \quad (1 \leqslant f \leqslant h). \tag{2}$$

When using the SIC technique, edge servers may receive signals at the same time if the SINR requirement is satisfied. Define β as the SINR threshold. When task $v_{pi}[k]$ is uploaded to edge sever s_j, we have

$$SINR^k_{p \to s_j} \cdot y_p(f) = \frac{P_{p,s_j} \cdot y_p(f)}{N_0 + \sum\limits_{\substack{p \geq q \\ P_p \neq P_q}} P_{q,s_j} \cdot y_q(f)} \geqslant \beta \cdot y_p(f), \tag{3}$$

where N_0 is the noise power and P_{p,s_j} is the transmission power of the task $v_{pi}[k]$ to s_j. For P_{p,s_j}, if CB technique is not used for transmitting, we have $P_{p,s_j} = (h_{i,s_j})^2 P$, and if CB technique is used, we have $P_{p,s_j} = (\sum_{d_g \in D_i(f)} h_{g,j})^2 P$, where $(h_{g,s_j})^2$ is the channel gain between the edge device d_g and the edge server s_j, and $D_i(f)$ is the set of edge devices assisting the transmission of device d_i by CB technique at time slot t_f.

When d_i broadcasts task $v_{pi}[k]$ to the surrounding devices for preparing the CB transmission, it also needs to meet the SINR requirement. Otherwise, there will be interference and the broadcasting can not be carried out smoothly. So we have

$$SINR^k_{p \to D_i(f)} \cdot x_p(f) = \frac{(h_{p,d_g})^2 P \cdot x_p(f)}{N_0 + \sum\limits_{\substack{p \geq l \\ P_p \neq P_l}} (h_{l,d_g})^2 P \cdot x_l(f) + \sum\limits_{\substack{p \geq q \\ P_p \neq P_q}} P_{q,d_g} \cdot y_q(f)} \tag{4}$$

$$\geqslant \beta \cdot x_p(f) \quad (d_g \in D_i(f)).$$

According to Shannon formula, we can get the broadcast transmission rate and the CB transmission rate. We have

$$r_{p \to D_i}(f) = r_{p \to s_j} = W log_2(1 + \beta). \tag{5}$$

Now we give the formula of the first time $T_u[p]$. Notice that when $v_{pi}[k]$ is being uploaded and if CB technique is used, the transmission time can be divided into three parts. One, waiting time $t_w[p]$ for other's broadcasting or CB transmitting. Two, broadcasting time $t_b[p]$. Three, CB transmitting time $t_c[p]$; Define $\mathcal{R}_p$ as the amount of data for the task $v_{pi}[k]$. For $t_b[p]$ and $t_c[p]$, we have

$$\begin{cases} t_b[p] = \dfrac{\mathcal{R}_p}{r_{p \to D_i}(f)}, \\ t_c[p] = \dfrac{\mathcal{R}_p}{r_{p \to s_j}}. \end{cases} \tag{6}$$

For $t_w[p]$, we can further divide it into two parts. The first part is the waiting time for other's broadcasting. The second part is the waiting time for other's CB transmitting. So we have

$$t_w[p] = \sum_{l=0}^{h}((1 - x_p(l)) \cdot (1 - e_p(l))) \cdot \tau + \sum_{l=0}^{h}((1 - y_p(l)) \cdot (1 - e_p(l))) \cdot \tau, \tag{7}$$

where τ is the length of a time slot. Then we can express $T_u[p]$ as

$$T_u[p] = t_b[p] + t_c[p] + t_w[p]. \tag{8}$$

For the second time $T_s[p]$, we know after a new task $v_{pi}[k]$ arrives at the server, it will be put into the server's task queue. The position in the queue is determined according to the priority of the task. Define $z_{p,j}(f)$ as

$$z_{p,j}(f) = \begin{cases} 1 : f \geqslant \frac{T_u[p]}{t} + k \\ 0 : \text{otherwise.} \end{cases}$$

Apparently if $z_{p,j}(f) = 1$, it means that task $v_{pi}[k]$ has arrived to s_j at t_f.

The waiting time $T_w[p]$ depends on $v_{pi}[k]$'s position in the task queue. The higher the position in the queue, the shorter the waiting time. We set a priority variable $\omega_p(f)$ for task $v_{pi}[k]$ in time slot t_f. The priority is affected by the remaining completion time. So in different time slots, the value of priority is different. When the priority of task is higher, its position in the queue is higher. At the same time, tasks that have arrived at edge server and have been completed before the time slot t_f must not exist in the queue. Define $fun_j(\mathcal{D}_p)$ as a function of the time taken by the task $v_{pi}[k]$ to calculate on s_j. Define $\mathcal{D}_l$ as calculation amount. Therefore, for the waiting time $T_w[p]$ of task $v_{pi}[k]$ in the queue, we have

$$T_s[p] = \sum_{\omega_l(f) > \omega_p(f)} \left(\sum_{\frac{T_l}{t} + k \leqslant f} fun_j(\mathcal{D}_l) \cdot z_{p,j}(f) \right), \tag{9}$$

where T_l is the time taken for task $v_{li}[k]$ to complete.

Now we give the expression of the third time $T_c[p]$. $T_c[p]$ can be expressed as

$$T_c[p] = fun_j(\mathcal{D}_p). \tag{10}$$

Define γ_p as the maximum completion delay of task $v_{pi}[k]$. If the time $T_p \leq \gamma_p$, we think $v_{pi}[k]$ is handled successful. Define N_c as the set of all successful tasks. Our optimization goal is to maximize the task completion rate C. We have

$$\begin{aligned}
\max \quad & C \\
\text{s.t.} \quad & C = \frac{|N_c|}{n} \\
& v_{pi}[k] \in N_c, \quad (T_p \leqslant \gamma_p) \\
& (1), (2), (3), (4), (5), (6), (7), (8), (9), (10).
\end{aligned} \tag{11}$$

In Eq. (11), variables such as $x_p(f)$, $y_p(f)$, $e_p(f)$ and $z_{p,j}(f)$ determine the time T_p taken to complete task $v_{pi}[k]$. The value of $e_p(f)$, $z_{p,j}(f)$ is affected by $x_p(f)$ and $y_p(f)$. If the values of $x_p(f)$, $y_p(f)$ can be determined, $e_p(f)$, $z_{p,j}(f)$ can be determined, the problem can be solved. But it's very difficult. The $x_p(f)$, $y_p(f)$ of these tasks cannot be determined directly. Therefore, it is difficult to determine the value of $e_p(f)$, $z_{p,j}(f)$ in each time slot. The queue condition on the edge server is also difficult to determine. This kind of problem is NP-hard and cannot be solved directly. Therefore, we design a heuristic algorithm, hoping to get a feasible solution.

3   Scheduling Algorithm

As Eq. (11) is NP-hard and can not be solved directly, we need to take other strategies to solve this problem. If we can determine the values of $x_p(f)$, $y_p(f)$, $e_p(f)$ and $z_{p,j}(f)$, the model can be solved. However, it is very difficult to get the values of these variables. We have three problems: (1) Which task is calculated on which server? (2) When is the task transferred? (3) How long does it take for a task to arrive at the server?

To solve these problems, variables can be determined. Therefore, we design a heuristic algorithm to solve these problem and determine variables in the Eq. (11), so as to get the solution of the model. Through the analysis of the model, we divide the whole algorithm into three steps: (1) Edge server selection; (2) Task transmission; (3) Build task queue. Next, we will introduce these three steps in detail.

3.1   Edge Server Selection

We now discuss the Edge Server Selection algorithm. Since there are multiple edge servers in the whole network, we need to select a suitable server for each task to perform its calculation. We first define a variable $\alpha_{pj}(f)$ to indicate the fitness of the edge server s_j for the task $v_{pi}[k]$. We have

$$\alpha_{pj}(f) = \frac{\gamma_p(f) - \sum_{v_{li}[k] \in M_j(f)} T_l}{T_c[p]}, \tag{12}$$

where $M_j(f)$ is the set of tasks on the s_j at t_f, $\gamma_p(f)$ is the remaining completion time of $v_{pi}[k]$ at t_f.

We will calculate $\alpha_{pj}(f)$ in each time slot for all tasks which have not yet transmitted to servers, and then select the most fitness server based on the following rules.

One, confirm that the selected edge server is in the transmission range of the now considered edge device. Notice that in our network, even when using CB technique, for some edge devices, some servers may not be reached. This transmissions should be excluded first.

Two, $\alpha_{pj}(f) > \alpha$, where α is a fitness threshold.

Three, if for a task there exists some servers can be reached directly, i.e., not using CB technique, we will selected the closest one for this task. Otherwise, we will select the one with the largest $\alpha_j(f)$ value for this task. Since comparing with direct transmitting, CB technique will cause more interference and will lead a complexity transmission. So we have this rule.

According to the above three rules, we can select the target edge server for each task. We have Algorithm 1.

Algorithm 1: Edge Server Selection

Input: the set of task V, the set of server S, fitness threshold α,
$\quad\quad M_j(f)(1 \leqslant j \leqslant m)$.
Output: Task's corresponding edge server $E[v, s]$
1 **for** *every server s_j in S* **do**
2 $\quad$ **for** *every task $v_{li}[k]$ in $M_j(f)$* **do**
3 $\quad\quad$ | get $\sum_{v_{li}[k] \in M_j(f)} T_l$
4 $\quad$ **end**
5 **end**
6 **for** *every task $v_{pi}[k]$ in V* **do**
7 $\quad$ $flag1 \leftarrow 0, flag2 \leftarrow 0;$
8 $\quad$ **if** *the task needs to select a server* **then**
9 $\quad\quad$ **for** *every server s_j in single-hop range* **do**
10 $\quad\quad\quad$ | find a server with biggest $\alpha_{pj}(f)$ and $\alpha_{pj}(f) > \alpha;$
11 $\quad\quad$ **end**
12 $\quad$ **end**
13 $\quad$ **if** *there is no suitable server in single-hop range* **then**
14 $\quad\quad$ **for** *every server s_j not in single-hop range* **do**
15 $\quad\quad\quad$ | find a nearest server with $\alpha_{pj}(f) > \alpha;$
16 $\quad\quad$ **end**
17 $\quad$ **end**
18 $\quad$ **if** *flag1=0,flag2=0* **then**
19 $\quad\quad$ | find nearest *server s_j; $E[v, s] \leftarrow v_{pi}[k], s_j;$*
20 $\quad$ **end**
21 **end**

3.2   Task Transmission

For the first step, we have confirmed edge servers for all tasks at current time slot. However, even using SIC technique, we can not realize all tasks be transmitted without interference. So in this step, we will decide which tasks will really be transmitted at current time slot, i.e., the Task Transmission algorithm. The main step of the Task Transmission algorithm is as following.

One, based on the remaining completion time $\gamma_p(f)$, sort all tasks from the smallest to the largest and get a task queue.

Two, check the task queue one by one, and based on SIC technique, decide the first transmitted task for each server. We give some explanations. Notice that the first task in the queue can be decided directly. Then for the second task, there may have three situations. First, the selected server is the same with the first one, then we skip this task and continue to check the following tasks. Two, the selected server is not the same with the first one, but this task will interference the first one even when using SIC, i.e., Eq. (3) or (4) will not be satisfied after adding this task, then we skip this task and continue to check the following tasks. Three, the selected server is not the same and this task will not interference with the first one, then we can decide this task. We will do it until all tasks in the queue have been checked.

Three, check the task queue again, and decide more transmitted tasks. In this step we will try to check the tasks in the queue which have not be decided again, and check if Eq. (3) or (4) can be satisfied when the task is added. If it can be satisfied, we will decide the task.

The detail steps can be found in Algorithm 2.

Algorithm 2: Task Transmission

Input: Task's corresponding edge server $E[v, s]$, the set of task V, the set of edge server S

Output: Updated task status

1   **for** *every unfinished transfer task* $v_{pi}[k]$ **do**
2   find a task $v_{pi}[k]$ with the least $\gamma_p(f)$;
3   find the corresponding server s_j in E[v,s];
4   transfer task $v_{pi}[k]$ to s_j;
5   **for** *every server in* S **do**
6   **if** *No tasks are transferred to the server* s_j **then**
7   find a task $v_{pi}[k]$ with the least $\gamma_p(f)$;
8         $v_{pi}[k], s_j$ in $E[v, s]$;
9   If there is no interference, transfer the task;
10   **end**
11   **end**
12 **end**
13 **for** *every unfinished transfer task* $v_{pi}[k]$ **do**
14   find the corresponding server in E[v,s];
15   If there is no interference, transfer the task;
16 **end**

3.3 Build Task Queue

Each time when a new task reaches to a server, instead of putting the task to the tail of the task queue directly, we want to give an algorithm to decide the suitable position in the queue, i.e., the Task Queue algorithm. To do that, denote a priority value $\omega_p(f)$ for task $v_{pi}[k]$ at time slot t_f, we have

$$\omega_p(f) = \frac{T_c[p]}{\gamma_p(f)}. \tag{13}$$

We will calculate each $\omega_p(f)$, and sort them from the largest to the smallest, then get a new queue. The detail steps can be seen in Algorithm 3.

Algorithm 3: Task queue update

Input: the set of task V, the set of edge server S, $M_j(f)(1 \leqslant j \leqslant m)$
Output: Task queue after update

1 **for** *every server in S* **do**
2   find the first task $v_{li}[k]$ in task queue;
3   calculates the first task $v_{li}[k]$;
4   **if** *the $v_{li}[k]$ is completed* **then**
5 | remove this task from the task queue; $M_j(f) \rightarrow v_{li}[k]$;
6   **end**
7 **end**
8 **for** *every server in S* **do**
9   **for** *every task $v_{pi}[k]$ arrived at the server* **do**
10 | $\omega_p(f) = \frac{T_p}{\gamma_p(f)}$;
11 | find the right location according to $\omega_p(f)$;
12 | insert task $v_{pi}[k]$ into task queue; $M_j(f) \leftarrow v_{pi}[k]$;
13 **end**
14 **end**

---

4 Simulation Result

In this section, we give simulation results. Consider 3 edge servers and 20 edge devices deployed randomly in a 1000 m × 1000 m square area. Edge devices generate tasks randomly at different time slots. The whole time T is divided into 100 time slots. For these 3 edge servers, we set the processing speed is 3 GHz, 4 GHz and 5 GHz, respectively. For edge devices, we set transmission power $P = 1$ W. For tasks, we set the range of data amount $\mathcal{R}_p$ from 1 and 3 MB, and the maximum completion delay γ_p from 25 and 30 timeslots. We set $N_0 = 10^{-15}$ W, $\beta = 1$ and $W = 1$ GHz. In the following we will first analyze the influence of fitness threshold α on the experimental results, and then compare our CB-SIC PRO scheduling scheme with CB-FIFO PRO, SIC PRO and SIC FIFO scheme in the same environment.

4.1   The Effect of Fitness Threshold α

In order to show the effect of the threshold α to the task completion rate and completion delay in different environments, we adjust the generated number of tasks randomly in the network. The number of tasks was 40, 50, 60 and 70 respectively. We first carry out the experiment according to CB-SIC PRO scheme. The experimental results are shown in the Fig. 2.

We can see that the change of α has a significant impact on the experimental results. In Fig. 2(a), we show the change of task completion rate under different α. We can see that when the number of tasks is 40, with the gradual increase of α, the task completion rate first rises slowly, then gradually decreases, and finally remains unchanged. When the $\alpha = 0$, the task completion rate is 98.2%. When the $\alpha = 14$, the task completion rate reaches 100%. It begins to decrease when the $\alpha = 22$. When the task completion rate drops to 98.2%, it remains unchanged. When the task number is 40, the completion rate remains at a high level, so the effect of α is not very obvious. With the increase of the task number, we can see that the fitness threshold α has a great impact on the task completion rate. Especially when the task number is 60, the lowest task completion rate is 79.1% while the highest is 94.8%. There is a 15.7% gap in task completion rate.

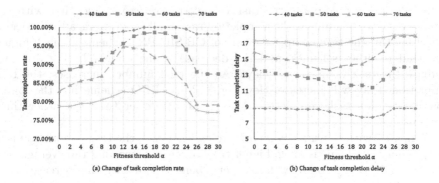

(a) Change of task completion rate   (b) Change of task completion delay

Fig. 2. The effect of the threshold α on the CB-SIC PRO scheme

We can also find that although the completion delay has a similar performance from Fig. 2(b). No matter how the number of tasks in the network changes, the task completion delay will first decrease, then slowly increase and finally remain unchanged with the increase of the threshold.

4.2   Comparison of Experimental Results

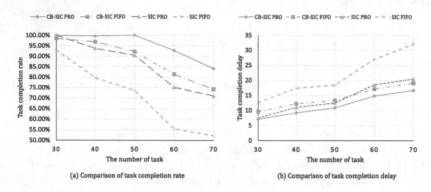

(a) Comparison of task completion rate   (b) Comparison of task completion delay

Fig. 3. Comparison of task completion rate

In Sect. 4.1, we find that when the fitness threshold $\alpha = 18$, CB-SIC PRO scheme can achieve good task completion rate and delay. Therefore, we set $\alpha = 18$ to carry out the following experiments. We generated the number of tasks randomly from 30 to 70, with the step 10. We get the change of task completion rate with different task number, and compare it with other schemes including CB-SIC FIFO, SIC FIFO and SIC PRO. The experimental results are shown in the Fig. 3.

In Fig. 3(a), we compare the task completion rate. We find that with the increase of the task number, the completion rate of all programs gradually begins to decline. But the task completion rate of CB-SIC PRO scheme is much higher than that of other schemes, and the decrease is the lowest. In Fig. 3(b), we compare the task completion delays. As the task number increases, the task completion delay will increase. However, CB-SIC PRO scheme has the lowest growth rate. It's task completion delay is always lower than the other three scheme.

Compared with the three comparative experiments, the task completion rate of our proposed scheme is much higher than other schemes, and the average task completion delay is also lower than other schemes. And with the increase of the number of tasks, the gap will become more and more obvious.

5   Conclusion

In this paper, a priority scheduling scheme is designed to improve the task completion rate for edge computing based on CB and SIC technique. When the computing resources of the nearest edge server are insufficient, edge devices can directly transfer tasks to remote idle edge server for computing. We first build a mathematical model according to the network structure. However, this model is NP-hard, which is difficult to solve directly. Therefore, we analyze the model and design a heuristic algorithm. In order to enable the task to be unloaded to a suitable edge server, we set the fitness threshold α and calculate the value of $\alpha_{pj}(f)$. We sort the task queue in edge server according to the task priority. In simulation experiments, we first show and analyze the influence of fitness threshold α. The results show that the task completion rate and completion delay will change with the change of α. Then the task completion rate and completion delay are compared. The results show that compared with other schemes, CB-SIC PRO scheme significantly improves the task completion rate and reduces the task completion delay.

References

1. Yu, L., Cai, Z.: Dynamic scaling of virtual clusters with bandwidth guarantee in cloud datacenters. In: IEEE INFOCOM 2016 - The 35th Annual IEEE International Conference on Computer Communications, pp. 1–9 (2016)
2. Xia, X., Chen, F., He, Q., Grundy, J.C., Abdelrazek, M., Jin, H.: Cost-effective app data distribution in edge computing. IEEE Trans. Parallel Distrib. Syst. **32**(1), 31–44 (2021)
3. Liu, Y., Li, Y., Niu, Y., Jin, D.: Joint optimization of path planning and resource allocation in mobile edge computing. IEEE Trans. Mobile Comput. **19**(9), 2129–2144 (2020)
4. Lin, L., Liao, X., Jin, H., Li, P.: Computation offloading toward edge computing. Proc. IEEE **107**(8), 1584–1607 (2019)
5. Dolui, K., Datta, S.K.: Comparison of edge computing implementations: fog computing, cloudlet and mobile edge computing. In: 2017 Global Internet of Things Summit (GIoTS), pp. 1–6 (2017)
6. Charyyev, B., Arslan, E., Gunes, M.H.: Latency comparison of cloud datacenters and edge servers. In: GLOBECOM 2020–2020 IEEE Global Communications Conference, pp. 1–6 (2020)
7. Wei, X., et al.: MVR: an architecture for computation offloading in mobile edge computing. In: 2017 IEEE International Conference on Edge Computing (EDGE), pp. 232–235 (2017)
8. Cai, Z., Shi, T.: Distributed query processing in the edge assisted IoT data monitoring system. IEEE Internet Things J. **7**(9), 1–1 (2020)
9. Zhu, T., Shi, T., Li, J., Cai, Z., Zhou, X.: Task scheduling in deadline-aware mobile edge computing systems. IEEE Internet Things J. **6**(3), 4854–4866 (2019)
10. Ding, Y., Liu, C., Li, K., Tang, Z., Li, K.: Task offloading and service migration strategies for user equipments with mobility consideration in mobile edge computing. In: 2019 IEEE International Conference on Parallel Distributed Processing with Applications, Big Data Cloud Computing, Sustainable Computing Communications, Social Computing Networking (ISPA/BDCloud/SocialCom/SustainCom), pp. 176–183 (2010)
11. Schäfer, D., Edinger, J., Breitbach, M., Becker, C.: Workload partitioning and task migration to reduce response times in heterogeneous computing environments. In: 2018 27th International Conference on Computer Communication and Networks (ICCCN), pp. 1–11 (2018)
12. Liu, Y., Peng, M., Shou, G., Chen, Y., Chen, S.: Toward edge intelligence: multi-access edge computing for 5g and internet of things. IEEE Internet Things J. **7**(8), 6722–6747 (2020)

13. Scherber, D., et al.: Coherent distributed techniques for tactical radio networks: enabling long range communications with reduced size, weight, power and cost. In: MILCOM 2013–2013 IEEE Military Communications Conference, pp. 655–660 (2013)
14. Marques, A.G., Wang, X., Giannakis, G.B.: Minimizing transmit power for coherent communications in wireless sensor networks with finite-rate feedback. IEEE Trans. Sig. Process. **56**(9), 4446–4457 (2008)
15. Shi, Y., Sagduyu, Y.E.: Coherent communications in self-organizing networks with distributed beamforming. IEEE Trans. Veh. Technol. **69**(1), 760–770 (2020)
16. Kong, J., Dagefu, F.T., Sadler, B.M.: Coverage analysis of distributed beamforming with random phase offsets using Ginibre point process. IEEE Access **8**, 134351–134362 (2020)
17. Liu, R., Shi, Y., Lui, K., Sheng, M., Wang, Y., Li, Y.: Bandwidth-aware high-throughput routing with successive interference cancelation in multihop wireless networks. IEEE Trans. Veh. Technol. **64**(12), 5866–5877 (2015)
18. Jiang, C., et al.: Cross-layer optimization for multi-hop wireless networks with successive interference cancellation. IEEE Trans. Wirel. Commun. **15**(8), 5819–5831 (2016)
19. Liang, Y., Wei, Z., Chen, Q., Wu, H.: Neighbor discovery algorithm in wireless ad hoc networks based on successive interference cancellation technology. In: 2020 International Conference on Wireless Communications and Signal Processing (WCSP), pp. 1137–1141 (2020)
20. Adhikari, M., Mukherjee, M., Srirama, S.N.: DPTO: a deadline and priority-aware task offloading in fog computing framework leveraging multilevel feedback queueing. IEEE Internet Things J. **7**(7), 5773–5782 (2020)

Dynamic Edge Computation Offloading and Scheduling for Model Task in Energy Capture Network

Xianzhong Tian(ID), Jialun Chen(✉)(ID), Zheng Zhao(ID), and Huixiao Meng(ID)

College of Computer Science and Technology, Zhejiang University of Technology,
Hangzhou, China
{txz,2111912145,2111912195}@zjut.edu.cn, menghx98@icloud.com

Abstract. As an emerging and promising technique, mobile edge computing (MEC) can significantly speed up the execution of tasks and save device energy by offloading the computation-intensive tasks from resource-constrained mobiles to the MEC servers. Besides, technological advances have promoted the emergence of novel applications task with a model framework. These model frameworks are indispensable and reusable: if the model task wants to execute on MEC, both the model and data need to offload; the model can store in the cache for the later execution of the same type of tasks. What's more, consider the limited capacity cache, it is a great challenge to replace the model dynamically to meet long-time requirements. In this paper, we jointly consider radio frequency (RF) energy capturing, computation offloading, and task scheduling in a multi-user cache-assisted MEC system. We formulate a replace algorithm and a global replacement scheduling algorithm (GRSA) to solve the mixed discrete-continuous optimization problem, which minimizes the total execution time subject to energy consumption and channel conflict. The simulation results show that our algorithm can effectively reduce computation latency.

Keywords: Mobile edge computing · Caching · Radio frequency energy capture · Task scheduling

1 Introduction

As we know, the time of 5G is coming, novel technology and applications are emerging. Despite the rapid development of central processors, user equipment still cannot meet the demand for computing-intensive applications with high real-time requirements. Mobile edge computing is an effective way to solve these problems by deploy computing and storage resources at the edge network to provide users with ultra-low latency and high computing power. Besides, the high energy consumption contradicts the limitation of device battery capacity, restricting the possibility that mobile devices deal with those applications alone. Scholars get an idea of capture energy from the environment to power some low-power devices. Therefore, the radio frequency energy capture network

Z. Liu et al. (Eds.): WASA 2021, LNCS 12937, pp. 429–440, 2021.
https://doi.org/10.1007/978-3-030-85928-2_34

(RF-EHN) emerges that nodes can capture energy from the radio frequency signals to maintain their long-term work.

Artificial intelligence, as a typical computing-intensive application, has been applied in image recognition, pattern recognition, natural language processing, and other fields. We found these application's tasks consist of two partitions: (1) Models, such as the framework and parameters of deep neural networks; (2) Data, such as an image of a recognized face. So, we call this kind of task a model task. Model tasks have these characteristics: (1) Indispensability. When the model task executes at the edge server, both the model and the data need offloading. Otherwise, the edge server does not know how to process the data. (2) Reusability. The same type of tasks has the same model, and the model can store in the cache for later execution. However, the cache capacity of the edge server is limited, it is impossible to save all the models, so some of them will be replaced out dynamically. Therefore, the offloading sequence of tasks will directly affect the content in the cache, thus affecting the efficiency of computation task offloading.

2 Related Work

As one of the core technologies of 5G [1], mobile edge computing is the technology to solve the deficiencies of devices in terms of resource storage, computation ability, and energy efficiency. The optimization objectives of offloading decisions are mainly in two categories: minimizing time delay and energy consumption. The literature [2] designed a computational offloading model to minimize the execution delay under energy consumption constraints. This model calculates transmission and computation time based on queuing theory, and it uses the Lyapunov method to make decisions using the current information of the system. Literature [3] investigates a scenario where multiple users share limited wireless channels and minimizes energy consumption.

Besides, wireless sensor networks have rapidly developed [2]. The author [4] proposes an RF charging station network architecture with three main components, i.e., information gateway, RF energy, and the network node. What's more, various modern beamforming technologies are focused on improving the efficiency of energy transformation in mobile devices [5–8]. The research of [9, 10] considering the impact of device battery on the offloading strategy. Regardless of local computing or task offloading to the MEC, the remaining battery energy must be sufficient.

Model tasks are different from common tasks: (1) Indispensability. In the literature [11], if mobile devices want to offload tasks to the server for calculation, the corresponding model must be existing in the server. IONN [12] proposed a partition-based offloading technology, which divides the DNN model into several partitions and offloads them to the edge server on demand. (2) Reusability. The literature [13] considers the results can be stored in the cache once calculated. There is no need to offloading again when the mobile device submits the same task. However, literature [12] doesn't consider the reusability of the model, and the literature [13] doesn't take the limited cache into account. In this paper, we will focus on these two features of the model task, and the user equipment will capture enough energy to calculate or offload. The models in the cache can replace dynamically according to the offloading sequences. Besides, we take the diversity of tasks into account. Even in the same type, the tasks require a different amount of computation.

3 System Model

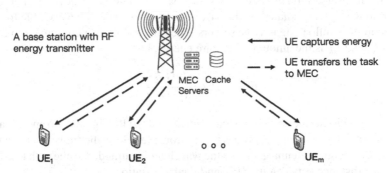

Fig. 1. System model of a single base station with multiple users

As illustrated in Fig. 1, we consider a multi-user cache-assisted MEC system with one base station and m single-antenna user equipment (*UE*), denoted by $\mathcal{M} \triangleq \{1, 2..., M\}$. The user equipment is equipped with an energy harvesting component and powered by the harvested energy from ambient RF signals. The base station contains RF emitters, MEC servers, and a cache that can store some models. The base station and the user equipment have only one antenna, so the number of channels is limited. At the same time, they can only broadcast (receive) radio frequency energy or receive (transmit) a task. All user equipment captures energy from RF signals radiated by the base station and then utilizes the energy to complete their tasks. Due to the model's repeatability and reusability, we need to make a scheduling scheme with the limited cache capacity. More details will be discussed in Sect. 4. Note that we assume the base station can observe all information. For ease of reference, we list the key notation of our system model in Table 1.

Table 1. Summary of key notations

Notation	Description
t_e	The time for user equipment to harvesting energy
E_k	Harvested energy by user equipment k
W_n	Model size of task type n
S_n^k	User equipment k generates a computation task of S bits and type of n
l_z	The user equipment's task is the z-th offloading
$X_n(z)$	Whether the model n cached when the base station receives the z-th task
f_k^l	Scheduled CPU-cycle frequencies of user equipment k for local execution
p^{tr}	Transmit power for computation offloading
$t_k^l (t_k^{mec})$	Execution delay of local (MEC server) execution for user equipment k
$e_k^l (e_k^{mec})$	Energy consumption of local (MEC server) execution for user equipment k
$T^l (T^{mec})$	Execution delay of local execution (MEC server execution)
x_k	Offloading decision of user equipment k
C	The capacity of the cache

3.1 Energy Capture Model

We assume the user equipment does not have a backup battery, so they must harvest the energy from RF signals radiated by the base station at first. It will be available for either local execution or offloading to edge servers. The time for all user equipment to capture energy is t_e, and E_k is the amount of capture energy, i.e.,

$$E_k = \eta P_b t_e \frac{G_T G_R \lambda^2}{(4\pi d_k)^2 L} \tag{1}$$

where $\eta \in (0, 1)$ is the energy conversion efficiency of the RF signals into energy, and P_b is the fixed transmit power by RF transmitter. Moreover, G_T is the transmission antenna gain, G_R is the receive antenna gain, λ is the wavelength emitted, L is the path loss factor, and d_k is the distance between the UE_k and the base station.

3.2 Task Model

In this paper, we consider N types of tasks. Each one is described by two parameters (W_n, S_n^k), n is the task type, $n \in \mathcal{N} \triangleq \{1, 2, \ldots, N\}$, k is the user equipment number. The W_n is the size of the model (in bits) and S_n^k is the size of the task (in bits). Additionally, the size of the task data follows a random distribution. Besides, considering the processing speed of computation tasks is different, we use J_n^k to represent the number of CPU cycles required to execute a 1 bit task of type n locally. Like image processing tasks on the device with the GPU run faster, we use K_n as the number of CPU cycles required for the edge server to execute a 1bit task of type n respective.

Due to the particularity of model tasks, user equipment needs to offload the model and the data together when they decide to offload the computation task to the MEC server for calculation. And the model cached in the base station is reusable for the later execution of the same type. Note that W_n, J_n^k, K_n are determined by model and user equipment, those can be estimated to a certain extent based on some prior measurements. The task model in this paper can be extended to a more general scenario by setting $W_n = 0$ for some tasks that do not require a model.

3.3 Caching and Offloading Model

Cache Model. The base station equips with a cache of size C (in bits), and it can make use of the reusable characteristics of the model task. Let $X_n(z) \in \{0, 1\}$ be a binary decision variable to denote whether the model type of n is cached or not when the base station receives the z-th task. When $X_n(z) = 0$ means the model of n is cached, and $X_n(z) = 1$ otherwise. Therefore, under the cache size constraint at the base station, we have

$$\sum_{p=1}^{N} W_p(1 - X_p(z)) \leq C, z \in \mathcal{Z} \tag{2}$$

Offloading Model. After the user equipment has captured the energy, the base station needs to decide the user equipment's tasks that are execute locally or offload to the MEC serve. Let x_k denote the offloading decision of UE_k, where $x_k \in \{0, 1\}$. Here $x_k = 1$ and $x_k = 0$ indicate that the computation task of user equipment k is offloading to the MEC server and executing at local. Thus, the offloading mode indicators should satisfy the following operation constraint:

$$x_k \in \{0, 1\}, \forall k \in \mathcal{M} \tag{3}$$

Note that the base station has only one antenna, so it can only receive one task uploaded by the user at the same time. Therefore, the task offloading sequence is important. Let l_z represent the scheduling sequence of tasks, $z \in \mathcal{Z} \triangleq \{1, 2, \ldots, L\}, L = \sum_1^m x_k$ where L is the total number of all offloaded computation tasks. We use $l_z = k$ to indicate that the z-th offloading task comes from UE_k.

3.4 Computation Model

Local Execution Model. The CPU frequency of mobile devices is f_k^l, which can be implemented by adjusting the chip voltage with DVFS techniques [14]. Besides, we assume the CPU-cycle frequencies cannot exceed the maximum f_k^{max}, i.e., $f_k^l \leq f_k^{max}, \forall k \in \mathcal{M}$. Therefore, the task execution time of UE_k on local computing can be expressed as $t_k^l = S_n^k J_n^k / f_k^l$. Accordingly, the energy consumption for local is given by [15]: $e_k^l = \kappa (f_k^l)^3 t_k^l$, where κ is the effective switched capacitance that depends on the chip architecture. In this paper, energy consumed for purposes other than local computation and transmission is ignored for simplicity. Moreover, local computing energy must be less than or equal to capture the energy, i.e., $e_k^l \leq E_k$, so we can get that CPU frequency as $f_k^l = min\left(\sqrt{\frac{E_k}{\kappa S_n^k J_n^k}}, f_k^{max}\right)$. Then we take the energy capture expression into the CPU frequency equitation and get the local executed time expressed as a function of the energy capture time as

$$t_k^l = max\left(\kappa^{\frac{1}{2}}\left(S_n^k J_n^k\right)^{\frac{3}{2}}\left(p_t^k t_e\right)^{-\frac{1}{2}}, (S_n^k J_n^k)/f_k^{max}\right) \tag{4}$$

where p_t^k is the energy captured by UE_k per unit time, $p_t^k = \eta P_b \frac{G_T G_R \lambda^2}{(4\pi d_k)^2 L}$. The user equipment for local computing in parallel and the time required to complete all the local computation depends on the longest. So, the completed time in the local is given by

$$T^l = max\left((1 - x_k)t_k^l\right), k \in \mathcal{M} \tag{5}$$

Mobile-Edge Execution Model. The task will be offloaded to the edge server for execution when the local computation takes too long. We assume that the task computation result is smaller than the input, so neglect the delay and energy consumption for results reception. According to the Shannon-Hartley formula, the achievable transmission rate can be expressed as $r^{mec} = Blog_2\left(1 + (p^{tr}H)/\sigma\right)$, where B is the system bandwidth, H is the channel quality, p^{tr} is the transmit power of user equipment and σ is the power of complex additive white Gaussian noise.

The transmission of tasks consists of two parts: the model and the data. When user equipment offloads a task, it needs to consider whether the correspond model is cached in the base station or not. So, the transmission time is expressed as $t_{l_z}^{tr} = \left(S_n^{l_z} + W_n X_n(z) \right)/r^{mec}$, and the time to process the task at the edge server is given by $t_{l_z}^{co} = \left(S_n^{l_z} K_n \right)/f^{mec}$. Note that there are multiple user equipment in the system, but base station only has one antenna to receive, so the offloaded task needs to queue. In other words, the user equipment cannot offload until the previous offloaded. Then, the time for UE_{l_z} to complete the task on the edge server can be expressed as

$$t_{l_z}^{mec} = (\sum_{p=1}^{z} t_{l_p}^{tr}) + t_{l_z}^{co}, l_z \in \mathcal{M} \tag{6}$$

In the procedure of user equipment offloading tasks to the edge device, we only consider the energy consumption of transmission. Thus, the energy consumed by the z-th offloaded is given by $e_{l_z}^{mec} = p^{tr} * t_{l_z}^{tr}$. Same as the local calculation, the mobile-edge execution user equipment satisfying the energy constrain, i.e., $e_{l_z}^{mec} \leq E_{l_z}$. The above are the transmission and calculation time of single-user equipment, so we can get the completed time by taking all device that offloading to the edge server into account is that

$$T^{mec} = max\left(x_{l_z} t_{l_z}^{mec} \right), l_z \in \mathcal{M} \tag{7}$$

4 Problem Formulation

To make it easy to understand, we use an example diagram to simulate the process from the beginning of energy capture to complete all tasks. As shown in Fig. 2, there are four user equipments: user equipment 1 and 2 generate A type of task, user equipment 3 and 4 have B type of task. The data of each task is different. Moreover, due to the limited cache capacity, we assume that the model A and model B cannot be stored at the same time.

In solution 1, four user equipments capture energy at first. Then they get the offloading decision and sequence where UE_3 executes the computation task locally and others offloading to MEC. When UE_1 offloads to MEC, there is no need to offload model A again because UE_2 had loaded the model before. We use END to represent the finishing time point. From three solutions, we can see the importance of the offloading decision to task completion time by comparing solution1 with solution 2. Besides, the comparison between solution 1 and solution 3 demonstrating the advantage of the offloading sequence.

As mentioned above, we aim to provide the optimum energy capture time t_e, CPU frequency control policy $\mathcal{F} = \{f_k^l, 1 \leq k \leq M\}$, computation offloading selection policy $\mathcal{A} = \{x_k, 1 \leq k \leq M\}$, offloading sequence policy $\mathcal{L} = \{l_z, 1 \leq z \leq L\}$, so that the total task execution time of all user equipment include energy harvesting time can be minimized. Consequently, we can formulate the problem as follows:

$$\mathcal{P}\text{：} \min_{t_e, \mathcal{F}, \mathcal{A}, \mathcal{L}} (t_e + max(T^l, T^{mec})) \ k \in \mathcal{M} \tag{8}$$

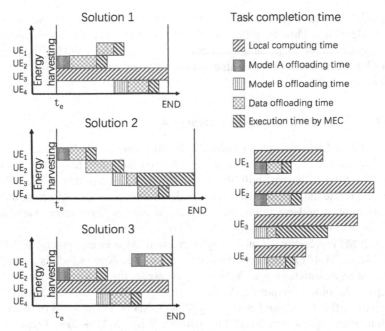

Fig. 2. Three different offloading and scheduling solutions

$$s.t.(1 - x_k)e_k^l + x_k e_k^m \leq E_k, \forall k \in \mathcal{M} \tag{9}$$

$$x_k \in \{0, 1\}, \forall k \in \mathcal{M} \tag{10}$$

$$\sum_{p=1}^{N} W_p X_p(z) \leq C, z \in \mathcal{Z} \tag{11}$$

$$f_k^l \leq f_k^{max}, \forall k \in \mathcal{M} \tag{12}$$

The expression of completion time on local and on MEC are shown in (5) and (7). And expression (9) is the battery energy constraint, the energy for computing cannot exceed the captured. Constraint (11) guarantees cached models do not exceed the caching capacity, and the maximum CPU-cycle frequency constraints are imposed by (12). Problem $\mathcal{P}$ is a non-convex mixed integer non-linear programming problem. The energy capture time is continuous, the offloading decision is discrete, and offloading sequence increases with the number of user equipment.

5 Proposed Global Replacement Scheduling Algorithm

5.1 CacheLRU Algorithm

The capacity of cache is limited, so the cached model will be replaced dynamically. The LRU method is a replacement strategy that has proved to be effective. When the cache is full, the model that the longest not used will be deleted to free up space. We propose the CacheLRU algorithm. This algorithm uses the hash table to find whether the model with task type n exists in the cache, and it can delete and add nodes quickly. The parameter input is task type n, and the return value represents whether the model of the z-th task in the cache.

5.2 Global Replacement Scheduling Algorithm

We can use CacheLRU algorithm eliminates the constraints (11), thus simplifying the problem. However, there are many variables involved, and they have complex logical relations. The time of harvest will affect the offloading decision, and the offloading sequence will cause the replacement of the model in the cache, thus affecting the user's energy consumption and execution time. So, we combine these optimized variables into a vector size of $(M + 2)$ represented by X.

The $X(1: M)$ represents the offloading decision of M user equipment, which value is 0 or 1. The $X(M + 1)$ represents the time of energy harvest, which is a continuous floating-point representation. And $X(M + 2)$ represents the order by an integer whose value maps to the offload sequence. As shown in Fig. 4, $X = [1,1,0,1,t_e,3]$ which mean $M = 4$ and the offload task number is $L = \sum_1^M X(1, M) = 3$. The kinds of orders are 3! $= 6$, each number represents a scheduling scheme. When $X(M + 2) = 3$ represents the first offloaded task from UE_2, the second offloaded task from UE_1, and the third from UE_4. In this way, each chromosome X can correctly express a task scheduling solution (Fig. 3).

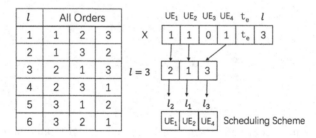

Fig. 3. The scheduling scheme represent by chromosome

Note that the $\mathcal{P}$ have energy limit (9). So, the fitness function is $f_{mec}(X) = t_e + \max\left(x_{l_z} d_{l_z}^{mec}\right) + g(x_{l_z} e_{l_z}^m - E_{l_z})$, the result of function $g(x_{l_z} e_{l_z}^m - E_{l_z})$ will be infinite when the variable is bigger than 0 and zero otherwise. Therefore, if energy consumption beyond the captured energy, the fitness function is infinite. When the next population iteration selects chromosomes, these poorly performing ones will be discarded, thus ensuring the correctness of the results. In the iteration of the population, individuals will experience cross variation, that is, change the energy capture time, offloading decision and scheduling scheme. To prevent meaningless population evolution, some pruning work is also done in this paper: first, assuming that all user equipments are executed locally, the offloading decision and sequence are not taken into account. By adjusting the energy capture time, we can get the shortest local computation time of all tasks denoted as T_l. So, the value range of X (M + 1) is $(0, T_l)$. Second, when the number of tasks offloaded to MEC is Z, the value range of Z is (1, M), and X (1:M) is {0,1}. Finally, X (M + 2) is an integer in the range of (1, Z!).

Integrated with local computation and MEC computation, the CacheLRU algorithm and global replacement scheduling algorithm (GRSA) are described as follows (Table 2):

Table 2. CacheLRU and global replacement scheduling algorithm

CacheLRU Algorithm	Global Replacement Scheduling Algorithm
Input: n	**Input: X**
Output: $X_n(z)$	**Output: $t_e, \mathcal{F}, \mathcal{A}, \mathcal{L}$**
if n in hashmap	initialization $ans = 0$;
used recently and move to tail;	**for** $Z \leftarrow 1$ to M
return 1;	Initialization pop1, threshold d, $T^l = 0$, $T^{mec} = 0$;
else	$X[1:M] \in \{0,1\}$, $\sum_{i=1}^M X[i] = Z$, $X[M+2] \in [1, Z!]$;
cur_cap = calculate now capacity;	**while** (pop1→d > d)
while（W_n + cur_cap > C）	**for** $i \leftarrow 1$ to M
node = hashmap[head];	**if** X[i] == 0
delete node from hashmap;	Calculate local delay using (7) as t_i^l;
cur_cap -= node. value;	$T^l = \max(T^l, t_i^l)$;
end while	**else**
add node to hashmap;	**for** k $\leftarrow 1$ to Z
end if	$t_{l_k}^{tr} += (S_{l_k} + \text{CacheLRU}(l_k \rightarrow n)W_n / r^{mec}$;
return 0;	$t_{l_k}^{all} = t_{l_k}^{tr} + d_{l_k}^{com}$;
	$T^{mec} = \max(T^{mec}, t_{l_k}^{all})$;
	end for
	end if
	end for
	$T_{tmp} = t_e + \max(T^l, T^{mec}) + g(x_{lz} e_{lz}^m - E_{lz})$;
	record $\min(T_{tmp})$ as T_Z and $\min(T_Z)$ as ans;
	record t_e, f_k^l, x_k, l_z when ans is the smallest;
	newpop1←select (pop1, T_{tmp});
	newpop2←crossover and mutation (newpop1);
	pop1← newpop2;
	end while
	end for
	return $t_e, \mathcal{T}, \mathcal{A}, \mathcal{L}$

6 Simulation Results

In this section, we present the simulation results to estimate the performance of the proposed algorithm. The simulation environment as follows: the number of UE is 6, the kind of task is 3, the model sizes are 1 MB, 3 MB, 7 MB and the capacity of cache is 7 MB. Moreover, the data of each take randomly from [1, 4] MB, and the model of tasks is random. The effective switched capacitance $\kappa = 10^{-28}$.The frequency of the edge server is 2 GHz and the user equipment is 0.5 GHz. In addition, the bandwidth is 1 MHz, $\sigma = 10^{-13}W$.

In order to evaluate the performance of the proposed algorithm (GRSA), we compare this with two benchmark algorithms. (1) All Offload (AO). In this algorithm, all tasks will offload to MEC for calculation, and the best task scheduling will be selected to complete. (2) No Schedule (NS). This algorithm does not consider the scheduling scheme, the offloaded tasks are sorted by the UE's number, but the offloading decision is optimized. The results were obtained from an average of 100 experiments.

6.1 Comparison with Different Number of UEs

The relationship between the total delay and the number of users is shown in Fig. 4. The increased users' number means that there are more tasks to calculate, and the execution delay also increases. What's more, we can see that the algorithm proposed in this paper always has a low delay and the gap between the three algorithms is growing with the increase of the number of users.

6.2 Comparison with Different Kinds of Tasks

In Fig. 5, we explored the influence of task's type on four strategies. We set the cache size to 4 MB and the size of each model is 2 MB. We can see that with the number of task types from 1 to 5, the total time to complete the task is slowly increasing. In this experiment, when the number of users remains the same, the increase of task types will reduce the reusability of the model and prolong the task completion time.

6.3 Comparison with Different Cache Sizes

The experiment studied the impact of cache sizes on the results in Fig. 6. Due to the diversity of tasks, we set the model sizes are 1 MB, 1.5 MB, 2 MB, 7 MB. At first, part of the tasks had to be computed locally, resulting in a long delay. With the increase of cache capacity, there are more decision possibilities, the selection of the offload scheme is abundant, and the delay is reduced rapidly. Finally, the delay line tends to level.

6.4 Comparison with Different Harvest Time

In this experiment, we explored the influence of energy harvest time. To achieve better results, we reduce the power of energy capture. First of all, the time to capture is not abundant, so some tasks can only be calculated locally. Secondly, with the harvest time increase, users have more computation offloading strategies and sequences, which can minimize the total execution time. Finally, each user equipment has captured enough energy, even the harvest time increasing cannot speed up the process of tasks (Fig. 7).

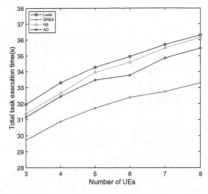

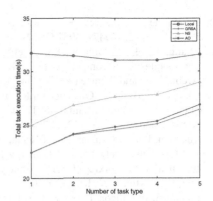

Fig. 4. Comparison with number of users

Fig. 5. Comparison with the kinds of tasks

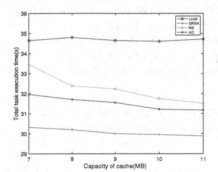

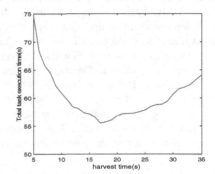

Fig. 6. Comparison with cache sizes

Fig. 7. Comparison with harvest time

7 Conclusions

In this paper, we investigated the dynamic offloading in a MEC system with multiple EH user equipment. All user equipment captures energy from RF signals radiated by the base station and then utilizes the harvested energy to finishing tasks. Besides, the model is repeatability and reusability. It is necessary to make a scheduling scheme with the limited cache capacity in the edge server. We proposed an optimized update algorithm (CacheLRU) and a global replacement scheduling algorithm (GRSA) to solve the mixed discrete-continuous optimization problem. The simulation results verified our proposed algorithm effectively improves the speed of the system.

Acknowledgment. This work was supported by the National Natural Science Foundation of China (Grant No. 61672465 and No. 61772472) and Zhejiang Provincial Natural Science Foundation of China (LY15F020027).

References

1. Sung, M., et al.: RoF-based radio access network for 5G mobile communication systems in 28 GHz millimeter-wave. J. Lightwave Technol. **38**(2), 409–420 (2020)

2. Nan, Y., et al.: Adaptive energy-aware computation offloading for cloud of Things Systems. IEEE Access **5**, 23947–23957 (2017)
3. Zhang, Y., He, J., Guo, S.: Energy-efficient dynamic task offloading for energy harvesting mobile cloud computing. In: 2018 IEEE International Conference on Networking, Architecture and Storage (NAS), Chongqing, pp. 1–4 (2018)
4. Choi, C.W.: Basic MAC scheme for RF energy harvesting wireless sensor networks: throughput analysis and optimization. In: TENCON 2018 - 2018 IEEE Region 10 Conference, Jeju, Korea (South), pp. 1317–1321 (2018)
5. Lakshmi, P.S., Jibukumar, M.G., Neenu, V.S.: Network lifetime enhancement of multi-hop wireless sensor network by RF energy harvesting. In: 2018 International Conference on Information Networking (ICOIN), Chiang Mai, pp. 738–743 (2018)
6. Lee, W.C., Min, B.W., Kim, C.Y., Kim, J.C., Yook, J.M.: A compact switched beam-forming network using silicon IPD technology for low-cost 5G communication. In: 2016 IEEE MTT-S International Microwave Symposium (IMS), San Francisco, CA, pp. 1–3 (2016)
7. Kim, Y., et al.: A Ka-band phase shifting low noise amplifier with gain error compensation for 5G RF beam forming array using 14nm FinFET CMOS. In: 2018 IEEE International Symposium on Circuits and Systems (ISCAS), Florence, pp. 1–4 (2018)
8. Lyalin, K.S., Oreshkin, V.I., Biryuk, A.A., Prikhodko, D.V., Dovgal, T.A.: The new beam-forming architecture of 5G wireless communication. In: 2019 IEEE Conference of Russian Young Researchers in Electrical and Electronic Engineering (EIConRus), Saint Petersburg and Moscow, Russia, pp. 2037–2039 (2019)
9. Wei, Z., Zhao, B., Su, J., Lu, X.: Dynamic edge computation offloading for Internet of Things with energy harvesting: a learning method. IEEE Internet Things J. **6**(3), 4436–4447 (2019)
10. Mao, Y., Zhang, J., Letaief, K.B.: Dynamic computation offloading for mobile-edge computing with energy harvesting devices. IEEE J. Sel. Areas Commun. **34**(12), 3590–3605 (2016)
11. Mao, Y., Zhang, J., Song, S.H., Letaief, K.B.: Power-delay tradeoff in multi-user mobile-edge computing systems. In: Proceedings of the IEEE Global Communications Conference (GLOBECOM), Washington, DC, USA, pp. 1–6 (2016)
12. Jeong, H.J., Lee, H.J., Shin, C.H., Moon, S.M.: IONN: incremental offloading of neural network computations from mobile devices to edge servers. In: Proceedings of the ACM Symposium on Cloud Computing, pp. 401–411. ACM (2018)
13. Cui, Y., He, W., Ni, C., Guo, C., Liu, Z.: Energy-efficient resource allocation for cache-assisted mobile edge computing. In: 2017 IEEE 42nd Conference on Local Computer Networks (LCN), Singapore, pp. 640–648 (2017)
14. Rabaey, J.M., Chandrakasan, A., Nikolić, B.: Digital Integrated Circuits: A Design Perspective, 2nd edn. Prentice-Hall, Upper Saddle River (2003)
15. Liu, P., Xu, G., Yang, K., Wang, K., Meng, X.: Jointly optimized energy-minimal resource allocation in cache-enhanced mobile edge computing systems. IEEE Access **7**, 3336–3347 (2019)

A Light-Weight Deployment Methodology for DNN Re-training in Resource-Constraint Scenarios

Shuting Sun, Songtao Guo, Chunhua Xiao[✉], and Zilan Liao

School of Computer Science, Chongqing University, Chongqing 400044, China
xiaochunhua@cqu.edu.cn

Abstract. Wireless smart devices with restricted resources in the IoT may need to update DNNs due to environmental changes. In order to alleviate the computational complexity of DNN updates and stringent requirements on the size and distribution of datasets when re-training, Deep Transfer Learning (DTL) is proposed for transferring the knowledge that DNNs can learn from large standard datasets and reducing the number of DNN layers that need to be re-trained. However, previous work has rarely reconciled the needs of the computational process with the advantages of the computational platform, resulting in sub-optimal performance of the system. To address this problem, we propose a Light-weight Deployment Methodology, which targets for agile deployment of DNN re-training in resource-constraint scenarios. We design a Hybrid Precision Light-weight Strategy to distinguish the general feature extractor layer from the others so that the different light-weight mechanisms are utilized for efficient computing. Besides analyzing the system performance from aspects of information loss, computational throughput, and resource utilization, our design is able to generate a system configuration guidance with NSGA-II, which compromises DNN performance and system efficiency. The evaluation shows the throughput of the computation module guided by NSGA-II reach 39.30 and 35.04 GOPs respectively for each quantization mechanism, with the relative errors of only 2.52% and 4.60% from the theoretical values. And the model size is reduced by 34.72% without accuracy loss.

Keywords: Deep Transfer Learning · Light-weight Strategy · Multi-objective optimization

1 Introduction

Wireless smart devices with restricted resources in the IoT may need to update DNNs due to environmental changes. Since the weather, angle, light, etc. have the possibility to degrade the accuracy of the initial model in the ground-truth deployment, DNN updates for specific scenario are essential.

Deep Transfer Learning (DTL) is proposed to allow even resource-constraint devices to update DNNs with target field dataset. When DNNs are re-trained

© Springer Nature Switzerland AG 2021
Z. Liu et al. (Eds.): WASA 2021, LNCS 12937, pp. 441–452, 2021.
https://doi.org/10.1007/978-3-030-85928-2_35

using DTL, there are no stringent conditions on the sample distribution and size of the dataset. Even the size of target field dataset is small, the ability of general feature extracting reserves owing to the practical knowledge that transferred from pre-trained models.

Although DTL can reduce the difficulty of DNN re-training in terms of computational process and dataset normality, implementing model updates on resource-constraint scenarios can still be challenging. First, DTL divides the network into 3 parts, frozen, fine-tune and re-training, each of which involves distinct computing regimes in the process of DTL and requires individual consideration. Besides, although a portion of the computation is mitigated in frozen layers, resource-constraint platforms are in dire need of computational efficiency improvement as the network depth and the iterations increase. Last but not least, during the process of DTL, layers are responsible for distinct operations. If the computation nature of DTL is finely considered, the resource-constraint wireless devices may have more potential to update DNNs.

A majority of the work has been done in designing training mechanisms based on FPGA with the workload of re-training the entire network of DNNs [3,4]. While deploying DTL on resource-constrained devices, the computational shrinkage benefits of the DTL approach should be perceived, so we proposed a Light-weight Deployment Methodology for DNN Re-training exploiting hardware acceleration advantages.

Therefore, we have proposed the following contributions in this work to tackle the above issues:

- A Hybrid Precision Light-weight Strategy is designed to segment the network by the feature extraction capability of the convolutional layer, focusing on both the DTL computation process and the capabilities of hardware properties to reduce the model size and the computation complexity.
- We also proposed a GA-based Search Scheme for system design. In order to avoid troubleshooting erroneous design solutions through a lengthy hardware development process, we provide a reliable model to predict the system performance before system implementation. Moreover, the NSGA-II is used to solve the multi-objective optimization problem, so that we can seek for the compromise configuration of a efficient system.
- We experiment on the guided configuration on FPGA platform to validate the reliance of the search scheme. By deploying the Light-weight Strategy for DTL, the size of YOLOv3-tiny we experimented on reduced by 34.72% without accuracy loss. The practical throughput of computing module for the two segments are 39.30 GOPs and 35.04 GOPs with relative errors of 2.52% and 4.60%.

2   Related Work and Motivation

Numerous efforts addressed light-weight deployment of DNNs in the prior. One of the dominant solution is model compression under tense resource constraints, and typical methods include bit-width reduction [5], weights sharing [6] and integer quantization [9].

Not only reducing size of DNN benefits for deployment of smart applications on wireless devices, it is also essential to ease the computational difficulty of the networks, and enable models to be re-trained on resource-constraint platforms. In terms of algorithms and software, the mixed-precision training mechanism [7] uses half-precision float numbers to store neural network parameters and proposed 3 mechanisms to prevent the loss of critical information. The model quantized to 2–5 bits is very close to the full precision model of baseline, even with a slight improvement. For low-power FPGA platforms, Fox proposes an 8-bit integer-based Training Acceleration prototype for Zynq All Programmable Chip(APSoC) devices that combines Block Floating Point Quantization and Stochastic Weight Averaging in Low-Precision Training(SWALP) [10] techniques to improve the accuracy of benchmarking by 0.5%.

While it may be beneficial to develop dedicated hardware acceleration for CNNs, there is a risk at scale if these accelerators do not yield the expected benefits due to performance bounds caused by offload-induced overhead. To determine such performance bounds early in the hardware design phase, plenty of work construct analytical models to predict the performance and bottleneck of SoC [1,2,8]. These efforts have varying degrees of attention to hardware detail, but all collectively make important contributions to reducing algorithmic and hardware co-design costs.

In summary, deploying DTL on resource-constrained platforms requires not only a compressed model design and a computation acceleration method from an algorithmic perspective, but also a well-designed circuit that can match the algorithm from a hardware perspective. In addition, an accurate evaluation of the on-chip system performance is also important for the algorithm and hardware co-design. Therefore, our work designs a Light-weight Deployment Methodology for DNN Re-training in Resource-Constraint Scenarios that is algorithm-aware and hardware-aware with the help of a multi-objective optimal model of performance evaluation.

3 Lightweight Deployment Methodology for DTL

In DNNs, it usually starts out with some regular pattern of computation process, and the features extracted have commonality among various dataset. In the re-training mechanism of DTL, those layers constitute *General Feature Extraction* process. The degree of specificity is most evident in last layers of the network, that needed random initialization and re-training in DTL, constitute *Result Generation* process. The remaining layers form the *Specific Feature Extraction* process to learn new data patterns from target field dataset, where pre-trained weights are finely tuned in DTL.

Therefore, based on the computation nature of DTL, we separately design a Light-weight Deployment Methodology as shown in Fig. 1. It includes 3 fundamental processes, which are Hybrid Precision Light-weight Strategy, Multi-Objective Problem Establishment, and GA-based Search Scheme.

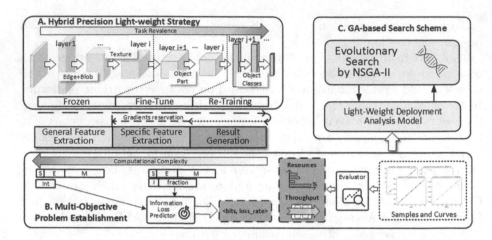

Fig. 1. An overview of Lightweight Deployment Methodology for DTL.

In Hybrid Precision Light-weight Strategy, we conclude all the computation layers of DTL into 2 segments according to the computational Complexity. All computational layers classified into the same functional layer adopt the same Light-weight mechanism. In order to provide a solution that cooperate the awareness of algorithm and hardware, we establish a Multi-Objective Problem with system performance optimal targets, including information loss, computational throughput and resources utilization. Finally, a GA-based Search Scheme is utilized for system configuration guidance. We apply the NSGA-II for solving the multi-objectives optimal problem for agile generation of excellent population, offering a finite set of configurations with compromise between DNN accuracy and Hardware efficiency.

The methodology is thoroughly described in the subsequent sections.

3.1 Hybrid Precision Light-Weight Strategy

In DNN re-training mechanism of DTL, we can separate DNN layers from feature generality and specificity. For general feature extractors, only forward inference are executed in DNN updating, while specific feature extractors and result generators have the responsibility to modify the model with operations of loss evaluation, gradients computing, and weights updating. Since the distinct computing tasks differ from computation complexity, quantization mechanisms deploying should cater to nature of DTL.

In terms of computation efficiency, the data computation efficiency of integer and fixed-point of the same length is comparable. In addition, the resources consumption rises with bitwidth. Conversely, float are far less efficient than the above two data types, with a single multiplication of a float with the same bit width being 4.19x slower than fixed-point data. Considering the different efficiency of data types on hardware, float calculations should be avoided.

Due to the apparent advantages of integer quantization for inference tasks, e.g. scaling down model size and calculative complexity, we apply it as the light-weight mechanism for segment of general feature extraction. For inference and weight update of the remaining layers, since the calculations involved in performing the gradient calculation and weight update require more precise data representation, if integer type is still used as the data representation type, it will inevitably lead to information loss and introduce extraneous float calculations to recover data precision. Therefore, we take fixed-point decimal as the data representation type for the latter segment. By flattening the training process on the time, a simplified diagram of the network training process is shown in Fig. 2, and the corresponding light-weight mechanism is marked under the dotted line as well.

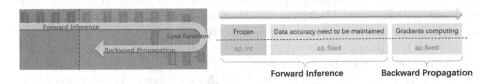

Fig. 2. The diagram of Hybrid Precision Light-weight Strategy.

3.2 Multi-Objective Problem Establishment

In order to analyze the system performance in terms of DNN and hardware, we focus on 3 optimal objectives, i.e. **a)information loss** to evaluate the discount in accuracy when data representation is reduced, along with **b)computational throughput** of the accelerated module to measure the system performance under the accelerate mechanism, and **c)resource utilization** to make sure the system design facilitate platform conditions. As for the Light-weight deployment methodology for DTL, with the SoC design based on the dynamic reconfigurable property of FPGA, optimal objectives need to be separately considered for two segment of DTL computation process. Importantly, under the scenario of resource-constraint, it is vital to take resource limitation into account, so that the system can be correctly deployed.

Next we analyze optimal objectives above to form a performance multi-objective optimal problem for the system design , and solve the problem using a genetic algorithm as well.

Information Loss. When we determine the reduction of weights representation to obtained a light-weight model, the accuracy loss should be carefully handled. However, it is prohibitive to evaluate accuracy for every single bit of representation. Thus, we convert the evaluation of accuracy into the magnitude of information loss during computation to predict the efficacy of the light-weight model.

To quantify the information loss, we separately analyze the information loss for integer and fixed-point quantization mechanism from two segment of the DTL computing process, denoted as $loss_{i,bit}$, where $i \in \{0,1\}$, 0 indicate the case of integer quantization and 1 for fixed-point, and bit represents the precision.

Since the computational process of DTL can be analogous to inference in the general feature extraction segment, we choose absolute error of inference performance as metric to evaluate information loss, compared accuracy of sampled acc_{bit} with that of full precision acc_0, formulated as

$$loss_{0,bit} = \frac{|acc_0 - acc_{bit}|}{acc_0} \tag{1}$$

After the general feature extractor segment, remaining DTL process including both forward and backward propagation, it is not adequate to evaluate only inference performance. Therefore, the gradient value obtained from the back propagation is selected as the evaluation metric.

In order to represent the $loss_{1,bit}$, we use the full-precision data representation for training, and record the gradient value every 10 epoch as baseline, noted as $G_0 = \{g_1, g_2, ..., g_i, ..., g_n\}$. Each element in the set g_i records the gradients of the network saved for the ith time. Then for each sampled bit, the computation is performed under the same training conditions. Once the number of epoch matches with records during the baseline training, we extract the corresponding gradients set g_i' for computation of loss. The average absolute error is used to represent the extent of information loss, formulated as:

$$g\_err_i = \frac{|grad_0 - grad_{bit}|}{|grad_0|}, grad_0 \in g_i, grad_{bit} \in g_i' \tag{2}$$

$$loss_{1,bit} = \frac{\sum g\_err_i}{N_{grad}} \tag{3}$$

where N_{grad} represents the number of gradients.

Computation Throughput. We choose the popular accelerator of Systolic Array with Output Stationary, calculating Matrix Multiplication with size of $A_{(PECOL \times K)} \times B_{(K \times PEROW)} = C_{(PECOL \times PEROW)}$ for analysis. The value of K is a parameter that is determined by the system designer and determines the number of small matrices into which the input and the weight matrix will be divided. We make a assumption of $PEROW = PECOL$ to simplify the model in the following.

As shown in the Fig. 3, the input will be sliced into several matrices that can be input to the systolic array for calculation, and the number of matrices divided determines the times the systolic array will be called recursively, which can be calculated by the following formula:

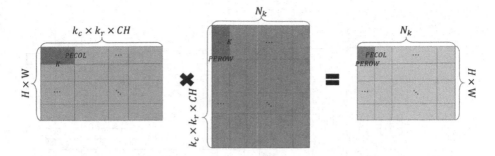

Fig. 3. Schematic diagram of input matrices slicing.

$$icp = \left\lceil \frac{k_c \times k_r \times CH}{K} \right\rceil , irp = \left\lceil \frac{H \times W}{PECOL} \right\rceil , wcp = \left\lceil \frac{N_k}{PEROW} \right\rceil \quad (4)$$

$$times = icp \times irp \times wcp \quad (5)$$

Since the complexity of small matrices loop is $O(n^3)$, we prefer to raise the value of K and $PEROW$ once the resources allow.

The time required to complete the convolution layer is formulated as

$$T = \frac{times \times cycles_{SA}}{F} \quad (6)$$

where $cycles_{SA}$ represents the time clocks for completing the Matrix Multiplication of $A_{(PECOL \times K)} \times B_{(K \times PEROW)} = C_{(PECOL \times PEROW)}$. F represents the Frequency of the hardware platform. Following that, we formulate $cycles_{SA}$ by combining the calculation principle of systolic array and process data I/O.

According to Fig. 4, we exhibit the computational schematic and Gantt Chart of the systolic array, taking a 3×3 systolic array as an example. The clock cycle of a single execution can be expressed as three phases and the time required for each phase can be accumulated to obtain $cycles_{SA}$:

$$cycles_{SA} = t_{read} + t_{compute} + t_{write} \quad (7)$$

Where the duration of t_{read} and t_{write} is related to the size of the two input matrices, proportional to the number of matrix elements.

$$t_{read} = k_{read} \left(PECOL \times K + K \times PEROW\right) = 2k_{read} \times K \times PEROW \quad (8)$$

$$t_{write} = k_{write} \left(PECOL \times PEROW\right) = k_{write} PEROW^2 \quad (9)$$

where k_{read} and k_{write} are on-chip cache read and write delay factors. When the K grows, t_{read} increases linearly, and K can be 2^{10} or even higher when the hardware on-chip storage resources allow. In such case, the growth trend of t_{read} can easily outpace the other two parts, causing the system a lot of time on reading, which is impractical. Therefore, we optimize the pipeline by intertwining

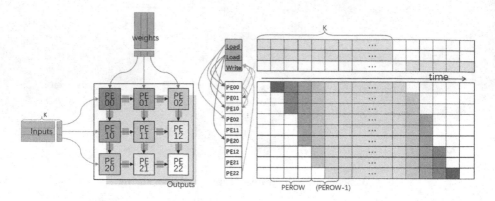

Fig. 4. systolic array calculation principle Gantt Chart.

the read, write and compute operations. According to the Gantt chart in Fig. 4, each time the data to be calculated is packaged and sent to the PE array, for PEs consuming. Only the first read operation is counted in, expressed as

$$t_{read} = k_{read} \left\lceil \frac{bit \times PEROW}{bandwidth} \right\rceil \tag{10}$$

The systolic array running with full workload after all the PEs are fed with data, and once K data finished transmitting, idle PE begins to write result right after that, so the $t_{compute}$ and t_{write} are denoted as

$$t_{compute} = k_{PE} \left(2 \times PEROW + K \right), t_{write} = k_{write} \left\lceil \frac{bit \times PEROW}{bandwidth} \right\rceil \tag{11}$$

k_{PE} is the coefficient of PE cell calculation.

Resource Utilization. According Fig. 4, logic resources (FF, LUT) are mainly provided to the computational functions of multiple PEs arranged neatly in the systolic array, with intermediate result caching. The remaining functional modules also include inter-module connections and on-chip storage. In systolic array, each PE performs the same task, so resources consumed by them are fixed under a certain data representation (bit). The FF and LUT resource consumption factors used by a single PE are denoted as R_{bit_t}, where $t = \{FF, LUT\}$.

$$Resources_{PEs\_t} = R_{bit\_t} \times \left(PEROW^2 \right) \tag{12}$$

In addition, there exists interconnection between the on-chip cache module and the computation module. The required on-chip resource consumption factor is denoted as $R_{bit\_connect}$, then the logical resources required for data interconnection between the on-chip storage can be expressed as follows

$$Resources_{mem\_t} = 2R_{bit\_connect\_t} \left[PEROW \times K + PEROW(PEROW - 1) \right] \tag{13}$$

The AXI-Stream interface encapsulates the entire systolic array into an IP core that carry the ready-to-process data package, consuming static resources, noted as $Resources_{wrapper\_t}$. By now, the total logic resource utilization required by the design of the systolic array IP core is formulate as

$$R = Resources_{PEs\_t} + Resources_{mem\_t} + Resources_{wrapper_t} \tag{14}$$

3.3   GA-Based Search Scheme

We phrase the problem of seeking to achieve an optimal SoC configuration in the form of multi-objective optimization. Because the multi-objective problem is hard to locate the solution that is optimal for all objectives, it usually returns a set of non-dominate solutions known as the Pareto solution set.

We define the genotype to be input as a binary string of 6 discrete variables, bit_{int}, bit_{fixed}, $PEROW_{int}$, $PEROW_{fixed}$, K_{int}, K_{fixed}, spliced by binary codes. The coded population is input to NSGA-II for searching the Pareto solutions and the optimal objective values, including minimum information loss for integer and fixed-point quantization $loss_i$, maximum computing module throughput for systolic arrays with 2 distinct configuration $Comp_i$, and the corresponding maximum resource utilization of FF and LUT for computing module $R_{i,t}$, subject to chip resource restriction. Where i indicates the integer or fixed-point quantization, and t indicates the type of logic resources(FF, LUT). We expressed the multi-objective optimization problem as

$$\begin{cases} \min loss_i(bit_i), \\ \max Comp_i(PEROW_i, K_i), \ s.t. R_{i,t} \leq Resource \ Limit. \\ \max R_{i,t}, \end{cases} \tag{15}$$

4   Experiments and Validation

4.1   Model Reliability

In order to verify the validity of the above theoretical analysis, we extracted some samples of $PEROW$ and K for practical validation, and the resulting points are plotted in the form of a scatter plot as in Fig. 5. The quantitative relationship functions of theoretical model were plotted as the curves as well. The alignment of the sampling points can be seen to be consistent with the quadratic trend of the analytical model.

We sampled points in the range of bit width between $[4, 16]$ for integer information loss fitting, and observed the pattern according to the experimental results, thus constructing maps through the general pattern to obtain $\langle bitwidth_0, loss\_rate_0 \rangle$. For the construction of the map between the data bitwidths of fixed-point quantization on the information loss, we sampled data at a fixed-point decimal bit width between $[8, 32]$ for experiments. The curve of information loss are exhibit in Fig. 6(a) and 6(b).

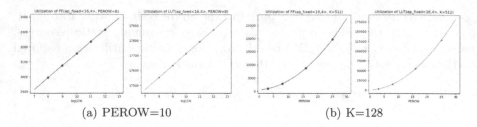

(a) PEROW=10   (b) K=128

Fig. 5. Comparison of analytical values and sampling point statistics for FF and LUT consumption.

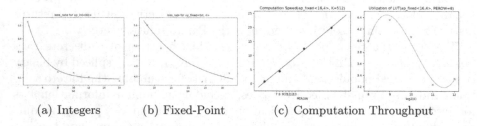

(a) Integers   (b) Fixed-Point   (c) Computation Throughput

Fig. 6. Fitting curves of Information loss and Computation Throughput.

The samples for computational throughput and the results of the fitted curve are shown in Fig. 6(c). When $PEROW$ is stationary, the reason for the fluctuation is the mutually constraining relationship between icp, irp, wcp and K, proving the prediction in Eq. 5.

4.2   NSGA-II Results

We experiment on a xc7z045-ffg900-3 chip with a clock frequency of 100 MHz, and a total of 437200 and 218600 FF and LUTs, respectively. The experimental DNN is chosen to be YOLOv3-tiny. Taking the capability of experimental chip into the constraints of the multi-objective optimization algorithm NSGA-II, a set of Pareto solutions can be obtained by combining a total of 8 optimization objectives. The objectives values corresponding to the 50 non-dominated individuals derived by the NSGA-II algorithm are shown in Fig. 7. For the output 50 non-dominated solutions, we first ranked them in descending order according to the computational throughput. Then, among the top ten individuals, those that meet the resource constraints are filtered, and the one with the least information loss is selected as the guiding configuration for this system design, as listed in Table 1 after decoding.

Table 1. Chroms and values of objectives generated by NSGA-II

	bit	PEROW	K	acc_{loss}	$Comp(GOPs)$	FF	LUT
int	11	32	4096	0.1056	40.32	27763	158028
fixed	21	30	4096	4.8321	36.73	23595	156598

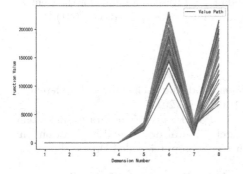

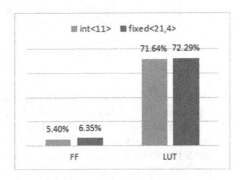

Fig. 7. Objective values for NSGA-II   **Fig. 8.** Resource utilization

Next, we used Xilinx's System-on-Chip development tool chain to synthesize and implement the system as well as the simulations for the experiments. By deploy the Light-weight Deployment Methodology for DNN Re-training in Resource-Constraint Scenarios, the size of weights of YOLOv3-tiny reduced by 34.72%, while the mAP maintains at 0.28, same with the result of full-precision version. In terms of computational performance, the practical throughput of computing module for integer and fixed-point quantization are 39.30 GOPs and 35.04 GOPs respectively, with relative errors of 2.52% and 4.60% compared with our theoretical prediction. Regarding the resource utilization, the statement given by Xilinx's System-on-Chip development tool chain is shown in the Fig. 8.

5 Conclusion

Deploying the DNNs which is capable of autonomous update on wireless devices in IoT confronts various challenges including limited storage resources, insufficient computational resources, and long hardware development cycles. Our work presents an innovative Light-weight Deployment Methodology for DTL in resource-constrained scenarios. By accounting for both the process of DNN re-training and the awareness of the hardware, a Light-weight Strategy for DTL is designed, and the performance of the whole system is analyzed based on this strategy and the design of the hardware computational acceleration module. The GA-based Search Scheme providing model in terms of both DNNs and platform performance, according to which the performance prediction and configuration guidance for the design of the hardware platform can be derived by NSGA-II. The experiments show that configuration we obtained by using the NSGA-II algorithm not only performs remarkably well, but also conserves the time and number of iterations for hardware development.

Acknowledgments. This work is supported by National Natural Science Foundation of China (No. 61772094), Chongqing Municipal Natural Science Foundation (No. cstc2020jcyj-msxmx0724), Venture & Innovation Support Program for Chongqing Overseas Returnees (cx2019094), and the Fundamental Research Funds for the Central Universities, (No. 2020cdjqy-a019, No. 2020cdj-lhzz-054, No. 2019cdxyjsj0021).

References

1. Beckmann, N., Sanchez, D.: Cache calculus: modeling caches through differential equations. IEEE Comput. Archit. Lett. **16**(1), 1–5 (2015)
2. Cong, J., Fang, Z., Gill, M., Reinman, G.: Parade: a cycle-accurate full-system simulation platform for accelerator-rich architectural design and exploration. In: 2015 IEEE/ACM International Conference on Computer-Aided Design (ICCAD), pp. 380–387. IEEE (2015)
3. Drumond, M., Lin, T., Jaggi, M., Falsafi, B.: End-to-end DNN training with block floating point arithmetic. CoRR abs/1804.01526 (2018). http://arxiv.org/abs/1804.01526
4. Geng, T., et al.: FPDeep: acceleration and load balancing of CNN training on FPGA clusters. In: 2018 IEEE 26th Annual International Symposium on Field-Programmable Custom Computing Machines (FCCM), pp. 81–84. IEEE (2018)
5. Gupta, S., Agrawal, A., Gopalakrishnan, K., Narayanan, P.: Deep learning with limited numerical precision. In: International Conference on Machine Learning, pp. 1737–1746. PMLR (2015)
6. Han, S., Mao, H., Dally, W.J.: Deep compression: compressing deep neural networks with pruning, trained quantization and Huffman coding. arXiv preprint arXiv:1510.00149 (2015)
7. Micikevicius, P., et al.: Mixed precision training. CoRR abs/1710.03740 (2017). http://arxiv.org/abs/1710.03740
8. Sriraman, A., Dhanotia, A.: Accelerometer: understanding acceleration opportunities for data center overheads at hyperscale. In: Proceedings of the Twenty-Fifth International Conference on Architectural Support for Programming Languages and Operating Systems, pp. 733–750 (2020)
9. Vanhoucke, V., Senior, A., Mao, M.Z.: Improving the speed of neural networks on CPUs. In: Deep Learning and Unsupervised Feature Learning Workshop, NIPS 2011 (2011)
10. Yang, G., Zhang, T., Kirichenko, P., Bai, J., Wilson, A.G., De Sa, C.: SWALP: stochastic weight averaging in low precision training. In: International Conference on Machine Learning, pp. 7015–7024. PMLR (2019)

Deep Reinforcement Learning Based Collaborative Mobile Edge Caching for Omnidirectional Video Streaming

Zengjie Tan and Yuanyuan Xu$^{(\boxtimes)}$

School of Computer and Information, Hohai University, Nanjing, China
{tzj1999,yuanyuan_xu}@hhu.edu.cn

Abstract. Omnidirectional virtual reality video streaming requires high data rate and low latency to provide immersive experiences. Caching video contents at collaborative wireless edge servers is a promising approach to enable omnidirectional video streaming. Given limited storage at edges and ultra-high rate of omnidirectional video streaming, collaborative caching is challenging. Although restricting caching to parts of field of views (FoVs) of omnidirectional videos can alleviate the problem, the FoV based collaborative caching is still difficult considering multiple video encoding versions, long-term benefits for multiple end users and possible FoV prediction error. In this paper, we propose a deep reinforcement learning (DRL) based scheme to learn a collaborative caching policy adaptively for tile-based omnidirectional video streaming, where watched tiles are cached with abundant storage space, and either discarded or replacing existing content when edge storages are full. The collaborative cache replacement is modeled as a Markov decision process (MDP). To address the problem of searching a large-scale action space in DRL, we designed an adaptive action-selection scheme utilizing FoV prediction results. Simulation results demonstrate the effectiveness of the proposed scheme.

Keywords: Omnidirectional video streaming · Collaborative edge caching · Deep reinforcement learning

1 Introduction

According to Cisco's Mobile VNI Forecast, virtual reality/augmented reality (AR/VR) mobile data traffic will grow nearly 12-fold from 2017 to 2022 [1]. Omnidirectional or 360° VR videos provide an immersive experience by allowing users to control the viewing orientation of the content. Since each omnidirectional video contains a 360° FoV and associated head mounted display (HMD)

This work is supported by National Natural Science Foundation of China under Grant No. 61801167, and the Fundamental Research Funds for the Central Universities under Grant No. B200202189.

Z. Liu et al. (Eds.): WASA 2021, LNCS 12937, pp. 453–464, 2021.
https://doi.org/10.1007/978-3-030-85928-2_36

has magnifying optical lens, resolution and frame rate of such video is much higher than the traditional videos. Furthermore, to avoid motion sickness of head rotations, the motion-to-photon (MTP) latency of the FoV region should be less than 20 ms [2]. Therefore, omnidirectional video streaming demands a high data rate and low latency.

Collaborative mobile edge caching [3] can be leveraged to enable high data rate delay-sensitive omnidirectional video streaming, with which wireless base stations, act as edge servers, collaborate to provide storage within the edge of the network. With the deployment of edge cache, a few users requested content can be fetched only once from the content delivery network (CDN), and the subsequent requests can be served from local or neighboring edge servers, which effectively reduces latency and traffic in the backhaul network [4]. However, limited storage at edge servers poses challenges for caching high-rate omnidirectional contents. Moreover, adaptive bitrate technologies [5] are widely applied to satisfy heterogeneous user requests and accommodate fluctuating network conditions, resulting in more encoded versions for an omnidirectional video. An efficient caching scheme needs to decide "what" and "where" to cache wisely [6].

For traditional omnidirectional video streaming [7,8], encoding each video according to particular viewport results in more encoded versions, and transmitting the content outside the viewer's FoV wastes the transmission bandwidth. Coding tools of the high efficiency video coding (HEVC) standard [9] can be used to encode each image into multiple independent tiles. Tiles overlapped with FoV are assigned more resources during streaming, while other tiles are not transmitted or delivered with a lower quality version. A few works [10–14] consider collaborative caching for tile-based omnidirectional video streaming utilizing the FoV prediction information. Besides, a non-cooperative FoV-aware edge caching has been proposed for multi-bitrate tile-based omnidirectional videos streaming in [15]. However, these schemes rely on accurate FoV prediction. Although restricting caching to tiles of FoVs of omnidirectional videos can alleviate the problem, these schemes suffer from inaccurate FoV prediction resulting in an unpleasant viewing experience. Obtaining an FoV based collaborative caching policy is complicated and difficult, considering multiple video encoding versions, long-term benefits for multiple end users and possible FoV prediction error.

To obtain a feasible solution, deep reinforcement learning (DRL) can be used to learn a caching policy automatically utilizing the data collected during interactions among viewers, edge servers and CDN. DRL-based edge caching has been used for general content in [16,17] and traditional video streaming [18]. Inspired by these works, we propose a DRL-based collaborative caching scheme for tile-based omnidirectional video streaming. The proposed scheme caches watched tiles with abundant storage space and guide the cache replacement when storages are full. The collaborative caching problem has been formulated aiming to reduce backhaul traffic and latency while satisfying user requests. Then the collaborative cache replacement policy is modeled as a Markov decision process. To address the difficulty of searching a large-scale action space in DRL, we designed an adaptive action-selection scheme utilizing FoV prediction results. Simulation results demonstrate the effectiveness of the proposed scheme.

2   Collaborative Edge Caching System

2.1   System Overview

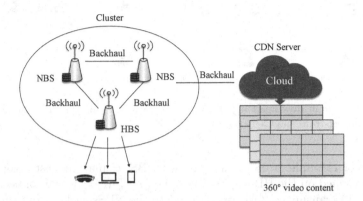

Fig. 1. Illustration of collaborative edge caching framework. A home base station (HBS) and multiple neighboring base stations (NBSs) collaborate to provide edge caching for omnidirectional video streaming.

The framework of collaborative edge caching is presented in Fig. 1. The network consists of M base stations (BSs) and the CDN server where the original video contents are stored. Each BS is associated with an edge caching server providing limited cache storage and can connect to another BS in one hop in the cluster. These BSs form an edge cluster and share resources via backhaul links. We denote the BS in the cluster as h_j whose total cache capacity is limited to B_j.

There are a set of omnidirectional videos in the video library $\mathcal{V}$. Each video frame is encoded into a fixed number of rectangular tiles with two quality versions (e.g., varying video resolution). If N is used to represent the total number of tiles in $\mathcal{V}$, there are $2N$ tile variants in the library. The ith tile variant in $\mathcal{V}$ is denoted as z_i whose size is v_i, where $i \in \{0, 1, 2, ..., 2N - 1\}$. The indexes of tile variants are arranged from the high-quality version of all the tiles to the low-quality versions, where N separates the indexes for each variant of a single tile. The other encoding version of v_i can be denoted as $v_{i'}$, where $i' = (i + N) \bmod 2N$. Besides, the caching state of z_i on BS h_j at time t can be represented by a binary variable $c^s_{z_i, h_j}(t) \in \{0, 1\}$, where the values 1 and 0 mean that z_i is cached and not cached in h_j, respectively. Therefore, the caching status of the whole cluster at time t can be represented by a matrix $C^s(t)$ as follows.

$$C^s(t) = \begin{bmatrix} c^s_{z_0, h_1}(t) & c^s_{z_0, h_2}(t) & \cdots & c^s_{z_0, h_M}(t) \\ c^s_{z_1, h_1}(t) & c^s_{z_1, h_2}(t) & \cdots & c^s_{z_1, h_M}(t) \\ \vdots & \vdots & \cdots & \vdots \\ c^s_{z_{2N-1}, h_1}(t) & c^s_{z_{2N-1}, h_2}(t) & \cdots & c^s_{z_{2N-1}, h_M}(t) \end{bmatrix}. \tag{1}$$

Depending on the caching status of the edge cluster, requested video content can be served by the HBS or one of the several NBSs or CDN, as shown in

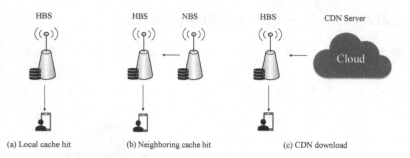

(a) Local cache hit   (b) Neighboring cache hit   (c) CDN download

Fig. 2. A user may download a particular tile variant from the HBS or one of the several NBSs, or from the CDN server.

Figure 2. For example, a user connected with BS h_j may request a tile variant z_i. If z_i is cached on the HBS h_j at time t, i.e., $c^s_{z_i,h_j}(t) = 1$, the connected edge server h_j will transmit z_i. Otherwise, if one of the NBSs caches z_i at time t, i.e., $\forall k \neq j, c^s_{z_i,h_k}(t) = 1$, the requested content will be delivered by the neighboring edge server h_k. If the edge cluster did not cache z_i but the other encoding version $z_{i'}$, the other version is delivered according to the above priority. If neither z_i nor $z_{i'}$ is cached at any edge server, z_i will be downloaded from CDN.

2.2 Problem Formulation

In this work, we consider a collaborative edge cache scheme that caches watched tile variants with abundant storage space, and guides the cache replacement when storages are full. The problem of cache replacement is formulated to reduce the amount of data transmitted in the backhaul network and enhance the quality of experience (QoE) for user requests in the long term.

A local cache replacement decision at time t is represented by $c^r_{z_k,z_i}(t) \in \{0,1\}$. If the decision is to replace the kth tile variant z_k with the ith tile variant z_i in video library at time t, then $c^r_{z_k,z_i}(t) = 1$; otherwise, the value is 0. When a cache replacement happens, the caching status changes as well affecting value of $c^s_{z_i,h_j}(t+1)$. For example, providing that z_k is cached in BS h_j at time t, if $c^r_{z_k,z_i}(t) = 1$, then accordingly $c^s_{z_k,h_j}(t+1) = 0$ and $c^s_{z_i,h_j}(t+1) = 1$. User request is represented by a binary variable $r_{z_i,h_j}(t) \in \{0,1\}$, where values 1 and 0 represent a user connected with h_j requests z_i or not at time t, respectively.

We assume that backbaul traffic between BSs within the edge cluster is neglectable, compared with the backhaul traffic associated with CDN. Thus, the transmission cost for a request $r_{z_i,h_j}(t)$ can be given by:

$$T_{i,j}(t) = v_i \cdot (\sum_{l=1}^{M} c^s_{z_i,h_l}(t) \cdot \mu_0 + (1 - \sum_{l=1}^{M} c^s_{z_i,h_l}(t))(1 - \sum_{l=1}^{M} c^s_{z_{i'},h_l}(t)) \cdot \mu_1)$$

$$+ v_{i'} \cdot (1 - \sum_{l=1}^{M} c^s_{z_i,h_l}(t)) \sum_{l=1}^{M} c^s_{z_{i'},h_l}(t) \cdot \mu_0, \tag{2}$$

where μ_0 and μ_1 ($\mu_0 < \mu_1$) are the corresponding unit price of bandwidth resources obtained from the edge and the remote CDN, respectively.

In this work, we mainly consider quality mismatch level and streaming delay for user QoE. In our caching system, an actual delivered variant of tile can be different from the target variant but satisfy users' other preferences, such as low streaming delay. Thus, as the quality mismatch happens when other variants of the same requested tile are cached instead of the target variant, the quality mismatch level for user request $r_{z_i,h_j}(t)$ can be defined as bellow.

$$M_{i,j}(t) = (1 - \sum_{l=1}^{M} c^s_{z_i,h_l}(t)) \cdot \sum_{l=1}^{M} c^s_{z_{i'},h_l}(t). \tag{3}$$

The streaming delay for user request $r_{z_i,h_j}(t)$ can be defined as:

$$D_{i,j}(t) = d_1 \cdot c^s_{z_i,h_j}(t) + d_2 \cdot (1 - \sum_{l=1,l\neq j}^{M} c^s_{z_i,h_l}(t)) + d_3 \cdot (1 - \sum_{l=1}^{M} c^s_{z_i,h_l}(t)), \tag{4}$$

where $d1$, $d2$, and $d3$ ($d1 < d2 < d3$) represent the transmission delay from the HBS, NBS, and CDN, respectively.

Based on the above analysis, the cache replacement problem can be formulated as minimizing the weighted sum of transmission cost, quality mismatch level, and streaming delay for user requests in a long term of T, subject to a limited cache caching storage capacity as follows.

$$\min_{C^r(0),C^r(1),...,C^r(T)} \sum_{t=0}^{T} \sum_{i=0}^{2N-1} \sum_{j=1}^{M} r_{z_i,h_j}(t) \cdot (k_1 \cdot T_{i,j}(t) + k_2 \cdot M_{i,j}(t) + k_3 \cdot D_{i,j}(t)),$$

$$\tag{5}$$

$$s.t. \sum_{i=0}^{2N-1} \sum_{j=1}^{M} c^s_{z_i,h_j}(t) \cdot v_i \leq B_j \tag{6}$$

$$\left\{ c^s_{z_i,h_j}(t), c^r_{z_k,z_i}(t), r_{z_i,h_j}(t) \right\} \in \{0,1\} \tag{7}$$

$$\sum_{i=0}^{2N-1} \sum_{j=1}^{M} c^s_{z_i,h_j}(t) \leq 1 \tag{8}$$

$$\sum_{i=0}^{2N-1} c^r_{z_k,z_i}(t) \leq 1 \tag{9}$$

$$c^s_{z_i,h_j}(t+1) = 1, c^s_{z_k,h_j}(t+1) = 0, if \ c^r_{z_k,z_i}(t) = 1 \tag{10}$$

$$c^r_{z_k,z_i}(t) \leq \sum_{j=1}^{M} c^s_{z_k,h_j}(t). \tag{11}$$

Equation (5) indicates the cache replacement policy of minimizing our objective function, where the cache replacement policy at time t is presented by $C^r(t)$, which is composed of a set of cache replacement decisions. k_1, k_2, and k_3 are the relative trade-off coefficients. Besides, Eq. (6) guarantees that the size of cached tiles does not exceed the storage capacity of each BS. Equation (7) states that the values of those variables can only take a value of 0 or 1. Equation (8) ensures that z_i can only be cached unless there is no replica in the edge cache. Equation (9) states that it can only take cache replacement operation once or do not take cache replacement operation at time t. Equation (10) ensures the caching states' corresponding changes brought by a cache replacement. Equation (11) ensures that only cached tile can be replaced or fetched.

With this policy, the system can decide whether and which item in the edge cache should be replaced when the caching storage capacity is not enough. Nevertheless, with users requesting different video content, views, and qualities, the cluster has a large number of various cache statuses. The multiple bitrate video caching problem that maximizes the perceived QoE has been proved to be NP-hard [19]. The QoE function in [19] is assumed to be positive and strictly increasing, while our problem has a more complicated objective function. It is crucial to develop a low-complexity solution to adapt to the complex environment.

3   DRL-Based Collaborative Edge Cache Replacement Solution

The process of cache replacement is modeled as a Markov decision process. A deep reinforcement learning approach is used to obtain a cache replacement solution. We use a robust version of DQN, Double DQN (DDQN), to train our DRL agents in the edge cluster. The DRL agent can collect the information automatically and be trained in the background. After enough iterations, the agent can make cache replacement decisions intelligently. Here, we introduce the state space, action space, and the reward function of the DRL agent applied in our caching system as follows:

State Space: The state space is generally a finite set of the state. We consider employing the viewing pattern of user FoV to improve cache efficiency. Thus, the system state at time t, $state_t$, consists of the current caching status $C^s(t)$ and the FoV weight status of the cached tiles $F(t)$. Specifically, we also use matrix to represent the latter, so the current system state can be expressed as $state_t = (C^s(t), F(t))$. Then, with given FoV information, an FoV weight can be defined as the percentage of FoV overlapped area in a tile as shown in Fig. 3.

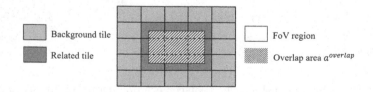

Fig. 3. Illustrations of tiles and FoV region.

The FoV weight of z_i $(0 < i < N)$ with higher quality level at $t = 0$ is calculated as $f_{z_i}(0) = \frac{a_i^{overlap}}{a}$, where a is the area of z_i, and $a_i^{overlap}$ represents the overlap area of z_i and the FoV region. Considering the user preference, we set each variant of a tile has same FoV weight at $t = 0$ and gradually changes its value with each arrival of request. Thus, the FoV weight of z_i at time t is:

$$f_{z_i}(t) = (1 + \left| sgn(\sum_{j=1}^{M} r_{z_i,h_j}(t)) \right| \cdot \frac{1}{N}) \cdot f_{z_i}(t-1). \tag{12}$$

Thus, the matrix of $F(t)$ can be displayed as below.

$$F(t) = \begin{bmatrix} f_{z_1}(t) \\ f_{z_2}(t) \\ \vdots \\ f_{z_{2N-1}}(t) \end{bmatrix}. \tag{13}$$

Therefore, as the state space is all the possible combination of the current caching status and the FoV weight status, it can be given as:

$$\mathcal{S} = \{(C^s(t), F(t)) | C^s(t) \in \mathbb{C}, F(t) \in \mathbb{F}\}, \tag{14}$$

where $\mathbb{C}$ is the set of all caching status and $\mathbb{F}$ is the set of all FoV weight status.

Action Space: The action space is the set of finite actions. In order to limit the action space size, we restrict that the DRL agent can only select one tile to replace by currently requested content, or keep the edge caching status the same. Therefore, in our caching system, the cache replacement is only available between the tile of the same quality in case the removal of one tile can not free up enough space for the newly added content. According to this, we define $\mathcal{A}$ as the action space, which also means the set of possible replacement choices, and it can be given as:

$$\mathcal{A} = \{c_{z_k,z_i}^r(t) | c_{z_k,z_i}^r(t) \in \mathbb{R}\}, \tag{15}$$

where $\mathbb{R}$ is the set of all cache replacement decisions.

Reward: The reward function defines the goal in an MDP problem. Instead of using our formulated objective function as the reward function directly, we assume that replacing more tiles of low FoV weight with the user requested tile variants will contribute more to maximize the system reward. Therefore, the reward function can be given by:

$$reward_t = \sum_{i=0}^{2N-1} \sum_{j=1}^{M} (1 - f_{z_k}(t)) \cdot r_{z_i,h_j}(t) \cdot (k_1 \cdot T_{i,j}(t) + k_2 \cdot M_{i,j}(t) + k_3 \cdot D_{i,j}(t)). \tag{16}$$

With the discount factor γ, the total reward through the whole process is:

$$\mathcal{R} = \sum_{t=0}^{T} \gamma^t \cdot reward_t. \tag{17}$$

Algorithm 1. DRL-based Collaborative Cache Replacement Algorithm

---

Input: Initialize the caching status $C^s(0)$, the experience replay memory $\mathcal{M}$, main $\mathcal{Q}$ network with random weight θ, and target $\hat{\mathcal{Q}}$ network with $\theta' = \theta$, the tile sets of all cached tiles in BS j at time t $\hat{A}_j(t)$ and a void tile set $\{\hat{a}\}$.

Output: The cache replacement policy $C^r(0), C^r(1), ..., C^r(T)$.

1: **for** t = 0, 1, ..., T **do**
2:      BS h_j receive a request of tile z_i at time t.
3:      **if** $\sum_{j=1}^{M} c_{z_i,h_j}^s(t) = 1$ **then**
4:          Transmit z_i from the edge cluster.
5:      **else**
6:          Download z_i from the CDN server and transmit it to user.
7:          **if** Edge cache storage is full **then**
8:              Observe the current state $state_t$, and preprocessed it as $\Phi(state_t)$.
9:              Generate p as random.
10:              **if** $p \leq \epsilon$ **then**
11:                  **for** $j = 1, 2, ..., M$ **do**
12:                      Add $argmin_{z_k \in \hat{A}_j(t)} f_{z_k}(t)$ to $\{\hat{a}\}$.
13:                  **end for**
14:                  Randomly select a tile $z_{\hat{k}}$ from the tile set $\{\hat{a}\}$.
15:                  $action_t = c_{z_{\hat{k}},z_i}^r(t)$.
16:              **else**
17:                  $action_t = argmax_{action_t}(\mathcal{Q}(\Phi(state_t), action_t); \theta_t)$.
18:              **end if**
19:              Execute $action_t$, obtain $reward_t$ and preprocessed new state $\Phi(state_{t+1})$.
20:              Construct transition $(\Phi(state_t), action_t, reward_t, \Phi(state_{t+1}))$.
21:              Store the transition into $\mathcal{M}$.
22:              Sample a random mini-batch of transitions $\hat{\mathcal{M}}_i \in \mathcal{M}$.
23:              Update the main $\mathcal{Q}$ network.
24:              Update the target $\hat{\mathcal{Q}}$ network periodically.
25:          **else**
26:              Cache z_i in the edge cluster.
27:          **end if**
28:      **end if**
29: **end for**

As depicted in Algorithm 1, in our caching system, if the requested content is not cached in edge cluster and the edge caching space is full at time t, the DRL agent would observe the state feature $\Phi(state_t)$ from the environment, and obtain actions and Q value from the Q network. Then, an ϵ-greedy policy is applied at selecting the execution action $action_t$. This policy can force the agent to explore more possible actions. Here, to overcome the difficulty of searching a large-scale action space, the action space has been narrowed with an adaptive action-selection scheme. We add the tile variant with the least FoV weight on each BS to $\{\hat{a}\}$, and randomly select one from $\{\hat{a}\}$ to replace. After $action_t$ is executed, the DRL agent would obtain the reward $reward_t$ and next state $state_{t+1}$ from the caching system, and the new state would be preprocessed as well. The transition $(\Phi(state_t), action_t, reward_t, \Phi(state_{t+1}))$ will be constructed and then stored to the memory buffer $\mathcal{M}$. In the end, the DRL agent would update the parameters with transitions that sampled from memory buffer $\mathcal{M}$. Thus, we can learn a DRL-based cache replacement policy to make proper cache replacement decisions and serve users with improved performance.

4   Experiment Result

4.1   Simulation Setup

We consider an edge cluster consisting of three edge cache servers. Each user randomly connects with a BS as HBS, while the remaining BSs in the cluster become NBSs. The unit price of bandwidth for edge servers is set to 20% of that of the CDN server using the pricing of Amazon AWS [20], where prices are represented by μ_0 and μ_1 in Eq. (2). As to d_1, d_2, and d_3, the latency of fetching video content from the HBS, the NBS and CDN server, are randomly generated from the ranges of [5, 10](ms), [20, 50](ms), and [100, 200](ms) according to a uniform distribution [21]. About trade-off weights k_1, k_2, and k_3, different combinations of varying values are tested, where empirical values are obtained which set $k_1 = 0.1$, $k_1 = k_2 = 0.45$ in our simulation, respectively.

The video library in [22] is used, which has ten one-minute omnidirectional videos accompanied by real viewing traces of 50 viewers. Each video has two encoded versions with bitrates of 1 Mbps and 3 Mbps, respectively. Requests for different videos follow a Zipf distribution with the skew parameter $\alpha = 0.5$. To test the proposed scheme with inaccurate FoV prediction, the average of all viewers' FoV positions in ten consecutive frames is used as the predicted FoV position for these frames.

In the DRL implementation, the constructed Q network has three hidden layers of fully connected units with 512, 128, and 32 neurons, respectively. The capacity of the experience replay buffer is set as 10000, and the mini-batch size is 64. Specially, to get a better long-term reward, we set the discount factor γ of reward as 0.99.

4.2   Performance Comparison

The DRL-based collaborative caching scheme, referred as DRL-CCS, is compared with the following schemes.

- DRL-based caching scheme (DRL-CS): A caching scheme that employed an DRL-based cache replacement algorithm. Different from our proposed scheme, DRL-CS does not enable collaboration between BSs.
- Collaborative least recently used caching scheme (LRU) [16]: A collaborative caching scheme employed the wide used least recently used cache replacement strategy. When the caching storage is full, the caching scheme will remove the tile whose last access time is the oldest compared with others.

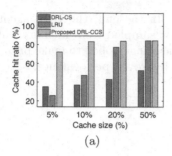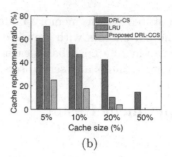

Fig. 4. The performance of all schemes with cache size from 5% to 50%: (a) cache hit ratio, (b) cache replacement ratio.

To evaluate the efficiency of these caching schemes, a performance comparison is conducted with the total cache size varying from 5% to 50% of the size of the video library, which is shown in Fig. 4. Generally, with the cache size increase, more tiles are cached in the edge server resulting in a higher cache hit ratio and lower cache replacement ratio. Compared with the DRL-CS and LRU schemes, the proposed scheme achieves up to 37.06%, and 46.40% performance gains in terms of the cache hit ratio, as shown in Fig. 4(a). Although the cache hit ratio of DRL-CS is higher than LRU, its cache replacement ratio is also higher because of the limited caching space compared with the collaborative caching scheme. Frequent cache replacement causes extra I/O expenses, which is not desirable. As shown in Fig. 4(b), with the cache size getting larger, the DRL-CCS scheme reduces up to 38.33% and 46% of the cache replacement operations compared with the DRL-CS and LRU schemes.

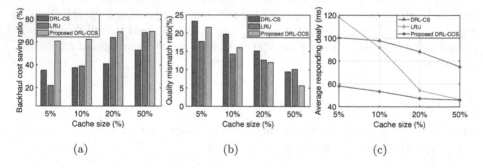

Fig. 5. The performance of all schemes with cache size from 5% to 50%: (a) backhaul cost saving ratio, (b) quality mismatch ratio, (c) average responding delay.

Since the proposed scheme aims to save backhaul costs and improve the user QoE jointly, relevant schemes are compared in terms of cost saving ratio, quality mismatch ratio, and average responding delay as shown in Fig. 5. For most conditions, our DRL-CCS could save backhaul cost up to 60.65%, and can also achieve at least 25.47% and 38.81% performance gains compared with the DRL-CS and LRU schemes, respectively, as shown in Fig. 5(a). Regarding the QoE performance, we can also see from Fig. 5(b), the proposed DRL-CSS scheme outperforms the DRL-CS and the LRU schemes, only showing a slightly worse quality mismatch performance when the cache size is small. The DRL-CS scheme also achieves a lower quality mismatch ratio than LRU by considering user preference. In Fig. 5(c), our proposed scheme reduced responding delay up to 49.05% and 57.82% compared with the DRL-CS and the LRU schemes, respectively. As the cache size increases, the performance of LRU gradually approaches DRL-CCS and has almost the same delay when the cache storage is sufficient.

5   Conclusion

In this paper, we propose a DRL-based collaborative mobile edge caching policy for omnidirectional video streaming. The problem of collaborative caching has been formulated, aiming to reduce backhaul traffic and latency while satisfying user requests. Due to the complexity of this problem, we proposed an efficient DRL-based method that to make online cache replacement decisions upon each user request arrival. Furthermore, an adaptive action selection scheme utilizing FoV prediction results has been designed to reduce the searched action space. Simulative results demonstrate the effectiveness of the proposed method.

References

1. Khurana, T.: Retail and AR and VR: 5G brings it home! (2019). https://blogs.cisco.com/sp/retail-and-ar-and-vr-5g-brings-it-home?dtid=osscdc000283
2. Dai, J., Zhang, Z., Mao, S., Liu, D.: A view synthesis-based 360° VR caching system over MEC-enabled C-RAN. IEEE Trans. Circuits Syst. Video Technol. **30**, 3843–3855 (2019)
3. Sukhmani, S., Sadeghi, M., Erol-Kantarci, M., El Saddik, A.: Edge caching and computing in 5G for mobile AR/VR and tactile internet. IEEE Multimedia **26**(1), 21–30 (2019)
4. Han, S., Su, H., Yang, C., Molisch, A.F.: Proactive edge caching for video on demand with quality adaptation. IEEE Trans. Wireless Commun. **19**(1), 218–234 (2020)
5. Wang, D., et al.: Adaptive wireless video streaming based on edge computing: opportunities and approaches. IEEE Trans. Serv. Comput. **12**(5), 685–697 (2019). https://doi.org/10.1109/TSC.2018.2828426
6. Tran, T.X., Hajisami, A., Pandey, P., Pompili, D.: Collaborative mobile edge computing in 5G networks: new paradigms, scenarios, and challenges. IEEE Commun. Mag. **55**(4), 54–61 (2017). https://doi.org/10.1109/MCOM.2017.1600863
7. Chakareski, J.: VR/AR immersive communication: caching, edge computing, and transmission trade-offs. In: Proceedings of the Workshop on Virtual Reality and Augmented Reality Network. VR/AR Network 2017, pp. 36–41 (2017). https://doi.org/10.1145/3097895.3097902
8. Song, Y., Zhao, Y., Li, C.: A user behavior aware immersive video caching algorithm. In: Proceedings of the 11th International Conference on Wireless Communications and Signal Processing. WCSP 2019, pp. 1–6 (2019). https://doi.org/10.1109/WCSP.2019.8927955

9. Sullivan, G.J., Ohm, J., Han, W., Wiegand, T.: Overview of the high efficiency video coding (HEVC) standard. IEEE Trans. Circuits Syst. Video Technol. **22**(12), 1649–1668 (2012)

10. Chakareski, J.: Viewport-adaptive scalable multi-user virtual reality mobile-edge streaming. IEEE Trans. Image Process. **29**, 6330–6342 (2020). https://doi.org/10.1109/TIP.2020.2986547

11. Maniotis, P., Bourtsoulatze, E., Thomos, N.: Tile-based joint caching and delivery of 360° videos in heterogeneous networks. In: Proceedings of the 21st International Workshop on Multimedia Signal Processing. MMSP 2019, pp. 1–6 (2019)

12. He, D., Jiang, J., Westphal, C., Yang, G.: Efficient edge caching for high-quality 360-degree video delivery. In: Ro, Y.M., et al. (eds.) MMM 2020. LNCS, vol. 11962, pp. 39–51. Springer, Cham (2020). https://doi.org/10.1007/978-3-030-37734-2_4

13. Yang, Y., Lee, J., Kim, N., Kim, K.: Social-viewport adaptive caching scheme with clustering for virtual reality streaming in an edge computing platform. Future Gener. Comput. Syst. **108**, 424–431 (2020). https://doi.org/10.1016/j.future.2020.02.078

14. Sun, L., Mao, Y., Zong, T., Liu, Y., Wang, Y.: Flocking-based live streaming of 360-degree video. In: Proceedings of the 11th ACM Multimedia Systems Conference. MMSys 2020, pp. 26–37 (2020). https://doi.org/10.1145/3339825.3391856

15. Mahzari, A., Taghavi Nasrabadi, A., Samiei, A., Prakash, R.: FoV-aware edge caching for adaptive 360° video streaming. In: Proceedings of the 26th ACM International Conference on Multimedia. MM 2018, pp. 173–181 (2018). https://doi.org/10.1145/3240508.3240680

16. Li, D., et al.: Deep reinforcement learning for cooperative edge caching in future mobile networks. In: Proceedings of the 2019 IEEE Wireless Communications and Networking Conference, pp. 1–6 (2019). https://doi.org/10.1109/WCNC.2019.8885516

17. Yang, Z., Liu, Y., Chen, Y., Tyson, G.: Deep reinforcement learning in cache-aided MEC networks. In: Proceedings of the 2019 IEEE International Conference on Communications. ICC 2019, pp. 1–6 (2019). https://doi.org/10.1109/ICC.2019.8761349

18. Wang, F., Wang, F., Liu, J., Shea, R., Sun, L.: Intelligent video caching at network edge: a multi-agent deep reinforcement learning approach. In: Proceedings of the IEEE Conference on Computer Communications. INFOCOM 2020, pp. 2499–2508 (2020). https://doi.org/10.1109/INFOCOM41043.2020.9155373

19. Qu, Z., Ye, B., Tang, B., Guo, S., Lu, S., Zhuang, W.: Cooperative caching for multiple bitrate videos in small cell edges. IEEE Trans. Mob. Comput. **19**(2), 288–299 (2020). https://doi.org/10.1109/TMC.2019.2893917

20. Amazon Web Services, Inc.: Amazon EC2 pricing (2021). https://aws.amazon.com/cn/ec2/pricing/on-demand/

21. Tran, T.X., Pandey, P., Hajisami, A., Pompili, D.: Collaborative multi-bitrate video caching and processing in Mobile-Edge Computing networks. In: Proceedings of the 13th Annual Conference on Wireless On-demand Network Systems and Services. WONS 2017, pp. 165–172 (2017). https://doi.org/10.1109/WONS.2017.7888772

22. Lo, W.C., Fan, C.L., Lee, J., Huang, C.Y., Chen, K.T., Hsu, C.H.: 360° video viewing dataset in head-mounted virtual reality. In: Proceedings of the 8th ACM on Multimedia Systems Conference. MMSys 2017, pp. 211–216 (2017). https://doi.org/10.1145/3083187.3083219

DNN Inference Acceleration
with Partitioning and Early Exiting
in Edge Computing

Chao Li[1], Hongli Xu[2], Yang Xu[2(✉)], Zhiyuan Wang[1], and Liusheng Huang[2]

[1] School of Computer Science and Technology,
University of Science and Technology of China, Hefei 230026, China
{lcccccc,cswangzy}@mail.ustc.edu.cn
[2] Suzhou Institute for Advanced Research,
University of Science and Technology of China, Suzhou 215123, China
{xuhongli,xuyangcs,lshuang}@ustc.edu.cn

Abstract. Recently, deep neural networks (DNNs) have been applied to most intelligent applications and deployed on different kinds of devices. However, DNN inference is resource-intensive. Especially, in edge computing, DNN inference demands to face the constrained computing resource of end devices and excessive data transmission costs when offloading raw data to the edge server. A better solution is DNN partitioning, which splits the DNN into two parts, one running on end devices and the other on the edge server. However, one edge server often needs to provide services for multiple end devices simultaneously, which may cause excessive queueing delay. To meet the latency requirements of real-time DNN tasks, we combine the early-exit mechanism and DNN partitioning. We formally define the DNN inference with partitioning and early-exit as an optimization problem. To solve the problem, we propose two efficient algorithms to determine the partition points of DNN partitioning and the thresholds of the early-exit mechanism. We conduct extensive simulations on our proposed algorithms, and the results show that they can dramatically accelerate DNN inference while achieving high accuracy.

Keywords: Edge computing · DNN inference · DNN partitioning · Early-exit

1 Introduction

In recent years, with the rapid development of machine learning (ML), intelligent applicants are becoming more and more prevalent [1]. As a result, Deep Neural Networks (DNNs), as the most widely used ML models, have been attracting more and more attention, and are adopted in many intelligent applications. Moreover, these applications can run on many Internet of Things (IoT) devices, such as mobile phones, wearables [2]. However, these end devices are embedded and heterogeneous. To provide high-quality services, many real-time AI applications, e.g., real-time voice and video processing [3], demand to respond within

© Springer Nature Switzerland AG 2021
Z. Liu et al. (Eds.): WASA 2021, LNCS 12937, pp. 465–478, 2021.
https://doi.org/10.1007/978-3-030-85928-2_37

a given time. Whereas, end devices may fail to support these applications with their limited resources, which may cause intolerable computing delays. To this end, traditional cloud computing [4] methods are used to provide powerful computing capability for end devices to meet the computing requirements of DNN inference of the real-time AI applications. These methods have been the research hotspot in the past decades [5]. In cloud computing, end devices usually forward data to the cloud server through the wireless links with low bandwidth, and the cloud server then performs the DNN inference tasks that are computation-intensive. As we can see, the main challenge faced by cloud computing is the intolerable delays caused by the excessive data transmission through low bandwidth between end devices and the cloud.

To prevent the unacceptable computing delay caused by performing DNN inference locally on end devices or the transmission delay caused by forwarding data to the cloud for execution, edge computing [6] comes into being. The principal idea of edge computing is to place edge servers at the network edge and provide computing capacity for nearby end devices with low transmission delay. Edge computing enables us to handle the latency-sensitive DNN inference tasks effectively. Recently, some researches have been proposed to accelerate DNN inference based on edge computing, such as edge caching [7] that caches and reuses the task results (e.g., the prediction of image classification at the network edge) to reduce the querying latency of AI applications. However, these works also encounter some difficulties. Since the wireless bandwidth often fluctuates widely in edge computing [8], uploading raw input data from end devices to the edge server may still cause significant latency.

To further improve the DNN inference performance of real-time tasks in edge computing, DNN partitioning is proposed. According to previous works [9], we note that the output data size at some intermediate DNN layers is much smaller than that of the raw input data. The observation motivates us to find an appropriate partition point to split a DNN into two parts to reduce the communication cost by offloading intermediate output to the edge server. Specifically, the part before the partition point is processed on the end device and the other in the edge server. [10] Since end devices have limited computing resources, executing excessive DNN layers on the end device will incur significant computing latency. Therefore, it is crucial to find an partition point to achieve an optimal trade-off between the computing latency and the communication cost.

Since the edge server has limited resources compared to the cloud, it will incur lots of queueing delays when multiple tasks need to be processed on the edge server simultaneously. To further improve DNN inference, we introduce another approach, called the early-exit mechanism, to reduce the queueing delay. Since the features learned in the former layers of a DNN may be sufficient to obtain satisfying inference results [11], the principle idea of early-exit is to terminate the inference process in an intermediate layer. According to the early-exit mechanism, the forward process of the entire DNN through the input layer to the final layer can be avoided. The existing early-exit methods include two categories. The first one modifies the standard DNN model structure by adding exit branches at certain layer locations and then trains the original model with the exit branches together, such as [11]. However, there are two shortcomings as follows. Firstly, it is hard to design exit branches for a given model structure. Secondly, it incurs a lot of additional costs to train the modified model, for example, training resnet50 on 8 T P100 GPUs requires 29 h [12]. The second category adds a linear classifier after each convolutional layer and monitors the output to decide whether a given sample can be correctly classified at the specific exit point, such as Condition Deep Learning (CDL) [13]. However, the second approach will sacrifice the classification accuracy. In this paper, we introduce the Support Vector Machine (SVM) [14] trained with hinge loss for the early-exit mechanism, in which SVM is regarded as the classifier. The method can be applied directly to the pre-trained model without modifying the structure, and it has been proven that there is almost no accuracy loss [15]. Besides, we perform quantitative analysis on the threshold value of our early-exit mechanism. The threshold value are employed to compare with classification probability to determine whether samples can be classified in advance, and which will be discussed in detail in Sect. 2. Compared with the existing methods mentioned above, this method has the advantages of generality, low computational cost, and high inference accuracy.

In this paper, we combine DNN partitioning and the early-exit mechanism to accelerate DNN inference in heterogeneous edge computing. To address the problem, we first propose a dynamic programming (DP) method to obtain partition decisions and then put forward an algorithm based on greedy adjusting and convex optimization (GACO) to compute optimal exit threshold for each end device. Furthermore, we design different partition points and threshold values for heterogeneous devices. The main contributions of this paper are as follows:

- We adopt DNN partitioning and early-exit mechanism to accelerate DNN inference in practical heterogeneous edge computing, where one edge server provides services for multiple heterogeneous devices simultaneously.
- We design a DP algorithm to split the DNN and quantitatively analyze the early-exit mechanism in the GACO algorithm.
- We conduct extensive simulations on our proposed algorithms, and the results show that they can dramatically accelerate DNN inference while achieving high accuracy.

The rest of the paper is organized as follows. Section 2 introduces the system model and provides the problem definition. In Sect. 3, we propose two algorithms to address the optimization problem. The simulation results are shown in Sect. 4. We summarize the paper in Sect. 5.

2   System Model and Problem Formulation

In this section, we first describe the system model, and then we formally define the optimization problem.

2.1   System Model

In the scenario of edge computing, since the number of end devices is more than that of edge servers, one edge server usually needs to provide services for multiple

Table 1. Notation summary

Notations	Summary
s	Edge server
U	A set of devices $\{u_1, u_2, ..., u_n\}$
D	DNN with layers $\{d_1, d_2, ..., d_m\}$
μ	Computing capacity of server s
χ_i	Output size of d_i
Φ	Total task arrival rate
ϕ_u	Task arrival rate on device u
c_i	Required CPU cycles for d_i
γ_i	Required CPU cycles for the classifier at the ith layer
r_u	Uplink transmission rate between device u and server
ζ_u	Required CPU cycles on edge server for device u
y_l^u	Threshold setting at lth layer on device u
x_l^u	Partition decision at the lth layer of DNN on device u
λ	Total required computing capacity on server s
p_s^u	The offloading probability on device u

end devices simultaneously. The mission of the end device is to accomplish DNN tasks under the latency requirements (Table 1).

For the arrival tasks, the end device can process them in three ways, i.e., computing with the local processing unit, offloading to the edge server through the transmission unit, or executing on the end device and edge server with DNN partitioning. As mentioned before, the edge server needs to process a lot of tasks from different end devices simultaneously. However, the resources of the edge server are limited, which will incur excessive queueing time for tasks on the edge server. Therefore, we introduce the early-exit mechanism to filter out samples that can be classified in advance to alleviate the pressure on the edge server. Next, we will formally define the problem in the above scenario.

2.2 Problem Formulation

We denote the set of devices as $U = \{u_1, u_2, u_3, ..., u_n\}$, where $n = |U|$ is the total number of the devices. The computing capability of the edge server s is defined as μ (i.e., CPU cycles per second). Without loss of generality, we assume that the tasks' arrival rate on device u ($u \in U$) follows a Poisson process with expected arrival rate ϕ_u (e.g. tasks/second). The total task arrival rate in the system is denoted as $\Phi = \sum_{u \in U} \phi_u$. We train a classifier for each convolutional layer of the pre-trained DNN and assume that the DNN is pre-loaded at all devices and the edge server. Considering a DNN $D = \{d_1, d_2, d_3..., d_m\}$, where m is the number of layers. Let c_i be the number of required CPU cycles for the ith layer of the DNN with standard input.

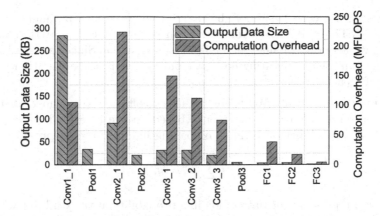

Fig. 1. The computation overhead and output data size of each layer of AlexNet.

DNN Partitioning. For better understanding the performance bottleneck of DNN inference, we obtain the computation overhead and the intermediate output data size of each layer of AlexNet through computation. As shown in Fig. 1, the output data size decreases with the depth of the DNN, which shows that the deeper on the DNN the partition point is set, the more expensive the computation overhead on the end device, and the less the communication overhead between the end device and the edge server. Based on the observation above, we should choose an appropriate partition point to utilize computing and bandwidth resources to accelerate DNN inference by DNN partitioning. Let $x_l^u = \{0, 1\}$ indicate whether to partition the DNN at the lth layer or not for device u, then we have $\sum_{i=1}^{m} x_i^u = 1, \forall u \in U$.

Early-Exit Mechanism. To cope with excessive queueing time on the edge server, we introduce the early-exit mechanism. The early-exit mechanism significantly reduces runtime and resource consumption by avoiding the processing of all layers. The input data passes the input layer and is classified into multiple class labels by the classifier in the early-exit mechanism. Each class label has a probability, and the classification probability is the maximum probability among them. To filter out the samples that can be classified by the classifier, we introduce the threshold value. Then we compare the threshold value and the classification probability. When the classification probability is greater than the threshold value, the samples will be classified by the classifier. Furthermore, the decrease of the threshold value will reduce the task completion time and decrease the accuracy. Therefore, it is significant to set the proper threshold value to obtain the trade-off between completion time and accuracy. In this paper, we adopt the SVM trained with hinge loss as the classifier. The hinge loss can be formulated as $L = \frac{1}{N}\sum_i L_i + \hat{\lambda}R(W)$, where N is the number of class labels, and $L_i = \sum_{j \neq l_i} \max(0, s_j - s_{l_i})$, here s_{l_i} represents the maximum score among all class labels and s_j represents the scores of class labels except the s_{l_i}. Besides, $\hat{\lambda}$ determines the trade-off between increasing the margin size and ensuring that the $\mathbf{x}_i$ lies on the correct side of the margin, where $\mathbf{x}_i$ is a p-dimensional real input vector. The $R(W)$ is the regularization penalty. Let $y_l^u \in [0,1]$ denote the threshold value of the classifier at the layer l for device u. Since the classifier will also bring additional computing costs, we only place it at the partition point of the DNN for each device.

Communication Model. We decide whether to offload the intermediate output to the edge server for processing or not based on the threshold value. Let p_s^u represent the probability of device u offloading intermediate output

$$p_s^u = \sum_{i=1}^m x_i^u p_i(y_i^u) \tag{1}$$

where $p_i(y_i^u)$ represents the data offloading probability at the ith layer when the threshold value is y_i^u, which can be obtained offline. Let h_u denote the channel gain between device u and edge server, and G_u be the transmission power. Then, the uplink transmission rate between the device and server can be derived by Shannon capacity $r_u = Blog_2(1 + \frac{G_u h_u}{\sigma^2})$, where B represents the channel bandwidth and σ^2 is the noise power. The communication latency between device u and the edge server is $T_u^s = \frac{1}{r_u} \sum_{i=1}^m x_i^u \chi_i$, where χ_i represents the intermediate output size of layer i. Since the data size of the result is negligible, the downlink transmission latency can be ignored.

Computation Model. After partitioning, the computing time of tasks comprises two parts, i.e., the computing time on the device and the edge server. As the task arrival process on each device follows a Poisson process, the task arrival at each device can be modeled as the M/M/1 system. Therefore, the expected completion time of one task on device u is $T_u^l = \frac{1}{\frac{1}{T_u^q} - \phi_u}$. T_u^q is the computing time of one task on device u, where $T_u^q = \sum_{i=1}^m x_i^u (f_i^u + \sum_{j=1}^i \frac{c_j}{F_u})$. Note that F_u represents the computing capability of device u (i.e., CPU cycles per second), and f_i^u represents the required computing time of the classifier at the ith layer of the DNN on device u. We have $f_i^u = \frac{\gamma_i}{F_u}$, where γ_i represents the number of required CPU cycles for the classifier at the ith layer. Let ζ_u represent the total required CPU cycles by device u on the edge server, where $\zeta_u = \sum_{i=1}^m c_i \sum_{j=1}^i x_j^u$. Moreover, the total expected computing capacity on the edge server required by device u can be expressed as $\varepsilon_u = p_s^u \zeta_u \phi_u$. Therefore, the total required computing capacity of the edge server is $\lambda = \sum_{u \in U} \varepsilon_u = \sum_{u \in U} p_s^u \zeta_u \phi_u$. As tasks' arrival on each device follows a Poisson process, the arrival process on the edge server will also follow the Poisson process according to the splitting property of Poisson processes [16]. Therefore, the task arrival at the edge server can be modeled as the M/GI/1-PS system [17]. The expected computing time of one task from device u on the edge server is

$$T_u^c = \frac{\zeta_u}{\mu - \lambda} \tag{2}$$

For device u, the expected completion time of one task is

$$T_u = T_u^l + p_s^u(T_u^s + T_u^c) \tag{3}$$

and the expected accuracy is

$$\psi_u = \sum\nolimits_{i=1}^{m} x_i^u q_i(y_i^u) \tag{4}$$

where $q_i(y_i^u)$ denotes the inference accuracy when the threshold value of the classifier at the ith layer is y_i^u. The inference accuracy $q_i(y_i^u)$ can be pre-calculated when training classifiers. To maximize the average inference accuracy of tasks in the system, we formulate the optimization problem as follows

$$\max \frac{1}{\Phi} \sum\nolimits_{u \in U} \psi_u \phi_u$$

$$s.t. \begin{cases} T_u^l + p_s^u(T_u^s + T_u^c) \le T_u^{lim}, \forall u \in U \\ \sum_{i=1}^{m} x_i^u \le 1, & \forall u \in U \\ x_i^u \in \{0, 1\}, y_i^u \in [0, 1], & \forall u \in U \end{cases} \tag{5}$$

The first set of inequalities signifies that tasks in device u should be accomplished under latency requirement T_u^{lim}. The second set of formulas indicates that the DNN should be partitioned into two parts at most for each device.

3   Algorithm Design

Since the objective in Eq. (5) can be transformed into a knapsack-like problem by combining knapsack constraints, it is an NP-hard problem. In this section, we propose two algorithms to address the problem.

3.1   DNN Partitioning Based on Dynamic Programming

In this subsection, we propose a dynamic programming (DP) algorithm to determine the partition points. The objective is to minimize the average task completion time in the system, which can be expressed as

$$\min \frac{1}{\Phi} \sum_{u \in U} T_u * \phi_u \tag{6}$$

To solve this problem, we first omit the early-exit mechanism here, and redefine some variables as $T_u = T_u^l + T_u^s + T_u^c$, where $T_u^c = \frac{\zeta_u}{\mu - \lambda}$ and $\lambda = \sum_{u \in U} \zeta_u * \phi_u$. According to the analysis in Sect. 2, the transmission time and local computing time are only related to the DNN partitioning decision on a single device, while the computing time on the edge server relates to all devices' partitioning decisions. Therefore, we rewrite the objective function as

$$\min \frac{1}{\Phi} (\sum_{u \in U} (T_u^l + T_u^s) * \phi_u + \sum_{u \in U} T_u^c * \phi_u) \tag{7}$$

According to Eq. (2) and $\lambda = \sum_{u \in U} \zeta_u * \phi_u$, we have

$$\sum_{u \in U} T_u^c * \phi_u = \frac{\lambda}{\mu - \lambda} \tag{8}$$

Therefore, Eq. (7) can be converted to

$$\min \frac{1}{\varPhi}\left(\sum_{u \in U} (T_u^l + T_u^s) * \phi_u + \frac{\lambda}{\mu - \lambda}\right) \tag{9}$$

Generally, DP is a method of solving complex problems by decomposing the original problem into relatively simple subproblems [18]. The original problem in this subsection is to determine partition points that minimize task completion time. We decompose the original problem into minimizing task completion time when there are only n' devices, where $n' \le n$. To solve the subproblem, we iterate the set of devices U from u_1 to u_n. For iteration i, the problem is to minimize the sum of task completion time from device u_1 to u_i, and in which we enumerate all possible partition points on u_i and the total local computing time from device u_1 to u_i. Then we define a function $f(u_i, p_i, \kappa_i)$ to indicate the minimum computing time on the edge server when the partition point of u_i is p_i and the total local computing time from u_1 to u_i is limited to κ_i. Upon the principal of DP, the $(i-1)$th iteration is a subproblem of the ith iteration. Therefore, we should calculate $f(u_i, p_i, \kappa_i)$ by adding $f(u_{i-1}, p_{i-1}, \kappa_i - \varpi_i)$ and the increased time on the edge server when the partition point of u_i is p_i, where ϖ_i represents the local computing time on u_i. In addition, $f(u_{i-1}, p_{i-1}, \kappa_i - \varpi_i)$ has been calculated at $(i-1)$th iteration. However, the computing time on the edge server is related to the partition decisions of all devices, therefore, the value of $f(u_{i-1}, p_{i-1}, \kappa_i - \varpi_i)$ will be changed when adding u_i to the device set containing u_1 to u_{i-1}. Next, we will make some transformations to solve the problem.

For Eq. (8), since $\frac{\partial(\frac{\lambda}{\mu-\lambda})}{\partial\lambda} = \frac{\mu}{(\mu-\lambda)^2} > 0$, the value of Eq. (8) increases with λ. Therefore, to minimize the computing time of tasks on the edge server can be transformed into minimizing the loads (i.e., λ) on the edge server. Based on the transformation, we define a function $g(u_i, p_i, \kappa_i)$ to represent the minimum loads on the edge server when the partition point of u_i is p_i and the total local computing time from u_1 to u_i is limited to κ_i. Then we have that $g(u_i, p_i, \kappa_i) = g(u_{i-1}, p_{i-1}, \kappa_i - \varpi_i) + l_i$, where l_i represents increased loads on the edge server when partition point of u_i is p_i. During the iterations, we store the partition points that minimize the function g into a recordset. Through the iterations, we can obtain the minimum loads of the edge server for any given local computing time constraints κ_i, which can be converted into the computing time on the edge server according to Eq. (8). Then, we can obtain the optimal partition points corresponding to the minimum computing time from the recordset. Through the DP algorithm, we can obtain a set of optimal partition points for all devices, which minimizes the sum of total local computing time and the computing time on the edge server.

3.2 Threshold Setting on Greedy Adjusting and Convex Optimization

After determining the partition points, we will set the threshold value for the classifier on each device. In this subsection, we propose an algorithm to obtain threshold values, which is based on greedy adjusting and convex optimization (GACO). The algorithm can be described as follows:

1) **Greedy adjusting.** We first sort the device set U in ascending order in terms of the task completion time on each device. After given the DNN partitioning strategy, there are some devices whose tasks have met the latency requirements. For these devices, we offload as few DNN layers as possible from the devices to the edge server for relieving the computation loads of the edge server, while meeting the latency requirements.

2) **Problem transformation.** According to the first set of inequalities in Eq. (5), the shorter the computing time on the edge server, the larger the threshold value can be set. Meanwhile, according to the relationship between the threshold value and the inference accuracy shown in Fig. 2, the inference accuracy will be improved with the increase of the threshold value. The relationship can be obtained in advance when training the classifiers. From Fig. 2, we can obtain the relationship between the data offloading probability $p_i(\omega)$ and the inference accuracy $q_i(\omega)$ of the classifier at layer i, which can be expressed as $q_i(\omega) = \vartheta p_i(\omega) + \varrho$ through approximate analysis. Therefore, we can use $p_i(\omega)$ to replace $q_i(\omega)$ in Eqs. (4)–(5). The objective can be converted to

$$\max \frac{1}{\varPhi} \sum_{u \in U} \sum_{i=1}^{m} x_i^u (p_i(y_i^u)\vartheta + \varrho)\phi_u \tag{10}$$

and according to Eq. (1) and Eqs. (2)–(3) the completion time constraint can be expressed as

$$T_u = T_u^l + \sum_{i=1}^{m} x_i^u p_i(y_i^u)(T_u^s + \frac{\zeta_u}{\mu - \sum_{v \in U} \sum_{j=1}^{m} x_j^v p_j(y_j^v)\zeta_v \phi_v}) \tag{11}$$

3) **Convex optimization.** We compute the partial derivative of T_u with respect to $p_i(y_i^u)$ as

$$\frac{\partial T_u}{\partial p_i(y_i^u)} = \sum_{i=1}^{m} x_i^u (T_u^s + \frac{\zeta_u(\mu-\lambda)+p_i(y_i^u)\zeta_u^2\phi_u}{(\mu-\lambda)^2}) = \sum_{i=1}^{m} x_i^u (T_u^s + \frac{\zeta_u(\mu-\lambda+\lambda_u)}{(\mu-\lambda)^2}) \tag{12}$$

and the second order partial derivative with respect to $p_i(y_i^u)$ as

$$\frac{\partial^2 T_u}{\partial p_i^2(y_i^u)} = \sum_{i=1}^{m} x_i^u (\zeta_u \frac{2(\mu-\lambda)\zeta_u\phi_u(\mu-\lambda+\lambda_u)}{(\mu-\lambda)^4}) = \sum_{i=1}^{m} x_i^u (\frac{2\zeta_u^2\phi_u(\mu-\lambda+\lambda_u)}{(\mu-\lambda)^3}) \tag{13}$$

where $\lambda_u = p_s^u \zeta_u \phi_u$. We assume that the computation capacity of the edge server meets the computing requirements of all tasks, thus $\mu > \lambda$, then $\frac{\partial^2 T_u}{\partial p_i^2(y_i^u)} > 0$. Therefore, Eq. (11) is a strictly convex function. In addition, since the objective function Eq. (10) is linear after determining x_i^u in Subsect. 3.1, Eq. (5) becomes a convex optimization problem and can be solved by deploying the CVXPY package [19] on the edge server. Then we can obtain a set of probabilities corresponding to the optimal threshold values.

4) **Threshold setting.** We can transform the data offloading probabilities to the optimal threshold values according to their relationship in Fig. 2.

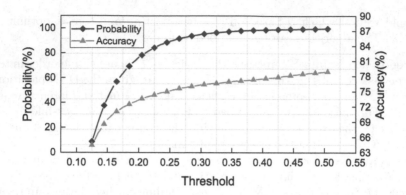

Fig. 2. The relationship among probability, accuracy and threshold.

4 Experiments and Evaluation

In this section, we first discuss the simulation settings in detail and then present the results. Finally, we provide a brief summary of those simulation results.

4.1 Simulation Settings

We simulate an edge computing scenario, where an access point (AP) is deployed exactly in the center of a square region. Furthermore, we simulate the number of devices as 50 randomly distributed in the area, and the devices are divided into five categories, each with different computing capabilities. For each device, its task generation follows a Poisson process. We conduct the simulation over a classical DNN AlexNet [20] and the real dataset CIFAR-10 [21]. For AlexNet, the computation overhead of each layer is different, which is obtained offline. The dataset CIFAR-10 is comprised of 60000 32 × 32 natural images (50000 for training and 10000 for testing) in 10 different class labels. The classifier we adopt here is described in Sect. 2. All simulations are performed on an AMAX workstation which carries an 8-core Intel(R) Xeon(R) CPU (E5-2620v4) and 4 NVIDIA GeForce RTX 2080Ti GPUs with 11 GB RAM.

In the simulation, we compare proposed algorithms DP-GACO with two baselines for performance evaluation under different resource (e.g., time and communication) constraints, including Device-Only and Edge-Only, where the first baseline executes tasks totally on end devices and the second baseline offloads all tasks to the edge server. Furthermore, we mainly adopt three metrics for performance evaluation. 1) *Completion proportion of tasks* is the proportion of the number of completed tasks within latency requirements to all tasks. 2) *Inference accuracy* is the proportion of correctly classified tasks to completed tasks. 3) *Inference speedup* denotes the ratio of task completion time of the Device-Only method to that of DP-GACO.

4.2 Simulation Results

In this subsection, the results are shown to evaluate the efficiency of the DP-GACO. All results are normalized to the Device-Only method.

Performance Comparison Under Different Latency Requirements.
We set the bandwidth as 30 Mbps and control latency requirement to 100 ms, 200 ms, 300 ms respectively to measure the performance of DP-GACO and baselines. Figure 3(a) shows that DP-GACO has a number of completed tasks 1.25–4.39× compared with the Device-Only method. For the low latency requirements, the Edge-Only method fails to accomplish tasks because of excessive transmission delay, however, DP-GACO can partition the DNN and adjust the threshold values to overcome the shortage. Figure 3(b) shows the inference accuracy under different latency requirements. For the low latency requirements, DP-GACO will adjust the threshold value to a small value for classifying more tasks on devices, as a result, the accuracy will suffer an apparent loss. Conversely, the threshold value can be adjusted to a large value when the latency requirement increases, and there is almost no loss of accuracy at this moment. According to the multiplication of the proportion of completed tasks and inference accuracy, we can obtain that the DP-GACO has a number of correctly classified tasks 1.25–3.25× compared with the Device-Only method.

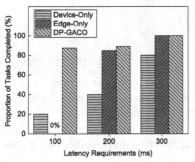
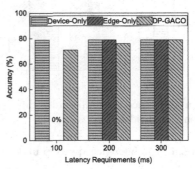

(a) Completion proportion of tasks   (b) Inference accuracy comparison

Fig. 3. The results under different latency requirements.

Performance Comparison Given Different Bandwidths. In this part, the latency requirement is set to 500 ms. We measure the performance of algorithms in inference speedup under different bandwidths of 20 Mbps, 50 Mbps, and 80 Mbps. From Fig. 4(a), we can observe that DP-GACO has an inference speedup of 1.1–2.58×, 1.04–1.5× compared with Device-Only and Edge-Only methods, respectively. For high bandwidths, DP-GACO offloads more tasks to the edge server to avoid excessive computing time on the devices, and meanwhile, DP-GACO also partitions the DNN to relieve the resource contention on the edge server. Therefore, DP-GACO can obtain better performance in inference speedup than Edge-Only and Device-Only methods. When confronted with the low bandwidths, the Edge-Only method will be inefficient by the data transmission delay. However, DP-GACO can adjust the partition points and threshold values to reduce data transmission amount to address these problems.

Performance Comparison Given Different Numbers of Devices. To test the scalability of proposed algorithms, we simulate different numbers of devices to evaluate the performance and set the latency requirement to 500 ms and the bandwidth to 50 Mbps. The results are shown in Fig. 4(b), from which we can observe that DP-GACO has an inference speedup of 1.68–4.73×, 1.19–1.71× compared with Device-Only and Edge-Only methods respectively. For the Edge-Only, the inference speed decreases with the increase of the number of devices because of the queueing time of tasks on the edge server. However, DP-GACO can adapt to the variations of the number of devices by setting the appropriate partition points and threshold values.

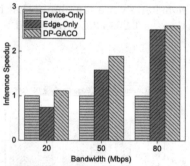   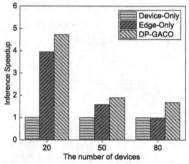

(a) Inference speedup under different bandwidths

(b) Inference speedup under different numbers of devices

Fig. 4. The inference speedup under different bandwidths and numbers of devices.

To summarize, our proposed algorithms substantially outperform two baselines in the following aspects. Firstly, under the stringent latency requirements, DP-GACO classifies more tasks correctly. Secondly, DP-GACO can also improve inference speedup 1.1–2.58× compared with the Device-Only method under low latency requirements while achieving high accuracy. Finally, Fig. 4 shows that DP-GACO can also dynamically adapt to the variations in bandwidth and the number of devices by adjusting the partition points and threshold values.

5   Conclusion

In this paper, we study the acceleration of DNN inference in heterogeneous edge computing. We propose two efficient algorithms to partition DNN and set the threshold values in the early-exit mechanism. The simulation results show that DP-GACO can maximize the average inference accuracy under the latency requirements. In the future, we will explore to optimize the offloading decisions for end devices in the scenario of multiple edge servers.

References

1. Liu, W., Wang, Z., Liu, X., Zeng, N., Liu, Y., Alsaadi, F.E.: A survey of deep neural network architectures and their applications. Neurocomputing **234**, 11–26 (2017)
2. Marjani, M., et al.: Big IoT data analytics: architecture, opportunities, and open research challenges. IEEE Access **5**, 5247–5261 (2017)
3. Jain, D.K., Jacob, S., Alzubi, J., Menon, V.: An efficient and adaptable multimedia system for converting PAL to VGA in real-time video processing. J. Real-Time Image Process. **17**(6), 2113–2125 (2019). https://doi.org/10.1007/s11554-019-00889-4
4. Yin, K.: Cloud computing: concept, model, and key technologies. ZTE Commun. **8**(4), 21–26 (2020)
5. Kang, Y., et al.: Neurosurgeon: collaborative intelligence between the cloud and mobile edge. ACM SIGARCH Comput. Archit. News **45**(1), 615–629 (2017)
6. Mao, Y., You, C., Zhang, J., Huang, K., Letaief, K.B.: A survey on mobile edge computing: the communication perspective. IEEE Commun. Surv. Tutor. **19**(4), 2322–2358 (2017)
7. Drolia, U., Guo, K., Tan, J., Gandhi, R., Narasimhan, P.: Cachier: edge-caching for recognition applications. In: 2017 IEEE 37th International Conference on Distributed Computing Systems (ICDCS), pp. 276–286. IEEE (2017)
8. Chen, W., Liu, B., Huang, H., Guo, S., Zheng, Z.: When UAV swarm meets edge-cloud computing: the QoS perspective. IEEE Netw. **33**(2), 36–43 (2019)
9. Li, E., Zeng, L., Zhou, Z., Chen, X.: Edge AI: on-demand accelerating deep neural network inference via edge computing. IEEE Trans. Wireless Commun. **19**(1), 447–457 (2019)
10. Hu, C., Bao, W., Wang, D., Liu, F.: Dynamic adaptive DNN surgery for inference acceleration on the edge. In: IEEE INFOCOM 2019-IEEE Conference on Computer Communications, pp. 1423–1431. IEEE (2019)
11. Teerapittayanon, S., McDanel, B., Kung, H.T.: BranchyNet: fast inference via early exiting from deep neural networks. In: 2016 23rd International Conference on Pattern Recognition (ICPR), pp. 2464–2469. IEEE (2016)
12. He, K., Zhang, X., Ren, S., Sun, J.: Deep residual learning for image recognition. In: Proceedings of the IEEE Conference on Computer Vision and Pattern Recognition, pp. 770–778 (2016)
13. Panda, P., Sengupta, A., Roy, K.: Conditional deep learning for energy-efficient and enhanced pattern recognition. In: 2016 Design, Automation & Test in Europe Conference & Exhibition (DATE), pp. 475–480. IEEE (2016)
14. Pisner, D.A., Schnyer, D.M.: Support vector machine. In: Machine Learning, pp. 101–121. Elsevier (2020)
15. Shafiee, M.S., Shafiee, M.J., Wong, A.: Dynamic representations toward efficient inference on deep neural networks by decision gates. In: CVPR Workshops, pp. 667–675 (2019)

16. Altman, E., Ayesta, U., Prabhu, B.J.: Load balancing in processor sharing systems. Telecommun. Syst. **47**(1), 35–48 (2011). https://doi.org/10.1007/s11235-010-9300-8
17. Gow, R., Rabhi, F.A., Venugopal, S.: Anomaly detection in complex real world application systems. IEEE Trans. Netw. Serv. Manage. **15**(1), 83–96 (2017)
18. Stuckey, P.J., Guns, T., Bailey, J., Leckie, C., Ramamohanarao, K., Chan, J., et al.: Dynamic programming for predict+ optimise. In: Proceedings of the AAAI Conference on Artificial Intelligence, vol. 34, pp. 1444–1451 (2020)
19. Diamond, S., Boyd, S.: CVXPY: a python-embedded modeling language for convex optimization. J. Mach. Learn. Res. **17**(1), 2909–2913 (2016)
20. Alom, M.Z., et al.: The history began from AlexNet: a comprehensive survey on deep learning approaches. arXiv preprint arXiv:1803.01164 (2018)
21. Ayi, M., El-Sharkawy, M.: RMNv2: Reduced MobileNet v2 for CIFAR10. In: 2020 10th Annual Computing and Communication Workshop and Conference (CCWC), pp. 0287–0292. IEEE (2020)

Available Time Aware Offloading for Dependent Tasks with Cooperative Edge Servers

Bingyan Zhou, Long Chen$^{(\boxtimes)}$, and Jigang Wu

School of Computer Science and Technology, Guangdong University of Technology,
Guangzhou 510006, China
lonchen@mail.ustc.edu.cn

Abstract. In most existing cases, the computing time of edge devices
are assumed consecutive. This is impractical because edge servers are
selfish in nature. As a consequence, edge servers have higher priority
to process their own tasks. This delays computing for both mobile end
users and neighboring edge servers, causing service quality degradation.
We design an offloading network with edge-edge collaboration accounting
for interrupted service time. Dependent subtasks of an application can
be offloaded to each available computing intervals on edge devices. Our
aim is to minimize the total application completion time. We formulate
the problem as a mixed integer non-linear programming, and prove it
is NP-hard. When global knowledge is known before offloading, we propose a greedy off-line algorithm GKGO to offload subtasks among edge
devices. Real-world trace experiments show that the proposed algorithm
outperforms benchmark algorithm by over 50% on the average application completion time.

Keywords: Edge computing · Offloading · Heterogeneous ·
Availability · Dependency

1 Introduction

Considering the delay drawback of cloud offloading, multi-access edge computing
(MEC) has emerged to bring services close to end users [3]. There are two main
edge computing models: device-edge and edge-edge cooperation models. For the
former, tasks of an application are divided and processed at both mobile devices
and edge servers. For the later edge-edge cooperation model, edge servers can
not only process their own private jobs, but also provide computing services for
neighboring edge servers [12]. In existing device-edge models [12], mobile devices
have to handle part of the computation intensive tasks such as DNN training
or inference, which is not suitable for the case when end devices are resource
constraint. Similar to [13], to fully exploit the computing capabilities of edge
servers, we account for the edge-edge cooperation model in MEC.

© Springer Nature Switzerland AG 2021
Z. Liu et al. (Eds.): WASA 2021, LNCS 12937, pp. 479–493, 2021.
https://doi.org/10.1007/978-3-030-85928-2_38

Most of prior arts on edge-edge collaboration assume edge servers are always ready to respond to the computing requests in a timely manner. However, edge servers are selfish in nature. They are dedicated to completing their own computing jobs first in the so called private or primary time slots[1], during which tasks originated from edge servers themselves have high priority to be processed and there are no executing for other jobs happen. After that, the remaining time slots can be used to help processing for other applications. In many cases, running applications in the primary processing time on edge servers should not be paused when new computing tasks arrive. For example, when the edge server is executing a time critical security check application based on face recognition, it should not be paused until the application has been finished. In vehicular ad hoc network, the real-time vision applications on edge servers [14] should be processed in high priority especially in autonomous driving. This causes the available computing service time intervals serving for other applications appear in an alternate manner with private processing time intervals. Existing works [3] and [4] assume consecutive available computing resources measured by computing slots or available computing time intervals. Those service intervals offered by edge servers are discrete [10] in general, having the following characteristics: (I) *The staring time slots are random.* Edge servers are private in nature, taking high priority to process their own jobs. This can delay computing for neighboring edge servers. (II) *Cross-edge resources lack coordination.* Each edge server has its own available computing time intervals. Those available computing resources across edge servers lack coordination.

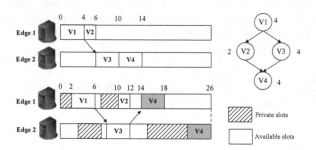

Fig. 1. A motivation example

If not properly handled, the above mentioned available computing intervals across different edge servers may be wasted. Take Fig. 1 as an example. There is an application with four subtasks $V_1 \sim V_4$, having computation time requirements of 4, 2, 4 and 4 slots accordingly. The edges in the task graph represent communication delay of two unit time slots if subtasks are scheduled onto two different edge servers. If all the available computation time intervals are coherent, the application completion time is $4+2+4+4 = 14$ slots. When some of the

---

[1] In the next paragraphs, we use private time slots and primary time slots interchangeably.

computing slots are unavailable, adopting the same offloading strategy, i.e., V_1, V_2 on edge server 1 and V_3, V_4 on edge server 2, the total application finishing time is 26 slots, because of the delay caused by private computing slots at edge servers. If proper adjustment is made, e.g., by offloading subtask V_4 (initially on edge server 2, marked by light purple) onto edge server 1 (marked by green), the total application finishing time can be reduced to 18 slots. This obtains a 30.8% improvement. Therefore, by carefully coordinating the available computing service intervals, we can make good use of edge resources while achieving high efficiency of task computing.

Observing the potential benefits, in this work, we expect to take full advantages of available computing capabilities of edge servers. In practice, the computing tasks at each edge servers in the vicinity of mobile users are posted by mobile devices. However, due to limited computing capabilities (e.g., CPU cycle-frequencies, computing time), edge servers cannot serve all the training or inference requests at one time. Therefore, we expect to minimize the total training or inference time of DNN models, coordinating the available time intervals on edge servers. There are two main challenges for task processing across the edge servers. In one aspect, it would be difficult to process all the computation intensive tasks on one single edge server. Therefore, the first challenge is how to handle more computing tasks on edge servers with respect to computation capability constraints. In the other aspect, DNN training and inference are subtask dependent. The requests from different users should be assigned to different edge servers. Since subtasks can be running in parallel on different edge servers. Thus the limited computing resources should be shared among edge servers. Inefficient task scheduling and offloading may result in longer execution delays, due to the dependency influence. The main contributions of this work are as follows:

- We optimize the total application completion time and formalize it as service interruption aware offloading for dependent tasks with cooperative edge devices (SENSE) problem, which is a mixed integer nonlinear programming. Besides, we prove it is NP-hard and unapproximable.
- For the case where global knowledge of the available computation intervals happens, we propose an offline greedy algorithm, termed global knowledge greedy offloading (GKGO). We show that it is effective to guarantee the computing resource capacity constraints.
- Google cluster dataset [9] based trace simulation results demonstrate that, the proposed algorithm outperforms benchmark algorithm HEFT-offline by over 50% on the average application completion time.

2   System Model

2.1   Network Model

We consider an MEC system with a set of $S = \{1, 2, \cdots, N\}$ multiple heterogeneous edge devices coordinated by an access point (AP) or a base station (BS), and $|S| = N$, $N > 2$. For simplicity, each edge device $n \in S$ possesses only one core or virtual machine (VM). If there are more than one VM on an edge device, the whole VMs can be spitted into multiple separate virtual edge devices with each possesses one VM. The edge devices can connect with each other via wired internet links or the wireless channels operated by the AP/BS. To save battery power, mobile devices themselves can fully offload their computation intensive computation tasks to edge devices directly.

2.2 Task Model

Similar to most existing works, we focus on a typical application with dependent subtasks in the aforementioned MEC system, because by adding virtual entry and exit nodes, different applications may be combined as a large application. Offloading priority based heterogeneous applications will be left for our future investigation. An application, (e.g., object detection for auto-driving, sample training for federal learning or path planning for reinforcement learning) is represented by a directed acyclic graph $G = (V, E)$, where V is set of M subtasks with $V = \{1, 2, \cdots, M\}$, $|V| = M$, and E is the set of Θ edges between subtasks. Each edge in E represents the precedence constraints. Each node $j \in V$ in the task graph G denotes a subtask and its weight W_j represents workload of task j, which means the number of CPU cycles needed to complete the task, its data size D_j that represents the communication data bits with its descendant subtasks.

2.3 Computation and Communication Model

1) *Computation on edge device*: Let f_n be the CPU computing rate (cycles/s) of the processor on edge device n, where $n \in S$. If one subtask j of the application, $j \in V$, is offloaded to be executed on the nth edge device during the kth available slots, the task computing time t_j^{nk} can be expressed as,

$$t_j^{nk} = \frac{W_j}{f_n}, \tag{1}$$

and the CPU speed of the nth edge device f_n should follows $0 < f_n \leq f_n^{\max}$, where $f_n^{\max}$ is the maximum CPU speed.

2) *Communication delay*: Let $R_{n,n'}$ be the transmission rate between two edge devices, where $n, n' \in S$ and $n \neq n'$. The communication delay between subtasks j and j', where $(j, j') \in E$, denoted as $C_{j,j'}^{n,n'}$, can be expressed as,

$$C_{j,j'}^{n,n'} = \Delta_j^n + D_j / R_{n,n'}, \tag{2}$$

where Δ_j^n is the extra delay of the nth edge device when transmitting the jth subtask due to coding and or re-transmission. The communication delay equals to zero when subtasks j and j' are scheduled and executed on the same edge server. That's because the intra-communication delay is much less than the inter-communication delay. Otherwise, $C_{j,j'}^{n,n'}$ in Eq. (2) means subtask j of the application is executed on the nth edge device while subtask j' is scheduled and executed on the n'th edge device.

3) *Available computation interval*: For each edge device n, its total time interval is T_n. Private edge devices may execute their own tasks first. When CPU cycle slots of VMs on those edge devices become available, they can be reused to handle tasks from end devices. As a consequence, T_n is divided by both available and unavailable time slots. Without loss of generality, we assume the kth available time slots on the nth edge device are represented by the interval between the available interval start time α_n^k and the available interval end time β_n^k. Therefore, there are K_n available intervals for edge device n, thus $k \in [1, K_n]$ for any $n \in S$, as shown in Fig. 2.

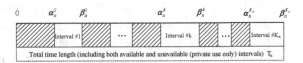

Fig. 2. Typical available computing slots

4) *Execution start time and Execution end time*: First, let x_j^{nk} be a binary variable that indicates whether subtask j of the application is executed on the kth available interval of edge device n. Thus, we have,

$$x_j^{nk} = \begin{cases} 1, & \text{the } j\text{th subtask is on the } k\text{th interval of } n, \\ 0, & \text{Otherwise.} \end{cases} \tag{3}$$

If $x_j^{nk} = 1$, then the jth subtask is executed on the kth interval of edge device n. Otherwise, $x_j^{nk} = 0$. The execution start time B_j^n is the time when the jth subtask begin to execute on edge device n and the execution finish time F_j^n is the time when it finishes. Therefore, we can obtain,

$$B_j^n = \begin{cases} \alpha_n^k \cdot x_j^{nk}, & for \quad j = 1, \\ \max \left\{ \max_{j' \in \max pre(j)} \left\{ F_{j'}^{n'} + C_{j',j}^{n,n'} (x_{j'}^{n'k'} \oplus x_j^{nk}) \right\}, \\ \alpha_n^k \cdot x_j^{nk} \right\}, & for \quad j > 1. \end{cases} \tag{4}$$

and

$$F_j^n = B_j^n + t_j^{nk} \cdot x_j^{nk}, \quad \forall j \in V. \tag{5}$$

In Eq. (4), when $j = 1$, $B_j^n = \alpha_n^k \cdot x_j^{nk}$. We schedule the first subtask (the root of the task graph G) at the start time of the available interval start time α_n^k, because we want to minimize the application finish time as soon as possible. For the remaining subtasks except for the root subtask, the subtask j ($j > 1$) can only begin when all its preceding subtasks j' have been finished and the results have been correctly received by subtask j. The term $x_{j'}^{n'k'} \oplus x_j^{nk}$ equals to 1 if and only if the two subtasks j and j' have been scheduled onto two different edge devices. Equation (5) means the task completion time F_j^n equals to the task start time plus the execution time.

Definition 1. *(Possible fit) The jth subtask of application i can only be executed on the kth available interval of the nth edge device if and only if all the following inequalities are met:*

$$\alpha_n^k \leq B_j^n \leq \beta_n^k, F_j^n \leq \beta_n^k, \tag{6}$$

and

$$(\beta_n^k - \alpha_n^k)x_j^{nk} \geq t_j^{nk} \cdot x_j^{nk} + \sum_{\pi(j')=\pi(j)} t_{j'}^{nk} \cdot x_{j'}^{nk}, j' \neq j. \tag{7}$$

where $\pi(j)$ is a schedule, and $\pi(j) = (n, k)$, which means subtask j of the application is offloaded to the kth available interval of edge device n. Equation (6) ensures task start time B_j^n should within the available computing interval and the subtask completion time F_j^n should not be overlong, larger than β_n^k. Finally, Eq. (7) means the kth available computing interval on edge device n for subtask j should hold not only j, but also any other subtasks j', $j' \neq j$, that have been offload and scheduled on the k th available computing interval of edge device n.

5) *Resource constraint*: For each edge device, its CPU or GPU may execute different applications for their own benefits. As a consequence, the number of computation time it can release for sharing is limited. Define the computation time that edge device n willing to help as Ψ_n, which can be used to balance the workloads, we obtain,

$$\sum_{k=1}^{K_n} \sum_{j=1}^{M} t_j^{nk} \cdot x_j^{nk} \leq \Psi_n. \tag{8}$$

It is worthy noting that, the total time length on the nth edge device is T_n. We introduce a variable $0 < \gamma_n < 1$ to represent the fraction ratio of the available time at edge device n, then we have $\Psi_n \leq \gamma_n T_n$. This means, the total available computing time is no less than the willing to help time.

3 Problem Formulation

Based on the preliminaries and definitions mentioned in Sect. 2, we give formal description of the resource availability-aware offloading problem SENSE with private cooperative edge devices.

Given a task graph G of one application with M dependent subtasks, the available time that each edge device willing to share, we try to propose a possible fit schedule (See Definition 1) and offload the subtasks to each of the edge devices in the network following the schedule. The objective is to minimize the total application completion time, as shown in $OPT - 1$:

$$\textbf{OPT-1} \quad obj : \min F_M^n \tag{9}$$

$$s.t. \sum_n x_j^{nk} \leq 1, \quad \forall n \in S \tag{10}$$

$$\sum_j x_j^{nk} \leq 1, \quad n \in S, \tag{11}$$

$$F_j^n - B_{j'}^n \geq 0, \quad \forall j' \neq j,$$
$$and \quad (1) \sim (8). \tag{12}$$

Where constraint (10) means that each subtask can only be served by one edge device while constraint (11) means that each subtask can only be served by one available interval on the corresponding edge device. The final constraint (12) ensures no overlapping happens for two different subtasks on a given available interval. Note that the problem defined in $OPT-1$ is a MINLP, which is NP-hard in general. Next, we show $OPT-1$ is NP-hard by reduction it to the famous open shop scheduling problem [5].

Corollary 1. *The scheduling problem $F_n, h_{n,k}|nr|C_{max}$, $n > 2$, $k > 1$ is NP-hard and is not approximable.*

Proof. In the open shop problem [5], there is a set T of τ tasks that should be executed for a period of time by each of the m machines in set M. In the scheduling, there are no precedence constraints between tasks. Following the notations in [6], denote $F_n, h_{nk}|r/nr|C_{max}$ as the scheduling problem with n machines, arbitrary number of k unavailable intervals on machine n, i.e., h_{nk}, and resumable/nonresumable cases r or nr. The objective is to optimize the makespan of all tasks C_{max}. As indicated by Kubzin et al. [7] and proved by Breit et al. [2], the problem $F_2, h_{1,k}, h_{2,k}|r|C_{max}$, for all $k > 1$, it is NP-hard and is not approximable unless $\mathcal{P} = \mathcal{NP}$. Then the harder problem $F_n, h_{n,k}|nr|C_{max}$, $n > 2$, $k > 1$ is also not approximable.

Theorem 1. *Problem SENSE defined in $OPT-1$ is not approximable within a constant factor unless $\mathcal{P} = \mathcal{NP}$.*

Proof. In the problem $OPT-1$, for one application, there are M subtasks. Then M corresponds to τ in Corollary 1. We relax the precedence constraint of $OPT-1$, keep other constraints remain and obtain $OPT-1'$, then the $OPT-1'$ problem corresponds to an open shop problem. The number of edge devices in $OPT-1'$, N corresponds to n in F_n of Corollary 1. We investigate a general case where there are multiple available intervals on each of the edge devices, hence there are multiple unavailable intervals for each edge device and $k > 1$ according to Corollary 1. In the edge-edge enabled MEC network, there are more than two edge devices as indicated in the network model, then the $OPT-1'$ can be termed with $F_{N>3}, h_{s_n \in S, k>1}|nr|C_{max}$. According to Corollary 1, $OPT-1'$ is NP-hard and is not approximable. Therefore, the original problem $OPT-1$ is also NP-hard and is not approximable, because it is harder when considering the precedence constraints.

4   Algorithm

The GKGO algorithm contains three phases: the greedy search phase, the interval adjust phase and the research constraint checking phase. These three subphases are coordinated by the main algorithm described in Algorithm 1.

Algorithm 1. Global Knowledge Greedy Offloading (GKGO)

Input: Task graph G of the given application

The start time and end time intervals for all edge devices $\{\left(\alpha_n^k, \beta_n^k\right)\}, k \in [1, K_n], n \in S$;

Output: Binary variable set of time intervals $\{x_j^{n,k} | j \in V, k \in [1, K_n], n \in S\}$;

1 Obtain visiting sequence Q for task graph G using breadth first traversal or search (BFS)

2 **foreach** q in Q **do**

3      $(\hat{n}, \hat{k}, x_q^{\hat{n},\hat{k}})$=Greedy_Search$(q, N, K_n)$;

4   Interval_Adjust$(\hat{n}, \hat{k}, x_q^{\hat{n},\hat{k}}, \{[\alpha_n^k, \beta_n^k]\})$;

5 $[x_q^{n,k}]$=Research_Constraint_Checking(τ, N, K_n); Return $\{x_j^{n,k}, j \in V, k \in [1, K_n], n \in S\}$;

As shown in Algorithm 1, GKGO first uses the breadth first traversal to obtain a visiting order for given task graph G. Then, for each available time interval on each edge device, GKGO computes it's start time and finish time of earliest task based on the visiting order of subtasks, as shown in lines 3–14 of Algorithm 3. In additional, for all the obtained task finish time on each time interval, the GKGO algorithm chooses the time interval that produces the minimum task completion time for each subtask. Then, the available time interval is adjusted as lines 1–7 in Algorithm 2. What's more, the resource constraint (8), each subtask that violates the resource constraint is added to the list of *need_reschedule_task*. Finally these rescheduled subtasks are offloaded to the edge device with the minimum completion time.

Algorithm 2. The Interval Adjust Phase Interval_Adjust

Input: $\hat{n}, \hat{k}, x_q^{\hat{n},\hat{k}}, \left\{[\alpha_n^k, \beta_n^k]\right\}$

Output: New available computing intervals

1 **if** $\alpha_{\hat{n}}^{\hat{k}} == minB_q^{\hat{n},\hat{k}}$ **then**

2      $\alpha_{\hat{n}}^{\hat{k}} \leftarrow \widetilde{F}_q^{\hat{n},\hat{k}}$;

3 **if** $\beta_{\hat{n}}^{\hat{k}} == \widetilde{F}_q^{\hat{n},\hat{k}}$ **then**

4      $\beta_{\hat{n}}^{\hat{k}} \leftarrow \widetilde{B}_q^{\hat{n},\hat{k}}$;

5 **if** $\alpha_{\hat{n}}^{\hat{k}} < \widetilde{B}_q^{\hat{n},\hat{k}}$ and $\beta_{\hat{n}}^{\hat{k}} > \widetilde{F}_q^{\hat{n},\hat{k}}$ **then**

6      $tmp \leftarrow \beta_{\hat{n}}^{\hat{k}}, \beta_{\hat{n}}^{\hat{k}} \leftarrow \widetilde{B}_q^{\hat{n},\hat{k}}$;

7   Add $\left(\widetilde{F}_q^{\hat{n},\hat{k}}, tmp\right)$ to $K_{\hat{n}}$;

---

1) *Greedy Search Phase*: Firstly, the greedy search phase obtain a visiting sequence Q for task graph G of the application. For each subtask $q \in Q$,

GKGO repeats the following operations in this phase. By setting $x_q^{n,k}$ as $x_q^{n,k} = 1$, GKGO uses Eqs. (4) and (5) to calculate the begin execute time B_q^n and finish time F_q^n on each intervals of edge devices. For each interval $k \in [1, K_n]$, if the subtask start time B_q^n is lagging behind the interval end time β_n^k or the kth interval length on edge device n is smaller than the execution time $t_q^{n,k}$, the subtask q cannot be scheduled on the kth available interval on n, which is referred to as $x_q^{n,k} = 0$. Using four variables $\widetilde{F}_q^n$, $\widetilde{B}_q^n$, $\hat{n}$ and $\hat{k}$, we are able to record the interval number $\hat{k}$ and the edge device number $\hat{n}$ that brings about the minimum B_q^n and F_q^n. For each subtask $q \in Q$, after NK_n iterations, the optimal computing interval $\hat{k}$ will be selected by setting $x_q^{\hat{n},\hat{k}}$ to 1.

2) *Interval Adjust Phase*: After offloading the qth subtask to the $\hat{k}$th available interval of device $s_{\hat{n}}$, the length of available computing intervals should be adjusted. Following the relative positions between the two intervals $[\alpha_n^k, \beta_n^k]$ and $[\widetilde{B}_q^{n,k}, \widetilde{F}_q^{n,k}]$, there are three cases. In case 1, if $\alpha_{\hat{n}}^{\hat{k}} == \widetilde{B}_q^{\hat{n},\hat{k}}$, $\alpha_{\hat{n}}^{\hat{k}} = \widetilde{F}_q^{\hat{n},\hat{k}}$. In practical, the new available computing interval $\hat{k}$ on edge device $\hat{n}$ lies on the right side of the new added computation interval for task q. In case 2, if $\beta_{\hat{n}}^{\hat{k}} == \widetilde{F}_q^{\hat{n},\hat{k}}$, $\beta_{\hat{n}}^{\hat{k}} = \widetilde{B}_q^{\hat{n},\hat{k}}$. In this case, the new interval lies on the left side of the new added computing interval. In case 3, the new available computing interval is $[\widetilde{F}_q^{\hat{n},\hat{k}}, \beta_{\hat{n}}^{\hat{k}}]$, when $\alpha_{\hat{n}}^{\hat{k}} < \widetilde{B}_q^{\hat{n},\hat{k}}$ and $\beta_{\hat{n}}^{\hat{k}} > \widetilde{F}_q^{\hat{n},\hat{k}}$.

Algorithm 3. The Greedy Search Phase $(\hat{n}, \hat{k}, x_q^{\hat{n},\hat{k}}) =$ Greedy_Search (q, N, K_n)

Input: q, N, K_n
Output: $\hat{n}$, $\hat{k}$, $x_q^{n,k}$

1    $\widetilde{F}_q^n \leftarrow +\infty$; $\widetilde{B}_q^n \leftarrow +\infty$;
2    $\hat{n} \leftarrow -1$; $\hat{k} \leftarrow -1$;
3   **for** $n \leftarrow 1$ to N **do**
4   **for** $k \leftarrow 1$ to K_n **do**
5        $x_q^{n,k} \leftarrow 1$; /*Enable to calculate using equations (4) and (5)*/ ;
6   Compute $B_q^{n,k}$, $F_q^{n,k}$ by (4) and (5) respectively;
7   **if** $B_j^k \geq \beta_n^k$ or $|\beta_n^k - \alpha_n^k| < t_q^{n,k}$ **then**
8          $x_q^{n,k} \leftarrow 0$;
9   break;
10   **else**
11          $x_q^{n,k} \leftarrow 0$;
12   **if** $F_q^{n,k} < \widetilde{F}_q^{n,k}$ **then**
13            $\widetilde{F}_q^{n,k} \leftarrow F_q^{n,k}$; $\widetilde{B}_q^{n,k} \leftarrow B_q^{n,k}$;
14            $\hat{n} \leftarrow n$; $\hat{k} \leftarrow k$;
15   $x_q^{\hat{n},\hat{k}} \leftarrow 1$; /*offloading the qth subtask to the $\hat{k}$-th available interval of edge device $\hat{n}$*/;

3) *Resource Constraint Checking Phase*: The phase first initializes a task queue *need_reschedule_task* and the total computing time for each edge device $\theta(n)$. For s_n, if there exists one subtask q, $x_q^{n,k} = 1$ and $\theta(n) + t_q^{nk} > \Psi_n$, the subtask and the tasks after q in the initial sequence set Q will be added to *need_reschedule_task*. After that, the occupied computing intervals of subtasks in *need_reschedule_task* will be de-allocated. The new available computing intervals on each edge device will be obtained after the de-allocation and interval adjust operations. When the *need_reschedule_task* is ready, for each task τ in this new list, GKGO algorithm checks the resource constraint. If $\theta(n) + W_\tau/f_n > \Psi_n$, then subtask τ cannot be offloaded to edge device s_n. By executing the sub-procedures in the greedy search phase, new offloading strategies will be obtained. Otherwise, the algorithm has no solution.

Theorem 2. *The time complexity of the GKGO algorithm is $O(MNK_{\max}+\Theta)$, where M is the number of subtasks, and Θ is the number of edges in application graph G. $K_{\max} = \max\{K_n\}$ and N is the total number of edge devices.*

Proof. The BFS procedure takes $O(M + \Theta)$. The basic operations of the GKGO algorithm are the comparisons between the task computing time and the available computing intervals. For each time interval, there is a comparison in need. For edge device s_n, there will be K_n comparisons. For the scheduling phase without computing constraints, which corresponds to Lines 1–15 in Algorithm 3, there are three 'for' circulations, $MN \max\{K_n\}$ operations. The adjust and resource constraint checking phases in Algorithms 2 and 4 have at most $MN \max\{K_n\}$ operations, which results in a total time complexity of $O(MNK_{\max} + \Theta)$, where $K_{\max} = \max\{K_n\}$.

Theorem 3. *Unless given a speed augmentation of at least γ_n, $0 < \gamma_n < 1$, the SENSE problem cannot be approximated better than $O(\max\{(1 - \gamma_n)T_n\} + M^{1-c})$, where $c \in [0,1)$.*

Proof. Considering the discrete unavailability computation intervals on each edge device n, we choose the maximum $(1 - \gamma_n)T_n$, $\forall n \in S$ among all edge devices, denoted by $\max\{(1 - \gamma_n)T_n\}$. Then problem SENSE solved by GKGO algorithm can be divided into one scheduling problem with continuous service intervals, plus one additional operation time cost $O(\max\{(1 - \gamma_n)T_n\})$ to imitate the additional delay caused by unavailable service intervals. According to Theorem 3.12 of [8], the unweighted flow time with precedence tasks cannot be approximated better than $\Omega(n^{1-c})$, for any constant $c \in (0,1)$ and n is the number of jobs in [8]. Therefore, as a special case of the unweighted flow time problem in this work, the precedence constraints are obtained via breadth first searching of GKGO algorithm, thus the total delay performance can be $O(\max\{(1 - \gamma_n)T_n\} + M^{1-c})$.

Algorithm 4. Research Constraint Checking Phase

Input: $\tau, N, K_n, \left\{[\alpha_n^k, \beta_n^k]\right\}$

Output: $x_q^{n,k}$

1 /*Calculate the total computing time $\theta(n)$ for each edge device n and obtain the edge devices that violate computing resource constraint*/ ;
2 $need\_reschedule\_task \leftarrow \emptyset; \theta(n) \leftarrow 0;$
3 **for** each n in S **do**
4   **for** each q in Q **do**
5   **for** $k \leftarrow K_n$ to 1 **do**
6   **if** $x_q^{n,k} == 1$ **then**
7           $\theta(n) \leftarrow \theta(n) + t_q^{nk};$
8   **if** $\theta(n) > \Psi_n$ **then**
9   Add q and the task sequence after q to $need\_reschedule\_task$;
10          $\theta(n) \leftarrow \theta(n) - W_q/f_n, x_q^{n,k} \leftarrow 0;$
11   Reset$\{\left(\alpha_n^k, \beta_n^k\right)\}, k \in [1, K_n], n \in S$ for the subtasks after the sequence number of τ based on $\{x_j^{n,k}, j \in V, k \in [1, K_n], n \in S\}$
         /*refer to line 1 to line 7 in Algorithm 2, the interval adjust phase. */;
12   Break;
13 **foreach** τ in $need\_reschedule\_task$ **do**
14   **foreach** edge device $n, n \in S$ **do**
15   **if** $\theta(n) + W_\tau/f_n > \Psi_n$ **then**
16   subtask τ cannot be offloaded to n;
17   Break;
18    $[x_q^{n,k}]=$Greedy_Search(τ, N, K_n);

---

5   Performance Evaluation

We conduct extensive simulation experiments based on real-world Google cluster traces [9], and compare the performance of proposed algorithm with benchmark algorithm.

5.1   Simulation Setup

The workload and data size values for each subtask are extracted from Google cluster data set [9]. Typical scientific workflow type is used in our experiments, it is Montage [1] shown in Fig. 3(a). For Montage, we choose the data of subtasks from the same numbered job_ID of the Google data set. All the values are averaged. The maximum CPU speed of the edge device is set as $f_n^{\max} = 10 \times 10^9$ cycles/s [4] and the default value is 4×10^9 cycles/s. By default, the transmission speed between edge devices is set as $R_{n,n'} = 100\,\text{Mbps} \approx 12.5$ MB/s, where $n \neq n'$, $s_n \in S$ and $n \in [1, N]$. Denote the total time T_n as a large number to represent both the sum available and unavailable time slots for the nth edge device, where $n \in [1, N]$. The first length of available computing interval is randomly chosen from $[0, 20]$ s in the generating window.[2] and the maximum length of $T_n = 300$ s.

---

[2] It is worthy noting that the size could be any possible size within T_n, because the real available interval start time is adjusted via some distributions within each generating window. And the total available computing time of edge device n is controlled by γ_n. As shown in Fig. 2.

The start time of the available interval, α_n^k follows uniform distribution on each of the generating window of 20 s over T_n. There are $\lfloor T_n/(20 - 0) \rfloor$ available generating windows on n. We set total time $T_n = 300$, CPU speed $= 4 \times 10^9$ cycles/s, available fraction ratio $\gamma_n = 0.5$, extra transmission delay $\Delta_j^n = 0.1$ s and number of edge devices $N = 5$ in the default parameters.

Since there is no resource-availability aware offloading algorithm in the MEC-enabled network, we modify the existing scheduling algorithm HEFT [11] for heterogeneous processors, to make it applicable to the offloading with cooperative edge devices. Note that the comparing benchmark algorithm can be constructed using different initial scheduling algorithms except for the HEFT. We adopt HEFT because it is a well-known parallel scheduling algorithm suitable for heterogeneous edge devices. Specifically, we compare the proposed algorithm GKGO with the following benchmark approach.

HEFT-offline: The scheduling results of HEFT algorithm is directly applied to the case when there are computing resource unavailable intervals. This corresponds to the scheduling and offloading with 23 slots application completion time shown in Fig. 1. It has a time complexity of $O(M_i^2 N + K_{\max} M_i)$.

5.2   Simulation Results

We conduct four groups of simulations to evaluate proposed algorithm on the application completion time. In the first group (as shown in Fig. 3(b)), we vary the number of edge devices while keeping other variables as default. Finally, in the remaining groups, we record the results of application completion time with CPU speed, extra transmission delay and the fraction ratio of available time, as shown in Figs. 3(c)–3(e).

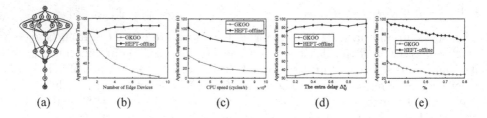

(a)   (b)   (c)   (d)   (e)

Fig. 3. (a) A scientific workflow type [1] called Montage and mapped in the Google cluster data set [9]. (b) Task completion time with number of edge devices. (c) Task completion time with CPU speed. (d) Task completion time with extra delay. (e) Task completion time with fraction ratio of available time.

More specifically, the results in Fig. 3(c)–3(e) show that under various conditions, the proposed algorithm GKGO outperforms benchmark algorithm. On average, GKGO outperforms HEFT-offline by 53.23% accordingly on the application completion time. From Fig. 3(c), we see that the application completion time decreases dramatically with CPU speed increases for all cases. However, simply increase CPU speeds may bring more costs, which anticipates a budget balanced scheme remains for our future investigation. Figure 3(d) depicts the uncertainty influence due to extra transmission or computation delays. We observe that application completion delay of the proposed algorithms GKGO, HEFT-offline increases as the extra delay Δ_{ij}^n increases. However, as shown in Fig. 3(e), a larger γ_n represents a greater computing capability, which can expedite the execution of hetero-applications. On average, the proposed algorithm GKGO outperforms the benchmark algorithm by over 50% on the total delay.

We further conduct experiments on the algorithm run time on a desktop computer with Intel core i7-6700 3.4 Ghz processor and 16 GB RAM. The results in Fig. 4(a) suggests that the proposed algorithm GKGO have almost linear run time with the number of edge devices. This complies with the time complexity analysis.

To study the possible influence caused by the available interval generation, we change the distribution of available interval start time within each generating window (see Fig. 2). It complies with norm distribution with $N(5,5)$, $N(5,10)$, and $N(10,10)$ respectively. As in Fig. 4(b), two typical algorithms are chosen to examine the robustness of proposed algorithm. We see that, in the norm distribution, when the average values are equal, a higher derivation will cause longer completion delay. This is because a higher derivation causes longer distance between adjacent available intervals, which results in longer delay.

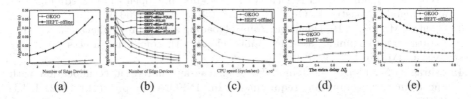

(a)   (b)   (c)   (d)   (e)

Fig. 4. (a) Algorithm run time with number of edge devices. (b) Application completion time with number of edge devices. When the available interval start time follows the distribution of N(5, 5) within each generating window. (c) Task completion time with CPU speed. (d) Task completion time with extra delay Δ_{ij}^n. (e) Task completion time with fraction ratio of available time γ_n.

Similarly, when the derivation stays constant, a higher average value will also cause longer delay due to the same reason. In the final group of experiments, we reexamine the delay performance with CPU speed, the extra delay and the fraction ratio γ_n, when the available interval start time follows the distribution of $N(5,5)$ within each available computing interval generating window. We observe that the Fig. 4(c) shows similar performance to Fig. 3(c). Figure 4(d) is similar to Fig. 3(d). Figure 4(e) is similar to Fig. 3(e) accordingly. Therefore, the proposed algorithm is robust.

6 Conclusions

We have studied the joint scheduling and computation offloading problem for applications with dependent subtasks under computing resource availability constraints. The objective is to offload the tasks full offloaded by mobile end users to each of the edge devices while minimizing the application completion time. We have proposed greedy algorithm GKGO for offline execution. Through real-world trace driven simulation, we have shown the proposed algorithm outperforms benchmark algorithm. Our future work includes extending this work with incentive mechanisms motivating edge devices under budget constraints. Delay-cost trade-off will also be investigated. Further more, we plan to test the effectiveness of the proposed schemes by deploying it on different platforms.

Acknowledgement. This work was supported by the Guangzhou Municipal Science and Technology Bureau Research Project on Basic and Applied Basic Research. Part of this work was supported by the National Natural Science Foundation of China under grant no. 62072118.

References

1. Abrishami, S., Naghibzadeh, M., Epema, D.H.: Cost-driven scheduling of grid workflows using partial critical paths. IEEE Trans. Parallel Distrib. Syst. **23**(8), 1400–1414 (2011)
2. Breit, J., Schmidt, G., Strusevich, V.A.: Two-machine open shop scheduling with an availability constraint. Oper. Res. Lett. **29**(2), 65–77 (2001)
3. Chen, M.H., Liang, B., Dong, M.: Joint offloading and resource allocation for computation and communication in mobile cloud with computing access point. In: INFOCOM, pp. 1–9. IEEE (2017)
4. Eshraghi, N., Liang, B.: Joint offloading decision and resource allocation with uncertain task computing requirement. In: INFOCOM, pp. 1414–1422. IEEE (2019)
5. Gonzalez, T., Sahni, S.: Open Shop Scheduling to Minimize Finish Time (1976)
6. Kubiak, W., Błażewicz, J., Formanowicz, P., Breit, J., Schmidt, G.: Two-machine flow shops with limited machine availability. Eur. J. Oper. Res. **136**(3), 528–540 (2002)
7. Kubzin, M.A., Strusevich, V.A., Breit, J., Schmidt, G.: Polynomial-time approximation schemes for two-machine open shop scheduling with nonavailability constraints. Naval Res. Logist. (NRL) **53**(1), 16–23 (2006)
8. Kulkarni, J., Li, S.: Flow-time optimization for concurrent open-shop and precedence constrained scheduling models. In: Blais, E., Jansen, K., Rolim, J.D.P., Steurer, D. (eds.) Approximation, Randomization, and Combinatorial Optimization. Algorithms and Techniques (APPROX/RANDOM 2018). Leibniz International Proceedings in Informatics (LIPIcs), vol. 116, pp. 16:1–16:21. Schloss Dagstuhl-Leibniz-Zentrum fuer Informatik, Dagstuhl, Germany (2018). https://doi.org/10.4230/LIPIcs.APPROX-RANDOM.2018.16. http://drops.dagstuhl.de/opus/volltexte/2018/9420
9. Reiss, C., Wilkes, J., Hellerstein, J.: Google cluster-usage traces: format+ schema google inc. Mountain View, CA, USA, White Paper (2011)

10. Shmoys, D.B., Wein, J., Williamson, D.P.: Scheduling parallel machines on-line. SIAM J. Comput. **24**(6), 1313–1331 (1995)
11. Topcuoglu, H., Hariri, S., Wu, M.Y.: Performance-effective and low-complexity task scheduling for heterogeneous computing. IEEE Trans. Parallel Distrib. Syst. **13**(3), 260–274 (2002)
12. Wang, X., Chen, X., Wu, W.: Towards truthful auction mechanisms for task assignment in mobile device clouds. In: IEEE Conference on Computer Communications (INFOCOM), pp. 1–9. IEEE (2017)
13. Yang, Y., Zhao, S., Zhang, W., Chen, Y., Luo, X., Wang, J.: Debts: delay energy balanced task scheduling in homogeneous fog networks. IEEE Internet Things J. **5**(3), 2094–2106 (2018)
14. Zhang, W., Li, S., Liu, L., Jia, Z., Zhang, Y., Raychaudhuri, D.: Hetero-edge: orchestration of real-time vision applications on heterogeneous edge clouds. In: IEEE Conference on Computer Communications (INFOCOM) (2019)

ECCR: Edge-Cloud Collaborative Recovery for Low-Power Wide-Area Networks Interference Mitigation

Luoyu Mei[1], Zhimeng Yin[2], Xiaolei Zhou[1,3(✉)], Shuai Wang[1], and Kai Sun[1]

[1] Southeast University, Nanjing, China
{lymei2002,shuaiwang,sunk}@seu.edu.cn
[2] City University of Hong Kong, Hong Kong, China
zhimeyin@cityu.edu.hk
[3] The Sixty-Third Research Institute, National University of Defense Technology,
Changsha, China
zhouxiaolei@nudt.edu.cn

Abstract. Recent advances in Low-Power Wide-Area Networks have mitigated interference by using cloud assistance. Those methods transmit the RSSI samples and corrupted packets to the cloud to restore the correct message. However, the effectiveness of those methods is challenged by the high transmission data amount. This paper presents a novel method for interference mitigation in a Edge-Cloud collaborative manner, namely ECCR. It does not require transmitting RSSI sample any more, whose length is eight times of the packet's. We demonstrate the disjointness of the bit errors of packets at the base stations via real-word experiments. ECCR leverages this to collaborate with multiple base stations for error recovery. Each base station detects and reports bit error locations to the cloud, then both error checking code and interfered packets from other receivers are utilized to restore correct packets. ECCR takes the advantages of both the global management ability of the cloud and the signal to perceive the benefit of each base station, and it is applicable to deployed LP-WAN systems (e.g. sx1280) without any extra hardware requirement. Experimental results show that ECCR is able to accurately decode packets when packets have nearly 51.76% corruption.

Keywords: Low-Power Wide-Area Networks (LP-WANs) ·
Edge-cloud collaborative · Interference mitigation

1 Introduction

Low-Power Wide-Area Networks (LP-WANs) are gaining increasing attention in both the industry and academia, because of the advantages of long-range coverage, low energy consumption, and low deployment cost. Among LP-WANs technologies, LoRa is one of the leading emergent technologies in the unlicensed

Z. Liu et al. (Eds.): WASA 2021, LNCS 12937, pp. 494–507, 2021.
https://doi.org/10.1007/978-3-030-85928-2_39

sub-GHz bands. It covers an area of several square kilometers from the base station and supports millions of end devices in the field [7]. However, with the widely application of different wireless technologies in daily life and industry [7–9,9–12], multiple wireless protocols might be densely deployed in the same area, such as LoRa, sigfox [28], and 802.11ah [8]. As a result, those wireless networks are inevitably overlapping, and lead to either isomorphism or heterogeneity interferences.

Most of the conventional approaches mitigate the LoRa interference by redesigning the Physical and MAC layers [3–6]. Transparent solutions are proposed in [5,6] to re-design and synchronize LoRa sender, while [1,6] take efforts to avoid corruptions at the base station side. Those efforts introduce extra hardware cost, deployment complexity, or are not compatible with deployed LoRa devices. Some recent efforts make use of the cloud resources to mitigate the LoRa interference, without any extra hardware. OPR [2] restores the corrupted packets by transmitting those packets and RSSI samples to the cloud, and cycles through alternative fragments matched in the error-detection fields. However, those cloud-based methods lead to excessive overhead of RSSI transmission and computation, which greatly limits their feasibility in practice.

Inspired by the cloud-based methods, we ask a natural question that can we further reduce the transmission and computation overhead. In this paper, we propose a novel method for LoRa interference mitigation in an edge-cloud collaborative manner, named as Edge-Cloud Collaborative Recovery (ECCR). Instead of directly transmitting the RSSI samples, we identify the corruptions by adding error checking codes at the base station side. Besides, we find that bit errors of the packet received by different base stations are disjoint with others. In a nutshell, corruptions are detected by the error checking code before decoding. And then, the packets from multiple receivers can be utilized to restore the packet at the cloud side. Since the errors in packets are located on the base station, there is no need to transfer RSSI samples to the cloud any more. Benefit from this, ECCR greatly reduces both the transmission and computation overhead in the conventional cloud-based approach.

To support edge-cloud collaboration, the challenge for ECCR in a LoRa base station is to rapidly detect packet corruptions quickly enough so that it ensures recovering packets in real-time communication. We design error checking code after the encoding of the LoRa physical payload, through which, the base station detects corruptions before decoding the packet. With such error checking code, ECCR successfully detects and reports corruption for using cloud resources to restore packets.

This paper presents the first edge-cloud collaborative design for LoRa interference mitigation. The features we provide and the challenges we address in this emulation-based design are indeed generic and applicable to a whole set of future interference mitigation. Specifically, the major contributions of ECCR are as follows:

- We propose ECCR, a novel interference mitigation approach for LoRa. To the best of our knowledge, it is the first edge-cloud collaborate method for interference mitigation. It takes the advantage of both clouds' global management ability and edges' signal perceive benefits. Without modifying any hardware, ECCR is a transparent design and hence is easily deployed in existing LoRa infrastructure.

- To mitigate interference in real-time, we address a few challenges including (i) detecting corruption before decoding the packets, (ii) collaborating multiple base stations for packet recovery. These techniques provide guidance for the range extension of edge-cloud collaborative interference mitigation.
- We conduct extensive experiments on commercial-off-the-shelf devices (sx1280 LoRa chip) and the USRP-N210 platform as the base station to evaluate the correctness and performance of ECCR. Experimental results show that ECCR is able to accurately decode packets even the corruption rate achieves 51.76%.

2   Background and Motivation

To explain ECCR, it is necessary to first introduce how LoRa and LoRa's Wide-Area Networking architecture (LoRaWAN) work. In this section, we first concisely introduce the architecture of LoRa and LoRa's Wide-Area Networking architecture (LoRaWAN) and then explain the principles of ECCR, finally, we conduct experiments to motivate our works.

2.1   How LoRa Works

LoRa is a new type of spread spectrum communication protocol released by Semtech in August 2013. It works in the unlicensed sub-GHz frequency. As shown in Fig. 1, LoRa employs the technology of Chirp Spread Spectrum. Since the characteristics of long-range and high robustness, it has been utilized for decades in military communications. Recently, it has become the de-facto mainstream technology for the Internet of Things (IoT) for both industrial and civilian networks worldwide.

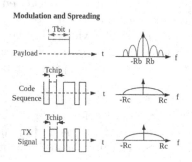

Fig. 1. Spread spectrum of LoRa [29]

2.2   How LoRaWAN Works

The architecture of LoRaWAN is shown in Fig. 2. It contains several functional modules: Receiver, Gateway, Network service, Application. Generally, LoRa end node utilizes sub-GHz band wireless for data transmission with base stations, and after receiving the mixed signals, the gateway demodulates them into packets. These packets are finally transmitted to the cloud for applicational usage.

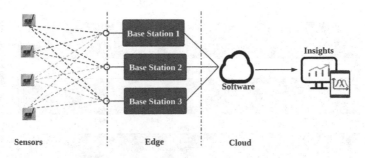

Fig. 2. LoRaWAN architecture

Table 1. Motivation of the ECCR

	Data Transmission amount	Error correction capability	Computational complexity
Standard [16]	Low	Low	Low
Cloud-based [2]	High	High	High
Edge-Cloud: ECCR	**Low**	**High**	**Low**

2.3   Motivations

Prior works has shown massive improvement in performance with modified hardware to coherently combine signals at the physical layer. However the extra hardware cost indeed limits the feasibility in real system. Balanuta et al. propose a cloud-based approach in [2] to leverage most likely corrupt bits across a set of packets that suffered failed CRCs at multiple LoRa LP-WAN basestations. After offloading the corrupted packets and RSSI samples, the failed packets might bo recovered with a probability of 72%. However, the offloading phase incurs excessive communication overhead and limits the large-scale application. We summarize the major performances of Standard LoRa [17], Conventional approach with specialized hardware, and Cloud-based approach in Table 1. In this paper, we ask a natural question that can we design an approach that achieves all the ideal performance at the same time, i.e., low data transmission amount, low computational complexity, high error correction capability and no extra hardware demand. To achieve this, we design an interference mitigation approach in a edge-cloud collaborative manner. The corruption is detected at base station side while the packets are restored at the cloud side. Such a design greatly reduces the data transmission amount. Besides, ECCR utilizes packets from multiple base stations, to achieve high error correction capability. With a carefully designed packet recovery algorithm, ECCR is able to restore packets with the time approaching LoRa (Table 2).

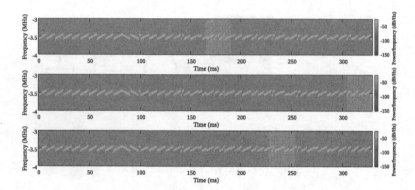

Fig. 3. In Phase/in Quadrature (I/Q) of a LoRa packet with Collision captured with a software defined Radio. (From top to bottom are Lab, Hallway, Library)

Table 2. Payload corruption in different receivers. (Bold part represent for corruptions).

	Payload received
Lab	74 86 111 ... 108 111 32 87 ... 114 108 100 33 ...
Hallway	72 101 108 ... 108 111 32 87 ... **98 108 117 49** ...
Library	72 101 108 ... **105 119 32 78** ... 114 108 100 33 ...

Disjoint Interference. Our design is based on an interesting finding. For different wireless devices, their coverage vary a lot due to the difference in protocols. We find that, the interference is disjoint among different LoRa base stations. To support this findings, we conduct a real experiment. Our first micro-benchmark shows the difference of interference in different receivers.

Figure 3 shows the corruptions in different receivers, which are disjoint. Table 1 also shows that the received payloads of LoRa are corrupted at different locations when facing interference.

We utilized a real-world, 10 km² test-bed in Southeast University, to collect LoRa packets with interference. We examine the interference of LoRa in different sites: (i) a laboratory room, (ii) a hallway, and (iii) a library. We set the transmission power at 10 dBm and put the sender in outdoor environments.

Benefit of Low Data Transmission Requirement. Received Signal Strength Indication (RSSI) is an indication of the strength of the received signal, and its realization is carried out after the baseband receiving filter of the reverse channel. Traditionally, RSSI is utilized to determine the link quality and whether to increase the signal sending power.

OPR [2] proposes a cloud-based error detecting method. It requires the base station sending RSSI samples as an index for detecting interference. Since, LoRa is able to work under the power level of the noise floor, burst interference increases RSSI level, and then corruptions can be identified in the cloud side. However, in LoRa protocols, RSSI is eight times of the length of the payload (e.g. 200 bytes for a 25-byte payload packet [2]). Compared to the payload, RSSI sample is still very long, even after compression. Clearly, transmitting the RSSI samples to the cloud leads to high the network throughputs of base stations.

3   Main Design

ECCR takes advantages of both the global management ability of the cloud and the signal awareness benefit of each base station. In this section, we first describe the overview of ECCR, then move forward and step into the key components of ECCR, i.e., error detection and error recovery, respectively.

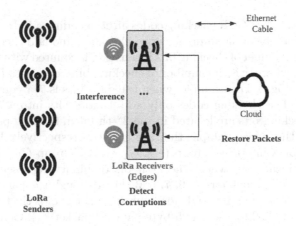

Fig. 4. The architecture of the ECCR

3.1   Overview of the ECCR

Figure 4 shows the architecture of ECCR. The LoRa senders send packets to the base stations in the field. ECCR adds error checking code after the encoding of LoRa physical payload for error detection, to detects corruption of the received packets in the base station and report them to the cloud. Since the corrupted parts of those packets are disjoint, when multiple packets form different base stations are available, the cloud restore the corrupted packets with a weight voting algorithm. Generally, the error correction capability of ECCR has a growth trend as the increasing number of base stations, because an increasing number of useful packets are collected by base stations.

3.2   Error Detection

Error Detection is the most important part of the ECCR design. ECCR adds error checking codes in the LoRa physical payloads so that the base station can identify whether a received packet is corrupted by the interference before decoding.

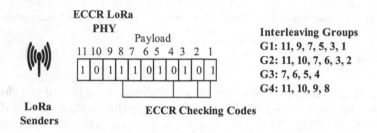

Fig. 5. How ECCR works in LoRa senders

Figure 5 shows the ECCR checking codes after encoding a LoRa physical payload. We take the idea of hamming for error checking, and add checking bits into the payload. The number of checking bits in a packet is counted with the Equation: $2^r \geq m + r + 1$, where, r is the number of checking bits, m is data bits.

As shown in Fig. 5. For example, when the data bits is 7, r equals to 4, since $2^4 \geq 7 + 4 + 1$. The checking codes only add 4 more bits into a 7-bit payload. Specifically, checking bits are located in the 2^k-th bit in the new payload, where $k = 1, 2, ...r$. In the above example, they are 1, 2, 4, 8, respectively. Each checking bit represents for a interleave group (e.g. $G_1 - G_4$). Group G_k indexes for the bits which are located in where the k-th bit of binary representation of the location is 1 (e.g. G_1 index for 11, 9, 7, 5, 3, 1). Although the packet length will slightly increas (4 bits in 7-bit payload). Our approach avoids the transmission of RSSI samples (add 200 bytes to a 25-byte payload packet [2]). Generally, ECCR reduces the computation overhead of error detection.

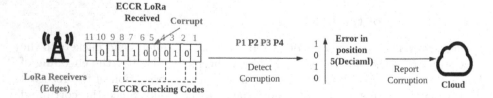

Fig. 6. How ECCR carries on error detection in LoRa receivers

Figure 6 show the error detection works in the base stations. The ECCR checking codes are used for detecting corruptions before decoding packets. After demodulating the signal, the base station utilizes ECCR checking to detect corruption, before decoding. If the bit in location k is wrong, the interleave groups with index it, will fail the error checking. In our design, "1" is used to represent for error, while "0" for correct, and the binary sequence of right and wrong cases of interleaving groups meets the error location when converted to decimal. ECCR takes advantage of this and detects error locations. For example, if the 5-th bit corrupted, the correct and wrong situation of the four interleaving groups are as the Eq. (1):

$$
\begin{cases}
Gb_1 = D_1 \oplus D_3 \oplus D_5 \oplus D_7 \oplus D_9 \oplus \\
Gb_2 = D_2 \oplus D_3 \oplus D_6 \oplus D_7 \oplus D_{10} \oplus D_{11} \\
Gb_3 = D_4 \oplus D_1 \oplus D_6 \oplus D_7 \\
Gb_4 = D_8 \oplus D_8 \oplus D_9 \oplus D_{10} \oplus D_{11}
\end{cases}
\tag{1}
$$

Here D_k represents the correct and wrong conditions of k-th bit, and Gb_{1-4} represents the Boolean value of interleaving groups.

Once a corruption packet is detected, the base stations reports to the cloud. Then the cloud is able to collaborate packets from multiple base stations and restore packets through voting. Although ECCR checking code is able to correct some error bits, it has restrictions when corruptions increase (e.g. When 7, 11 corrupted, four interleave groups all come to failure, the error cannot be recovered by ECCR checking code), so that ECCR further utilizes the cloud to recovery packets.

3.3   Error Recovery

We have demonstrated in Sect. 2.3 that the received payloads of LoRa are corrupted at a different location when facing disjoint interference in multiple base stations. ECCR further utilizes the error checking code to detect corruptions in packets, then the error is reported to the cloud through reliable ethernet connections during which LoRaWAN utilizes 128 bits AES for integrity protection and data encryption. The cloud collaborates packets from multiple base stations, assigns weight to them according to the proportion of corruption, and utilizes a weight voting algorithm to restore the correct packet. Specifically, the weight of symbols is signed according to the Eq. (1):

$$
\begin{cases}
W_k = \dfrac{\sum_{i=1}^{L_k} k(2)[t] - \sum_{i=1}^{L_k}(k(2)[t]==1 \wedge G_i)}{\sum_{i=1}^{L_k} k(2)[t]} \\
L_k = \sum_{i=1}^{p} k(2)[i] \vee 1(\exists k(2)[p] \wedge \nexists k(2)[p+1]) \\
G_i = \wedge_{n=1}^{\cup(D \ in \ G_i)} D_n
\end{cases}
\tag{2}
$$

Where W_k represents for the weight of the k-th symbol, $k(2)$ for the binary representation of k, L_k for the length of $k(2)$, and G_i for the ECCR checking result for i-th interleaving group, D_n for the correct and wrong conditions of the n-th bit. D in G_i are shown in Eq. (1).

Table 3. Voting Result (Bold part represent for corruptions).

	Payload received	Symbol weights
Lab	**74 86 111** ... 108 111 32 87 ... 114 108 100 33	0 0 0 ... 100 0 50 33 ... 100 50 50 33
Hallway	72 101 108 ... 108 111 32 87 ... **98 108 117 49**	0 0 0 ... 100 0 50 33 ... 0 0 0 0
Library	72 101 108 ... **105 119 32 78** ... 114 108 100 33	0 0 0 ... 0 0 0 0 ... 100 50 50 33
	Voting Result	
Voting	72 101 108 ... 108 111 32 87 ... 114 108 100 33	

ECCR utilizes the weight Eq. (1) to assign weights for each symbols. The weights are also utilized to measure the reliability of packets during the weight voting process. A higher weight means the packet is closer to the correct one. In that way, the correct information of multiple packets are collaborated to restore the ture packet (an example of weight voting process is shown in Table 3). Note that, if all the weights of the symbols in those packets are 0, in other words, interleaving groups that index the symbol location all come to error, ECCR treats every packet equally at that symbol location. (e.g. 1, 2 and 3-th symbol in Table 3)

4   Performance Evaluation

To evaluate the correctness and performance of the proposed ECCR approach, we conduct extensive experiments with emulation. Our evaluations include different situations of Wi-Fi interference. To ensure limit-testing the performance of ECCR, we emulated In-Phase/Quadrature (I/Q) of LoRa packets using LoRaMatlab [13] and utilize WLAN Waveform Generator [14] to generate Wi-Fi packets as interference. We control the degree of interference by extending the time of Wi-Fi packets. Our test covers multiple scenarios, including: (i) Standard LoRa, (ii) LoRa and ECCR checking code, (iii) ECCR (Figs. 7, 8, 9 and 10).

Fig. 7. Lab   **Fig. 8.** Hallway   **Fig. 9.** Library   **Fig. 10.** Outdoor site

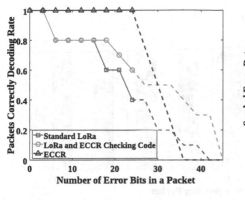
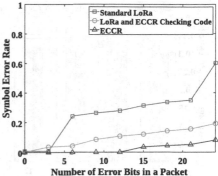

Fig. 11. Packets decoding rate   **Fig. 12.** Symbol Error Rate (SER)

Performance of Packets Correctly Decoding Rate. Figure 11 shows the Packets correctly Decoding Rate of three scenarios when the interference duration increases. Packets correctly decoding rate of (i) and (ii) both decline when the interference extend. ECCR maintains 100% correctly decoding rate until there are more than 30 error bits in a packet. Notice that because both (i) and (ii) utilize forward error correction code for interference mitigation the decoding rates steadily declines when increasing the duration of the interference. ECCR takes advantage of the correct information from multiple receivers so it faces a drop of correctly decoding rate when the duration of interference exceeds a boundary (30 error bits in our experiments).

Performance of Symbol Error Rate. Figure 12 compares the Symbol Error Rate (SER) in three different scenarios. Notice that adding ECCR checking codes reduces SER, and ECCR achieves the lowest SER. Specifically, the error correction capability of LoRa is increased by adding ECCR checking codes (see Sect. 3.2 error detection). Besides, the use of weight voting algorithm further reduces SER.

Figure 11 and Fig. 12 show that ECCR maintains accurately decodes packets when packets have 51.76% corruption (in original LoRa) and it also reduces SER by 51.76%.

Average Computation Time. Figure 13 shows the computing time performance of three different scenarios, where adding ECCR checking code contributes 17% computation time and weight voting algorithm contributes 10% computation time. ECCR, which costs 27% of average computation time, achieves to accurately decode packets when packets have nearly 51.76% corruption (In the strongest interference situation, 27 ms).

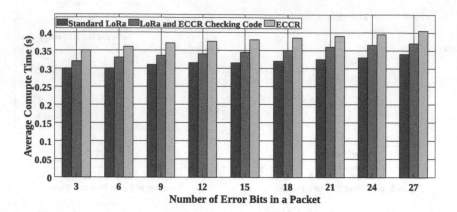

Fig. 13. Average computation time

5   Related Works

This section summarizes the most related works of this paper. Most of the efforts on the LP-WANs interference mitigation fall into the following two categories. LP-WANs interference mitigation mostly on re-designing LoRa base stations and end devices [3–6], is protocol-based. Recently, using cloud computing resources for recovering corrupted packets has emerged as a mechanism for information collaboration for interference mitigation, these cloud-based methods show great compatibility to deployed LP-WANs systems.

Protocol-Based Approaches. Early efforts on interference mitigation in LP-WANs have focused on solutions to physical, and MAC layers, including SCLoRa [17], Choir [23], FTrack [24], mLoRa [25], etc. in physical layer and S-MAC [26], LMAC [27], etc. in MAC layer. These protocol-based solutions require re-designing LP-WANs senders and/or base stations. The requirement on dedicated devices greatly limits the large-scale application for those approaches.

Cloud-Based Approaches. Benefit from the architecture of the LP-WANs system, it is feasible to utilize cloud resources for interference mitigations. For example, OPR [2] offloads RSSI samples and the corrupted packets together send to the cloud, and utilizes the cloud to compute and restore packets. Taking advantage of the ample computational resources and the global management ability of the cloud, cloud-based approaches achieve great progress in recent researches. Besides, those approaches show great compatibility to deployed LP-WANs systems, since they don't require any hardware modification. However, offloading all the RSSI samples to the cloud incurs excessive communication overhead in the uplink bandwidth.

ECCR proposed in this paper is the first work to realize error detecting at the base station side without transmitting RSSI sample to the cloud. It greatly reduces the data transmission amount. Also, ECCR utilizes a weight voting algorithm to collaborates correct information from multiple base stations, so that it has the capability to recovery packets with low compute complexity.

6 Conclusion

This work presents ECCR, an edge-cloud collaborative recovery design for interference mitigation. Taking the advantage of both the global management ability of the cloud and the signal to perceive the benefit of each base stations, ECCR is the first work, to the best of our knowledge, to implement the interference mitigation based on edge-cloud collaborative recovery, which achieves to accurately decode packets when packets have nearly 50% corruption and reduce SER for 50%. Our experiments show that ECCR achieves correctly decoding packets when there is 50% corruption.

In the future, we will further focus on the case with insufficient receivers (e.g., two base stations). ECCR, explores a new methodology to achieve interference mitigation with edge-cloud collaboration, and achieves a nice balance among reliability, flexibility, deployability, and complexity.

Acknowledgement. This work was supported in part by National Natural Science Foundation of China under Grant No. 61902066, Natural Science Foundation of Jiangsu Province under Grant No. BK20190336, China National Key R&D Program 2018YFB2100302 and Fundamental Research Funds for the Central Universities under Grant No. 2242021R41068.

References

1. Knight, M., Seeber, B.: Decoding LoRa: realizing a modern LPWAN with SDR. In: Proceedings of the GNU Radio Conference, vol. 1, no. 1 (2016)
2. Balanuta, A., Pereira, N., Kumar, S., Rowe, A.: A cloud-optimized link layer for low-power wide-area networks. In: Proceedings of the 18th International Conference on Mobile Systems, Applications, and Services, pp. 247–259 (2020)
3. Dongare, A., et al.: Charm: exploiting geographical diversity through coherent combining in low-power wide-area networks. In: 2018 17th ACM/IEEE International Conference on Information Processing in Sensor Networks (IPSN), pp. 60–71 (2018)
4. Eletreby, R., Zhang, D., Kumar, S., Yağan, O.: Empowering low-power wide area networks in urban settings. In: Proceedings of the Conference of the ACM Special Interest Group on Data Communication, pp. 309–321 (2017)
5. Hessar, M., Najafi, A., Gollakota, S.: NetScatter: enabling large-scale backscatter networks. In: 16th USENIX Symposium on Networked Systems Design and Implementation (NSDI 2019), pp. 271–284 (2019)
6. Xia, X., Zheng, Y., Gu, T.: FTrack: parallel decoding for LoRa transmissions. In: Proceedings of the 17th Conference on Embedded Networked Sensor Systems, pp. 192–204 (2019)
7. Mikhaylov, K., Petaejaejaervi, J., Haenninen, T.: Analysis of capacity and scalability of the LoRa low power wide area network technology. In: European Wireless 2016; 22th European Wireless Conference, pp. 1–6. VDE (2016)

8. Li, L., Ren, J., Zhu, Q.: On the application of LoRa LPWAN technology in sailing monitoring system. In: 2017 13th Annual Conference on Wireless On-Demand Network Systems and Services (WONS), pp. 77–80 (2017)
9. Petäjäjärvi, J., Mikhaylov, K., Yasmin, R., Hämäläinen, M., Iinatti, J.: Evaluation of LoRa LPWAN technology for indoor remote health and wellbeing monitoring. Int. J. Wireless Inf. Netw. **24**(2), 153–165 (2017)
10. Jawad, H.M., Nordin, R., Gharghan, S.K., Jawad, A.M., Ismail, M.: Energy-efficient wireless sensor networks for precision agriculture: a review. Sensors **17**(8), 1781 (2017)
11. Sartori, D., Brunelli, D.: A smart sensor for precision agriculture powered by microbial fuel cells. In: 2016 IEEE Sensors Applications Symposium (SAS), pp. 1–6 (2016)
12. Ilie-Ablachim, D., Pǎtru, G.C., Florea, I.M., Rosner, D.: Monitoring device for culture substrate growth parameters for precision agriculture: acronym: MoniSen. In: 2016 15th RoEduNet Conference: Networking in Education and Research, pp. 1–7. (2016)
13. MATHWORKS Help Center. https://ww2.mathworks.cn/help/. Accessed 5 Apr 2021
14. WLAN Waveform Generator. https://ww2.mathworks.cn/help/wlan/. Accessed 5 Apr 2021
15. Wi-Fi Alliance. Wi-fi halow. http://www.wi-fi.org/discover-wi-fi/wi-fi-halow. Accessed 5 Apr 2021
16. LoRa Alliance. LoRaWAN. https://lora-alliance.org/about-lorawan/. Accessed 5 Apr 2021
17. Hu, B., Yin, Z., Wang, S., Xu, Z., He, T.: SCLoRa: leveraging multi-dimensionality in decoding collided LoRa transmissions. In: 2020 IEEE 28th International Conference on Network Protocols (ICNP), pp. 1–11. IEEE (2020)
18. Wang, S., Yin, Z., Li, Z., He, T.: Networking support for physical-layer cross-technology communication. In: 2018 IEEE 26th International Conference on Network Protocols (ICNP), pp. 259–269. IEEE (2018)
19. Wang, S., Kim, S.M., Yin, Z., He, T.: Correlated coding: efficient network coding under correlated unreliable wireless links. In: 2014 IEEE 22nd International Conference on Network Protocols, pp. 433–444. IEEE (2014)
20. Jiang, W., Yin, Z., Liu, R., Li, Z., Kim, S.M., He, T.: BlueBee: a 10,000x faster cross-technology communication via PHY emulation. In: 15th ACM Conference on Embedded Network Sensor Systems, pp. 1–13 (2017)
21. Kim, S.M., He, T.: FreeBee: cross-technology communication via free side-channel. In: 21st Annual International Conference on Mobile Computing and Networking, pp. 317–330 (2015)
22. Jiang, W., Yin, Z., Kim, S.M., He, T.: Transparent cross-technology communication over data traffic. In: IEEE INFOCOM 2017-IEEE Conference on Computer Communications, pp. 1–9 (2017)
23. Eletreby, R., Zhang, D., Kumar, Yağan, S.: Empowering low power wide area networks in urban settings. In: Proceedings of the Conference of the ACM Special Interest Group on Data Communication, pp. 309–321. ACM (2017)
24. Xia, X., Zheng, Y., Gu, T.: FTrack: parallel decoding for LoRa transmissions. In: Proceedings of the 17th Conference on Embedded Networked Sensor Systems, pp. 192–204. ACM (2019)
25. Wang, X., Kong, L., He, L., Chen, G.: mLoRa: a multi-packet reception protocol in LoRa networks. In: IEEE 27th International Conference on Network Protocols, pp. 1–11. IEEE (2019)

26. Xu, Z., Luo, J., Yin, Z., He, T., Dong, F.: S-MAC: achieving high scalability via adaptive scheduling in LPWAN. In: IEEE INFOCOM 2020-IEEE Conference on Computer Communications, pp. 506–515. IEEE (2020)

27. Gamage, A., Liando, J.C., Gu, C., Tan, R., Li, M.: LMAC: efficient carrier-sense multiple access for LoRa. In: Proceedings of the 26th Annual International Conference on Mobile Computing and Networking, pp. 1–13. IEEE (2020)

28. Shahid, A., et al.: A convolutional neural network approach for classification of LPWAN technologies: Sigfox, LoRa and IEEE 802.15. 4g. In: 2019 16th Annual IEEE International Conference on Sensing, Communication, and Networking (SECON), pp. 1–8. IEEE (2019)

29. SEMTECH. https://www.semtech.com/. Accessed 5 Apr 2021

Scheduling and Optimization I

A Stay-Point-Based Charger Placement Scheme for Nondeterministic Mobile Nodes

Lingyun Zhong[1], Shitong Duan[2], Yingjue Chen[1], and Feng Lin[1(✉)]

[1] College of Computer Science, Sichuan University, Chengdu 610065, China
{zhonglingyun,chenyingjue}@stu.scu.edu.cn, linfeng@scu.edu.cn
[2] College of Software Engineering, Sichuan University, Chengdu 610065, China
duanshitong@stu.scu.edu.cn

Abstract. Wireless rechargeable sensor networks (WRSN) provide an approach to address the energy scarcity problem in wireless sensor networks by introducing static or mobile chargers to recharge the energy-hungry sensor nodes. Most of the existing studies on WRSN focus on optimizing the charging schedule to static nodes or mobile nodes with deterministic mobility. In this work, we aim to provide charging service for nodes with nondeterministic mobility by deploying the minimal number of static chargers. We propose a novel charger placement scheme by using the mobility characteristics reflected by the node's stay points. In the proposed scheme, we first generate one candidate location based on every stay point exacted from the nodal historic trajectories. And then, we weigh each candidate location by the energy gain of placing a charger on it. Then we prove it is an NP-hard problem to select the minimal subset of candidate locations to place chargers and propose a greedy algorithm to address this problem. The simulation results show the proposed algorithm outperforms the existing algorithm.

Keywords: Wireless rechargeable sensor network · Stay point · Nondeterministic mobile node · Charger placement

1 Introduction

Wireless rechargeable sensor networks (WRSN) can prolong the lifetime of wireless sensor networks by employing one or multiple chargers to recharge the sensor nodes with wireless power transfer technology [1]. As a possible solution for the energy scarcity problem in wireless sensor networks, WRSN has been attracting a lot of interest.

Most of the existing researches on WRSN have focused on recharging static nodes, while a small number of studies have explored recharging mobile nodes. However, these studies on mobile charging all assume the nodal trajectories are deterministic or the movements of the nodes are controlled. Thus, chargers know

© Springer Nature Switzerland AG 2021
Z. Liu et al. (Eds.): WASA 2021, LNCS 12937, pp. 511–522, 2021.
https://doi.org/10.1007/978-3-030-85928-2_40

exactly the locations where to encounter and recharge the sensor nodes. However, in many applications, this assumption is not true. One typical example is the chronic-disease-patient surveillance systems, where the sensors are attached to and moving with each monitored patient. In these cases, the movements of sensors are nondeterministic.

In this work, we aim to recharge nondeterministic mobile nodes with static chargers. This task essentially is to choose some optimal locations to place the static chargers. Thus, the mobile nodes can get charged automatically when approaching the chargers. According to the studies of wireless power transfer, there are two fundamental requirements for wireless energy transferring: one is the energy transfer lasts for a period of time; the other is the distance between the charger and the charged node must be limited. Therefore, in the problem of charging nondeterministic mobile nodes with static chargers, the locations to place static chargers have the following constraints:

1. Mobile nodes are likely to visit or approach these locations at some points in the future.
2. Once a mobile node visits or approaches them, it is likely to stay at these locations for some time.
3. For each node, at least one of these locations satisfies both constraint 1 and constraint 2.

Constraints 1 and 2 ensure that static chargers are deployed in compliance with wireless energy transfer requirements, while constraint 3 ensures that all mobile nodes have the opportunities to be charged. In our work, under the above three constraints, we choose to minimize the number of static chargers as the optimal goal. Therefore, we named the problem as the problem of charging nondeterministic mobile nodes with the minimal number of static chargers (CMMC).

The existing researches [2,3] have shown that, because the importance of locations is different, there are some regions, called stay points, where people have stopped for a while and have a high likelihood of visiting multiple times, such as shopping malls and tourist attractions. Stay points reflect nodal mobility characteristics and indicate the particularity of locations. Obviously, to our problem, constraint 1 and constraint 2 would be satisfied simultaneously if we generate candidate locations of chargers based on the stay points. Then we can pursue the optimal goal on the candidate locations only under constraint 3.

Based on the above analysis, we propose a stay-point-based charger placement scheme. Firstly, we generate one candidate location for a possible charger based on every stay point extracted from the nodal historical trajectories and then weigh each candidate location by the energy gain of placing a charger on it. Then we prove that the problem of selecting the minimal subset from the candidate locations is NP-hard and propose a greedy algorithm to solve it.

The rest of this paper is organized as follows. Section 2 reviews related work. Section 3 introduces the network model and formulates our problem. Section 4 presents the proposed scheme. Section 5 conducts simulations for performance evaluation. Section 6 concludes our work.

2   Related Work

Most of the existing work on charging mobile sensor nodes assumes that the trajectories of sensor nodes are deterministic. For instance, [4] proposed a scheme to adapt the working power of the static charging pile to charge the sensor nodes moving nearby. [5] designed a generic framework for charging mobile nodes with optimization of the charging path and charger scheduling. [6] proposed a tree-based charging scheme to charge the mission-critical robots while the charger can communicate with the charged robot at any time to determine the future travel trajectory and charging needs of the robots.

Up to now, several works investigate providing charging service for nodes with nondeterministic mobility. [7,8] addressed this problem with a single mobile charger. Unfortunately, due to using a single mobile charger, these two algorithms cannot work well in a network in which the nodes move widely or rapidly. To our best knowledge, [9] is the only work to explore charging nondeterministic mobile nodes with static chargers. In order to provide charging services with a limited energy budget, [9] celled the area through which the nodes pass, and then selected some of the cell centers to place static chargers through two heuristics. However, the algorithm in [9] does not consider the characteristics of node movement and does not guarantee that all mobile sensors will get a chance to be charged.

3   Preliminaries

In this section, we present the network model and formulate the CMMC problem.

3.1   Network Model

We consider a two-dimensional target area Z with a base station (BS), and n mobile nodes. Let $S = \{s_1, s_2, ..., s_n\}$ denotes the set of mobile nodes. The mobile node $s_i \in S$ is powered by a rechargeable battery with the energy capacity b.

The mobile node s_i is equipped with GPS to record its location $l_i(t) = (x_i(t), y_i(t))$ at time t and send this location with the timestamp to the BS every ΔT via a long-distance communication tech like LPWAN. Let $T_i^{(t)}$ denotes the trajectory of the node s_i at time t. Thus, we have $T_i^{(t)} = \{(0, l_i(0)), (\Delta T, l_i(\Delta T)), ..., (t', l_i(t'))\}$, where $\Delta T | t'$ and $0 < t - t' < \Delta T$.

The BS is the control center of the network, and responsible for receiving sensing data and the location report from nodes.

Based on the analysis of historic trajectories, we can select a certain number of locations for placing static chargers. These locations are denoted by a set $C = \{c_1, c_2, ..., c_m\}$. The coordinate of the location $c_i \in C$ is $(x(c_i), y(c_i))$. Without causing confusion, we also use c_i to denote the static charger placed at $(x(c_i), y(c_i))$.

We assume the nodes are attached to and moving with people. The only energy consumption of nodes consists of the following two parts: the energy consumed by sensing and the energy consumed by data transmission. Let p_i

denotes the energy consumption rate of node s_i. If a node runs out of energy, we consider it is a dead node and cannot work anymore.

The static chargers have unlimited energy capacities and are always in the working state with the same transmission power P_0. The chargers are working in an omnidirectional charging model which is widely adopted in existing studies [10]. The effective charging radius of static chargers is R, and chargers use RF to provide charging service. When node accesses the charger's charging range, it will receive power from the charger immediately. Base on [11], we use the wireless recharge model as follows

$$P(c_j, l_i(t)) = \begin{cases} \frac{P_0 \cdot \alpha}{(d(c_j, l_i(t)) + \beta)^2}, d(c_j, l_i(t)) \leq R \\ 0, d(c_j, l_i(t)) > R \end{cases}, \tag{1}$$

where $P_{(c_j, l_i(t))}$ is the power that node s_i at location $l_i(t)$ received from charger c_j. α and β are constants determined by hardware of the charger and environment. Node s_i at location $l_i(t)$ within the charging range of charger c_j equals to $d(c_j, l_i(t)) \leq R$. The distance $d(c_j, l_i(t)) \leq R$ is the Euclidean distance between the charger c_j and the location $l_i(t)$, and it is

$$d(c_j, l_i(t)) = \sqrt{(x_{c_j} - x_i(t))^2 + (y_{c_j} - y_i(t))^2}. \tag{2}$$

Note that the node's battery capacity limits the amount of energy the node can receive. Therefore, if the total energy transmitted to node s_i is more than it needs to be replenished, the maximum energy received by node s_i is the energy capacity, otherwise, the energy received by node s_i is the energy charged from the charger. According to (1), (2), we can calculate the received energy by node s_i at location $l_i(t)$ from charger c_j as:

$$E(c_j, l_i(t)) = min\{b - R_i, P(c_j, l_i(t)) \cdot t_j\}, \tag{3}$$

where R_i denotes the residual energy of node s_i, $P(c_j, l_i(t))$ is the received power of s_i from charger c_j, and t_j denotes the stay time of node s_i at location $l_i(t)$.

3.2   Problem Definition

As analyzed in Sect. 1, there are three constraints on the CMMC problem. We were expecting to use the characteristics of the stay points to deploy chargers at the stay points that satisfy constraint 1 and constraint 2 simultaneously. Unfortunately, we find the stay points cannot be used as the candidate locations of chargers in practice (see Sect. 4.1). We have to generate candidate locations of chargers based on the stay points. Then, we can try to find the minimal subset of the candidate locations to place chargers under the constraint that at least one of the stay points is kept for any node (constraint 3).

According to the above analysis, the CMMC problem can be deduced into two sub-problems, namely the candidate charger generation problem (CCGP) and the charger selection problem (CSP).

The main task of CCGP is to generate the candidate chargers based on extracting the stay points from the historic trajectory of each node. The definition of CCGP is given as follows:

CCGP. *Given all the historical trajectory T_i, where $s_i \in S$, the objective of CCGP is to generate a set of candidate chargers C' based on the union of the stay points set Λ_i of node s_i. The formulation of CCGP is depicted as below:*

$$C' = G\left(\bigcup_{s_i \in S} \Lambda_i\right) = G\left(\bigcup_{s_i \in S} = F(T_i)\right), \tag{4}$$

where G denotes the algorithm to generate the set of candidate chargers and F denotes the algorithm to extract Λ_i from T_i.

After getting the candidate chargers, we should select a minimal subset of them to place chargers under the constraint 3. There are two requirements to perform this task. First, we should introduce a positive weight metric $W(c'_i)$ for each candidate charger $c'_i \in C'$, thus we can determine which charger should be selected. On the other hand, we should relate nodes with each candidate charger $c'_i \in C'$, so we can check if constraint 3 is met when selecting c'_i.

To easily depict, we introduce two definitions to show the relationship between stay points and candidate chargers and the relationship between nodes and candidate chargers, respectively.

Definition 1 (stay-point-coverage). *Given the stay point set Λ_i of node s_i and one candidate charger location c'_k. Let $\lambda_{i,j} \in \Lambda_i$ denotes the jth stay point of node s_i, $l(\lambda_{i,j})$ is the location of $\lambda_{i,j}$, and $d(c'_k, l(\lambda_{i,j}))$ denotes the distance between c'_k and $l(\lambda_{i,j})$. If $d(c'_k, l(\lambda_{i,j})) < R$, we call the stay point $\lambda_{i,j}$ is covered by the candidate charger c'_k and denote this relationship as $\lambda_{i,j} \in V(c'_k)$, where $V(c'_k)$ denotes the set of all the stay points covered by c'_k.*

Definition 2 (node-coverage). *Given the stay point set Λ_i of node s_i and one candidate charger location c'_k. If $\lambda_{i,j} \in V(c'_k), \exists \lambda_{i,j} \in \Lambda_i$, we call the node s_i is covered by the candidate charger c'_k and denote this relationship as $s_i \in H(c'_k)$, where $H(c'_k)$ denotes the coverage set of c'_k.*

Based on above definitions, we have $H(c'_i) \subseteq S$ and the constraint 3 can be represented as $\bigcup_{c_i \in C} H(c_i) = S$. We can give the definition of CSP as follows:

CSP. *Given the set of candidate chargers C', and the set of sensor nodes S to find the minimal subset $C \subseteq C'$ to place chargers, such that each node has to be covered by elements in C at least once while the network may get maximum weight. The problem formulized as follows:*

$$min|C|, \tag{5}$$

$$max \sum_{c_i \in C} W(c_i), \tag{6}$$

$$s.t. \bigcup_{c_i \in C} H(c_i) = S, C \subseteq C'. \tag{7}$$

Theorem 1. *The charger selection problem (CSP) is NP-hard.*

Proof. Define $M(c_i') = \frac{1}{W(c_i')}$ as the weight of c_i'. Since $W(c_i')$ is positive, $M(c_i')$ is positive. Since each candidate charger has its own coverage set, $M(c_i')$ can be view as the weight of $H(c_i')$. The CSP can be restated as that: Given the set S and a collection $\{H(c_i') \subseteq S\}$, where $\bigcup_{c_i' \in C'} H(c_i') = S$ and each $H(c_i')$ has a positive weight $M(c_i')$. The goal of CSP is to find a subcollection $\{H(c_i)\} \subseteq \{H(c_i')\}$, such that $\bigcup_{c_i \in C} H(c_i) = S$ and its weight $\sum_{c_i \in C} M(c_i)$ is minimized. Obviously, the CSP becomes a standard minimum weight set cover problem (MWSCP). Since the MWSCP is NP-hard [12], we proof the CSP is NP-hard.

4   Proposed Charging Scheme

We have analyzed and formulized the two subproblems of CMMC so far. In this section, we present our charging scheme named SPCPS (stay-points-based charger placement scheme), to solve the two subproblems one by one. The proposed scheme works in two phases. In phase I, to address CCGP, we propose a candidate location generating algorithm that generates one candidate location for each stay point detected by the stay point detection algorithm in [2]. In phase II, we weigh each candidate location by the energy gain of placing a charger on it and propose a greedy algorithm to choose the locations of chargers from the set of candidate locations based on the energy gain, so as to the CSP is addressed.

4.1   Candidate Chargers Generation

We use the stay points detection algorithm in [2] to extract the stay points in a given trajectory by defining two constants, namely *timeThresh* and *disThresh*, respectively. The *timeThresh* is the time threshold for detecting stay points. The *disThresh* is the spatial threshold for detecting the stay points that limits the maximum distance of two locations belonging to the same stay point. By running the stay points detection algorithm, we can get the stay point set from each trajectory and present them as follows:

$$\Lambda_i = \{\lambda_{i,j}\} = \{(t_j, l(\lambda_{i,j}))\}, \tag{8}$$

where t_j is the residence time of the node s_i at the stay point $\lambda_{i,j}$, and $l(\lambda_{i,j})$ is the coordinate of $\lambda_{i,j}$.

It is important to note that there are two reasons why we cannot use $\lambda_{i,j}$ as the candidate charger directly. The first reason is the results of the stay points detection algorithm are time-dependent while the candidate chargers are not. For example, considering one node may intermittently stay in the same location several times, which means multiple stay points for the stay points detection algorithm while they represent only one candidate location of chargers in our case. The other reason is that $\lambda_{i,j}$ may represent the region nodes often stay precisely. We note that one stay point is a geographic region and $\lambda_{i,j}$ only contains one location. For example, let's assume there are two stay points we got $\lambda_{i,j}$ and $\lambda_{s,t}$. The distance between $l(\lambda_{i,j})$ and $l(\lambda_{s,t})$ is pretty small. Obviously, the $\lambda_{i,j}$ and $\lambda_{s,t}$ represent the same geographic region, and the medium point between $l(\lambda_{i,j})$ and $l(\lambda_{s,t})$ may represent the region more precisely than these two stay points.

Based on the above consideration, we propose an algorithm to generate the candidate locations of chargers based on the stay points we got. In the proposed algorithm, for each raw stay point $\lambda_{i,j}$, we first generate a candidate charger c_k' at the $l(\lambda_{i,j})$ where $k = \sum_{u=1}^{i}|\Lambda_u| + j - 1$. Then we calculate the medium point of $V(c_k')$ like follows:

$$f(c_k') = \frac{\sum_{\lambda \in V(c_k')} l(\lambda)}{|V(c_k')|}. \tag{9}$$

Then we move c_k' to $f(c_k')$. Repeat this process until c_k' does not change.

The details of the generating candidate location algorithm are depicted in Algorithm 1.

Algorithm 1. Generate Candidate Locations (GCL)

Input: stay point set Λ
Output: chargers' candidate location set C'
1: $C' \leftarrow \varnothing$
2: **for** $i \leftarrow 1$ to n **do**
3:    **for** $j \leftarrow 1$ to $|\Lambda_i|$ **do**
4:        $k = \sum_{u=1}^{i}|\Lambda_u| + j - 1$
5:        $c_k' = l(\lambda_{i,j})$
6:        **repeat**
7:            calculate the stay point set $V(c_k')$
8:            $c_k' \leftarrow f(c_k')$
9:        **until** c_k''s coordinate does not change
10:       $C' \leftarrow C' \cup \{c_k'\}$
11:   **end for**
12: **end for**
13: **return** C'

4.2   Charger Selection

As we mentioned in Sect. 3.2, we solve the CSP by selecting a part of candidate chargers with the weight metric $W(c'_i)$.

According to (3), the energy transfer from one charger to its covered node is relevant to the distance between the node and the charger, as well as the staying time of the nodes. Therefore, the different nodes covered by the same charger may have different energy gain. In our case, we use the energy gain as the weight metric $W(c'_i)$. Let $E(c'_k, \lambda_{i,j})$ denotes the energy gain the node s_i get at $\lambda_{i,j}$ from the charger c'_k. We can have the energy gain $W(c'_k)$ of the candidate charger $c''_k \in C'$ as below:

$$W(c'_k) = \sum_{\lambda_{i,j} \in V(c'_k)} E(c'_k, \lambda_{i,j}). \tag{10}$$

According to (3), $E(c'_k, \lambda_{i,j})$ can be calculated by follows:

$$E(c'_k, \lambda_{i,j}) = min\left\{b - R_i, P(c'_k, \lambda_{i,j}) \cdot t_j\right\}, \tag{11}$$

where $P(c'_k, \lambda_{i,j})$ is the received power of s_i from c'_k at $\lambda_{i,j}$.

The CSP essentially is a weighted set cover problem. In this work, we propose a greedy algorithm to solve this problem. In the proposed algorithm, for the node set S, the candidate charger set C', and the set of stay points $\Lambda = \bigcup \Lambda_i$, we first calculate the $V(c'_k)$, $H(c'_k)$ and $W(c'_k)$ for each candidate charger c'_k. Then, we select c'_k with the maximum $W(c'_k)$ to the result set C and delete c'_k from C'. Specially, for all the $s_i \in H(c'_k)$, we delete s_i from S and Λ_i from Λ. Repeat this process until $S = \varnothing$. Finally, we get the charger set C.

The detailed of selecting proper locations are depicted in Algorithm 2.

Algorithm 2. Select Charger Locations(SCL)

Input: node set S, stay point set Λ, candidate location set C'
Output: charger location set C
1: $C \leftarrow \varnothing$
2: **while** $S \neq \varnothing$ **do**
3:     **for** $c'_k \in C'$ **do**
4:         update $W(c'_k)$, $H(c'_k)$ and $V(c'_k)$
5:     **end for**
6:     find c'_k with the maximum weight $W(c'_k)$
7:     $C \leftarrow C \cup \{c'_k\}$
8:     $C' \leftarrow C' \setminus \{c'_k\}$
9:     $S \leftarrow S \setminus H(c'_k)$
10:    $\Lambda \leftarrow \Lambda \setminus V(c'_k)$
11: **end while**
12: **return** C

---

5   Performance Evaluation

We evaluate the performance of the SPCPS scheme by comparing with the TCA approach [9]. To the best of our knowledge, TCA and our scheme are the only two schemes for placing static chargers to recharge nodes with nondeterministic mobility. To ensure the effectiveness of comparison, the sum power of chargers selected by SPCPS is regarded as the power budget of TCA.

We conduct two groups of simulations. These simulations evaluate the performance of SPCPS and TCA based on the energy consumption rate and initial energy of the node respectively.

We first introduce the simulation set (Sect. 5.1), and show the simulation results of SPCPS and TCA (Sect. 5.2).

5.1   Simulation Setup

We carry out the simulation by replaying mobility from the CRAWDAD dataset [13]. In our simulation, we choose 13 students as mobile nodes from the data set that stores the human mobility trace of 36 students in NCSU, whose trajectories are over 22000 s and long enough to extract stay points.

We set the time interval between two continuous locations is 30 s. The staying time threshold of stay points is 60 s and the distance threshold is 100 m. The default capacity energy of node is 10 J. The static energy consumption rate for each node is uniformly set in the range of $[8.3 \times 10^{-4}\,\mathrm{J/s}, 3.3 \times 10^{-3}\,\mathrm{J/s}]$. We use 0–12000 s to select charger locations and 12000–22000 s to simulate the charging process (the simulation lasts for 10000 s). At the beginning to simulate the charging process, we set the residual energy of each node is uniformly range from 1 J to 4 J.

We set the parameters in the charging model as follows: $P_0 = 100\,\mathrm{w}$, $\alpha = 0.64$, $\beta = 30$ and $R = 100\,\mathrm{m}$. To filter the GPS error of locations, we use the power level to represent the received power of each node. The radii of different power levels R_1, R_2, R_3, R_4 are 10 m, 30 m, 60 m, 100 m, respectively.

To save the calculating time, we use the trajectory data with the time interval 30 s to select the charger set. For the accuracy of the simulation, we smooth the original trajectory data into the data with a time interval of 1 s for simulation.

5.2   Simulation Results

Under different variables, we present the performance of SPCPS and TCA algorithms in the number of chargers, the nodal survival ratio and the death time of 30% nodes. The number of chargers is the number of selected chargers by algorithms which is our optimization goal. The nodal survival ratio is the ratio of the number of surviving nodes to the total number of nodes at the end of the simulation, while the death time of 30% nodes specifies when the network performance starts to degrade significantly. Thus, these three metrics illustrate the performance of charger placing algorithms.

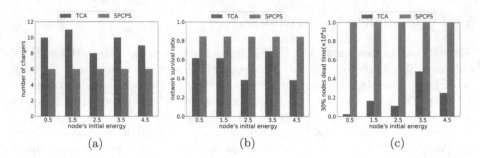

Fig. 1. Impact of nodes' initial energy

Varying the Initial Energy of Nodes. In Fig. 1, we compare the performance of the different nodal initial energy on SPCPS and TCA. We carry out simulations where the static average initial energy of each sensor is multiplied by 0.2, 0.6, 1.0, 1.4, 1.8 and set the expectations as the horizontal coordinates of figures.

Figure 1(a) shows that the initial energy of the node has no effect on the number of chargers in SPCPS, which is because SPCPS does not consider the initial energy of the node. TCA also does not consider the initial energy of the node, but since its optimization goal is to provide charging services with a limited energy budget. Therefore, TCA is sensitive to the nodal residual energy, which results in the number of chargers varying with the nodal initial energy. In addition, since SPCPS exploits the mobility characteristics of nodes to deploy chargers, it selects a smaller number of chargers although SPCPS considers the charging coverage of all nodes.

In Fig. 1(b), the results show that SPCPS achieves better results, which is 23%–46% higher than TCA, effectively extending the network lifetime. This is because TCA does not consider the movement characteristics of the nodes and treats all movement trajectories of the nodes equally. In contrast, the proposed algorithm generates candidate locations based on stay points, which effectively reflects the movement characteristics of nodes. Therefore, although the TCA algorithm deploys more chargers (Fig. 1(a)), our algorithm achieves better results. We also notice that the result of TCA fluctuates because of the fewer selected chargers when the expectations are 2.5 and 4.5 (see Fig. 1(a)).

Figure 1(c) presents the results of the death time of 30% nodes of the two algorithms. Since the proposed scheme always achieves beyond 70% at the survival ratio, the death time of 30% nodes of the proposed scheme always is ∞. As the initial energy of the node increases, the death time of 30% of the nodes in TCA is delayed. The reason is obvious, the initial energy of the node becomes larger and the node's lifetime in the network becomes longer.

Varying the Energy Consumption Rate of Nodes. Figure 2 shows the performance of SPCPS and TCA under different energy consumption rates of nodes. We carry out simulations where the static average energy consumption

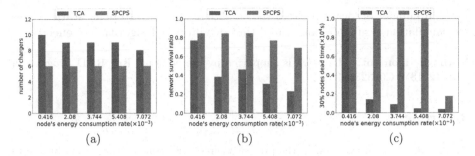

Fig. 2. Impact of nodes' consumption rate

rate of each sensor is multiplied by 0.2, 1.0, 1.8, 2.6, 3.4 and set the expectations as the horizontal coordinates of Fig. 2(a), Fig. 2(b) and Fig. 2(c).

In Fig. 2(b), the number of chargers selected by SPCPS does not vary with the energy consumption rate. This is because the chargers selected by SPCPS depend only on the trajectories and the charging radius and are not affected by the energy consumption rate. When the energy consumption rate increases, the number of chargers selected by the TCA generally decreases. This is because the TCA considers the energy consumption rate when selecting the charger locations. The lower the energy consumption rate, the less energy the node can receive, and the energy capacity of the node is limited. And since the TCA will exhaust its power budget, it tends to select more chargers.

Figure 2(c) illustrates that the survival ratios of both SPCPS and TCA decrease, which is due to the increase in the consumption rate causing the nodes to die faster. The survival ratio of TCA on the expectation 3.744×10^{-3} is a little higher than it on the expectation 2.08×10^{-3}, because of the random value of the energy consumption rate. The survival ratio of SPCPS is 8%–46% higher than TCA, which means SPCPS has a better charging efficiency, since SPCPS considers the charging coverage of all nodes, it could take care of more nodes.

According to Fig. 2(c), the death time of 30% nodes of TCA gradually gets earlier with the increase of the energy consumption rate. One reason is that the number of chargers decreases and the energy consumption rate increases result in the death rate of nodes accelerate. Compared with the expectation of node energy consumption rate that varies from 4.16×10^{-4} to 2.08×10^{-3}, the death time of 30% nodes significantly delays. When the expectation of energy consumption rate at 7.072×10^{-3}, there is the first time that over 30% of nodes die in SPCPS. However, the proposed scheme still outperforms TCA.

6   Conclusion and Future Work

In our work, we have studied the problem of charging nondeterministic mobile nodes with the minimal number of static chargers. We used the stay points to find the mobility characteristics and generated the candidate charger locations based on the stay points. And then we proposed a greedy algorithm to select the minimal number of locations from the candidate locations to place static chargers. Simulation results demonstrated that our proposed algorithm is effective.

Acknowledgement. This work is supported by the National Key R&D Program of China(2018YFC0832303).

References

1. Roselli, L., et al.: Review of the present technologies concurrently contributing to the implementation of the internet of things (IoT) paradigm: RFID, green electronics, WPT and energy harvesting. In: 2015 IEEE Topical Conference on Wireless Sensors and Sensor Networks (WiSNet), pp. 1–3. IEEE (2015)
2. Li, Q., Zheng, Y., Xie, X., Chen, Y., Liu, W., Ma, W.Y.: Mining user similarity based on location history. In: Proceedings of the 16th ACM SIGSPATIAL International Conference on Advances in Geographic Information Systems, pp. 1–10 (2008)
3. Gonzalez, M.C., Hidalgo, C.A., Barabasi, A.L.: Understanding individual human mobility patterns. Nature **453**(7196), 779–782 (2008)
4. Madhja, A., Nikoletseas, S., Voudouris, A.A.: Adaptive wireless power transfer in mobile ad hoc networks. Comput. Netw. **152**, 87–97 (2019)
5. Chen, L., Lin, S., Huang, H.: Charge me if you can: Charging path optimization and scheduling in mobile networks. In: Proceedings of the 17th ACM International Symposium on Mobile Ad Hoc Networking and Computing, pp. 101–110 (2016)
6. He, L., Cheng, P., Gu, Y., Pan, J., Zhu, T., Liu, C.: Mobile-to-mobile energy replenishment in mission-critical robotic sensor networks. In: IEEE INFOCOM 2014-IEEE Conference on Computer Communications, pp. 1195–1203. IEEE (2014)
7. Liu, T., Wu, B., Xu, W., Cao, X., Peng, J., Wu, H.: Learning an effective charging scheme for mobile devices. In: 2020 IEEE International Parallel and Distributed Processing Symposium (IPDPS), pp. 202–211. IEEE (2020)
8. Li, Y., Zhong, L., Lin, F.: Predicting-scheduling-tracking: Charging nodes with non-deterministic mobility. IEEE Access (2020)
9. Zhang, S., Qian, Z., Wu, J., Kong, F., Lu, S.: Wireless charger placement and power allocation for maximizing charging quality. IEEE Trans. Mob. Comput. **17**(6), 1483–1496 (2017)
10. Fu, L., Cheng, P., Gu, Y., Chen, J., He, T.: Minimizing charging delay in wireless rechargeable sensor networks. In: 2013 Proceedings IEEE INFOCOM, pp. 2922–2930. IEEE (2013)
11. Yeager, D.J., Powledge, P.S., Prasad, R., Wetherall, D., Smith, J.R.: Wirelessly-charged uhf tags for sensor data collection. In: 2008 IEEE International Conference on RFID, pp. 320–327. IEEE (2008)
12. Vazirani, V.V.: Approximation Algorithms. Springer, Heidelberg (2013). https://doi.org/10.1007/978-3-662-04565-7
13. Injong, R., Minsu, S., Seongik, H., Seongjoon, L., Song, C.: CRAWDAD dataset ncsu/mobilitymodels (2009)

Practical Bandwidth Allocation for Video QoE Fairness

Wanchun Jiang[✉], Pan Ning, Zheyuan Zhang, Jintian Hu, Zhicheng Ren, and Jianxin Wang

School of Computer Science and Engineering, Center South University, Changsha 410083, Hunan, China
{jiangwc,jxwang}@csu.edu.cn

Abstract. Nowadays, the QoE unfairness problem exists under the scenario of multiple clients sharing bottleneck links, as clients just maximize their Quality of Experience (QoE) independently via adaptive bitrate algorithm and congestion control algorithms provide only connection-level fairness. Improving the QoE fairness among clients, the video providers would jointly optimize the QoE of multiple clients. Nevertheless, existing solutions are impractical due to either deployment issues or heavy computation overhead. Therefore, we propose the practical bandwidth allocation (PBA) mechanism for video QoE fairness in this paper. Specifically, PBA formulates QoE by considering the impacts of both network conditions and devices and reconfigures congestion control algorithm according to the piggybacked QoE. In this distributive manner, PBA can rapidly converge to the bandwidth allocation with good QoE fairness. Real-world experiments confirm that PBA improves the QoE fairness and accordingly increases the minimum QoE of video streams by at least 13% and 15% compared with Copa and Cubic, respectively. Moreover, the performance advantage of PBA becomes significant under dynamic wireless networks.

Keywords: Quality of Experience (QoE) · Fairness · Bandwidth allocation

1 Introduction

Nowadays, the proportion of video streaming in IP traffic is expected to be 82% in 2022 [1]. Moreover, the popularity of various short video apps also increases rapidly. Accordingly, the improvement of Quality of Experience (QoE) for users under complex Internet draws more and more attention. Over the past decades, many adaptive bitrate (ABR) algorithms have been developed for clients to optimize the video QoE [2,14,18] and congestion control algorithms are improved for video transmission [5,6,8,9] under dynamic network conditions.

Because ABR algorithms are independently adopted by different clients, the impacts of devices on QoE is ignored at clients. Moreover, when multiple devices share a bottleneck link, e.g., smartphones and laptops share the same WiFi, each

© Springer Nature Switzerland AG 2021
Z. Liu et al. (Eds.): WASA 2021, LNCS 12937, pp. 523–534, 2021.
https://doi.org/10.1007/978-3-030-85928-2_41

client will compete for the maximum possible bandwidth. Under this condition, each client is blind to the bandwidth requirement of others, which is directly associated with the devices. Meanwhile, the underlying congestion control algorithms allocate bandwidth equally among different clients, being unaware of their QoEs [5,8,9]. In total, the QoEs of clients are unfair. With the popularity of video traffic, the probability of multiple video flows sharing bottleneck links increases, and the QoE unfairness problem would become more significant.

Improving the QoE fairness among clients, the video providers would jointly optimize the QoE of multiple clients. To address the QoE unfairness problem, work [11] suggests allocating bandwidth based on the QoE information of clients at the bottleneck router. However, this solution suffers from deployment issues, as routers can hardly identify the bottleneck in reality and are usually blind to both the number of video streams and the client QoEs. In contrast, Minerva [6] reconfigures the parameter of CUBIC [5] at servers according to the piggybacked QoE information of clients and thus improves the QoE fairness with the distributive bandwidth allocation of CUBIC. However, Minerva suffers from heavy computation overhead, because the calculation of both the QoEs of each chunk under all possible states and the VMAF values of each frame of each chunk is needed in advance. Besides, the convergence speed of Minerva, which is important under dynamic networks, has not been discussed.

In this paper, we design and implement the practical bandwidth allocation (PBA) mechanism for video QoE fairness. Specifically, PBA is easy to deploy as it distributively reconfigures the parameter of congestion control algorithms for QoE-fair bandwidth allocation. Moreover, the complex computation about VMAF is replaced by a direct and simple formulation of the device-dependent factors, such as screen size and resolution, during the calculation of video QoE in PBA. Furthermore, PBA adapts to dynamic network conditions by ignoring the QoE collected a long time ago and replacing the congestion control algorithm CUBIC with Copa [9] for better convergence speed. Consequently, PBA can rapidly converge to the bandwidth allocation with ideal QoE fairness and accordingly improve the minimum QoE of video streams significantly.

To evaluate PBA, we build a video system, where clients employ dash.js [3] and the server is based on caddy [4], and implement PBA. Experimental results confirm that PBA respectively improves the minimum QoE by at least 13% and 15% compared with Copa and Cubic and performs well under dynamic networks.

2   Background and Related Work

The user-perceived QoE is the most critical performance index for video traffic transmission, as it is directly associated with the video providers' revenue [7]. Generally, the QoE is affected by both the device-dependent factors, such as screen size and resolution, and the network-dependent factors, such as bitrate, rebuffer time, and the switching of bitrates. To improve the video QoE under the complex Internet environment, various ABR algorithms are proposed to maximize the QoE of clients [2,14,18]. Furthermore, new underlying congestion control algorithms, such as BBR [8], Copa [9], and PCC Vivace [10], are developed recently to improve the data transmission performance. For example, experimental results in [9] show that Copa can achieve similar throughput and 2–10 lower queueing delays than CUBIC by ensuring σ inflight packets for each flow. By the way, the portion of bandwidth grasped by each Copa flow is in directly proportional to the value of parameter $\bar{\delta}$. With a better network, the corresponding video QoE would also be greatly improved.

However, when multiple users compete independently within a bottleneck link, the QoEs of clients may become unfair. The reasons are twofold. Firstly, the underlying congestion control algorithms are unaware of QoE and allocate bandwidth fairly among all competing flows. Secondly, the QoEs of users are different from each other due to device-dependent factors even with the same bandwidth. This QoE unfairness problem would become more significant, as the probability where multiple users share the same bottleneck link increases with the increase of video traffic. Addressing this QoE unfairness problem, the video providers would jointly optimize the QoE of multiple users.

The existing solutions to the QoE unfairness problem can be roughly divided into the following two categories.

Centralized Bandwidth Allocation. According to work [11, 20], the band-width allocation at the bottleneck-router according to clients' QoE information can solve this problem. Specifically, the QoE is qualified by the network-dependent factors including bitrate, rebuffer time, and switching of bitrates in every 2 s. Moreover, the average QoE up to now is employed to guide the band-width allocation. Furthermore, smart routers are supposed to identify the bot-tleneck link and execute the bandwidth allocation actions for QoE fairness.

However, the device-dependent factors are not involved in the definition of QoE in [11]. When the bandwidth allocation is guided by this QoE, the users with different devices may receive the same bandwidth and thus their QoE is still unfair. Moreover, the number of video flows sharing the same bottleneck link varies, while the QoE measured before the variation of flow number may still influent the average QoE and the corresponding bandwidth allocation. Therefore, the time scale of ensuring QoE fairness should be chosen carefully under dynamic network environment. Furthermore, most routers can't identify the bottleneck link or know the number of video flows sharing this bottleneck link in reality.

Distributed Bandwidth Allocation. Aware of the impractical assumption on the prior knowledge of bottleneck link and the number of video streamings in [11], work [6] proposes the Minerva scheme, which adjusts the bandwidth allocation distributively via dynamically reconfiguring congestion control algorithms with the QoE information. Specifically, both the rebuffer time and the perceptional quality of chunks influence the QoE of Minerva. Wherein the calculation of perceptional quality is based on VMAF [12] or PSNR [13], both of which take all the network-dependent factors and device-dependent factors into consideration. Based on the QoEs collected both in history and predicted in the future, Minerva constructs a utility function and utilizes it to reconfigure congestion control algorithms. In this way, congestion control algorithms adjust the bandwidth allocation in a distributed manner for QoE fairness. What's more, there is no need to identify the bottleneck link or modify routers.

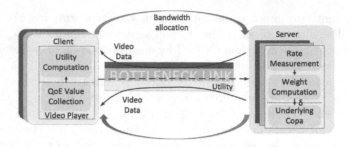

Fig. 1. The framework of PBA

Although Minerva is easy to deploy, it's still impractical due to the heavy computation overhead. Specifically, to facilitate the prediction of future QoE, Minerva needs to compute the QoE of each chunk under all possible network environments and buffer occupancy status in advance. Wherein, during the computation of QoE, the VMAF value of each frame in each video chunks should be computed and the highest bitrate video version is needed as the reference. On the other side, the dynamic number of video flows also influences both the computation overhead and the bandwidth allocation, as the utility function of Minerva is calculated based on the QoEs of all chunks in history.

In total, the device-dependent factors are either overlooked as in the QoE formulation of ABR algorithms [2,14,18] and work [11], making it hard to achieve QoE fairness, or overemphasized as in Minerva [6], resulting in large computation overhead. What's more, the time scale of QoE fairness has not been considered properly and thus existing works can hardly adapt to dynamic wireless networks.

3   Design

Motivated by the above insights, we design the Practical Bandwidth Allocation (PBA) algorithm for QoE fairness in this section.

3.1   Framework

In brief, the PBA algorithm achieves QoE fairness by distributively reconfiguring the parameter of congestion control algorithms according to the QoE of clients similar to Minerva, but pays special attention to the formulation of QoE and the time scale of QoE fairness. In details, the framework of PBA is shown in Fig. 1, which is composed of clients and servers.

Client. Each client monitors the QoE of chunks to construct the convex utility function and sends the utility to video server for bandwidth allocation. Meanwhile, client employs the default MPC algorithm [14] for adaptive bitrate selection, and the prediction results on the rebuffer time and bitrate for the future chunks in MPC are also utilized for the future QoE estimation in PBA.

Server. Each server measures its sending rate, calculates the weight with both sending rate and utility, and reconfigures the parameters of congestion control protocol according to the weight. The Copa algorithm is chosen to replace the default CUBIC algorithm due to its good performance and the convenience of adjusting parameter δ for bandwidth allocation.

In this distributive manner, PBA can guide the bandwidth allocation of congestion control algorithms with the QoE of clients and accordingly improve the QoE fairness. Consequently, the minimum QoE would be significantly improved.

3.2 Device-Sensitive QoE Formulation

The QoE formulation of PBA should be device-sensitive, but avoids large computation overhead. Specifically, both the network-dependent factors including bitrate, switching of bitrates, rebuffer time, and the device-dependent factors, including screen resolution and screen size, are considered, as defined below.

$$QoE = f(B) + \gamma g(S) - \lambda |f(B) - f(B_{old})| - \mu R \tag{1}$$

Here B stands for the bitrate, S denotes the screen size and R is the rebuffer time. Function $f(B)$ and $g(S)$ respectively reflects the impact of bitrate and screen size, and the term $|f(B) - f(B_{old})|$ is the switching of bitrates. Parameters γ, λ, and μ are the weights of these impact factors.

In details, the term $f(B)$ is formulated as follows

$$f(B) = min\{\frac{ppi_{video}}{ppi_{screen}}, 1\} In \frac{B}{B_{min}} \tag{2}$$

wherein B_{min} denotes the minimum bitrate. On the one hand, the QoE increases with the increase of bitrate in general. But when the bitrate is large enough to provide most details for the video clip, a higher bitrate will have a smaller impact on QoE. Therefore, the relationship between QoE and bitrate conforms to the characteristics of concave function. Accordingly, the logarithmic function is used similar to [18] in Eq. (2). On the other hand, the impact of resolution on QoE is associated with bitrate. Under the same bandwidth, devices with larger screen sizes and higher resolutions often need a larger bitrate for better QoE. This impact of resolution is quantified by pixels per inch (ppi) of video and screen in Eq. (2). Specifically, when the video ppi is smaller than the screen ppi, the QoE increases with the increase of the video ppi. Conversely, when the video ppi is larger than the screen ppi, the increase of video ppi would have few impacts on QoE according to Eq. (2).

Moreover, the term $g(S)$ is used to abstract the impact of screen size on video playback. It should be constant for any given screen size. But when the video is played on devices with different screen sizes, users will have a different viewing experience [21]. Based on literature [17], we list the values $g(S)$ of common devices used in our experiments in Table 1. The values reflecting the viewing experience of other devices can be studied in future work.

In sum, PBA formulates QoE by considering the impacts of both network conditions and devices in a simple but practical way.

Table 1. The $g(S)$ of devices with different screen sizes

Screensizes (inch)	4	6	10	13
$g(S)$		2.9	3.4	4.0	4.4

3.3 Time Scale of QoE Fairness

PBA seeks to optimize the max-min QoE fairness [6], which captures the idea of improving the experience of the worst-performance clients, i.e., maximize the minimum QoE of clients. Here the QoE of client refers to the average QoE of all chunks received by this client. Because PBA focuses on the average QoE in long term, it constructs the following utility function for the kth chunk, instead of utilizing the QoE of current chunk directly for the configuration of congestion control algorithm.

$$U(k) = \frac{1}{2 * m + 1} \sum_{i=k-m}^{k+m} \alpha^{|i-k|} * QoE(i) \tag{3}$$

where both m and α are parameters. The reasons for Eq. (3) are as follows. First of all, the QoEs of chunks $\{1, 2, \ldots, k - m - 1\}$ in history, which is considered in [6] and [11], will have no impact on the following bandwidth allocation of PBA. This is because the number of video flows sharing the bottleneck link may have changed since the $k - m - 1^{th}$ chunk. In other words, this characteristic makes PBA adaptive with dynamic networks. Moreover, the utility U changes with the variation of the estimated QoEs of future chunks. i.e., the utility U is sensitive to the change of bandwidth allocation. Furthermore, considering the QoEs of recent m chunks, the utility U would not change suddenly. Accordingly, the corresponding bandwidth allocation would become smooth. The last but not the least important, the utility U is a linear composition of QoEs, the QoE is a convex function of the bitrate, and the bitrate changes linearly with the change of bandwidth. In total, the utility U is a convex function of the bandwidth. This characteristic will ensure the bandwidth allocation of PBA converges to the QoE fairness point, as discussed in Sect. 3.4.

The parameter m in Eqs. (3) should be set according to whether the number of flows sharing the bottleneck link changes. However, this is unknown in the real dynamic network. Without information of the number of flows, PBA sets the parameter $m = 4$ by default. In this way, the prediction results of MPC [14] can be directly used for the calculation of Eq. (3).

The parameter α reflects the influence of historical chunks and future chunks. With parameter $\alpha < 1$, the older chunk has a smaller impact on the utility U. This is because the network status reflected by the older chunk may have changed. Moreover, the QoE of the future chunk is predicted. The further the chunk is, the larger the prediction error. With these consideration, the larger the time interval, the smaller the value of $\alpha^{|i-k|}$ used in Eq. (3), no matter whether it is a historical chunk or a future chunk.

3.4   Bandwidth Allocation

In PBA, the bandwidth allocation is achieved by reconfiguring the underlying Copa algorithm according to the piggybacked utility U received at servers. Specifically, when the server receives a utility U, it will calculate a weight w based on U and the sending rate $Rate$ to this client as follows:

$$w = Rate/U \tag{4}$$

Subsequently, the weight w is used to reconfigure the parameter δ of Copa, which stands for the number of packets of this flow in the bottleneck link [9].

$$\bar{\delta} \leftarrow w * \delta \tag{5}$$

With the new parameter $\bar{\delta}$, the Copa flow would grasp a new portion of bandwidth. In total, the bandwidth of client is reallocated based on the received utility U. Note that $Rate$ is always measured after Copa converges to a stable bandwidth allocation with parameter $\bar{\delta}$. By the way, the exponential weighted moving average of the sending rate is used for the smooth measurement results.

With the above equations, PBA would eventually converge to bandwidth allocation for ideal QoE fairness. Specifically, when the QoE of a client is small, the utility U is small and the corresponding weight is large. Accordingly, the bandwidth allocated to this client will be increased. Consequently, the QoE of this client will increase with increased bandwidth. Moreover, the utility U is a convex function of the bitrate, which increases linearly with the increase of bandwidth. It indicates the utility U increases faster than the sending rate at the beginning, and then eventually becomes slower and slower. Therefore, the weight w would increase after the new bandwidth allocation, until the increase of utility U is slower than the sending rate. On the contrary, if the QoE of a client is large, the bandwidth allocated to this flow would become smaller and the QoE will decrease similarly. Recursively, the bandwidth allocation would converge to the portion where the QoEs among clients are fair. By the way, the bottleneck link is always fully utilized because the parameter δ of Copa solely influences the queueing delay [9].

3.5   Discussion

PBA is easy to deploy, because it just distributively reconfigures Copa algorithm according to the piggybacked QoE information. Moreover, the overhead of collecting QoE information is small, as all the factors in Eqs. 1–5 are easy to obtain. The largest computation overhead is the prediction of future QoE in Eq. (3). This overhead is reduced by reusing the results of MPC. Finally, PBA is adaptive with dynamic networks, as the impact of QoEs in history decays quickly in Eq. (3). In total, PBA is a practical solution to maintain QoE fairness.

Table 2. Information of videos and devices

Videos	(240p, 150 kbps) (360p, 400 kbps) (480p, 600 kbps)
	(720p, 1500 kbps) (1080p, 2700 kbps) (1080p, 4200 kbps)
Devices	(4 in., 480p) (6 in., 720p) (10 in., 1080p) (13 in., 1080p)

4   Evaluation

4.1   Setup

The video client is based on Google Chrome browser (version 86) with QUIC support enabled. Each client uses the MPC algorithm [14] in dash.js (version 3.3) to choose the bitrate of the next chunk and uses selenium (version 3.141.0) to automatically control the start and pause of video. Moreover, dash.js is modified to track the playback buffer, rebuffer time, bitrate, switching of bitrates, screen size and resolutions of video and screen, and calculate QoEs and utility.

The video server is based on Ubuntu 18.04 LTS, which provides HTTPS service with caddy (version 1.0.0). Moreover, the quic-go (version 0.10.2) employed by the video servers is modified to retrieve the piggybacked utility, monitor the sending rate and compute weight for the reconfiguration of congestion control algorithm. Of course, Copa is also embedded into quic-go for experiments.

The scenario of multiple video streams sharing a single bottleneck link is emulated by Mahimahi [15]. The "BigBuckBunny" video in the DASH dataset [16] is played for 500 s by each device. The video is encoded by H.264/MPEG-4 AVC codec. The resolution and bitrate of this video, and the screen size and resolution of the user devices are shown in Table 2 respectively. We set parameters $\alpha = 0.9, \gamma = 0.1, \lambda = 0.25$, and $\mu = 0.08$. Works [6] and [11] are not compared to PBA because we can hardly implement them.

4.2   The QoE Fairness

At first, we conduct simulations to show the advantage of PBA on improving QoE fairness. In details, the video is simultaneously played by all 4 different devices. Moreover, the bottleneck link capacity is respectively fixed at 4 Mbps, 6 Mbps and 8 Mbps in different runs of experiments to show the ability of QoE-aware bandwidth allocation. When different congestion control algorithms are employed, the average QoE of all chunks is collected for each video flow and Fig. 2 shows the maximum and minimum average QoEs of these flows. When the link bandwidth is 8 Mbps, PBA improves the minimum QoE by 17.5% and 14.9% respectively, compared with Cubic and Copa. The improvement percentage changes to 18.6% and 17.5% when the link bandwidth is 4 Mbps, and 15% and 14.4% when the link bandwidth is 6 Mbps. Meanwhile, the whiskers in Fig. 2 also show that PBA significantly narrows the gap between the maximum and the minimum QoEs of clients compared to both Cubic and Copa, no matter what the link capacity is.

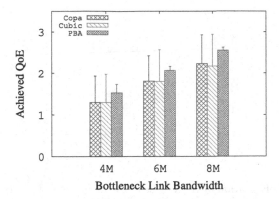

Fig. 2. The Max-min QoE fairness with different bottleneck link bandwidths where the whiskers extend from the minimum to maximum QoEs

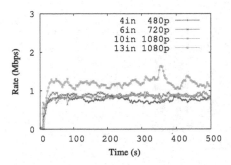
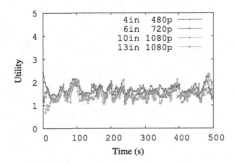

Fig. 3. Evolution of flows' rates in PBA   **Fig. 4.** Evolution of utility in PBA

Next, we show how PBA achieves a better QoE fairness by treating the 4 Mbps link bandwidth condition as an example. Specifically, we collect the evolution of sending rates and utilities in PBA, as shown in Fig. 3 and Fig. 4. At the beginning, the sending rates of video streams increase simultaneously such that the bottleneck link is fully utilized. Though the sending rates of video flows are similar, their utility are different from each other due to the device differences. In details, the video flow of the 4 in. device has the largest utility and the 13 in. device has the smallest utility under the same bandwidth. After initiation, the utilities of video flows are eventually adjusted to the same value by PBA and the corresponding sending rates of video flows disperse to different levels. In other words, PBA allocates the bottleneck link bandwidth such that the utilities, which reflect the QoEs, of different video flows are similar. Note that the difference between the 10 in. device and the 13 in. device exhibits the impact of screen size, as they have the same screen resolution. In total, this experiment confirms that PBA can improve max-min QoE fairness by reconfiguring Copa according to the piggybacked QoE.

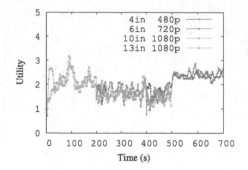

Fig. 5. Evolution of utilities in PBA under dynamic network

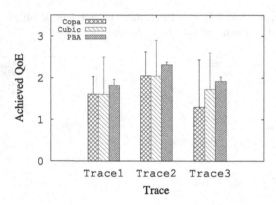

Fig. 6. The max-min QoE fairness with real traffic traces where whiskers extend from the minimum to maximum QoEs

4.3 PBA in Dynamic Video Streaming

Subsequently, we consider the condition that the video is played at different times. In details, the 10 in. and 13 in. devices play the video at the beginning, the 6 in. device starts to play the video at 200 s, and the 4 in. device starts to play the video at 400 s. The evolution of the utilities of different video flows are shown in Fig. 5. In the beginning, the utilities of the 10 in. and 13 in. devices converge to the same value under the adjustment of the PBA algorithm. Therefore, their QoEs are fair before the 200 s. After the 6 in. device starts at 200 s, the bottleneck link is shared by three video flows and should be reallocated. Because the utilities of the 10 in. and 13 in. devices are not influenced by the QoEs before 200 s, the utility of all these three video flows eventually converge to another common value again in the time interval [200 s, 400 s]. A similar phenomenon occurs when the 4 in. device starts at 400 s. At 500 s, the 10 in. and 13 in. devices finish playing the video and the remaining video flows continue to adjust their utilities such that their QoE are fair. In total, it confirms PBA ensures QoE fairness under dynamic networks.

(a) Cubic   (b) Copa   (c) PBA

Fig. 7. Video images comparison of each strategy in Trace1 (Color figure online)

4.4 LTE Trace-Driven Experiments

To be more realistic, the fixed bottleneck link bandwidth of the mahimahi shell is replaced by 3 real LTE network traces provided by [19]. We repeat the experiments where all 4 devices start to play video concurrently at the beginning and the result is shown in Fig. 6. Similar to the result in Fig. 2, PBA significantly improves the minimum QoE by 13% and 25% on average, compared with Copa and Cubic, respectively. In other words, the worst QoE is greatly improved by PBA. Moreover, PBA also reduces the gap between the maximum QoE and the minimum QoE, compared with Copa and Cubic, according to the whiskers shown in Fig. 6. In details, the average gap between the maximum and minimum QoE is respectively 0.85 with Copa, 0.77 with Cubic. In contrast, the average gap between the maximum QoE and the minimum QoE with PBA is less than 0.15, i.e., an improvement of 82% and 80% compared to Copa and Cubic, respectively.

On the other hand, we randomly choose a video frame when the video is played at screen with the Trace 1. As shown in Fig. 7, the quality of the video frame with either Cubic or Copa is low, as the regions circled in red are blurred. In contrast, the corresponding video frame with PBA is always clear. This is consistent with the Max-min QoE fairness shown in Fig. 6. In other words, PBA significantly improve the minimum QoE of video streams.

5 Conclusion

In this paper, we propose the PBA algorithm, which is easy to deploy. Specifically, PBA formulates QoE by taking both the impacts of devices and the network conditions into consideration, and uses it to guide the configuration of the congestion control algorithm. In this distributive manner, PBA clients can make bandwidth allocation with ideal QoE fairness. Experiments confirm that PBA respectively improves the minimum QoE by at least 13% and 15% compared with Copa and Cubic and greatly narrows the gap between the maximum and minimum QoEs. Moreover, PBA is adaptive with dynamic wireless networks.

Acknowledgments. This work is partly supported by CERNET Innovation Project under Grant No. NGII20190112 and National Science Foundation of China under Grant No. 61972421, Innovation-Driven Project of Central South University under Grant No. 2020CX033.

References

1. Cisco, Visual Networking Index: Forecast and Methodology 2016–2021, September 2017
2. Akhtar, Z., Nam, Y.S., et al.: Oboe: auto-tuning video ABR algorithms to network conditions. In: Proceedings of SIGCOMM, pp. 44–58, August 2018
3. Akamai. dash.js. https://github.com/bbc/dash.js
4. Mholt. Caddy. https://github.com/caddyserver/caddy
5. Ha, S., Rhee, I., Xu, L.: CUBIC: a new TCP-friendly high-speed TCP variant. ACM SIGOPS Oper. Syst. Rev. **42**(5), 64–74 (2008)
6. Nathan, V., Sivaraman, V., et al.: End-to-end transport for video QoE fairness. In: Proceedings of ACM SIGCOMM, pp. 408–423 (2019)
7. Mok, R.P.K., Chan, E.W.W., et al.: Inferring the QoE of HTTP video streaming from user-viewing activities. In: Proceedings of the First ACM SIGCOMM Workshop on Measurements up the Stack, pp. 31–36, August 2011
8. Cardwell, N., Cheng, Y., et al.: BBR: congestion-based congestion control. Queue **14**(5), 20–53 (2016)
9. Arun, V., Balakrishnan, H.: Copa: practical delay-based congestion control for the internet. In: NSDI, pp. 329–342 (2018)
10. Dong, M., Zarchy, D., et al.: PCC vivace: online-learning congestion control. In: NSDI, pp. 343–356 (2018)
11. Yin, X., Bartulović, M., et al.: On the efficiency and fairness of multiplayer HTTP-based adaptive video streaming. In: 2017 American Control Conference (ACC), pp. 4236–4241, May 2017
12. Li, Z., Katsavounidis, I., et al.: Toward a practical perceptual video quality metric. The Netflix Tech Blog **6**, 2 (2016)
13. Salomon, D.: Data Compression: The Complete Reference. Springer, Heidelberg (2004)
14. Yin, X., Jindal, A., et al.: A control-theoretic approach for dynamic adaptive video streaming over HTTP. In: Proceedings of ACM SIGCOMM, pp. 325–338, August 2015
15. Lederer, S., Mueller, C., et al.: Distributed DASH dataset. In: Proceedings of the 4th ACM Multimedia Systems Conference, pp. 131–135, February 2013
16. Netravali, R., Sivaraman, A., et al.: Mahimahi: accurate record-and-replay for HTTP. In: USENIX ATC, pp. 417–429 (2015)
17. Triyason, T., Krathu, W.: The impact of screen size toward QoE of cloud-based virtual desktop. Comput. Sci. **111**, 203–208 (2017)
18. Spiteri, K., Urgaonkar, R., et al.: BOLA: near-optimal bitrate adaptation for online videos. IEEE/ACM Trans. Networking **28**(4), 1698–1711 (2020)
19. Abbasloo, S., Yen, C.Y., Chao, H.J.: Classic Meets Modern: a Pragmatic Learning-Based Congestion Control for the Internet, pp. 632–647. SIGCOMM, New York (2020)
20. Mansy, A., Fayed, M., Ammar, M.: Network-layer fairness for adaptive video streams. In: IFIP Networking, Toulouse, France, pp. 1–9 (2015)
21. Brunnström, K., et al.: Qualinet white paper on definitions of quality of experience. In: European Network on Quality of Experience in Multimedia Systems and Services (COST Action IC 1003), March 2013

Controller Placements for Optimizing Switch-to-Controller and Inter-controller Communication Latency in Software Defined Networks

Bo Wei, Yuqi Fan[✉], Lunfei Wang, Tao Ouyang, and Lei Shi

School of Computer and Information Engineering, Anhui Province Key Laboratory of Industry Safety and Emergency Technology, Hefei University of Technology, Hefei 230601, Anhui, China
{2019110966,cxwlf,ouyangtao}@mail.hfut.edu.cn,
{yuqi.fan,shilei}@hfut.edu.cn

Abstract. The logically centralized control plane in large-scale SDN networks consists of multiple controllers, and the controllers communicate with each other to keep a consistent view of the network status. Inconsistent controllers or controllers failing to maintain the network state in time may severely degrade the network performance. However, most of the existing research focuses on the switch-to-controller communication latency by ignoring the communication latency between the controllers. In this paper, we formulate a novel multi-objective SDN controller placement problem with the objectives to minimize both the switch-to-controller and the inter-controller communication latency. We propose an efficient Multi-Objective Controller Placement (MOCP) algorithm. Algorithm MOCP generates the new controller placement solutions with crossover and mutation operations. The switches are assigned to the controllers with the greedy strategy initially, and then mapped to the other controllers via the local search strategy. Our simulation results show that algorithm MOCP can effectively reduce the latency between the controllers and from the switches to controllers simultaneously.

Keywords: Software defined networks · Latency · Multi-objective optimization · Non-dominated solution

1 Introduction

In Software Defined Networks (SDNs), network switches (nodes) are only responsible for data forwarding, while controllers determine the paths of network packets across the switches. Upon the arrival of an unknown flow, the switch sends

L. Shi—This work was partly supported by the National Key Research and Development Plan (2018YFB2000505), the Key Research and Development Project in Anhui Province (201904a06020024), and the Open Project of State Key Laboratory of Complex Electromagnetic Environment Effects on Electronics and Information System in China (CEMEE2018Z0102B).

© Springer Nature Switzerland AG 2021
Z. Liu et al. (Eds.): WASA 2021, LNCS 12937, pp. 535–546, 2021.
https://doi.org/10.1007/978-3-030-85928-2_42

a flow set-up request to the controller which responds to the request with a flow entry to be installed in the flow table of the switch. Therefore, the switch-to-controller latency is critical for the performance of SDNs.

Some work has been done to improve the latency performance in SDNs, which is important in computer networks [1–3]. The network was split into several sub-networks using community partitioning and a controller was deployed in each sub-network [4]. A capacitated controller placement problem was introduced to minimize the propagation delay, whereas the load of each controller does not exceed its capacity [5]. The controller placement problem in an edge network was formulated with the objectives of delay and overhead minimization; the problem was converted to a Mixed Integer Programming (MIP) problem using linearization techniques, and approximation solutions were presented using the theory of supermodular functions [6]. A Pareto-based optimal controller placement method (POCO) was proposed to consider maximum node-to-controller latencies and resilience in terms of failure tolerance and load balancing [7]. The POCO framework was extended with heuristics to support large-scale networks or dynamic networks with the properties changing over time [8]. The controller placement problem was investigated by jointly taking into account both the communication reliability and the communication latency between controllers and switches if any link in the network fails [9]. A metaheuristic-based Reliability-Aware and Latency-Oriented controller placement algorithm (RALO) was proposed to minimize the switch-to-controller communication delay for both the cases without link failure and with single-link-failure [10].

Inter-controller and controller-node traffic overheads can be at the same order of magnitude [6], and existing research indicates that inconsistent controllers or the controllers that fail to maintain the state of the network in time, will not only affect network performance, but also severely degrade the performance of some application layer applications [11]. Existing research on communication latency oriented controller placements focuses on how to reduce the switch-to-controller latency, without considering the communication latency between the controllers.

In this paper, we address the controller placement problem to reduce the communication latency from the switches to the controllers and between the controllers. We formulate a novel multi-objective SDN controller placement problem with the aim to minimize both the average switch-to-controller delay and the maximum inter-controller communication latency. We propose an efficient metaheuristic-based Multi-Objective optimization Controller Placement algorithm (MOCP) for the problem. Algorithm MOCP generates the new controller placement solutions with crossover and mutation operations. The switches are assigned to the controllers with the greedy strategy initially, and then mapped to the other controllers via the local search strategy. Finally, we conduct experiments through simulations. Experimental results demonstrate that algorithm MOCP can effectively reduce the latency between the controllers and from the switches to controllers simultaneously.

2   Problem Formulation

Table 1. Table of symbols and notations

s_i, s_j	i-th, j-th switch/node
c_k	k-th controller
C	The set of controllers
K	The number of controllers
u_k	The capacity of controller c_k
r_i	The number of requests from switch s_i
$x_{i,k}$	Indicate whether switch s_i is associated with controller c_k ($= 1$) or not ($= 0$)
$y_{i,k}$	Indicate whether controller c_k is co-located with switch s_i ($= 1$) or not ($= 0$)
$l_{i,j}$	The shortest path latency between nodes s_i and s_j

For a given SDN network $G = (V, E)$, where V is the set of switches/nodes and E denotes the set of edges between the switches. Each controller is co-located with one and only one switch [7], and the total number of requests processed by each controller should be within its processing capacity. Each switch is mapped to exactly one controller. When a switch is mapped to a controller, we say the switch and the controller are associated with each other. The symbols and notations used in the paper are listed in Table 1.

The communication between two nodes goes through the shortest path between the two nodes. In this paper, we aim to determine where to place each controller and the exact association relationship between the controllers and the switches, with the objectives to optimize both the average switch-to-controller delay and the maximum inter-controller communication latency. In other words, our optimization objectives are to

Minimize:
$$[l^c, l^s] \tag{1}$$

Subject to:
$$l^c = \max_{c_k \in C, c_{k'} \in C} d_{k,k'} \tag{2}$$

$$l^s = \frac{\sum_{i=1}^{|V|} \sum_{k=1}^{K} l_{i,k} \cdot x_{i,k}}{|V|} \tag{3}$$

$$\sum_{k=1}^{K} x_{i,k} = 1, \quad \forall s_i \in V \tag{4}$$

$$\sum_{i=1}^{|V|} y_{i,k} = 1, \quad \forall c_k \in C \tag{5}$$

$$y_{i,k} \leq x_{i,k}, \quad \forall c_k \in C, \; \forall s_i \in V \tag{6}$$

$$\sum_{i=1}^{|V|} x_{i,k} \cdot r_i \leq u_k, \quad \forall c_k \in C \tag{7}$$

$$x_{i,k} \in \{0,1\}, y_{i,k} \in \{0,1\}, \quad \forall c_k \in C \tag{8}$$

Equations (2) and (3) define the maximum latency between controllers and the average latency from the switches to the associated controllers, respectively. Equation (4) ensures that each switch is mapped to one and only one controller. Equation (5) mandates that each controller can only be co-located with one switch. Equation (6) dictates that switch s_i must be mapped to controller c_k, if controller c_k is co-located with switch s_i. Equation (7) signifies that the controllers cannot be overloaded. Equation (8) requires that $x_{i,k}$ and $y_{i,k}$ are binary integer variables.

3 Controller Placement Algorithm

In this section, we propose an efficient metaheuristic-based Multi-Objective Controller Placement (MOCP) algorithm to obtain a set of non-dominated solutions. Each solution determines the locations of the controllers. Algorithm MOCP shown in Algorithm 1 first randomly generates an initial solution set P_0 with N solutions, and performs crossover and mutation operations to get another solution set Q_0 with N solutions (lines 1–2). The algorithm then proceeds iteratively. In each iteration, the algorithm merges the last obtained solution sets P_w and Q_w to get a new solution set R_w with $2N$ solutions (line 4). After assigning the switches to the controllers for each solution in R_w, the algorithm performs solution ranking and solution evaluation to find the best N solutions in R_w as the new solution set P_{w+1}. A new solution set Q_{w+1} is also generated by performing crossover and mutation operations on P_{w+1} (line 7). The procedure continues until the maximum number of iterations is reached. The algorithm returns O_1 obtained by solution ranking as the Pareto optimal solution set.

3.1 Solution Construction

Assuming P is the existing set of N solutions, the algorithm constructs Q, a new set of N solutions, by performing crossover and mutation operations on the solutions in P.

With crossover, two solutions exchange the controller placement locations between two designated crossover points. Mutation places one of the controllers

Algorithm 1. *MOCP algorithm*

Input:
  $G = (V, E)$; K; Solution set size N; Number of iterations I.
Output:
  The controller locations and the mapping relationship between the switches and
  the controllers.
 1: Randomly generate the initial population P_0 with N solutions;
 2: Perform crossover and mutation on P_0 to obtain a new solution set Q_0, $w = 0$;
 3: **while** $w \leq I$ **do**
 4:    $R_w = P_w \cup Q_w$;
 5:    Run Algorithm *Switch Assignment* on R_w;
 6:    Perform *Solution Ranking, Congestion Degree Calculation* on R_w, and select the
       best N solutions among R_w to obtain solution set P_{w+1};
 7:    Perform crossover and mutation operations on P_{w+1} to get another solution set
       Q_{w+1} with N solutions;
 8:    $w = w + 1$;
 9: **end while**
10: Return O_1.

in the current solution at another node. Assuming the position of controller c_k
to be mutated is node s_i in the current solution, the position of controller c_k
is mutated to another node which is adjacent to s_i. If there are multiple such
nodes, we randomly select one as the new controller location of c_k.

3.2 Evaluation of the Solutions

For two solutions p and p', we say p dominates p' ($p \prec p'$), if solution p is
better than p' in both of the objectives. If there is no solution in solution set
P dominates p ($\nexists p' \prec p, p' \in P$), p is called a non-dominated solution. The set
of all non-dominated solutions is called the non-dominated solution set or the
Pareto optimal solution set.

For an existing solution set P, solution ranking shown in Algorithm 2 ranks
the solutions by the ascending order the number of solutions dominate the solutions. The solutions of the same rank are put in the same solution subset. The
algorithm first puts the solutions which cannot be dominated by any other solution in P in the same subset O_1 (lines 1–4). For each solution o in O_1, the
algorithm finds all the solutions that can be dominated by o, and denotes the
collection of the found solutions as Q_o. For each solution $q \in Q_o$, the algorithm
deceases the value of e_q by 1. If $e_q = 0$, we put solution q in subset O_2. Obviously, the solutions in O_2 are worse than those in O_1. The algorithm continues
the process of putting each solution in P into a subset, until all the solutions are
classified in the subsets. We denote $Rank(p) = r$, if solution $p \in O_r$.

Congestion degree of solution p, denoted as $Cong(p)$, is used to estimate the
intensity of other solutions around solution p, which can be expressed graphically
as the side length of the largest rectangle around solution p. For each of the two
objective functions, Algorithm 3 sorts the solutions in solution set P by the

Algorithm 2. *Solution Ranking*

Input:
     Solution set P.
Output:
     The ranked solution subsets.
 1: **for** each solution $p \in P$ **do**
 2:     Calculate e_p, the number of the solutions in P dominating solution p;
 3: **end for**
 4: Put each solution $p \in P$ with $e_p = 0$ in solution subset O_1; $r = 1$;
 5: **while** $O_r \neq \phi$ **do**
 6:     $r = r + 1$;
 7:     **for** each solution $o \in O_{r-1}$ **do**
 8:         Find the solution collection Q_o dominated by solution o;
 9:         **if** $Q_o \neq \phi$ **then**
10:             **for** each solution $q \in Q_o$ **do**
11:                 $e_q = e_q - 1$;
12:                 **if** $e_q = 0$ **then**
13:                     Add solution q into solution subset O_r;
14:                 **end if**
15:             **end for**
16:         **end if**
17:     **end for**
18: **end while**
19: **Return** each O_r.

---

non-ascending order of the objective function values. Denote the two objective function values of solution p as $f_1(p)$ and $f_2(p)$, respectively. Let the congestion degrees of the two solutions with the smallest and largest objective function values be ∞. For each of the other solutions, the congestion degree of solution p is calculated as the total side length of the rectangle around solution p on the two objective functions.

After performing solution ranking and congestion degree calculation, each solution p in current solution set P has two attribute values: solution rank $Rank(p)$ and congestion degree $Cong(p)$. For solutions p and p', we say p is better than p' if one of the two conditions is satisfied: (1) $Rank(p) < Rank(p')$, or (2) $Rank(p) = Rank(p')$ and $Cong(p) > Cong(p')$.

3.3   Switch to Controller Assignment

Algorithm 4 shows the process of allocating the switches to the controllers given the controller locations. Each controller maintains a list b_k of the switches, and the switches in each list are sorted in the non-descending order of the shortest path lengths between the controller and switches (lines 1–4). Algorithm 4 selects the switch $s_{i'}$ with the smallest distance to its corresponding controller from all the header nodes of the K lists (lines 6–12). Algorithm 4 then assigns the selected switch $s_{i'}$ to the controller $c_{k'}$, such that the path length between $s_{i'}$

Algorithm 3. *Congestion Degree Calculation*

Input:
    Solution set P.
Output:
    The congestion degree of each solution $p \in P$.
1: Initialize each $Cong(p) = 0$;
2: **for** $g = 1..2$ **do**
3:    Sort the solutions in P by the non-ascending order of the objective function
      values $f_g(p)$; Denote the sorted solutions as $p_1, p_2, \ldots, p_{|P|}$;
4:    $Cong(p_1) = \infty$, $Cong(p_{|P|}) = \infty$;
5:    **for** $m = 2..|P - 1|$ **do**
6:      $Cong(p_m) = Cong(p_m) + f_g(p_{m+1}) - f_g(p_{m-1})$;
7:    **end for**
8: **end for**
9: **Return** each $Cong(p)$.

---

and $c_{k'}$ is the shortest among all the paths between $s_{i'}$ and the controllers (line 13). After switch $s_{i'}$ is mapped to a controller, the algorithm updates each list b_k by deleting the mapped switch $s_{i'}$ and the switches with more requests than the remaining capacity of controller c_k (line 14). When all the switches are mapped to the controllers, Algorithm 4 performs the operations of remap and swap to find other switch-controller association which can reduce the average switch-to-controller latency.

Operation $remap(i, k, q)$ reassigns switch s_i from the originally mapped controller c_k to another controller c_q ($k \neq q$) to generate a new association relationship, under the condition that controller c_q is not overloaded. The benefit of the remapping operation is defined by Eq. (9).

$$\pi_1(i, k, q) = l_{i,k} - l_{i,q} \tag{9}$$

where $\pi_1(i, k, q) > 0$ indicates that the switch-to-controller delay will be reduced, if switch s_i originally assigned to controller c_k is re-associated with controller c_q.

Operation $swap(i, j)$ remaps switch s_i originally assigned to controller c_k to controller c_q, and reassigns switch s_j ($i \neq j$) originally mapped to controller c_q to controller c_k ($k \neq q$), under the condition that controllers c_k and c_q are not overloaded. The benefit of the swap operation is defined by Eq. (10). If $\pi_2(i, j, k, q) > 0$, we can decrease the switch-to-controller delay by swapping the mapping relationship between the switches and the controllers.

$$\pi_2(i, j, k, q) = (l_{i,k} + l_{j,q}) - (l_{i,q} + l_{j,k}) \tag{10}$$

4 Performance Evaluation

4.1 Simulation Setup

We evaluate the proposed algorithm MOCP against the state-of-the-arts: PSA [8] and EA [12]. The communication latency between two nodes in the network

---

Algorithm 4. *Switch Assignment*

Input:
  $G = (V, E)$; K; Controller locations set $CL = \{c_1, c_2, \ldots, c_K\}$.
Output:
  Mapping relationship between the controllers and the switches.
 1: Each controller c_k maintains a list b_k which is initialized as $b_k = \phi$;
 2: **for** each $c_k \in C$ **do**
 3:     Calculate the shortest path lengths between controller c_k to all the switches, and
        put all the switches in list b_k in the non-descending order of the path lengths;
 4: **end for**
 5: **while** $\exists\, b_k \neq \phi$ **do**
 6:     $k' = 0, i' = 0, l' = \infty$;
 7:     **for** $k = 1..K$ **do**
 8:         Select the head switch s_i of list b_k;
 9:         **if** $l_{i,k} < l'$ **then**
10:             $l' = l_{i,k}, \quad i' = i, \quad k' = k$;
11:         **end if**
12:     **end for**
13:     Assign switch $s_{i'}$ to controller $c_{k'}$;
14:     Update each list b_k by deleting the mapped switch $s_{i'}$ and the switches with
        more requests than the remaining capacity of controller c_k;
15: **end while**
16: **for** $i = 1..|V|$ **do**
17:     $k' = 0, \quad j' = 0, \quad h' = 0$;
18:     **for** $j = i + 1..|V|$ **do**
19:         Assume switches s_i and s_j are assigned to controllers c_k and c_q, respectively;
20:         **if** $h' < \pi_2(i, j, k, q)$ **then**
21:             $h' = \pi_2(i, j, k, q), \quad j' = j, \quad k' = q$;
22:         **end if**
23:     **end for**
24:     **if** $h' > 0$ **then**
25:         swap(i, j');
26:     **end if**
27: **end for**
28: **for** $i = 1..|V|$ **do**
29:     $k' = 0, \quad h' = 0$;
30:     **for** $q = 1..K$ **do**
31:         Assume s_i is mapped to c_k;
32:         **if** $h' < \pi_1(i, k, q)$ **then**
33:             $h' = \pi_1(i, k, q), \quad k' = q$;
34:         **end if**
35:     **end for**
36:     **if** $h' > 0$ **then**
37:         remap(i, k, k');
38:     **end if**
39: **end for**

---

is approximated by the shortest path distance between the two nodes [13]. Two real network topologies of ATT and Internet2 [14] are used in the simulations. We also use network topology generator GT-ITM [15] to randomly generate two networks of Gnet1 and Gnet2. The processing capacity of the controllers is set as 1800 kilo-requests/s. The average number of requests from the switches is 200 kilo-requests/s, with the minimum being 150 kilo-requests/s and the maximum as 250 kilo-requests/s. The number of search times for the algorithms in the simulations is set as about 2.5% of the total feasible solution space [8]. The parameters of the networks and algorithm MOCP are shown in Table 2. We run each algorithm for 30 times, and merge the obtained non-dominant solution sets into a large set. The non-dominant solution set which has the largest intersection with the large set is taken the final result. We denote the solution sets obtained by algorithms MOCP, PSA and EA as P^M, P^P and P^E, respectively.

Table 2. Table of the parameters of networks and algorithm MOCP

Network	Number of nodes	Number of edges	Number of controllers	Number of iterations	Solution set size
ATT	25	57	4	6	50
Internet2	34	42	5	50	140
Gnet1	40	52	6	100	1000
Gnet1	51	64	7	3000	1000

The performance metrics are: Coverage (C) [16], Spacing (S) [17] and Maximum Spread (MS) [18], the number of solutions, and the optimal single-objective values. Coverage reflects the dominance relationship between two Pareto solution sets. Assuming P and Q are two Pareto optimal solution sets, the coverage of P over Q, $C(P,Q)$, is the ratio of the number of solutions which are in Q and dominated by the solutions in P to the total number of solutions in Q. $C(P,Q) = 1$ indicates that all solutions in Q are dominated by those in P. $C(P,Q) = 0$ indicates that no solution in Q is dominated by those in P. A large $C(P,Q)$ value shows that P is better than Q. Spacing evaluates the uniformity of the solution distribution in the Pareto optimal solution set. Assuming P and M are the Pareto solution set and the number of optimization objectives, respectively, $f_g(p)$ is the g-th objective function value of solution p. A smaller S value indicates that the solution set is more evenly distributed than a larger S value. Maximum spread measures the breadth of the solution distribution in the Pareto optimal solution set. The larger the MS value, the wider the distribution of the solution set.

4.2 Performance Evaluation of the Proposed Algorithm

Figures 1(a)–(d) depict the Pareto optimal solutions sets obtained by the three algorithms under the four networks. Algorithm MOCP achieves the best performance among the three algorithms. It is calculated that both $C(P^M, P^S)$

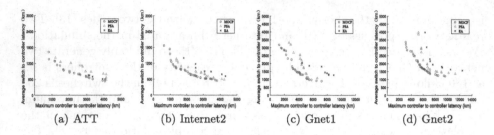

(a) ATT   (b) Internet2   (c) Gnet1   (d) Gnet2

Fig. 1. Pareto sets under different networks.

and $C(P^M, P^E)$ are 1 in all the four networks, which demonstrates that the solutions of algorithm MOCP always dominate those of algorithms PSA and EA. Algorithm MOCP also leads to the smallest optimal single-objective values among the three algorithms. It can also be observed that algorithm MOCP gets more solutions than the other two algorithms, and the solutions of algorithm MOCP are more evenly distributed than those of algorithms PSA and EA.

Table 3. Table of performance of the algorithms

Network	Algorithm	Number of solutions	S	MS
ATT	MOCP	21	105	3422
	PSA	14	213	3046
	EA	5	113	978
Internet2	MOCP	37	87	3444
	PSA	22	123	2975
	EA	7	449	2594
Gnet1	MOCP	30	272	6341
	PSA	20	372	4522
	EA	8	574	4533
Gnet2	MOCP	37	165	6886
	PSA	20	378	6594
	EA	9	893	6593

Table 4. Table of optimal single-objective values of the algorithms

Network	Algorithm	Minimum $f_1(p)$ (km)	Minimum $f_2(p)$ (km)
ATT	MOCP	527	816
	PSA	585	1201
	EA	599	3094
Internet2	MOCP	539	634
	PSA	591	1370
	EA	718	1809
Gnet1	MOCP	892	1281
	PSA	1078	2651
	EA	1271	4436
Gnet2	MOCP	1202	3072
	PSA	1362	5221
	EA	1574	6310

Table 3 shows the simulation results of the three algorithms in different performance metrics. For the performance of the number of solutions, algorithm MOCP finds the largest size of optimal solution set among the three algorithms, and algorithm PSA obtains more solutions than algorithm EA. For the performance of spacing, algorithm MOCP outperforms algorithms PSA and EA in the four networks. The S value of algorithm MOCP is 26.8%–56.3% smaller than that of algorithm PSA. Algorithm MOCP algorithm achieves 7.1% better performance than algorithm EA in ATT network, while algorithm MOCP is about 80% better than algorithm EA in Internet2 and Gnet2 networks. It can be seen from the performance of the number of solutions and spacing metric that algorithm MOCP achieves better performance than algorithms PSA and EA in searching for local non-dominated solutions. For the performance of maximum spread, algorithm MOCP leads to bigger MS values than algorithms PSA and EA. A big MS value indicates that the solution set spreads across a large solution space. In Gnet1 network, the MS value of algorithm MOCP is 40.2% larger than that of algorithm PSA. In ATT network, algorithm MOCP achieves 249% larger MS value than algorithm EA. In Gnet2 network, the MS values of algorithms PSA and EA are similar, while algorithm MOCP obtains 4.4% larger MS value than algorithm PSA. From the performance of maximum spread and the number of solutions, it can be observed that algorithm MOCP outperforms algorithms PSA and EA in searching for global non-dominated solutions.

Table 4 lists the optimal single-objective values obtained by the three algorithms under different networks, which demonstrates that algorithm MOCP achieves smaller optimal single-objective values than algorithms PSA and EA in both of the objectives. Specifically, for the performance of the average switch-to-controller latency, algorithm MOCP is 8.7% and 17.2% better than algorithm PSA in the networks of Internet2 and Gnet1, respectively; while algorithm MOCP obtains 29.8% and 12% better results than algorithm EA in the networks of Gnet1 and ATT, respectively. For the performance of maximum inter-controller communication latency, algorithm MOCP performs 32% and 53% better than algorithm PSA in the networks of ATT and Internet2, respectively; while algorithm leads to 51.3% and 73.6% better results than algorithm EA in the networks of Gnet2 and ATT, respectively.

5   Conclusions

Both switch-to-controller latency and inter-controller communication delay have great impact on the network performance. In this paper, we formulated a novel multi-objective SDN controller placement problem with the objectives to minimize both the switch-to-controller and the inter-controller communication latency. We proposed an efficient metaheuristic-based Multi-Objective Controller Placement (MOCP) algorithm. We conducted experiments through simulations. Experimental results showed that algorithm MOCP could effectively reduce the latency between the controllers and from the switches to controllers simultaneously.

References

1. Cai, Z., Chen, Q.: Latency-and-coverage aware data aggregation scheduling for multihop battery-free wireless networks. IEEE Trans. Wirel. Commun. **20**(3), 1770–1784 (2021)

2. Chen, Q., Gao, H., Cai, Z., Cheng, L., Li, J.: Energy-collision aware data aggregation scheduling for energy harvesting sensor networks. In: IEEE Conference on Computer Communications (INFOCOM), pp. 117–125 (2018)
3. Chen, Q., Cai, Z., Cheng, L., Gao, H.: Low latency broadcast scheduling for battery-free wireless networks without predetermined structures. In: The 40th International Conference on Distributed Computing Systems (ICDCS), pp. 245–255 (2020)
4. Liao, J., Sun, H., Wang, J., Qi, Q., Li, K., Li, T.: Density cluster based approach for controller placement problem in large-scale software defined networkings. Comput. Netw. **112**, 24–35 (2017)
5. Yao, G., Bi, J., Li, Y., Guo, L.: On the capacitated controller placement problem in software defined networks. IEEE Commun. Lett. **18**(8), 1339–1342 (2014)
6. Qin, Q., Poularakis, K., Iosifidis, G., Tassiulas, L.: SDN controller placement at the edge: optimizing delay and overheads. In: IEEE INFOCOM 2018-IEEE Conference on Computer Communications, pp. 684–692. IEEE (2018)
7. Hock, D., Hartmann, M., Gebert, S., Jarschel, M., Zinner, T., Tran-Gia, P.: Pareto-optimal resilient controller placement in SDN-based core networks. In: Proceedings of the 2013 25th International Teletraffic Congress (ITC), pp. 1–9. IEEE (2013)
8. Lange, S., et al.: Heuristic approaches to the controller placement problem in large scale SDN networks. IEEE Trans. Netw. Serv. Manag. **12**(1), 4–17 (2015)
9. Fan, Y., Ouyang, T.: Reliability-aware controller placements in software defined networks. In: The 21st IEEE International Conference on High Performance Computing and Communications (HPCC), pp. 2133–2140. IEEE (2019)
10. Fan, Y., Wang, L., Yuan, X.: Controller placements for latency minimization of both primary and backup paths in SDNs. Comput. Commun. **163**, 35–50 (2020)
11. Levin, D., Wundsam, A., Heller, B., Handigol, N., Feldmann, A.: Logically centralized? State distribution trade-offs in software defined networks. In Proceedings of the First Workshop on Hot Topics in Software Defined Networks, pp. 1–6 (2012)
12. Zhang, T., Bianco, A., Giaccone, P.: The role of inter-controller traffic in SDN controllers placement. In: 2016 IEEE Conference on Network Function Virtualization and Software Defined Networks (NFV-SDN), pp. 87–92. IEEE (2016)
13. Heller, B., Sherwood, R., McKeown, N.: The controller placement problem. ACM SIGCOMM Comput. Commun. Rev. **42**(4), 473–478 (2012)
14. Knight, S., Nguyen, H.X., Falkner, N., Bowden, R., Roughan, M.: The Internet topology zoo. IEEE J. Sel. Areas Commun. **29**(9), 1765–1775 (2011)
15. Thomas, M., Zegura, E.W.: Generation and analysis of random graphs to model internetworks. Tech. rep., Georgia Institute of Technology (1994)
16. Zitzler, E., Thiele, L.: Multiobjective evolutionary algorithms: a comparative case study and the strength pareto approach. IEEE Trans. Evol. Comput. **3**(4), 257–271 (1999)
17. Schott, J.R.: Fault tolerant design using single and multicriteria genetic algorithm optimization. Tech. rep., Air force inst of tech Wright-Patterson afb OH (1995)
18. Zitzler, E., Deb, K., Thiele, L.: Comparison of multiobjective evolutionary algorithms: empirical results. Evol. Comput. **8**(2), 173–195 (2000)

Fat Topic: Improving Latency in Content-Based Publish/Subscribe Systems on Apache Kafka

Shiyou Qian[1(✉)], Jiawei Xu[1], Jian Cao[1], Guangtao Xue[1], Junshen Li[1,2], and Wenyi Zhang[1]

[1] Shanghai Jiao Tong University, Shanghai, China
{qshiyou,titan_xjw,cao-jian,gt_xue,eureka_zwy}@sjtu.edu.cn,
lmz6131@sina.com
[2] Shanghai Municipal Tax Service, State Taxation Administration, Shanghai, China

Abstract. Apache Kafka is a mainstream message middleware that can provide topic-based data distribution with high throughput. Some existing works have explored building a large-scale content-based publish/subscribe system on Kafka. However, when the number of subscribers is large, the time overhead for matching the message with a large number of subscriptions and forwarding the message to the matched subscribers is large, which greatly affects the latency of message distribution. In this paper, we propose a new type of topic called the fat topic in Kafka to improve the latency of content-based data distribution. In addition, we modify Kafka's code to provide Consumer and Provider APIs to access fat topics. We conducted extensive experiments to evaluate the performance of fat topics. The experiment results show that the fat topic can improve the latency of content-based event distribution by about 3.7 times compared with the original Kafka topic.

Keywords: Data distribution · Kafka · Performance · Fat topic

1 Introduction

The publish/subscribe (pub/sub) communication paradigm can rapidly and stably distribute events (or messages)[1] from the source (publisher) to the destination (subscriber). The pub/sub system can achieve complete decoupling of communication parties in terms of time, space and synchronization [6]. Pub/sub systems can be roughly divided into two categories: topic-based and content-based. For topic-based pub/sub systems [1,2,8,17], each message is marked as a topic. Subscribers who are interested in a topic will receive all messages about that topic. Content-based pub/sub systems [4,11,12,16] provide subscribers with fine-grained expression, but at the cost of performing expensive event matching.

Apache Kafka [9] is an open-source distributed event streaming platform used by thousands of enterprises for high-performance data pipelines, streaming

---

[1] In Kafka, events are termed as messages. In our paper, event and message are interchangeable.

Z. Liu et al. (Eds.): WASA 2021, LNCS 12937, pp. 547–558, 2021.
https://doi.org/10.1007/978-3-030-85928-2_43

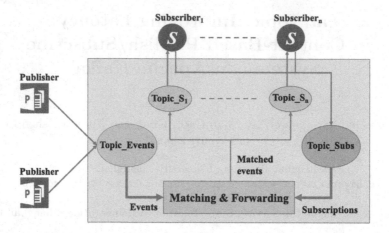

Fig. 1. The framework of content-based pub/sub systems based on Kafka

analysis, data integration, and mission-critical applications. 80% of Fortune 100 companies use Apache Kafka to respond in real time to every customer event, transaction, user experience and market movement[2]. For topic-based data distribution, Kafka can achieve a million-level high throughput.

Some work has focused on building large-scale content-based pub/sub systems on Kafka [3, 10, 18]. The framework of these systems is summarized in Fig. 1. Events and subscriptions are stored in two topics respectively. For each subscriber who submits a subscription, an individual topic is created to store the events that satisfy his subscriptions. Events are matched with subscriptions and forwarded to the individual topics of the matched subscribers. In this framework, when there are a large number of subscribers, such as in the stock market [16] and mobile e-commerce [4], events are forwarded to many subscribers. This forwarding operation is very expensive and severely affects event distribution latency.

In this paper, we address this issue by proposing a new type of topic called the fat topic to improve the event distribution latency of content-based pub/sub systems on Kafka. Forwarding events from a topic to many subscriber topics not only increases latency, but also consumes a lot of network and storage resources. The basic idea of our solution is that after the event is matched, the event and its match list will be stored together in a fat topic. In this way, storage consumption and network traffic can be greatly reduced, thereby reducing event distribution latency. To evaluate the performance of fat topics, we conducted a series of experiments. The experiment results show that the fat topic can improve event distribution latency by about 3.7 times compared with the original Kafka topic. The main contributions of this paper are as follows:

- We propose the fat topic in Kafka to reduce the latency of event distribution.
- We implement the fat topic in Kafka to provide Consumer and Provider APIs.
- We conduct experiments to evaluate the performance of the fat topic.

---

[2] http://kafka.apache.org.

The rest of the paper is organized as follows. Section 2 discusses the related work. Section 3 details the design of the fat topic. Section 4 describes the implementation of the fat topic in Kafka. Section 5 analyzes the experiment results. We conclude the paper in Sect. 6.

2   Related Work

2.1   Kafka Overview

Apache Kafka [5,9] is a distributed open-source streaming platform, which is widely used as a message queue by enterprises to distribute or transform message streams. The Kafka architecture is composed of three parts: *Kafka Cluster*, *Producer* and *Consumer*. The *Kafka Cluster* consists of one or more brokers that store messages and subscriptions in topics. Each message consists of a key and a value. The *Producer* is an API used by publishers to push messages to the topic in the *Kafka Cluster*, and subscribers use *Consumer* API to fetch messages from the topic.

2.2   Content-Based Pub/Sub Systems on Kafka

A large volume of work focuses on building content-based pub/sub systems on Kafka [3,10,18]. For the three matching algorithms including REIN [14], TAMA [20] and OpIndex [19], a lightweight parallelization method PhSIH is proposed [10]. They implemented a content-based pub/sub system prototype on Kafka to evaluate the parallelism effect of PhSIH. The work in [3] proposes a subscription-classifying and structure-layering (SCSL) method to optimize the real-time performance of content-based pub/sub systems. The SCSL method is also evaluated on Kafka. Xu et al. designed a real-time on-demand data aggregation framework called Roda [18]. They implemented the matching algorithm OpIndex [19] as the filter of Roda based on Kafka.

2.3   Matching Algorithms

Matching algorithms are critical to the performance of large-scale content-based pub/sub systems. Researchers have proposed many effective matching algorithms in the last two decades, such as TAMA [20], REIN [13], PS-Tree [7] and H-tree [15]. These algorithms rely on different data structures to efficiently index subscriptions to improve matching performance and subscription maintenance. For example, TAMA and REIN use table structures to index subscriptions. Table data structures support the counting-based matching strategy. In addition, PS-Tree and H-Tree store subscriptions in tree-like data structures and utilize pruning strategies in the matching process.

Our work is orthogonal to these studies. We focus on improve the forwarding performance of large-scale content-based pub/sub systems on Kafka. As far as we know, this issue has not been discussed in the existing work.

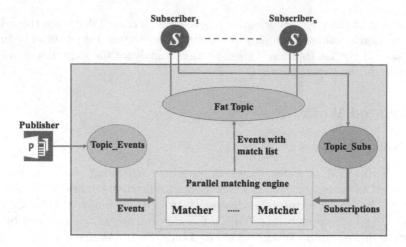

Fig. 2. The content-based pub/sub system framework with the fat topic

3   Optimization Model

3.1   Basic Idea

In the content-based pub/sub framework proposed in [10], an individual topic is created for each subscriber to store the matched messages. For a message with N interested subscribers, this framework needs to forward the message from one topic to N individual topics, as shown in Fig. 1. This scheme requires a lot of storage and network resources, and significantly affects the latency of message distribution. Therefore, for large-scale content-based pub/sub systems, the forwarding process is a potential performance bottleneck. In addition, event matching is also expensive in large-scale content-based pub/sub systems.

The basic idea of our solution to improve forwarding performance is that after matching an event with a set of subscriptions, we store the event together with the match list in a topic, instead of forwarding the event from one topic to many topics. In this way, we not only reduce the storage consumption of events, but also reduce network traffic. We call the topic for storing the event with its match list the *fat topic*.

3.2   Framework

Based on the fat topic, we design a content-based pub/sub framework on Kafka, as shown in Fig. 2. The framework is mainly composed of two components: the fat topic and the parallel matching engine. In our framework, publishers publish events and subscribers submit subscriptions in the original Kafka topics. The process is similar to that in [10]. After matching the event, we first combine the event with its match list to form a fat event, and then push it to the fat topic. In this way, the storage usage and network traffic can be greatly reduced.

For each event type, there are three topics and a parallel matching engine. *Topic_Subs* is an original Kafka topic to which subscribers submit subscriptions through the Kafka Producer API. The parallel matching engine obtains subscriptions from *Topic_Subs* through the Kafka *Stream* API. Subscriptions are maintained in local memory to speed up the matching. When an event producer publishes events to *Topic_Events* through the Kafka Producer API, the parallel matching engine also fetches events through the Kafka *Stream* API. After matching the event with the locally stored subscriptions, the parallel matching engine sends the event with its match list to the *Fat Topic* through the extended *FatTopicProducer* API. When a subscriber sends a *FatTopicFetch* request to extract its matched events from the *Fat Topic* through the extended *FatTopicConsumer* API, its ID will be checked against the match list and the corresponding response will be sent back. The implementation details of the fat topic are described in Sect. 4.1.

3.3   Parallel Event Matching

Since event matching is critical to the performance of large-scale content-based pub/sub systems, we consider parallel matching in the framework. There are two parallel mechanisms which can be deployed in a stream group manner to increase system throughput and reduce event distribution latency.

The first is the subscription division mechanism, which is suitable for time-sensitive events. Under this mechanism, the entire subscription set is divided into n subsets. A stream matcher is responsible for a subset. In this way, each event should be dispatched to all matchers. Each matcher matches the event with its local subscription subset and pushes the event together with the partial match list to the fat topic. The advantage of the subscription division mechanism is that it reduces the number of subscriptions maintained by each matcher, thereby reducing the matching time. In addition, this mechanism avoids the need to summarize the matching results of all matchers by storing the event multiple times in the fat topic, which is a trade-off between storage cost and performance. Another mechanism is to replicate the matcher that maintains all subscriptions. Events are dispatched to the matchers in a round-robin way. Through this mechanism, the system throughput can be improved, which is suitable for situations where events are generated very quickly. In our framework, we can support different matching algorithms and different parallel mechanisms.

4   Implementation

We modified Kafka's code to support fat topics and provide parallel matching through the Stream API.

4.1   Fat Topic

The fat topic is a new type of topic we have extended in Kafka. The layout of the fat topic is shown in Fig. 3. The fat topic is used to store events combined with the

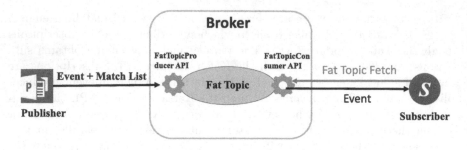

Fig. 3. Fat topic implementation in Kafka

The same as the original Kafka topic

......	IsFat	SubscriberName

Fig. 4. The fields of the fat topic fetch protocol

match list. The implementation of fat topics is transparent to subscribers. The difference between the fat topic and the original Kafka topic is that when a subscriber fetches events from the fat topic, the broker needs to check whether the subscriber is in the match list of the event. Three parts of Kafka are extended to realize the fat topic: broker, *FatTopicProducer* API and *FatTopicConsumer* API.

The *FatTopicProducer* API is provided for the matching engine to store events with their match list in fat topics. The original Kafka *Producer* API has three main arguments: *topic name*, *key* and *value*. *Topic name* indicates the target topic of the event. *Value* is the actual data of the event. *Key* is hashed at the producer side to select the topic partition. In the implementation of the *FatTopicProducer* API, we store the match list of the event as a string in the *key* argument. The match list consists of the names of the matched subscribers. The names in the string are separated by a special delimiter. For example, suppose that the match list is $\{s1, s2, s3\}$, and we choose @ as the delimiter, the value of the *key* argument is set to @s1@s2@s3@.

The *FatTopicConsumer* API issues the *FatTopicFetch* request, which is a new communication protocol in Kafka for consumers to read data in the fat topic. As shown in Fig. 4, two fields are added to *FatTopicFetch*. The *IsFat* field indicates whether the consumer is accessing a fat topic. The *SubscriberName* field is set by the consumer. This field should be unique to each consumer group in Kafka. The limitation is that since we introduce a delimiter in the match list of the *FatTopicProducer* API, the *SubscriberName* field cannot contain the delimiter. Consumers in a group can share a *SubscriberName*. Usually, *SubscriberName* should be set to be the same as the ID of the consumer group to which the consumer belongs.

On the broker side, when the broker receives a fetch request through the *FatTopicConsumer* API, the broker will check the event to which the consumer offset points to determine whether *SubscriberName* is in the match list of the event. We adopt a sub-string search algorithm to improve efficiency. If the match list contains string @*s1*@ which is the combination of delimiter and *SubscriberName*, the check result is true; otherwise, it is false. According to the search result, the broker will respond in two ways. If *SubscriberName* is in the match list, the broker will send the event to the consumer. Otherwise, the broker will add empty data to the response body. When the consumer does not receive the event, it merely records the event offset in the response. When the consumer issues the next *FatTopicFetch* request, the offset indicates the right event to access. The purpose of the two different fetch responses is to correctly track the event position of the consumer in the fat topic. Kafka uses consumer offset to accelerate the data location search. Our implementation does not affect Kafka's reading efficiency in the log files. In addition, other features of Kafka topics such as load balance and data replications remain.

4.2   Parallel Matching Engine

The parallel matching engine is implemented through the Kafka *Stream* API. Matchers in the engine use the API to pull subscriptions and events. After matching an event, the matcher sends the event with its match list to a fat topic, as shown in Fig. 2. We realize the two parallel mechanisms mentioned in Sect. 3.3.

The subscription-division mechanism is implemented by deploying a group of n matchers. All matchers use the same stream ID to pull subscriptions in *Topic_Subs*. In this way, subscriptions are evenly dispatched to the n matchers. In addition, each matcher in the group uses a unique stream ID to pull events in *Topic_Events*. Each matcher will obtain all events. After matching the event with its local subscription subset, the event is sent to a fat topic with its match list. The event is stored n times in the fat topic.

The matcher replication mechanism is also implemented by deploying a group of n matchers. Each matcher uses a unique stream ID to pull subscriptions from *Topic_Subs*, which means that each matcher maintains all subscriptions. All matchers use the same stream ID to pull events from *Topic_Events*. Thus, events are evenly dispatched to all matchers. Each matcher performs event matching on the entire subscription set and sends the event with its match list to a fat topic. The event is stored only once in the fat topic.

5   Performance Evaluation

5.1   Evaluation Settings

We conducted a series of experiments to evaluate the performance of fat topics. We modified the code of Kafka_2.12-2.2.0 to implement the fat topic. The experiment system topology is shown in Fig. 5. We deploy Kafka on three virtual machines (VM) with each one having 4 vCPUs and 8 GB RAM. We use three VMs (32 vCPUs and 64 GB RAM) to realize the parallel matching engine which employs the matching algorithm REIN [14]. In each stream matcher, we

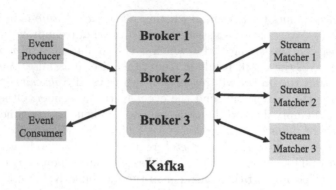

Fig. 5. The topology of the experiment system

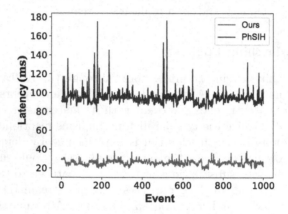

Fig. 6. Event distribution latency

use 4 threads to match. The stream matcher is implemented in Java 11.0.7. In addition, we use one VM (4 vCPUs and 8 GB RAM) as the event producer to publish events at a high rate and one VM (4 vCPUs and 8 GB RAM) as the event consumer to submit subscriptions. In the deployed Kafka system, each topic has three partitions to increase system parallel performance.

In our experiments, each event has 50 attributes. We simulate 100,000 consumers who submit a total of 250,000 subscriptions. Each subscription contains 5 predicates which define conditions on attributes. The attributes of these subscriptions are uniformly selected from the 50 attributes in events. The average matching probability of events is 0.4% which means that each event has about 1,000 matched subscribers. We implemented the stream matchers through REIN which is suitable for running multiple threads.

5.2   Latency Improvement of Fat Topic

Based on the original Kafka topic, PhSIH [10] builds a content-based pub/sub system which has low performance and high storage cost. We compare our

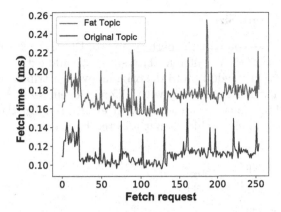

Fig. 7. The fetch cost of the fat topic and the original Kafka topic

content-based framework based on fat topics with PhSIH in which each event is forwarded from the event topic to the individual topics of its matched subscribers. As there are 1,000 matched subscribers on average for each event, the end-to-end latency of events varies with the forwarding sequence. In the experiment, we use one stream matcher and measure the tail end-to-end latency. The experiment results are shown in Fig. 6. The average end-to-end latency of PhSIH is 94.795 ms while it is only 25.642 ms for our system. These results verify that the fat topic can improve event distribution latency by about 3.7 times compared with the original Kafka topic. In addition, many network sending requests exist in PhSIH while there is only one in our system. Therefore, the performance of our system is more stable than PhSIH. The standard deviation of latency of PhSIH and our system is 7.51 and 2.54, respectively.

5.3   Fetch Cost of Fat Topic

As described in Sect. 4.1, we implemented the fat topic to improve event forwarding efficiency in large-scale content-based pub/sub systems. At the broker that stores the fat topics, an extra verification step is performed compared with the original Kafka topic. To evaluate the fetch cost of fat topics, we create an original topic and a fat topic in Kafka and then publish 23,804 messages to each topic. For the fat topic, we add a fixed number of consumers in the match list. Then, we launch an original Kafka consumer and a fat topic consumer to fetch messages in each topic, respectively.

In the experiment, the consumer requests a batch of messages in each fetch. We first measure the batch fetch time from sending the consumer request to receiving the response. Then, we compute the average cost of fetching a message by dividing the batch fetch cost by the batch size. The results are shown in Fig. 7. The average fetch time of the original Kafka topic is about 0.1118 ms and the one of the fat topic is 0.1733 ms. The verification step takes about 0.0615 ms which can be ignored compared with the improvement of event distribution latency shown in Fig. 6.

5.4   Effect of Event Size

In this experiment, we compare the performance of PhSIH with our system in the situation where events are of different data sizes. We add extra data (from 1 KB to 10 KB) to the event in addition to the original event attribute values. Figure 8 shows the event distribution latency with different event sizes. We observe that the latency of PhSIH increases linearly with event size. On the contrary, our system has a stable latency which is not affected by event size.

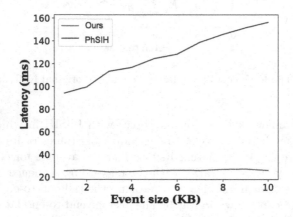

Fig. 8. Event distribution latency with different event sizes

5.5   Parallel Matching Performance

We evaluate the two parallel matching mechanisms described in Sect. 3.3. We measure the system throughput and event matching time of the two parallel mechanisms. In Fig. 9 and Fig. 10, blue bars represent the event parallel mechanism (for short Parallel Event), yellow bars represent the subscription parallel mechanism (for short Parallel Sub) and the black bar is the baseline which does not use any parallel mechanism. For example, $E3$ means that there are 3 matchers in the event parallel mechanism. The same is for the subscription parallel mechanism. Figure 9 shows the system throughput of the two mechanisms, which indicates that the event parallel mechanism can increase system throughput more significantly than the subscription parallel mechanism. Figure 10 shows the event matching time of the two mechanisms. The event parallel mechanism does not improve matching performance. On the contrary, the subscription parallel mechanism greatly reduces matching time as the number of subscriptions in each stream matcher is reduced.

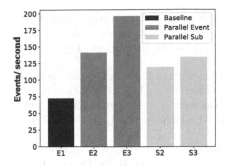

Fig. 9. System throughput of different parallel mechanisms (Color figure online)

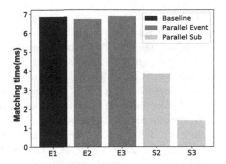

Fig. 10. Matching time of different parallel mechanisms (Color figure online)

6 Conclusion

In this paper, we propose a new type of topic called the fat topic to optimize the forwarding performance of large-scale content-based pub/sub systems on Kafka. Based on the fat topic, we design an efficient content-based pub/sub framework. We conducted a series of experiments to evaluate the effect of the fat topic. The experiment results show that the fat topic improves event distribution latency by 3.7 times compared with the original Kafka topic.

Acknowledgments. This work was supported by the National Key Research and Development Program of China (2019YFB1704400), the National Natural Science Foundation of China (61772334, 61702151), and the Special Fund for Scientific Instruments of the National Natural Science Foundation of China (61827810).

References

1. Chockler, G., Melamed, R., Tock, Y., Vitenberg, R.: SpiderCast: a scalable interest-aware overlay for topic-based pub/sub communication. In: Proceedings of the 2007 Inaugural International Conference on Distributed Event-based Systems, pp. 14–25 (2007)
2. Detti, A., Funari, L., Blefari-Melazzi, N.: Sub-linear scalability of MQTT clusters in topic-based publish-subscribe applications. IEEE Trans. Netw. Serv. Manage. **17**(3), 1954–1968 (2020)
3. Ding, T., Qian, S., Cao, J., Xue, G., Li, M.: SCSL: optimizing matching algorithms to improve real-time for content-based pub/sub systems. In: 2020 IEEE International Parallel and Distributed Processing Symposium (IPDPS), pp. 148–157. IEEE (2020)
4. Ding, T., et al.: MO-Tree: an efficient forwarding engine for spatiotemporal-aware pub/sub systems. IEEE Trans. Parallel Distrib. Syst. **32**(4), 855–866 (2020)

5. Dobbelaere, P., Esmaili, K.S.: Kafka versus RabbitMQ: a comparative study of two industry reference publish/subscribe implementations: industry paper. In: Proceedings of the 11th ACM International Conference on Distributed and Event-based Systems, pp. 227–238 (2017)
6. Eugster, P.T., Felber, P.A., Guerraoui, R., Kermarrec, A.M.: The many faces of publish/subscribe. ACM Comput. Surv. (CSUR) **35**(2), 114–131 (2003)
7. Ji, S., Jacobsen, H.A.: Ps-tree-based efficient Boolean expression matching for high-dimensional and dense workloads. Proc. VLDB Endowment **12**(3), 251–264 (2018). https://doi.org/10.14778/3291264.3291270
8. Jokela, P., Zahemszky, A., Esteve Rothenberg, C., Arianfar, S., Nikander, P.: LIPSIN: line speed publish/subscribe inter-networking. ACM SIGCOMM Comput. Commun. Rev. **39**(4), 195–206 (2009)
9. Kreps, J., Narkhede, N., Rao, J., et al.: Kafka: a distributed messaging system for log processing. Proc. NetDB. **11**, 1–7 (2011)
10. Liao, Z., et al.: PhSIH: a lightweight parallelization of event matching in content-based pub/sub systems. In: Proceedings of the 48th International Conference on Parallel Processing, pp. 1–10 (2019)
11. Martins, J.L., Duarte, S.: Routing algorithms for content-based publish/subscribe systems. IEEE Commun. Surv. Tutorials **12**(1) (2010)
12. Muhl, G., Fiege, L., Gartner, F.C., Buchmann, A.: Evaluating advanced routing algorithms for content-based publish/subscribe systems. In: 10th IEEE International Symposium on Modeling, Analysis and Simulation of Computer and Telecommunications Systems, MASCOTS 2002. Proceedings, pp. 167–176. IEEE (2002)
13. Qian, S., et al.: A fast and anti-matchability matching algorithm for content-based publish/subscribe systems. Comput. Netw. **149**, 213–225 (2019)
14. Qian, S., Cao, J., Zhu, Y., Li, M.: REIN: a fast event matching approach for content-based publish/subscribe systems. In: IEEE INFOCOM 2014-IEEE Conference on Computer Communications, pp. 2058–2066. IEEE (2014)
15. Qian, S., Cao, J., Zhu, Y., Li, M., Wang, J.: H-Tree: an efficient index structure for event matching in content-based publish/subscribe systems. IEEE Trans. Parallel Distrib. Syst. **26**(6), 1622–1632 (2015). https://doi.org/10.1109/TPDS.2014.2323262
16. Qian, S., Mao, W., Cao, J., Le Mouël, F., Li, M.: Adjusting matching algorithm to adapt to workload fluctuations in content-based publish/subscribe systems. In: IEEE INFOCOM 2019-IEEE Conference on Computer Communications, pp. 1936–1944. IEEE (2019)
17. Saito, T., Nakamura, S., Enokido, T., Takizawa, M.: A topic-based publish/subscribe system in a fog computing model for the IoT. In: Barolli, L., Poniszewska-Maranda, A., Enokido, T. (eds.) CISIS 2020. AISC, vol. 1194, pp. 12–21. Springer, Cham (2021). https://doi.org/10.1007/978-3-030-50454-0_2
18. Xu, J., et al.: Roda: a flexible framework for real-time on-demand data aggregation. In: Qiu, M. (ed.) ICA3PP 2020. LNCS, vol. 12453, pp. 587–602. Springer, Cham (2020). https://doi.org/10.1007/978-3-030-60239-0_40
19. Zhang, D., Chan, C.Y., Tan, K.L.: An efficient publish/subscribe index for e-commerce databases. Proc. VLDB Endowment **7**(8), 613–624 (2014)
20. Zhao, Y., Wu, J.: Towards approximate event processing in a large-scale content-based network. In: 2011 31st International Conference on Distributed Computing Systems, pp. 790–799. IEEE (2011)

Communication-efficient Federated Learning via Quantized Clipped SGD

Ninghui Jia[1], Zhihao Qu[1(✉)], and Baoliu Ye[2]

[1] Hohai University, Nanjing, China
jianinghui@hhu.edu.cn, quzhihao@hhu.edu.cn
[2] Nanjing University, Nanjing, China
yebl@nju.edu.cn

Abstract. Communication has been considered as a major bottleneck of Federated Learning (FL) in mobile edge networks since participating workers iteratively transmit gradients to and receive models from the server. Compression technology like quantization that reduces the communication overhead and hyperparameter optimization technology like Clipped Stochastic Gradient Descent (Clipped SGD) that accelerates the convergence are two orthogonal approaches to improve the performance of FL. However, the combination of them has been little studied. To fill this gap, we propose Quantized Clipped SGD (QCSGD) to achieve communication-efficient FL. The major challenge of the combination lies in that the gradient quantization essentially affects the adjusting policy of step size in Clipped SGD, resulting in the lack of convergence guarantee. Therefore, we establish the convergence rate of QCSGD via a thorough theoretical analysis and exhibit that QCSGD has a comparable convergence rate as SGD without compression. We also conduct extensive experiments on various machine learning models and datasets and show that QCSGD outperforms state-of-the-art methods.

Keywords: Federated learning · Gradient quantization · Clipped gradient descent

1 Introduction

Since its inception by Google [13], Federated Learning (FL) has shown great promises in protecting the privacy-sensitive data and alleviating the cost of the computation and communication of the traditional learning paradigm. Its core idea is to let mobile devices cooperatively train a global model without exposing their own data [11]. The most widely used training method in FL is Stochastic Gradient Descent (SGD). Under SGD, each mobile device separately trains the local model and uploads the local model or the local gradient to a server for aggregation. Then, the server updates the global model and sends it to each mobile device. The above steps run iteratively until a target accuracy is achieved.

Z. Liu et al. (Eds.): WASA 2021, LNCS 12937, pp. 559–571, 2021.
https://doi.org/10.1007/978-3-030-85928-2_44

FL has shown significant successes in many edge applications. However, in a highly dynamic mobile edge network, the scarcity of radio resources will significantly affect the performance of FL [6,8,18,19]. Moreover, On account of the iterative update for SGD and the massive model size, the communication traffic is still the bottleneck of FL.

To address the communication challenge in FL, communication compression is an effective way to alleviate the overhead. Two mainstream approaches of communication compression are quantization [2] and sparsification [1]. Quantization transforms the gradient represented by 32 or 64 bits into fewer bits. QSGD [2] is the representative method that can quantize the gradient into arbitrary bits and guarantee the variance bounded. Sparsification is another compression method that drops out some coordinates of gradients and utilizes the remains of the gradient as representation. Top-k [17] is one typical methods that simply choose the largest k elements of the gradient.

On the other hand, hyperparameter optimization techniques can improve the convergence speed of SGD in FL, also yielding communication efficiency. Recently, Clipped Stochastic Gradient Descent (Clipped SGD [22]), which is designed to improve the SGD training, has been proposed to adaptively adjust the step size for faster convergence. The basic idea is to adjust the step size according to the L_2-norm of the gradient.

Though the above-mentioned methods have attracted much attention in communication-efficient FL, the combination of compression and hyperparameter optimization has been little studied. To fill in this gap, in this paper, we propose the method named Quantized Clipped SGD (QCSGD) that combining the quantization with Clipped SGD to reduce the communication overhead of FL. The combination is not easy since compression on the gradient essentially affects the adjusting policy of step size in Clipped SGD. Moreover, the convergence rate of quantized Clipped SGD is still unknown. Therefore, we establish the convergence rate via a thorough analysis. Extensive experiments on various machine learning models and datasets show that QCSGD outperforms state-of-the-art methods. The contribution of this paper is summarized as follows:

- We propose a new method named QCSGD that integrates quantization and Clipped SGD to accelerate the convergence rate and meanwhile reduce the communication overhead of FL.
- To the best of our knowledge, we are the first to establish the convergence rate of the Clipped SGD with quantization. Our theoretical analysis shows that QCSGD exhibits a comparable convergence rate as SGD without compression. In additional, our analysis does not rely on the convexity assumption of the training problem, thus suitable to popular deep neural networks.
- We conduct extensive experiments on various machine learning models including Logistic Regression, MnistCNN, and AlexNet. Experimental results show that QCSGD can reduce the communication traffic up to 2.0× and improve the convergence speed up to 1.5×.

2   Preliminary

2.1   Problem Formulation

In this section, we introduce the empirical risk minimization problem typically used in FL. Given a dataset $\mathcal{D}$, the local dataset of each participating worker n is denoted by $\mathcal{D}_n$, and $D_n = \mathcal{D}_n$. Let N be the total number of workers, then $D = \sum_{i=1}^{N} D_n$. Let $f_i(w)$ be the loss function in worker i, where $w \in \mathbb{R}^d$ represents the model parameter vector. The gradient vector and the model parameter vector have the same dimension d. The objective is to seek the optimal solution to minimize the global loss function.

$$\min_{w \in \mathbb{R}^d} F(w) = \sum_{i=1}^{N} \frac{D_i}{D} f_i(w) \tag{1}$$

2.2   SGD and DSGD

The optimization object (1) is the weighted average of the loss values. It is generally impossible to get the closed-form optimal solution since the machine learning model has a complex loss function. Using the gradient to seek the optimal model parameters iteratively is widely applied in the training problem because gradient indicates the direction to the optimal solution which makes the model finally converge to an expected accuracy.

Since the data size is massive, traditional gradient descent methods need to compute the gradient with respect to the whole dataset which incurs huge computation cost. To tackle this issue, Stochastic Gradient Descent (SGD) has been proposed to solve (1). SGD randomly selects one sample and computes the stochastic gradient instead of the full gradient to decide the updating direction. In this paper, we adopt the mini-batch SGD, in which gradients are computed with respect to a mini-batch of samples. Thus, the update rule of the model in iteration t is:

$$w_{t+1} = w_t - \eta_t \mathbf{g}(w_t; \xi), \tag{2}$$

where η_t is the step size, ξ is the randomly selected mini-batch, w_t and w_{t+1} are model in t-th and $(t+1)$-th iteration, respectively. In FL, each worker has a subset of the training data. We use distributed SGD (DSGD) to tackle this problem. In DSGD, workers compute the local gradient using their local data and sent the result to the server. Server aggregates the gradient from workers and updates the model:

$$w_{t+1} = w_t - \eta_t \sum_{i=1}^{N} \frac{D_i}{D} \mathbf{g}(w_t; \xi_t^i) \tag{3}$$

where $\mathbf{g}(w_t; \xi_t^i)$ represents the local gradient with respect to a local mini-batch ξ_t^i and the model parameter w_t.

2.3   Quantization

In this paper, we employ the most widely used QSGD [2] as the compressed operator. Assuming the L_2-norm of gradient is m, for any element e of the gradient, the quantization rules are:

$$Q_s(e) = m \cdot \mathbf{sgn}(e) \cdot \mathbf{q}(e) \tag{4}$$

$$\mathbf{q}(e) = \begin{cases} l/s & \text{with probability } 1 + l - \frac{s|e|}{m}, \\ (l+s)/s & \text{otherwise}, \end{cases} \tag{5}$$

where s is the quantization level, l is an integer between 0 and s, and $\mathbf{sgn}(\cdot)$ is the sign of each element.

QSGD is unbiased, i.e., $\mathbb{E}[Q(g)] = g$. Meanwhile, the error of quantization is bounded by ϵ such that $\mathbb{E}[\| Q(g(w, \xi)) - g \|] \leq \epsilon \|g\|$, where $\epsilon = \sqrt{min\left\{ \frac{d}{s^2}, \frac{\sqrt{d}}{s} \right\}}$ and d is the dimension of the gradient.

2.4   Clipped Gradient Descent

In this part, we introduce a method of hyperparameter optimization to improve the performance of vanilla SGD, named Clipped GD. Vanilla SGD has a fixed learning rate η, while Clipped GD performs the following updates:

$$w_{t+1} = w_t - h_c \nabla f(w_t), \quad where \ h_c := min\left\{ \eta_c, \frac{\gamma \eta_c}{\|\nabla f(w)\|} \right\} \tag{6}$$

where $\nabla f(w_t)$ is the gradient with respect to w_t, η_c is the step size, and γ is a constant scale factor. Instead of fixed learning rate, Clipped GD uses L_2-norm of the gradient to adaptively adjust the hyperparameter of the iterative updates.

3   Algorithm

In this section, we introduce the algorithm named QCSGD. We first introduce the detail of the algorithm and then give the theoretical analysis on the convergence rate of it:

3.1   Quantized Clipped SGD

In this paper, we propose an algorithm named QCSGD that integrates gradient compression and hyperparameter optimization techniques. Quantization efficiently reduces the communication traffic but leads to the loss of accuracy. Clipped GD is the method that adaptively adjusts the descending step size for SGD to accelerate the model training.

To adaptively adjust the step size, we should compute the L_2-norm of the gradient which is sent from workers. In our method, the gradients received by the server have been quantized into fewer bits. Therefore, in the server, we aggregate

---

Algorithm 1 Quantized Clipped SGD

Input: Initial point w_0, clipped coefficient γ, learning rate η, iteration number T, Training dataset $\mathcal{D}$

1: **for** $t = 1, 2 \cdots, T$ **do**
2:     Randomly select a mini-batch of samples ξ_t^i from local data $\mathcal{D}_i$ of the ith worker
3:     Compute the local gradients: $g(w_t, \xi_t^i)$ with respect to ξ_t^i and model parameters w_t
4:     Compress $g(w_t, \xi_t^i)$ into $Q(g(w_t, \xi_t^i))$ using quantization compressor Q
5:     Aggregate the local gradients from different workers: $\bar{g}(w_t, \xi_t) = \sum_{i=1}^{N} \frac{D_i}{D} Q(g(w_t, \xi_t^i))$
6:     Compute the $h_c \leftarrow min\left\{\eta_c, \frac{\gamma\eta_c}{\|\bar{g}(\cdot)\|}\right\}$, using (7)
7:     Update the model parameters: $w_{t+1} = w_t - h_c\bar{g}(w_t, \xi_t)$
8: **end for**
    Output: Updated model parameters w_T

---

the compressed gradient $Q(g(w_t, \xi_t^i))$ instead of origin gradient $\mathbf{g}(w_t; \xi_t^i)$. Thus, the updating rule of the global model in QCSGD is:

$$w_{t+1} = w_t - \sum_{i=1}^{N} \frac{D_i}{D} h_t Q(\mathbf{g}(w_t, \xi_t^i)), \quad where \ h_c := min\left\{\eta_c, \frac{N\gamma\eta_c}{\|\sum_{i=1}^{N} \frac{D_i}{D} Q(\mathbf{g}(w_t, \xi_t^i))\|}\right\}$$
(7)

Our method QCSGD same as the formulation above can alleviate the communication overhead and accelerate the convergence speed.

3.2 Algorithm Description

In this paper, we mainly focus on the PS architecture which is a typical framework for FL. In summary, QCSGD which is described in Algorithm 1 can be implemented as follows.

At iteration t, the server broadcasts current model parameters w_t to all workers. Workers calculate the local gradients $g(w_t, \xi_t^i)$ based on w_t and local minibatch ξ_t^i. Then, our method compresses the gradient into $Q_i(\mathbf{g}(w_t, \xi_t^i))$ using the quantization compressor Q. Server receives the compressed gradients from all workers and aggregates them into $\bar{g}(w_t, \xi_t)$ for the global model updating every few rounds. The step size for QCSGD needs to take the minimum value of the learning rate and the value of $\frac{\gamma\eta_c}{\|\bar{g}(w_t, \xi_t)\|}$. After determining the step length, server updates the model parameters and send them back to workers for the next iteration.

4   Convergence Analysis

In this section, we establish the convergence rate of QCSGD. We first make the following assumptions which are widely adopted in SGD-based methods for FL and distributed machine learning [2,12]:

(1) (*L*-smooth) The objective function is Lipschitz continuous and for any $\omega_1, \omega_2 \in \mathbb{R}$, we have $\|\nabla F(\omega_1) - \nabla F(\omega_2)\| \leq L\|\omega_1 - \omega_2\|$.
(2) (**Bound Value**) F is bounded below by a scalar F^*, i.e., for any iteration t, $F^* \leq F(\omega_t)$. w
(3) (**Unbiased Gradient**) The stochastic gradient is unbiased for any parameter w, i.e., $\mathbb{E}_\xi[g(w, \xi)] = \nabla F(w)$.
(4) (**Bound Variance**) The variance for stochastic gradient is bounded by σ^2, i.e., for any parameter w, $\mathbb{E}_\xi[\| g(w, \xi) - \nabla F(w) \|^2] \leq \sigma^2$.

Then, we establish the convergence rate of QCSGD in the following theorems.

Theorem 1. *Under the assumptions (1)–(4), considering that Algorithm 1 runs with a fixed stepsize $\eta = \eta_t$ for each iteration t, when the step size satisfies that $\eta \leq \frac{1}{4LNG(1+\epsilon^2)}$, where L is Lipschitz constant, N is the number of workers, ϵ is the parameter bounding the quantization error, and $G = \sum_{i=1}^{N} \frac{D_i^2}{D^2}$, for any integer $T > 1$, we have*

$$\frac{1}{T} \sum_{t=1}^{T} \| \nabla F(w_t) \|^2 \leq \frac{2|F^* - F(w_1)|}{\eta \cdot T} + 4L\eta\sigma^2 GN(1 + \epsilon^2) + L\gamma^2\eta \quad (8)$$

Theorem 2. *Let $\eta = \sqrt{\frac{2|F^* - F(w_1)|}{[4L\sigma^2 GN(1+\epsilon^2)+L\gamma^2] \cdot T}}$, then for sufficient large T such that*

$$\sqrt{\frac{2|F^* - F(w_1)|}{[4L\sigma^2 GN(1 + \epsilon^2) + L\gamma^2] \cdot T}} \leq \frac{1}{4LNG(1 + \epsilon^2)} \quad (9)$$

we have $\frac{1}{T} \sum_{t=1}^{T} \| \nabla F(w_t) \|^2 \preceq O(\frac{1}{\sqrt{T}})$, where $\preceq$ denotes order inequality, i.e., less than or equal to up to a constant factor.

Due to the page limitation, we remove the proofs to a technical report [9]. According to Theorem 1 and 2, we show that QCSGD can achieve a convergence rate of $\frac{1}{\sqrt{T}}$, which is same as SGD without compression. Thus, QCSGD can reduce the communication of FL due to gradient quantization. We further verify the convergence acceleration via extensive experiments. Notably, our analysis does not rely on the convexity assumption of the training problem, thus suitable to the popular deep neural networks with non-convex objectives.

5   Performance Evaluation

We conduct experiments on various machine models and datasets to show the performance of QCSGD. Experiment results show that QCSGD not only alleviates the communication overhead but also improves the convergence speed. The codes can be found on github [9].

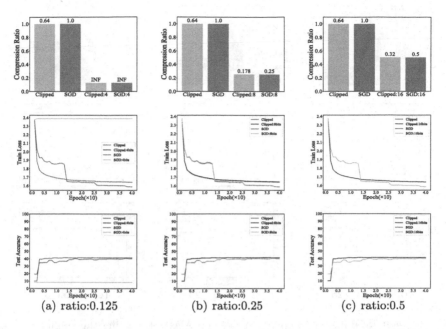

Fig. 1. Results of different compression ratio on LR. Setting the vanilla SGD as the baseline of communication traffic with 1.

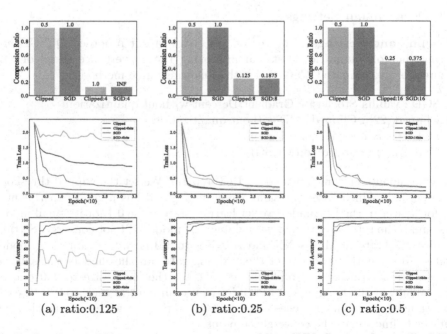

Fig. 2. Results of different compression ratio on MnistCNN. Setting the vanilla SGD as the baseline of communication traffic with 1.

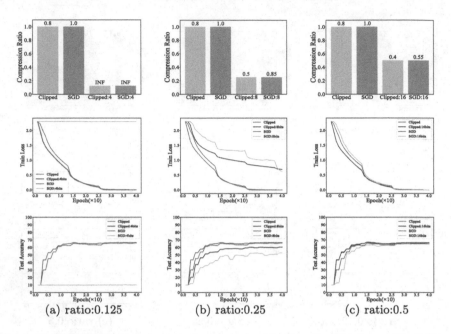

Fig. 3. Results of different compression ratio on AlexNet. Setting the vanilla SGD as the baseline of communication traffic with 1.

5.1 Experiment Settings

Baseline and Settings. Two major objectives of our proposed QCSGD are saving the communication cost and improving the convergence speed of FL. Therefore, we compare QCSGD with the following three methods:

(1) SGD : vanilla Stochasitc Gradient Descent without quantization
(2) Clipped [22] : Clipped SGD without quantization
(3) SGD:(-) : SGD with quantization.
(4) Clipped:(-) : our method QCSGD

All experiments are implemented on PyTorch 1.0. We set the clipped threshold γ to be 0.25, which takes the same value in [22] and has a good experimental performance. In the LR model, we set learning rate to be 0.1 for its small model size and if the rate is set to a larger volume, the model will not converge. Setting the learning rate in MnistCNN and AlexNet to 1.0 is suitable for their model scales. Along with the decay of the learning rate, all the models can achieve an acceptable convergence performance. We set the batch size to 200 due to the amount of the training data in order to use all data in each epoch. In each experiment, the training process runs 10000 iterations in which all models have sufficient time to get the convergence point.

Datasets and Models. We consider *Mnist* and *Cifar*10 as the training datasets. *Mnist* has $60K$ 28×28 training data and *Cifar*10 has $50K$ 32×32 training data. In order to better verify our method, convex and non-convex machine learning models are considered in our experiments. We adopt Logistic Regression (LR) as the convex model and MnistCNN and AlexNet as the non-convex models.

Metrics. Model convergence, communication traffic and test accuracy are the evaluation metrics. Convergence rate demonstrates descent speed of the loss value. Communication traffic indicates the required communication size between server and workers until convergence. The compression ratio in the figures means the reduced traffic in each iteration compared with naive SGD. The size of communication traffic is defined by the size of original transferred data while the loss of the model achieves to a target value. We set the target value in LR as 1.7, in MnistCNN as 0.9 and in AlexNet as 1.

5.2   Experiment Results

Figure 1 shows the results of training LR on *Cifar*10. It has three subfigures with different compression ratios, i.e., 0.125, 0.25 and 0.5. From the training loss figures, we observe that Clipped SGD is better than SGD without quantization and can save traffic by 1.5×. Meanwhile, Clipped SGD can improve the convergence speed by 3× since Clipped SGD can reach the loss of 1.8 at 5 epochs while SGD needs 15 epochs. If the compression ratio is 0.125, both our method and vanilla quantized SGD can not converge since training LR easily causes overfitting and a small compression ratio usually degrades the model accuracy. Under the compression ratio of 0.25 or 0.5, our method converges faster than SGD by 3× and reduce the communication overhead by 1.4–1.5×. In the loss pictures, when the number of the epochs is larger than 15, the loss of SGD is less than our method since Clipped SGD adjusts the step length to an extremely small value and leads to the loss descending slower than SGD. From the accuracy pictures, it can be seen that Clipped SGD is better than SGD in all cases and can achieve the accuracy of 40%.

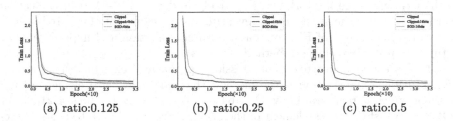

(a) ratio:0.125   (b) ratio:0.25   (c) ratio:0.5

Fig. 4. Results of different compression ratio on AlexNet. Setting the vanilla SGD as the baseline of communication traffic with 1.

In Fig. 2, we plot the trends of four algorithms when training MnistCNN. Compared to the baseline, Clipped SGD without quantization can save 2× communication traffic and accelerate training by at least 4×. With the compression ratio of 0.125, SGD can not converge but QCSGD can converge at the eleventh epoch with test accuracy of 85%. Under the compression ratio of 0.25 or 0.5, QCSGD achieves a similar result as Clipped SGD due to the minimal loss of accuracy and saves the communication traffic by 2× and improves the training speed by 4×.

Figure 3 plots the results of training AlexNet on $Cifar10$. In contrast to SGD, Clipped SGD without quantization can reduce 1.25× traffic and accelerate the convergence by 2 epochs. After ten epochs, the clipped coefficient is close to learning rate, so the descent speed of SGD and Clipped SGD is similar. When compression radio is 0.125, quantiaztion methods are not convergence. Under the compression ratio of 0.25, the acceleration effect is more clear and speeds up 1.4×. QCSGD can achieve better performance in terms of testing accuracy especially when the compression ratio is 0.25, i.e., 60% under QCSGD and 50% under SGD.

We also conduct experiments in which each worker runs multiple local updates in each global iteration, similar to FedAvg [13]. In such setting, each worker runs 4 local updates according to its local model and then uploads the updates to the server for global model updating. The training trends are plotted in Fig. 4. The results also demonstrate that our method outperform SGD in terms of convergence speed and the communication cost.

We can conclude that our proposed QCSGD can reduce the communication overhead and improve the convergence speed of FL. In the case of training small models like LR, the effectiveness of QCSGD in training acceleration is not significant due to the training process rapidly getting convergence or overfitting, but the communication overhead is still reduced. This phenomenon indicates that QCSGD is more applicable to large-scale models like deep neural networks.

6   Related Work

FL has been proposed to protect the privacy of users and alleviate the cost of computation and communication of the traditional learning paradigm. Due to the dynamic edge network and iteratively updates of SGD, communication overhead has been the main factor preventing the development of FL. To improve the training efficiency of FL, communication compression and hyperparameter optimization are two efficient methods.

There are two mainstream compression approaches, e.g., quantization and sparsification. Quantization is the method that quantizes each element of the gradient which is represented by 32 or 64 bits float with fewer bits [4,21]. 1-Bit SGD [16] transforms each element of the gradient using only 1-bit via sign function. In [20], TernGrad is proposed which quantizes each element with a ternary $\{-1, 0, 1\}$. The representative and widely used quantization method is QSGD [2] which can quantize the element into arbitrary bits and firstly give the bounded error of quantization. FetchSGD [15] and SketchML [10] utilize sketch to quantize the gradient which match the distribution of gradient value and can reduce the compression error. Sparsification is another way to reduce the communication overhead. The core idea is to transmit a subset of dimensions instead of the entire gradient vector to the server [12,14]. One typical sparsification method is top-k that selects the k largest values of the gradient elements to represent the whole gradient [17]. In FL, a modified method is proposed to adaptively adjust k to accommodate the characteristic of non-IID data distribution[7]. To improve the convergence rate, error feedback has been applied in sparsification methods to compensate the error incurred by compression [1,3,5,12].

Hyperparameter optimization that adjusts the hyperparameter in SGD can improve the convergence speed and thus reduce the communication rounds. Momentum [23] and Nesterov's Acceleration [14] have been proved to have a faster convergence rate than SGD. The momentum method updates an additional part of the previous iteration and Nesterov's Acceleration uses the second-order information to correlate the gradient. Clipped gradient Descent (Clipped SGD) [22] is different from these methods in that Clipped SGD adjusts the step length via L2-norm of the gradient. In our paper, we firstly combine Clipped SGD with quantization and establish its convergence rate.

7   Conclusion

FL has been proposed to enable individual mobile devices to cooperatively training a global model. It has shown great advantages in preserving privacy and leveraging resources in the edge environment. On account of the iterative updating of SGD and huge model size, FL in mobile edge networks with unstable wireless links and limited bandwidth still faces the challenge of communication overhead. To address this problem, in this paper, we firstly combine quantization with hyperparameter optimization and proposed a communication-efficient method named QCSGD. We establish the convergence rate of QCSGD and show that QCSGD exhibits a comparable convergence rate as SGD without compression. Experimental results demonstrate that QCSGD outperforms state-of-the-art methods.

Acknowledgements. This work was supported in part by National Key R&D Program of China (Grant No. 2018YFB1004704), Fundamental Research Funds for the Central Universities (Grant No. B200202176 and B210202079).

References

1. Aji, A.F., Heafield, K.: Sparse communication for distributed gradient descent. In: Proceedings of the 2017 Conference on Empirical Methods in Natural Language Processing, pp. 440–445 (2017)
2. Alistarh, D., Grubic, D., Li, J., Tomioka, R., Vojnovic, M.: QSGD: communication-efficient SGD via gradient quantization and encoding. In: Advances in Neural Information Processing Systems, vol. 30, pp. 1709–1720 (2017)

3. Alistarh, D., Hoefler, T., Johansson, M., Konstantinov, N., Khirirat, S., Renggli, C.: The convergence of Sparsified Gradient methods. In: NeurIPS (2018)
4. Bernstein, J., Zhao, J., Azizzadenesheli, K., Anandkumar, A.: SignSGD with majority vote is communication efficient and fault tolerant. arXiv preprint arXiv:1810.05291 (2018)
5. Chen, C.Y., Choi, J., Brand, D., Agrawal, A., Zhang, W., Gopalakrishnan, K.: ADaComP: adaptive residual gradient compression for data-parallel distributed training. In: Proceedings of the AAAI Conference on Artificial Intelligence, vol. 32 (2018)
6. Chen, M., Yang, Z., Saad, W., Yin, C., Poor, H.V., Cui, S.: A joint learning and communications framework for federated learning over wireless networks. IEEE Trans. Wireless Commun. (2020)
7. Han, P., Wang, S., Leung, K.K.: Adaptive gradient sparsification for efficient federated learning: an online learning approach. arXiv preprint arXiv:2001.04756 (2020)
8. Huang, T., Ye, B., Qu, Z., Tang, B., Xie, L., Lu, S.: Physical-layer arithmetic for federated learning in uplink MU-MIMO enabled wireless networks. In: IEEE INFOCOM 2020-IEEE Conference on Computer Communications, pp. 1221–1230. IEEE (2020)
9. Jia, N.: https://github.com/jianinghui/WASA2021.git
10. Jiang, J., Fu, F., Yang, T., Cui, B.: SketchML: accelerating distributed machine learning with data sketches. In: Proceedings of the 2018 International Conference on Management of Data, pp. 1269–1284 (2018)
11. Kairouz, P., et al.: Advances and open problems in federated learning. arXiv preprint arXiv:1912.04977 (2019)
12. Lin, Y., Han, S., Mao, H., Wang, Y., Dally, B.: Deep gradient compression: reducing the communication bandwidth for distributed training. In: International Conference on Learning Representations (2018)
13. McMahan, B., Moore, E., Ramage, D., Hampson, S., y Arcas, B.A.: Communication-efficient learning of deep networks from decentralized data. In: Artificial Intelligence and Statistics, pp. 1273–1282. PMLR (2017)
14. Murata, T., Suzuki, T.: Accelerated Sparsified SGD with Error Feedback. arXiv preprint arXiv:1905.12224 (2019)
15. Rothchild, D., et al.: FetchSGD: communication-efficient federated learning with sketching. In: International Conference on Machine Learning, pp. 8253–8265. PMLR (2020)
16. Seide, F., Fu, H., Droppo, J., Li, G., Yu, D.: 1-bit stochastic gradient descent and its application to data-parallel distributed training of speech DNNs. In: Fifteenth Annual Conference of the International Speech Communication Association (2014)
17. Shokri, R., Shmatikov, V.: Privacy-preserving deep learning. In: Proceedings of the 22nd ACM SIGSAC Conference on Computer and Communications Security, pp. 1310–1321 (2015)
18. Tran, N.H., Bao, W., Zomaya, A., Nguyen, M.N., Hong, C.S.: Federated learning over wireless networks: optimization model design and analysis. In: IEEE INFOCOM 2019-IEEE Conference on Computer Communications, pp. 1387–1395. IEEE (2019)
19. Wang, S., et al.: Adaptive federated learning in resource constrained edge computing systems. IEEE J. Sel. Areas Commun. 37(6), 1205–1221 (2019)
20. Wen, W., et al.: TernGrad: ternary gradients to reduce communication in distributed deep learning. arXiv preprint arXiv:1705.07878 (2017)

21. Wu, J., Huang, W., Huang, J., Zhang, T.: Error compensated quantized SGD and its applications to large-scale distributed optimization. In: International Conference on Machine Learning, pp. 5325–5333. PMLR (2018)
22. Zhang, J., He, T., Sra, S., Jadbabaie, A.: Why gradient clipping accelerates training: a theoretical justification for adaptivity. In: International Conference on Learning Representations (2020). https://openreview.net/forum?id=BJgnXpVYwS
23. Zhao, S.Y., Xie, Y.P., Gao, H., Li, W.J.: Global momentum compression for sparse communication in distributed SGD. arXiv preprint arXiv:1905.12948 (2019)

A Node Preference-Aware Delegated Proof of Stake Consensus Algorithm With Reward and Punishment Mechanism

Yuanyuan Sun[1], Biwei Yan[2(✉)], Jiguo Yu[2,3], and Xincheng Duan[2]

[1] School of Computer Science, Qufu Normal University, Rizhao 276826, China
[2] School of Computer Science and Technology, Qilu University of Technology
(Shandong Academy of Sciences), Jinan 250353, China
jiguoyu@sina.com
[3] Shandong Laboratory of Computer Networks, Jinan 250014, China

Abstract. Blockchain is a distributed data structure that ensures data security and reliability, and has been widely used in different application scenarios. As the core part of blockchain, consensus algorithm has become the bottleneck of blockchain development, which directly determines the performance of blockchain system. Therefore, considering the preference of nodes, we propose a node preference-aware delegated proof of stake consensus algorithm with reward and punishment mechanism (NPRP-DPoS) to improve the reputation of witness nodes. NPRP-DPoS designs a reward and punishment mechanism to reward or punish generators and voters, and constructs a reputation mechanism to motivate the positive behavior of nodes. At the same time, NPRP-DPoS uses Borda count to select the witness nodes which are more in line with the preference of the voting nodes. The experimental results shows that NPRP-DPoS algorithm can quickly eliminate exception nodes and motivate nodes to vote effectively. Also, NPRP-DPoS algorithm makes the election more fair and reasonable, ensures the interests of nodes and enhances the security of system.

Keywords: Blockchain · Consensus algorithm · Reward and punishment mechanism · Node preference

1 Introduction

Blockchain, as an infrastructure that can realize a secure peer-to-peer transaction system, has attracted attention from academia [1,2], finance [3], industry [4], and different technologies [5,6]. As a peer-to-peer network, there is no trusted

This work was partially supported by NSF of China under Grants 61832012, 61672321, 61771289 and 61373027, and the Science, Education and Industry Integration Innovation Program of Qilu University of Technology (Shandong Academy of Science) under Grant 2020KJC-ZD02.

Z. Liu et al. (Eds.): WASA 2021, LNCS 12937, pp. 572–583, 2021.
https://doi.org/10.1007/978-3-030-85928-2_45

central authority to determine the order of transactions and even blocks. Instead, a consensus mechanism is needed to manage the blockchain. The peers submit valid transactions to the locked blocks, which determine who will propose the next block through the consensus between nodes and form a chronological chain.

At present, PoW (Proof of Work) accounts for more than 90% of the total share of the existing digital currency market, but it is often criticized to varying degrees because of the huge waste of resources and the long generation block cycle. Therefore, PoS (Proof of Stake) is proposed, which can reduce resource waste and transaction delay in PoW. And the time of generating blocks is reduced from 10 min to 60 s. However, it uses the stakes of nodes to compete for the computing power of generating blocks, which can easily lead to the phenomenon that nodes have stakes and do not often participate in competition but can get the accounting right. So, in order to solve this problem, DPoS (Delegated Proof of Stake) select some witness nodes through stake-based voting to represent all nodes to generate blocks in turn, so the time of generating blocks is reduced to 3 s. But in DPoS, there may be exception nodes in the witness node of election, or some nodes controlled by the voters with more stakes. This election method is relatively unreasonable and unfair, ignoring the interests and powers of nodes.

Considering the preference of nodes, we propose a node preference-aware delegated proof of stake consensus algorithm with reward and punishment mechanism (NPRP-DPoS) to improve the reputation of witness nodes, thus ensuring the consensus efficiency of system. First, in election candidate nodes phase, the reputation mechanism is set up, and the reputation value and the number of votes are used as the reference index of node election. It can avoid the nodes with low reputation value participating in consensus, thus realizing the rapid demotion of exception nodes and ensuring the efficiency of system. Then, in election witness nodes phase, Borda count is used to score the preference of candidate nodes, and the nodes that are more consistent with the preference of voting nodes are selected. It makes the selected node more fairer and more in line with the actual situation, thus ensuring the interests of blockchain nodes. Finally, a reward and punishment mechanism based on node role is constructed, and the generators and voters involved are rewarded and punished according to the rules, thus encouraging the nodes to vote and generate blocks actively and effectively.

2   Related Work

To solve the problems of waste of resources, slow trading speed and easy concentration of power in the hands of the rich in PoW [7] and PoS [8], Larimer put forward a consensus algorithm based on stakes voting, which is called DPoS [9]. The node votes according to its own stakes, selects some nodes that participate in election and get the top N number of votes to become the witness nodes, and entrusts them to participate in the transaction verification and accounting. DPoS improves the throughput and verification speed of transaction, but the witness nodes are relatively fixed and generates blocks for a period of time, and can only troubleshoot the problem by skipping exception nodes. This mechanism will bring a lot of security threats. To solve the problems existing in DPoS, Luo et al. [10] improved the ring-based coordinator election algorithm to elect agent nodes, which greatly reduced the transaction cost. In 2019, on this basis, Luo et al. [11] introduced Yao's millionaire algorithm to conduct the second election to achieve secure multi-party computing. Yang et al. [12] proposed a DPoS algorithm with downgrade mechanism, which makes malicious nodes quickly detected and degraded. Meanwhile, the consensus framework proposed by Wang et al. [13] can eliminate malicious nodes and encourage nodes to vote actively in time. Moreover, a randomized delegated proof of stake algorithm proposed by Fan et al. [14] and a hybrid consensus algorithm based on modified proof of probability and DPoS proposed by Wang et al. [15] respectively improve the scalability, security and efficiency of DPoS.

3   The NPRP-DPoS Consensus Algorithm

3.1   Module Framework

The consensus process of NPRP-DPoS consists of three phases: candidate nodes election, witness nodes election, generation block and reward and punishment mechanism. The main modules of NPRP-DPoS are shown in Fig. 1.

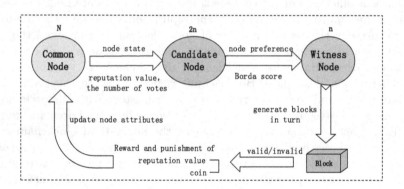

Fig. 1. Module framework of NPRP-DPoS consensus algorithm.

Assume N_{common} represents a set of all N common nodes, that is $\forall N_i, N_i \in N_{common}$. Use $N_{candidate}$ to represent a set of all $2n$ candidate nodes, and use $N_{non-candidate}$ to represent a set of all $N - 2n$ non-candidate nodes, that is $N_{common} = N_{candidate} \cup N_{non-candidate}, N_{candidate} \cap N_{non-candidate} = \varnothing$. For the set of candidate nodes $N_{candidate}$, $N_{witness}$ represents a set of all n witness nodes and $N_{non-witness}$ represents a set of all n non-witness nodes, that is $N_{candidate} = N_{witness} \cup N_{non-witness}, N_{witness} \cap N_{non-witness} = \varnothing$. Thus, the following relationships exist:

$$N_{witness} \subset N_{candidate} \subset N_{common}$$

$$\begin{cases} N_i \in N_{common}, & i \in [1, N] \\ N_i \in N_{candidate}, & i \in [1, 2n] \\ N_i \in N_{non-candidate}, & i \in [1, N - 2n] \\ N_i \in N_{witness}, & i \in [1, n] \\ N_i \in N_{non-witness}, & i \in [1, n] \end{cases}$$

3.2   Candidate Node Election Phase

This phase has two purposes, one is to ensure that the elected candidate nodes have a high credibility, the other is to ensure that exception nodes can achieve rapid detection and demotion. In order to select trusted nodes, we add a reputation value attribute *Reputation* and a state attribute *State* for each node, and classify the state of nodes according to reputation value. Then, all nodes are sorted according to the proposed reputation mechanism and $2n$ candidate nodes are selected. Different constraints on participation of nodes whose states are different in the consensus. The reputation value is counted using a percent system, and the reputation value of all nodes N_{common} is initialized to 50. And according to the reputation mechanism, the state of nodes can be divided into the following three types:

1) Exception State (ES): The malicious behavior state of a node, indicating that the reputation value is located between $[0, 50)$. The node of this state indicates that it is poor in the process of generating blocks and voting, and has the behavior of generating invalid blocks many times.
2) Normal State (NS): The initial state of all nodes, indicating that the reputation value is located between $[50, 100]$. The node of this state indicates that it has just joined the network or is general in the process of generating blocks and voting, and has no obvious positive and malicious behavior.
3) Good State (GS): The good behavior state of a node, indicating that the reputation value is located between $(100, 150]$. The node of this state indicates that it performs well in the process of generating blocks and voting, and does not produce invalid blocks behavior many times.

In order to effectively measure the good or exception of nodes through the reputation value, after the end of each election cycle, the reputation value and state can be updated in combination with the reward and punishment mechanism of the third phase. During the current election cycle, the state of nodes should be transformed according to the generating blocks behavior and voting behavior of nodes, as shown in Fig. 2.

Specific steps at this phase are as follows:

(1) **Step 1. Initialize:** Update the reputation value attribute *Reputation* and state attributes *State* of all nodes N_{common} in the blockchain network during the current election cycle $Round_r$. Assume $Reputation_{N_i}$ represent the reputation value of the node N_i and $State_{N_i}$ represent the state of N_i.

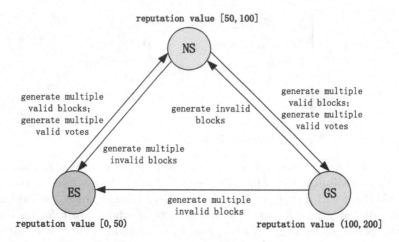

reputation value [50, 100]

NS

generate multiple
valid blocks;
generate multiple
valid votes

generate invalid
blocks

generate multiple
valid blocks;
generate multiple
valid votes

generate multiple
invalid blocks

ES

generate multiple
invalid blocks

GS

reputation value [0, 50)

reputation value (100, 200]

Fig. 2. Node state transition.

(2) **Step 2. Vote:** Any node N_i will vote on its own approved node N_j and broadcast messages about voting $< Hash(N_j, VOTE_{N_i}, Round_r), N_i >$ to the network. $VOTE_{N_i}$ represents the number of votes of N_i. In this voting behavior, the number of votes N_j obtained is proportional to the stake of N_i, and each node is allowed to vote only once.

(3) **Step 3. Count:** After receiving multiple voting messages, the system counts the number of votes obtained by each node. The formula for calculating the number of votes obtained by N_i is $TotalVote_{N_i} = \sum_{k=1}^{|Voter_i|} VOTE_{N_k}$, where $Voter_i$ represents the set of nodes that all votes to N_i.

(4) **Step 4. Sort:** First, according to the number of votes, the nodes in the same state are sorted. And then sort the node state in GS, NS, ES order. That is to say, the overall order is: GS and the number of votes is not 0, NS and the number of votes is not 0, GS and the number of votes is 0, NS and the number of votes is 0, ES and the number of votes is not 0, ES and the number of votes is 0. And construct the final set of node rankings $N_{common-sort}$.

(5) **Step 5. Elect candidate nodes:** Select the top $2n$ nodes from the above sorted $N_{common-sort}$ to become the candidate nodes $N_{candidate}$ for the current election cycle $Round_r$.

3.3   Witness Node Election Phase

In this phase, we consider the preference of nodes in order to further make the election conform to the actual situation and be fair. Borda count is introduced to quantify this value. Meanwhile, $2n$ candidate nodes are sorted and n nodes are selected as witness nodes.

Borda count [16] is an election system that aggregates the whole preference and can be calculated in linear time, which requires low time and calculation cost, so it is often used in a variety of environments [17,18]. In this method, each voter sorts the candidates according to their preferences and sets the corresponding scores according to the ranking order. For example, 10 candidates are ranked, the first candidate is assigned 10 points, the second candidate is assigned 9 points, and so on. Then, the individual preferences of all voters are aggregated into an overall preference. Borda count is different from the majority voting method, it does not tend to choose one of the most popular nodes, but tends to choose that are more in line with the preference of voting nodes and are more easily recognized by widely voting nodes. In this algorithm, assume $2n$ candidate nodes are $N_1^C, N_2^C, N_3^C, ..., N_{2n}^C$ and the weight of Borda count is set to $2n, 2n - 1, ..., 3, 2, 1$.

Specific steps at this phase are as follows:

(1) **Step 1. Initialize**: The system broadcasts messages about candidate nodes $< Round_r, N_{candidate} >$ to each node in the blockchain network, where $Round_r$ represents the current election cycle and $N_{candidate}$ represents a set of all candidate nodes in the current election cycle.

(2) **Step 2. Count**: When the node in non-candidate node set receives the message $< Round_r, N_{candidate} >$, all non-candidate nodes N_i^{NC} sort a preference ordering $Order_{N_i^{NC}}$ according to $N_{candidate}$ and broadcast the message $< Hash(Round_r, N_{candidate}, Order_{N_i^{NC}}), N_i^{NC} >$. After receiving this message, the system needs to verify that $Round_i$ is true. If true, this message is received and the preference ordering information of N_i^{NC} for candidate nodes set $N_{candidate}$ is counted; otherwise, this message is rejected and discarded.

(3) **Step 3. Construct preference matrix and single Borda score**: For each non-candidate node N_k^{NC} ($k \in \{1, 2, ..., N - 2n\}$), there are the following preference rules:

$$b_{ij}^k = \begin{cases} 1, & N_k^{NC} \; prefer \; N_i^C \; to \; N_j^C \\ 0, & N_k^{NC} \; do \; not \; prefer \; N_i^C \; to \; N_j^C \end{cases}$$

If $i = j$, then $b_{ij}^k = 1$. The preference matrix of N_k^{NC} is constructed as follows:

$$B^k = \begin{bmatrix} b_{11}^k & b_{12}^k & \cdots & b_{1(2n)}^k \\ b_{21}^k & b_{22}^k & \cdots & b_{2(2n)}^k \\ \cdots & \cdots & \cdots & \cdots \\ b_{(2n)1}^k & b_{(2n)2}^k & \cdots & b_{(2n)(2n)}^k \end{bmatrix}$$

According to the above preference matrix, the Borda scores of the current nodes N_k^{NC} for the candidate nodes N_i^C can be calculated: $b_i^k = \sum_{j=1}^{2n} b_{ij}^k$.

(4) **Step 4. Construct Borda score matrix and cumulative Borda score**: The Borda scores of all non-candidate nodes for all candidate nodes are calculated according to the above rules, and the Borda score matrix of all non-candidate nodes for all candidate nodes is constructed based on $(N - 2n) \times (2n)$ Borda scores:

$$B = \begin{bmatrix} b_1^1 & b_1^2 & \cdots & b_1^{N-2n} \\ b_2^1 & b_2^2 & \cdots & b_2^{N-2n} \\ \cdots & \cdots & \cdots & \cdots \\ b_{2n}^1 & b_{2n}^2 & \cdots & b_{2n}^{N-2n} \end{bmatrix}$$

Then, the cumulative Borda scores of all non-candidate nodes on the candidate nodes N_i^C are calculated according to the above Borda score matrix: $b_i = \sum_{k=1}^{N-2n} b_i^k$.

(5) **Step 5. Elect witness nodes**: Rank the final cumulative Borda score and select the top n nodes as the witness nodes $N_{witness}$ for the current election cycle $Round_r$.

3.4   Block Generation Phase

In this phase, in order to solve the problem that most nodes in DPoS do not vote actively, we construct a reward and punishment mechanism based on node role. The witness nodes generated in phase 2 alternately generate blocks and broadcast blocks to other witness nodes for verification. At the same time, a validity mark is defined for each block, which is located in the head of block, indicating that the block is valid or invalid, marked as $Valid$ or $Invalid$ respectively.

For the witness node generating blocks, if the generated block is valid, reward the node with a reputation value of 5 points and 10 coins. If the block is invalid, punish the node with a reputation value of 10 points and 20 coins. And in order to encourage the node to strive for the right to account and get the income, it is necessary to pay a deposit of 50 coins when the node joins the network. Therefore, it urges the witness nodes to reduce the generation of invalid blocks, motivate the node to continuously generate effective blocks, and improve the reliability of witness nodes and the security of system. For the nodes participating in the voting, when a valid block is generated, the reliability of the elected witness node is higher. Then all the voting nodes voting to the witness node will be rewarded with coins and reputation values according to the corresponding voting number ratio. When an invalid block is generated, it is proved that the reliability of the elected witness node is not high, so it is necessary to punish all the voting nodes with a certain proportion of coins and reputation value. It positively motivates the nodes to vote effectively and suppresses the nodes to vote invalidly. The formula of reward and punishment for voters is as follows:

$$\begin{aligned} RewardCoin_i &= VOTE_i/TotalVote \times 10 \\ PunishmentCoin_i &= VOTE_i/TotalVote \times 20 \\ RewardReputation_i &= VOTE_i/TotalVote \times 5 \\ PunishmentReputation_i &= VOTE_i/TotalVote \times 10 \end{aligned}$$

where $VOTE_i$ represents the number of votes of the current node N_i and $TotalVote$ represents all the votes obtained by the node that N_i votes to.

Specific steps at this phase are as follows:

(1) **Step 1. Generate block**: The witness node N_i^W in the witness node set $N_{witness}$ generates a block $Block_{N_i^W}$. The block consists of a hash of the previous block $HASH(PreBlock)$, a timestamp $TimeStamp$, a mining difficulty value set by the system D, a random value $nonce$, a Merkle tree root $MerkleTreeRoot$, and a number of transactions Txs. $Block_{N_i^W}$ expressed as follows:

$$Block_{N_i^W} = \langle HASH(PreBlock), TimeStamp, D, nonce, MerkleTreeRoot, Txs \rangle$$

(2) **Step 2. Broadcast and verify**: The witness nodes that take turns with accounting rights will generate blocks in turn and broadcast their own generated blocks to the blockchain network. After the remaining witness nodes receive the $Block_{N_i^W}$ message, verify that the block is valid. If more than 50% of the nodes are verified, the state of $Block_{N_i^W}$ is $Valid$, and the block is appended to the blockchain; otherwise, the state of $Block_{N_i^W}$ is $Invalid$.

(3) **Step 3. Reward**: If the state of $Block_{N_i^W}$ is $Valid$, N_i^W will be rewarded. Update $Balance_{N_i^W}$ and $Reputation_{N_i^W}$ attributes as follows: $Balance_{N_i^W} = Balance_{N_i^W} + 10$; $Reputation_{N_i^W} = Reputation_{N_i^W} + 5$. At the same time, all the nodes voting to N_i^W (nodes in $Voter_{N_i^W}$) are rewarded as follows: $Balance_{N_i^V} = Balance_{N_i^V} + VOTE_{N_i^V}/TotalVote_{N_i^W} \times 10$; $Reputation_{N_i^V} = Reputation_{N_i^V} + VOTE_{N_i^V}/TotalVote_{N_i^W} \times 5$.

(4) **Step 4. Punish**: If the state of $Block_{N_i^W}$ is $Invalid$, N_i^W will be punished. Update $Balance_{N_i^W}$ and $Reputation_{N_i^W}$ attributes as follows: $Balance_{N_i^W} = Balance_{N_i^W} - 20$; $Reputation_{N_i^W} = Reputation_{N_i^W} - 10$. At the same time, all the nodes voting to N_i^W (nodes in $Voter_{N_i^W}$) are punished as follows: $Balance_{N_i^V} = Balance_{N_i^V} - VOTE_{N_i^V}/TotalVote_{N_i^W} \times 20$; $Reputation_{N_i^V} = Reputation_{N_i^V} - VOTE_{N_i^V}/TotalVote_{N_i^W} \times 10$.

In this phase, in order to ensure that the reputation value meets the standard range of node state classification, when $Reputation_{N_i^W}$ value reaches 150 upward, the node will no longer be rewarded with the reputation value, and $Reputation_{N_i^W}$ value will remain at 150, but can be punished. When $Reputation_{N_i^W}$ value reaches 0 down, this node no longer punishes the reputation value, and $Reputation_{N_i^W}$ value will remain at 0, but can be rewarded.

4   Performance and Experimental Analysis

The experimental environment of this algorithm is Intel(R) Core(TM) i5-5200U CPU @ 2.20 GHz processor, 12.0 GB memory, 64-bit Ubuntu 16.04 system. Under this configuration, the blockchain system based on NPRP-DPoS algorithm is simulated on the Goland using Go language. This system builds a distributed network with 6 nodes, in which the number of election candidate nodes is 4, and the number of election witness nodes is 2. In this experiment, 30 rounds of simulated random voting are carried out, and it is assumed that the exception node is node 1 between the 11th and 20th rounds, and the exception node is node 4 between the 21st and 30th rounds. And each node has 9 important attributes. The reputation value and balance of the node are initialized to 50 and 100, respectively. The initialization of node preferences is shown in Table 1.

Table 1. Initialization of preferences of each node.

Node preference ordering	1st	2nd	3rd	4th	5th	6th
Node 1	Node 5	Node 1	Node 3	Node 2	Node 6	Node 4
Node 2	Node 2	Node 6	Node 4	Node 1	Node 3	Node 5
Node 3	Node 2	Node 4	Node 3	Node 1	Node 5	Node 6
Node 4	Node 1	Node 6	Node 5	Node 2	Node 4	Node 3
Node 5	Node 6	Node 4	Node 3	Node 5	Node 1	Node 2
Node 6	Node 4	Node 5	Node 1	Node 2	Node 6	Node 3

4.1 Security

In NPRP-DPoS, the block is safe and legal as long as $n/2+1$ good witness nodes can verify and reply. First of all, assume that the blocks that are originally in *Invalid* condition can be maliciously validated as *Valid*. And then, because in the process of validating the block, only more than 50% of confirmation reply is received to consider the block as *Valid*. That is, if the number of good witness nodes is greater than $n/2+1$, the *Invalid* block estimation will not be maliciously verified as *Valid*. At this point, the maximum number of malicious witness nodes is $n - (n/2 + 1) = n/2 - 1$. This is in contradiction with the above hypothesis. Therefore, it is proved that as long as there are $n/2 + 1$ good witness nodes that can verify and reply, more than 50% of correct reply can be received, and the validity or invalidity of the block will not be misjudged, which ensures the security and legitimacy of the block.

4.2 Reputation Mechanism Verification

The comparison of election ranking of exception node 1 in 30 rounds of voting in Fig. 3(a) shows that the evaluation value ranking of node 1 in NPRP-DPoS is obviously lower than that in DPoS. From the state change of exception node 1 in Fig. 3(b), it can be seen that when node 1 has exception behavior in exception rounds, the state of node will be degraded quickly in just a few rounds, although it will be upgraded because of effective voting. But once invalid blocks appear, there is a tendency to lower state levels. According to this, the reputation mechanism proposed in NPRP-DPoS can reduce the ranking of exception nodes and realize the rapid demotion of exception nodes, thus further reducing the probability of exception nodes becoming witness nodes.

4.3 Node Preference Mechanism Verification

As can be seen from the comparison of the number of selected as witness nodes in Fig. 4, most of the number of selected as witness nodes has changed, which indicates that the use of node preference mechanism does change the election result of node. Meanwhile, according to the initialization of node preference ranking in Table 1, we can calculate the overall preference ranking: (node1, node4), node2,(node5, node6), node3, where the brackets indicate that the Borda scores of the two nodes are the same and can not distinguish the ranking order. It can be seen from the change of the number of selected as witness nodes of each node that the initial preference ranking of all nodes is considered in the election of witness nodes, and the ranking order is relatively consistent. This shows that the node preference mechanism proposed in NPRP-DPoS can effectively follow the preference intention of node and be more in line with the actual situation, so that the node can be elected more in line with the public opinion.

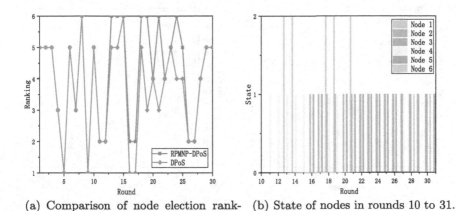

(a) Comparison of node election rankings of exception node 1.

(b) State of nodes in rounds 10 to 31.

Fig. 3. Validation of reputation mechanism.

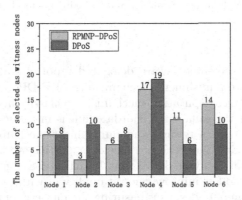

Fig. 4. Comparison of the number of selected as witness nodes.

4.4   Reward and Punishment Mechanism Verification

From Fig. 5(a) and Fig. 5(b), we can see that the reputation value and balance of all nodes in NPRP-DPoS show an overall growth trend. It shows that as long as the node produces a valid block or makes a valid vote, the reputation value and balance are rewarded. From the change trend of the assumed exception node 1 and exception node 4, it can be seen that the reputation value and balance of exception node 1 show a downward trend in round 11–20 and the reputation value and balance of exception node 4 also show a downward trend in round 21–30. This shows that as long as an invalid block is generated in a specified round, the reputation value and balance of the node that generates the block are punished. After the reward and punishment mechanism is introduced, the credibility of the witness node is improved by effective block generation and effective voting. The higher the credibility, the more the node gains, thus encouraging the node to vote effectively and generate the block effectively.

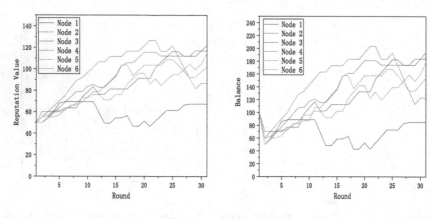

(a) Reputation value change for all nodes.   (b) Balance change for all nodes.

Fig. 5. Validation of reward and punishment mechanism.

5   Conclusion

We propose a node preference-aware delegated proof of stake consensus algorithm with reward and punishment mechanism (NPRP-DPoS) to improve DPoS. This algorithm designs a reputation mechanism to classify node states based on reputation value. At the same time, Borda count is introduced to calculate the preference of nodes, and a reward and punishment mechanism is designed to reward or punish nodes that generate blocks or participate in voting. Theoretical and experimental analysis shows that NPRP-DPoS algorithm can quickly eliminate exception nodes, improve the rationality of witness node election and the voting enthusiasm of nodes, thus ensuring the interests of nodes and enhancing the security of system.

References

1. Wang, H., Zheng, Z., Xie, S., Dai, H.N., Chen, X.: Blockchain challenges and opportunities: a survey. Int. J. Web Grid Services **14**(4), 352 (2018)
2. Sun, Z., Wang, Y., Cai, Z., et al.: A two-stage privacy protection mechanism based on blockchain in mobile crowdsourcing. Int. J. Intell. Syst. **36**(5), 2058–2080 (2021)
3. Kabra, N., Bhattacharya, P., Tanwar, S., Tyagi, S.: MudraChain: blockchain-based framework for automated cheque clearance in financial institutions. Future Gener. Comput. Syst. **102**, 574–587 (2020)
4. Bodkhe, U., et al.: Blockchain for industry 4.0: a comprehensive review. IEEE Access **8**, 79764–79800 (2020)
5. Zhu, S., Cai, Z., Hu, H., et al.: zkCrowd: a hybrid blockchain-based crowdsourcing platform. IEEE Trans. Industr. Inf. **16**(6), 4196–4205 (2019)
6. Zhu, S., Li, W., Li, H., et al.: Coin hopping attack in blockchain-based IoT. IEEE Internet Things J. **6**(3), 4614–4626 (2018)
7. Nakamoto, S.: Bitcoin: a peer-to-peer electronic cash system (2009). https://bitcoin.org/bitcoin.pdf/
8. King, S., Nadal, S.: PPcoin: peer-to-peer crypto-currency with proof-of-stake. Self-published paper (2012)
9. Gramoli, V.: From blockchain consensus back to Byzantine consensus. Future Gener. Comput. Syst. Available (2017). https://doi.org/10.1016/j.future.2017.09.023
10. Luo, Y., Chen, Y., Chen, Q.: A new election algorithm for DPos consensus mechanism in blockchain. In: 2018 7th International Conference on Digital Home (ICDH), Guilin, China, pp. 116–120 (2018)
11. Luo, Y., Wu, Y., Wang, J.: MPC-DPOS: an efficient consensus algorithm based on secure multi-party computation. In: 2019 2nd International Conference on Blockchain Technology and Applications, pp. 105–112 (2019)
12. Yang, F., Zhou, W., Wu, Q.: Delegated proof of stake with downgrade: a secure and efficient blockchain consensus algorithm with downgrade mechanism. IEEE Access **7**, 118541–118555 (2019)
13. Wang, B., Hu, Y., Li, S.: A blockchain consensus mechanism for educational administration system. In: 2019 IEEE 2nd International Conference on Electronics Technology (ICET), Chengdu, China, pp. 603–608 (2019)
14. Fan, X., Chai, Q.: Roll-DPoS: a randomized delegated proof of stake scheme for scalable blockchain-based internet of things systems. In: The 15th EAI International Conference on Mobile and Ubiquitous Systems: Computing, Networking and Services, NY, USA, pp. 482–484 (2018)
15. Wang, B., Li, Z., Li, H.: Hybrid consensus algorithm based on modified proof-of-probability and DPoS. Future Internet **12**(8), 122 (2020)
16. Borda, J.: A paper on elections by ballot (English translation). Condorcet Found. Soc. Choice Polit. Theor., 114–119 (1994)
17. Bag, S., Azad, M., Hao, F.: E2E verifiable borda count voting system without tallying authorities. In: 14th International Conference on Availability, Reliability and Security, pp. 1–9 (2019)
18. Chao, T., Liang, X.: DPoSB: delegated Proof of Stake with node's behavior and Borda Count. In: 2020 IEEE 5th Information Technology and Mechatronics Engineering Conference (ITOEC), Chongqing, China, pp. 429–1434 (2020)

Minimizing Energy Consumption with Devices Placement and Scheduling in Internet of Things

Chuanwen Luo[1,2], Yi Hong[1,2(✉)], Zhibo Chen[1,2], Deying Li[3], and Jiguo Yu[4,5]

[1] School of Information Science and Technology, Beijing Forestry University,
Beijing 100083, People's Republic of China
{chuanwenluo,hongyi,zhibo}@bjfu.edu.cn
[2] Engineering Research Center for Forestry-oriented Intelligent Information
Processing of National Forestry and Grassland Administration,
Beijing 100083, People's Republic of China
[3] School of Information, Renmin University of China,
Beijing 100872, People's Republic of China
deyingli@ruc.edu.cn
[4] School of Computer Science and Technology,
Qilu University of Technology (Shandong Academy of Sciences),
Jinan 250353, Shandong, People's Republic of China
jiguoyu@sina.com
[5] The Shandong Laboratory of Computer Networks,
Jinan 250014, People's Republic of China

Abstract. The Internet of Things (IoT) is an emerging paradigm which makes billions of IoT devices integrate to the Internet, and enables them to gather and exchange information. The Low-Power Wide Area Network (LPWAN) technologies, such as LoRa, SigFox, NB-IoT, bring new renovation to the wireless communication between end devices in the IoTs, which can provide larger coverage and support a large number of IoT devices to connect Internet with few gateways. Based on these technologies, we can directly deploy IoT devices on the candidate locations to cover targets without considering multi-hops data transmission to the base station like the traditional wireless sensor networks. In this paper, we investigate the problem of the Minimum Energy consumption of IoT devices through Placement and Scheduling (MEPS), where we consider both the placement and scheduling of IoT devices to monitor all targets such that all targets are continuously observed for a certain period of time. The objective of the problem is to minimize the total energy consumption of the IoT devices. We first propose the mathematical model for the MEPS problem and prove that the MEPS problem is NP-hard. Then we study two sub-problems of the MEPS problem, Minimum Location Coverage (MLC) and Minimum Energy consumption Scheduling Deployment (MESD), and propose an approximation algorithm for each

Supported in part by the National Natural Science Foundation of China under Grants (62002022, 32071775), also supported by the Fundamental Research Funds for the Central Universities (No. BLX201921).

of them. Based on these two sub-problems, we propose an approximation algorithm with the approximation ratio $2(\ln m + 1)$ for the MEPS problem, where m is the number of targets.

Keywords: Coverage problem · Internet of Things · Network placement and scheduling · Approximation algorithm

1   Introduction

The Internet of Things (IoT) is a flourishing paradigm in the scenario of modern wireless telecommunications, which has been provided a wide diversity applications for all walks of life in modern time, such as mobile devices applications [13], smart systems [4] and so on. IoT applications are required a growing number of technologies to offer low-power operation, low-cost and low-complexity IoT devices that will be able to communicate wirelessly over long distances. As the development of the Low Power Wide Area Network (LPWAN) technologies, such as SigFox, NB-IoT and LoRa, long-range and wide-area communication at low power has become reality [8]. Since the long range communication of the LPWAN technologies are gradually used in the IoTs, the IoT devices can only communicate with LPWAN gateways and do not need to communicate directly with each other. Taking LoRa for example, a single gateway can support as many as 10^5 IoT devices, and three gateways are enough to cover all devices in urban area within an approximately 15 Km radius [12]. The architecture of the LPWAN-based Internet of Things is shown in Fig. 1, in which IoT devices are deployed in the monitoring area to observe targets or to detect the environment and few gateways over the territory gather data from IoT devices that are placed at different miles from the gateways. Then the received data by the gateways is transmitted to the users through the Internet or Satellite for further computational analysis to determine the appropriate response mechanism.

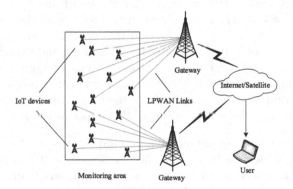

Fig. 1. The architecture of the LPWAN-based Internet of Things.

From the architecture of the LPWAN-based Internet of Things, we can directly deploy IoT devices to monitor all targets in any region with LPWAN-based network without considering other data transmission methods such as virtual backbone networks [6] and mobile data collectors [3,9]. Since many IoT devices are battery-powered sensors, for example, in Wireless Sensor Networks (WSNs), the power usage profile should be carefully designed in order to extend the battery lifetime. How to prolong the network lifetime is a classic problem in WSNs, which is called the coverage problem [10]. Researches on coverage problem benefit a lot of applications, such as environment monitoring, battlefield surveillance, and military facility [2]. Recently, many researches proposed various problems and corresponding algorithms for the coverage problem. In [5], Cardei et al. studied the target coverage problem with the objective of maximizing the network lifetime of a power constrained WSN deployed for detecting of a set of targets with known locations. However, they did not consider the placement of sensors in the problem. In [1], Akhlaghinia et al. studied the heterogeneous point coverage problem in sensor placement to cover a large number of targets with various coverage requirements using a minimum number of heterogeneous sensors. In the problem, they only investigated the placement of sensors without considering network lifetime. In [11], Mini et al. considered both the deployment locations and scheduling of the given IoT devices to maximize the network lifetime with the required coverage level. However, they deployed all available IoT devices to cover targets randomly without considered candidate sites of them. Although they proposed algorithms to solve the placement problem and coverage scheduling problem of IoT devices, they ignored the corresponding theoretical analysis for the algorithms.

In the above literature, they only considered one of the deployment and scheduling of IoT devices or ignored the factor that candidate sites can be placed by IoT devices which has to be considered in some applications, such as smart city. Actually, to minimize the total energy consumption of IoT devices, we need to consider not only the deployment of IoT devices but also the scheduling of them. Meanwhile, due to the emergence of wireless charging technologies and natural energy charging methods (e.g. solar charging) for the IoT devices, the current applications of IoTs have shifted from maximizing the network lifetime to working for a certain period of time. In this paper, we study the Minimum Energy consumption of IoT devices through Placement and Scheduling (MEPS) problem, where we consider both the placement and scheduling of IoT devices to monitor all targets in a region such that all targets are continuously observed for a certain period of time, and the total energy consumption of all used IoT devices is minimized. The contributions of this paper are shown as below.

(1) We propose a new practical model of minimizing the total energy consumption of all IoT devices by placing the IoT devices and scheduling them for continuously observing all targets for a certain period of time. Then we define the problem as the Minimum Energy consumption of IoT devices through Placement and Scheduling (MEPS) problem, and prove that it is NP-hard.

(2) To solve the MEPS problem, we introduce two other problems, Minimum Location Coverage (MLC) problem and Minimum Energy consumption Scheduling Deployment (MESD) problem. Then we present an approximation algorithm for each of them. Afterwards, an approximation algorithm for the MEPS problem is proposed on the basis of the solutions for the MLC and MESD problems.

(3) We illustrate the effectiveness of the proposed algorithm by theoretical analysis.

The remainder of this paper is organized as follows. Section 2 introduces some models and definition for the MEPS problem. Section 3 proposes an approximation algorithm to solve the MEPS problem. Section 4 concludes the paper.

2   Model and Problem Definition

Let $\mathcal{A}$ be represented as a two-dimensional plane area. There are m targets located on $\mathcal{A}$, which need to be observed by IoT devices. Let $Q = \{r_1, r_2, \cdots, r_m\}$ represent the set of m targets located on $\mathcal{A}$. Due to the particularity of some detection areas, such as smart cities, IoT devices can only be deployed on some fixed locations. We call these fixed locations as *candidate sites* of IoT devices. Let $L = \{L_1, L_2, \cdots, L_N\}$ denote the set of N candidate sites. Suppose that there exists n available IoT devices that can be deployed candidate sites to monitor targets in Q. We use $S = \{s_1, s_2, \cdots, s_n\}$ to represent the set of n IoT devices, in which each IoT device s_i can be active continuously at most E_i time slots. Without loss of generality, we assume that there are enough candidate sites to put IoT devices for observing all targets in Q. In this paper, we assume that each IoT device $s_i \in S$ continuously works E_i time slots once it starts working, and $E_i \leq T$, where T is the minimum required continuous working time of IoT devices for observing targets. For any pair of $s_i \in S$ and $r_j \in Q$ (or $L_k \in L$ and $r_j \in Q$), let d_{s_i, r_j} (or d_{L_k, r_j}) denote the Euclidean distance between s_i and r_j (or L_k and r_j).

In this paper, we aim to find a subset $C \subseteq S$ of IoT devices which are deployed on the some candidates sites in L to observe all targets in Q, and to minimize the total energy consumption of all IoT devices by scheduling IoT devices in C such that all targets can be continuously observed at least T time. More formally, we call the research problem as the Minimum Energy consumption of IoT devices through Placement and Scheduling (MEPS), whose detailed definition is shown in Definition 1.

Definition 1 (MEPS). *Given a set $Q = \{r_1, r_2, \cdots, r_m\}$ of m targets, a set $S = \{s_1, s_2, \cdots, s_n\}$ of n IoT devices in which all IoT devices have the same coverage range R and each IoT device $s_i \in S$ can work E_i time slots, a set $L = \{L_1, L_2, \cdots, L_N\}$ of N candidate sites to be put IoT devices, a positive time T, the Minimum Energy consumption of IoT devices through Placement and Scheduling (MEPS) problem aims at finding a subset $C \subseteq S$ of IoT devices placed on the candidate sites in L and scheduling the IoT devices in C such that*

(1) *for any candidate site $L_k \in L$, it can be placed more than one IoT device from C,*

(2) *for arbitrary target $r_j \in Q$, it is continuously observed by IoT devices in C at least T time,*

(3) *for each IoT device $s_i \in C$, it keeps working E_i time slots once it starts working, and,*

(4) *the total energy consumption of IoT devices in C, $M = \sum_{s_i \in C} E_i$, is minimized.*

Next, we will introduce the mathematical formulation for the MEPS problem. The problem can be formulated into an Integer Programming (IP) problem as below. We first introduce some notations as follows.

i: index of IoT devices, where $1 \le i \le n$.
j: index of targets, where $1 \le j \le m$.
k: index of candidate sites, where $1 \le k \le N$.
t: index of active time slots, where T time is divided into T time slots.
We define the binary variables x_{ik}, a_{jk} and y_{it} as below.

$$x_{ik} = \begin{cases} 1, & \text{if } s_i \text{ is placed at } L_k, \\ 0, & \text{otherwise.} \end{cases} \tag{1}$$

$$a_{jk} = \begin{cases} 1, & \text{if } d_{L_k, r_j} \le R, \\ 0, & \text{otherwise.} \end{cases} \tag{2}$$

$$y_{it} = \begin{cases} 1, & \text{if } s_i \text{ is active at } t \text{ time slot,} \\ 0, & \text{otherwise.} \end{cases} \tag{3}$$

We can obtain the following mathematical formulation of the MEPS problem.

$$Minimize \ \sum_{k=1}^{N} \sum_{i=1}^{n} x_{ik} \cdot E_i \tag{4}$$

s.t.

$$\sum_{k=1}^{N} \sum_{i=1}^{n} a_{jk} \cdot x_{ik} \cdot y_{it} \ge 1 \qquad j = 1, 2, \cdots, m, \ \ t = 1, 2, \cdots, T \tag{5}$$

$$\sum_{k=1}^{N} \sum_{t=b_i}^{b_i + E_i - 1} x_{ik} \cdot y_{it} = E_i \quad \exists b_i \in \{1, 2, \cdots, T\}, \ i = 1, 2, \cdots, n \tag{6}$$

$$x_{ik} \in \{0, 1\} \qquad\qquad i = 1, 2, \cdots, n, \ k = 1, 2, \cdots, N \tag{7}$$

$$a_{jk} \in \{0, 1\} \qquad\qquad j = 1, 2, \cdots, m, \ k = 1, 2, \cdots, N \tag{8}$$

$$y_{it} \in \{0, 1\} \qquad\qquad i = 1, 2, \cdots, n, \ t = 1, 2, \cdots, T \tag{9}$$

The function (4) is to minimize the total energy consumption of IoT devices for continuously observing all targets at least T time. Constraint (5) ensures that for each target $r_j \in Q$, there at least exists an IoT device $s_i \in S$ located at some candidate site $L_k \in L$ to cover r_j at any t-th time slot. Constraint (6) guarantees that the IoT device $s_i \in S$ located on $L_k \in L$ will run out of energy as soon as it starts working. Constraints (7)–(9) define the domains of the variables.

In the following, we will prove that the MEPS problem is NP-hard. We consider a special case of the MEPS problem, in which we set $T = 1$, $N = n$, $E_i = 1$ for any IoT device $s_i \in S$. At this point, the objective of the MEPS problem can be transformed into finding a subset $C \subseteq S$ of IoT devices with minimum cardinality such that all targets are covered. Since for any $s_i \in C$, it needs to be placed at corresponding candidate site to cover targets, the objective of the MEPS problem changes from finding the minimum subset C to looking for the minimum subset $L' \subseteq L$ of candidate sites, where $|C| = |L'|$. Therefore, the special case of the MEPS problem can be equivalently transformed into the Minimum Point Coverage (MPC) problem, as shown in Definition 2.

Definition 2 (MPC). *Given a set $Q = \{r_1, r_2, \cdots, r_m\}$ of m targets, a set $L = \{L_1, L_2, \cdots, L_N\}$ of N candidate sites to be put IoT devices, all IoT devices have the same coverage range R, the Minimum Point Coverage (MPC) problem is to find a subset $L' \subseteq L$ of candidate sites such that all targets are covered by IoT devices located on the candidate sites in L' and $|L'|$ is minimized.*

In the MPC problem, for each candidate site $L_k \in L$, we use U_k to denote the set of targets covered by L_k where for each target r_j, $r_j \in U_k$ if and only if $d_{L_k, r_j} \leq R$. Let $F = \{U_1, U_2, \cdots, U_N\}$. Then the MPC problem can be equivalently transformed into the Set Cover (SC) problem, which is a classic NP-hard problem.

Theorem 1. *The MPC problem is NP-hard.*

Proof. According to the definitions of SC and MPC problems, we can obtain that the decision version of the MPC problem has a YES answer if and only if the decision version of the SC problem has a YES answer and $|F'| = |L'|$. Since the SC problem was proved NP-hard [7], the MPC problem is NP-hard.

Theorem 2. *The MEPS problem is NP-hard.*

Proof. According to the Theorem 1, we can obtain that the MPC problem is NP-hard. Since the MPC problem is a special case of the MEPS problem, the MEPS problem is also NP-hard.

3   Algorithm for the MEPS Problem

According to the definition of the MEPS problem, we can obtain that the total energy consumption of IoT devices depends on the number of placed IoT devices with their corresponding initial energy. Therefore, we need to deploy IoT devices as few as possible to cover targets, and schedule the deployed IoT devices to minimize the total energy consumption such that every target in Q is continuously observed at least T time slots by IoT devices. Based on these considerations, we can find that the MEPS problem consists of two sub-problems, Minimum Location Coverage (MLC) and Minimum Energy consumption Scheduling Deployment (MESD), as shown in Definitions 3 and 4. In this section, we first propose an approximation algorithm for each of the MLC and MESD problems. Then based on the problems MLC and MESD, we propose an approximation algorithm for the MEPS problem.

Definition 3 (MLC). *Given a set $Q = \{r_1, r_2, \cdots, r_m\}$ of m targets, a set $L = \{L_1, L_2, \cdots, L_N\}$ of N candidate sites to be put IoT devices with coverage range R, the Minimum Location Coverage (MLC) problem is to find minimum subset $L' \subseteq L$ of candidate sites such that all targets are within the coverage range of candidate sites in L'.*

Definition 4 (MESD). *Given a set $S = \{s_1, s_2, \cdots, s_n\}$ of n IoT devices in which each IoT device $s_i \in S$ carries E_i active time slots, a set $P = \{L_1, L_2, \cdots, L_K\}$ of K sites to be put IoT devices, a positive time T, the Minimum Energy consumption Scheduling Deployment (MESD) problem is to find a subset $C \subseteq S$ of IoT devices placed at the sites in P and to schedule the IoT devices in C such that*

(1) for any site $L_k \in P$, it can be placed more than one IoT device from C,
(2) for arbitrary site $L_k \in P$, the IoT devices located at L_k can cumulatively work at least T time,
(3) for each IoT device $s_i \in C$, it keeps working E_i time once it starts working, and,
(4) the total energy consumption of IoT devices in C, $M = \sum_{s_i \in C} E_i$, is minimized.

3.1   Algorithm for MLC Problem

In this subsection, we propose a greedy algorithm, called MLCA, to solve the MLC problem. Let U_k denote the set of targets within the coverage range of L_k, which is called the coverage set of L_k. The MLCA algorithm contains two steps. Firstly, for arbitrary $L_k \in L$, we compute its coverage set U_k. For any $r_j \in Q$, if $d_{L_k, r_j} \leq R$, then $U_k = U_k \cup \{r_j\}$. Secondly, we repeats the following steps until one of the conditions $L = \emptyset$ and $Q \neq \emptyset$ is satisfied.

– Select L_k with the maximum U_k from L.
– Execute the operations $L' = L' \cup \{L_k\}$, $L = L \setminus \{L_k\}$ and $Q = Q \setminus U_k$.
– For arbitrary $L_i \in L$, update its coverage set by deleting targets in $U_k \cap U_i$ from U_i.

After executing the above algorithm, if there exists solution for the MLC problem, we can obtain a set $L' \subseteq L$ of candidate sites, which can cover all targets in Q. The pseudo code of the MLCA algorithm is shown in Algorithm 1. Then we will analyze the performance of the MLCA algorithm.

Algorithm 1. MLCA

Input: $Q = \{r_1, r_2, \cdots, r_m\}$, $L = \{L_1, L_2, \cdots, L_N\}$, R;
Output: L';
1: Sets of $L' = \emptyset$, $U_k = \emptyset$ for any $L_k \in L$;
2: **for** arbitrary $L_k \in L$ **do**
3:     **for** any $r_j \in Q$ **do**
4:         **if** $d_{L_k, r_j} \leq R$ **then**
5:             $U_k = U_k \cup \{r_j\}$;
6:         **end**
7:     **end**
8: **end**
9: **while** $L \neq \emptyset$ && $Q \neq \emptyset$ **do**
10:     Pick $L_k = arg\max_{L_k \in L} U_k$, $L' = L' \cup \{L_k\}$, $L = L \setminus \{L_k\}$, $Q = Q \setminus U_k$;
11:     **for** any $L_i \in L$ **do**
12:         $U_i = U_i \setminus U_k$;
13:     **end**
14: **end**
15: **if** $Q \neq \emptyset$ **then**
16:     There is no solution for the MLC problem;
17: **end**

Theorem 3. *If there exists solution for the MLC problem, then we suppose L^* is an optimal solution for the MLC problem. We can obtain the approximation ratio of the MLCA algorithm is $\ln m + 1$, where m is the number of targets.*

Proof. If there exists solution for the MLC problem, according to the MLCA algorithm, we can observe that the while loop terminates after executing at most m steps, since in each iteration of the while loop, at least one target is covered by candidate site L_k. Let Q_k denote the number of targets that are still not covered at iteration k of the while loop. In each iteration k, we can use all $|L^*|$ candidate sites in the optimal solution to cover all targets in Q. Therefore, there must exist a candidate site in L^* that covers at least $Q_k/|L^*|$ targets, which means at least $Q_k/|L^*|$ targets are covered in every iteration. In other words, we can obtain after iteration k, there are left at most $Q_k - Q_k/|L^*|$ targets that have not been covered by candidate sites, that is

$$Q_{k+1} \leq (1 - \frac{1}{|L^*|}) \cdot Q_k \leq (1 - \frac{1}{|L^*|})^2 \cdot Q_{k-1} \leq, \cdots ,$$
$$\leq (1 - \frac{1}{|L^*|})^{k+1} \cdot Q_0 = (1 - \frac{1}{|L^*|})^{k+1} \cdot m, \tag{10}$$

where the last equality depends on the fact that $Q_0 = m$, since all m tragets are not covered by candidate sites before the first iteration of the while loop. Notice that there exists $1 \leq i \leq m$ such that after executing i iterations of the while loop, $Q_i \leq 1$. Based on the fact that $1 + x \leq e^x$ for any $x \in (-\infty, +\infty)$, we have

$$(1 - \frac{1}{|L^*|})^i = ((1 - \frac{1}{|L^*|})^{|L^*|})^{\frac{i}{|L^*|}} \leq e^{-\frac{i}{|L^*|}} \tag{11}$$

Based on inequations (10) and (11), we can obtain

$$m \cdot e^{-\frac{i}{|L^*|}} \leq 1 \iff i \geq |L^*| \cdot \ln m \tag{12}$$

Therefore, we can obtain that after $i = |L^*| \cdot \ln m$ iterations, the remaining number of targets in Q_i is less than or equal to 1. Thus, the algorithm will terminate after at most $|L^*| \cdot \ln m + 1$ iterations, which can obtain $|L'| \leq |L^*| \cdot \ln m + 1 \leq (\ln m + 1) \cdot |L^*|$, since $|L^*| \geq 1$ and only one candidate site is added into L' in each iteration based on the algorithm MLCA.

3.2   Algorithm for the MESD Problem

In this subsection, we propose an approximation algorithm for solving the MESD problem, called MESDA. Before describing the algorithm, we introduce some notations. For any $1 \leq k \leq K$, we use C_k to denote the set of IoT devices placed at location L_k, and let $\Phi = \{C_1, C_2, \cdots, C_K\}$. Let M_k represent the total energy consumption of IoT devices in C_k.

Algorithm 2. MESDA

Input: $S = \{s_1, s_2, \cdots, s_n\}$, E_i for each $s_i \in S$, $P = \{L_1, L_2, \cdots, L_K\}$, T;
Output: C, M, Φ;
1: Sets of $C = \emptyset$, $M = 0$, $C_k = \emptyset$ and $M_k = 0$ for each $1 \leq k \leq K$;
2: **while** $P \neq \emptyset$ && $S \neq \emptyset$ **do**
3:     Pick $s_i = arg\max_{s_i \in S} E_i$;
4:     Pick $L_k = arg\min_{L_k \in P} M_k$;
5:     $C_k = C_k \cup \{s_i\}$, $M_k = M_k + E_i$, $S = S \setminus \{s_i\}$;
6:     **if** $M_k \geq T$ **then**
7:         $P = P \setminus \{L_k\}$;
8:     **end**
9: **end**
10: **while** $S \neq \emptyset$ **do**
11:     Pick $s_i = arg\max_{s_i \in S} E_i$;
12:     Select $< s_j, k > = arg \min_{s_j \in C_k, 1 \leq k \leq K} (M_k - E_j + E_i)$ such that $M_k - E_j + E_i \geq T$;
13:     **if** $E_i \geq E_j$ **then**
14:         $S = S \setminus \{s_i\}$;
15:     **else**
16:         $C_k = C_k \cup \{s_i\} \setminus \{s_j\}$, $M_k = M_k - E_j + E_i$, $S = S \setminus \{s_i\}$;
17:     **end**
18: **end**
19: $\Phi = \bigcup_{1 \leq k \leq K} \{C_k\}$, $M = \sum_{C_k \in \Phi} M_k$, $C = \bigcup_{C_k \in \Phi} C_k$;

The MESDA consists of three phases. The first phase is to find a subset $C_k \subseteq S$ of IoT devices for any $1 \leq k \leq K$ such that $\sum_{s_i \in C_k} E_i \geq T$. The second phase is to optimize M_k by replacing the high energy consumption IoT devices in

C_k with low energy consuming ones from the remaining IoT devices in S for any $1 \leq k \leq K$. Finally, we compute $\Phi = \{C_1, C_2, \cdots, C_K\}$, $C = \bigcup_{1 \leq k \leq K} C_k$ and $M = \sum_{C_k \in \Phi} M_k$. The detailed description of the algorithm is shown as below.

The first phase of the MESD algorithm repeats the following four steps until one of the conditions $P = \emptyset$ and $S = \emptyset$ is satisfied.

- Select s_i with the maximum E_i from S, where if there exists two IoT devices $s_i, s_j \in S$ such that $E_i = E_j$, then the minimum ID of them is selected.
- Pick L_k with the minimum M_k for any $1 \leq k \leq K$, where if there exists M_k and M_l such that $M_k = M_l$, then the minimum ID of them is selected.
- Add s_i into C_k, and execute the operations $M_k = M_k + E_i$ and $S = S \backslash \{s_i\}$.
- Compare M_k with T. If $M_k \geq T$, then $P = P \backslash \{L_k\}$.

After executing the first phase of the algorithm, we can obtain a set C_k of IoT devices for any $L_k \in P$, in which the total working time M_k of IoT devices is greater than or equal to T. In the second phase, for any $1 \leq k \leq K$, we optimize M_k by replacing the high energy consumption IoT devices in C_k with low energy consuming ones in S.

The second phase of the algorithm repeats the following steps until $S = \emptyset$.

- Select s_i with the maximum E_i from S.
- Compute a tuple $< s_j, k > = arg \min_{s_j \in C_k, 1 \leq k \leq K} (M_k - E_j + E_i)$ such that $M_k - E_j + E_i \geq T$.
- Compare E_i with E_j. If $E_i \geq E_j$, then s_i is deleted from S, otherwise, $C_k = C_k \cup \{s_i\} \backslash \{s_j\}$, $M_k = M_k - E_j + E_i$ and s_i is removed from S.

After executing the second phase of the algorithm, we can obtain a set C_k of IoT devices located on each $L_k \in P$ and the total energy consumption $M_k = \sum_{s_i \in C_k} E_i$ of IoT devices in C_k such that all targets covered by site L_k are continuously observed at least T time. Finally, we can obtain $\Phi = \{C_1, C_2, \cdots, C_K\}$, $M = \sum_{C_k \in \Phi} M_k$ and $C = \bigcup_{1 \leq k \leq K} C_k$. The pseudo code of the algorithm is shown in Algorithm 2.

In the following, we will analyze the performance of the MESDA algorithm. We use C^* to represent the optimal set of IoT devices placed at sites in P for the MESD problem. Let M^* denote the total energy consumption of IoT devices in C^*. Without loss of generality, we use C_k^* to be the optimal set of IoT devices placed at $L_k \in P$ when C^* has been confirmed. Let M_k^* represent the total energy consumption of IoT devices in C_k^*.

Theorem 4. *If the MESDA algorithm has the feasible solution, then we can obtain the approximation ratio of the algorithm is 2.*

Proof. According to the definition of the MESD problem, we have $M_k^* \geq T$ for any $1 \leq k \leq K$, and $M^* = \sum_{1 \leq k \leq K} M_k^* \geq K \cdot T$.

For any $1 \leq k \leq K$, we let $<s_i, E_i> = arg \max_{s_j \in C_k} E_j$, where C_k is obtained by the MESDA algorithm. We analyze the performance of the algorithm in the light of the following two cases.

(1) $0 < E_i < \frac{T}{2}$. Then we can obtain that for any $s_j \in C_k$, $E_j < \frac{T}{2}$. Based on the algorithm, the last IoT device added into C_k makes M_k be greater than or equal to T, which means $M_k \leq T + E_j < \frac{3T}{2} \leq 1.5M_k^*$.

(2) $\frac{T}{2} \leq E_i < T$. If there exists $E_j \in C_k$ such that $\frac{T}{2} < E_j \leq E_i$, then based on the algorithm, we can obtain $C_k = \{s_i, s_j\}$ and $M_k = E_i + E_j < 2T < 2M_k^*$. Otherwise, we have $M_k \leq T + E_j \leq 1.5M_k^*$.

From what have been discussed, we can obtain $M_k < 2M_k^*$. Therefore, we have $M = \sum_{1 \leq k \leq K} M_k \leq \sum_{1 \leq k \leq K} 2M_k^* \leq 2M^*$, which means the approximation ratio of the MESDA algorithm is 2.

3.3   Algorithm for the MEPS Problem

In this subsection, we propose an approximation algorithm, called MEPSA, to solve the MEPS problem based on the algorithms for the MLC and MESD problems. The algorithm consists of two steps corresponding to Algorithms 1 and 2, respectively, as shown in Algorithm 3.

After executing the Algorithm 3, we can obtain the total energy consumption of IoT devices M, the subset $C \subseteq S$ of IoT devices that are placed at candidate sites to keep observing all targets at least T time slots and the set $\Phi = \{C_1, C_2, \cdots, C_{L'}\}$, in which each C_k is the set of IoT devices placed at L_k, where $1 \leq k \leq |L'|$.

Algorithm 3. MEPSA

Input: $Q = \{r_1, r_2, \cdots, r_m\}$ $S = \{s_1, s_2, \cdots, s_n\}$, E_i for each $s_i \in S$, $L = \{L_1, L_2, \cdots, L_N\}$, R, T;
Output: C, M, Φ;
Step 1: Compute the set L' of candidate sites to cover all targets in Q by executing Algorithm 1;
Step 2: Compute Φ, C, M based on L' by executing Algorithm 2, where $P = L'$;

In the following, we will analyze the performance of the MEPSA algorithm. Suppose C_{opt}^* is an optimal subset of S for the MEPS problem. Let M_{opt}^* be the total energy consumption of IoT devices in C_{opt}^*. Since each $r_j \in Q$ needs to be continuously observed at least T time, we divide T time into equal T time slots. We use c_t^* to represent the minimum energy consumption of all active IoT devices for the MEPS problem such that all targets are covered in the t-th time slot, and let L_t^* denote the set of sites which are placed the active IoT devices in the t-th time slot.

Lemma 1. *For any $1 \leq t \leq T$, we have $c_t^* \geq |L^*|$, where L^* is the minimum set of candidate sites for the MLC problem.*

Proof. In the MEPS problem, all targets need to be covered by IoT devices placed at candidate sites in L for any $1 \leq t \leq T$, which means that there exists a subset $L_t \subseteq L$ that can cover all targets for the arbitrary t-th time slot. Thus, based on the definitions of MEPS problem and MLC problem, we can obtain that for any such subset L_t, it is a feasible solution for the MLC problem. Therefore, we have $|L_t^*| \geq |L^*|$, since L_t^* is a feasible solution for the MLC problem. Therefore, we can obtain $c_t^* \geq |L^*|$ since $c_t^* = |L_t^*|$.

Lemma 2. *We can obtain $M_{opt}^* \geq |L^*| \cdot T$.*

Proof. According to the Lemma 1, we can obtain $c_t^* \geq |L^*|$ for arbitrary $1 \leq t \leq T$. Based on the definition of the MEPS problem, we have $M_{opt}^* \geq \sum_{1 \leq t \leq T} c_t^* \geq |L^*| \cdot T$.

Theorem 5. *The performance ratio of the MEPSA algorithm is $2\ln m + 2$, where m is the number of targets.*

Proof. According to the MEPSA algorithm, we have $M = \sum_{L_k \in L'} M_k$, where M_k is the energy consumption of IoT devices located on L_k obtained by the MEPSA algorithm. On the basis of Theorems 3 and 4, we can get $|L'| \leq \ln m \cdot |L^*| + 1$ and $M_k < 2T$ for any $1 \leq k \leq |L'|$. Based on Lemma 2, we can obtain

$$M = \sum_{L_k \in L'} M_k \leq |L'| \cdot \max\{M_k | L_k \in L'\}$$
$$\leq (\ln m \cdot |L^*| + 1) \cdot 2T \leq 2(\ln m + 1) \cdot M_{opt}^*.$$

4   Conclusion

In this paper, we investigate the Minimum Energy consumption of IoT devices through Placement and Scheduling (MEPS) problem. We first propose the mathematical model for the MEPS problem and prove that the MEPS problem is NP-hard. Then we study two sub-problems of the MEPS problem, Minimum Location Coverage (MLC) and Minimum Energy consumption Scheduling Deployment (MESD), and propose an approximation algorithm for each of them. Based on these two sub-problems, we propose an approximation algorithm for the MEPS problem.

References

1. Akhlaghinia, R., Hashemi, S., Shadgar, B.: Sensor placement for heterogenous point coverage. IEEE (2010)
2. Cai, Z., Chen, Q.: Latency-and-coverage aware data aggregation scheduling for multihop battery-free wireless networks. IEEE Trans. Wirel. Commun. **20**(3), 1770–1784 (2021)
3. Cai, Z., He, Z.: Trading private range counting over big IoT data. In: 2019 IEEE 39th International Conference on Distributed Computing Systems (ICDCS), pp. 144–153. IEEE (2019)

4. Cai, Z., Zheng, X.: A private and efficient mechanism for data uploading in smart cyber-physical systems. IEEE Trans. Netw. Sci. Eng. **7**(2), 766–775 (2018)
5. Cardei, M., Thai, M.T., Li, Y., Wu, W.: Energy-efficient target coverage in wireless sensor networks. In: Proceedings IEEE 24th Annual Joint Conference of the IEEE Computer and Communications Societies (2005)
6. Chen, Q., Cai, Z., Cheng, L., Gao, H.: Structure-free general data aggregation scheduling for multihop battery-free wireless networks. IEEE Trans. Mob. Comput. (2021)
7. Feige, U.: A threshold of ln n for approximating set cover. J. ACM (JACM) **45**(4), 634–652 (1998)
8. Ismail, D., Rahman, M., Saifullah, A.: Low-power wide-area networks: opportunities, challenges, and directions. In: Proceedings of the Workshop Program of the 19th International Conference on Distributed Computing and Networking (2018)
9. Luo, C., Satpute, M.N., Li, D., Wang, Y., Chen, W., Wu, W.: Fine-grained trajectory optimization of multiple UAVs for efficient data gathering from WSNs. IEEE/ACM Trans. Netw. **29**(1), 162–175 (2021)
10. Luo, C., Hong, Y., Li, D., Wang, Y., Chen, W., Hu, Q.: Maximizing network lifetime using coverage sets scheduling in wireless sensor networks. Ad Hoc Netw. **98**, 102037 (2020)
11. Mini, S., Udgata, S.K., Sabat, S.L.: Sensor deployment and scheduling for target coverage problem in wireless sensor networks. IEEE Sens. J. **14**(3), 636–644 (2014)
12. Yousuf, A.M., Rochester, E.M., Ousat, B., Ghaderi, M.: Throughput, coverage and scalability of LoRA LPWAN for Internet of Things. In: 2018 IEEE/ACM 26th International Symposium on Quality of Service (IWQoS) (2018)
13. Zhu, T., Shi, T., Li, J., Cai, Z., Zhou, X.: Task scheduling in deadline-aware mobile edge computing systems. IEEE Internet Things J. **6**(3), 4854–4866 (2018)

Optimized Adversarial Example Generating Algorithm Based on Probabilistic Graph

Chaochao Li, Yu Yang$^{(\boxtimes)}$, Yufei Man, Junyu Di, and Rui Zhan

School of Cyberspace Security,
Beijing University of Posts and Telecommunications, Beijing 100876, China
{lichaochaohao,yangyu,manyf,dijunyu,zhanrui}@bupt.edu.cn

Abstract. Deep learning technology is widely used in various fields. Once the deep model is attacked, it will cause huge economic losses and security problems. Therefore, the security of deep model has become a research hotspot. For attacking the depth model and detecting the robustness of the depth model, the adversarial examples is the core technology. And stAdv is one of the most advanced adversarial examples generation technologies. It has the advantages of a high success rate of attack and small visual distortion of adversarial examples, but it also has the problems of long generation time of adversarial examples and low efficiency. Aiming at the above-mentioned shortcomings, this paper improves the efficiency of adversarial examples generation algorithm, and proposes an optimized adversarial examples generation algorithm P&stAdv based on probabilistic graph. This method combines the steganography algorithm and CAM technique. P&stAdv perform attack evaluation on each pixel of the image, and introduces a method of obtaining the "appropriate point" of the image based on the steganography algorithm to generate the adversarial examples. Then the cost matrix of image modification is obtained and the image probabilistic graph is generated. Finally, use adversarial examples to attack images according to probabilistic graph. The experimental results show that the proposed algorithm has high efficiency. Compared with stAdv, the generation time of adversarial examples is reduced by 35%. This algorithm can modify the minimum number of pixels while ensuring a high success rate of attack. Moreover, it can make more effective attacks on complex texture images.

Keywords: Adversarial examples · Spatial transformation · Deep neural network · Probabilistic graph · Color channels

1 Introduction

In recent years, the rapid development of artificial intelligence-related research has became one of the most popular research directions in cyberspace security. China's artificial intelligence market has already reached 6 billion U.S. dollars in 2019 and 9.1 billion U.S. dollars in 2020 [1]. The Artificial Intelligence Institute of China also predicts that the annual growth rate of the artificial intelligence market will reach 50% in the next few years [2]. The industry of artificial intelligence grew bigger and its prospects for the

© Springer Nature Switzerland AG 2021
Z. Liu et al. (Eds.): WASA 2021, LNCS 12937, pp. 597–607, 2021.
https://doi.org/10.1007/978-3-030-85928-2_47

future are also bright [3]. Both national scientific research institutions and many Internet companies in the limelight are accelerating the innovation and research of artificial intelligence [4]. The development of artificial intelligence is generally optimistic. However, new research demonstrates that the neural networks can be attacked due to its vulnerabilities. Currently there are adversarial attack technologies which are a severe threat to the deep learning models [5]. Generally speaking generates adversarial examples by adding small disturbances that are imperceptible by the human eye to the original image, and then transfers the adversarial examples as input to the deep learning model, which leads to erroneous output results of the learning model, and even controllable [6].

This article mainly studies the technologies in the related fields of adversarial examples generation. The current mainstream adversarial examples generation method is based on gradient attack [7]. There are two problems with this method. One is that the quality of the generated adversarial examples image is poor, and the other is that the human eye can easily detect its difference from the original image. In addition, the existing defense strategies are mainly focused on gradient attack, which are diverse and tend to mature. The attack method based on gradient is difficult to achieve better attack effect under defense strategy. The method based on constrained optimization attack has favorable visual effects [8]. The attack ability of stAdv [9] algorithm proposed by Chaowei Xiao performs well in multiple models with different data sets. The visual effect of the adversarial examples image generated by this algorithm is also very excellent. Most importantly, the principle of the algorithm is to perform spatial transformation perturbation on the image, which is different from the traditional method of changing pixel values. At present, there is no research result of defense strategy for this kind of attack method, so it shows strong robustness under different defense strategies. However, a big problem with this algorithm is that it takes more time to generate adversarial examples. The algorithm adopts the global search and traversal solution method when calculating the optimal solution, which causes a huge amount of calculation and leads to insufficient algorithm efficiency.

Aiming at the problems of the above methods, this paper combines the leading-edge steganography algorithm and the CAM [10] technology, and proposes an optimized spatial transformation adversarial examples generating algorithm based on probabilistic graph with high accuracy and high attack efficiency.

2   Related Work

Szegedy [11] first pointed out that adding small noise to the example can make the classifier based on deep neural network output the wrong category, thus proposed the concept of adversarial examples. The research directions in the field of adversarial examples research at home and abroad are mainly divided into attacks and defenses against convolutional neural networks. The research on the attack direction is to study the method of adversarial examples generation that can make the classification model produce wrong results. At present, there are many advanced achievements in the directions of attack and defense, and at the same time the attack and defense have also achieved mutual promotion. After a new attack method appears, scholars will study new defense methods to make it invalid. Meanwhile, after the new defense method appears, scholars will also study new attack methods to break it. The advancement of adversarial examples technology is promoted in this way, therefore the research on the attack direction in this article also has practical significance. Some visual quality assessment parameters related to adversarial examples technology are introduced below.

SSIM (Structural SIMilarity) [12], namely structural similarity index, is a method to measure the subjective perception of digital images. Compared with other indicators, it considers the visual characteristics in design, so it can well reflect the visual sense of people eyes. The SSIM index mainly measures the similarity between the two images from the three directions of brightness, structure and contrast. Assuming there are images x and y, the SSIM index of the two is calculated as follows.

$$SSIM(x, y) = [l(x, y)]^{\alpha}[c(x, y)]^{\beta}[s(x, y)]^{\gamma} \tag{1}$$

Mutual information [13] is an important parameter in information theory to measure the relevance of the information contained between two systems. It is also used in many papers related to images to measure the degree of mutual inclusion of information contained in two images. In the image matching process, entropy and joint entropy are usually used to reflect the degree of interdependence of information between images. That is the mentioned mutual information. Entropy can be interpreted as a random variable. Mutual information is inversely proportional to image similarity. Taking images F and R as an example, the mutual information value between them is expressed as follows.

$$MI(F, R) = H(F) + H(R) - H(F, R) \tag{2}$$

3 Spatial Transformation and Improvement Based on Probabilistic Graph

3.1 Problem Analysis of stAdv Algorithm

As one of the frontier attack algorithms for adversarial examples, stAdv [14] has good performance in terms of the quality of the generated adversarial examples, the success rate of attacks, and the robustness of the defense strategy. However, the author did not analyze and experiment on its attack efficiency in the original paper. Higher efficiency means shorter adversarial examples generation time which is also an important indicator for evaluating adversarial examples algorithms. This article uses ResNet and CNN as the attacked models to conduct targeted attacks on the MNIST dataset. Both stAdv and FGSM are analyzed from such three aspects as the attack time which is the generation time of the adversarial examples, the SSIM value used to measure the visual effect and the success rate of the attack. From the experimental data, stAdv is highly close to the original image in terms of image visual effects, and the SSIM value exceeds 0.8. In contrast, FGSM is only about 0.5–0.6. This is consistent with what the original text mentioned that stAdv can produce better and more realistic results. And the attack success rate of stAdv is better than FGSM. But both are more than 95%, and the difference between them is not particularly obvious. It is not particularly meaningful to compare the attack success rate. Finally, it is worth noting that stAdv consumes nearly 5 times as much time as FGSM in terms of adversarial examples generation time, and its efficiency is significantly lower than FGSM.

3.2   Proposal of Improved Algorithm Based on Probabilistic Graph

This paper proposes a new spatial transformation adversarial examples generation method P&stAdv based on probabilistic graph and CAM (Class Activation Mapping) positioning mechanism. First of all, the algorithm uses the function $h(x)$ to process the image x in order to convert it from a three-channel image to a grayscale image, and uses the WOW adaptive steganography algorithm to extract the image cost matrix $Cost[]$. Secondly, use the CAM positioning mechanism for the image to filter out the areas $m(x)$ that have a greater impact on the visual effect. Thirdly, select the "appropriate" predetermined point in the expected area, and use it together with the cost matrix to enlarge the image probabilistic graph. Finally, perform spatial transformation processing based on the obtained probabilistic graph.

Image Filter Design.   The purpose of image filtering is mainly to screen out suitable areas for adversarial attacks. The image filter is mainly composed of the filter and the cam locator. The filter includes cost function extraction. At the same time, it is responsible for finding a safer area for image steganography, which is usually invisible to the human eye and can be used as an attack area for spatial transformation. Using this principle to construct an image filter can better find the image area that needs to be processed, greatly reducing the computational cost and ensuring that the image has a better visual effect. The first thing the image filtering needs to do is to extract the pixels in the image and get the value of each point. This article uses the getpixel method under the python image processing class image to extract pixel values. After extracting the pixel value, this paper uses a steganography algorithm based on wavelet design to determine the region in the image suitable for spatial transformation attack. In the following Fig. 1, the carrier image has been filtered in different directions. It can be seen that the residual images in the three directions are quite different in the processing results. The horizontal image result mainly highlights the contour in the horizontal direction. Similarly, the vertical and diagonal processing are to highlight the image contour in the corresponding direction. The region with bright light after extracting the residual is suitable for information embedding, and this region is also suitable for adversarial examples processing.

Use the following formula to calculate the embedded information cost of the image which is the cost matrix. The lower the cost, the more suitable for adversarial examples attack processing. And then save the extracted cost matrix as $Cost[]$.

$$\text{rho} = \left((\text{xi}\{1\}.^\wedge p) + (\text{xi}\{2\}.^\wedge p) + (\text{xi}\{3\}.^\wedge p) \right).^\wedge \cdot (-1/p) \tag{3}$$

In the second part, the CAM positioning mechanism is used to select an area with a large amount of image information. CAM is also known as heat map of class activation. It can be understood in this way: Suppose that a classifier ResNet is used to classify an image, and the input image contains a computer and a globe. There are multiple probability components in the output, among which there are two corresponding to the image classified as a computer and a globe. The two different classifications are related to some regions of the image more and some regions less. In other words, the correlation between pixels in different regions of the image and the image category is different. CAM is the heat map that reflects this correlation. For the region which is more sensitive to classification, the darker the color and the higher the temperature. As shown in the

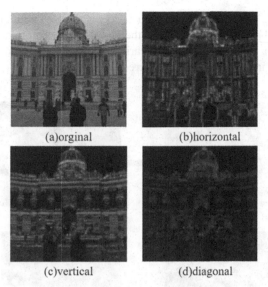

(a)orginal   (b)horizontal

(c)vertical   (d)diagonal

Fig. 1. The carrier image is decomposed from three directions using the WOW algorithm.

Fig. 2 below, the original label of the image on the left is a police car. The color is darker and the temperature is higher at the wheel and alarm. It means that these two areas have a greater impact on the classification of police vehicles. The image on the right is classified as smoke. The darker color at dense smoke indicates that this area has a greater influence on the classification result of smoke. According to this, the main classification sensitive area of the image under the correct category can be judged and changed. Such an attack is highly targeted.

Fig. 2. CAM images of different categories.

After passing through the image filter, the cost of changing the corresponding pixels of the entire image and the key sensitive areas of the image can be obtained. The experiment uses an image originally classified as playing basketball. The lower left corner of the figure below shows that CAM will display the basketball area and the face area in a darker color, representing that the region contains more information and contributes more to the classification results of basketball. It is thus judged that, if it is to be misclassified, mainly attacking the area will be more targeted. Observe the lower right corner of the Fig. 3 below. The area with more black dots is the area with higher change cost, and the background part has little effect on the visual effect. Through the analysis of the two graphs, the area suitable for the adversarial attack can be picked up, and the attack cost and attack pertinence are fully considered.

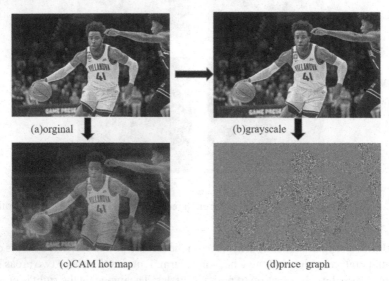

(a)orginal   (b)grayscale

(c)CAM hot map   (d)price graph

Fig. 3. Sample image processing results

Appropriate Pixel Selection Based on the Difference of RGB Color Channels.
After extracting image-related information it is necessary to determine the specific area of the spatial transformation according to the information, and then select specific pixels to attack. The method used in the original stadv algorithm is to calculate the spatial distance between any two adjacent points in the whole image and select the smallest distance scheme. This method has a larger amount of calculation and more redundancy. This article optimizes it. Select the appropriate points using the principle of steganography-related algorithms to select the undisputed points. Finally, the probabilistic graph is calculated by combining the cost function.

This chapter uses the RGB color model of color images to propose a selection strategy for "appropriate" pixels. By comparing the following figure, it can be found that when the same image embeds information on different color channels, the embedding position selected by the algorithm is quite different. The white area in (a) in the figure below shows the difference in the embedding position of the R channel and the G channel. The difference between the embedding positions of the R channel and the B channel is shown in Fig. 4(b). And the embedding position difference between G channel and B channel is shown in Fig. 4(c). The difference of the three color spaces is combined and the result is shown in the Fig. 4.

It can be considered that using the same steganography algorithm to embed the same information in the three color spaces can determine the attack value of a pixel. If a certain pixel is selected by the three color spaces more times, it means that the pixel has more

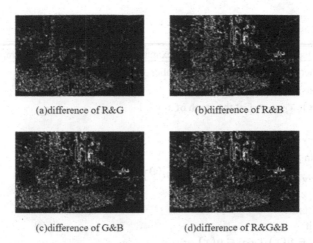

(a)difference of R&G   (b)difference of R&B

(c)difference of G&B   (d)difference of R&G&B

Fig. 4. The difference in channel location.

attack value and the attack on this pixel is less observable. Combined with the filtered area of the image, the specific pixels suitable for attack can be specifically determined. A pixel can be defined as an "inappropriate" pixel when it is selected once to embed information, a "smaller fit" pixel when selected twice, and an "appropriate" pixel when selected three times. The focus of the algorithm is to pay close attention to the loss changes of the image attack. Taking different pixels to attack can obtain different attack loss values.

Probabilistic Graph Generation and Use. After obtaining the cost matrix and the filtered area of the image, the probabilistic graph is calculated and used for spatial transformation. The formula for calculating the probabilistic graph is shown below.

$$p(x) = \varepsilon \cdot Cost(x) + \rho \cdot \sum_{i=0}^{w} W[x_i] \tag{4}$$

Among them, is the weight taken by the cost function, and is the point in the area filtered by the image filter. The combination of these two parameters can represent the probability of using a pixel in an adversarial examples attack. The higher the probability, the lower the cost of changing the point and the more worthy of the change. The probabilistic graph is essentially a weight that combines visual effects and change costs. The larger the value, the easier it is to perceive the information embedding at that position, and the greater the visual effect of the adversarial examples processing. Determine the visual balance effect of the examples combined with the perceptual loss equilibrium function when performing iterative transformation. Set the objective function as follow.

$$f^* = argmini * L_{adv}(x, f) + j * L_{flow}(f) + argmin(L_{per}) + minp(x) \tag{5}$$

The new objective function considers the selection of modified pixels instead of modifying the entire image. This improvement guarantees the visual effect and greatly reduces the amount of calculation.

The following Table 1 gives the algorithm flow.

Table 1. The algorithm flow.

Algorithm: optimal generation of adversarial examples based on probabilistic graph
Input: A classifier F; a clean image x and Number of iterations M
Output: An adversarial example x*
1: $x_{Cost[]}, p(x), x_{CAM}$ ←Get the graph of x
2: $x* ← x$
3:   while $p(x) \neq NULL$ do
4:      for x_i in $p(x)$ do
5:          $x_{adv}^i = \sum_{q \in N} x^q (1 - |u^{(i)} - u^{(q)}|)(1 - |v^{(i)} - v^{(q)}|)$
6:          if $F(x*) \neq F(x)$ then
7:              return x*
8:          end if
9:      $x_{Cost[]} \in p(x)$ $x_{CAM} \in p(x)$
10:   end while
11: return θ

In the algorithm, a classification model F of the target to be attacked, the image sample x, and the number of iterations M are known. First, extract the probabilistic graph and the heat map area of the image to get the probabilistic graph $p(x)$. And then select a certain and appropriate point in the probabilistic graph to conduct the adversarial attack every time the image is transformed in the spatial domain. After the attack, it is judged whether the expected attack effect is achieved, and if it does not continue to select more points to attack. After selecting the appropriate points, add $x_{Cost[]}$ and x_{CAM} to $p(x)$ in sequence until the image is successfully misclassified by the classifier.

4   Simulation and Result Analysis

4.1 Experimental Data Set and Model

The data sets used in this simulation are ImageNet [15] and CIFAR10 [16]. In order to study and compare the performance improved in stAdv, this article uses its attack model VGG16 network [17] as the target to be attacked model which has been well pre-trained in the CIFAR10 data set. Due to the use of multiple small convolution kernels and the increase in the number of network layers of the model, the VGG16 network has a relatively good generalization effect on the test set and can achieve a high classification accuracy rate under multiple data sets.

4.2 Result Analysis

Attack Ability Assessment.   In order to verify the performance of P&stAdv, this article has been tested under multiple models. At the same time, in order to further test the attack effect of P&stAdv under traditional defense measures, this paper also conducted experiments under three defense measures using the cifar10 data set, and compared with the classic methods FGSM and C&W [18]. The results of targeted attacks under the normal model are shown in Table 2.

Table 2. P&stAdv attack experiment results.

Model	ResNet32	Wide ResNet	VGG16
Accuracy	93.16%	95.82%	94.57%
Attack success rate	98.79%	97.62%	97.85%

Accuracy in the above table represents the classification accuracy of the target model tested on the CIFAR10 data set. The classification accuracy rates of ResNet32, Wide ResNet and VGG16 are respectively about 93%, 96% and 95%, which are in line with the benchmark classification capabilities of these three models. It can be seen that the benchmark model is working normally. On this basis, the attack algorithm P&stAdv proposed in this paper is used to carry out targeted attacks on the benchmark model. The data shows that the attack success rate of this algorithm has reached more than 97%. The algorithm proposed in this paper can effectively generate adversarial examples and interfere with the classification ability of the target model.

Adversarial Aample Generation Time Evaluation. The generation time of adversarial examples is also a good indicator of algorithm performance. On the premise that the attack success rate is reasonable and the P&stAdv attack success rate is higher than stadv, this paper compares the adversarial examples generation time of the two algorithms before and after optimization on the three data sets. The results are shown in Table 3.

Table 3. The results of the experiment on the generation time of adversarial examples.

Data	MNIST	CIFAR10	ImageNet	MNIST	CIFAR10	ImageNet
Algorithm		stAdv			P&stAdv	
Attack Success Rate	99.80%	96.92%	90.85%	99.95%	98.64%	93.50%
Attack Time	18.28s	18.65s	19.98s	10.71s	11.85s	12.71s

The experimental results show that the optimizated algorithm based on probabilistic graph has faster examples generation time under the premise that the attack success rate is better than stAdv, which is reduced by 34.8% on average compared to stAdv. And it has consistency on the three data sets which greatly reduces the generation time of adversarial examples. This result is also in line with experimental expectations, indicating that P&stAdv has a higher attack efficiency.

The Visual Effect of Adversarial Examples. This article compares with stadv and other methods using the specific visual effect measurement indicator SSIM. The results are shown in Table 4.

Table 4. Image visual quality experiment results.

Network	SSIM on stAdv	SSIM on P&stAdv	SSIM on FGSM	SSIM on C&W
VGG16	0.8525	0.9152	0.5645	0.6535
ResNet	0.8654	0.9176	0.5728	0.6629

Four attack methods were compared under the same network. P&stAdv obtained the best experimental indicators indicating that it has the best visual effects. P&stAdv is optimized on the basis of stAdv, and a spatial transformation attack is performed on fewer pixels. The results of this experiment are in line with expectation. This shows that P&stAdv has higher attack performance in all aspects than traditional spatial transformation algorithms.

5 Conclusion

This paper mainly studies the optimized spatial transformation algorithm based on probabilistic graph. Although the classic stAdv algorithm has good attack and visual effects, it takes more time to generate adversarial examples which leads to lower efficiency of the algorithm. There are still many optimizations in this algorithm. This paper proposes a new optimized type of spatial transformation adversarial attack method P&stAdv based on probabilistic graph using steganography algorithm. Compared with stAdv, the method in this paper first processes the image with gray scale, and then uses the image filter to obtain the cost matrix of the image. Secondly, use CAM technology to find sensitive areas of the image. At the same time use adaptive steganography algorithm to detect all three channels of the image to select pixels suitable for adversarial attack. Finally, the obtained image information is used to synthesize the probabilistic graph of the image, and then the probabilistic graph is used for spatial transformation adversarial examples generation. Several experiments are designed to evaluate the performance of the algorithm, mainly to evaluate the attack ability, the generation time and the visual effect of the adversarial sample. Experimental results show that the proposed P&stAdv algorithm has better performance. The attack capability of the algorithm inherits the characteristics of stAdv that also performs well under defensive measures. The adversarial examples generation time of this algorithm is reduced by about 35%, and the image quality effect is also excellent.

The follow-up work of this article can be carried out in the following areas:

1) Research on black box attack methods based on spatial transformation;
2) In the direction of defense, it could conduct research on defense methods of spatial transformation adversarial examples that are not yet available.

References

1. Moosavi-Dezfooli, S.M, Fawzi, A., Frossard, P.: Deepfool: a simple and accurate method to fool deep neural networks. In: Proceedings of the IEEE conference on computer vision and pattern recognition (2016)
2. Zhang, R., Isola, P., Efros, A.A.: Colorful image colorization. In: Leibe, B., Matas, J., Sebe, N., Welling, M. (eds.) ECCV 2016. LNCS, vol. 9907, pp. 649–666. Springer, Cham (2016). https://doi.org/10.1007/978-3-319-46487-9_40
3. Goodfellow, I., Pouget-Abadie, J., Mirza, M., et al.: Generative adversarial nets. In: Advances in Neural Information Processing Systems, pp. 2672–2680 (2014)
4. Baluja, S., Fischer, I.: Adversarial transformation networks: learning to generate adversarial examples. arXiv preprint arXiv:1703.09387 (2017)
5. Goodfellow, I., Shlens, J., Szegedy, C.: Explaining and harnessing adversarial examples. In: Proceedings of ICLR (2015)
6. Kurakin, A., Goodfellow, I., Bengio, S.: Adversarial examples in the physical world. In: 5th International Conference on Learning Representations, ICLR 2017, Toulon, France, 24–26 April 2017
7. Papernot, N., McDaniel, P., Jha, S., et al.: The limitations of deep learning in adversarial settings. In: 2016 IEEE European Symposium on Security and Privacy (EuroS&P), pp. 372-387. IEEE (2016)
8. Papernot, N., McDaniel, P., Goodfellow, I., et al.: Practical black-box attacks against deep learning systems using adversarial examples. In: Proceedings of the 2017 ACM on Asia Conference on Computer and Communications Security, pp. 506–519 (2017)
9. Carlini, N., Wagner, D.: Adversarial examples are not easily detected: bypassing ten detection methods. In: Proceedings of the 10th ACM Workshop on Artificial Intelligence and Security, pp. 3–14 (2017)
10. Papernot, N., McDaniel, P., Wu, X., et al.: Distillation as a defense to adversarial perturbations against deep neural networks. In: 2016 IEEE Symposium on Security and Privacy (SP), pp. 582-597. IEEE (2016)
11. Madry, A., Makelov, A., Schmidt, L., et al.: Towards deep learning models resistant to adversarial attacks. In: International Conference on Learning Representations (2018)
12. Chunpeng, G., et al.: Secure keyword search and data sharing mechanism for cloud computing. IEEE Trans. Dependable Secure Comput. (2020)
13. Tanay, T., Griffin, L.: A boundary tilting perspective on the phenomenon of adversarial examples. ArXiv preprint arXiv:1608.07690 (2016)
14. Chunpeng, G., Liu, Z., Xia, J., Liming, F.: Revocable identity-based broadcast proxy re-encryption for data sharing in clouds. IEEE Trans. Dependable Secure Comput. (2019)
15. Papernot, N., McDaniel, P., Goodfellow, I.: Transferability in machine learning:from phenomena to black-box attacks using adversarial samples. ArXiv preprint arXiv:1605.07277 (2016)
16. Ge, C., et al.: Revocable attribute-based encryption with data integrity in clouds. IEEE Trans. Dependable Secure Comput. (2021)
17. Ge, C., Susilo, W., Fang, L., Wang, J., Shi, Y.: A CCA-secure key-policy attribute-based proxy re-encryption in the adaptive corruption model for dropbox data sharing system. Des. Codes Crypt. 86(11), 2587–2603 (2018). https://doi.org/10.1007/s10623-018-0462-9
18. Liming, F., Willy, S., Ge, C., Wang, J.: Public key encryption with keyword search secure against keyword guessing attacks without random oracle. Info. Sci. 221–241, Elsevier (2013)

CDVT: A Cluster-Based Distributed Video Transcoding Scheme for Mobile Stream Services

Cheng Xu[1], Wei Ren[1,2,3(✉)], Daxi Tu[1], Linchen Yu[4], Tianqing Zhu[1], and Yi Ren[5]

[1] School of Computer Science, China University of Geosciences,
Wuhan, People's Republic of China
`weirencs@cug.edu.cn`
[2] Key Laboratory of Network Assessment Technology, CAS, Institute
of Information Engineering, Chinese Academy of Sciences,
Beijing 100093, People's Republic of China
[3] Guizhou Provincial Key Laboratory of Public Big Data, Guizhou University,
Guiyang 550025, China
[4] School of Cyber Science and Engineering, Huazhong University of Science
and Technology, Wuhan, People's Republic of China
[5] School of Computing Science, University of East Anglia, Norwich NR4 7TJ, UK

Abstract. Distributed video transcoding has been used to huge video data storage overhead and reduce transcoding delay caused by the rapid development of mobile video services. Distributed transcoding can leverage the computing power of clusters for various user requests and diverse video processing demands. However, it imposes a remaining challenge on how to efficiently utilize the computing power of the cluster as well as achieve optimized performance through reasonable system parameters and video processing configurations. In this paper, we design a Cluster-based Distributed Video Transcoding System called CDVT using Hadoop, FFmpeg, and Mkvmerge to achieve on-demand video splitting, on-demand transcoding, and distributed processing, which can be applied to large scale video sharing over mobile devices. In order to further optimize system performance, we conducted extensive experiments on various data sets to find relevant factors that affect transcoding efficiency. We dynamically reconfigure the cluster and evaluate the impacts of different intermediate tasks, splitting strategies, and memory configuration strategies on system performance. Experimental results obtained under various workloads demonstrate that the proposed system can ensure the quality of transcoding tasks while reducing the time cost by up to 50%.

Keywords: Distributed transcoding · Hadoop · Video processing · FFmpeg

© Springer Nature Switzerland AG 2021
Z. Liu et al. (Eds.): WASA 2021, LNCS 12937, pp. 608–628, 2021.
https://doi.org/10.1007/978-3-030-85928-2_48

1   Introduction

Nowadays, mobile devices with media playback capabilities are very common in our daily life [1,2]. The mobile devices can provide various services [3] and applications, including video and audio[4]. People are getting used to watching videos on their mobile devices, e.g., smartphone, pad, etc. Terminals with diverse Technological specifications and heterogeneous network environment raise new challenges to streaming media services [5]. Various mobile devices needs videos of different qualities, e.g., 240p, 1080p, to meet personalized user requirements [6]. So that video service providers need to prepare video data in multiple bitrates and multiple packaging formats for the same video content on the server-side [7]. In order to provide such services, video transcoding technology was proposed which is now widely used in media services. Traditional video transcoding methods are relatively inefficient and expensive, and it is difficult to support the huge demand for multimedia traffic. Research on new and efficient video transcoding methods has begun to attract attention.

Earlier research relies on multi-node computing power to process transcoding tasks parallelly to reduce transcoding time [8–10]. These methods target special user scenarios, which fail to provide theoretical guidelines and general recommendation paradigms for different user tasks. In the case of a given system, it is desirable to have general recommended configurations which can be friendly adapted to different scenarios. Compared with usual parameter choices, finding options that fit the characteristics of the distributed transcoding method will be more likely to stimulate the system to achieve optimized performance.

In this paper, we propose a Hadoop-based distributed video transcoding system. Our system can transcode a variety of video data according to user's requirements, such as encoding method, video bit rate, and packaging format. In the system, huge volume user-created video data are stored in the distributed file system of the Hadoop cluster. Then, the video data are processed in a distributed manner, where FFmpeg [11] and Mkvmerge [12] are used for efficient transcoding. Moreover, we conduct extensive experiments to determine the insights and the key points, which have significant impacts on the transcoding efficiency. Our experiment results help us to tune potential factors, process control, system parameter configuration, and segmentation strategies, of the system for optimized system performance. Based on our findings, transcoding algorithms and parameters are well tuned and configured. The experimental results show that the system can obtain notable manifestation by using appropriate segmentation strategy and parameter configuration under the condition of constant cluster size. That is, traditional distributed transcoding increases the speed by 1.35 times compared to single machine transcoding, while our suggested strategies can increase the transcoding rate to 2.06 times.

Based on the aforementioned introduction, the most significant contributions we have made in this paper are as follows:

1) We proposed the architecture of a distributed video transcoding system with optimized performances by evaluating various processing parameters such as cluster size, split size, memory allocation to MapTask.

2) We implemented and extensively evaluated the system CDVT and obtain design parameters and generally recommended transcoding configurations.

3) We designed and initially deployed two key algorithms to enable the user transcoding configuration to adaptively obtain the optimized transcoding performance.

The rest of this paper is organized as follows: Sect. 2 surveys related work. In Sect. 3, we introduces our system. Section 4 proposes the performance analysis. Finally, Sect. 5 presents conclusions with some future work.

2   Related Work

In recent years, in order to provide users with a good viewing experience and reduce costs for video service providers, distributed video transcoding has become an effective measure to address this challenge [13,14]. Video transcoding based on distributed clusters can effectively solve the corresponding problems of high hardware and time costs [15]. In this way, computing nodes are added to the distributed computing environment, and the hardware cost of common computing nodes is low, so as to enhance the parallelism of task processing and achieve the purpose of improving transcoding efficiency [16,17]. Hadoop, as a distributed computing framework proposed by Apache [18], can provide a distributed computing capability by simply deploying it on computer clusters. It has two important frameworks: Hadoop Distributed File System (HDFS) and MapReduce. As a Distributed File System, HDFS has strong scalability and high fault tolerance [19]; MapReduce, as a distributed programming framework, can effectively screen out the underlying details and provide a good environment for developers [20].

For example, Yang et al. [21] proposed a Hadoop-based distributed transcoding system that transcodes video files in units of 32MB in size, and concluded that parallel transcoding can reduce transcoding time by about 80%. This study mainly explored the feasibility of a distributed transcoding scheme based on the MapReduce framework, but failed to give more details in terms of system design. Ryu et al. [22] designed a Hadoop-based scalable video processing framework to parallelize video processing tasks in a cloud environment. By implementing face tracking experiments, it has been shown that video processing speed can be significantly improved in a distributed computing environment. Moreover, it emphasizes that this video processing framework has good scalability. Kodavalla et al. [23] proposed a distributed transcoding scheme for mobile devices. By using DVC and H.264 advanced video encoders to transcode in the network, the transcoding method has met its key objective of low complexity encoder and the decoder at both mobile devices of video conference application. In addition, researchers such as Sameti et al. [17] still want to complete distributed video transcoding on the Spark platform. As a successor of Hadoop, Spark may be found to perform better on distributed transcoding.

While implementing distributed transcoding to reduce video transcoding time, researchers have also begun to explore the factors that affect distributed transcoding. For example, Chen et al. [24] proposed a transcoding system based on MapReduce and FFmpeg, which can achieve efficient video transcoding work. On the other hand, this work attempts to introduce a third-party file system in the system, and wants to further improve the transcoding efficiency by reducing the disk I/O and network time overhead during the MapReduce process of the cluster. Song *et al.* [25] also implemented a distributed video transcoding system based on MapReduce and FFmpeg, and experimentally analyzed that the system has different transcoding speed promotion rates for videos of different sizes. It can achieve a speed increase of 1.38 times, 1.51 times, and 1.64 times for 500 MB, 1 GB, and 2 GB video processing respectively. In addition, the effect of the number of cluster nodes on the improvement of transcoding efficiency is demonstrated in a mathematical model. In some transcoding schemes, the video is divided into chunks of equal size and the chunks are distributed across multiple virtual machines for parallel transcoding [26, 27]. However, Zakerinasab *et al.* [28] analyzed the impact of chunk size on coding efficiency and transcoding time. They [29] propose a distributed video transcoding scheme that exploits dependency among GOPs by preparing video chunks of variable size. The scheme effectively reduces bitrate and transcoding time. Kim *et al.* [30] also proposed a Hadoop-based system that can transcode various video formats into the MPEG-4 format. In the experimental part, the experimental scheme is designed for the cluster size, HDFS block size, and backup factor size. Then the impact of the three factors mentioned above on the cluster transcoding speed is evaluated.

In general, the above researches [17, 21, 22, 24, 25, 28–30] have proposed a variety of ideas for the application of processing large-scale video data transcoding, and revealed the advantages of distributed transcoding for traditional transcoding methods when processing large-scale data. On the other hand, they did not further explore the factors affecting the efficiency of distributed transcoding under the proposed mechanism. Therefore, this paper proposes a distributed transcoding system based on Hadoop, and tries to figure out the optimal strategy to adapt the transcoding efficiency of the proposed mechanism while evaluating the system performance through a set of experiments.

3 CDVT: Cluster-Based Distributed Video Transcoding System

In this section, we will introduce the overall architecture and workflow of the proposed system in detail, which will include several core components of the system and the functions of each component.

3.1 System Structure Design

Since the system we designed is based on the Hadoop cluster model, the working mode of the cluster nodes is mainly the master/slave mode. When processing video transcoding tasks, the core design of the system consists of placing tasks into the MapReduce framework for processing and generating multiple subtasks for parallel processing to improve the transcoding efficiency of the system.

As shown in Fig. 1, the system is divided into three main domains according to different responsible functions, which are the Video Data Preprocessing and

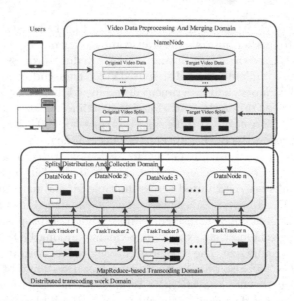

Fig. 1. The overall architecture of the proposed system

Merging Domain (VDPAMD), the Splits Distribution and Collection Domain (SDACD), and the MapReduce-based Transcoding Domain (MTD). The solid and dashed lines in the figure represent the transfer of source data and target data respectively. The main components and functional domains of the proposed system are explained as follow:

NameNode. This role is the only global manager in the entire cluster, and its functions include: job management, status monitoring, and task scheduling. More specifically, it is responsible for processing submissions from users in the system, which includes the original video data and XML parameter files that are eager to transform the data. On the other hand, it will start the entire process after accepting user submission as the main program entrance, which includes splitting the original data according to XML content, generating the corresponding index file for each segment, uploading the original segment set to HDFS, invoking the deployed JAR package containing the MapReduce program, downloading the target fragment set to the local, and finally merge the target fragment set and store target data in the specified path.

DataNode. This role stores files on HDFS in the form of data blocks in the cluster. Its functions include responding to read and write requests to HDFS and synchronizing data storage information with NameNode. Explaining in more detail, it is responsible for receiving and centrally storing the original and target segment sets in the proposed system. At the same time, when the MapReduce program is invoked, the video fragment and their indexes on the DataNode will be distributed in parallel to the task performers in the cluster. Then, after any task executor finishes transcoding the video fragments, the target fragments will be returned to the DataNode for concentration.

TaskTracker. This role is responsible for accepting each subtask job in the cluster, starting and tracking task execution. In other words, after a Map Task is generated, TaskTracker is responsible for executing the task, which includes reading the corresponding splits according to the index file distributed to the task, transcoding the read splits, and writing the transcoded data back to HDFS.

Video Data Preprocessing And Merging Domain. The video data preprocessing and merging domain will not only accept video data collection to be transcoded from users such as video surveillance, video service providers, etc., but also collect the transcoded video data collected from the distributed transcoding work domain. Source video splits set and target video splits set, both types of them need to be collected and stored in this domain. When the source data to be transcoded is collected, VDPAMD will process those data according to the parameter submitted by the user. The processing work includes splitting the video according to the configured size, extracting the transcoding parameters from the XML file, and submitting related tasks to the Hadoop cluster. Similarly, when the transcoded splits are collected, the area needs to complete the merging of those splits.

Distributed Transcoding Work Domain. The distributed transcoding work domain consists of two parts: the splits distribution and collection domain (SDACD) and the MapReduce-based transcoding domain (MTD).

(1) One between the two, SDACD is implemented based on HDFS, and it will collect the source video splits obtained by VDPAMD and the target video splits completed by MTD. Simultaneously, SDACD also needs to allocate splits for the Map Task on each transcoding node of the MTD according to the index, which is the split distribution function of the domain.
(2) The other between the two, MTD is responsible for executing multiple transcoding subtasks in parallel. Each computing node in the Hadoop cluster will be set up with FFmpeg, then all the nodes with video processing capabilities form MTD. During the execution of the entire MapReduce task, every node of MTD will be assigned one or more Map Tasks, and then the node will find the split that needs to be processed according to the previously generated index and download it to the local for transcoding. Finally, what MTD needs to do is to upload the transcoded splits to SDACD after the Map Task ends.

3.2   System Workflow

After elaborating on the system components and the main functions of each component through the Sect. 3.1, this section hopes to further introduce how they work together through Fig. 2 in order to show the main workflow. Firstly,

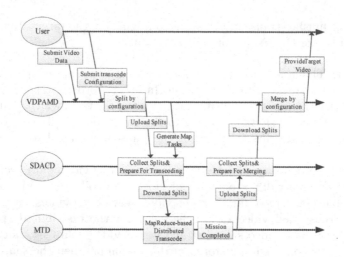

Fig. 2. The flowchart of the transcoding service

users can access the VDPAMD and submit the original video data that needs to be transcoded to this domain. When the video data is submitted, the transcoding options (including bit rate, spatial resolution, temporal resolution, compression standard conversion, packaging format, etc.) selected by the user will be made into the corresponding XML and submitted to VDPAMD together. Secondly, the system processes the video in VDPAMD according to the user's configuration, which includes splitting the original video into multiple fragments and uploading all the fragments to SDACD, and generating a corresponding index for every video fragment. After that, when all the fragments are collected in SDACD, the parameter configuration parsed from the XML submitted by the user will be passed to the MapReduce task and submitted to the Hadoop cluster.

Subsequently, transcoding nodes in the MTD need to transcode the original video fragments. Because of the MapReduce-based working mechanism, it allows every transcoding node to receive one or more Map Tasks. Every Map Task will be assigned an index and transcoding parameters, and they will read the video segment from SDACD according to the data storage information in the index, and then transcode according to the transcoding parameters. Afterwards, when the transcoding task is finished in a distributed computing manner, all nodes in MTD will upload the currently processed segments to SDACD, and then delete all intermediate files. Immediately afterwards, all transcoded shards will be collected on VDPAMD, and they will be cleared in SDACD after they are collected. Finally, VDPAMD merges the fragments completed by the transcoding task, deletes all the fragments after the merge phase is completed, and stores the final target video file to the specified path to meet the needs of the user.

3.3   Key Algorithm Design

Algorithm 1: Algorithm for selecting optimized splitting size

---

Input:

    α: cluster nodes size participating in MTD

    β: HDFS block size in cluster pre-configuration

    κ: user-configured split size in XML

    ω: user submitted dataset size

Output:

    μ: optimized split size for current systems

1: **while** system available **do**

2:    **if** κ != null **then**

3:      $\mu \leftarrow \kappa$

4:      **if** $\lceil \frac{\omega}{\mu} \rceil < \alpha$ and $\lceil \frac{\omega}{\beta} \rceil < \alpha$ **then**

5:        $\mu \leftarrow \lceil \frac{\omega}{\alpha} \rceil$

6:      **end if**

7:      **if** $\lceil \frac{\omega}{\mu} \rceil < \alpha$ and $\lceil \frac{\omega}{\beta} \rceil \geq \alpha$ **then**

8:        $\mu \leftarrow \min\{\mu, \beta\}$

9:      **end if**

10:     **if** $\lceil \frac{\omega}{\mu} \rceil \geq \alpha$ and $\lceil \frac{\omega}{\beta} \rceil \geq \alpha$ **then**

11:      $\mu \leftarrow \beta$

12:     **end if**

13:     **if** $\lceil \frac{\omega}{\mu} \rceil \geq \alpha$ and $\lceil \frac{\omega}{\beta} \rceil < \alpha$ **then**

14:      $\mu \leftarrow \max\{\lceil \frac{\omega}{\alpha} \rceil, \beta\}$

15:     **end if**

16:    **else**

17:      $\mu \leftarrow \beta$

18:    **end if**

19: **end while**

20: **return** μ

Regardless of the design parameter level or the transcoding configuration parameter level, the selection that is more in line with the system characteristics can make the CDVT show optimized performance compared to selections that are not suitable. So it should be noted that in terms of video splitting size in VDPAMD and how much computing memory is allocated to each MapTask in MTD, we proposed splitting strategies and memory allocation methods respectively, ensuring CDVT performs as best as possible.

Algorithm 1 provides a pseudo-code to select the optimized split size which was a general recommended configuration obtained through our extensive evaluation of the system CDVT. This method is triggered when the user-defined split size is parsed. The optimized split size for current systems μ are determined by the combined influence of cluster nodes size participating in MTD α, the HDFS block size β in the system configuration, the user selected partition size κ, and the submitted dataset size ω.

$$\lceil \frac{\omega}{\mu} \rceil < \alpha \; and \; \lceil \frac{\omega}{\beta} \rceil < \alpha \tag{1}$$

When condition (1) is satisfied, the computing nodes in current system cannot be fully utilized no matter whether dataset is split by μ or β, which may be the reason why the dataset submitted by users are too small. Then, with the destination of making the utmost of system resources, the video spliting size at this case is suitable to be adjusted to $\lceil \omega/\alpha \rceil$.

$$\lceil \frac{\omega}{\mu} \rceil < \alpha \ and \ \lceil \frac{\omega}{\beta} \rceil \geq \alpha \qquad (2)$$

When condition (2) is satisfied, it is appropriate for current system that user submitted the dataset at a suitable scale but the system's available computing nodes are underutilized. Correspondingly, it is necessary to properly straighten out the split size so that it approaches β from a larger value.

$$\lceil \frac{\omega}{\mu} \rceil \geq \alpha \ and \ \lceil \frac{\omega}{\beta} \rceil \geq \alpha \qquad (3)$$

When condition (3) is satisfied, it is the case that both the scale of user submission tasks and the utilization rate of the computing nodes are appropriate for the current system. At this time, the optimized split size for current systems μ be configured as β preferentially;

$$\lceil \frac{\omega}{\mu} \rceil \geq \alpha \ and \ \lceil \frac{\omega}{\beta} \rceil < \alpha \qquad (4)$$

When condition (4) is satisfied, a more extreme case is considered which the size of dataset submitted by the user is small and the split size is also smaller than expected. This situation is also a configuration that is not conducive to the full advantage of current system. The split size needs to be properly corrected in such circumstances so that it approaches β from a smaller value.

Algorithm 2 : Pseudo-Code for checking MapTak Memory Allocation

---

Input:
　　　λ: configurable memory size for nodes in MTD
　　　γ: memory the user wants to allocate for each MapTask in XML
Output:
　　　ϵ: memory allocated to MapTask optimized for the current system
　1: **while** system available **do**
　2:　　**if** $\gamma! = null$ and $\gamma \leq \lambda$ **then**
　3:　　　　$\epsilon \leftarrow \gamma$ parse and validate user configuration parameters
　4:　　　　**if** $\lambda \mod \epsilon! = 0$ **then**
　5:　　　　　　resize ϵ to take full advantage of configurable memory
　6:　　　　　　$p \leftarrow \lceil \frac{\lambda}{\gamma} \rceil$ maximum parallel MapTask numbers under γ
　7:　　　　　　$\epsilon \leftarrow \frac{\lambda}{p}$ calculate final recommended allocation
　8:　　　　**end if**
　9:　　　　$\epsilon \leftarrow \lambda$
10:　　**end if**
11: **end while**

Algorithm 2 provides the pseudo-code for checking MapTask allocated Memory. The algorithm is triggered when the memory size γ defined by the user in

XML allocating for each MapTask is parsed. Assuming that the configurable memory of all nodes in the MTB is indiscriminate, if γ obtained from the configuration is greater than λ, the configuration will lose efficacy unquestionably. In such circumstances, the ϵ is adjusted to the maximum configurable memory by default. Conversely, the γ configured by user is possibly effective when $\gamma \leq \lambda$. Then the algorithm needs to check whether the allocation ϵ can make the available resources fully profitable by the corresponding method (line 4 in Algorithm 2). When the configurable memory is not fully allotted, the strategy (lines 5–7 in Algorithm 2) readjusts ϵ to allocate the largest possible memory for each MapTask while each node obtains the maximum MapTask parallelism.

4   Experiments and Evaluation

4.1   Experimental Design

Under the premise of ensuring the integrity and validity of the transcoded data, we focus on taking the task completion time and speedup as performance evaluation metrics. In experimental design, our main purpose is to evaluate the performance of the proposed system and explore the configuration factors that affect the transcoding efficiency of the system.

More detail, we will first verify the efficiency advantages of distributed transcoding compared to single machine transcoding through experiment in Sect. 4.3.1, and then compare distributed transcoding and distributed transcoding under different system configurations through Sects. 4.3.2, 4.3.3, 4.3.4. The experiment takes time as an observation variable, and uses the data set size, the number of cluster slave nodes, each stage of the service process, video segmentation size, and task memory allocation [31] as control variables.

Finally, we implemented and extensively evaluated the system CDVT, and obtained design parameters and general recommended transcoding configurations.

4.2   Experimental Setup

We set up a Hadoop cluster consisting of 5 computing nodes to conduct this experiment. One of the computers can serve as the master (NameNode) and the remaining 4 as slaves (DataNode and TaskTracker). Tables 1 gives these software and hardware parameters.

In addition, in order to verify the performance of transcoding source video data of different scales into target data, we give the source and target data parameters used in this experiment in Table 2.

4.3   Experimental Results

In the following experiments, we took time as an observation variable, and uses the data set size, the number of cluster slave nodes, each stage of the service process, video segmentation size, and task memory allocation as control variables.

Table 1. Configuration of nodes

Components	Configurations and releases
OS	Ubuntu_14.04_LTS
JDK	Oracle JDK 1.8 Update 171
Hadoop	Apache Hadoop 2.7.6 stable release
FFmpeg	ffmpeg 3.3.8
MKVmerge	mkvmerge v6.7.0 64bit
CPU	Main frequency: 3.20 GHz, Intel Core i5 4460
RAM	Capacity: 4 GB, Kingston DDR3 (800 MHz)

Table 2. Parameters of source and target data

Parameter	Source data	Target data
Codec	Avc1	MPEG-4
Resolution	1920 × 800	720 × 480
Container	mkv	avi
Frame rate	30	25
Aspect ratio	16:9	16:9

Table 3. Total transcoding time(s) and speedup(SU) with different cluster size

Nodes	1	2		3		4	
Dataset(GB)	Time(s)	Time(s)	SU	Time(s)	SU	Time(s)	SU
0.25	97.84	72.01	1.36	70.16	1.39	70.90	1.38
0.5	205.36	149.82	1.37	148.74	1.38	148.07	1.39
1	482.72	344.80	1.40	335.22	1.44	312.86	1.54
2	1030.54	682.48	1.51	599.15	1.72	551.09	1.87
4	1920.94	1178.49	1.63	1032.76	1.86	934.86	2.06

4.3.1 Experiment of Cluster Size Affecting Performance

In the first experiment, we took 0.25 GB, 0.5 GB, 1 GB, 2 GB, and 4 GB video files as inputs, and measured the time-consuming and speedup ratios for different cluster sizes. The speedup is used to describe the increase in the processing rate of distributed transcoding methods relative to single-point transcoding, so it is defined as: Speedup(n) = transcoding time for single-node/transcoding time for n nodes.

Table 3 reveals the transcoding time-consuming and speed-up ratios of different size datasets under different cluster sizes. For example, when the number of slave nodes in the system is 4, it takes 934.86 s for 4 GB of video data, which has speedup as 2.06 times compared with the completion time of a single machine transcoding of 1920.94 s. It also means a reduction in time costs by more than 50%.

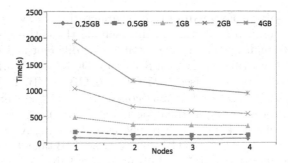

Fig. 3. Transcoding time under different cluster nodes

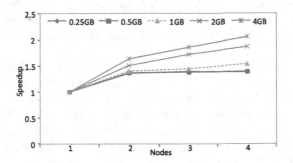

Fig. 4. Speedup under different cluster nodes

Figure 3, 4 can visually illustrate the effect of various cluster nodes on transcoding performance through the relationship between transcoding time and cluster size. They also reveal as following: (1) when the source video size is constant, the system can use more nodes to obtain less time-consuming and higher speedup; (2) when the cluster size is constant, larger source video can be obtained better transcoding efficiency.

Table 4. Time consuming at each stage of the transcoding service

Task	Time(s)				
	0.25 GB	0.5 GB	1 GB	2 GB	4 GB
Receive and parse XML configuration files	0.51	0.53	0.54	0.50	0.58
Split process of the source data in VDPAMD	0.89	8.97	22.66	41.95	73.47
Create a corresponding index for each split	0.03	0.02	0.03	0.03	0.03
Upload splits and indexes to specific folder in HDFS	11.90	23.93	59.52	121.06	221.66
Transcode on MapReduce-based Transcoding Domain	53.85	105.74	208.87	346.68	565.42
Download and collect all target segments in VDPAMD	3.84	8.55	20.40	39.17	72.13
Merge and get final target data	0.41	0.89	1.39	2.26	4.19
Total	70.90	148.07	312.26	551.09	934.86

4.3.2 Task Analysis Experiment in Transcoding Service

In the second experiment, we start to disassemble the entire transcoding service workflow into multiple stages, that is, multiple different tasks, according to the system details described in System Structure Design (Sect. 3.1) and System Workflow (Sect. 3.2). We also used 0.25 GB, 0.5 GB, 1 GB, 2 GB, and 4 GB video files as input to measure the time consumption of tasks in each stage of the transcoding process, and put the experimental data in Table 4.

For example, for the same task of receiving and parsing XML configuration files, 0.25 GB data takes 0.51 s, 0.5 GB takes 0.53 s, 1 GB takes 0.54 s, 2 GB takes 0.50 s, and the last 4 GB takes 0.58 s. This means that throughout the workflow, the time it takes to process the task of receiving and parsing the XML configuration is not much different, and it does not fluctuate significantly due to changes in the size of the original data. Similarly, the task with minimal time fluctuations throughout the workflow also has the task of creating a corresponding index for each split.

In contrast, for the same task of transcoding on the MapReduce-based Transcoding Domain, 0.25 GB data takes 53.85 s, 0.5 GB takes 105.74 s, 1 GB takes 208.87 s, 2 GB takes 346.68 s, and the last 4 GB takes 565.42 s. It means that throughout the workflow, the time it takes to process the task of transcoding on the MapReduce-based Transcoding Domain is much different, and it fluctuated significantly due to changes in the size of the original data. Finally, according to Fig. 5, in the input data processing of all sizes, the task of transcoding on the MapReduce-based Transcoding Domain has the largest time-consuming component and the largest fluctuation. Therefore, we can reduce the overall execution time by focusing on further improving the performance of transcoding on the MapReduce-based Transcoding Domain, which is also the most important work in the next section.

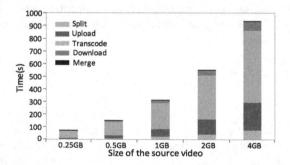

Fig. 5. Time cost for different tasks in transcoding services

Table 5. Time cost for different tasks under different split sizes and viarous data sizes

Dataset	Main task	Time(s) cost at different split sizes				
		64 MB	100 MB	128 MB	150 MB	256 MB
0.25 GB	Split	1.42	1.39	0.89	1.12	0.89
	Upload	20.13	16.47	11.90	10.51	9.78
	Transcode	71.16	62.36	53.85	56.71	60.51
	Download	7.87	6.27	3.84	3.57	1.96
	Merge	0.20	0.18	0.41	0.19	0.18
	Total	100.78	86.67	70.90	72.09	73.31
0.5 GB	Split	6.38	7.83	8.97	9.25	8.86
	Upload	45.04	28.89	23.93	21.86	19.99
	Transcode	129.34	118.61	105.74	110.62	115.72
	Download	17.97	10.74	8.55	8.25	7.18
	Merge	0.99	0.67	0.88	0.90	0.67
	Total	199.73	166.74	148.07	150.87	152.42
1 GB	Split	34.24	26.07	22.67	19.61	21.31
	Upload	98.40	70.03	59.53	52.69	51.10
	Transcode	257.67	227.96	208.87	222.86	239.10
	Download	40.20	25.15	20.40	18.77	11.08
	Merge	1.55	1.42	1.40	1.34	1.55
	Total	432.01	350.63	312.86	315.26	324.13
2 GB	Split	43.65	41.85	41.95	45.00	45.79
	Upload	189.46	137.58	121.04	112.06	98.97
	Transcode	475.23	416.13	346.68	384.00	412.45
	Download	74.24	47.76	39.16	33.53	20.24
	Merge	2.58	2.29	2.26	2.25	2.58
	Total	785.16	645.62	551.09	576.85	580.03
4 GB	Split	81.35	75.97	73.47	73.27	74.77
	Upload	352.15	267.26	221.66	206.52	188.21
	Transcode	862.39	730.45	565.42	635.30	688.99
	Download	119.91	94.63	72.13	57.87	41.82
	Merge	4.99	4.23	4.19	4.45	4.15
	Total	1420.79	1172.54	934.86	977.40	997.94

4.3.3 Experiment of Split Size Affecting Performance

In the third experiment, we are inspired by the second experiment, which will mainly discuss the factors affecting the performance of transcoding on the MapReduce-based Transcoding Domain. We also took 0.25 GB, 0.5 GB, 1 GB, 2 GB, and 4 GB video files as input and measured the time-consuming tasks of each stage in the transcoding workflow, but we added a control variable: split size. Split size is the unit of data processing during the video splitting phase, and it will also be the bigness of each task processed by MapTask. Here, we performed five sets of tests on each data set according to the XML file with the split sizes of 64 MB, 100 MB, 128 MB, 150 MB, and 256 MB, and finally put the obtained data into Table 5. For instance, for the same stage of transcoding with 4 GB dataset (Transcode), it takes 862.39 s under split size is 64 MB, takes 730.45 s under split size is 100 MB, takes 565.42 s under split size is 128 MB, takes 635.30 s under split size is 150 MB and takes 688.99 s under split size is 256 MB.

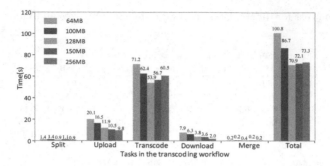

Fig. 6. Time cost for different tasks under different split sizes and 0.25 GB data

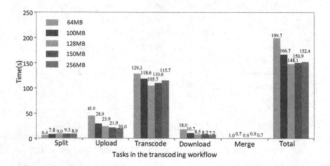

Fig. 7. Time cost for different tasks under different split sizes and 0.5 GB data

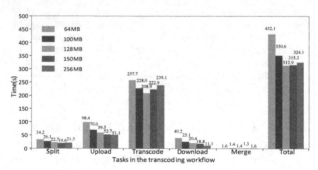

Fig. 8. Time cost for different tasks under different split sizes and 1 GB data

Figures 6, 7, 8, 9 and 10 more vividly reflect the impact of split size on transcoding performance. Taking Fig. 10 as an example for illustration, we find that as the split size is changed, the time-consuming in the stages of Split and Merge jitter small and this fluctuation has almost no effect on the transcoding time (Total). The Upload and Download tend to decrease as split size increases. It is because the larger the partition size, the smaller the number of data blocks and the smaller the overhead of file transfer. And under various datasets, Fig. 11 shows the global impact of different split sizes on the total transcoding time.

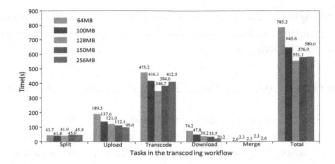

Fig. 9. Time cost for different tasks under different split sizes and 2 GB data

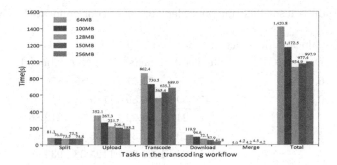

Fig. 10. Time cost for different tasks under different split sizes and 4 GB data

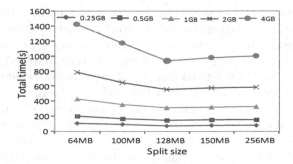

Fig. 11. Transcoding time under different split sizes and various dataset

Most notably, however, as the split size changes, the jittering trend of the transcoding task (Transcode) approaches the convex function and is similar to the trend of total time consumption (Total). It means that the system can improve the performance of the stage of transcoding on the MapReduce-based Transcoding Domain through proper split size configuration, thereby minimizing the total time overhead. The reason why we choose to slice with 128 MB of data for the optimized performance may be that the default size of the HDFS data storage unit is 128 MB, which can be manually configured. Therefore, we recommend configuring the split size configuration as much as possible to the size of the distributed storage data block in the system design to obtain the optimized system performance.

4.3.4 Experiment of MapTak Allocated Memory Affecting Performance

To further discuss the impact of memory allocation on transcoding performance, the last experiment will be performed with a fixed size of slave nodes (4 nodes) and a splitting strategy of 128 MB. There are also five sizes of data sets to be transcoded.

Table 6. Total transcoding time(s) under various memory allocated to MapTask

Allocated memory Dataset(GB)	1 GB Time(s)	2 GB Time(s)	3 GB Time(s)	4 GB Time(s)
0.25	71.88	71.77	72.88	70.90
0.5	170.50	160.89	179.68	148.07
1	366.24	335.22	312.86	312.86
2	631.20	581.36	666.49	551.09
4	1051.20	1006.86	1125.33	934.86

Before discussing the experimental results, we want to introduce what is allocated memory to MapTask. In the MapReduce working framework, there is a parameter named mapreduce.map.memory.mb in its configuration file, which is used to control the processing memory allocated to each MapTask. For example, suppose that on a node with 4 GB memory, if memory allocated to MapTask is set to 1 GB, then theoretically, at most four tasks can be run simultaneously; if this value is set to 3 GB, only one task can be run. Then, the dilemma is that the smaller the allocation of memory, the more parallel the processing of tasks on each node will be, but at the same time the ability to process the same tasks will be weakened. In this case, getting the appropriate compromise is even more important for computationally intensive video transcoding tasks.

Table 6 and Fig. 12 show the results of transcoding makespan in the final experiment with 0.25 GB, 0.5 GB, 1 GB, 2 GB, and 4 GB video data as input under different memory allocated to MapTask. It can be found that the transcoding performance of the system is the worst when the allocated memory is 3 GB. It is because 3 GB is not a factor of the system node memory (4 GB), which results in insufficient memory usage. When the memory is allocated to 1 GB, 2 GB, and 3 GB respectively, the system transcoding performance fluctuates small. When the size of the processed data is large, the allocation of memory as large as possible will make the system's transcoding performance the best. It shows

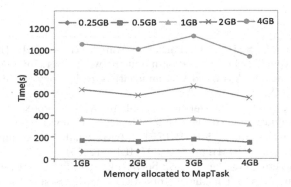

Fig. 12. Time cost under different allocated memory and various dataset

that in an effective parallel processing framework, equipping computing nodes with stronger computing capabilities is more beneficial to system transcoding performance.

5   Conclusion and Future Work

In this paper, we proposed the architecture of a distributed video transcoding system that can efficiently transcode non-real-time large-scale video on users' demand, which can be applied to video-on-demand and video sharing over mobile devices. In particular, we expounded the system design and workflow in detail, and discussed the effect of cluster size, intermediate task flow, split strategy, and memory allocation to MapTask on system performance through four sets of experiments. Experimental results show that larger cluster size or befitting memory allocation can produce the optimized system performance and shorter transcoding completion time at the system design parameters level. At the transcoding configuration level, users choose a larger dataset to be processed, or select split size that is closer to the current system storage unit, which can maximize the advantages of the proposed system and will enlighten subsequent applications. In addition, the proposed system can ensure the quality of transcoding tasks while reducing time-to-cost by up to about 50%, when the system is running under optimized configuration parameters.

Future research includes implementing distributed processing of real-time video data or combining transcoding tasks with crowdsourcing under limited computing resources.

Acknowledgement. The research was financially supported by National Natural Science Foundation of China (No. 61972366), the Foundation of Key Laboratory of Network Assessment Technology, Chinese Academy of Sciences (No. KFKT2019-003), Major Scientific and Technological Special Project of Guizhou Province (No. 20183001), and the Foundation of Guizhou Provincial Key Laboratory of Public Big Data (No. 2018BDKFJJ009, No. 2019BDKFJJ003, No. 2019BDKFJJ011).

References

1. Hong, S.-I., Lyu, H.-S., In, C.-G., Park, J.-C., Lin, C.-H., Yoon, D.-H.: Development of digital multimedia player based on mobile network sever. In: 2012 14th International Conference on Advanced Communication Technology (ICACT). IEEE, pp. 1280–1283 (2012)
2. Petrangeli, S., Bouten, N., Dejonghe, E., Famaey, J., Leroux, P., De Turck, F., Design and evaluation of a dash-compliant second screen video player for live events in mobile scenarios. In: 2015 IFIP/IEEE International Symposium on Integrated Network Management (IM), pp. 894–897. IEEE (2015)
3. Davis, D., Figueroa, G., Chen, Y.-S.: SociRank: identifying and ranking prevalent news topics using social media factors. IEEE Trans. Syst. Man Cybern.: Syst. **47**(6), 979–994 (2016)
4. Liu, Y., Liu, A., Xiong, N.N., Wang, T., Gui, W.: Content propagation for content-centric networking systems from location-based social networks. IEEE Trans. Syst. Man Cybern.: Syst. **49**(10), 1946–1960 (2019)
5. Xu, C., Ren, W., Yu, L., Zhu, T., Choo, K.-K. R.: A hierarchical encryption and key management scheme for layered access control on H. 264/SVC bitstream in Internet of Things. IEEE Internet Things J. **7**, 8932–8942 (2020)
6. Hentati, A.I., Fourati, L.C., Rhaiem, O.B.: New hybrid rate adaptation algorithm (HR2A) for video streaming over WLAN. In: 2017 Sixth International Conference on Communications and Networking (ComNet), pp. 1–6. IEEE (2017)
7. Li, Z., Huang, Y., Liu, G., Wang, F., Zhang, Z.-L., Dai, Y.: Cloud transcoder: bridging the format and resolution gap between internet videos and mobile devices. In: Proceedings of the 22nd International Workshop on Network and Operating System Support for Digital Audio and Video, pp. 33–38. ACM (2012). https://doi.org/10.1145/2229087.2229097
8. Gao, G., Zhang, W., Wen, Y., Wang, Z., Zhu, W., Tan, Y.P.: Cost optimal video transcoding in media cloud: insights from user viewing pattern. In: 2014 IEEE International Conference on Multimedia and Expo (ICME), pp. 556–571. IEEE (2014). https://doi.org/10.1109/ICME.2014.6890255
9. Tan, H., Chen, L.: An approach for fast and parallel video processing on apache Hadoop clusters. In: 2014 IEEE International Conference on Multimedia and Expo (ICME), pp. 1–6. IEEE (2014). https://doi.org/10.1109/ICME.2014.6890135
10. Kim, H.-W., Mu, H., Park, J.H., Sangaiah, A.K., Jeong, Y.-S.: Video transcoding scheme of multimedia data-hiding for multiform resources based on intra-cloud. J. Ambient Intell. Humaniz. Comput. **11**, 1809–1819 (2019). https://doi.org/10.1007/s12652-019-01279-1
11. FFmpeg: A complete, cross-platform solution to record, convert and stream audio and video (April 2019). http://ffmpeg.org/
12. Mkvmerge: mkvtoolnix-matroska tools for linux/unix and windows (April 2019). https://mkvtoolnix.download/doc/mkvmerge.html
13. Huh, J., Kim, Y.-H., Jeong, J.: Ultra-high resolution video distributed transcoding system using memory-based high-speed data distribution method. In: 2019 34th International Technical Conference on Circuits/Systems, Computers and Communications (ITC-CSCC), pp. 1–4. IEEE (2019)
14. Hsu, T.-H., Wang, Z.-Y.: A distributed SHVC video transcoding system. In: 2017 10th International Conference on Ubi-Media Computing and Workshops (Ubi-Media), pp. 1–3. IEEE (2017)

15. Li, X., Salehi, M.A., Joshi, Y., Darwich, M.K., Landreneau, B., Bayoumi, M.: Performance analysis and modeling of video transcoding using heterogeneous cloud services. IEEE Trans. Parallel Distrib. Syst. **30**(4), 910–922 (2018)

16. Li, X., Salehi, M.A., Bayoumi, M., Tzeng, N.-F., Buyya, R.: Cost-efficient and robust on-demand video transcoding using heterogeneous cloud services. IEEE Trans. Parallel Distrib. Syst. **29**(3), 556–571 (2017). https://doi.org/10.1109/TPDS.2017.2766069

17. Sameti, S., Wang, M., Krishnamurthy, D., Stride: distributed video transcoding in spark. In: 2018 IEEE 37th International Performance Computing and Communications Conference (IPCCC), pp. 1–8 (2018). https://doi.org/10.1109/PCCC.2018.8711214

18. Apache: The apache Hadoop project develops open-source software for reliable, scalable, distributed computing (December 2018). http://hadoop.apache.org/

19. Apache: HDFS architecture guide (December 2018). http://hadoop.apache.org/docs/stable/hadoop-project-dist/hadoop-hdfs/HdfsDesign.html

20. Apache: MapReduce tutorial (December 2018). http://hadoop.apache.org/docs/stable/hadoop-mapreduce-client/hadoop-mapreduce-client-core/MapReduceTutorial.html

21. Yang, F., Shen, Q.-W.: Distributed video transcoding on Hadoop. Comput. Syst. Appl. **11**, 020 (2011)

22. Ryu, C., Lee, D., Jang, M., Kim, C., Seo, E.: Extensible video processing framework in apache Hadoop. In: 2013 IEEE 5th International Conference on Cloud Computing Technology and Science, vol. 2, pp. 305–310. IEEE (2013). https://doi.org/10.1109/CloudCom.2013.153

23. Kodavalla, V.K.: Transcoding of next generation distributed video codec for mobile video. In: 2018 Second International Conference on Advances in Electronics, Computers and Communications (ICAECC), pp. 1–7. IEEE (2018)

24. Chen, M., Chen, W., Cai, L.: Data-driven parallel video transcoding for content delivery network in the cloud. In: 2018 5th IEEE International Conference on Cyber Security and Cloud Computing (CSCloud)/2018 4th IEEE International Conference on Edge Computing and Scalable Cloud (EdgeCom), pp. 196–199. IEEE (2018). https://doi.org/10.1109/CSCloud/EdgeCom.2018.00042

25. Song, C., Shen, W., Sun, L., Lei, Z., Xu, W.: Distributed video transcoding based on MapReduce. In: 2014 IEEE/ACIS 13th International Conference on Computer and Information Science (ICIS), pp. 309–314. IEEE (2014). https://doi.org/10.1109/ICIS.2014.6912152

26. Heikkinen, A., Sarvanko, J., Rautiainen, M., Ylianttila, M.: Distributed multimedia content analysis with MapReduce. In: 2013 IEEE 24th Annual International Symposium on Personal, Indoor, and Mobile Radio Communications (PIMRC), pp. 3497–3501. IEEE (2013)

27. Kim, M., Han, S., Cui, Y., Lee, H., Cho, H., Hwang, S.: CloudDMSS: robust Hadoop-based multimedia streaming service architecture for a cloud computing environment. Cluster Comput. **17**(3), 605–628 (2014)

28. Zakerinasab, M.R., Wang, M.: Does chunk size matter in distributed video transcoding?. In: 2015 IEEE 23rd International Symposium on Quality of Service (IWQos), pp. 69–70. IEEE (2015)

29. Zakerinasab, M.R., Wang, M.: Dependency-aware distributed video transcoding in the cloud. In: 2015 IEEE 40th Conference on Local Computer Networks (LCN), pp. 245–252. IEEE (2015)

30. Kim, M., Cui, Y., Han, S., Lee, H.: Towards efficient design and implementation of a Hadoop-based distributed video transcoding system in cloud computing environment. Int. J. Multimed. Ubiquit. Eng. **8**(2), 213–224 (2013). https://doi.org/10.1109/icce-tw.2015.7216972

31. Yang, J., Li, R.-F.: A container resource configuration method in Hadoop transcoding cluster based on requirements of a sample split. In: 2017 IEEE 2nd International Conference on Cloud Computing and Big Data Analysis (ICCCBDA), pp. 108–112. IEEE (2017). https://doi.org/10.1109/ICCCBDA.2017.7951893

Author Index

Printed in the United States
by Baker & Taylor Publisher Services

Printed in the United States
by Baker & Taylor Publisher Services